MONSIGNOR WILLIAM BARRY MEMORIAL LIBRARY
BARRY UNIVERSITY
DA576 .S35 1970
Scott, Charles Prestwich,   010101 000
The political diaries of C. P.

0 2210 0003571 9

DA
576
.S35   127128
1970

Msgr. Wm. Barry Memorial Library
Barry College
Miami, FL   33161

SCOTT

POLITICAL DIA...

The Political Diaries of C. P. Scott, 1911-1928

By the same author
The Downfall of the Liberal Party 1914-1935

The Political Diaries of C. P. Scott 1911-1928

Edited with an introduction and commentary by Trevor Wilson

Cornell University Press, Ithaca, New York

Barry University Library

Miami, FL 33161

© Trevor Wilson 1970

First published 1970

Standard Book Number 0-8014-0569-6

Library of Congress Catalog Card Number 75-110993

Printed in Great Britain

All rights reserved. Except for brief quotations in a review, this book, or parts thereof, must not be reproduced in any form without permission in writing from the publisher. For information address Cornell University Press, 124 Roberts Place, Ithaca, New York 14850.

DA
576
. S35
1970

127128

To Jenny and Sara

Contents

List of Plates

Preface

For thirty years after his death in 1932, the diaries of C. P. Scott remained closed from the public gaze (apart from the passages included
in J. L. Hammond's rather unsatisfactory biography of Scott, published
in 1934). This was not because the diaries contained anything scandalous, being as they were political and not personal records. But they
contained a certain amount which might cause agitation to individuals
concerned in politics, including utterances by or about persons (or
their close relatives) still living. And anyway it was usual until lately to
adopt a quite exaggerated reserve towards political documents of
recent origin. In this respect there has been a merciful change of
attitude in the last decade; and this volume is one product of the change.

Scott's diaries, with many of his letters, reside in the British
Museum.[1] I encountered them there soon after they had been opened to
scholars in the early 1960s, while researching for a book on the British
Liberal party. Seen as a whole, they seemed to me valuable in a way
that was not true of most other collections of private papers. The
insight which they provided into the careers of certain politicians, and
into a whole range of crucial political events, appeared to warrant their
publication *in extenso*. I put this suggestion to Mr. L. P. Scott, who on
behalf of the Scott family is the executor of his grandfather's estate, and
he readily assented.

What follows is not the whole of the diaries. For one thing, they
are in no sense an exhaustive record of Scott's political encounters, so
that publishing them *in toto* would not provide the satisfaction (such as
it is) of completeness. And the diaries do include a certain amount that
is just too tedious to inflict on the general reader: material that is
repetitious, or over-detailed, or concerned with what must be considered the blind alleys of politics. (Those with a specialist interest in
the period can now secure on microfilm a complete copy of the diaries

---

[1]Other letters are still held by the *Guardian*, but these will probably be transferred to the
British Museum in due course.

if they want it.) Hence what follows is a selection, but a generous selection, containing—at a rough estimate—more than half of the diaries, together with appropriate extracts from Scott's letters (particularly the correspondence with his close friend L. T. Hobhouse, one-time leader-writer on the *Manchester Guardian* and from 1907 to 1929 Professor of Sociology at London University). The principle governing inclusion of material is simple enough in broad terms, though sometimes difficult to apply—and another editor would doubtless have selected rather differently. Only at one point, indicated by a footnote, has something been left out on grounds of taste. For the rest, everything that seemed to illuminate the main issues and individuals of politics has been in-cluded. Material that appeared not to do this has been left out.

This does not mean that all that follows will instantly appear to throw new light on the great questions of the day. Many diary-entries will appear of only minor importance. But often the value of a journal like this lies less in its startling revelations than in the cumulative effect of dozens of tiny incidents which it records. Standing alone these incidents may not amount to very much. Taken together they throw a quite new light on the character of politicians or the nature of the issues over which they were struggling. That is the real justification for publishing these diaries as an entity, rather than leaving them to be used simply as an aid to various pieces of research.

Just how reliable are Scott's diaries? They contain minor in-accuracies (for example of dating—these have been indicated where noticed), but no glaring errors or inventions which I have been able to detect. Moreover they stand up well to cross-checking. Thus where Scott provided more than one record of the same incident, for example in a letter as well as in a diary-entry, the two accounts have proved consistent with each other. More than this, where there exists another account of a conversation recorded by Scott (e.g. in the diaries of Lord Riddell, the biography of C. F. G. Masterman, and the papers of Lord Gladstone) the two versions prove to be substantially similar. Of course there are differences, depending on how the participants viewed each other and the issues they were discussing; and certainly we are left wishing for many more opportunities of verifying Scott's narrative. One would dearly like, for example, to have accounts by Asquith of those encounters with Scott from which, in Scott's version, Asquith emerged so badly. But this is not because Asquith's account would probably be more accurate (nor, from such diary-records as he kept, more illuminating); only that it would help us to get a stage nearer to the whole of a truth of which Scott, inevitably, provides only a part.

But as long as we are forced to make do with only one record of these encounters, we are not likely to get a better one than that which Scott provides.

Admittedly one must never forget Mr. Malcolm Muggeridge's warning about the unreliability of eye-witness history.[2] Eye-witnesses, he reminds us, are not detached observers seeing all that takes place and setting it down impartially and in due proportion. They are people with axes to grind and causes to foster (including the cause of their own self-esteem), and this will certainly colour their recollection of any event—let alone the recollection which they are prepared to commit to paper. But the limitations of which Mr. Muggeridge speaks apply to most of the raw materials from which the political historian (himself no wholly detached observer) must construct his account. It has not, fortunately, been felt that these limitations are sufficient to require the political historian to close up shop and seek some other occupation. In reading what Scott wrote it is certainly necessary to bear in mind the shortcomings as a witness of a man with his prejudices and convictions. Nevertheless, as long as we continue to believe that political history should be written at all, and as long as we do not suspend our capacity for disbelief, we shall find Scott a powerful aid to a clearer understanding of the men and the issues which made up the politics of his time.

[2] "The Eye-Witness Fallacy" in *Tread Softly For You Tread on My Jokes* (Collins, London, 1966).

Acknowledgements

Editing this volume has proved a more complex task than initially I had reckoned on. In bringing it to fruition I have been generously assisted by a number of individuals and institutions to whom I am grateful. I have three debts in particular: to Mr. L. P. Scott for granting me permission to prepare this edition of Scott's diaries and correspondence, and to include correspondence of other members of the staff of the *Manchester Guardian*; to the Australian Research Grants Committee, which provided me with a generous grant to secure microfilms of Scott's diaries and letters and of the relevant files of the *Manchester Guardian*; and to the University of Adelaide, which enabled me to visit England in order to seek out the material I needed.

I also wish to thank Mr. David Ayerst, who drew generously on his store of information on the history of the *Manchester Guardian* for my enlightenment; Mr. A. J. P. Taylor, who by allowing me to see a draft of parts of his forthcoming life of Lord Beaverbrook saved me from perpetuating a number of historical fallacies; Mr. and Mrs. Malcolm Muggeridge, who provided me with a view of Scott not quite the traditional one and, in support of it, allowed me to read Mr. Muggeridge's suppressed novel *Picture Palace*; and Professor M. R. D. Foot, Mr. John Grigg, and Mr. Michael Turnbull, who in the course of conversations provided me with a number of useful ideas. I must also record my gratitude to Mr. Richard Ollard, who has again made the relationship between writer and publisher one of unfailing enjoyment; and to my wife and children, who endured a great deal that the undertaking might be completed.

The following individuals and institutions have kindly allowed me to consult private papers in their possession, or to quote letters to Scott of which they hold the copyright: the British Museum, the Beaverbrook Library and Beaverbrook Newspapers, the Bodleian Library, the *Guardian* Library, the British Library of Political and Economic Science, the National Library of Scotland, Mrs. Jennifer

Balme, Mrs. Mary Bennett, Mrs. Sylvia Blelloch, Mrs. Margaret Bone, Miss M. V. Bryce, Professor Myles Dillon, Lord Harcourt, Rt. Hon. Malcolm MacDonald, Miss Pegeen Mair, Mrs. Lucy Masterman, Lady Mottistone, Mr. Maurice Phillipps, Viscount Runciman of Doxford and Sir Stephen Runciman, Mr. Richard Scott, Lord Simon, Mr. J. C. Smuts and the Smuts Archive Trust, Sir George Trevelyan, Mr. Henry H. Villard, and Dr. Meyer W. Weisgal and The Trustees of the Weizmann Archives.

Note on the Principles of Editing

I have reproduced Scott's text as faithfully as possible consistent with producing a volume that is readable. For example I have retained his sometimes cranky and erratic use of punctuation marks (particularly quote marks, which he appeared to include or withhold without rhyme or reason) and capital letters. Where something has been omitted from within a passage this has been indicated by three dots if the omission remains within a sentence, and four dots if the omission extends beyond a sentence. And where a letter or diary passage is incomplete in the sense that something has been omitted before or after the passage reproduced, this has been indicated either by the word "Extract" or by a row of four dots at the beginning or end. (On the other hand I have made no attempt to indicate where whole conversations, or indeed whole diary-entries, have been omitted, because although the reader may wish to know that a conversation as reproduced here is incomplete, it seems purposeless to indicate that an entire conversation with a person or persons unknown has been left out).

Nevertheless, while trying to reproduce Scott faithfully, I have thought it desirable to take some minor liberties with his text, remembering that this book is intended for a wider audience than historical researchers. Scott's diaries present certain problems to the editor: they consist of large slabs of material with few if any paragraphs, they contain numerous abbreviations and even short-hand devices, and they have occasional misspellings or inconsistencies of spelling. In addition there is the problem presented by Scott's footnotes. Having written up his diary he would frequently go through adding points which he had forgotten to include. These are usually not footnotes proper, that is they are not asides or minor points of information which were excluded from the main body of the text because they would have hung up the flow of the narrative. They are additional information which simply got overlooked by Scott the first time through. To relegate them to the bottom of the page would in many instances be as inappropriate as it would be in other cases to bring them into the text at the point Scott indicated.

In all these minor respects I have been somewhat cavalier with Scott's text. I have made paragraphs-breaks where the sense appeared to require them, because it seemed to me that the reader's need for them outweighed the danger that I might marginally alter Scott's meaning by putting them in. I have corrected or standardised spelling, and have unscrambled every abbreviation (without trying to decide whether a speaker did in fact say "Ll.G." or "M.G." instead of "Lloyd George" or "Manchester Guardian"). As for Scott's footnotes, I have done with them what seemed appropriate. Some, if they contained little of value, have been left out altogether. (No indication is given of these omissions. After all, to include in this book a footnote which consisted of nothing but a set of dots might seem a trifle precious.) The rest have been left as footnotes, or brought into the text—sometimes in brackets—at the point Scott indicated, or brought into the text somewhere else. In each case, the sense of the passage, and the question of readability, have decided the issue. For example, sometimes Scott indicated a footnote in the middle of a sentence, yet the footnote itself consisted of several sentences. This has usually been brought into the body of the text at the nearest appropriate point, perhaps becoming a paragraph on its own, but not quite at the position Scott had suggested.

In another way I have tinkered slightly with Scott's text. Sometimes he would try to make his diary-entries easier for his readers (and he did intend the diaries to be read by people like Hobhouse) by the use of underlinings, either of the names of the people he was talking to or of the main topics of their conversation. These are a hindrance rather than a help. He was very erratic in using underlining, employing it at some stages of his narrative and not at others, so that to the unsuspecting reader it looks as if he was providing emphasis for certain names or points when he was doing nothing of the sort. I have simply omitted these underlinings, and kept his underlinings only when he was indeed using them for emphasis. Similarly, Scott's enumeration of points in a conversation has been omitted on those occasions where it has seemed more likely to provide confusion than illumination.

Finally, to set the record straight, it may be noted that in order to make Scott's sense clearer, brackets or dashes have been inserted into his text at the following places: page 52, lines 30 and 32; page 60, lines 8 and 9; page 65, lines 2 and 3; page 65, line 17; page 73, lines 7 and 8; page 94, lines 20 and 21; page 155, lines 24 and 26; page 161, lines 19 and 22; page 190, lines 31 and 32; page 264, lines 15 and 17; page 268, line 3; page 279, lines 29 and 30; page 313, lines 12 and 14; page 317, lines 15 and 16; page 348, lines 1 and 2; page 372, lines 3 and 7; page 395, lines 22 and 23; page 403, lines 3, 37 and 38; page 412, lines 4 and 5; page 485, lines 5 and 10; page 486, lines 1 and 2; and that the last paragraph on page 48 and the first on page 49 have been brought in from later in Scott's text.

Introduction

I

In February 1911, C. P. Scott started keeping a diary. The date has no significance and the diary no conscious beginning. Its first entry is a minor tale of a cabinet minister fallen among furious ladies; the minister in question does not re-appear in its pages. Perhaps there were earlier entries which have been lost, but there is no compelling reason to suppose so. Scott came upon diary-keeping by chance, took to the practice slowly and erratically, and then allowed it to become a habit. It required another four years before the diaries developed any continuity or solidity. But by the time the First World War was entering its second year, Scott, unwittingly, was committing to paper a political narrative of first-class importance.

II

At the beginning of 1911, Charles Prestwich Scott was 64 years old. His wife was dead, his family grown up. He had edited the *Manchester Guardian* for nearly forty years, and for four had been its principal proprietor. He had reached an age where most men's careers are coming to a close. But for Scott, this was the reverse of true. He was if anything at the height of his powers, and entering on his period of greatest influence. By 1911 he had become the close companion of men who were deciding the destinies of the nation, as well as being himself the editor of a newspaper with which (in J. L. Garvin's phrase) the whole world had to reckon.

The political stance of the *Manchester Guardian*, as of its editor, was unequivocal. It was a journal of the Liberal left, espousing causes like social reform, the alliance between Liberalism and Labour, the female suffrage, Irish Home Rule, and a pacific foreign policy. Among the things it opposed were the excesses of British imperialism, the Russian autocracy, the pretensions of the House of Lords, and lavish expenditure on armaments. In the disputes which had racked the Liberal party regarding the Boer war, it had come down unreservedly on the side of the "pro-Boers" against the "Imperialists"—Liberal or Conservative.

Scott had himself participated in the political struggles of the turn of the century. He had entered Parliament in 1895 as Liberal member for a Lancashire constituency, and had retained his seat until the beginning of 1906. But although he had done good service in advocating proposals like old age pensions, and in attacking Britain's "forward" policy in China and South Africa, Scott as a parliamentarian had not been a success. Certainly his protest in 1899 against the conduct of British forces in the Soudan had attracted the attention of the young Winston Churchill.[1] But for the most part he had lacked the voice and the manner to command the attention of a hostile House. Moreover, Scott had never been able to devote himself single-mindedly to the affairs of Parliament. The needs of a great newspaper situated in the north of England, and the care of a dying wife, had made great claims upon him. In 1903 he had announced that he would not re-contest his seat at the next general election.

Yet the years in Parliament had not been wasted. In 1905, during Scott's last months there, the Conservative grip on office which had lasted for most of twenty years was finally broken. The men with whom he had sat in opposition moved on to the government benches. Some of his close associates received posts in the new Liberal government. In January 1906 the Liberals won a smashing electoral victory. Although hereafter Scott was no longer in the House, or even resident in London for more than a few days at a time, he maintained his ties with former colleagues. They welcomed his advice, and no doubt hoped to gain his journalistic support. Hence they encouraged him to visit them in London, unburdening their hearts and revealing their secrets. One day in the train going back, Scott jotted down an account of the conversations he had just had with members of the government. So began the diaries.

III

These are, then, diaries in a particular sense. They are not a record of Scott's day-to-day life, and only rarely recount conversations in the northern city where he lived and worked. Strictly speaking, they are

[1] See Winston Churchill, *My Early Life* (The Reprint Society, London, 1944), p. 241.

not a document about Scott at all. They are an account of what, during his periodic visits to the south, he learned about the affairs of state. Thus their chief interest lies in what they reveal about the decisions that were being taken at the top and the men who were taking them.

Where the diaries are personal to Scott is, first, in the choice of issues which he particularly wanted to hear discussed, and secondly in the choice of individuals with whom he wanted to discuss them. Not all doors were equally open to him, nor did he seek the company equally of all politicians. Although a journalist, he was not looking for news when he went calling in London. His intention was political. He wished to know what the government was proposing to do, and where possible to influence its actions—to adapt Bagehot, he wanted to be consulted, to encourage, and to warn. So he spent little time with those who, though they might have provided him with information, were unlikely to respond to his advice. He did not cultivate leaders of the Conservative party,[2] who in his view had misgoverned the country during his years in Parliament. And he tended to regard with suspicion that section of Liberals who had condoned the worst actions of the late Conservative regime. Instead he looked most readily to the anti-imperialist Liberals who had been his allies during his parliamentary career.

This does not mean that the individuals who figure prominently in Scott's diaries are exclusively those with whom he had worked as an M.P. He sought the company of anyone who might assist the causes dear to his heart. Some examples will show this. Shortly before the war, when he was opposing increases in naval expenditure, and again during the first years of the war, when he was opposing conscription, Scott saw much of Reginald McKenna and Sir John Simon, two Liberal ministers who shared his views on these matters. But in other respects Scott was far removed from these men, who belonged on the *laissez-faire*, "business" wing of the party; so thereafter he saw little or nothing of them. Similarly, he had many conversations in 1916 with Winston Churchill, because he believed that the nation was in grave danger and that it ought to be employing Churchill's services fully; after that he met him rarely.

Yet having said this, it is still the case that some of the people he visited most frequently in and after 1911 were allies from an earlier stage: men to whom he was tied by past association as well as present concern. Especially is this true of the individual who figures in the diaries most prominently of all.

[2] Or Unionist party, as it was then often called.

IV

One man dominates Scott's pages. Many times it seemed that he would finally be driven (or expel himself) from them, but always he recovered the centre of the stage. Indeed it may be thought that the chief interest of this volume lies in the insights it provides into the career and character of David Lloyd George.

Such insights are none too common. Admittedly a vast amount has been written about Lloyd George. Yet the detailed scrutiny needed to understand him—the study in depth of his conduct during a series of key episodes—has largely been lacking. Those memoirs and diaries which have been published (no doubt there are others of importance yet to appear) have offered much external information but little unravelling of his character. Scott takes us a stage further. Admittedly he deals only with certain years of Lloyd George's career, and certain events within those years. But some of these events were crucial for an understanding of Lloyd George, and Scott recounts them in detail. More than this, he approached Lloyd George with a rare blend of sympathy and dispassion, of personal involvement offset by cool detachment. Hence his narrative makes possible a deeper comprehension of the man who dominated his political life.

There is a question here, though it is certainly no new question. During Scott's lifetime, it was often wondered how a man of his probity and rigid principles could continue to associate with a politician whose name was a byword for deviousness and inconstancy. The mystery was deepened by the part which Scott played in the personal rivalry which racked the Liberal party: the feud between Lloyd George and the Liberal leader H. H. Asquith. That Scott should have taken Lloyd George's side at every crucial stage in this struggle seemed to many good Liberals past comprehending.

Scott's attitude was not always interpreted to his credit. It was sometimes claimed that Asquith maintained a proper reticence in his relations with the press, whereas Lloyd George employed all his resources of flattery and charm to seduce journalists to his cause. Scott, it was sometimes suggested, was not immune from such blandishments.

One of the most trenchant statements to this effect is provided in the following extract from the autobiography of Vivian Phillipps. Phillipps was at various stages private secretary to Asquith and Liberal chief whip, and his devotion to his leader caused him to figure in some painful disputes with Scott. In a chapter entitled "At Liberal Headquarters" he writes:

One of my frequent visitors was C. P. Scott, the famous Editor of the *Manchester Guardian*. Scott had been one of the victorious Manchester Liberals in the Liberal landslide of 1906, but during his four years in the House, from 1906 to 1910, he had failed to make the mark which had been expected of him by many who took his *Manchester Guardian* leaders as their political bible.

Whether this produced in him some sort of antipathy to the Liberal Government of those days, and, possibly, to Asquith as its head, I know not, but by the time that I began to meet him in 1917, he was distinctly Coalition-minded and strong in his approval of Lloyd George as the head of the then Coalition Government.

Lloyd George was fully alive to the importance of keeping the *Manchester Guardian* friendly, and spared no pains to pay special attentions to Scott. Every now and then he would have C.P. to breakfast with him at 10 Downing Street, and this was almost invariably followed by a visit to me from C.P. who would spend some time explaining to me what a good and true Liberal Lloyd George was, in spite of his predominantly Tory Cabinet, and hinting that it was very unfortunate that Asquith should adopt a critical attitude to a Coalition of which Lloyd George was the head.

More than once, on these occasions, I suggested to him that perhaps he would like to have a talk with Asquith, adding that I was sure that I could arrange it at some time to suit him, but he always found some reason why he was unable to manage it.

At a later stage, when the Coalition was rocking from one blunder to another, he became more and more uncomfortable, and his anxiety to assure me (presumably for transmission to Asquith) that Lloyd George, in spite of the Coalition's performances, was "just as good a Liberal as he had always been", was almost pathetic.

The fact was that there was a streak of vanity in C.P. on which Lloyd George was not slow to play. Whenever Lloyd George spoke in Manchester, C.P. must always be given a seat on the platform close to him and Ll.G. would never miss referring to his presence as that of "the world's greatest living journalist".

On the other hand, Asquith, with his rooted dislike of anything like currying favour with the Press, would use none of these arts, and there it was.

Poor old C.P.! During the final somersaults of the Coalition in

1922, he was hard put to it to find a saving word for Ll.G., and I remember H. W. Massingham, at that time Editor of *The Nation*, saying at lunch at the Club one day, "To me there are few spectacles more melancholy than that of dear old C. P. Scott drearily dredging in a foul pond for the soul of Ll.G.".[3]

Is this a fair assessment? Some of it, clearly, is nonsense. Scott did not sit in the Parliament of 1906-10 at all, so he can hardly have been resentful of Asquith's success as Prime Minister because he himself was making no great impression. Certainly when he was in the House (from 1895 to 1905) he may have recognised that Asquith was his superior as a parliamentarian. But Asquith's political stature had become apparent before Scott ever entered the Commons, for Asquith had been the one real success of the short-lived Rosebery government from 1893 to 1895. The Liberal who made his reputation while Scott sat in Parliament was not Asquith, but Lloyd George; which pretty effectively disposes of Phillipps's "jealousy" conjecture.

Yet for all its inaccuracies and exaggerations, Phillipps's account cannot simply be ignored. It is a fact of significance that an old-style Liberal like himself and a left-wing radical like Massingham, who can have agreed on precious little else, were at one in deploring Scott's un-abated sympathy for Lloyd George. Apparently Scott, whether from vanity or some more noble cause, was able throughout his career to see merits in Lloyd George which escaped many other Liberals. No doubt Lloyd George's deference towards him in part explains this. But it is not certain that Scott was wrong to respond positively to what, after all, seems to have been a pretty genuine display of respect. And it cannot justly be said that Lloyd George's show of respect robbed Scott of his critical faculties. Indeed the reader of the diaries is more likely to be impressed by his often quite disenchanted view of Lloyd George than by any excessive indulgence.

Where Scott differed from a fellow-radical like Massingham—not to say a committed Asquithian like Phillipps—was that he could never bring himself utterly to lose faith in Lloyd George. He saw his faults, but not to the exclusion of his other qualities. He recognised his un-trustworthiness and condemned his violations of Liberal beliefs. But these never quite convinced Scott that Lloyd George was incorrigible. Other Liberals, while perhaps agreeing with him in all else, did come to feel this. Lloyd George seemed to them so devious, and his actions

[3] Vivian Phillipps, *My Days and Ways*, n.d. (c 1943), printed "for private circulation only", pp. 54-5.

so deplorable, that they eventually regarded him as beyond redemption. And the important question, at least in the present context, is not why they felt like this, but why Scott did not.

V

Three points need to be taken into account here. In the first place, it is possible to exaggerate the differences in character between Scott and Lloyd George. Appearances favoured Scott. With his piercing blue eyes and commanding white beard, he looked like a prophet descending from the mountain to rebuke unrighteousness. In this respect it was probably to his advantage that, in the period covered by his diaries, he lived in the north and only came to London on special occasions. But to those who worked with him on the *Manchester Guardian*—who were immersed in the daily affairs of the newspaper, its policies and its personalities—he seemed a more complex character. Scott is best remembered for having uttered the dictum, "Comment is free, but facts are sacred". But (if Mr. Malcolm Muggeridge's recollection is correct) he also wrote on one occasion, "Truth like everything else should be economised".[4] These two statements are not, as they might seem at first, necessarily contradictory. But they do suggest that Scott's personality—like truth itself—was complex and many-sided rather than simple and straightforward. That is, he was not at all out of his depth when dealing with men whose business it was to master the arts of the possible.

Probably the most perceptive remarks on Scott's character have been made by Kingsley Martin (who, like Malcolm Muggeridge, was on the staff of the *Guardian* during Scott's last years).[5] Mr. Martin considers it unfortunate that commentators on Scott have dealt so exclusively with "his courage and integrity, his humanitarianism and his championship of unpopular causes." He points out that there were additional qualities to Scott which need to be taken into account:

> his remarkable astuteness, his diplomatic gift, his caution, his capacity for compromise, his knowledge of when to strike and when to forbear. C. P. Scott had something of the fox in him, as well as much of the lion. He was no champion of lost causes: he

[4] The quotation appears in Mr. Muggeridge's suppressed novel *Picture Palace* (1934), where Scott appears as Old Savoury and his newspaper as the Accringthorpe Courier.
[5] See Kingsley Martin, *Father Figures* (Hutchinson, London, 1966), p. 168.

27

was, on the contrary, the benignly Machiavellian advocate of causes which less far-sighted men thought lost or utopian.

This pen-portrait suggests that Scott was composed of many of the same elements as Lloyd George. Certainly the elements were mixed in markedly different proportions; and the difference in proportions resulted in very different characters. But even so, Scott had enough in common with Lloyd George that, as he was not likely to be gulled by Lloyd George's flattery, neither was he separated from him by any sort of a gulf separating righteousness from unrighteousness.

The second point is this. Great Britain, during the period covered by these diaries, passed from one severe crisis to another. Scott was bound to ask who was the man best equipped to lead it through its difficulties—and to do so in a way which would both preserve the state and advance the causes for which his newspaper stood. Was Asquith, the Liberal leader and (from 1908 to 1916) Prime Minister as well? Was Balfour, or Bonar Law, or Baldwin, the successive leaders of the Conservative party? Was Ramsay MacDonald, the principal figure in the Labour party? In Scott's view, all were seriously wanting. Compared with them, only Lloyd George—the "dynamic force" whom Baldwin was to condemn for that very quality—possessed the initiative, flair, and courage to bring the nation through its troubles. Admittedly it was never quite certain that he would give the required lead, or give it in the right direction; and when he did not, Scott was prompt to condemn him. But, compared with his contemporaries, Lloyd George seemed incomparably the nation's best hope.

This leads to the third point. Scott's conviction that Lloyd George possessed the capacity to direct the nation in the way it ought to go, at whatever cost and even danger to himself, was not based on conjecture. During what to Scott had been the supreme political test, Lloyd George had done it. In the fiery ordeal of the Boer War, Lloyd George and Scott had stood together against the fierce antagonism of the whole Conservative party, many Liberals, and the weight of public and press opinion. These events had formed a bond between the two men which Lloyd George's subsequent back-slidings never quite severed.

There are many indications of the union which this experience created between them. In November 1901 Lloyd George appeared in Scott's constituency to speak of him as "one of the heroes of the struggle", "one of the ablest men they had and the most courageous Member who had ever been returned. . . . He had made sacrifices and had run risks which few realised in the part which he had taken in this struggle—the greatest that England had passed through, he thought, for a century."[6] Two years later, when Scott announced his decision not again to contest his seat, Lloyd George wrote to him:

> I am very sorry to learn that you have made up your mind not to be in the next Parliament. We shall miss you sadly for the work of the "Pro-Boers" is only beginning. It will need as much pressure to keep a Liberal Government straight as a Tory.[7]

In a letter written near the end of his life, Scott recurred to these events. In April 1930, at the age of 83, he was presented with the freedom of the city of Manchester, and Lloyd George sent a telegram expressing his delight "that my native city is honouring itself today by conferring its highest distinction upon the greatest Liberal publicist of the day." Scott wrote in reply:

> Very many thanks for your kind message today. It was good of you to remember the occasion. I think the best thing the Manchester Guardian has done in my time was to oppose the Boer War, and I thought of that when your telegram was read. We were together there.

VI

If Scott's alliance with Lloyd George originated in the Boer War, so in a measure did his suspicion of Asquith. Clearly Asquith was one of those Liberals who, in the eyes of "pro-Boers", needed to be kept "straight". He had been one of the principal "Liberal Imperialists"; that is, he had supported Conservative policy in South Africa not only against out-and-out opponents of the Boer War like Lloyd George, but against moderate critics like Sir Henry Campbell-Bannerman (the leader of the Liberal party from 1899 to 1908). This for Scott was a grave misdemeanour. Thereafter, he regarded Asquith as a doubtful asset to the Liberal cause. Scott's attitude on the matter was made quite evident in February and March 1908. Campbell-Bannerman, who since 1905 had been Liberal Prime Minister, fell gravely ill, and it was everywhere assumed that Asquith would succeed him. The *Manchester Guardian*, alone among Liberal papers, declined to welcome the prospect. It did not put up a rival candidate to Asquith—though it had

[6]Press cutting in the Lloyd George Papers.
[7]Lloyd George to C.P.S., 12 October 1903.

initially hoped that Campbell-Bannerman would survive long enough to make this possible[8]—but it demanded guarantees of Asquith's good behaviour before he should become leader. In a letter to Scott on 3 March, L. T. Hobhouse, who was probably Scott's closest confidant in these matters, wrote:

> I am clear now that we cannot directly oppose Asquith for the present. But I think we ought at the outset to indicate reserves, and to press in the direction George suggests. I have drafted something which might perhaps serve as the basis of an article, a letter or possibly a leader. . . . pray alter it as you think best.

In a pungent editorial on 6 March 1908, which was presumably the product of the Scott-Hobhouse collaboration, the *Manchester Guardian* gave its reasons for doubting Asquith.

> From the beginning of the Armenian troubles to the close of the Boer War [it stated] the Liberal party in every effort that it made for justice and humanity found upon its flank men of high position in its own ranks raking its attack with a cross-fire. The culminating point was reached when it was proclaimed that the Liberal slate was to be wiped clean of its old formulae, and that in particular the Irish policy for the sake of which the party had virtually wandered in the wilderness for twenty years was to be abandoned and the central contention of its opponents to be upheld. At the same time a Liberal League was formed to uphold these new principles, or rather negations of principle. Of this League Mr. Asquith was a distinguished vice president. He has doubtless since dissociated himself from its founders. Nor did he ever go so far as some of his distinguished colleagues in the advocacy of Unionism and the Imperial idea. But that through the long years of Opposition, and particularly in the crisis of the Boer War, his influence told in that direction is not a matter which admits of controversy. . . . It would be ungracious and untimely to emphasise a personal contrast. Mr. Asquith is laying the party under real and present obligations for his masterly exposition of the Licensing Bill and for his able conduct of business. But the fact remains that those Liberals who look to the party for the resolute championship of democratic ideas at home and abroad cannot entrust him with their political destinies with the kind of confidence which they extend to the present Prime Minister. They can accept his leadership only under reserve, and, it

[8]See the leading article in the *Manchester Guardian*, 19 February 1908.

seems to us, only with adequate guarantees for the fuller representation in the councils of the party of the sounder and more decided
Liberal traditions.

This last sentence gives the clue to the line of attack proposed by
Lloyd George ("the direction George suggests"): that Asquith could
only be accepted as Liberal leader if the radical element in the cabinet
was strengthened. It would shake "the foundations of party confidence", continued the *Guardian*, if the present cabinet, minus Campbell-Bannerman, should continue. In order to avoid this, "the most
trusted Liberal leaders" must be "more fully recognised in the distribution of offices."

> Men like Mr. Lloyd-George, for example, whose official career has
> been one unbroken series of brilliant successes, would, if their
> authoritative position was adequately recognised, serve as a guar-
> antee to the party at large.

The paper went on to name other individuals worthy of advancement,
and to put in a claim for "some of the younger men . . . whose presence
would be a pledge of vital Liberalism." "A reconstruction on such lines
as these would seem to us a necessary corollary of any such change of
leadership as is now suggested. The alternative would be a position of
highly unstable equilibrium."

The paper did not recur to this subject for a month. When it did (on
Campbell-Bannerman's resignation) it seemed reconciled to Asquith's
succession.[9]

> Mr. Asquith's Ministerial experience, his splendid services to Free
> Trade, his Parliamentary skill, the success with which he has during
> this session acted as Sir Henry Campbell-Bannerman's deputy, and
> . . . the advice which Sir Henry Campbell-Bannerman has no doubt
> given to the King—all these considerations have rendered it certain
> that Mr. Asquith would be asked to form the new Ministry.

But the *Manchester Guardian* still thought it necessary to face certain
facts: that Campbell-Bannerman had enjoyed the full trust of the party,
having "stood fast by essential Liberalism in its darkest days" and
"championed the cause of freedom when it was most unpopular";
and that Asquith would only succeed in his new post if he managed to
restore this situation. He would do so, argued the paper, only if he
gave a proper place in the counsels of the party to the men in whom it

[9] *Manchester Guardian*, 6 April 1908.

reposed full confidence. The implication was clear that, for Scott, Asquith did not possess such confidence; and it was again stated explicitly that Lloyd George, above all others, did.

VII

Yet it would be wrong to conclude that Scott's allegiance in the subsequent conflicts between Asquith and Lloyd George had been wholly determined in advance, by the attitude of the contestants towards the Boer War. In June 1901, when the conflict within the Liberal party was at its height, Scott had written to Hobhouse: ". . . I detest personal quarrels and I would do nothing whatever to make it more difficult than it need be for any of these men [i.e. the Liberal Imperialists] to take the right course. [Sir Edward] Grey I fancy is hopeless by conviction; Asquith, I should say, not at all so but much corrupted by his surroundings—a great Parliamentary force, possible yet to be utilized." And although in 1908 the *Manchester Guardian* regarded Lloyd George as the best Liberal available, this did not mean that its editor was uncritical of him. In August of that year Scott was very concerned about some of his attitudes to Germany. Writing to Hobhouse, Scott made remarks like: "I think Lloyd George is on a very dangerous track. He is trying to force the German Government into a definite agreement for the limitation of naval armaments and as an alternative would apparently favour the wild scheme of a 100 million naval loan. He won't succeed and we at least will oppose the loan scheme tooth and nail."

The situation, then, may be summed up as follows. The struggle over the Boer War had predisposed Scott strongly in favour of Lloyd George and against Asquith; but it had not settled his attitude for good and all. It rested with their conduct during the ensuing years to decide whether Lloyd George would ever quite exhaust the credit balance he had laid up for himself, and whether Asquith would ultimately atone for his early misdemeanours. Only during the period covered by Scott's diaries did these issues work themselves out to a final conclusion.

1. The Liberal Government and Its Problems, 1911-1914

When Scott made his first diary-entry, the Liberal government was nearly six years old. It had survived the transition from Campbell-Bannerman to Asquith, and was starting to build up a formidable record of legislation. In 1910 it contested two general elections, fought largely over the powers of the House of Lords. The results of these elections deprived the Liberal party of an independent majority in Parliament; but with the support of the small Labour party and the Irish Nationalists, Asquith was returned securely to office. His first action was to curtail decisively the powers of the Upper House. With the passage of the Parliament Act in 1911 the Lords could only delay a measure for three years, not veto it indefinitely. This was a mighty triumph for the Liberals.

But the government was beset by serious difficulties, and some of these grew in intensity after 1911. There was the problem of the suffragettes—those supporters of the female suffrage who were tired of trying to proceed by constitutional means, and instead resorted to violence. There was a wave of industrial unrest, and the spread of anti-parliamentary views amongst a section of the working class. Further, the Irish problem had entered a new phase. By curtailing the veto of the House of Lords, the government had made it possible to enact Home Rule by 1914. Asquith's dependence on the Irish Nationalists, and the Home Rule proclivities of his own party, made it certain that he would proceed with this measure. His decision raised serious difficulties, which the government was loath to face. The Irish Nationalists demanded Home Rule for all of Ireland. Ulster (i.e. the counties in the north-east) was prepared to resist this by force. The Conservatives, made reckless by their persistent failure at the polls and deeply anti-pathetic to Ireland, backed up Ulster's defiance; so did a section of the army. These were problems enough for any government, but there remained another more serious than all the rest: the menacing international situation, and the government's divisions about what measures should be taken to meet it.

Scott was profoundly concerned about all these issues. But as a novice at diary-keeping, he did not attempt to make a consecutive record of the government's actions during the last years of peace. This chapter is episodic, and makes no mention of some large questions which were certainly engaging Scott. It may

Barry University Library

Miami, FL 33161

further be noted that a good many diary-entries are not reproduced here, because they are too fragmentary to be very informative. But allowing for this, what follows still throws important light on some of the principal issues and individuals of the day.

1] THE WILD WOMEN

On the face of it, the issue of votes for women was one of the minor problems of the day. Yet in its time it generated a deal of controversy. For one thing the Liberal government was divided on the matter: thus Lloyd George and Sir Edward Grey, the Foreign Secretary, supported the female suffrage, but Asquith strongly opposed it. Again, the suffragists were themselves deeply divided. Some wanted only a mild measure, confining the vote to women of property. Others (including Lloyd George) argued that this would favour the Conservatives, and that women must receive the vote on the same terms as men. Even more serious was the division over tactics. Most suffragists, including Scott, wished to proceed by constitutional means. But they were overshadowed by the small section of militants led by Mrs. E. Pankhurst. This group favoured "direct action", believing that only by intimidating members of the government (whether friendly or hostile to their cause), creating a public nuisance, and enduring suffering themselves, would they bring the male sex to heel.

Militancy had a dual effect. It roused those taking part in it to a high pitch of fervour and devotion. This is reflected in several of Mrs. Pankhurst's letters to Scott, two of which are quoted below. But it provoked fierce resentment not only among the opponents but also among the more tepid supporters of female suffrage. This becomes apparent in the first diary extract, recording an interview with Augustine Birrell, the amiable Secretary of State for Ireland and victim of a militant "outrage".

Mrs. E. Pankhurst to C.P.S., 21 July 1909 (Extract)

I am surprised that you should quibble as to what is a political offence when the leaders of your Party and the Government itself are fêting men from Turkey who by violence have just secured Constitutional rights! Why bomb throwing shooting and stone throwing are time honoured masculine political arguments! The long boycott by your own paper of woman suffrage which persisted until we began in a very mild way to make ourselves unpleasant is evidence that so long as women relied on the justice of their demands they were treated with contempt.[1]

[1]Until Scott became proprietor of the *Manchester Guardian*, he was not free to advocate woman's suffrage. The paper's change of policy owed nothing to the militants.

Mrs. Pankhurst to C.P.S., 16 August 1910

You have known Mrs. Elmy so long as a devoted worker in the Woman's Movement and also as a contributor to the "Guardian" that I am sure you will like to know what we are doing to show appreciation of her work. She will not live much longer[,] indeed I fear that she will be soon numbered with those who have died heartbroken and despairing of ever obtaining justice at the hands of hypocritical politicians. Well some of us mean to make a good fight for it before we are old and helpless as she is. . . .

You have taken my criticism so kindly in the past that I venture to say how disappointed I am that there was no leader in the "Guardian" commenting on Mr. Lloyd George's dishonest speech made to the Liberal Women at Carnarvon. Can you and other Liberals wonder that we have come to the conclusion that we must take up again the weapons we laid down after the General Election? Unless there is a Governmental change of front in November this is what we mean to do and it is certain that the general public understanding and sympathising with our disappointment will not blame us.

Already names are pouring in for a deputation and many women are joining who have hitherto held aloof but who feel they cannot with self respect do so any longer.

Diary, 2 February 1911

Birrell at Irish Office 12.30—1.
My object was to enlist his interest in the Cabinet for the solution of the Women's Suffrage question. I found him friendly and genial to me but deeply exasperated against the women who had attacked and injured him—perhaps permanently—and evidently quite prepared to see the suffrage question shelved in this Parliament and indefinitely postponed. When I pointed out the great danger that then might happen he said it was just what he expected would happen.

He said I could have little idea of the great and increasing exasperation caused by the methods of the militants and said he had, after the attack on him, been overwhelmed with letters from people resenting it in the most violent language, and saying now he would surely no longer support the Suffrage agitation. I don't think he will go back on his pledges and convictions in this matter but evidently no active support can be looked for from him. He will take no further concern in the matter.

On the merits he is in favour of the sort of solution proposed in the Conciliation Bill[2] and dead against adult suffrage. He is against it for men no less than for women—thinks we have gone quite far enough in the extension of the franchise. . . .

As to what should be done to press forward the Conciliation Bill he gave no advice. . . .

The attack on him. He gave me full particulars. He was walking alone from the House to his club (the Athenaeum) and had got within a few yards of the steps leading up to the Duke of York's monument. He was still on the roadway—not the pavement—when a body of about 20 suffragettes on their way to take the Prime Minister's house from the rear—Horse Guard's Parade side—came right on to him. Some one cried "Here's Mr. Birrell" (it is false, he said parenthetically, to pretend they didn't know me and mistook me for somebody else) and the whole body immediately swarmed round me. I was not kicked, but they pulled me about and hustled me, "stroked" my face, knocked off my hat and kicked it about and one whose unpleasant features yet dwell in my memory harangued me with "Oh! you wicked man; you must be a wicked man not to help us" and so forth. I didn't like to use my fists and I couldn't swing my umbrella, I couldn't even get it up to swing, and I had that heavy coat on (pointing to a heavy fur-lined coat) but I struggled to get free and in so doing I twisted my knee (pointing to his left knee) and slipped the knee-cap (I had done the same thing before to my right knee). It was excessively painful and I was in terror at the same time that they would knock off my spectacles in which case I should have been absolutely blind. I don't know what I should have done when happily at this moment Lionel — Lord (Crewes?) secretary[3] drove up in a motor, saw [what] was taking place and jumping out scattered the women right and left and rescued me. I felt like a man attacked by pygmies who overcome him by their numbers. They then left me.

There was no attempt to do me any serious physical injury and if I had lain down on the ground I don't suppose they would have jumped upon me but it was a brutal, outrageous and unprovoked assault and it may lame me for life. Can I walk? Oh! yes I can walk but I can't take any strong exercise on which I depend for health. I've just been to

[2]This bill proposed giving the vote only to those women who occupied domiciles in their own right—generally the elderly and Conservative.
[3]The omission and question-mark are Scott's.

Switzerland and I haven't enjoyed myself a bit—couldn't climb or do anything. The doctors tell me the knee may get right in a few months but it will be more liable to slip again and if it does I may have to have the cap removed and that may mean a stiff leg. I couldn't stand that. In any case I shall probably be, like a good many others, a weak-kneed politician to the end of my life. And so he ended on a joke.

He seemed to me in a nervous state though he looked well and all the time after the first few words he kept wringing his hands in a way I have never seen a man do before.

11] WARSHIPS

British foreign policy revolved around the German navy. Germany was the greatest industrial power on the Continent; and the greatest military power in the world. With the invention of the super-battleship—the Dreadnought—the Germans were theoretically in a position to overtake Britain's naval strength, and so destroy Britain's security. Inevitably British foreign policy was geared to preventing this happening.

In 1909, anxiety over German naval-building became acute among the government's naval advisers. Their case was pressed strongly in the cabinet by Reginald McKenna, the First Lord of the Admiralty. The Liberal government became acutely divided. McKenna and his associates insisted that the number of new Dreadnoughts to be built in the coming year should exceed the four originally projected. Their adversaries claimed that the German menace was a myth and that the money was needed for social reform. The chief exponents of the latter view at this time were Lloyd George, Chancellor of the Exchequer, and Winston Churchill, then President of the Board of Trade. Asquith wrote regarding them in February 1909: "Winston and Lloyd George by their combined machinations have got the bulk of the Liberal press into the same camp. . . . [They] go about darkly hinting at resignation (which is bluff) . . . . but there are moments when I am disposed summarily to cashier them both."[4]

Ultimately, with the aid of strong Conservative pressure and a public outcry, the advocates of an increased navy were successful. Instead of the four battleships which Lloyd George and Churchill had been prepared to concede, and the six originally demanded by McKenna, eight were built. Scott was not pleased.

The controversy revived sharply in February 1911. McKenna had to admit that his fears of two years earlier regarding the rate of German naval-building had been proved unfounded. The "economists" in the cabinet used this as ground for demanding a reduction either in the number of ships to be built immediately,

[4]J. A. Spender and C. Asquith, *Life of Herbert Henry Asquith, Lord Oxford and Asquith* (Hutchinson, London, 1932),vol. I, p. 254.

or else in the long-term naval expenditure. Once again, Lloyd George took the lead.

Diary, 16 February 1911

Lloyd George

Breakfast 9.15—11. C. F. G. Masterman[5] and his wife also there. Before they came in Lloyd George briefly explained situation. Naval Construction Programme had to be settled. McKenna wholly in the hands of the Admirals and both threatening resignation if the whole of their demands were not satisfied. It was a question whether or not he should threaten to do the same if they were.

Conversation on this situation went on freely throughout breakfast-time and afterwards and hardly anything else was discussed. Masterman was all for letting things slide and postponing the decisive stand till after the Parliament Bill was through: "then I should not much mind what happened". Lloyd George was evidently longing to fight now but not sure of his ground. He would not "bluff"—I cordially agreed—but if he threatened resignation must be prepared to carry it through. It appeared that he is practically alone in the Cabinet; even Churchill would probably not resign with him.

I urged that it was incredible that Asquith should venture to sacrifice him but he was not sure of this—as against McKenna certainly, but as against him and all the naval Lords perhaps no. The precise demands of these last were never definitely stated, but I assumed that they wanted 5 or 6 Dreadnoughts (as stated by the "Daily Mail") and that Lloyd George might fairly concede 4, though that was much more than was necessary[,] and this was not contradicted. "If I go out" said Lloyd George "I go out to fight and carry the war into the country".

Masterman declared that if he resigned the Government would be so weakened that it could not carry the Parliament Bill; then, rather inconsistently, warned Lloyd George of the fate of Randolph Churchill.[6] Lloyd George disputed the parallel which would only have applied if Churchill had been defending traditional Toryism and Salisbury attacking it. I put it to George that his position was far

---

[5] Active Liberal social reformer and Under-Secretary for the Home Department.
[6] In 1886 Lord Randolph Churchill, Winston Churchill's father and one of the rising stars of the Tory party, had precipitately resigned as Chancellor of the Exchequer from Lord Salisbury's Conservative ministry because he could not secure reductions he was demanding in naval and military estimates. He never returned to office—an experience which haunted political aspirants for many years to come.

stronger now than when an election was pending and any division would have been fatal. George evidently feeling about for a compromise. The time no doubt inopportune, "but when", he asked, "is the time opportune for breaking up a Government and if there were strong reasons this session there would be strong reasons also next session and the session after." Meanwhile the policy and expenditure of the country were being dictated by the Sea Lords whose demands grew and their power with it and who must be met and defeated if a tolerable state of things was to be restored. (He mentioned incidentally that under the existing practice they were required to sign the naval estimates certifying them to be adequate for the security of the country —a most improper thing).

How if power were taken to build 5 ships and two of them were to be treated as contingent so as to postpone the conflict till September when the Parliament Bill would be passed [?] I pointed out that if power were taken experience seemed to show that it would almost certainly be used and that it would be far more effective to knock off one ship definitely than two contingently. I said somebody had got to make a stand, that the Government would have to be attacked as false to Liberal principles and he with the rest if he stood in with them. He agreed. I begged him not to allow us to be forced into such a position.

When I left he was to see Asquith in a few minutes. He had already pointed out to him, he told me at the beginning, that the Government is becoming virtually a Liberal Imperialist Government.

Lloyd George to C.P.S., 16 February 1911

I think I have accomplished something which was worth the risk I actually took. I felt I could not go on assenting meekly to this growth of expenditure on the mechanism of butchery. After you left I made up my mind to take the decisive step. Tonight I have an offer which is so substantial an approximation to my own proposal that I have concluded it would be impossible for me to reject it.

Can you come along about 10.45. . . .

Many thanks for your kind help.

Diary, 17 February 1911

Called [on Lloyd George] by appointment 10.45, stayed about half an hour. George in great spirits. "After you left me yesterday", he said, "I made up my mind I must make a stand. I put it in this way to the

Prime Minister: 'if I were only, say, President of the Board of Trade and merely shared the collective responsibility of the Cabinet I should be willing to subordinate my personal view to that of the majority but as Chancellor of the Exchequer I am responsible for the finance of the country and I cannot accept these estimates. Rather than do so I tender my resignation. I shall not attack you. I shall help you all I can to carry the Parliament Bill, but I must ask you to find another Chancellor of the Exchequer'." Asquith replied that, even so, George's resignation would be fatal to the Parliament Bill and to the Ministry. He also pointed out that nearly all the expenditure for the current year was consequential on construction already authorised or "automatic". George said that was so and that in so far as it was consequential he was prepared to meet it, though he had often thought he ought to have resigned two years ago rather than accept the decisions then come to. But what of next year and the year after? It was the programme now to be authorised with which he was concerned. He must see his way to substantial reductions in these years.

With that he left and Asquith saw McKenna. McKenna was very obstinate and neither he nor the Admirals would at first give way. It was only when Asquith let it be seen that he was prepared to part with them both rather than with George that they were willing to come to terms. There were negotiations in which George took part. McKenna was plaintive and asked what he was to do if his naval advisers resigned. "Alter your whole system" said George "and in particular that part of it which makes the signature of the naval lords to the naval estimates necessary". They tried to go into the whole question of the relative strength of navies—the number and size of the ships of this power and of that—but George declined altogether to enter into these details. He put the matter simply in this way. "You say you will want so much money; I tell you I haven't got it and am not prepared to provide it. If it is to be provided it must be by somebody else".

Finally at 10 o'clock at night the matter was reduced to concrete terms and it was agreed that the increase of 4 millions in this year's naval estimates over last year's should be wiped out and rather more than wiped out in the next two years, that there should be a substantial reduction in each of the two years and that the total reduction in the second year should be $4\frac{1}{2}$ millions. McKenna asked that the saving should be on army and navy together and George said that was indifferent to him. His agreement was with McKenna and if McKenna could get part of the money from Haldane it was all right.[7]

[7] R. B. Haldane was Secretary of State for War in the Liberal government.

C. P. Scott and Winston Churchill
driving to a meeting in the Manchester
Free Trade Hall, 22 May, 1909

Redmond (left) and Dillon outside
Buckingham Palace

This agreement George got *in writing*. The programme of construction to be adapted accordingly. "I am not concerned", said George, "as to how you do it. You know best about that; I know nothing. I simply ask for delivery of the goods—the money". "They liked that", George said to me, "they like to be told that they are the only people who know anything about the navy, and once you put them on their honour to keep within a certain figure it's wonderful how they will make it do and prove to you up to the hilt that the British navy can lick Creation". So we had a good laugh and his last words were "I think your journey is worth 4 millions to the nation—and a half."

In the event, matters turned out less favourably than Lloyd George had expected. For one thing, he had conceded McKenna's demand of five new ships for the coming year; the savings of four-and-a-half millions were not to come into effect until 1913. And McKenna subsequently insisted that the full reduction was dependent on either (a) the army agreeing to share in these economies or (b) the German government agreeing to slow down naval building. Neither condition was fulfilled.

III] BRITAIN AND GERMANY

When Lloyd George argued in March 1911 for limiting expenditure on the navy, one reason he put forward— in a letter to McKenna—was that: "There is a much better feeling with Germany now."[8] If this feeling existed, events in the next few months quite dispelled it—and even carried Lloyd George out of the camp of German sympathisers.

The origins of the Agadir crisis of 1911 went back to the entente which Britain formed with France in 1904. Under one of its secret provisions, Britain agreed to support French colonial ambitions in Morocco. The agreement was soon put to the test. In 1905, shortly after the Liberals came into office, the Kaiser made a flamboyant speech supporting Moroccan independence. In the ensuing international conference, Britain took the French side. The outcome, in addition to strengthening the entente, was that France secured police powers in a considerable part of Morocco. However Moroccan independence was nominally preserved.

In 1911 the French decided to complete their acquisition of the territory. On the pretext of quelling disorders there they sent in troops. The German government reacted sharply. On 1 July it sent a gunboat to the Moroccan port of

[8] A. J. Marder, *From the Dreadnought to Scapa Flow* (Oxford University Press, London, 1961), vol. 1, p. 218.

Agadir, and made it clear that France would have to pay for its advance in Morocco by lavish grants of territory in the Congo to Germany. (Many of the conversations that follow provide an uncomfortable reminder of the vanished world in which European powers assumed that territories in Africa and Asia were theirs for the taking).

Germany's action threw British opinion into a ferment. Fear of the German navy gave rise to the suspicion that Germany was seeking, by establishing a naval base in Morocco, to cut Britain's trade-routes. Moreover, it seemed that Germany was once more attempting to disrupt the entente by subjecting France to a diplomatic humiliation. Worst of all, Germany was apparently bent on overturning an international agreement to which Britain was a signatory without letting the British government have any say. (France's attempts to upset the agreement were not similarly resented). On 4 July 1911, at the direction of the cabinet, the Foreign Secretary, Sir Edward Grey, warned the German ambassador that Britain "could not recognise any new arrangement which was come to without us."[9] The German government took no notice.

One of the few members of the cabinet who felt no sympathy for French colonial ambitions, and who believed that Britain was quite misguided in aligning with France against Germany, was the Lord Chancellor, Lord Loreburn. Loreburn was no thorough-going radical. He opposed women's suffrage, was accused of favouring Conservatives in the appointment of magistrates, and upheld Russia's violations of Persian independence (a matter about which Scott felt very strongly, especially as he believed that the British government was condoning Russia's actions). But on the issue of relations with Germany, Loreburn agreed with those radicals who deplored the government's policy.

Diary, 20 July 1911

Breakfast with Lord Chancellor and after at House of Lords 9-12. He talked mainly of the question of the appointment of magistrates, the attacks on him in the Liberal press and the proposed vote of censure by [Neil] Primrose[10] in the House of Commons. Went through the returns of appointments supplied by Primrose to the "Daily Chronicle" and showed them to be wrong in every case, often wildly and grotesquely. Promised to send me the corrected figures for publication.

He spoke also gravely and warningly of the immediate danger of a quarrel with Germany on the Moroccan question. "Take care we don't get into a war with Germany. Always remember that this is a Liberal League Government. The Government of France is a tinpot Govern-

[9] Grey of Fallodon, *Twenty-Five Years* (Hodder and Stoughton, London, 1925), vol. I, p. 222.
[10] Well-connected Liberal M.P.

ment. Germany has but to stamp her foot and they will give way. They are capable of leaving us in the lurch. It would suit them admirably that we should be involved in a war with Germany".

[Loreburn:] "Do you know Asquith well?" [C.P.S.:] "He is very friendly and ready to see me". "Then I advise you to go and see him at once, but don't tell him I have said anything to you". "Is it urgent or would next week do?" "Better this week than next week. Better today than tomorrow."

After lunch called at House of Commons and talked to Geoffrey Howard one of the Whips[11] (Chief Whip away in Scotland). Said he was a Peace-man but strongly upheld Asquith's rather menacing statement on the Agadir incident in the House of Commons. We could not possibly afford to let Germany have a Naval station on the West African coast, "cutting our two great trade-routes" (to South Africa and India?). It would mean "the addition of millions to the naval Estimates." I asked if he then understood Asquith's action to be directed to the protection not of French but of specifically British interests. He said he had no special information, but that it was generally understood in the House to be so intended and was so taken, he believed, by Germany.

Afterwards saw Vaughan Nash, the Prime Minister's secretary and he tried to get me an interview but reported the Prime Minister unable today or tomorrow; desperately occupied with Parliament Bill and other matters. Monday as bad. I did not like to press the matter. He agreed to try for Tuesday.

Later had tea with Lord Courtney[12] in House of Lords and discussed the same matter. He regarded the telegram in today's "Times" as to Germany's demand for part of French Congo and a port on the coast (much better one than Agadir) as very serious[,] and wholly distrusted Grey's probable attitude in such a matter. He also had heard the talk about the cutting of trade-routes and joined me in mocking at it. We could not expect to have all the naval stations in the world to ourselves. As to the alleged consequence of a great increase in the naval estimates it could happen no doubt but only if we had the folly to invite it.

Having failed to secure an interview with Asquith, Scott—either before leaving London or during the same train journey to Manchester in which he made the fore-

[11]Howard was a member of an old-established political family (his father was the Earl of Carlisle) most of whom—unlike himself—had broken with the Liberal party over the Home Rule question.
[12]Prominent anti-imperialist Liberal, who had gained national stature (and lost his seat in Parliament) by his opposition to the Boer War.

going diary-entries—wrote the Prime Minister a strong letter on the international situation:

C.P.S. to Asquith, 20 July 1911 (Extract)

I hope you will forgive me if, as officially responsible for the Liberal organisation in Manchester, I write just a few lines about the possibility of our coming to a quarrel with Germany on the Moroccan (Agadir) question or matters arising out of it. That we should go to war in order to prevent Germany from acquiring a naval station on the West African coast has I believe not occurred to most Liberals as even a possibility, but what I have no doubt of is that if such a thing were to happen it would pulverise the party. There is no feeling among Liberals here against Germany—it is generally recognised that her policy of the open-door in Morocco has even been of material service to us—and that there would be any deadly danger to our interests in her acquiring a West-African port would be wholly disbelieved. I can imagine no more foolish war and none more fatal alike to party and to national interests than one with Germany on this matter.

The day after Scott wrote the above letter to Asquith, a new turn was given to events by Lloyd George.

As explained earlier, Grey had intimated to the German ambassador that Britain expected to be consulted on the Moroccan situation, and the cabinet was now becoming concerned at Germany's failure to reply. Lloyd George was due to speak at a bankers' dinner at the Mansion House. Apparently on his own initiative, he proposed to Grey that he should issue a warning to the German government that Britain could not be ignored in this way. Grey was only too happy to have such action taken by one of the cabinet's supposed pro-Germans. So on 21 July Lloyd George told his audience of bankers—and the world—that "if a situation were to be forced upon us in which peace could only be preserved" by allowing Britain to be treated "as if she were of no account in the Cabinet of nations, then I say emphatically that peace at that price would be a humiliation intolerable for a great country like ours to endure."

This menacing utterance was a prime example of what a friendly Liberal journalist had once described to Scott as Lloyd George's "tendency to become the advocate of what he has to defend". The expression had been used by Harold Spender during the first crisis over naval estimates in 1909, when, after saying how he had been urging Lloyd George against resignation, he admitted that he could not press him too far. "It is not worth his while to emerge as the great Pro-Great-Navy Chancellor, and to be the defender of a policy which involves heavy taxation without social reform. You know his tendency to become the advocate of what he has to defend—a legal tendency—and therefore along that line he might become a second Chamberlain."[13] *Fears that Lloyd George might go the way of Joseph Chamberlain, who had begun his career as a Liberal social reformer and ended up a right-wing Imperialist, had been present among Lloyd George's supporters from early in his career. And as they were present in Spender's mind in 1909, so they were powerfully revived by the Mansion House speech in 1911. This utterance, which profoundly angered the German government, also caused amazement to some of Lloyd George's Liberal allies. Hoping to head off criticism from at least one quarter, he went to considerable lengths to stay Scott's hand.*

R. H. Gretton (of the "Manchester Guardian's" London staff) to C.P.S., n.d. [21 July 1911]

I have a message from the Chancellor of the Exchequer to you. He asks you not to write anything about the German business without seeing him. This is *urgently* requested as a personal matter. The Chancellor asks if you could come up to breakfast with him tomorrow at 9.15. He regrets very much having to suggest your returning to town, but he and the master of Elibank[14] feel it of the utmost importance that nothing should be written without your seeing him. The Chancellor asks me to send him a message to the bankers' dinner giving him your reply.

Scott, having no idea what Lloyd George was preparing to say at the bankers' dinner, must have been somewhat puzzled by the foregoing and the following "urgent" messages.

Gretton to C.P.S., n.d. [21 July 1911]

Urgent

Further message from the Master of Elibank. Your letter has only just been received by the Prime Minister though it appears to have been sent yesterday. The Prime Minister is most anxious that you should not misapprehend the situation, and hopes very much that you will be able to come up to town when he would see you after your breakfast with the Chancellor.

The "breakfast with the Chancellor" took place on the morning following the Mansion House speech. Here are two views of it:

[13] Harold Spender to C.P.S., 29 January 1909.
[14] Alexander Murray, the Master of Elibank, Liberal chief whip 1910-12.

Diary of A. C. Murray [15], 22 July 1911 [16]

I breakfasted today with Lloyd George. The latter was engaged in an endeavour to inculcate a little common-sense and patriotism into the head of Scott, (Editor of the Manchester Guardian) in respect of the Morocco situation.

Diary, 22 July 1911

Breakfast with Lloyd George. Chief Whip and his brother and Miss Lloyd George also there. Afterwards alone with Lloyd George; then Churchill joined and Murray came back. Then saw Prime Minister and lastly some talk with the other 3 and with Lloyd George alone before leaving.

They were all civil and apologetic for bringing me up. Churchill said to Lloyd George that I ought to be kept constantly informed as to all important matters. Lloyd George said that was just what he tried to do and rather reproached me for not coming to him sooner now.

Lloyd George rather laid it on about "Manchester Guardian"—it would smash party if we and Government were at odds. "Manchester Guardian" he had found much more considered in Germany than any other Liberal paper and if we let Government down in international controversy it would be inferred that they had no sufficient backing in the country and give a dangerously false impression of their actual determination which up to a certain point was fixed and practically unanimous, Loreburn being the only exception.

Their present demand was simply to be made parties to any re-settlement of the Moroccan question. They were bound by treaty with France to give her diplomatic support and under Algeciras convention had treaty rights which they were entitled to assert. 17 days ago Grey had sent despatch to Berlin making this request in the most un-provocative manner; the despatch had not even been acknowledged.[17] Metternich's attention had just been called to this neglect. He replied that he had heard nothing from his Government on the subject. A second despatch was therefore sent yesterday repeating the request. There had been a question of doing more than this and sending

---

[15]Liberal M.P. and brother of the Master of Elibank. [16] Elibank Papers.

[17]It was not a despatch, but a spoken communication to Count Metternich, the German ambassador.

warships to Agadir. I gathered that Grey had wished to do this and Lloyd George opposed and that Grey had withdrawn the suggestion.

Lloyd George spoke warmly of Grey and said he was very good in showing him (Lloyd George) everything[,] and that he (Lloyd George) had got him only yesterday to modify his despatch (to Berlin). A despatch had also been sent to our ambassador at Paris instructing him to inform the French Government that we were not prepared to give them support in regard to the French Congo.

The feeling of the government was that looking to the enormous possessions of France and of Great Britain in Africa and to the relatively very small possessions of Germany[,] Germany might reasonably claim a larger share and that it would be policy so far as possible to satisfy her. Her demands on the French Congo and the French reversionary right to the Belgian Congo were extravagant but they were not opposed to any British interest, though in any general settlement we might look for some concession from her in turn. . . . But as to Morocco we had a strong interest not in preventing the acquisition by Germany of territory[,] even of considerable territory[,] on the South Moroccan coast and hinterland—a very rich district—on the contrary it would give her useful occupation and take up some of the money that might otherwise go into Dreadnoughts; but in preventing the formation of a great naval base right across our trade routes.

I represented that as Germany could not afford to divide her battleships the worst she could do would be to detach a cruiser squadron and that the worst consequence to us would be that we must detach twice as many cruisers to watch them. He thought this would be a serious weakening of our forces but had no real reply.

On the whole he was strongly in favour of proceeding in the most conciliatory manner possible but of insisting unflinchingly that no change in the status quo in Morocco should take place without our being made parties to it. Asquith was quite conscious of the anti-Germanism of the Foreign Office staff and was prepared to resist it. But neither he nor Grey nor himself (Lloyd George) would consent to hold office unless they were permitted to assert the claim of Great Britain to have her treaty rights and her real interests considered and to be treated with ordinary diplomatic civility as a Great Power. The whole correspondence would have hereafter to be published and it would be fatal even to our party interests if it should be found that we had not maintained the clear rights and the dignity of the country.

I of course agreed with him about this. I did not think it conceivable that Germany should resist such a demand temperately pressed, but the

47

question was what interests had we for which in the last resort we were prepared to go to war and was the prevention of a German naval station at Agadir one of them. I got no clear answer to this.

Repeatedly in the course of the conversation Lloyd George spoke of France's weakness and terror in face of Germany. She had her eyes ever fixed on "those terrible legions across the frontier". "They could be in Paris in a month and she knew it." Then Germany would ask not 200 millions[18] but 1,000 millions as indemnity and would see to it that France as a Great Power ceased to exist. There was real danger that Prussia (it was Prussia really, not Germany, which was in question) should seek a European predominance not far removed from the Napoleonic.

I said I had hoped that recently there had been a movement the other way and that the German Emperor's visit to this country had been used to bring about better relations. He flared up and said the German Emperor when our guest had behaved "like a cad" and actually used his opportunity of meeting the representatives of other nations also our guests in order to influence their minds against us, as "this comes of trusting Great Britain". The present German Chancellor he described as a coarse bully[19] and he said his opinion of the Emperor had considerably changed since he had found he was the sort of man thoroughly to enjoy this person's company, drinking quantities of beer with him and roaring over the smutty stories which formed the staple of his conversation. He did not tell me his authority for all this. The impression I got was that he is not immune from the microbe of Germanophobia.

He was very much down on Loreburn whom he described as "petulant, unreasonable" and always "rubbing Grey the wrong way"; practically alone in the Cabinet. When I spoke of the Cabinet as a "Liberal League Cabinet" he repudiated the description—there had been a great change in the last year or two. I said no doubt the Radicalism of the party was influencing the Government; he suggested that it was rather the Budget that had done it.[20]

Churchill's only contributions to the discussion, beyond his remark about me, were highly rhetorical denunciations repeated at intervals

[18]As after the Franco-Prussian war of 1870-71 (when Alsace-Lorraine was also annexed from France).

[19]Lloyd George seems to be describing Kiderlen-Wachter, the dissolute German Foreign Secretary, not the limited but upright Chancellor, Bethmann-Hollweg.

[20]That is Lloyd George's "People's Budget", which the House of Lords initially had rejected.

of the insolence of Germany and the need of asserting ourselves and teaching her a lesson. Every question with him becomes a personal question.

Murray left before the end of breakfast with his brother and Miss George and only came in for a moment or two at intervals afterwards. He concurred generally with all that Lloyd George said and was particularly emphatic about the present Government not being a Liberal League Government, it was a Radical Government.

My interview with Asquith was comparatively brief—perhaps 20 minutes. As to the facts he did not add much to what Lloyd George had told me and which he assumed that I knew. I pressed him as to the essential point of the extent of our interest at Agadir. I repeated what I had said to Lloyd George and he did [not] materially disagree with me. "If you ask me", he said, "whether, to put it brutally, it is worth our while to go to war about Agadir (i.e. its being made into a fortified port) I should say it is not". Apart from this question we should have no objection to Germany's acquiring territory in South Morocco provided always that she maintains the "open door" to trade. . . . There would be no objection on our part to the acquisition by Germany of territory and a port—Libreville—in the French Congo. That lies far to the east of the trade-routes and she might do what she liked there. Another reason why we could not object is that she already possesses by the terms of a secret treaty (one of the many to which the late Government were parties) certain contingent rights to a port on the West African coast. What we should really like if it came to a division of spoils would be Tangiers—"one of the few desirable spots which we do not already possess". But we should strongly resist the acquisition by Germany of a port on the South Mediterranean coast.

Speaking generally he strongly concurred in Lloyd George's view that Germany's desire for expansion in Africa should be satisfied. He had a large map, coloured according to protectorates, hanging [on] the wall and invited me to consider the enormous disparity between the English and French and the German possessions. . . .

One may wonder why Asquith thought it worthwhile to point out to Scott the relative sparseness of German colonial possessions vis-à-vis those of Britain and France. But that is by the way.

Within a matter of days Scott returned to London, still striving to coax the government back from the brink of a showdown with Germany. His next visit was to the Foreign Secretary.

Diary, 25 July 1911

Breakfast 9-10.30. Sir Edward Grey referred at once to my conversation of Saturday with Lloyd George. I said there was one point which he had left obscure; was, or was not the question of the fortification of Agadir as a naval base a vital interest for us. "The *fortification*. Oh! yes. That is certainly a vital interest". But I replied what does it amount to? "It is very undesirable no doubt and would place us at a certain disadvantage in the event of war with Germany, but would it be worth while to go to war in order to prevent a relatively slight disadvantage in case we were at war?" He did not pretend that it would, but merely contended that the disadvantage might be greater than I had suggested. . . .

As to the present position of affairs: I had spoken of our "despatch" to Germany of nearly 3 weeks ago; there had been no despatch but merely a conversation between himself and the German ambassador— a very formal one no doubt and Metternich had taken down in writing the material words of his statement for communication to his Government. At last—yesterday—Metternich had telephoned asking to see him and there had been a further conversation. He attributed even this tardy response to Lloyd George's speech on Saturday[21] which had had a considerable—what diplomatists called—"retentissement".[22] As to the effect of this communication now it had come I gathered that no admission had been made of the claim we had made to be consulted in case the direct negotiation with France should fail. (There had been no demand for immediate consultation). All the satisfaction he had got was a statement that Germany had not landed troops at Agadir but when Grey asked if he would give permission to make this fact public he declined to do so.

Grey also told me that the negotiation with France was being conducted under pledge of secrecy—i.e. that France was not at liberty to inform us of its progress. A new point to me and a rather grave one was the general contention[,] which I understood from Grey to be put forward by Germany[,] that by our agreement giving France a free hand politically in Morocco we had estopped ourselves from interfering in any direct political negotiations into which she might enter with another power, just as France would be estopped from interfering under similar circumstances in Egypt. It was this I gathered which made him so anxious that it should be at once and clearly under-

[21]A mistake for Friday. [22]That is, reverberation or repercussion.

stood in Germany that we should regard the presence of a great naval power like Germany on the Atlantic coast of Morocco as constituting a new situation and giving us a right which we meant to assert to be considered and consulted. He did not wish Germany through ignorance of our real intentions to commit herself so far that she could not withdraw, as happened with Russia before the Crimean war.

As to the capabilities of Agadir as a naval base his information from the Admiralty was that it is better than Mogador but that to make it really formidable would be very expensive. . . .

All through he spoke of the importance of getting Germany to moderate her demands so as not to compel France to reject them, but he never alleged a corresponding need that France should be prepared to make really big concessions in order to pay off Germany as she had already paid off us. He did not deny when I put it to him that Germany had just as good (or bad!) a right to compensation for giving France a free hand politically in Morocco as we had claimed and received.

I spoke incidentally of the importance to us of getting Germany to abandon any political interests in Morocco[,] or at least the northern part of it[,] so as to exclude her from interference on the Mediterranean sea-board; and he admitted at once that for Germany to acquire a naval base on the Mediterranean would be infinitely more serious than for her to acquire one on the Atlantic as it would involve a great and permanent increase of our naval force in the Mediterranean (which we had been able by our agreement with France to reduce) in order to prevent our communications with Egypt from being cut. . . .

Note. At one point in the conversation I tried to get at the more general and underlying ground of our policy. He at once admitted that this was to give to France such support as would prevent her from falling under the virtual control of Germany and estrangement from us. This would mean the break-up of the triple entente[,] as if France retired Russia would at once do the same and we should again be faced with the old troubles about the frontier of India. It would mean also the complete ascendancy of Germany in Europe and some fine day we might have the First Lord of the Admiralty [McKenna] coming to us and saying that instead of building against two powers we had to build against six. (I remarked that I could well imagine his saying so). But the history of the Napoleonic wars showed that any power which achieved European dominance in the last resort came to a check against England, which so long as she retained her sea-power could not be coerced, and that would be the inevitable sequel to a German as to a French supremacy.

As the danger of war with Germany receded, Scott and his associates became free with recriminations concerning the British government's part in the affair. Loreburn, conscious of his isolation in the cabinet, was outspokenly critical of colleagues he seemed powerless to influence. A principal object of their disfavour was Lloyd George. In addition to his being suspect for his actions in this matter, it was now becoming known that in 1910 he had concocted a scheme for solving the impasse over the House of Lords by the setting up of a coalition government. Both incidents aroused doubts about his political stability.

In the following conversation, Loreburn mentions several Liberal cabinet ministers who have not been referred to hitherto. These may be briefly identified: Lewis Harcourt, son of a former Liberal leader, was Secretary of State for the Colonies.

Lord Morley, biographer (and one-time colleague) of Gladstone and an opponent of the Boer War, was Lord President of the Council.

John Burns, a former Labour leader and the first artisan to enter the cabinet (where he did not distinguish himself), was President of the Local Government Board.

Lord Gladstone, son of the former Liberal leader, had left the government in 1910 to become Governor-General of South Africa.

Lords Bryce, Elgin, and Ripon were all distinguished figures from the Gladstone era who had retired from the cabinet between 1906 and 1908.

J. A. Pease was President of the Board of Agriculture, Walter Runciman President of the Board of Education, and Herbert Samuel Postmaster-General.

Diary, 6-8 September 1911

LORD LOREBURN

Many conversations during a two days' visit at Kingsdown House.

Foreign Policy. Loreburn less alarmed than when I saw him previously in London about Morocco, but still uneasy. Advised that if the difficulty became acute President Taft should be asked to offer his good offices. Had never heard of the secret treaty mentioned to me by Asquith as to Portuguese West Africa (by which in certain eventualities we assented to the acquisition by Germany of a port on that coast) and complained that this was only one instance among many of the way in which he was ignored in the Cabinet.

Spoke of Harcourt as the man on whom on the whole he could most rely in the Cabinet for support to a peace policy. Was eager that I should see Lloyd George and have it out with him. Morley very little use—weak and very captious. Burns well-meaning but counting for little. Pointed out the great weakening of the {real Liberal element in Radical the Cabinet since Campbell-Bannerman's death. Besides the substitution of Asquith for Campbell-Bannerman there had been the loss of Bryce, Elgin (of whom he spoke warmly)[,] Ripon and Gladstone (weak but still well-meaning). In their places Churchill (unstable), Pease (a nobody), Runciman and Samuel (men owing promotion to and dependent on Asquith[,] and Runciman at least an avowed Liberal Leaguer)—altogether an almost purely Liberal League Cabinet.

I explained to him Grey's statement to me of his policy—a mere revival of the old Palmerstonian policy of the Balance of Power—and he agreed that it was rotten to the core. He himself is tired and disheartened and eager to get out of office, but I put it to him strongly that it was his duty to stay until at least some critical issue arose on which he could make a protest which would be understood in the country and which he could afterwards defend and fight upon and appeal to all good Liberals to back him. He did not dispute this. . . .

[Regarding] Lloyd George. Told a naughty story. A year ago Lloyd George was opposed to the keeping on of the 3/9d. spirit duty, to which the Irish were opposed, in the held-up Budget of 1909-10 and was outvoted in the Cabinet. A month or two later on the 1910-11 Budget he quite forgot this and publicly declared that to abandon the duty would be a crime against civilisation.

Again: he told me of a conversation he had had with "a distinguished Liberal journalist"—this I afterwards found was Alfred Spender[23]—who told him that[,] when taken to task (by the Chief Whip) for his rather hostile attitude towards Lloyd George[,] retorted by telling him that he had it on unimpeachable authority that at the time of the Conference last year Lloyd George had taken on himself the task of negotiator and had gone straight to [A.J.] Balfour[24] with proposals for a Coalition. The concessions on the Tory side are not stated—the conversation naturally related only to those offered by Lloyd George—but these last included (1) Universal military service (2) a hundred million loan for the Navy (3) [Tariff] Retaliation. Loreburn expressed scepticism but Spender was positive as to the correctness of his information. You should ask him about it, said Loreburn.

[23] J. A. Spender was editor of the Liberal *Westminster Gazette* and a close friend (and subsequent biographer) of Asquith. Unlike his brother Harold, he usually viewed Lloyd George with disfavour.
[24] Leader of the Conservative party from 1902 to 1911.

Diary, 7 November 1911

Sir Frank Lascelles (Our ambassador at Berlin 1895 to 1908)
Called by appointment at his house, 14 Chester Square, on Lady
Courtney's introduction. My principal object was to get his interpretation of the original object of the Entente with France. He said emphatically that its point was *not* directed against Germany. But he said
that was the interpretation they [the Germans] put on it and I had great
difficulty in persuading them to the contrary. But my instructions were
that it had no hostile bearing. The Germans are an extremely sensitive
people. As Lord Salisbury put it to me "They are like a jealous woman".
"But tell them", he added[,] "we are not monogamists; we are polyg-
amists". . . .

Lloyd George's Mansion House speech had caused extreme
irritation. Yet when Asquith said substantially the same thing a few
days later in restrained language it was regarded as quite correct.
(Lloyd George himself now realised that he had gone too far, but
claimed that his speech none the less had *prevented a war*). Lascelles was
at Berlin in August (a month later) and saw the Emperor. An aide-de-
camp to whom he spoke said the indignation in Germany was extreme
and beyond control. The Emperor himself was very angry. "I was on
the point" he said "of coming to terms with France when you interfered and spoilt everything". . . . Then I went on, said Sir F. Lascelles,
to say something which I knew would provoke an outburst and I got it.
"On our side, Sir," I said, "there was an impression that you were
taking advantage of our internal divisions in order to steal a march on
us". "How dare they say any such thing?" stormed the Emperor at the
top of his voice.

Sir F. Lascelles' own opinion about Agadir is that it was a mistake
—"ever since von Bulow[25] came into office", he said, "he has in my
opinion made a series of mistakes and he has shown his cleverness
chiefly in getting out of their consequences"—but its importance was
greatly exaggerated. It was just a move in the game and need not greatly
have alarmed us. The result of the whole negotiation between France
and Germany is in his opinion a distinct defeat for Germany. This is
recognised and felt in Germany and the fact is emphasised by the
resignations of the two important Colonial officials.[26]

[25]Presumably an error for von Bethmann-Hollweg, who had replaced von Bulow as German
Chancellor in 1909.

[26]Von Lindequist, the German colonial secretary, and von Danckelmann, one of the permanent officials in the Colonial Office, had—to the Kaiser's disgust—resigned in consequence of the terms on which Germany had agreed to settle the dispute.

I asked him what he thought could now be done to bring about a better state of feeling and relations between Germany and England. He agreed that the first thing needful was to go back to the original meaning and intention of the Entente and was greatly interested when I told him that I believed a strong effort was being made within the Cabinet to bring this about. He said he knew nothing of this but that Haldane he did know would be strongly in favour of it and also the Lord Chancellor. The proper course would be for a declaration to that effect to be made in Parliament and he understood there was to be a discussion and that that would give Grey the opportunity for a statement. It was of the utmost importance that it should be clear and reassuring. . . .

Speaking generally he deprecated English nervousness in regard to Germany as uncalled for and undignified. The gross error in regard to German naval construction for which McKenna was responsible last year[27] and which had never been confessed as it ought to have been was probably due to this cause. A more recent example was the scare (of which he happened to have information through a friend in the navy) that we were on the point (a month ago) of being attacked by Germany which had no better foundation than that the Admiralty had lost sight of two German gunboats. . . .

Incidentally he remarked that the Germans were delighted at Churchill's appointment to the Admiralty [in place of McKenna] which they took as a compliment to the Emperor of whom he is a personal friend! . . .

Loreburn's dubious value as an ally of the radicals in foreign policy matters becomes clear in the following conversation. He remained unmoved by the circumstances of Persia, whose independence was being threatened by Russia. (The economic adviser to the Persian government, an American named Morgan Shuster, had recently been forced from office by a Russian ultimatum). And Loreburn could think of nothing which might reverse the cabinet's policy towards Germany. The nearest he got to a positive proposal was when he argued that the Liberal ministry should be broken up and its place taken by a Conservative regime under Bonar Law, the party leader, and Lord Lansdowne, formerly Conservative Foreign Minister.

Diary, 1 December 1911

Loreburn. Friday, December 1 dined with Loreburn, Lady Loreburn

[27]Probably an error for 1909.

as usual leaving us alone for the evening after dinner. Talk mainly on Germany, also on Persia.

As to Persia found him quite uninterested and indifferent. He regarded the modern Persians as a corrupt and hopeless lot, the Majlis[28] as an absurd and incompetent body and the country as only to be governed by a strong ruler. Shuster was a pushing American who had taken a strong anti-Russian line and ought to go. He did not seem to know that Russia had demanded that all European officials should in future be approved by her[,] or to have reflected on what were the necessary conditions of any sort of Persian national independence. He merely said that unless Russia was absolutely deceiving us she had no sort of design of annexing or assuming a protectorate over Northern Persia and that seemed to satisfy him. . . .

As to Germany he said the recent statements would tell me a good deal, but not half or a tithe of what had really happened—he meant of course in the way of folly and provocation on our side. As to what should now be done he was rather in despair. Grey was hopeless and impervious to any argument. It was impossible for the Cabinet to control him in detail, yet everything depended in diplomacy on the handling of detail. . . .

He agreed with me that the root of the recent mischief was the perversion of the friendly understanding with France into an alliance but that was a subtle thing and how could you prevent it except by changing the Minister? You could not take a vote in the Cabinet on an abstract proposition. Grey no doubt ought to go, but who was there to take his place? Either Churchill or Haldane would be worse, the one irresponsible the other with his closed mind and passion for intrigue. Morley was now really senile and [Lord] Crewe[29] was not at all the same man since his illness. Birrell, honest and able fellow, would be the best. But in any case the resignation of Grey would mean the break-up of the Cabinet as probably George, Churchill and Haldane would go with him. He saw nothing for it but a change of government. Bonar Law and Lansdowne would be far better. They would not be deeply committed, like Grey, to an extravagant championship of France and would have no difficulty in going straight to Germany and establishing a parallel understanding with her. The tone of both their speeches had been far better than Grey's and Law's especially had been remarkable. (He did not believe Law had the stuff in him for a leader, but this speech was on a high level.)

[28]The elected assembly.
[29]Government leader in the House of Lords and Secretary of State for India.

Augustine Birrell

The Suffragettes' attack on
Buckingham Palace, 21 May, 1914.
Mrs. Pankhurst being carried away by
the police has gone limp, the
Suffragette form of passive resistance.

Morley arriving for the Cabinet
Meeting on 2 August, 1914

L. T. Hobhouse

His own judgment counted for nothing with Grey so he had gone to see Asquith (this needed an effort as there is a coolness between them owing to Asquith's not having backed him as Loreburn thinks he ought on the Magistrates question) and begged him to wrestle with Grey. . . . Asquith was friendly and said he largely agreed with [him] but whether he would really exert himself was another matter. The fatal thing was that the Prime Minister who alone was in constant communication with Grey and alone could really influence him never attempted to influence him at all. In this as in everything else he was as wax— "putty" rather is Loreburn's familiar metaphor. . . .

IV] THE SUFFRAGE

On 26 October 1911 Lloyd George broached to Scott "an entirely new proposal in regard to Women's Suffrage." The government intended to introduce a Reform Bill in the following session applying to male voters and virtually embodying manhood suffrage. Lloyd George suggested "that an amendment should be introduced providing that 'man' should include 'woman'—i.e. converting the Bill at a stroke into an Adult Suffrage Bill."

Scott took this proposal to the leaders of the National Union (the non-militant women's suffrage organisation) and they were delighted. However H. N. Brailsford, secretary of the Conciliation Committee which sought to bring together all the suffrage bodies, foresaw difficulties from two quarters: the Conservative M.P.s who supported female suffrage, because they were unlikely to agree to it on so large a scale; and the militant organisation, because it entertained "the deepest suspicion of Lloyd George". Christabel Pankhurst, said Brailsford, "envisaged the whole suffrage movement in its present phase as a gigantic duel between herself and Lloyd George whom she designed to destroy. She had lost all sense of proportion and honestly believed she could force the Government to yield." Still, Brailsford did not see how a suffrage society could resist a proposal to give men and women the vote on equal terms.

Scott took this information back to Lloyd George, who was "quite satisfied" with it.

But the problem posed by militant tactics continued during the following months to oppress the Chancellor of the Exchequer.

Diary, 2 December 1911

Lloyd George. Breakfast December 2, 9.15-10.45. Alone at first (with Mrs. Lloyd George and the elder daughter), afterwards Chief Whip came in and later Donald of the "Chronicle"[30] for golf. We talked almost entirely of the Women's Suffrage movement and the damage done to it by the militant outrages. I regretted Grey's letter in yesterday's paper practically throwing up the sponge if there should be a continuance of these proceedings[,] and said I supposed it was written from a sense of loyalty (exaggerated as I thought) to Asquith on his being attacked by the militants—a non suffragist by suffragists—and was glad to hear that this was the case since it gave the letter only an incidental importance. As a matter of fact the militants did not attack Asquith as an anti-suffragist at all and liked him better than many of the suffragist members of the Government, but simply as a member of the Government. "But what can they hope to achieve by attacking him?", he asked, "they can't expect to make him change his mind". "Oh! yes, they do; they are quite hopeful of converting him". (I had this the previous day from Brailsford). "Then they must be mad". "They are mad, Christabel Pankhurst has lost all sense of proportion and of reality". "It's just like going to a lunatic asylum"[,] said George, "and talking to a man who thinks he's God Almighty". "Yes, very much like that."

Afterwards we discussed what should be done. I urged that the militants should be ignored and the suffrage campaign pressed on as though they didn't exist. "That's all very well for us", said George, "though it's difficult. I don't mind and it doesn't put me out much at meetings or irritate me, I'm used to the rough and tumble and have had to fight my way, so is Churchill (though he is sensitive about his perorations) but it's different with Grey, he isn't accustomed to interruption and can't do with it. But what really matters is the effect on the audiences and on the public. At Bath I had very hard work. The people were already irritated with previous interruptions when I rose to speak; my task of persuasion was made very much more difficult". I replied that that was no doubt the case but we were in for a fight and must go through with it. The public would of course be furious; the problem was to turn their fury into the right channel. At present they said "these people are suffragists; let us wreck the suffrage"; the reply was "not at all; they are suffrage-wreckers; let us disappoint them". He agreed, but said it wasn't easy. . . .

Diary, 23 January 1912

Lunched with Churchill and discussed suffrage among other things.

[30]Robert Donald, editor of the Liberal *Daily Chronicle*.

He still declares himself a suffragist, though a quite impracticable one. Is opposed both to Conciliation Bill and to larger measure. Would admit the women who really want and need it—graduates, doctors[,] poor law Guardians and members of town councils—by categories, as many as could be devised perhaps 100,000 in all. I discussed the general question with him of the need of a big change affecting the whole position of women and shook him a bit—a queer emotional creature. He practically admitted that his present wrecking tactics are the outcome of resentment at the treatment he has received from the W.S.P.U.[31] He is not to be despaired of if tackled.

v] THE CABINET AND FOREIGN POLICY

The Agadir crisis caused some members of the cabinet to learn for the first time that Britain and France had been concerting their naval and military arrangements. This led to vigorous protests. Matters came to a head at cabinet meetings in November 1911, at which resolutions were passed in effect rebuking the Foreign Minister for his acts of concealment.

A principal supporter of this protest was McKenna, who had recently lost his post as First Lord of the Admiralty. (There had been a dispute between the naval and military chiefs which had been settled in the latter's favour). McKenna had strongly resented Asquith's decision to replace him at the Admiralty by Churchill, and had come near to refusing the new post offered him—the Home Office. Eventually he decided to stay in the government, but on 20 October he visited Asquith at Archerfield and let him know that he proposed to reveal the facts about the military conversations with France to the cabinet members who had been kept in the dark. Asquith did not try to dissuade him; but thereafter the cat was truly out of the bag.[32]

Loreburn discussed these events with Scott in January 1912. Scott was able to make only a scrappy, episodic account of the discussion. In October 1914 Loreburn again rehearsed the whole matter, and this time Scott recorded the conversation in full. The following pages include extracts from both sources. In reading the second account it is necessary to bear in mind the lapse in time, and the fact that the war had recently broken out; even so, this account is still of interest.

[31]Women's Social and Political Union, the militant organisation.
[32]There is a memorandum by McKenna recounting his conversation with Asquith on 20 October 1911 in the McKenna Papers.

Notes of a conversation with Loreburn at his home (Kingsdown House, Deal) on 7 January 1912[33]

"Preparing a formula".

Germany for years has been trying to make friends. "Incredible" the way she has been repulsed. For 3 years have been pressing for information. Questions constantly evaded sometimes with actual falsehoods. Later read me memorandum on the subject—would consult Harcourt. This would form substance of his statement in the Cabinet (when Grey made his statement which he had promised to do) and the concluding words declaring that this country was not under any obligation direct or indirect, express or implied[,] to support France against Germany by force of arms would form the substance of a statement in which he would ask the Cabinet to concur and possibly move as a resolution to be voted on. He should resign if it were rejected and explain publicly his reasons for doing so. Probably Harcourt would do the same.

The Cabinet rotten. Asquith nerveless. Grey obsessed about Germany. Lloyd George unstable. . . . Haldane an intriguer. Morley a wreck. Crewe not much less so. The solid ground is touched in (a) Harcourt, right judging at every critical point, wise, courageous, but does not cut any figure and is physically not a strong man (b) [Lord] Pentland[34] though he has little force or weight (c) McKenna, has rather come over, though personal feeling may enter here—felt very much his removal from Admiralty. It is the *way* Asquith does these things that hurts, more than the things themselves—as also in the case of Elgin's dismissal, a most undeserved thing[,] and [Lord] Carrington's removal from the Board of Agriculture [in October 1911].

Germany. I said I had heard from a foreign source on which I could rely that at the time of the Morocco dispute the French Minister of War and Foreign Minister and Prime Minister regarded the military force of England as absolutely at their command. He said go to Grey and tell him and ask him if it is true. He implied he knew it was true that they had a reasonable expectation of this though as a matter of fact he said the Cabinet had never sanctioned it and would probably have refused to give the support requested—or at least many of them would have resigned sooner. But what a terrible position for us to be in—to have either to sanction a war with Germany or leave France in the lurch.

[33]The order in which these notes appear here is not always that of the original; other sections have been omitted.
[34]Secretary of State for Scotland.

I added that it was notorious that plans had been discussed with the French Minister of War for the landing of British troops—"not with the knowledge of the Cabinet" he said. Well he added now you know pretty well the cause of our anger and of our protests and why I am no longer so isolated.

Speaking of the division of parties in the Cabinet he said McKenna would probably now wish to be on the anti-alliance or commitment side, but that he was probably too much bound by his past actions and declarations to take a strong part. Nevertheless he said before the October Cabinet he told Asquith's secretary that if the resolutions (insisting on the Cabinet being kept better informed on questions of foreign policy) were not carried there would be 8 resignations including his own. He was wrong for on a division they were 15 to 4. It is not usual to have formal resolutions in the Cabinet but on this occasion he clearly implied that there was one and he said he should ask for a copy of it, though not from Asquith but from somebody else. There are of course no minutes of Cabinet meetings.

Resolution of October 20.[35] The dissentients were Grey, Haldane, Lloyd George—and the Prime Minister.

Sequel of October Cabinets. It remains to determine the future policy towards Germany. This would naturally have been discussed in November, but the Insurance Bill Railway strike etc. occupied attention and also it seemed better to postpone any positive action till after the German elections. It will come on before Parliament meets.

German Emperor anecdote. On a recent visit to Windsor the Emperor was shown to his room by a high court official who, according to custom, walked upstairs before him *backward*. The Emperor looked at him and then proceeded to walk up backwards *himself*. Entreaties from Official. Emperor says come along and walk beside me.

Mrs. Asquith.[36] (1) When Loreburn in conversation let on that he knew of Lloyd George's proposal as to Coalition exclaimed "Why you don't mean to say you know about that"—a clear confirmation.
(2) On one occasion wrote a very angry letter to Lloyd George accusing him of working against Asquith—virtually of trying to supplant him. Lloyd George was furious, wrote an indignant letter, "would not submit to dictation from 10 Downing Street", would clear out rather.

[35]Loreburn's dating, though very explicit, seems to have been astray. The cabinet meetings on this matter took place on 1 and 15 November. On 20 October Asquith was at Archerfield, talking with McKenna.
[36]Asquith's second wife, Margot, was a formidable person who wrote many indiscreet letters and made many indiscreet remarks.

Morley. Extraordinary pettiness and exaggerated vanity—a dotage. . . . would do nothing unless put to the front and given all the credit. Was therefore selected to move the resolution on October 20—else would probably have opposed it.

The following conversation took place two months after the outbreak of the First World War, but the section presented below concerns the events dealt with in the preceding conversations.

Diary, 23 October 1914

Loreburn. Dined October 23. He started off directly after dinner to tell me "the whole story" of the relations of the Cabinet to Foreign Policy since he became a member of it. . . .

The crisis came at the time of the Agadir affair in August [1911]. Lyttelton[37] happened to be on a visit to Loreburn and in the course of conversation remarked that it was a good thing that at least on foreign affairs the two parties were united. He then went on to speak of the Unionist leaders having been approached and asked if their support could be relied on in the event of war with Germany, assuming that Loreburn as a member of the Cabinet must know all about it. This was the first Loreburn had heard of it (although he took care not to let this appear) and it afterwards appeared that everything had been arranged for the landing of a force of 150,000 men on the French coast down to the minutest detail of the time of departure and arrival of the trains and the stations at which they should get refreshments. This had all been arranged by members of the Committee of Imperial Defence. . . .

Loreburn was furious and consulted Morley and Harcourt. The same information had reached Harcourt. Neither had been consulted, though Morley was a member of the Committee of Imperial Defence. It was decided at once to bring the matter up in the Cabinet and Morley as the senior member of the Cabinet was chosen to lead off which he did, Loreburn said, very well. Practically there was no defence, though every effort was made to divert the discussion to the merits of the action taken and away from the fact of its concealment. Finally as the meeting was breaking up Loreburn remarked that he took for granted that it was agreed nothing of the kind should ever occur again. Churchill rather hotly demurred. Then, said Loreburn, clearly we must meet again and have the matter out.

[37]Rt. Hon. Alfred Lyttelton, Colonial Secretary in the Conservative government from 1903 to 1905.

In preparation for this two resolutions were drawn up together with a statement of the facts which had given rise to them. A long and unpleasant discussion took place in which Loreburn again pressed for an answer to the question "Why were we not told?" Asquith went as white as a sheet but no answer was forthcoming. Finally both resolutions were accepted without dissent. The first, which was the material one, was to the effect that no military conversations with any foreign power should in future take place without the previous knowledge of the Cabinet. "Previous" was insisted upon. "You are very suspicious", said Asquith. "We have reason to be" retorted Loreburn. The other resolution Loreburn could not recall—he had mislaid his documents! —but he thought it was merely consequential.[38] Then the statement of facts was initialed as correct by the delinquents Asquith, Grey, Lloyd George, Churchill—I am not sure about Haldane. Throughout this discussion Grey had remained silent. As he got up he said, almost as it were abstractedly, "I always said we ought to be fair to the Cabinet".

After this Loreburn put it to Morley and Harcourt whether they ought not all three to resign as a protest. Morley declined, as also did Harcourt. . . . Loreburn reluctantly acquiesced. It was his intention to have brought forward in the Cabinet resolutions laying down certain lines for our foreign policy, but soon after that he became seriously ill and, under doctor's orders, was compelled to resign.[39]

One more note from Scott's conversation with Loreburn in January 1912 deserves to be preserved here.

Churchill. He remarked that Churchill had been very quiet of late. I replied that he felt he was being outpaced by George[,] and told him the anecdote I had heard (I couldn't remember at the moment from whom) of his lament that he had left the Tory party as otherwise he would now be its leader and his indignation at being told that he couldn't change twice. [Loreburn] said it was new to him, but evidently regarded this attitude as in character and even as excusable.

In October 1914, Scott made a fuller record of what he then recalled of the Churchill "anecdote". Obviously the story cannot, on such remote authority, be regarded as necessarily authentic, but it is a good tale, and is valuable as a revelation of a widely-held attitude to Churchill.

[38]Loreburn had in fact given Scott the second resolution. The first stipulated that no communications should take place between the General Staffs of Britain and other countries "which can, directly or indirectly, commit this country to military or naval intervention."
[39]In June 1912.

Sir F. Lascelles. I called on him and had a long conversation (on introduction from Lord Courtney) at the time, if I remember rightly of the Agadir difficulty. . . .

He told me—I am almost certain it was he and of course the whole conversation was in confidence—an extraordinary anecdote about Churchill. It was at the time immediately after Balfour's resignation of the leadership and Bonar Law's adoption as his successor. Churchill was in the billiard-room of a club—I think a Conservative club— stretched on one of the settees. He said to a friend sitting beside him "Every politician makes one great mistake in his life. I made mine when I left the Tory party. If I hadn't I should now be its leader". "That may be so", the friend replied, "but you can't change sides twice". Churchill leapt up as if he had been shot and shouted "Not change twice!" in violent protest. Afterwards the other men asked what Churchill was making such a row about and the friend told them.

VI] THE WOMEN'S SUFFRAGE AMENDMENT

Two of the causes nearest Scott's heart were Irish Home Rule and women's suffrage; one of his closest friends politically was John Dillon, whose standing in the Irish Nationalist party was second only to that of John Redmond, the Nationalist leader.

In January 1913 Scott found that the Irish M.P.s for whose cause he was struggling might be planning to act against women's suffrage. As explained earlier, Lloyd George's strategy was to introduce an amendment to a government bill dealing with the male suffrage so as to include women under it as well. But the Irish held the balance in Parliament between Liberals and Labour on the one hand and Conservatives on the other. Even though women's suffrage was not a strictly party matter, the mass of Conservative M.P.s opposed it. If the Irish members did the same they would probably secure its defeat. Scott was distressed by this prospect.

Diary, 15-16 January 1913

Dillon (lunch both days at House of Commons)
Women's Suffrage. Declared himself now definitely an anti-suffragist (a year or so ago he had told me he was pulled two ways on the subject, that *quâ* democrat he was in favour and *quâ* Catholic opposed, but now he would not admit that any question of democratic principle was involved) but discussed the whole matter dispassionately and fairly.

He said an immense change in Irish feeling had been caused by the attacks of the militants in Ireland, particularly on Asquith in Dublin; (and Devlin,[40] who is a suffragist, afterwards spoke in the same way about the attack on Churchill on his visit to Belfast). Apart from this two motives weighed with the Nationalists (1) Gratitude and loyalty to Mr. Asquith. Two years ago there had been great mistrust of him. But that feeling had entirely disappeared and had been replaced by one of warm attachment. They would not willingly do anything to hurt or wound him.

(2) They felt that his personal position and authority was involved —that he had placed himself in an almost impossible position and that, as the maintenance of his personal credit and authority were vital to the prospects of Home Rule, it was clearly to their interest to rescue him from his difficulties.

I pointed out that there were powerful considerations to be taken into account on the other side: that important sections of opinion— the Labour party and many Radicals—would be outraged if the Irish members (having secured the determination of their own franchise) should interfere to determine in a reactionary sense a vital question in ours. . . .

He admitted that these were considerations not to be ignored and said the whole question was still completely open and would probably remain so till the last moment and might be largely determined by Asquith's speech. There would be no party resolution and he did not even know if there would be a party meeting. . . .

Home Rule. . . . As to Ulster (he begged me to regard this as strictly confidential) he himself would be prepared to go almost any length in the direction of Home Rule within Home Rule for the 4 North-Eastern counties[,] provided always that Ulster remained within the Bill as a part of Ireland and not as cut out of the Bill and a part of England. But terms in this sense would have to be asked for, not offered. . . .

Diary, 20 January 1913

J. Redmond

Women's Suffrage and the Irish Party. Saw him by appointment in his room in order to represent to him the impolicy of defeating the suffrage amendments to the Reform Bill by Nationalist votes. At first he met me with the stereotyped answer that every member of the party would be "free" to vote as he thought proper. . . . Then we got more

[40] Joe Devlin was leader of the Catholic and Home Rule minority in Ulster.

to the realities of the matter and he put his case and I put mine. I put it to him that it would be a horrible position for Home Rulers like myself to be torn between our allegiance to Home Rule and our determination to resist the ruin of the suffrage cause—to desire the success of the Government on the one ground and its defeat on the other—but that undoubtedly that was what would happen if the suffrage amendments were defeated and the Bill afterwards persisted in. That moreover if they were defeated by Irish votes we should feel that there had been a betrayal by the Home Rule party of the very principle of Home Rule[,] and that emancipation for Irishmen had been purchased at the cost of its refusal for English women. Our allegiance would be shaken and our ardour cooled.

He admitted that he was conscious of this and he earnestly hoped that such a situation would not arise. At the same time he had to look at the alternative. For the Prime Minister who had denounced women's suffrage as a "national disaster" to be compelled not only to accept it but to press it through under the exceptional powers of the Parliament Act would be an impossible position. . . .

Incidentally he mentioned that as a young man 30 years ago when he first entered Parliament he had been in favour of Women's Suffrage and given votes for it. Then for a period he abstained. Finally about 4 years ago he began to vote against it. Ireland on the whole women's question was 50 years behind England. In England the demand for the franchise had arisen through the great advance in women's education and their entry into all kinds of public positions and activities. In Ireland nothing of the kind had occurred and there was no demand for the franchise except to a small extent in some of the great cities. Women took no part in elections as they did here and, though there was nothing in the Catholic religion which prohibited the enfranchisement of women, the whole attitude of mind inculcated by it—that of reserve, retirement, modesty—was adverse to it.

We parted cordially. . . .

The Prime Minister. I afterwards had a short interview with Asquith in his room. I asked Illingworth[41] to arrange this and he brought back what he described as the "characteristic" answer that he "would be glad to see me at any time and on any subject—except women's suffrage".

Nevertheless I went but assured him at once that I wished to discuss nothing with him except the political situation as affected by Women's

[41]Percy Illingworth was Liberal chief whip from 1912 until his sudden death in January 1915.

Suffrage. This I put to him in something the same way as I had to Redmond and pointed out that if a comprehensive and almost final measure of franchise reform were passed definitely excluding women, it must alienate considerable forces of opinion and those among the most energetic in the party and produce coolness and even hostility. He admitted this but, like Redmond, presented the alternative as much more undesirable and even ruinous. . . .

We parted on a conciliatory observation by him that I had put the matter in rather a new light to him and he would consider it.

A week after Scott's interviews with Redmond and Asquith, the hopes of the supporters of women's suffrage were shattered—not by a vote in the House but by a decision of the Speaker. The Speaker ruled that any amendment seeking to introduce votes for women into the government's manhood suffrage bill would be out of order. The government, protesting that it had not intended to mislead the supporters of the women's vote, thereupon withdrew its bill altogether. But at the same time it offered to make parliamentary time available for a private member's bill embodying female suffrage. (This stood little chance of success without government backing.)

Scott breakfasted with Lloyd George on 3 February. According to Lloyd George, the Speaker's decision was "entirely unexpected", "a sudden thought. [The] Speaker had said to himself 'They are getting on too fast with this Parliament Act. I must pull them up.' " (Scott, however, heard differently from members of the National Union, who "had information on which they could rely that the Government had known of the danger several weeks before").

The only course which Lloyd George could now suggest was a "private member's bill with full facilities for all its stages and for the use of the Parliament Act." This proposal had already been rejected by Christabel Pankhurst, who declined "everything short of [a] Government Bill." Scott felt the same:

Diary, 3 February 1913 (Extract)

I said on his own showing no chance for private member's bill. Better drop it. He had no reply except the merely formal one that "discussion would do good". (Really he wanted the Government to seem to keep its pledge and cared nothing whether the Bill were defeated or not).

I said complete failure of Liberal party would be to throw whole suffrage movement into the hands of Labour party. He paused a moment and then said he should not regret that. It would do the Labour party good—give it an ideal aim. He had been disappointed with the Labour party in Parliament. They had not fought for a single thing really worth fighting for—only for narrow trade [union?] interests. No leader worth anything. [Philip] Snowden much the best man among them. . . .

VII] THE LAND FOR THE PEOPLE

Whatever his showing on the suffrage question, Lloyd George had been instrumental in achieving two major pieces of legislation between 1909 and 1912: the "People's Budget" and National Insurance. In 1912 his thoughts were turning in a new direction. He announced that there was a "bigger task in front of us". "You have got to free the land—the land that is to this day shackled in the chains of feudalism." He followed this up by himself appointing a committee of Liberals, most of them land reformers and single taxers, to investigate fully the system of rural and urban land-holding. (Its reports appeared in 1913 and 1914).

Apparently Lloyd George contemplated launching his land crusade separate from the Liberal cabinet. The Liberal M.P. A. C. Murray, who did not sympathise with Lloyd George's views on this matter, discussed the subject with the Foreign Secretary in September 1912. Grey told him that "Lloyd George is prepared to leave the Cabinet and go out and preach the gospel of land reform on his own." But in Grey's view, if he did so he would find that he had made a big mistake: Lloyd George's star did not stand as high in the political firmament as it had done three years before, and he did not appreciate the tremendous hold which the Prime Minister had acquired over Liberals in Parliament and the country.[42]

When Scott saw Lloyd George the following January, the latter's views had moderated. It seems that earlier, in a conversation of which we have no record, Lloyd George had talked to him of resignation. He did not do so now. Perhaps the fact that his career was endangered by an injudicious speculation, and the scandal which ensued from it, had driven thoughts of resignation over land policy from his mind. Lloyd George, in company with two other ministers, had purchased shares in the American Marconi company at a time when its English counterpart was being awarded a government contract, and the propriety of their action was being scrutinised by a parliamentary committee of inquiry.

Diary, 16 January 1913 (Extract)

Lloyd George
Land Reform. Proposes now to take up the campaign in the country in March. Had not intended to start till rather later. But Haldane's magniloquent speech in Manchester leading people to suppose that

[42]A. C. Murray's diary, 3 September 1912.

Education and not the Land was to be the next great subject to be taken up by the Government had forced his hand. Was very severe on Haldane who he said had indeed consulted himself and Pease and the Prime Minister, but had spoken quite vaguely to each, representing to each in turn that he had fully consulted the other two and had their sanction for his proposals thus obtaining an easy assent from the third[,] whereas in fact not one of the three had had more than the vaguest and most perfunctory explanation and the Cabinet had of course not been consulted at all. The Prime Minister had merely cautioned him not to be too precise—an injunction which the Prime Minister sarcastically added he had amply observed. Interminable verbiage was George's description of the speech[,] and he added something more scathing about "a barrel of tallow"—a picturesque description of Haldane's physical peculiarities—which when set fire to could indeed produce "any amount of smoke but no flame—no sort of illumination".

He would not however start on his campaign till he had £50,000 at his back. For it was not a case for speeches alone; the country must be flooded with pamphlets and relevant facts. Asked how long the campaign could be effectively kept up he said he thought as much as two years. No attempt should at first be made to formulate a scheme of reforms, but the evils of the existing conditions should be explained and enforced and out of the discussions thus raised a scheme of reform could gradually be evolved.

But he was already clear as to the general lines on which it should proceed. (1) Wages of agricultural labourer must be raised. 14/- to 18/- a week was not a living wage. This was already recognised in the fact that the labourer was not asked to pay an economic rent for his cottage. There must be a minimum wage and this would help to solve (2) the Housing question. This was vital. Present conditions[,] as shown e.g. in report of Diocesan Committee for diocese of Carlisle, make decency and morality practically impossible. A case of 14 people of all ages living practically in one room and girl of 14 pregnant. These horrors difficult to speak of in public but it must be done. (3) The Use of the Land in the public interest. At present three dominant objects of landlord class were first Power, then Amenity, last profitable use of the land in the public interest. The order must be reversed.

He touched on two points (a) Game Preserving. Sport in the old style was all right where a man was content to follow the dogs and come back with a modest bag but the battue with all that it involved was a monstrosity and bred mischief. (b) The system, almost universal in England, of annual tenancies was inconsistent with good husbandry.

69

In farming a man ought to be able to look ten years ahead and to have full security. The evidence already in his hands on all these matters was overwhelming. It was directed not against individuals but against a system.

His Personal Position. He had no idea now, as he had when I last saw him, of leaving the Cabinet in order to have a free hand. He counted confidently on carrying the Cabinet with him. There were of course people in the party who in their hearts hated all reforms and he constantly came across nominal Liberals whose one cry was "Why not let it alone?" They did not realise that for Liberalism stagnation was death. The worst kind of Tory was the nominal Liberal.

Lloyd George to C.P.S., 3 June 1913

Are you likely to be up in town soon? I should very much like to have a talk with you on one or two matters. I have to decide amongst other things within the next few days whether to start the Land Campaign at the latter end of June or to postpone it till the beginning of October. . . .

I should also like a talk with you as to the best line to take when the Marconi report comes before the House.

C.P.S. to Lloyd George, 7 June 1913[43] (Extract)

Your letter of June 3rd has been sent on to me here [Switzerland] . . . . Writing here in ignorance of so much that you would have told me I can only have general opinions probably of little or no value. My feeling has always been that the Land campaign should not be hurried. The more it is examined the bigger appear the issues involved—a minimum wage no doubt and arising out of that presumably a land court to adjust rents by way of compensation—tremendous issues which once invoked must be fought right through and would tax the full power of the strongest Government. . . .

About the Marconi business I write with even greater diffidence. There will I imagine be two Reports—a majority and a minority Report. Both must one imagines whole-heartedly acquit Ministers of all the grosser charges brought against them. But what reservations will the Minority make? A good deal depends on that. My own feeling would be for complete frankness and an unreserved expression of regret for whatever you feel you have to regret. That you have regrets I know because you have told me so and these I think were not based solely on

[43] Lloyd George Papers.

the fact that trouble had resulted to your colleagues and to the party. If you had thought more about it you wouldn't have done it though every honest and impartial person would I believe wholly acquit you of any sort or kind of improper motive and those who know you best will also know how little the desire of money-making enters into your composition. There has been an attempt [i.e. by Lloyd George's critics] to set up altogether new standards of conduct for Ministers in regard to their private investments[,] but probably most of us would admit that very speculative investments—that is investments which are liable to very great and sudden changes of value—are not desirable for them and the Marconis were of this kind. I believe that a simple and candid statement of this kind would meet with an immediate and cordial response both from the House and from the country.

VIII] BATTLESHIPS AGAIN

In January 1914 the Liberal cabinet was once more fiercely divided over the issue of Dreadnoughts.

Churchill had set the ball rolling in October and November 1913 by delivering public warnings that, unless the great powers agreed on a "naval holiday", Britain would have to increase substantially the naval budget for 1914-15. This produced a storm of protest from the Liberal press and many Liberal M.P.s. It also aroused much dissent in the cabinet.

One of the dissenters did not keep his views to himself. On 1 January 1914 the Daily Chronicle *published an interview with Lloyd George. In it, he spoke fulsomely of the improved relations between Britain and Germany, and called strongly for a reduction in expenditure on armaments. In order to make quite explicit the target of his remarks, he recalled that Lord Randolph Churchill (the First Lord's father) had resigned as Chancellor of the Exchequer rather than agree to "bloated" expenditure on weapons of war.*

Churchill was invited by a newspaper to comment on this utterance. He declined, in terms which constituted a clear rebuke to Lloyd George for his ill-manners.

The struggle in the cabinet centred on two issues: the number of battleships to be built in the coming year (four as against two); and the prospects of off-setting any increase in estimates for 1914-15 by substantial reductions in 1915-16. Once again, Lloyd George allowed his attention to become focussed on the second issue: that is, he would agree to increased expenditure for the present if he could secure a promise of reductions in the future. Other enthusiasts for economy, like McKenna and Sir John Simon, preferred something more immediate.

McKenna's role in this conflict is noteworthy. In 1909 he had been First

Lord of the Admiralty and the principal advocate in the cabinet of increased expenditure on the navy, whereas Churchill had been a leading opponent. But in 1911 Churchill had succeeded to his post and his opinions. McKenna now returned the compliment. In January 1914 he proved a more intrepid opponent of Churchill's naval estimates than did Lloyd George.

Churchill's position was complicated by doubts about his political intentions. It was widely suspected that in moving from a little-navy to a big-navy position, he was also planning to desert Irish Home Rule—and perhaps leave the Liberal party altogether. This suspicion, which ultimately Lloyd George (if we are to accept his statements to Scott) voiced to Churchill direct, is well brought out in the two letters on the Home Rule question which follow. They were written by T. P. O'Connor, who sat for a Liverpool constituency but was a member of the Irish Nationalist party, deriving his support from Irishmen resident in England.

T. P. O'Connor to C.P.S., 17 October 1913 (Extract)

I am extremely anxious as to the character of the speech which Winston will deliver in Manchester tomorrow. He has already enormously, I had almost said disastrously, complicated the situation by his foolish and disloyal speech at Dundee.[44] You know already that he delivered that speech without authority; and perhaps you know the feelings of resentment it has created among his own colleagues. It has confirmed the impression, which is pretty general, that he casts longing eyes over to his old party where a man of his conspicuous abilities, would have a much greater chance of getting to the top than in our ranks. Whether it would be better in the long run that a man with his views about the Navy and a friend of conscription in some form, should go over to the Tories, is a question I will not debate just now; for me it is sufficient that the addition of his energy and power to the Orange crusade at this moment, would be an enormous increase of the difficulties of our position.

But all the same if he persist in preaching this intolerable and impracticable idea of the mutilation of Ireland, there will have to be plain speaking, whatever the cost. I believe the Cabinet as a whole is perfectly sound; and that in pressing this solution against us, Winston would stand alone. As I gather, the guiding and inflexible principle of the Cabinet is that they will loyally stand by us; and [as] they now know that rather than consent to the mutilation of Ireland, we would

[44]Churchill had said that the claim of Ulster for special consideration could not be ignored.

prefer to see the postponement of Home Rule for some years longer, I assume that we may take their position as settled.

O'Connor to C.P.S., 20 October 1913 (Extract)

I believe he [Churchill] stands practically alone, though Lloyd George occasionally shows a little weakening.

Diary, 15 January 1914

Breakfast with Lloyd George. Simon (now Attorney-General and member of Cabinet) also there. Illingworth came in for a few minutes, also Rufus Isaacs, now Lord Chief Justice,[45] but neither stayed or took part in the general conversation which lasted over 2 hours. Found letter on table from Illingworth: "much will turn on the nature of the advice you give this morning. *Weigh your words:* I need not say more".

Navy Estimates. Question at issue. Should 2 capital ships be laid down or 4. If not 4 then Churchill will resign and carry most, if not all, his sea-lords with him. . . . Simon was in favour of pressing for two ships only and letting Churchill resign. It was not thought that any other member of the Cabinet would go with him. Both he and Lloyd George strongly of opinion that Churchill was only waiting for a favourable opportunity to leave the party and Simon thought that if he resigned on Home Rule and the coercion of Ulster it might be more damaging.

Lloyd George not inclined to stand out on this point [i.e. the number of ships] provided that by reduction in other directions he could get lower estimates for the following year and keep the total of the naval estimates for this year under 50 millions. I agreed. Obviously however a stringent and public undertaking to this effect would be necessary and it seemed unlikely that this could be got. Illingworth reported that Churchill would say no more than that he would do his best.

Simon undertook to prepare a memorandum for circulation among the Cabinet. This to be considered at another meeting on the following day. . . .

[45]Isaacs, formerly Attorney-General, had now become Lord Reading.

[Scott again discussed the issue of naval estimates with Simon on the following day.]

Diary, 16 January 1914 (Extract)

Simon did not raise again the question of the number of ships to be laid down, but we agreed that it was hopeless to get from Churchill any approach to moderation in expenditure and that he ought if possible to be forced to resign. Simon promised to complete his memorandum by Sunday morning [17 January] and I was asked to meet him and Lloyd George at midday on Sunday.

Going away I asked Simon if he thought it was any use my coming again, but he insisted on it very strongly.

Diary, 17 January 1914

Lord Morley

Morley had asked me to come and see him and I offered to go to lunch. The conversation seemed to spread itself out and I stayed till past 5.

Navy Estimates. He was very unsatisfactory about these—deplored their extravagance and the policy leading up to them, but did not propose to do anything to check either. Had no idea of voting against the 4 ships of this year's programme or of supporting George if he should make a stand. Said the naval expenditure for the following year would be even greater and that new taxation was inevitable. Thought Churchill's Cabinet Memorandum unanswerable on the point of our being committed, was angry with Lloyd George for his "Chronicle" interview and said Grey was incensed and would certainly now support Churchill and if he threatened resignation go with him. Thought Lloyd George would have no support of any weight if he resigned, but forgot all about Simon.

Irish Question. Equally unsuggestive here. Did not appear to approve of Home Rule within Home Rule. Thought Carson[46] and the Covenanters ought to have been checked earlier. But heartily agreed when I said that come what may we must give the Nationalists no ground for thinking that we have in any shape or form played them false. Treated negotiation and conference as definitely at an end. Said Law had demanded that there should be no Irish Parliament.

Yet he was charming and there were flashes of the old Morley.

[46] Sir Edward Carson, leader of Ulster in its resistance to Home Rule.

Diary, 18 January 1914

Lloyd George

I kept my appointment (changed by wire last night to 11 o'clock) and waited ¾ of an hour. Then George turned up, said that Simon was not coming and our meeting was off—that he had McKenna and Samuel downstairs and they were going into the Naval estimates with some Treasury Officials. Since Friday[47] he had discovered that the real naval expenditure to be provided for in the estimates for 1914-15 was between 55 and 56 millions. . . . He and McKenna and Samuel had agreed that Churchill must go. Asquith returning probably tomorrow. Expected to see him on Tuesday. Would like to see me afterwards on the same day.

Thinking the matter over have written urging him to make a stand even to the point of resignation.

C.P.S. to Lloyd George, 18 January 1914

I have been thinking over our conversations and in particular over what you told me this morning. In face of the enormous liabilities incurred by Churchill without authority it seems to me that it is hardly possible any longer to temporise. I don't know what you will think it right to do but I don't see how a Chancellor of the Exchequer holding your views is to submit to treatment of that kind and to acquiesce in a naval expenditure running up next year to far above 50 millions with no assurance of future reduction, and that at a time when our relations with Germany are particularly good and no danger threatens us. It is impossible to justify it. From the point of view alike of your personal credit and of the power and credit of the party I would far rather see you out of office. There need be no damage to Home Rule. Home Rule and other good causes will be damaged when Liberalism ceases to be true to itself and somebody it seems to me has got to save it now.

Diary, 21 January 1914

Lloyd George

Breakfast alone, 9.30-11. Began at once on events of yesterday. Interviews with Churchill and Prime Minister (returned previous evening from Riviera). 5 hours with Churchill and with Churchill and Prime Minister together—some very straight talk, "polite but deadly" as

[47] 16 January.

Churchill put it to the Prime Minister. Position: Lloyd George prepared to face all present obligations including the 4 ships, but only on condition (1) that a clean breast is made of everything to Parliament and (2) that there is a great and assured reduction for the following year (1915-16). On this basis estimates for this year (1914-15) would be over 53 millions and there must be 2d. on the income tax to meet the deficit. . . .

The conflict with Churchill was in regard to reductions in 1915-16. At first Churchill was obdurate and would give no pledge, as he had been also on Sunday. Then Lloyd George made a home thrust: "You will resign. What will you resign upon? Everything has been conceded to you. You have your 4 ships; your estimates are up to over 53 millions. You are not satisfied. You want more. And you go out of office on the top of that and expect the country to support you".

On that Churchill's tone completely altered and for the first time he began seriously to give his mind to the question of reductions. He made some concessions—ships could be put out of commission instead of so vast a proportion being kept always ready for sea, acceleration of "Canadian["] ships could be made nominal rather than real, and there could be minor economies. But the aggregate was not enough. Lloyd George required altogether 6 or 7 millions, so as to bring down the 1915-16 estimates to 46 or 47 millions, the figure estimated for in the current year (1913-14). Churchill could not see his way. Did not know if he could carry his Board, especially Prince Louis of Battenberg[48] who, being a German, would be bound to take the high (British) patriotic line. [Sir John] Jellicoe,[49] a far abler man, easier to deal with.

Conference with Prime Minister. Asquith declared that if Lloyd George resigned he would not carry on but should dissolve Parliament within a week. . . . Here Lloyd George delivered his second home thrust. In the presence of the Prime Minister he stated there was a strong impression among important people, and those not merely Churchill's opponents on the question of naval armaments, that if he did not resign on that he would resign on the Irish question and that therefore it was useless to make concessions to him, and Lloyd George challenged him to say if this were so or not. Churchill greatly confused and taken aback. Had no such intention, but could not commit himself in advance etc. Asquith expressed his full confidence in him and so the matter ended, but the effect will be to make it far more difficult for Churchill to take the course which had been foretold.

[48]First Sea Lord, a naturalised Englishman of Austro-German origin.
[49]Second Sea Lord.

Nothing definitely settled as to amount of reductions for 1915-16. Lloyd George demand[ing] estimates of 46 millions, but would not reject 47. He would, however, require a pledge not from Churchill but from the Prime Minister. "Why?" asked Churchill. "Because I do not trust you" was the reply. "I had your promise for this year and you have broken it; my whole Budget was based on your estimate and now it has proved wholly delusive". This ended the interview.

To me Lloyd George said that, though he asked for estimates in 1915-16 of 46-7 millions[,] he would not actually resign if he got a pledge for 49. Asked me to stay in town over the Cabinets tomorrow and on Friday and to see him again with Simon. Naval estimates not likely to come on till Friday's Cabinet. . . .

Diary, 22 January 1914

Lloyd George, Simon, Masterman
Met at Treasury (6.30) after Cabinet. Lloyd George very tired; Simon alert, incisive, distrustful of all pledges which came from Churchill. Interview brief and hurried. Lloyd George called out for part of time.

Crucial question put to me would the Liberal party in the country stand a 54 million estimate [in 1914-15] with merely a promise of reduction in 1915-16. Replied that I did not think they would push revolt so far as to turn out the Government; there was too much at stake, but that to acquiesce in that or anything like that as a standard would wreck the party.

Simon obviously dissatisfied, and left rather hastily soon after. Had some talk with him afterwards on telephone. He urged (1) that to put { keep a spendthrift in a great spending department meant of necessity extravagant expenditure (2) that if there were any reality in the proposed reductions there was no sense in postponing them till next year; they ought to take effect at once in this year's estimates.

Diary, 23 January 1914

Lloyd George
Breakfast. . . . I pressed Simon's point about immediate reductions. Lloyd George replied that he was getting them so far as was possible, but that most of the economies would only apply to commitments which would only fall to a small extent into this year.

I said I agreed with Simon that no general undertaking to reduce was of the slightest value, that the pledge must be in relation to specific items of expenditure. On this basis what economies could he [see] his way to in 1915-16 as compared with 1914-15 for which the estimate was 54 millions? How did he propose to reach what he called "normal" estimates, i.e. 46-47 millions? He gave particulars [totalling 6¼ millions] .... Asked if he thought Simon would retire rather than accept the 54 million estimate. He thought certainly not. He was out for Churchill's head—a kind of Robespierre—and McKenna, Runciman, Samuel and Hobhouse[50] were with him, but they could not act alone. Beauchamp[51] also very strong. Mrs. Churchill a good Radical and was doing all she could with Churchill. She said Admirals weren't helping him at all, but sat there "like a row of stuck pigs".

Ireland. Asquith decided to make statement as to terms offered to Ulster immediately on meeting of Parliament. These go so far that impossible for Opposition to abet rebellion in face of them. Cabinet united in determination to meet force by force. Churchill had now finally agreed to stand in with the rest of the Cabinet in this. . . .

Diary, 25 January 1914

Lunched with Lloyd George at his house, Walton Heath. McKenna and Hawtrey of the Treasury also there. Masterman (Financial Secretary to the Treasury) looked in after lunch. Lloyd George opened up freely on the Naval estimates at lunch. . . .

Lloyd George had spent the morning in bed with a headache and though he was lively enough at lunch seemed tired and slack afterwards. McKenna on the other hand confident and pugnacious. Said to me "You know I am a big navy man, but I am against waste". He contended all through that we were getting nothing for the extra expenditure and declared that the vote for construction was actually less today than in his day when the estimates were 6 and 8 millions lower. The difference—apart from sheer waste—was practically all due to the policy of keeping almost the whole fleet instantly ready for sea. This was the Beresford policy and came in with Churchill. . . .[52]

Lloyd George had to leave to see a caller before we broke up and we all three remarked on his spiritlessness. Probably it was only due to fatigue and he will be all right after a good night, but he certainly

[50]Sir Charles Hobhouse, Chancellor of the Duchy of Lancaster.
[51]Lord Beauchamp, First Commissioner of Works.
[52]Lord Charles Beresford, Commander-in-Chief of the Channel Fleet from 1907 to 1909, had been an outspoken critic of admiralty policy prior to Churchill's accession to this office.

showed very little fight. At one moment indeed he said it was more the Prime Minister's business than his and he thought he should just leave him to settle it. McKenna protested that this would mean certain defeat and finally he said there must be a meeting of those members of the Cabinet who felt strongly with him and asked McKenna to call it at the Treasury tomorrow afternoon.

I remarked that we should have to remind him of a certain passage in a famous interview[53] and of the "bold and independent initiative" then called for. On way back to Manchester wrote letter to Lloyd George appended.

C.P.S. to Lloyd George, 25 January 1914

The conversation this afternoon seemed to me to go a long way towards showing a way out. McKenna's statement that construction is actually less than in his time though estimates (apart from arrears) are 6 to 8 millions higher seems to me immensely important because construction—the number of our ships as against German ships—is what everybody talks about and is the only thing the public understands. If then we can maintain the full programme of construction and at the same time, by reverting to the old pre-Churchill standard of preparedness for sea, save ultimately some 5 or 6 millions, and immediately an appreciable instalment of that sum, the problems would be solved. . . .

If you carry your point as to the standard of preparedness (which in view of present relations with Germany it would be monstrous if you don't) there would be not merely the promise but the virtual certainty of substantial economies this year and much larger ones next year. This would be better than any paper promises and the beauty of it is that it violates no undertaking of any kind and is not open to effective public attack. . . .

I feel it in my bones that the fight has got to be now or never— and that despite all adverse conditions. And it doesn't seem such a difficult fight. I can't quite imagine the Prime Minister dissolving because he won't accept the pre-Churchill standard of preparedness, to which for years he was a party, and that is the key of the whole situation.

Perhaps inspired by Scott's letter (or by others in similar vein from associates like Simon) Lloyd George made a final attempt to curtail Churchill at a cabinet

[53]Presumably Lloyd George's own interview with the *Daily Chronicle* on 1 January 1914.

meeting on 29 January. But McKenna clearly felt that, already on the 25th, the fight had gone out of Lloyd George. Certainly by early February the Chancellor of the Exchequer was no longer struggling. Churchill got his four battleships and estimates of over £50 millions for that year, with only a contingent promise of reductions for the following year. He was "in high spirits" at this solution.[54] *McKenna and Simon were not.*

Diary, 6 February 1914

McKenna

Saw McKenna primarily about the Press Competition Bill. Then he opened up on subject of the Naval Estimates taking it up at the point we had left it on the Sunday week previous at Walton Heath. Reminded me that he had at last been actually rude to Lloyd George on the subject of his ridiculously inadequate proposal to be satisfied with the promise —and not even the promise, but the hope—of reductions in 1915-16, without any serious attempt to secure reduction in 1914-15, and how, thus goaded, Lloyd George had proposed a meeting next day at the Treasury of the party of economy in the Cabinet. The meeting was held, but, instead of any improvement in Lloyd George's attitude, it was as bad as ever, or worse. So much so that after the meeting was over McKenna wrote and told him that he could not undertake to follow his lead in the Cabinet and must hold himself entirely free to take his own line. I gathered that Simon and Hobhouse had taken similar action.

Lloyd George, McKenna said, had now given up the fight and was not troubling himself further in the matter. "What does it mean?", asked McKenna, "he is now Churchill's man". I suggested that perhaps it was because he had put his resignation on the table and did not want to leave it there. "Resignation!", cried McKenna with infinite scorn. "You don't mean to say he has offered his resignation to the Prime Minister." I said I understood he had threatened to resign. But McKenna only dissolved in Homeric laughter.

The only explanation he could himself suggest was that Lloyd George was acting as bell-wether to bring the stalwarts into the Churchill fold.

The fight in the Cabinet he said would go on. Nothing had been decided and nothing would be decided for the present. He was working hard at the detailed figures and was in good hopes of getting the estimates well below 50 millions (I think he said 47 or 48 and this to include

[54]See A. J. Marder, *From the Dreadnought to Scapa Flow*, vol. 1, pp. 323-6.

arrears of construction). "Two years ago", he said, "I was fighting one against 19 in the Cabinet for estimates 10 millions less than those now proposed and now it seems the position is reversed, though the estimates are 10 millions higher. I am, you know, a big navy man, but just because I want a big navy I hate waste and we are not getting ships for our money". I rather liked him. He was so game. . . .

IX] THE HOME RULE TIMETABLE

With the issue of battleships out of the way, attention turned to the increasingly urgent problem of Ireland.

By 1914, a Home Rule Bill had twice passed the House of Commons and been rejected by the Lords. Under the Parliament Act of 1911, if it went through the Commons a third time it would become law. The Bill treated Ireland as a whole. The Protestants in the north-east of Ireland rejected this notion of Irish unity, and were prepared to resist any attempt to bring them under a Dublin Parliament. For this purpose they had set up their own armed force, known as the Covenanters or Ulster Volunteers. The Conservative party, according to its leader Bonar Law, would go to any lengths in supporting Ulster's resistance. And it was apparent that the military forces of the crown could not be relied on to coerce Ulster if it rebelled.

The response of the Asquith government seemed pusillanimous. The ministry took no firm action against the setting up of a private army in Ulster or the gun-running which accompanied it. Nor did it prosecute the Conservative leaders for flagrantly seditious speeches. Worst of all, it offered to amend the Home Rule Bill to meet some of Ulster's objections, but did not state which amendments it would accept. Thus Ulster was inspired to increase its show of resistance in order to extract from the government as many concessions as possible.

Yet Asquith's policy was also the policy of the leading Irish Nationalists. They believed that Ulstermen, presented with the impending fact of Home Rule, would be obliged to moderate their position. They felt it contrary to the spirit of Irish self-government that British forces should act to suppress the Volunteers in the north. And they did not want the Liberal government, or themselves, to begin the process of granting concessions to Ulster, lest they should be denounced as traitors by their own followers in Ireland. Hence they could only propose inaction, as they waited for the Home Rule timetable to run its course.

Diary, 7 February 1914

Lunched with Dillon at Bath Club and had two hours with him. He argued strongly and persistently against any statement by the Prime

Minister at this stage of the particular concessions he was prepared to offer to Ulster. To do so, he said, would be

(1) to create an impossible Parliamentary position. The Opposition would at once say "we cannot consider these proposals till we see them in black and white in the form of clauses to the Bill. Produce your clauses". Then, if clauses were produced, they would say "Oh, but this is a new Bill. Withdraw your Bill; you admit it is unsatisfactory. At the least let the electors say whether they think so too". Thus the demand for a dissolution would be greatly strengthened. The Opposition both in Parliament and in Ulster would be in the wildest spirits. "Now", they would say, "at last we have got them on the run".

(2) In Ireland the effect would be disastrous. Already on the mere rumour of concessions protests pour in. If they were announced on authority meetings and resolutions would follow especially from the Ulster Catholics. "Intolerable", it would be said, "that our Catholic archbishop (of Armagh) should be subject to Orange domination[55] and that Catholic education in the northern counties should be at the mercy of the same power". Redmond could not stand against such protests. He would have either to declare against the proposed concessions or to remain silent in the House, which would be nearly as bad. If on the other hand the concessions were only announced on the Suggestion Clause after the Bill was through Committee and was practically safe, then Redmond could always say "Well I dislike the changes; I accepted them with the greatest reluctance, but they were the price I had to pay, and at any rate I have got the Bill".

His view was that [of] the *policy* of the Ladybank speech[56] which expressed willingness to make concessions but threw the onus of making proposals onto the other side. He admitted that a "development" of this might be needed, but that could only mean that the direction in which the concessions should be made, the subjects to which they should relate, should be indicated. But he was very nervous about going any distance in the way of particulars.

He urged that the Unionists should be challenged to say what they mean by Ulster and did not believe they could give any practicable definition. If they said the four predominantly Protestant counties that would never be accepted by the excluded Protestants and Covenanters in the other counties, not even by the small Protestant minority in Donegal. If on the other hand they took the barony as the unit then

[55]Orangemen was a name (probably derived from William of Orange) applied to the ultra-Protestants of the north-east.
[56]By Asquith.

there would be found predominantly Catholic baronies in every county. The puzzle was really insoluble.

Then again how could the Catholic population even in the predominantly Protestant districts be expected to accept Orange domination. I remarked that there might be some Imperial control to secure fair-play. He replied, if that were done, how could they resist the claim of Protestant minorities in the rest of Ireland to similar Imperial protection?

Altogether his whole line was to make difficulties, not to solve them. . . .

C.P.S. to L. T. Hobhouse, 21 April 1914 (Extract)

I've had one or two interesting communications lately which I'll tell you about when you next come along. One was a visit from [Geoffrey] Robinson, Buckle's successor in the Editorship of the "Times",[57] who wrote asking to see me and did actually motor over from some place in Yorkshire to Portinscale where I was staying for the Easter weekend. He wanted to confer on the Ulster question and we had quite an interesting "conversation" and didn't really much differ—rather a new thing for the Thunderer[58] to do!

Scott's account of his discussion with Robinson, from which the following is a very brief extract, seems only to demonstrate the impasse which the situation had reached:

Diary, 13 April 1914 (Extract)

We talked all round question and agreed as to hopelessness of Bonar Law as negotiator and superiority of Carson's frank realism. Finally I suggested that there was in principle pretty much agreement between us as to following points:

(1) Irish question has to be tackled now, not postponed. Cannot wait for general scheme of "Federation" or Devolution.

(2) Nobody really wants a divided Ireland. Any arrangement for excluding Ulster must be provisional only.

[57]Robinson (who in 1917 was to change his name to Dawson) had been editor of *The Times* since 1912. The paper was at this stage owned by Lord Northcliffe, the founder of the "popular" press in Britain—in particular the *Daily Mail*.
[58]Nickname for *The Times*.

(3) Compulsion on a resisting Ulster is and must always be morally and politically impracticable as a permanent policy.
[The next diary-entry explains the context of the exchange of letters between Scott and Hobhouse which follows:]

Diary, 26 April 1914

Dillon called on me at my house, having been at meeting in Manchester previous evening. We spoke of landing of arms and other illegalities in Ulster on previous day. I said we had perhaps made mistake in not checking volunteer movement sooner. He dissented and strongly deprecated any action even now which might lead to actual conflict between army and volunteers—fearing effect on future of Ireland. . . . [The rest of this interview is summarised in Scott's reply to the letter from Hobhouse which follows.]

Hobhouse to C.P.S., 2 May 1914 (Extract)

I was, with you, all in favour of coming to terms with Carson, provided always that the Government would make it clear that in the end they would not bow to physical force. But now I fear that is precisely what they have done. To make overtures, fresh overtures and unsolicited, to Carson on the morrow of the gun-running can only be taken as a surrender—a surrender which I anticipated from the moment when I read Asquith's sonorous declaration about vindicating the law. He always talks like that when he means to do nothing.

We said last month that the question then raised was a much greater one than that of Home Rule. I am afraid that question is now settled. This government at least will not fight the forces of society when these really make up their minds to a stand. Better far, to my mind, to lose Home Rule than to accept a compromise based on the dictation of Carson with the backing of the army and society. . . .

In itself I am in favour of the voluntary principle[59] and therefore of inclusion by county option. But that should have been carried through earlier, not under coercion. As it is we have given in after a fashion which must have permanent and most serious reaction on political methods.

Perhaps I am too pessimistic—I hope so.

[59]That is, the principle that the various parts of Ireland should have the right to choose whether or not to enter a Home Rule Ireland.

C.P.S. to Hobhouse, 4 May [60] **1914 (Extract)**

I quite understand your feeling and largely share it, but the situation is not simple and there is some excuse I think to be made for the Government. Of course Asquith is strong only in words and in a situation needing immediate decision and action would always fail. But his natural timidity has been re-enforced by strong pressure from the Irish.

It chanced that Dillon was in Manchester on the day (Sunday) the news came and he came to my house to see me. He was dead against any strong display of force, or any prosecutions, but was quite in favour of a gradual strengthening of the military force in Ulster as he feared bad riots later and said it was essential the police should be adequately supported as otherwise they might cave in altogether. More than half of them (including the chief of police in Belfast) are in active sympathy with the Carsonites, but he thought they would do their duty if they were supported.

In the leader today I have put the case for action a little more strongly. I have had a summons today from George to lunch with him tomorrow and as it's Budget day the matter must be rather urgent.

The summons from Lloyd George, with whom Scott lunched on 4 May, did not prove to be of great moment. Lloyd George wanted Scott to find out what the Irish leaders thought of proposals for a federation (in which other parts of Britain, such as Scotland and Wales, would share the same measure of self-government as Ireland). Dillon, whom Scott saw the next day, told him precisely what he thought of it. He was "dead against anything on this line, realising that any arrangement suitable to other parts of the Kingdom would involve great reduction in terms offered to Ireland. His great anxiety was to knock the whole proposal on the head."

Two days later Scott lunched with Lord Esher, with whom he had been corresponding about Ireland and foreign policy. (Esher insisted on writing to Scott as "My dear Sir Charles", apparently unaware of his firm resolve against accepting any form of enoblement). Esher was an important figure in government circles, having been involved since 1902 in army reforms. He was a principal member of the Committee of Imperial Defence, which consisted of certain cabinet ministers (chosen by the Prime Minister) and military advisers. It was a body of undefined powers having oversight of all naval and army affairs.

Diary, 6 May 1914 (Extract)

Had an interesting 2 hours with Lord Esher. He had asked me primarily

[60]This appears to be an error for 3 May.

in order to discuss the powers and action of the Imperial Defence Committee, of which he is a permanent member. But we discussed chiefly the Ulster question. He is in intimate communication with both army and navy men, and was strongly of opinion that neither service could be trusted to take any active steps against rebellion in Ulster. It would not matter, he thought, to them what the precise merits of the case were on which trouble arose. There was in both services a strong feeling that Nationalists were disloyal and against the flag and that the Ulstermen were just the opposite. In the army feeling was strengthened by the sort of way in which the troops were cold-shouldered in the south of Ireland, particularly by the women who would not look at them.

I said probably the navy would be quite sufficient to bring Belfast to reason and that a short blockade would be effective. He doubted if the navy would fire a shot at vessels entering the port, but admitted when I put it to him that they might stop merchantmen if food ships were admitted. As a single gunboat would suffice for the whole operation his view seemed to me rather extravagant, but he stuck to it.

As to the Defence Committee he admitted when I pressed him that the contention he had made to me in writing, that the Committee had nothing to do with policy, and knew nothing about it, but only were concerned with hypothetical preparations for hypothetical contingencies[,] was not strictly correct. We discussed the events of August, 1911, when without the knowledge of the country or even of the cabinet (he assumed I knew this last, as I did) we had come within an ace of war with Germany. I had assumed that this came about through the action of the Defence Committee, but he denied this. The Defence Committee, other than members of the cabinet, were mostly away on their holidays, and the whole business was carried through by a small junta of cabinet members of the Committee. . . . It consisted in fact of the Prime Minister, Lloyd George, Churchill, Grey, General French and Lt. Gen. Ewart and two admirals, I think Admiral Seymour and Prince Louis of Battenberg. But he admitted that it was known to the Defence Committee that intimate communications were going on between the army and navy chiefs of France and England with a view to a possible war with Germany, and he added that they are still going on, in spite of the tremendous row in the cabinet and of the pledge given that nothing of the kind should happen again without the cabinet's knowledge—strange that he should speak so freely about these matters unless he knew that I already knew, as I did, which he may partly have inferred from the tone of the conversation. What was new to me was that in his view the pledge given was worthless.

Below is the account of the chance first meeting between Scott and Lord Fisher, the great naval administrator whose cause Scott was to champion so vigorously in the next few years. Fisher, an outspoken, flamboyant, controversial figure, had been First Sea Lord from 1904 to 1910 and was to be recalled to that post by Churchill soon after the outbreak of the war.

Diary, 15 June 1914

Saw Churchill at Admiralty. . . . As I was going in to Churchill's room Lord Fisher was coming out. Churchill introduced me and immediately he heard the name of the Manchester Guardian he became extremely cordial and begged me to come and see him, which I promised to do.

In retaliation against the establishment of a private army in Ulster, the Nationalists also began setting up and arming a force of "Volunteers." Dillon told Scott on 16 June "that it was nonsense for the National Volunteers to be deprived of the opportunity of arming themselves when the Ulster volunteers were already armed."

Scott seemed to be more concerned than members of the government about the way in which the law was being taken into other people's hands:

Diary, 17 June 1914

Breakfasted with Lloyd George next day, but only had a few minutes private conversation with him. He evidently sympathised with Dillon about the arming of the National Volunteers whose formation he greatly welcomed. I protested in the strongest way that to allow this by repealing the Arms Proclamation, or openly refraining from enforcing it, would be a complete abnegation of the responsibilities of government.[61] He seemed surprised, but did not attempt to controvert this.

C.P.S. to Hobhouse, 19 June 1914 (Extract)

Have you seen [J. A.] Hobson's scathing pamphlet, "Traffic in Treason"?[62] There is a tremendous lot of truth in it though I think he takes a very one-sided view of the immediate situation.

[61]The Irish administration, following the formation of the National Volunteers (but not earlier when Ulster began arming), had issued a proclamation forbidding the importation of arms into Ireland.

[62]Hobson was a prominent writer (from a left-wing position) on political and economic matters.

I confess I am beginning to feel with him that the existing Liberal party is played out and that if it is to count for anything in the future it must be reconstructed largely on a labour basis.

C.P.S. to Hobhouse, 25 June 1914 (Extract)

I lunched with Lord Fisher on Tuesday[63] and found him most interesting. He just stands and orates about all manner of things and one has little to do but let him run on; but he is very frank and jolly and strangely enough has a great opinion of the Manchester Guardian.

Diary, 30 June 1914

Breakfasted with Bryce. . . . We talked a good deal about Russia. He thought she was rapidly becoming a menace to Europe with her vast and rapidly increasing population and her also rapidly increasing prosperity. The Duma[64] was no check on the ambitions of the official classes. Germany, he thought, was right to arm and she would need every man . . . .

Met Dillon at his club at 11 o'clock. He spoke of Crewe's speech in introducing the Amending Bill[65] and actually inviting root and branch amendments[,] and his abject thanks to Carson for keeping order[,] as monstrous. The Nationalists had been anxious about it and had received an assurance that Crewe would speak strictly on instructions. . . . He had just had a long interview with Morley. Personally he was as delightful as ever but politically incredibly weak. He had actually said "Carson has won and the sooner the public knew it the better". . . .

[63] 23 June 1914.
[64] The Russian Parliament.
[65] A measure amending the Home Rule Bill to meet Ulster's objections.

2. *The Decision to Intervene,*
July-October 1914

Between 1911 and 1914, the international situation seemed markedly to improve —notwithstanding Germany's intransigent response to Britain's appeal for a "naval holiday". The Russian annexation of Persia which Scott had freely anticipated did not take place. Far more important, the great powers weathered upheavals in the Balkans in 1912 and 1913 which threatened to embroil them, partly because Germany was prepared to act with Britain to localise the conflict.

The following letter from Hobhouse to Scott in 1913 reflects the satisfaction felt by radicals at this trend.

Hobhouse to C.P.S., 4 June 1913 (Extract)

Our Foreign Policy Committee has been considering what we should do in view of the changed situation, whether to dissolve or continue to urge the questions upon which we are not yet satisfied. Neither course seemed desirable. Grey has done a great deal towards meeting us, and on the whole, we thought the best thing would be to proclaim our existence, and also our satisfaction at the turn things have taken, by a dinner. . . . [We feel] that much the best form that the function could take would be that of a dinner to you, as being a recognition of the line which the Guardian has taken all the way through, of the fact that a good deal of its policy has now been accepted by the Government, and as an indication or an argument that the rest of its policy will have to be accepted in due course.

But in July-August 1914, the painfully-won harmony which the great powers seemed to have achieved collapsed. What destroyed it was the refusal of the German government again to act with Britain as arbiter in a Balkan crisis. Instead Germany threw its weight on the side of conflict.

In June 1914 the heir to the Austrian throne was assassinated on Austrian territory by a Serb patriot. The Austrian government seized on this incident as grounds for crushing Serbia. In so doing it disregarded the fact that Russia, which

89

had its own ambitions in the Balkans, was committed to preserving Serbian independence.

Scott was in Jena during July for reasons of health. He returned to England late in the month to a darkening situation. In the first place there had been a serious occurrence of bloodshed in Ireland. On 26 July the Irish Volunteers, following Ulster's example, landed a consignment of arms. They were apprehended by a force of police and soldiers, but mostly got away. When the soldiers returned to Dublin they were stoned by the crowd, and opened fire in retaliation. Three people were killed and thirty-eight wounded. This show of sternness by the authorities seemed much in contrast to their lax treatment of Ulster.

Meanwhile the European situation was fast deteriorating. On 23 July the Austrian government sent a savage ultimatum to Serbia; Grey's reading of it at a cabinet meeting next day was for most ministers the first indication of approaching disaster. The Serbian reply, in Grey's words, "went further than we had ventured to hope in the way of submission."[1] But it availed nothing. On 25 July Austria-Hungary broke off diplomatic relations with Serbia and ordered partial mobilisation. On 26 July Grey appealed for an international conference. He was rebuffed by Germany next day.

Scott's conversation with Lloyd George at this point is of particular interest. It reveals the Chancellor of the Exchequer's ambivalent position in the days before the emergence of the Belgian question. He did not, in effect, want Britain to become involved, at least to begin with. Yet he recognised that Austria was bent on war, and that Germany would, for its convenience, convert a Balkan war into a European war (a clear appreciation of the Schlieffen tactics, whereby the German government had decided that in the event of war becoming likely it would overrun France—whatever the French attitude might be—before Russia was able to mobilise). In such circumstances, Lloyd George's sympathy lay with France.

Diary, 27 July 1914

Dillon. Met Dillon at Bath Club by appointment at 10.45 on my return from Jena. Found him strongly excited by the Dublin shootings and just starting to see Birrell at Irish Office where I afterwards heard from Illingworth [that] Redmond and Asquith were also present. Went with him to Irish office and talked by the way and for some time outside.

He said he had warned Birrell of the trouble there might be if attempt were made to seize arms after once they had been landed and begged him not to leave Ireland till he had made quite sure this would not be done. Birrell promised no attempt should be made to follow up arms once they had passed the customs officers' area. This promise

[1] Grey of Fallodon, *Twenty-Five Years*, vol. I, p. 311.

completely violated. The subsequent shootings in Dublin monstrous and would excite the most violent indignation among all Nationalists.

The whole proceeding deliberately intended to be provocative and to cause division between Government and Nationalists by the police official concerned (Arnold). General conviction in Ireland that the Government were deliberately dealing out different measure to Ulster and to rest of Ireland. Position as to Amending Bill difficult before, now impossible. Nationalists could not vote for it. Fixed for tomorrow but must be postponed. Asquith had told them quite needless for Nationalists to vote for 2nd reading of Bill but had since told them that if they abstained whole Labour party and a great many Liberals would abstain also and Government would be in peril. Party meeting had been called for 12 today to consider this situation. It would still be held, but would deal with very different matters. Adjournment would be moved on meeting of the House and Redmond would demand explanations.

We spoke briefly about European situation. He agreed as to monstrous character of "Times" leader promising England's support to Dual Alliance [i.e. France and Russia] in event of war. I said we should do our utmost to turn out the government, whatever the cost, if they took such a course. He said prevention better than cure. Keep them out of it.

Lloyd George. Saw him shortly afterwards at the Treasury. As to the attempt by police and men of Scotch border regiment to seize guns from Irish volunteers action had been taken by Arnold entirely on his own responsibility without consulting his chief or the Lord Lieutenant. He had already been suspended. Only first line of volunteers had been disarmed when, finding there would be resistance, the rest were allowed to disperse. The grave matter of the firing on the crowd in Dublin was done by the returning soldiers without any order from their officers. A stringent enquiry into the whole of the circumstances of both collisions would be held. Incidentally mentioned only 6,000 rifles landed at Larne not 50,000.

As to the European situation there could be no question of our taking part in any war in the first instance. Knew of no Minister who would be in favour of it and he did not believe the "Times" article represented the views even of the Foreign Office officials. But he admitted that a difficult question would arise if the German fleet were attacking French towns on the other side of the Channel and the French sowed the Channel with mines. He also evidently contemplated our going a certain distance with France and Russia in putting diplomatic pressure on Austria. Then if war broke out we might make it

91

easy for Italy[2] to keep out by as it were pairing with her. This would be a service to Italy, who hated Austria much more than she did France and no more wanted to be in the war than we did, also a service to France by relieving her of one antagonist.

As to the prospect of war he was very gloomy. He thought Austria *wanted* war—she had wanted it before during the Balkan crisis—and not an accommodation. She wanted to "teach Servia a lesson" and suppress her ambitions. Germany did not want war, but would be bound to support Austria. He thought if there was to be war it would come quickly so that Germany which could mobilise in a week could gain the initial advantage over France which took a fortnight and Russia which took a month. Germany would probably seek to strike hard at France and cripple her in the first instance, then swing back and strike at Russia. By sea she might use her superiority in order (1) to land a force behind the French force advancing to meet the German invasion across Belgium, (2) to join the Austrian fleet in the Mediterranean and cut the French communications with Algeria where she has a large force of very serviceable native troops.

I pointed out the danger of bluffing—of pretending to stand by the "Triple Entente" in order that we might claim as a price for retiring from it the corresponding retirement of Italy from the Triple Alliance, but he defended it on the ground of its serviceableness to France, remarking "You know I am much more pro-French than you are".

Illingworth. Had a good deal of talk with Illingworth while waiting for Lloyd George and he stayed in a tiresome way most of the time that I was talking with Lloyd George. Traversed a good deal of the same ground. He was emphatic that we could not be parties to the war as we have no interest in the Servian quarrel, but this would only apply to the first stage in which as he said Russia and France would be the aggressors, and I don't think he meant anything beyond this. He abused the "Times" article, however, and said Northcliffe wasn't fit to have a paper. I said I didn't care a pin about Northcliffe and his press, but that the article was not inspired by Northcliffe but by what the Times believed to be the views of the Foreign Office, that experience on a score of occasions had shown that in regard to naval and military affairs "Times" was semi-official and that as he knew a "Times" man actually was allowed a room at the Foreign Office. He could only say that on this occasion he thought it was not so.

I insisted that the only course for us would be to make it plain from the first that if Russia and France went to war we should not be in it.

[2] Italy was still nominally a member of the Triple Alliance with Germany and Austria.

I hoped Grey would keep them out of this war as he had of the war they threatened last year, but if he let us into it there would be an end of the existing Liberal combination and the next advance would have to be based on Radicalism and Labour.

C.P.S. to Hobhouse, 29 July 1914 (Extract)

What a monstrous and truly hellish thing this war will be if it really brings the rest of Europe into it. It ought to sound the knell of all the autocracies—including that of our own Foreign Office.

Loreburn to C.P.S., 31 July 1914 (Extract)

I send a line to express my most hearty sympathy and admiration of the line you are taking about this threat of war. It is the time of trial which we have thought of as possible after the worship of the "Entente".

I have come back today from London. The Cabinet is I believe, by a majority, quite against our intervening. You know what are the elements on the wrong side.

.... I have been in touch with Bryce and am ready in concert with him to write or speak in Parliament when it seems right to move—in concert with you.

By the time Scott visited London again, a week later, the die was cast. The course of events, briefly, was as follows.

On 28 July Austria attacked Serbia. Russia, as Serbia's protector, began mobilising against Austria, and on 31 July (anticipating German intervention) the Russian government ordered general mobilisation. This caused Germany to invoke the military timetable foreseen by Lloyd George. Up until the end of July there had been only one actual declaration of war: Austria's on Serbia. Now Germany declared war on Russia on 1 August, sent an ultimatum to Belgium on 2 August, and declared war on France on 3 August.

The speed and ruthlessness of Germany's actions alike against probable opponents, possible opponents, and innocent bystanders shocked the British cabinet into firm decision. As late as 2 August Asquith had been writing to Bonar Law (who was demanding British intervention) in terms much like those used by Lloyd George to Scott on 27 July. "We are under no obligation," Asquith wrote, "express or implied, either to France or Russia to render them military or naval help." He conceded that Britain had a "long standing and intimate friendship with France" and that it was "a British interest that France should not be crushed as a great Power." But "we do not think that these duties

93

impose upon us the obligation at this moment of active intervention either by sea or land." Britain's only effective obligations, therefore, were first to keep the German fleet away from the French coast,[3] and secondly "our treaty obligations" towards Belgium. "It is right, therefore, before deciding whether any and what action on our part is necessary to know what are the circumstances and conditions of any German interference with Belgian territory."[4]

Almost as Asquith was writing, the uncertainty over Belgium was being dispelled. With the news of Germany's violation of that country, the non-interventionist section in the British cabinet disintegrated. Only two members, Morley and Burns (both of negligible importance by this time), persisted in resigning. The rest either came down firmly for intervention, as did Lloyd George, or were reduced to helpless lamentation. Sir John Simon was to be found among the latter.

Telegram, C.P.S. to Lloyd George, 3 August 1914

Feeling of intense exasperation among leading Liberals here at prospect of Government embarking on war. No man who is responsible can lead us again.

J. A. Hobson to C.P.S., 3 August 1914

Learn from Ramsay MacDonald[5] and elsewhere Government likely to make a war committal this afternoon in which case several ministers—probably Harcourt Simon Burns—resign. Coalition Government might then be announced. Massingham intends to commit Nation to opposition policy and would like to get cooperation of Guardian with Daily News, and to consider formation of cooperative action with labour party. Could you empower someone to discuss policy today, if possible.

Address British neutrality,

19 Buckingham Street,
Strand.

Will you personally join committee?

Hobson to C.P.S., n.d. "Monday 9 p.m." [3 August 1914] (Extract)

Grey *appears*, so far as we know yet, to have carried the cabinet and the

---

[3] The German government offered no objection to this demand.

[4] This important letter is to be found in Robert Blake, *The Unknown Prime Minister* (Eyre and Spottiswoode, London, 1955), pp. 223-4.

[5] Chairman of the parliamentary Labour party (he resigned two days later).

House with him. This, of course, may turn out not to be so. . . . If there is war tomorrow, as seems pretty certain, our Neutrality Committee will drop that name, and lie low as a watching Conciliation Committee, waiting some opportunity to press for peace. Grey's speech appears to have converted some even of our friends to regard the war as justified.[6] What Grey said about the French defenceless north coast makes it clear we had a real obligation to defend that coast. But that would have been met by accepting Germany's undertaking not to cross the Straits of Dover. When we refused that bargain for neutrality, and insisted further on the preservation of neutrality of Belgium, we virtually made *that* the *casus belli*. This I personally regard as indefensible, though Germany's brutal behaviour to Belgium merits every reprobation. However the harm appears to be done.

G. H. Mair (London Office of the "Manchester Guardian") to C.P.S., n.d. [probably night of 3-4 August 1914]

Am informed that Lichnowsky[7] has told some of his friends today that his Government has got into the hands of the crown prince's party and lost reason altogether. Ultimatums have been issued not only to Belgium but to Norway and Sweden and Denmark.[8] I have this directly from one who talked with the Ambassador. I am informed that the Government papers when published will as Grey said throw a fresh light on the efforts of the Government to keep peace and on the impossibility of preventing Germans from taking provocative action.

Mair to C.P.S., 3 August [1914], "1.30 a.m." [probably in fact the morning of 4 August]

I have talked both to Dillon and Gilbert Murray[9] on the Government policy. Dillon says he considers that the Government is in honour bound to go in even though he has consistently opposed the policy which has led them to that position. Murray says he finds it difficult to resist Grey's case and he confirms what I wired tonight re the German Ambassador. He feels it very difficult to oppose Government action when the German Government has plainly run amok.

[6] Grey's points had been that Britain was under no *obligation* to intervene, except to protect the defenceless French coast and to preserve Belgian neutrality.
[7] Prince Lichnowsky, German ambassador to Britain 1912-14.
[8] One wonders who was the source of this extraordinary piece of misinformation.
[9] Prominent Liberal academic, initially a supporter of the Neutrality Committee.

[The diary-entry that follows is dated 3 August 1914, but from other items of Scott's correspondence this seems clearly a mis-dating for 4 August.]

Diary, [4] August 1914

Went to London, at Lloyd George's request to see him "as early as possible", by morning train. On reaching Downing Street found members of Cabinet just leaving. Simon turned back with me and we walked for a few minutes in the garden of No. 11 till Lloyd George came out.

He [Simon] was looking terribly worn and tired. He began at once by saying he had been entirely deceived about Germany and that I ought to know that the evidence was overwhelming that the party which had got control of the direction of affairs throughout the crisis had deliberately played for and provoked the war. The Emperor was away on his yacht and in his absence the Crown Prince and the War Party—Tirpitz[10] and the rest—had brought things to a point at which they were beyond control. "William is back from his yachting, but he is too late" is the remark attributed to the dutiful Crown Prince. Besides, said Simon, the Emperor is getting old—not in years, but prematurely. Beyond question Germany could have held Austria in check and moderated her demands had she wished to do so, but the party in power did not wish to do so.

At this point George came up and then Illingworth and after waiting a short time Simon went off. George asked if I had not got his telegram asking me to come at 3 instead of then, but none had reached Nottingham Place[11] when I got there. He talked rapidly for a few minutes and then had to leave for an appointment. He confirmed all that Simon had said about the provocative attitude of German diplomacy and said the despatches when they were published would prove it up to the hilt. Up to last Sunday only two members of the Cabinet had been in favour of our intervention in the War, but the *violation of Belgian territory* had completely altered the situation. Apart from that it would have been impossible to draw us into war now. (He had gone so far, however, as to urge that if Germany would consent to limit her occupation of Belgian territory to the extreme southerly point of Belgium—the sort of nose of land running out by Luxemburg—he would

[10]Alfred von Tirpitz, German Minister of Marine 1897-1916, and the driving-force behind Germany's "big-navy" policy.
[11]Where Scott used to stay in London.

resign rather than make this a *casus belli*. Presumably therefore some such offer was made to Germany and declined).

At the same time he said we could not have tolerated attacks on the French coast of the Channel and had the Government done so public opinion would have swept them out of power in a week. He had done his utmost for peace but events had been too strong for him. Was then called off and asked me to come to his room at the House of Commons at 3.

Went on to the House and found Simon in his room and afterwards lunched with him. I was more than ever impressed with his utter prostration. Morally and physically he was like a man half-dead though his mind was keen as ever. He began at once by saying "If you want any help from me I have none to give. I don't know what to suggest or what to do". We talked for a little and then I offered to go away, but he said "No—come and lunch". He was very silent so I had to talk and stated case for non-intervention. When I had done "Yes", he said, "I think you have not made a single point which I have not thought of again and again for a week". It was just bitterness.

We discussed the possibility of limited intervention confined to the protection of Belgian neutrality as provided by one clause in the temporary 1870 treaty. But he thought it impracticable. How could we protect Belgium except by landing troops? Against the despatch of troops he was opposed under any circumstances whatever. For one thing we should want them all at home. Carson had taken care of that.

I asked what explanation he could give of the desire of the German military party for war at this time. He said he thought it was due partly to the dread of the rapid growth of Russian power, partly to the publicly acknowledged defects in the French preparations—heavy guns, equipment etc.—the weakness of a new Government and the as yet incompleteness of the 3 years service, partly to a wholly erroneous impression of British embarrassment from the talk of "civil war" for which we had to thank Lord Northcliffe.

He spoke also of Germany's extreme confidence in her power which he believed to be largely justified. Her preparations were extraordinarily complete. Everything had been thought of and prepared for, including the financial situation. She had actually in hand an accumulated reserve of £100,000,000 in gold in addition to the normal supply. By the finessing of the last few days she was believed to have gained about 4 days start of France in mobilisation in addition to the 3 or 4 days which she has normally. We might he thought in a few days see some extraordinary events. France on the other hand was in terror and had been moving heaven and earth in vain to avert the war.

Finally just as I was leaving we stopped at the doorway of the Terrace and he spoke sadly of his position. Resignation would be for him by far the easiest course. On the other hand by staying in the Cabinet he might do some little good. He had he thought on one point even that morning. Previously he had asked me Did I think it would be possible if we engaged in this war to carry on the kind of agitation against it in the country which had been carried on during the Boer war and I said I thought not; the stakes were too great. That was evidently his own view. On the other hand he saw no line of action within the Cabinet which could avail to change the now destined course of events.

Lloyd George was engaged when I got to his room and then had to prepare the statement he was to make shortly in the House so I decided not to wait and saw him only to say good-bye. I spent the interval with Masterman in his room downstairs.[12]

He confirmed what Simon had said of the unwillingness of the German Emperor personally to enter upon the war—of all three Emperors indeed—and pointed to the significance of the publication in Berlin of the series of pathetic telegrams given in today's papers in which the German Emperor and the Tsar entreat each other vainly to stop the war. He confirmed also the secrecy and deliberation with which the war had been prepared for by German military camarilla. The German ambassador Prince Lichnowsky in London had been entirely deceived and he believed intentionally in order that he might deceive us. He [i.e. Lichnowsky] could give no explanations and had been almost in tears for the past week.

He asked if under existing circumstances I were in the Cabinet I should resign and I said I thought I should on the ground that there was no effective obligation to fight for the neutrality of Belgium and that from the point of view of British interests the dominance of Russia would be worse than the dominance of Germany. He pointed out that the occupation of Belgian territory by German troops, whatever promises might be given, would probably become permanent if Germany were victorious, just as our occupation of the Transvaal became permanent in spite of the declarations with which we entered on the war. I admitted the risk, but thought it less than others on the other side. . . .

[12]Masterman was at this time Chancellor of the Duchy of Lancaster and a member of the cabinet.

As to the German excuse for violating Belgian territory that they knew for certain that the French plan of campaign contemplated an advance through Belgium on the weak German-Belgian frontier he said it was absolutely baseless. The Cabinet knew this because the French plans had been fully communicated to us and they contemplated nothing of the kind.

He spoke strongly of the way in which George had fought in the Cabinet all through the week for peace. He also paid a strong tribute to Grey's sincerity and deep sense of the responsibility he was incurring. On one occasion at a Cabinet meeting Grey had burst into tears—an extraordinary and moving thing in a man so reserved. Very different was Churchill's light-hearted irresponsibility.

Mair to Scott, 4 August [1914]

I am informed tonight that a serious split has taken place in the Labour party. Ramsay MacDonald's leadership is in very serious danger. A considerable number of men including Crooks Roberts Hodge Walsh etc. are in favour of absolute support to the Government.[13]

C.P.S. to Hobhouse, n.d. [soon after 4 August 1914] (Extract)

Many thanks for your letters. I am so glad you approve of what we have done. I was working desperately all Saturday and Sunday [1 and 2 August] to work up opposition to the War and we had got the Chamber of Commerce well started and other movements on foot but events moved too fast for us and it was all in vain. It reminded me terribly of all that went before the Boer War.

I sent a wire to George on Monday [3 August] almost exactly in the sense of your own letter and he wired me urgently to come and see him. I went on Tuesday and you may like to see the notes (enclosed) I made on the way back of my interviews.

C.P.S. to W. Mellor (of Manchester and Salford Trades and Labour Council), 7 August 1914 (Extract)

I don't know if you are holding your meeting [protesting against British participation in the war] on Sunday but I'm afraid I can't be there. I am strongly of opinion that the war ought not to have taken place and

[13]Will Crooks, G. H. Roberts, John Hodge, and Stephen Walsh were all (unlike MacDonald) labourers and trade unionists by origin.

that we ought not to have become parties to it, but once in it the whole future of our nation is at stake and we have no choice but do the utmost we can to secure success. Of course there are principles at stake and there will be an account to settle, but the account must be held over till men have time to think and political action becomes again possible. Then indeed a good many of us may have something to say.

C.P.S. to Dillon, 9 August 1914 (Extract)

We have I think no longer a Liberal Government—had we really one before?—and to all intents and purposes there is a coalition, the first symbols of which are the appointments of [Lord] Kitchener[14] as a member of the Cabinet and (a minor matter) of F. E. Smith[15] as press-correspondent in intimate association with the Admiralty and War Office. This state of things is likely to continue and develop and will have tremendous reactions on our politics, including all that relates to Ireland. I should like to discuss the outlook with you.

C.P.S. to E. D. Morel,[16] 18 August 1914 (Extract)

I will write quite frankly as you ask me but only for the eyes of yourself and your co-signatories. As to (1):—The best mechanical means I can think of [for preventing war] is that no treaty shall be valid without the assent of Parliament. This would do something because it would be a notice to all concerned that informal understandings and arrangements, however intimate, are of no effect, and would enlist the self-respect of Parliament in giving effect to that position.

But the only real remedy is in the force of public opinion and the more effective general control of the House of Commons over the Government and the constitution of the Government. What is the use of having great Liberal majorities in the country and the House of Commons if the Government in its higher and its lower ranks is simply stuffed with Imperialists and we have hardly a genuine Liberal Minister even in training.

Another point:—You have now to deal not merely with the Government but with a body more powerful on the whole question of peace and war than the Government, that is, the Committee of Im-

---

[14]Britain's best-known soldier, who had just been appointed Secretary of State for War.
[15]Prominent Conservative, disliked by Liberals for his extreme support of Ulster.
[16]A prominent critic of pre-war diplomacy, Morel had taken a leading part in exposing European misrule in the Congo.

perial Defence. This new and anomalous body includes the whole of the "inner Cabinet", the leading personages at the War Office and the Admiralty, and any additions which to the Prime Minister of the day may seem good. Thus Lord Haldane is, I believe, still a member and Lord Esher and Lord Fisher are permanent members. Are any of the leading men of the Opposition now members? If not, no doubt they soon will be. Nominally this body has no control over policy and is supposed in ordinary times merely to discuss hypothetical situations. That, of course, is a sham; it is very much more than that and has at certain moments played a decisive part.

With a real Liberal Government resting on Radicalism and Labour and a real Liberal Foreign Policy free from the preposterous claim of "continuity", this body could be put into its proper place, but in no other way that I can see.

As to immediate steps, I don't see that much can be done beyond getting together, as you are doing, the nucleus of an organisation and preparing written matter for publication when the appropriate time comes and when the public is ready to listen. . . . at least we can do something towards preparing a sound and generous public opinion in our own country and resisting the all too potent working of hate and of greed.

If you will kindly send me a dozen copies of your appeal I will send them as opportunity offers to any of my friends who are likely to be sympathetic.

C.P.S. to Hobhouse, 27 August 1914 (Extract)

No chance I hope yet of universal military service. At least the "Morning Post"[17] yesterday said that *at present* it would be useless because our organization couldn't cope with it, but if the war goes on long no doubt some form of compulsory training will be proposed and whatever is proposed by the Government would, under existing conditions, be adopted. We have already what is virtually a coalition Government and it seems to me that in some ways it would be better to have one that was avowedly such. It might help toward greater independence and cooperation of Radicalism and Labour.

A month after the outbreak of war, Liberal minds were still churning over the events which had brought Britain into it. Simon was as distracted as before, in the cabinet but not of it. Lloyd George too had not yet become totally absorbed

[17] The organ of rigid and unbending Toryism.

in the conflict. His tone remained regretful, and his alignment was still with those who would have stood out if they could.

Another group—both Labour and Liberal—adhered firmly to the view that Britain ought never to have gone in. They were soon (if not quite accurately) to be dubbed "pacifists," and they included Ramsay MacDonald, who had lost the chairmanship of the Labour party on account of the war, and C. P. Trevelyan, who had resigned a junior post in the government for the same reason. The concern of this group was with Britain's "diplomatic errors" over the previous decade rather than with the events of August which had decided Lloyd George and neutralised Simon.

Scott moved uneasily between these sections. He believed that Britain had been guilty of diplomatic errors, and in due course he would have "something to say" about them. But he could not set aside as easily as MacDonald the events of August. Nor could he ignore the war as a reality which had to be coped with and not merely deplored. A German army stood in Belgium and much of France; neither hand-wringing nor historical retrospect would remove it. So even though some of Scott's letters seemed to place him close to the "pacifists", he was to see little or nothing of them after the interviews of early September recorded below. Nor for that matter did he see much more of Simon, until the conscription issue again brought them briefly together. Once more Scott found himself following in the footsteps of Lloyd George. For though he found it less easy than Lloyd George to wipe clean the slate of past misgivings and former principles, Scott recognised in the Chancellor of the Exchequer the capacity to grapple positively with the crushing problems of the present.

C.P.S. to Lloyd George, 31 August 1914[18]

Shall you be in London on Friday and, if so, may I come to see you any time that morning? Everything has changed since the day when last I saw you for those few minutes. Now it is not a question of going or not going into the war but of what is to come after it.

Diary, 3-4 September 1914

Went to London on Philip Morrell's invitation to dine and meet Trevelyan's Watching Committee on the War (Trevelyan, Ramsay MacDonald, E. D. Morel, Norman Angell) and others who had opposed the war.[19] Saw the first three at Trevelyan's house in afternoon. Found

---

[18] Lloyd George Papers.

[19] Angell, a business man by origin, had won fame with the publication in 1910 of *The Great Illusion*. In it he had argued that war could never be waged with profit, and that, as commerce spread throughout the world, wars between nations would become obsolete.

that the Watching Committee was fast developing into an acting committee part of whose function was to expose the diplomatic errors which had involved us in the war. Morel had prepared a long statement for this purpose among others and MacDonald proposed to call a conference shortly, probably in Manchester, of sympathisers with whom they had had relations.

At the evening meeting I strongly opposed the second proposal (which was practically abandoned) and took exception to the change of policy which had converted a movement for establishing a skeleton organization to act later when the time came for ending the war and for dealing effectively with the whole position then into one for influencing opinion now. Next morning met Hobhouse and Hobson at the National Liberal Club and found that, strongly as they felt about the war, they entirely agreed and Hobhouse was particularly emphatic. Called at Trevelyan's house. Both he and Morel gone away for weekend. In afternoon saw both Angell and MacDonald. Both agreed— Angell strongly and MacDonald quite definitely—to my surprise.

Had arranged to breakfast with Lloyd George but he asked me to come on to Lord Reading's. Simon, [E.S.] Montagu and Matthews, a big banker, also there. They discussed moratorium and banking arrangements. No talk with Lloyd George so he asked me to lunch. Had some talk with Simon in another room and went on with him to law courts where he was to open first prize court. He explained his position as a member of the Government. He and Lord Beauchamp and Morley and Burns had all resigned together on the Saturday before the declaration of war (August 1) on the ground that they could not agree to Grey's giving pledge to Cambon[20] to protect North coast of France against Germans, regarding this as equivalent to war with Germany. Grey intensely anti-German. Asquith greatly influenced by him. Lloyd George then, as more than once before[,] failed at the pinch. "That old windbag" Haldane counted for nothing. Churchill reckless. On urgent representations of Asquith he and Beauchamp agreed on Monday evening to remain in the Cabinet without in the smallest degree, so far as he was concerned, withdrawing his objection to the policy but solely in order to prevent the appearance of disruption in face of a grave national danger. That remains his position. He is, as it were, an unattached member of the Cabinet and sits very lightly.

He said it would be possible for him to speak in North West Manchester if he were challenged to do so, though he would much rather

[20]Paul Cambon, the French ambassador.

not.[21] I said I thought there was no demand for anything of the sort at present and that as a matter of fact all the leading Liberals in the [Manchester] Federation, so far as I had been able to ascertain their views, had been against our joining in the war. He said he was very glad to hear it. . . . He remarked that at the moment when I last saw him early in the afternoon of August 3 [i.e. 4], he was actually no longer a member of the Government.

With Lloyd George at lunch-time I had again only a few minutes alone in the garden before lunch, as Lord Reading was with him at lunch. He remarked that perhaps those members of the Cabinet who had been so ready to enter on the war would now realise why some of them had been eager to avoid it. Confirmed what Simon had said of Grey's anti-Germanism. Asquith's latent emotionalism had burst out in the same direction. He had never seen him so moved and he had never made such effective speeches. Churchill caring for nothing but to get to work with his fleet.

I asked him to what point he had pushed his opposition to our taking part in the war. He said he would have resigned rather than consent to our going to war if Germany would have agreed not to violate Belgian territory or if even she would have agreed only to pass over the small projecting piece between Luxemburg and France, and he said Grey had, under pressure, agreed that if Germany would respect Belgian neutrality he would not insist on supporting France (perhaps, George said, he knew she wouldn't), but he admitted that these terms had never been presented to Germany and said he "regretted it"—a very weak position. . . .

As to the prospects of the War I got two reports one from Paris, one from Berlin. George said a lady just back from Paris who had talked with numbers both of officers and men said there was only one feeling expressed—"*c'est fini*". Also there was complete distraction of counsels. Half the military men were hotly in favour of the defence of Paris, half as hotly against it. A whole division in Southern France had taken to its heels and a General Officer had been court-martialled and shot. Great numbers of French soldiers had taken refuge in Swiss territory. The Swiss were doing their best to repatriate them, but they weren't at all keen to come back.

On the other hand I gathered from Dudley Ward,[22] also on very

[21]Before war broke out Simon had been in the process of moving his candidature from West Ham, for which he then sat, to North West Manchester, which was held by the Conservatives.
[22]Well-connected Liberal M.P.

recent information, that in Berlin there is the most complete confidence, also from more than one person that the English in Germany are being extremely well treated. Ramsay MacDonald quoted some bad examples to the contrary in this country and what is more he added the proofs will later be forthcoming to put us to shame.

Trevelyan to C.P.S., 13 September 1914[23]

MacDonald, Morel and I, and I think that Angell agrees, have come pretty decisively to the conclusion that we ought to publish the full statement of our case and opinions contained in Morel's pamphlet. Two things have occurred in the last week. The tide of war has decisively turned. England is no longer in any sort of danger. Our troops are victorious. Before very long even some who oppose the war will be considering the possibility of peace. The other thing is that the Tory press (Morning Post and Express) is beginning to say that the movement is "secret." Of course they say we are pro-German. That is necessary. But we had better not let it be supposed that we are afraid of coming into the open. I see no reason now for delay, and I gather from your letter to Morel last week that you are at least not as averse to it as you were.

C.P.S. to MacDonald, 14 September 1914 (Extract)

There's a mighty difference certainly between the prospect of the war as it is today and as it was a week ago, and things are possible now which were hardly possible then. My feeling none the less is quite definite that nothing will be gained by raising now the question of the origin and merits of the war. People won't listen and it will only weaken greatly your influence on what is already the practical and will I hope soon become the urgent question of the settlement. . . . Therefore, if you ask what I think, I should say avoid altogether at the present stage all question of merits and origin and deal with the war as a tremendous fact out of which it should be our object to extract the best results possible but the issues of which are still largely uncertain.

C.P.S. to Morel, 25 September 1914

I think I ought to tell you definitely what I think about publication—

[23]This is one of several letters from members of the "pacifist" section seeking to enlist Scott's support for a campaign critical of Britain's role in the international crisis.

not that it matters, only I shouldn't like not to have done it. I think it would be a fatal error to attempt to deal with anything controversial at present. It seems to me our clear duty to make the country safe first and to adjust our domestic differences afterwards. Further I believe that by a contrary course now you will destroy most of your power of usefulness later when the questions of the time and terms of the settlement come up. Even these can at present only be considered in the most general manner, because we don't know what will be the conditions with which we shall then have to deal. Of course I don't know what you have written or may write. I can only say that I hope you mean to draw a clear line between the controversial and the non-controversial and, while preparing for the future, to let alone the past. Forgive this perhaps needless expression of opinion.

Loreburn to C.P.S., 25 September 1914 (Extract)

In regard to the end of the war and the terms, I am greatly distressed. I hold silence about the beginning of it and avoid all that class of subject because we are now in a fight which taxes all our resources and energy and we ought all to encourage those who are fighting. And whatever may be said about it, no one can deny that Germany has behaved extremely ill and that if she persisted in attacking Belgium there was a just cause for us to defend Belgium. It can do no good and may do harm to discuss the origin now.

Loreburn to C.P.S., 14 October 1914 (Extract)

I feel sure that Grey and the others did earnestly desire to avoid war but they had tied themselves up with France. I feel very sorry for them in a way and would be more sorry but for the consequences of what they have done.

Diary, 23 October 1914 (Extract)

[In conversation with Loreburn.]
He thought the war could have been prevented by a resolute policy of co-operation with Germany and a plain warning to France and Russia that they would not receive our support in a war with Germany. There were the two parties in Germany—the military and the civil. By alarming and irritating Germany we played into the hands of the first. When the war came it would have been kinder to Belgium to have

advised her to let the Germans through under protest. Instead of that we urged her to resist though we knew we could not protect her from disaster. As for Alsace-Lorraine if Germany were compelled to surrender them she would never rest till she got them back. It would be the "revanche" over again.

One result of the war would he feared be to bring us permanently into the field of international politics in Europe. We could not resume a policy of non-intervention.

3. The Fact of War, October 1914-February 1915

What were Liberal ideals worth in wartime? Two which soon came under attack were freedom of the press and the rights of aliens. The right-wing press was shameless in whipping up popular hatred against people of German birth or descent, and turned its fire against the Manchester Guardian when it protested.

Meanwhile, a change was coming over Lloyd George. When Scott last saw him, "the war" still meant the events which had brought it about. Now Lloyd George was turning his attention from its origins to its execution: to that complete absorption in its conduct which was to change the shape of his career.

For the moment it was the naval rather than the military aspect which concerned him. The shortcomings of Kitchener, who had become War Secretary, and of Sir John French, the Commander-in-Chief in France, were not yet apparent; neither was the grim stalemate which was developing in the west. The navy on the other hand had suffered some minor, but humiliating, setbacks. The German battleship Goeben had escaped to Turkey, so encouraging the Turks to take the German side. A German submarine had sunk one of the outmoded Cressy cruisers, and when two others came to pick up survivors had disposed of them as well. Meanwhile a German squadron in the Pacific was playing havoc with British merchant shipping, and on being attacked by a smaller force under Rear-Admiral Cradock had decisively defeated him. (This brought prompt action from Admiral Fisher, who had been recalled by Churchill as First Sea Lord. Fisher dispatched a strong naval force which destroyed all but one of the German raiders on 8 December).

There is detectable in some of Lloyd George's remarks a note of antipathy to Churchill. No doubt this was partly caused by disappointment with the war at sea, as well as by exasperation at Churchill's rash attempt to persuade the Belgians to hold Antwerp after it had ceased to be defensible. But there was a larger issue dividing them. Who in this conflict would emerge as the 20th-century Chatham, the saviour of his nation? Both men saw the war as a great challenge, and felt called to give a decisive lead. Hence their position was inherently one of rivalry. They could hardly be expected to foresee that they would have a war apiece.

C.P.S. to Hobhouse, 26 September 1914 (Extract)

Last night there came an instruction from the Press Bureau so stringent that it will almost prevent any sort of comment on the War. It is the result of the "Times" and "Daily Mail" giving away the flanking movement of the allies. They actually stated which of the French Divisions had been moved to the left flank—most important information for the Germans. So now we are forbidden to make any comments on movements for 4 days back or speculations on any for 7 days forward and all maps showing positions have to be censored!

At a time of nationalistic fervour, and with concern widespread about the activities of spies, aliens in Britain were subject to two forms of harassment; internment by the government (this came within Simon's province as Attorney-General), and assaults by a public spurred on by the popular press. Liberal consciences were stirred on both matters.

Hobhouse to C.P.S., 27 October 1914

About the alien question, I wrote to Simon the other day and you may like to see his reply. The Government have in fact modified their policy. Massingham tells me that Asquith was personally much concerned and has visited the concentration camps.

Simon's letter only partly answers mine, for I urged that the Press campaign was more dangerous than the Government action, and that Grey or Asquith ought to be asked to say a word to the country to point out the evil effect of rioting etc.

I wish a little more could be said in the Manchester Guardian about the thing, but I know the difficulties. You collect from the close of Simon's letter that careful expression of the milder view would by no means be unwelcome to him. . . .

Sugar users tell me I let the Government off much too lightly in my last short.[1] They have made a regular mess of it.

C.P.S. to Hobhouse, 2 November 1914 (Extract)

The scurril press is still yapping at our heels and I suppose will continue to do so. The truce of parties certainly doesn't apply to the party press. And it is all done by innuendo and epithets. However we must

[1] Journalists' expression for one of the smaller leading articles.

just put up with it and say what has to be said on the side of fairness and moderation.

Feeling is worse I gather in the south than it is here—partly I suppose because the war seems closer. . . .

Many thanks for sending me Simon's letter which is re-assuring. I will keep it till you come. Would it not be possible to have the German pastor here released at once? It would have an excellent effect as a proof that the Government don't mean to keep *all* the arrested people permanently in confinement.

In the discussion of the Goeben *incident that follows, it is interesting to note Lloyd George's assumption that inferior British vessels ought to have attacked the German battleship. The possibility that they might have suffered heavy defeat (with far greater damage to British prestige than was caused by the* Goeben's *escape) is not really entertained. Similarly, he discusses British setbacks in terms of incompetence and "society jobs" rather than of the military and naval might on which Germany was able to call—an indication that even a perceptive statesman like Lloyd George still had far to travel before he would appreciate all of war's realities.*

Diary, 27 November 1914

Breakfasted with Lloyd George, alone. As to the War he remarked on the reversal of expectations. The Army which we regarded as capable of little had done wonders. On the other hand in the conduct of the Navy on which we thought we could implicitly rely there had been some very uncomfortable incidents. Lord Fisher had described the state of things he found on taking office in place of Battenberg as "a perfect muddle".[2] This description did not I gathered apply to the operations of the main fleet under Jellicoe,[3] but to the conduct of affairs elsewhere.

(1) The loss of the three cruisers. Jellicoe not responsible for this. They were under Admiralty orders and had no business to be where they were. (This no doubt was part of the "perfect muddle", as they were undoubtedly taking part in the general scheme of operations which Jellicoe was directing).

(2) The escape of the *Goeben* from Messina—a dreadful business, which was directly responsible for the entry of Turkey into the War and indirectly for the defeat of Cradock's squadron in the South

[2]Battenberg had been forced to retire on account of his German origins.
[3]Now Commander of the Grand Fleet.

Pacific, since the fast cruisers which ought to have been there were detained off the Dardanelles in watching for the *Goeben*. [Rear-Admiral] Troubridge,[4] who was in command off Messina[,] had four ships each inferior both in speed and in armament to the *Goeben* and he simply allowed her to escape without attempting to give battle. The Admirals at home at once said he must be court-martialled and he was, but the court martial acquitted him on the ground that it was not clear that his four ships could have successfully engaged the German one. But that only throws the responsibility further back. Sir Berkeley Milne, in command of the Mediterranean squadron[,] was at Malta distant only 30 hours steam and with his flag-ship the *Inflexible*—not quite so swift as the *Goeben* but equally powerful—and submarines. Why had he not instantly gone himself to Messina? And why was he not court-martialled for this disastrous failure of duty? He has not been and he is still in command. He has powerful social connections. [“]Then it's a society job[”] said Lloyd George in conversation with Churchill and Fisher. "That's exactly it" retorted Fisher to Churchill's face. "Would you have court-martialled him?", said Lloyd George. "I would have hung him" Fisher answered.

(3) The South Pacific defeat. This due to Cradock's folly. The *Canopus* was only 200 miles off, but instead of waiting till he could effect a junction he engaged recklessly at once with a sort of bold British tar regardlessness of odds. Cradock was another society person, known not to be up to the mark. McKenna just before his supersession had determined on his recall. Churchill, on taking office, cancelled the decision.

(4) The Antwerp expedition. This was Churchill's special enterprize, though in this, as in other matters, he has of late had Grey's support. I asked if so serious a step had been taken without the assent of the Cabinet and gathered that this had been given only after the event, though I should infer that the question had been raised and not decided. Matters developed more quickly than was expected. Churchill had actually started for Belgium to confer with the King when the news came that the Belgian Government had decided at once to evacuate Antwerp and withdraw its whole army while there was still time and before the city had been bombarded. Churchill was instantly recalled, the Cabinet had dispersed for the week-end (it was on Friday) and the decision to send a relieving force appears to have been taken by Churchill, Grey and Asquith. Kitchener, under pressure, consented, but declined to send any troops. The force was to consist of marines and

[4]Commander of the Mediterranean Cruiser Squadron.

THE FACT OF WAR

bluejackets. As a matter of fact it consisted of about 3,000 blue-jackets and marines and of about 9,000 men of the "marine reserve"—the marine reserve being wholly, or mainly, a body of untrained or half-trained recruits. Churchill went off again to Belgium and told the King that an army was coming. The King thereupon agreed to postpone the [Belgian] retirement. Battenberg was left to carry out the arrangements for the relief-force to which the term "perfect muddle" would perfectly apply. So muddled were they that the pilot was forgotten though the transports would have to pass through a portion of the mine-field. A destroyer was despatched with all speed to stop them and turned back all the ships except one, which went right through the mine-field un-piloted and by a miracle escaped unharmed. Churchill went to the front waving his sword, but the net result was that the evacuation was delayed a few days, that the Belgians lost 20,000 men interned and we about 2,000 and that Antwerp was half ruined. But, I asked, was there no important strategical gain from the delay? George answered "none".

As to Battenberg he evidently regarded him as incompetent for so great a position, though most courteous, well-meaning and loyal. But he could exercise no real authority and was as clay in Churchill's hands. That was why Churchill liked him. Through all this narrative there was obvious a strong personal antagonism to Churchill. It may in some degree have coloured the statements, but the facts are there.

As to the War with Turkey, Lloyd George partly blamed Churchill also for that. The situation was not desperate even after the attacks by the *Goeben* on Russian Black-Sea ports. They did not concern us, and it was open to Russia to ignore them but the perfectly useless bombard-ment by the fleet of one of the Dardanelles forts and the seizure of Akaba brought us at once into war. Our whole endeavour should of course have been for postponement. The effect of bringing Turkey in has been to lock up 50,000 of our troops—including the Australians, some of the best of the Indian troops, besides our territorials (including a Lancashire regiment) and 300,000 Russian troops, both of which forces would have been invaluable elsewhere.

We went on to discuss some aspects of the future settlement. In feeling George is not strongly anti-German. He said he should have much greater pleasure in smashing Turkey than in smashing Germany. What about the Kiel Canal?, he said, evidently contemplating its cession to Denmark. But that could only be in case Denmark took a hand in the war. . . .

In regard to Italy he spoke much more definitely.[5] Italy, he said, is playing the part of the jackal or hyena. She wants to have her meat killed for her. She thinks she can come in after the war and pick up some fragments. But she won't; she will get nothing whatever unless she risks something for it. Of Servia he spoke warmly, but thought that Austria was on the point of killing her.

I spoke of the hardly noticed statement by Asquith at the Guild Hall that the Turkish dominion in Asia must now come to an end as well as that in Europe and of the enormous questions which that raised. He admitted their difficulty but thought the time had come to deal with the whole matter (though obviously he—and probably the rest of the Cabinet—had given it only the most cursory consideration). Russia he assumed would take Constantinople and Armenia and Great Britain Mesopotamia. When I asked what was to become of the rest of Asia Minor and the 10 million Turks in it he thought it would be a good plan to give it to Germany as a solatium. When I remarked that it might not suit Russia to have Germany on the other side of the Bosphorus, he said he meant that she [presumably Russia] should have control of the whole of the straits with enough territory to secure that.

Before leaving I raised the question of Palestine, and the Zionists.[6] It was not quite new to him as he had seen the article in the "New Statesman" and mentioned also that he had had a "whole hearted" i.e. "heart to heart" conversation with [Herbert] Samuel and had been astonished to find how that cold and dry person suddenly kindled and they had sympathised on the common ground of the small nationality. He was interested therefore at the suggestion of a partly Jewish buffer state, but thought France would have strong objections. As to Russia she might prefer Jews to Catholics in the Holy Places. But he was interested and when I mentioned Weizmann said he would like to see him and he would ask Samuel too and perhaps I would come. . . .

The war widened the divisions within southern Ireland. On the one hand, Redmond and the Irish Nationalists believed that by fighting on the British side, Irishmen would win self-government through gratitude. At the other extreme, the followers of Sinn Fein (the party which sought to sever all links with Britain and

[5] Italy had not yet entered the war on the side of the Allies, and was driving a hard bargain with them before doing so.

[6] In Manchester Scott had met Chaim Weizmann, the brilliant chemist and ardent Zionist, i.e. advocate of the establishment of a Jewish national home in Palestine. Weizmann's attainments as a chemist were soon to become important to Lloyd George as Minister of Munitions.

establish an independent Ireland) regarded Britain as Ireland's enemy and oppressor, and favoured a German victory. One who took this view was Sir Roger Casement, formerly a renowned British consular official, now a fanatical convert to the cause of Irish independence. Casement reached Berlin from the U.S.A. on 31 October 1914.

Outwardly Ireland remained loyal to the British connection. But the disappointing rate of recruiting in Ireland suggested that much of the country was not whole-heartedly behind Redmond's policy.

T. P. O'Connor. Later had an hour and a half with O'Connor at his flat. We talked a good deal at large about the War and then I asked him about Casement and the treasonable Irish weekly press—the "Irish Volunteer" and others. As to Casement he set him down as "both mad and bad" and he was open to prosecution on either score should he venture again on English or Irish soil which he understood it was his intention to do.

As to the treasonable press their attacks were directed primarily against the Nationalist party and only secondarily against Great Britain. He had no doubt they were subsidised by German money through America. They were largely distributed gratis and by seeking to stir up all the old hatreds bred by 100 years of wrong they were producing an effect and were interfering with recruiting both in Ireland and among the Irish in England. He did not think it possible, or safe, to ignore them and anticipated that action would be taken by the Government within a few days. The simplest plan would be to proceed by martial law and seize the presses and lay the persons responsible by the heels. That would be better than a prosecution. The question was whether it would not be best to give these gentry a "straight tip" to make themselves scarce and so get them out of the way. He seemed to incline to this course. . . .

As to recruiting in Ireland they could only look for a moderate success. Great numbers of Irish, it must be remembered, were already in the Army. Devlin was the only man who was having a real success and could deliver the goods. He did it by pointing out to the Nationalists in Ulster that the Covenanters had gone and would come back trained soldiers and, if they wanted to hold their own against them, they must get trained too. In the south and west the Sinn Feiners told the peasants that they were only asked to enlist in order that they might be conveniently killed off.

So far there was no improvement in the feeling between north and south. If anything it was worse. Personally he would be prepared to say that no man should be asked to come under Home Rule who did not wish to but others did not share his view. He did not explain how this principle was to be applied. . . .

Loreburn. His first and last word was "make peace", "make peace quickly". He thought France could not stand the strain of a long war, but quite apart from that he saw nothing to be gained from an attempt to push things to extremities. The old policy of non-interference in European combinations and intrigues, the policy of Disraeli, Salisbury and Gladstone, was essentially right, but it had been fatally abandoned with the result we see today and it could not be revived. We should now be compelled to take our place with the great military nations and he saw no escape from our being militarised—not to the same extent, but up to a certain point—also. All we needed now was a few years interval in which to prepare a thorough and effective system of home military defence, in the preparation of which no money should be spared. We could no longer trust to the navy. We should require also to make ourselves absolutely safe by land, so that no invader, even if he succeeded in effecting a landing would have a chance. That once done we should be more independent of alliances. . . .

Lord Morley. Lunched at the Courtneys—Morley, L. T. Hobhouse, H. N. Brailsford and Bertrand Russell there. Conversation general and did not come to much. An indiscreet remark by Morley was to the effect that if Germany had delayed her violation of Belgian territory 48 hours the Cabinet would have broken up and there would have been a *coalition Government*. One knew that more than once during the last days before the war we had been on the brink of that result.

C.P.S. to Hobhouse, 6 December 1914 (Extract)

My visit to London on Thursday[7] was rather a frost. The dinner and the discussion after it were thoroughly badly managed. . . . [Bernard] Shaw made an amusing speech and [Sidney] Webb an extraordinarily silly one. His point, enforced with ferocious emphasis, was that the war must by no means be allowed to finish when the military men and politicians wanted a patched-up peace, but that these gentlemen must have their noses kept to the grindstone till war for the future had been made impossible—he didn't tell us how. What he desired was to put a really pacific spirit into the Germans and he seemed to think this could be done by a sufficient amount of drubbing—like the schoolmaster with his "Be pure in heart, my boy, or I'll flog you". Still I'm not sorry

[7]Presumably 3 December 1914. No diary account of this visit has been preserved.

I went. These things are always illuminating. Nobody seemed to think much of Webb's deliverance.

C.P.S. to Hobhouse, 12 December 1914 (Extract)

I think it is stupid of me to have held off from writing [leaders on the war] so long. I don't quite know why I did it, but at first it seemed impossible to write honestly at all without raising questions which we had decided to leave alone, and then there was what seemed the impossibility of getting any harmony of feeling between what I could write and what [C. E.] Montague had written and was writing.[8] However I think I was wrong and I've started again these last few days. . . .

C.P.S. to Hobhouse, 20 December 1914 (Extract)

We had our first little warning (enclosed) the other day from the Press Censor. I was doubtful at first whether to acknowledge it, but on the whole thought I would in order to enter a caveat.

The Censor has also sent out a general prohibition—or request nearly equivalent—against comment on the Mission to the Vatican. This is carrying things rather far, but as we had the other little controversy on hand I thought I wouldn't take on another at the same time.

E. D. Morel to C.P.S., 6 February 1915 (Extract)

If Churchill's "unconditional surrender" interview represents the mind of the Government and the intentions of the Government, then we are laying up for this people and this nation of ours, a heritage of woe which will curse our grandchildren and, in my belief, digging England's grave. The other day, I saw a written account of an interview (not for publication) between a well-known Englishman who lives in Paris and a British diplomatist in active service, resident in one of the neutral capitals. . . . The diplomatist's language was staggering. All Germans were liars. Germany was to be "put out of action for a generation"; and not only in a political sense, but in an economic sense: even her

[8]Montague, as the *Manchester Guardian*'s chief leader writer, had since August 1914 been deciding the line taken by the paper (a line condemnatory of Germany) much more than had Scott. However in December 1914 Montague, despite his 47 years, succeeded in persuading a reluctant army to enlist him.

ports were to be dismantled, and her factories destroyed. Then comes Churchill.

I have not yet fully grasped the significance of the development of the past few days. But on the face of it, I can imagine that no country of 65 millions is going to consent to be starved, if it can help it. Lord! how we shall curse the course of our diplomacy from 1906 to 1914 one of these days.

I see the U.D.C.[9] is "out in the open" now. We did not precipitate it. I am glad. Our adherents grow and many working class organisations are rallying round us.

My feeling is that the sooner the Government can be forced to state the terms upon which it would discuss a settlement the better.

[9]The Union of Democratic Control, organisation of the critics of British intervention in the war.

4. *Munitions, March-June 1915*

By March 1915, Lloyd George's displeasure had switched from Churchill to Kitchener, as his concern had moved from the war at sea to the war on land. Even though without departmental responsibility in the matter, Lloyd George was already deeply immersed in those questions of munitions production and labour relations which were to loom so large in the war. It was this involvement which for the first time revealed him as a potential war leader.

The first diary conversation that follows gives a preview of one of the great personal vendettas of wartime politics—that between Lloyd George and McKenna. The government had decided to suspend for the duration the operation of its Act disestablishing the Anglican Church in Wales—a matter of keen interest to Welsh members, and hence to Lloyd George. The handling of the matter came within McKenna's jurisdiction as Home Secretary.

C.P.S. to Bryce, 7 March 1915[1] (Extract)

I never met such a ferocious old sea-dog as Fisher. One of the things he said when I saw him a short time before the war was that if he caught the crew of a submarine he would "boil them in oil"—picturesque but not quite prudent!

C.P.S. to Hobhouse, 17 March 1915 (Extract)

I am glad to see that at last the workmen's representatives are being called in. It is a supreme emergency and if we are to win this war within any tolerable time the whole force of the nation must be concentrated on the production of—shells! When I saw Lloyd George on Monday. . . . [Account follows]

[1]Bryce Papers.

Diary, 15 March 1915

Breakfasted with Lloyd George March 15. T. P. O'Connor also there almost all the time. We spoke first of Bill to postpone operation of Welsh Church Act for 6 months after war which was coming on in House of Commons that evening. He was strongly of opinion that the Bill was quite fair placing each party at the end of the war in as nearly as possible the same position as if there had been no war, but said Bill had been badly mismanaged by McKenna. Welsh members who could easily have been pacified had they been properly consulted had been ignored. He thought the Opposition to the Bill not really serious and that it would have been better to press it through now instead of postponing it till after Easter as the Government intended to do. He himself had had no part in the negotiations on the Bill as McKenna was extremely jealous of any interference on his part. Nevertheless he had told the Welsh members that he would be ready to meet any of them on any platform in Wales and defend the Bill and he did not think any of them would care to accept the challenge.

In regard to the war he was pessimistic (O'Connor told me he had been all through). He thought it would last another two years. I said that might depend on the terms which we were prepared to accept. He replied that at least we must have Alsace-Lorraine and we could not ask for that till the Germans had been driven back to the Rhine—and how near were we to that? We acclaimed it as a great victory when we had gained 1200 yards. And then there was Poland also to be reclaimed. It was not a question of "crushing" Germany but of defeating her. Personally he would rather crush Turkey than Germany.

Things would be different if we had a full supply of ammunition and equipment. If we could produce 12 million shells a month instead of three the whole situation would be transformed. Instead of having, as at present[,] 2 million men in the field against the Germano-Austrian three million, Russia could place 6 million and we could place a million instead of 400,000. He did not know how many shells Russia was producing—perhaps 2 million a month. France was the only one of the Allies, he believed, which was "pulling her weight". He was immensely impressed, on his recent visit to France, with the energy, resource and cleverness of the French. They had increased their output of shells sixfold since the beginning of the war. We were getting a good deal of war material from America but the Americans had no great existing factories for the manufacture of explosives. The production was now at last being organized in America as it was in

England, but the supply was precarious. At any moment the President of the U.S. might, in retaliation for the detention of some American vessel, stop the whole export of war material. President Wilson in private expressed sympathy with the Allies, but his public action did not correspond.

The supreme need in this country was to organise the production on business lines and speed it up to the utmost. He was looking out for a business man of commanding force and ability to direct the whole thing. (O'Connor had apparently come in order to discuss this matter and made various suggestions one of which—a Scotch Canadian who landing as a lad with 10/- in his pocket had become the greatest railway contractor in America—Lloyd George said was the best he had yet had).

The difficulty was with Kitchener. Six months ago he had urged the adoption of the very measures which were now being taken and Kitchener had blocked them. When in the debate on the Emergency Bill last week Bonar Law asked why, if the need was so great these steps had not been taken long before[,] he simply had no answer to make. Evidently his feeling against Kitchener was very strong—a man without imagination, jealous of his own authority and distrustful of all civilian interference. And this was the man whom everybody praised because he made no mistakes. But he made no mistakes because he made no experiments whereas a man like Churchill who tried to do new things and used new methods naturally did make mistakes and instantly incurred censure. . . .

Of Fisher on the other hand he expressed the highest opinion. People spoke of him as a blatherer but it was the greatest possible mistake to put him down as a mere talker. He was extraordinarily ingenious and contriving and with immense driving force. It was one of his new machines which the Clyde strikers had delayed for a fortnight. The Liverpool coal-heavers strike had held up six Atlantic liners which ought to have been fetching war material from America and a number of ships which ought to have been carrying supplies and explosives to the Dardanelles.

As to the political situation in Eastern Europe he said that the reason why Greece did not intervene was not the personal opposition of the King, but the fact that by the most competent military judges in Greece Germany was still expected to win—a rather serious fact, as he remarked, since Neutrals can form a more judicial estimate than we can. The same impression was influencing the other neutral countries —Bulgaria, Roumania, Italy. It required a man of real imagination and insight like Venizelos [the Greek Prime Minister] to realise the immense staying power of Great Britain which in the end would determine the issue. Bulgaria would come in the moment she was satisfied the Allies were going to win. . . . As to Turkey it might have been possible to temporise even after the proceedings of the *Goeben* in the Black Sea but Churchill gave us the final push into war by his attack on Akaba.

Lloyd George went a further stage in involving himself in war production when he resolved to deal with drunkenness among munitions workers. "We are fighting Germany, Austria and Drink," he stated on 29 March 1915, "and, as far as I can see, the greatest of these deadly foes is drink". He proposed to overcome it by state purchase of the trade, at a cost of £250 millions. His colleagues were not enthusiastic. Asquith felt that Lloyd George "has completely lost his head" on the drink question, and that his purchase scheme "would ruin our finances".² Ultimately little came of it.

This disgusted Scott. He saw it as further evidence of the Prime Minister's pusillanimity and unfitness for his task, especially when contrasted with Lloyd George's vigour and daring. Indeed Scott and Lloyd George were closer in attitude at this stage than at any other time during the war. For the moment, Scott was won over by Lloyd George's vision of a nation organised and mobilised for war, irrespective of the cost in individual liberty or liberal principle. In a letter to Hobhouse (unfortunately not preserved in toto) discussing the change of government in May 1915, Scott wrote approvingly of the ideal of "a nation marshalled and regimented for service".

This sharp move towards a "total war" outlook, combined with his exasperation at Asquith, probably explains Scott's rather indulgent attitude towards the Conservatives when, in May, they forced their way into the government. For some time Conservative attacks on ministers had been growing in severity. Then on 17 May Bonar Law demanded that Asquith dissolve the Liberal ministry and form a coalition. Asquith quickly agreed. Fisher had just resigned as First Sea Lord after a protracted falling-out with Churchill over the Dardanelles operation, and a crisis was approaching over the shortage of munitions, so that the Prime Minister felt himself in no position to argue. It is clear from correspondence that Lloyd George played a crucial part in these events: on 17 May Bonar Law was conveying to him the terms of the Conservative leaders' ultimatum to Asquith; later that day Lloyd George discussed with Simon the post the latter might have in the new ministry; a week later Lord Crewe was writing to him about the apportionment of key offices in the coalition.³

²Quoted in Roy Jenkins, *Asquith* (Collins, London, 1964), p. 338.
³See Bonar Law to Lloyd George, 17 May 1915; Simon to Lloyd George, 18 May 1915; and Crewe to Lloyd George, 24 May 1915, all in the Lloyd George Papers.

Other Liberals were not so well-informed. On 19 May Runciman wrote to McKenna: "If we are honoured with invitations to come in. . . ."; and later the same day he wrote: "E. Grey knows nothing more. Neither he nor R. B. Haldane have seen or heard from the Prime Minister."[4]

To Scott, only one change of office really mattered: that Lloyd George should head the newly-created Ministry of Munitions. But not for the last time, he found Lloyd George hesitant to take the chance which he had apparently created for himself—that is, to leave the security of the Exchequer for the hazards and opportunities of Munitions. When at last Lloyd George took the plunge—handing over the Exchequer to McKenna—it was with the explicit proviso that he might return whenever he pleased.

C.P.S. to Lloyd George, 7 March 1915

I was delighted, as I should fancy most other people were, with your Bangor speech—particularly with what you said about restrictions on the sale of intoxicants. The present partial and haphazard restrictions imposed by the police or the military can have little general effect, but I believe the nation is perfectly prepared for a little compulsory temperance and that the Government might go a long way in that direction during the war without the slightest risk. . . . Of course [abstinence] can only be treated, as you treat it, as a purely war measure and for the duration of the war. That is where you will get the big backing, but all the same there will be the permanent gains.

C.P.S. to Hobhouse, 23 April 1915 (Extract)

You will have judged from various indications that George's scheme of national purchase has come to grief. I wrote to him in some bitterness of soul, assuming that the Unionist leaders had given way to party pressure. In reply he says: "the difficulties are not altogether on the Opposition side, not even the most formidable obstacles which have presented themselves"—and indeed that became tolerably apparent when one read Asquith's Newcastle speech.

It's a wretched business and unhappily one can never make the truth known. Really Asquith gets worse as he gets older and it is time he were dead and buried—politically!

[4]Runciman to McKenna, 19 May 1915, McKenna Papers.

The Bishop of Lincoln to C.P.S., 7 May 1915 (Extract)

May I thank you for the firm and honourable line the *Manchester Guardian* has taken right through these devious and dangerous proposals about the Drink? The Cabinet would have done wisely for itself and for the Country (and wider still) by supporting Lloyd George at first and throughout. He is the biggest and best man of them all. What a touchstone the "Drink" question is! Asquith will not give up his liquor: this is the bottom of it. Then the Irish party! We always knew how it depended on the Whisky trade: *now* the cloven foot is exposed indeed.

The point of the following remark about Hobhouse and Dunkirk is not clear —presumably it concerns some sort of wartime employment—but this does not much matter. What makes the letter interesting is its revelation of Scott's almost total commitment to the position Lloyd George was now adopting on state direction of the nation in wartime.

C.P.S. to Hobhouse, 7 May 1915 (Extract)

You'll let me know what you decide about Dunkirk—won't you? I feel as if there were a far bigger work waiting here to be done by a man of your power . . . than anything you can possibly achieve directly in connection with the war. There is this whole vast question of national organization and of the rousing and disciplining of the working-class. The Government have no time and also not too much courage or statesmanship and most of the thinking has to be done for them. . . . It is being steadily borne in upon me that unless this country pulls itself together and submits to something not unlike a Prussian organization for the period of the war, the war may be almost indefinitely prolonged, the issue possibly even jeopardised, with the loss necessarily of innumerable lives precious to us which might be saved.

C.P.S. to J. L. Garvin,[5] 18 May 1915

I saw Lloyd George the other day after seeing you and had a few words with him alone,[6] but the Vanderveldes[7] were at lunch so I couldn't get very far and shall have to try to see him again. It is plain

[5] Editor of Conservative newspapers, especially the *Observer*.
[6] Regrettably there is no record of Scott's conversations with Lloyd George at this time.
[7] Possibly Emile Vandervelde, the Belgian Socialist leader, and his wife.

that we are nearing a Coalition, but I see no gain in that unless we are to have a new spirit and a new impulse at the centre of authority.

We shan't get that unless we make a push for it and the present drift is merely towards a reshuffling of the cards with an appearance of comprehension but, so far as I can see, no guarantee of greater effectiveness which can only come from a courageous initiative and an organizing mind.

I should like to see you again some time soon. . . . Your papers seem to me far the best in London and the only ones in which independence takes a really useful form.

C.P.S. to Hobhouse, 23 May 1915 (Extract)

About the political situation it seems to me that we must take what Lloyd George said as to the Tories "putting a pistol at the heads" of the Government *cum grano*. After all what had happened? The Government had failed most frightfully and discreditably in the matter of munitions. Kitchener was no doubt primarily to blame, but the matter was so vital that no Government which neglected to make itself thoroughly informed as to the facts could be absolved from grave responsibility. The Tories may well have said to themselves "This won't do. We can no longer trust this Government. We must either come in so as to have some control or the country must know the full facts—damaging as they would be to our credit." I'm not sure that in their place, with thousands of lives uselessly sacrificed, including some of the most precious, I shouldn't have felt like that. Party feeling may have come in. Very likely it did. It is certainly operative enough just now, and on *both* sides. But I feel inclined to "put the best construction" on the motives and action of at least the chief men of the Opposition. The question for us—you and me—now is how to get the best results from the change. . . .

But everything depends on a good start. If this Government fails and falls as grossly short in spirit and in action as the last, then indeed we may look for dark days.

Francis Hirst[8] to C.P.S., 21 May 1915 (from Tavistock)

Do you feel as much stirred as I do about the wickedness, and folly, and shame of introducing compulsory service? I feel that this, with

[8] Editor of the *Economist*; formerly on the *Manchester Guardian*. Outspoken representative of *laissez-faire*, anti-war liberalism.

Protection, the Censorship, and a military bureaucracy would make England no place for people like me. . . .

I am enjoying a little rest at this delightful place, and am not sorry to see the organised hypocrisy of Liberal Imperialism based upon the unholy alliance of Jingoism with Socialism falling to pieces.

Will not this Coalition Government be weak and discredited from the start, without any common purpose or object?

Will not a general election be necessary after all?

Are not horror and disgust about the war prevailing everywhere? and is there not a reaction against the foul Northcliffe pogrom of people with German names.

P.S. Why should all of us Britons be ruined because a little group of Liberal and Tory Imperialists has taken the idiotic resolution of destroying the German nation?

What a poor thing is the Cadbury Press![9]

C.P.S. to Hirst, 24 May 1915

I am glad you're taking a refresher in the country. I wish I could. Surely England can never have looked more beautiful. The war hardly bears thinking about, but I think I feel more strongly than you that the aggressive imperialism of Germany had to be resisted. I also feel that, however the war may end, that is likely to remain and to be a permanent menace to the Liberal and pacific civilization of the Western Powers (including the United States and Italy). It also seems clear to me that the Channel and the fleet are likely in the future to be less— much less—complete a defence than they have been hitherto and that we must be prepared to defend ourselves on land. How are we to do it? I see no reason to doubt that it can be done effectively without compulsion, but it cannot evidently be done without military training on a far greater scale and for a far longer time than was contemplated in the old territorial force. If we can get enough volunteers to train for six months and keep themselves efficient afterwards that would be the ideal solution, but they will have to be got so long as the danger to European peace and to our own security continues. That is as far as I can see at present, but of course the situation may alter. If the temper of Germany ever did alter really and fundamentally and Junkerism became a thing of the past and Social Democracy—or better still a revived Liberalism —came by its own, the cloud would at once lift and anything would be possible, but till something like that happens I think we shall have to

[9] The Liberal *Daily News* was owned by the Cadbury family.

remain armed and on something like the European scale. It is a dire and hateful necessity.

Hirst to C.P.S., 28 May 1915

Thank you so much for your letter. . . .

The present outcry for compulsion is clearly manufactured—the object being to discipline and enslave the working classes and to keep down Ireland. Dr. Clifford[10] who with Lloyd George preached the Holy War now renounces the idea of transplanting German institutions and especially the curse of military conscription.

As to the war compulsion would I think break down our finances pretty soon. One Dardanelles expedition on the top of Flanders and on the top of financing *all* the allies and all our colonies is more than we can stand. Even Pitt drew the line at a conscript army.

If patriotism means love of our national characteristics and institutions and of individual liberty surely we ought to fight stoutly against Milnerism,[11] supported as we are by these tremendous economic and political arguments.

What right has the state to enslave men and ship them to unknown destinations to be slaughtered?

We should be far better off fighting Germany alone than employing two continental armies—one in Turkey the other in Flanders.

. . . . From the sole standpoint of winning the war and emerging without a complete social and economic disaster at home I see every reason to combat conscription with all the forces in our power. There is nothing I think in your letter which goes against this view.

C.P.S. to Lloyd George, 24 May 1915

Forgive me for bothering you with a wire today. I was deeply concerned at the report that you might keep the Exchequer and leave the great work of organizing munitions to some one else. I think that would be fatal. For many reasons you are obviously and pre-eminently cut out for the new and essential work. Of course you ought to retain the Exchequer as well and if a Protectionist takes it very grave trouble may follow. But if that is refused—and I know you won't make claims for yourself even where the public interest demands it—then at least let us have the one great gain which Reconstruction promised us—your

[10]Baptist leader and active supporter of the Liberal party.
[11]Lord Milner was regarded as the embodiment of right-wing imperialism.

control with full powers of the one business that really matters. That is the public aspect of the matter; the personal one is small beside it, yet your friends will wish that, having made your reputation in one great post, you should go on to make it in another, for the time being and in the eye of the nation, far greater. Any other solution would appear childish and impossible.

[P.S.] It isn't munitions alone that you will have before long to organize, I expect, but the nation for war.

C.P.S. to Lloyd George, 25 May 1915[12]

You are of course overwhelmed with work, but I think it might be worth your while to see the bearer of this note (Charles Renold) and hear what he has to say (1) about the organization of the great armament firms which he regards as extremely defective (2) about certain tendencies in the whole engineering trade under the stimulus of the war demand which he regards as contrary to the public interest (3) certain constructive proposals he would like to lay before you. Charles Renold is a young fellow of ability and great public spirit for whose thorough disinterestedness and patriotism I can answer. He is a director of Hans Renold & Co. the largest firm of chainmakers in the country. . . .

Hans Renold—and Charles Renold as his substitute—are members of the Manchester Armaments Committee and young Renold can tell you some things which perhaps you ought to know as to the working of this sort of body.

Diary, 16 June 1915

Lunched with Lloyd George and saw him for a few minutes alone before and after. Told me he had just left Committee of Trade Union representatives and they had agreed to the following conditions as to Armament Workers.

1. All Trade Union rules to be suspended in Munitions workshops.
2. All workers in them to be placed under military discipline and made punishable for breaches of regulations.
3. Acceptance of service to be voluntary provided Trade Unions can within a week enlist a sufficient number of workers.
4. All private firms engaging munitions workers to be compelled to require a certificate from previous employer so as to prevent desertion from munitions works.

[12]Lloyd George Papers.

5. On the other hand war-profits to be annexed by the State.
Failing the enlistment voluntarily of a sufficient number of workers I gathered that Lloyd George's original scheme of universal compulsory service for home defence would take effect, such service to be in either a home defence army or in industrial service sanctioned by the State.

Dardanelles.[13] Was extremely pessimistic as to prospect. A mad enterprise. His conviction personally was that the Germans in command were simply playing with us, that it suited them admirably that we should go on wasting men and shells, and they would keep us at it, but that when it suited them they could drive us into the sea.

As to Russia she was "done for". Lemberg would be captured all right.

As to a General Election the rumour was absurd. They were just going to introduce a Bill prolonging the existence of Parliament for one year provisionally. Spoke with the utmost disgust of Sir Robertson Nicoll's article in the "British Weekly"[14]—an extravagant and hysterical performance calculated to do great harm and injurious to him personally as he would be held to have inspired it. When he looked at it he felt he really couldn't read it.

At lunch told him a good deal about Dr. Weizmann. He seemed interested and took me afterwards to see Dr. Addison at the Munitions Office.[15]

---

[13]The British, acting on Churchill's inspiration, were now committed to a full amphibious operation aimed at seizing the Gallipoli peninsula and ultimately driving Turkey out of the war.

[14]On 10 June 1915 the Nonconformist *British Weekly* (whose editor, Sir William Robertson Nicoll, was known to be friendly to Lloyd George) indulged in lavish praise of Lloyd George's controversial speech at Manchester foreshadowing industrial conscription. The article said that if the government, or the House of Commons, hampered him in his work he should refuse to go on. This was widely interpreted as a warning by Lloyd George to his colleagues.

[15]Christopher Addison, a doctor of medicine and Liberal M.P., was parliamentary secretary to the Minister of Munitions and in close relations with Lloyd George.

5. Compulsion, August-September 1915

The question of freedom—versus—organisation came to a head in September 1915 over the issue of military conscription. After a year of war the rate of recruiting had begun noticeably to slacken; the consumption of men in France and at Gallipoli was increasing. Up to this point Lloyd George had wanted industrial rather than military compulsion. Now he turned his attention to employing state powers to gather men into the army.

It was clear that this proposal would have to be forced upon the Liberal and Labour sections of the government, only Churchill among the Liberals supporting Lloyd George. But the Conservative party (now a substantial element in the government) was strong for conscription. Admittedly Balfour—ex-Conservative leader and former Prime Minister—was lukewarm, and Bonar Law, the present leader, was estranged from Lloyd George. But Lloyd George had a powerful ally in Lord Curzon, who saw himself as a potential Conservative leader, and strong backing from the Tory rank and file in Parliament. He also had the support of the Upper House, which was to prove of great tactical importance.

The uncertain quantity was Kitchener. He agreed that conscription might be necessary sometime, but would not say when. It is possible to guess why. He had failed as War Secretary, except in one respect: attracting men into the army. Most of his other functions had been taken from him. If he was no longer needed as a recruiting-officer, he would have no job left.

Where did Scott stand? In 1899, and again in August 1914, he had opposed conscription. But during 1915 he had moved far towards the compulsionist views of Lloyd George. Now that Lloyd George had gone the whole way, it might be expected that Scott would follow him. But at this point he drew back. Even though he had written approvingly in May of a nation "marshalled and regimented", he was coming to conclude that organisation was one thing, compulsion another—and that though a liberal state might be compatible with the former, it was not with the latter. It may also have been dawning on him (as the Manchester Guardian was to admit eight months later) that Lloyd George did not fully appreciate the difference.

Scott's position was made plain in a leading article of 8 September 1915. Its main points were as follows. The Guardian *could imagine no event so disastrous to civilisation as a definite victory for Germany, and would pay any price—including conscription—to avoid it. But it was first necessary to know that the price was justified. The advocates of conscription had not shown that it was. Many of them favoured conscription* per se, *believing in military discipline and a hierarchy of classes. There was, the* Guardian *concluded, only one certain effect that conscription would have: it would divide the nation.*

From this position Scott did not budge. He held that the necessity for conscription had not been proven, and that the matter was being decided not on its merits but in response to political pressure.

C.P.S. to Hobhouse, 24 August 1915 (Extract)

Many thanks for your letter. . . . Thank you also for your offer to take a few days on duty here early in next month. It will help me very much to do what I feel I ought to do, which is to go and see some of the big-wigs in London and come, if possible, to a definite understanding on the question of compulsory service. I want to know what they really need and intend and then, if the need be proven, we can perhaps do as much as anybody to make straight the way for what has to come and also may be able to influence the form it is to take and the manner of presenting it. What they have got to understand is that, if some very serious consequences are to be avoided, the case has got to be a clear one and to be frankly and clearly stated and the nation must not be tricked in any way nor taken by surprise.

I am not sure that it might not be well, under the new conditions, for me to see some of the leading people on the other side—say Balfour (whom I could easily see) and Kitchener to whom I might ask him to introduce me—a queer encounter!

Of Lloyd George I have heard nothing for some time and I must try of course to see him also. I think it very unlikely that there is anything much the matter [with his health]. He has immense buoyancy—it is one of his great assets—of spirit and along with it of bodily vigour, and, though he is not what you would call physically a strong man, he has great nervous power which enables him quickly to conquer any minor bodily afflictions and which braces rather than depresses him in difficult and trying situations. The Marconi business was probably by far the worst trouble he ever met in his public life and he came through that all right.

About Russia, serious as are her defeats, I can't feel that her resolution is in doubt. In less than 2 months winter will come to her aid and I believe she will fight on, even if she loses Petrograd, so long as we are undefeated in the West.

C.P.S. to Hobhouse, 1 September 1915 (Extract)

The temper in South-Wales[1] is rather ugly and seems to have taken even the men's leaders by surprise. I hope it's true that the terms secured were not fully understood, but I doubt it. We had to cancel a congratulatory short at the last moment last night. What an incompetent Runciman seems to be.[2] I never could understand why he was chosen for high office except on the strength of his Liberal Imperialism. He always seemed to me a small man and a pretentious one.

P.S. Just got a wire from Lloyd George asking me to breakfast on Friday.

Diary, 3 September 1915

Lloyd George wired me to come to breakfast. He was alone. Stayed an hour. He at once broached subject of prospects of the war and probable need of compulsory service. Russia done for. Germans would probably take both Petrograd and Moscow (and if they were wise would give autonomy to Finland; neither Poles nor Lithuanians were actively hostile to them and by their recent successes they had gained ample supplies of oil, wood, corn—of everything they needed). The Russians were desperately short not only of munitions but of rifles. . . .

Germany's next move would be to break through Servia to Constantinople. Bulgaria would present no obstacle. Germany would make her a present of Macedonia and merely ask a right of way which would be given. Once direct communication was established she could mobilise Turkey. The Turks have now about 500,000 men under arms. . . . With German help they could mobilise 3 million and make it necessary for us to send half a million men to Egypt. Even without these, when Russia had been put out of action the Central Powers would be in a majority as regards numbers, even counting in Italy because Italy, like the other allied powers, was short of munitions. She

[1]The scene of much industrial unrest.
[2]Runciman was at this time President of the Board of Trade, and the minister most concerned with industrial disputes.

was fully balanced by Turkey and the Turk was the better fighting man, partly because he was a barbarian.

As to munitions Germany was now producing 320,000 shells a week against our 30,000, but by next year we should be producing, with the addition of what we could import, nearly as many shells as Germany now.

As to men we were already running rather short. We were getting about 25,000 a week. Kitchener wanted 30,000. Then there were 100,000 munition workers now in the field who must be brought back. Under the voluntary system it was almost impossible to prevent the enlistment of these men. The recruiting officer wanted *men* and did not care what they were and would enlist without asking questions or give an incorrect description. 25,000 munitions workers had been enlisted even since May. He was confident we should have to come to compulsion; the danger was that we should adopt it too late. Kitchener's mind moved slowly and he did not easily rise to a new idea. His present view was that we should need compulsion in about 3 months; George would evidently like to go for it at once, or very shortly, largely I think because of the great indirect assistance he expected to get from it in supplying munitions workers—which at present is his great difficulty.

As to the Cabinet it is acutely divided. The Prime Minister is against it, but not so decidedly that he would not accept it if the majority of the Cabinet were in favour of it. In Churchill's phrase, said Lloyd George a little maliciously[,] "The Prime Minister is the man in the 'howdah'—wherever the elephant goes he will go". Like Palmerston in his later days nothing to him matters so much as that he should stay where he is, and quite unlike Gladstone he is never seized with a sudden impression that "something must be done". Balfour is much the same. He ruined his party in 1902-5 by his halting between two opinions and that is his attitude now. He can find nothing better to do than to hold up his hands and say he thinks the Germans must be mad.

I put a few points to him:

(1) The attitude of the Labour party and danger of serious resistance, but he was inclined to make light of this. If it were a question of calling up two millions of men at one time there might be danger, but not if they were called up only 30,000 or so at a time.

(2) The difficulty of discrimination. How are you going to determine whether a man is or is not wanted, not merely for the obvious purposes of munitions, coal etc., but for keeping our industries going. He said the problem was solved in Germany and in France and he did

not see why it should not be here. It could not of course be dealt with centrally, nor by the recruiting officers; there would have to be local Committees. General principles would have to be laid down for general application—e.g. as to exemption of one son in a family if several had already enlisted—and then applied with discretion by the local authority.

(3) I asked what method he would propose for selecting his monthly class or quota. Oh! he said "the ballot". Apparently he had so little considered the matter as to contemplate a general levy of all eligible men as indicated by the "pink papers" and then a preliminary selection by lot. I suggested that it would be better to call the men up by classes, starting with the unmarried and of these those under a certain age. He agreed that that might be better.

There was no time to thrash the thing out. He had a Cabinet Committee "the Dardanelles Committee" at 10.30 and it was already 10.45, so he asked me to come to Walton Heath on Sunday.

Lord Robert Cecil.[3] I had an appointment at 12.30. . . . I took the opportunity of broaching the question of compulsion. He said he was not in the secrets of the Cabinet, but entirely agreed with the letter of his brother, Lord Hugh Cecil, in "The Times".[4] He said there were differences of opinion among Conservatives, as among Liberals, though much less marked, and that if Kitchener declared for compulsion there would be practically no dissent. He spoke strongly of the mischief done by the Northcliffe press in stirring up strife, but feared nothing could be done to check them. . . .

He asked me if I had seen Lloyd George and I said I had. He then advised me to see Austen Chamberlain[5] who in temperament he said was the direct converse of his father, who was a man of impulse, whereas Austen was above all things cautious. "If ever I have a wild idea," he said, "I always take it to Austen in order to hear everything that can be said against it". He offered to introduce me there and then, but I said if I might use his name that would be sufficient.

Sir J. Simon and Arthur Henderson.[6] Met them at lunch at the

[3]Robert Cecil (Under Secretary for Foreign Affairs) and his younger brother Hugh were sons of the late Conservative Prime Minister Lord Salisbury. They were prominent members of the free trade, Anglican wing of the Conservative party.
[4]The letter called for a cessation of the conscription campaign as seriously impairing national unity.
[5]Son of Joseph Chamberlain, and a leading contender for the leadership of the Conservative party in 1911; Secretary of State for India in the Asquith coalition.
[6]Henderson was secretary of the Labour party and its principal representative in the government.

National Liberal Club—both keen against compulsion and full of suspicion and anger against Lloyd George—especially Simon. Henderson much cooler. Simon did almost all the talking.

Among the points which emerged were: (1) That differences in the Cabinet were so acute that both anticipated that we might be driven to a general election in a few weeks. (2) That the out and out opponents of compulsion were, besides the two present, first and foremost McKenna (who goes so far as to say that the one thing which could lose us the war is conscription—he appears to base himself largely, or mainly, on economic grounds) and Runciman. Also the Prime Minister, as at present disposed. (3) That relations between Lloyd George and the Prime Minister are very strained—that the first which the Prime Minister had heard of Lloyd George's conscription movement was from Bonar Law, who had gone to the Prime Minister and told him he thought it was his duty, if he didn't know, to inform him. (4) That the protagonist for conscription on the Conservative side in the Cabinet is Curzon, whom Simon and Henderson both disliked, but felt compelled to admire. "He is the brazen pot", said Simon, "among the earthen vessels." (5) That they regarded Curzon as the destined leader of the Tory party and thought if a dissolution were precipitated it would be his doing and that he might then seize the first place. Bonar Law they both liked but did not admire. (6) When I put it to Henderson whether organized labour would be irreconcilably opposed to compulsion, he said: No. He thought that if the Cabinet were unanimous in supporting it and Kitchener recommended it, the workmen would accept it.

I explained my own position to Simon and said I thought it was the duty of all of us, in the Cabinet and out of it to examine the thing purely on its merits, with an open [mind] and without any sort of partizanship. He said frankly he couldn't rise to that and asked me whether I was prepared for conscription after the war. I said certainly not for compulsory *service* but that compulsory *training* on the Swiss model might be necessary and almost certainly would be if Germany were undefeated. He said he would like to go to America. Altogether he gave me the impression of a man who had not really faced the facts and who was carried away by the ardour of the political fight.

Diary, 5 September 1915

Lunched with Lloyd George at Walton Heath and had a couple of hours or so with him walking and talking before and after lunch. The new points which emerged were:

(1) That, though he had not unlimited faith in compulsion he regarded it as practically our only chance of winning the war.

(2) He was dissatisfied with Kitchener who aimed only at a total Army of 70 divisions, or about 1,400,000 men, whereas in order to succeed we needed a much larger force and, with energy, it could be trained and equipped, but would demand new methods.

(3) He had quite made up his mind that if defeated on compulsion he would decline to be further responsible for the war.

(4) He recognised that this would mean the break-up of the Government with an immediate general election.

(5) It would also mean the break-up of the Liberal party and his own temporary secession from it.

(6) It was obvious that in all this he was thinking quite sincerely and simply of the military situation and the winning of the war. But when I put it to him he said at once that of course conscription would simplify very much his difficulties with labour (a) by enabling him to recall the 100,000 enlisted munition workers who were constantly promised but never came (b) as a means of discipline of the small minority who made all the trouble in the munitions works.

(7) Profits in these works were limited by agreement with the Labour leaders themselves to a maximum of 10 per cent or the pre-war rate if it exceeded that. As a matter of fact they were only allowing 8 per cent, but it made no difference to the attitude of the men.

(8) He agreed that all war profits should be heavily taxed and believed it would be done in the new financial proposals.

(9) As to the Register[7] he thought we could not afford to wait for the results of a canvass based on it but that if once the power of compulsion were granted it might not be necessary to apply it, but that enough men would come forward if they knew they could be compelled.

(10) As to the division of parties in the Cabinet he thought that if the Prime Minister supported Kitchener (with whom the question of compulsion was only one of time—at the outside 3 months) the Cabinet would be unanimous with the possible exception of Simon. McKenna and Runciman, the other two leaders of opposition, were both Asquith's men and had no future apart from him. Simon *might* hold out, but it was doubtful. If the Prime Minister opposed—which he did not seem to think likely—it might be that he and Churchill would be the only Liberal Ministers who would persist, but he anticipated that 40 or

[7] The National Register of manpower then being compiled.

50 Liberal members in the House of Commons would take the same course.

(11) He derided the idea that the financial resources of the country were insufficient. We had £4,000,000,000 of foreign securities which could be pledged.

(12) He would disregard therefore the needs of foreign trade and would exempt only the necessary proportion of those engaged directly or indirectly in war work (in which he included agriculture as well as coal mining) and a certain number of the textile workers.

Diary, 9 September 1915

Called [on Balfour] by appointment in afternoon at Admiralty[8] and stayed about 20 minutes. Put main points of my position which believed to be largely representative of many Liberals and Labour men.

(1) Opposed on {principle / general} grounds to compulsion, but prepared if it can be shown to be necessary in order to win the war, not only to accept but to advocate it.

(2) But essential conditions are

(a) that voluntary system should have been tried out to the full,

(b) that no attempt should be made to impose compulsion by authority, to hustle us into it, but that all the facts which may make it necessary should be fully stated.

(3) that before the voluntary system could be considered to have failed full use should have been made of the National Register and an appeal addressed individually to those who were judged suitable for enlistment on a considered and well thought-out system.

(4) that if this had been done and had failed and the need for more men was clear I believed the objection of organized labour would no longer be pressed, but that on any other terms it would be insuperable.

(5) that national unity was vital and it was essential to proceed cautiously.

(6) that I understood the immediate deficiency in the number of men enlisting as compared with the number whom it was possible to equip and train was not great and ought easily to be made good by a more effective method of recruitment based on the information supplied by the Register.

Balfour seemed to be surprised and pleased that I should be willing

[8]Balfour was First Lord of the Admiralty in the Asquith coalition—an appointment which came under increasing criticism during the following year.

to go so far in the direction of compulsion on cause shown. He said he himself disliked compulsion, though he could not say he was opposed to it on principle. I said I had used the word carelessly and meant only that I was opposed to it on general grounds. So he said was he. He asked on what evidence I based my opinion that there would be vehement resistance by Labour to any attempt to impose compulsory service by authority and without adequate cause shown[;] and I explained that I had no direct evidence beyond that of Arthur Henderson who, as he said, being a member of the Cabinet was not quite an outside witness, but rested my belief on indirect evidence derived from men like Hobhouse who had been in lifelong sympathy and contact with working-class opinion. He seemed himself to be satisfied and indeed agreed with me cordially point by point on the whole position. So there was nothing further really to discuss. . . .

Hobhouse to C.P.S., 24 September 1915

I managed at length to see McKenna this afternoon and had a talk inter alia upon conscription. It was interesting to get so completely different a view from that which we have had. McKenna's objection is not so much that it would divide the country, as that we are unable to stand it industrially. He argues "We have to provide 1,590 millions viz about 2/3 of the national income for the war. All the Allies make calls on us, and here is Greece coming in and we are trying to prop Roumania and hold on [to] Bulgaria (this *en passant*).[9] The Allies have plenty of men, but not equipment. There is a limit to what you can get from the U.S.A. You must in any case pay for what you get. . . . Therefore you must keep our own industry going. Now every time you withdraw men on a large scale you give it a shock. It recovers slowly as new workers, women and older men and boys, are gradually drawn in and slowly made efficient. But then you come and draw more men and industry runs down again." I said "Would you then actually stop recruiting?" He said, No, but I would go slowly. We can get on as long as only 5 or 10,000 a week are being drawn away, but if it goes much faster exports fall, the exchange goes against us etc. . . . He wholly scouts defeat. Where are we touched? We can go on ten years if they will only leave industry alone. . . . There are 100 ways of winning the war and only one of losing—conscription.

. . . . I found by the way he rather regarded us as converts to con-

[9] These expectations of fresh allies in the Balkans proved ill-founded. Greece and Rumania refused to enter the war at this stage, and Bulgaria intervened on the side of the enemy.

scription, which I pointed out was rather unjust in view of what we have actually written, but people always will put their own interpretation and I expect he goes more by what other journalists have said to him than by his own reading.

C.P.S. to Hobhouse, 26 September 1915

Many thanks for your very interesting account of interview with McKenna. George (who had come into rather violent collision with him) told me of his attitude but rather misrepresented it I think, as timid and obstructive. Thus he said McKenna objected to his spending £100 millions on guns in the U.S. on the ground that we could not afford it, and as making a bogey of the adverse American exchange.

George himself was for enlisting *all* the able-bodied men not needed for his munitions work and financing the war by our investments—i.e. our four thousand millions invested abroad and the French two thousand millions. I should think McKenna has a much saner judgment than he on a question of that kind and I am glad to know what is his real position—particularly as to our ability to stand a long war.

I'm not surprised that Fleet Street doesn't understand our attitude on conscription because it hasn't realised that the voluntary system can be made almost, perhaps quite, as effective. Thus we are not concerned to defend the existing system of indiscriminate enlistment and they don't see that in conceding so much we are not conceding everything, but in reality are, as I think, taking up a stronger defensive position. Still one must take care not to give ground for misunderstanding. I was very glad you emphasized in the Saturday article the distinction between pressure and compulsion, which is vital.

[P.S.] By the bye 5 to 10 thousand men a week must be insufficient even to supply wastage. Kitchener says he can do with 30,000 and I should think he ought to get as many as he can train and arm. It's no use carrying on a land war with insufficient forces and our allies would get tired if we don't.

6. The Issue of Strategy, October 1915

While the Allies were still attempting a break-through in the west, the Germans in 1915 made their main efforts elsewhere. Their aim was, while holding the line in France, to drive Russia out of the war (a reversal of the Schlieffen strategy with which they had begun the conflict). Although they fell short of their full objective, they inflicted massive losses on the Russians and penetrated deep into their territory. In September the Germans turned their attention to Serbia. They persuaded Bulgaria—now convinced that the Gallipoli expedition was a failure— to come in on their side, and in October the Central Powers fell on Serbia and crushed it. The British and French sent a force to Salonika which they hoped would persuade Greece to come to Serbia's aid, but without success.

Meanwhile, on 25 September the Allies launched a fresh offensive in the west. It was principally a French operation, but the British (at Kitchener's insistence) made a supporting attack at Loos. These assaults continued until early November, at great cost and with no strategic gain; nor did they cause the Germans to suspend their operations in the Balkans. However the Loos attack did have one important personal consequence: it was so badly bungled that French, the British Commander-in-Chief, was relieved of his post and replaced by Sir Douglas Haig.

Diary, 1 October 1915

Went to London by night. . . . Lunched with Lloyd George [on 1 October]. Churchill also there. Both very hostile to the policy of attack now being carried out on Western front, any considerable success from which they regarded as impossible. The whole of Cabinet had been opposed to it except one man—Kitchener. The whole of French Ministry also opposed except one man—Millerand [the Minister of War]. Joffre and Kitchener responsible. It was Joffre's last throw to recover his waning credit. Its failure would probably mean his fall.[1]

[1]This was a miscalculation. Joffre (the French Commander-in-Chief) was not superseded until November 1916.

The older French generals had been in favour—including Foch—the younger opposed—notably the ablest of them, Castelnau. In the War Council on the subject Foch was able to say all he had to say in 5 minutes, Castelnau in an exhaustive examination of the whole position was said to have taken 4 hours. This information not official, but communicated to Churchill by a French officer of distinction.

Both Lloyd George and Churchill insisted on the far greater possibilities of the Eastern front. As Churchill put it the same effort and expenditure which had given us the village of Loos would have given us Constantinople and the command of the Eastern world. Our policy in the Balkans had been persistently futile. We had missed some six excellent diplomatic chances. Even now we were without a considered policy and merely waiting on events. Bulgaria was obviously only playing for time till the Central powers were ready to attack.

Our attack in the West had probably settled a difficult question of strategy for the Germans. They had to determine how far to push their advance in Russia and how far to divert their forces for an advance in the Balkans. They might have continued the one and undertaken the other both with insufficient forces. Now they would no doubt dig themselves in as soon as they could straighten their line in Russia, and, after sending any necessary re-inforcements to the West, turn the whole weight of their attack on the Balkans. "I venture on that", said Churchill, "as a prophecy" and—appealing to Lloyd George—"you will bear witness that I have not been unsuccessful as a prophet". Thus by our present mistaken policy we may actually assist Germany to a sound one. We have at the same time gone far to use up the effective military superiority of France. Her losses have been very great and she has no reserves from which to make them good. She has already, said Lloyd George, according to the official information we have received, enlisted seven million men from first to last for the purposes of the war.

At this point [Robert] Donald of the "Chronicle" came in and soon after Lloyd George left for his office and asked me to go with him. . . .

Lloyd George spoke extremely seriously of his own position and virtually repeated what he had said to me on September 5, at Walton Heath, of his intention to resign if strong steps were not taken. He had seen the Prime Minister and told him, but had agreed to wait 3 weeks for the development of events. By about Tuesday next we should practically know the result of the Western offensive and he would ask me to see him again. I gathered that by that time he would have to take his decision. There was no time to discuss the matter further. I gathered that it was still for compulsory service that he was making his stand, but that may not be all.

I went back to Downing Street, as Churchill had asked me to go with him to his office,[2] and spent an hour with him in going through the confidential papers relating to (1) the loss of the 3 cruisers in the North Sea (2) Cradock's defeat in the Pacific (3) the Antwerp expedition (4) the attack by sea on the Dardanelles. He made out a conclusive case for himself on the first two and a fairly good defence on the other two. At first he offered to let me take away the papers to study, but thought better of it. He is chafing desperately at having virtually no work to do and spoke of perhaps resigning and joining his regiment. He said that so far as his difference with Lord Fisher [in May 1915] was concerned the Prime Minister had promised to back him, but when at the same time, in face of the munitions scandal, Lloyd George forced on a coalition Government it was inevitable that he should be sacrificed. He did not complain of that—it was the fortune of war. What he did strongly resent was that he should be held responsible for errors which he had done his best to prevent and he longed for the day when he could publish the whole of the facts.

On the general question of the conduct of the war I put it to him, as I had already put it to Lloyd George, that a mere increase in numbers, even supposing you could get any important increase by compulsion, would make little difference and that the really decisive things were first brains and secondly munitions. He did not dispute this but said all three were needed.

When I put it to him what would he do to bring about a real change for the better he hesitated a moment and then said, in absolute confidence, first get rid of Kitchener who is well qualified for many great positions but not for his present one. Even the Tory section of the Cabinet who came in believing in him have all given him up. (The French however still believe in him, partly because he talks French and fought with them as a volunteer in the Franco-German war). But whom would he put in his place? He said Lloyd George—this not even to be hinted at—with Sir Douglas Haig as military director at the War Office. The combination of the two offices of Secretary of State and military director was now seen to have been a mistake and would never be re-

[2]When the coalition government was formed in May, Churchill had been demoted from First Lord of the Admiralty to Chancellor of the Duchy of Lancaster—a change of status about which (given the attacks which had already been made on his direction of naval affairs) he felt very strongly.

peated. In addition there should be an inner Cabinet responsible for the conduct of the war and meeting daily.

C.P.S. to Hobhouse, 13 October 1915

Many thanks for your two letters. I entirely agree with what you say about the need for a steady flow of recruits and the positive danger of a mere spate and the supreme need of a better command. A wounded man—an *educated* corporal—just back from Loos sends a letter to us— too damaging for publication—from which it appears that in that engagement again we shelled our own men and that we *lost* hill 70 after winning it in that way. Otherwise we might have got through to Lens. . . .

[P.S.] Just heard from Lloyd George. Shall be lunching with him tomorrow.

7. The Political Crisis (1), October 1915

Lloyd George's drive for conscription was moving according to plan. The supporters of conscription were growing in number: most important, Kitchener had now withdrawn his opposition. And Lloyd George held the trump card of being able to force an appeal to the country. The life of the House of Commons was due to expire in January 1916; and any measure to extend its duration required the consent of the House of Lords. Acting on Lloyd George's inspiration, the Upper House made it plain that it would not extend the life of Parliament unless conscription was enacted simultaneously. Asquith sought to resolve this difficulty by making a "final" attempt to keep the voluntary system alive—the point about a final attempt being that it held out to men of military age, not the alternatives of accepting or escaping military service, but only the alternatives of volunteering or being conscripted. To direct this recruiting campaign he chose Lord Derby, the leader of Lancashire Conservatism.

Diary, 14-15 October 1915

Called by appointment at Downing Street at 1.30 [on 14 October]. Lloyd George indisposed, sent his motor car to take me to Walton Heath after lunch with his Secretary (Sutherland). A lovely day and he was lying on the verandah in his hammock enjoying the air and the roses. To his disgust summons came to Army Committee of Cabinet at 5.30 and after tea he motored me back to Downing Street. . . .

As to the political crisis it was acute and might probably come to a head at next day's Cabinet. Eight of them were determined to press the question of Compulsory Service to an issue. The names he gave were: besides himself, Churchill, Curzon, Carson, Bonar Law, [Walter] Long,[1] Lansdowne and Kitchener—a formidable group if they really stood together.

---

[1] Prominent Conservative, representative of the landed interest, and at this time President of the Local Government Board.

I represented that there was no case for compulsion till the Voluntary system had been tried out by aid of the Register, and that to divide the Cabinet and perhaps break up the Government at this time would be unpatriotic. He replied that he had proposed a compromise—that a Bill should be passed providing for compulsion in case in the opinion of the Government the need had arisen, but that this should not take effect till it had been approved by a vote both of the House of Commons and of the House of Lords—that is Contingent Compulsion. This would not satisfy Curzon or Carson, but they would probably not resign if it were accepted. I said the difference between Contingent Compulsion now and Compulsion when the need really arose, which could then be got by consent, was not worth fighting for, to which he replied that that was always what happened when you made a concession—you were told that the balance of your demand was not worth fighting for. Further it was no use to say you should have compulsion when the need arose because opinion would always differ as to whether the need had arisen and it would always be possible to say that the voluntary system had not really had a fair chance. The alternative was to get nothing and accept defeat and that they were not prepared for.

It was evident that there was more involved in the controversy than the immediate matter in dispute and that it had been made a battle ground of parties one object of which was either to get rid of Asquith (of whom Lloyd George spoke with great bitterness) or to break his influence, and another object was to get rid of Kitchener whom George proposed to send to France as Commander in Chief in place of French. This latter object, however, he thought might perhaps now be attained even without the previous dispossession of the Prime Minister. He [i.e. Asquith] had hitherto been very thick with Kitchener and depended much too much upon him, but Kitchener was now out of favour since he had declared in favour of compulsion.

I probed him as to whom he could suggest as Secretary of State for War in place of Kitchener, but he evaded the question. . . . I think he desired the office for himself.

Next day (October 15) saw McKenna in the morning at the Treasury. He developed very interestingly and ardently the financial argument against compulsion. The lack, he urged, is not of men but of munitions and of money or rather commodities to pay for them. Russia has half a million men ready and trained and is praying on her knees for rifles in order to put them in the field. Russia can carry on the war indefinitely if we can supply the munitions, or rather the goods and services needed to pay for munitions, and so can France. Our part in the war should be to act as paymaster for the rest. . . .

His point all through was that munitions and goods needed for the war could not be paid for by the sale of securities but only by goods and that we alone of the Allies were in a position to produce these in adequate quantity. He thought we had already gone far enough in withdrawing men from industry, but in order to keep up the existing force in the field would go so far as to allow enlistment up to 20,000 a week. This was considerably above the average rate of wastage.

He mocked at the idea of Lloyd George resigning and treated it as mere bluff. He had done the same thing several times before—notably in 1909 when he opposed McKenna's demand for a programme of 18 Capital ships in 3 years—and nothing had come of it.

In the afternoon saw Lord Derby at the War Office and he explained the plan which, after consultation with the Parliamentary Recruiting Committee and the Recruiting Committee of the Trades Union Congress[,] he had decided to adopt. It was very disappointing. There was to be a personal written summons to every man of military age married or single. All were to be summoned at once, and every man was to be called upon and asked, if unwilling to serve, to give his reasons which would be entered on his form. This work was to be entrusted to the local branch of the Parliamentary Recruiting Committee. A start was to be made with it at the end of October and it was to be completed by the end of November. It was to be clearly understood that this was the last chance of the Voluntary System. If that failed there would be nothing for it but compulsion.

I asked what would be held to constitute failure. How many men were required. He could not tell me. I asked how such a mass of men— say half a million—were to be trained. The outside figure which Kitchener had hitherto suggested was 35,000 a week. He said Kitchener had guaranteed he could train any number. They could be drafted into the existing cadres which were somewhat depleted, and clothed and equipped at once and supplied with rifles by degrees. I asked what was to happen when this first big draft was exhausted. He had no reply, but thought if it were big enough we need not trouble about that. I asked whether, if he were applying a compulsory system, he would proceed in this wholesale fashion. He said he should not, because in that case he should know he could get the men when he wanted them. I said he would get them also by a regulated voluntary system and that the total he would get in that way would be much greater. He replied that he had consulted the two Recruiting Committees and the general opinion was that to make the thing go it must be universal, "like a general election". He took great credit for having taken the matter out of the hands of the soldiers and put it in the hands of civilians.

My impression is that the thing is being rushed in order to get over the immediate political difficulty. It is only a week since Lord Derby was appointed and it is obviously impossible that he should have studied the matter otherwise than in the most superficial manner.

Diary, 17 October 1915

Soon after my return from London on Friday received wire from Lloyd George asking me to see him again on Sunday. Went to Walton Heath and had a walk with him before lunch. He was doubting whether to bring matters to a crisis at the Cabinet next day. Said conditions in Russia were far worse than supposed. Government had received a telegram to say that total losses of Russian armies were 6 millions (2 million prisoners) and they had left only 700,000 fighting men.

Showed me confidential document, signed by the whole of Unionist members of the Cabinet except Balfour (and of course Kitchener), in which formal request by Kitchener was quoted for 35,000 men a week —30,000 for the ranks and 5,000 (who need not necessarily be of military age) as navvies etc. for field work. The signatories strongly urged that this request must be complied with. Apparently the figure proposed on the other side is the 20,000 a week which McKenna told me he would reluctantly consent to. This document it was proposed to send to all the members of the Cabinet.

I put to him McKenna's argument that Russia had 500,000 men trained and ready to take the field if they could be supplied with rifles and that it would be far more effective to arm these than to begin to train fresh men who in any case would be better employed in making munitions and in carrying on the trade which enabled us to finance the war. He denied that Russia had such trained men and in any case they would need very much more than rifles. Moreover you could not set money against blood. Sacrifice must be equal.

He thought that the two parties in the Government as at present constituted neutralised each other and that either would carry on the Government far better without the other. If the conscriptionists retired the voluntaryists would be spurred to great efforts. He believed that Asquith who now refused any sort of compromise was riding for a fall. He saw things were going from bad to worse and wished to throw on to others the responsibility of facing the situation. For his part he would decline to relieve him. He and the others who thought with him, not having a majority in the House of Commons, would refuse to form a Government but would undertake to give to their late colleagues full support in the prosecution of the war and the constitutional course was for the Prime Minister who had a majority to accept this assurance and carry on.

He asked me what I, C.P.S., would do if I were Lloyd George. I replied that the question wasn't an easy one, but that I believed the voluntary system if pressed to its furthest point would give nearly as good a return of men as compulsion and that the difference which might remain would not be worth splitting the nation for. In any case I thought the nation was totally unprepared for a break-up of the Government on the issue of compulsion and for a possible general election as a consequence. He agreed as to this, but said they would keep the possibility of a general election in reserve and would not agree to the proposed extension of the life of this Parliament by a suspension of the Parliament Act for the present.

F. E. Smith[2] and Churchill came in unexpectedly to lunch, having motored over from London, and stayed for a consultation. They talked quite freely of the possibilities of the situation, F. E. Smith though not in the Cabinet being evidently as fully consulted by his party as if he were. They went over much the same ground that I had done with Lloyd George, but I went early so as to leave them free.

Before October was out, the pressure on Asquith was temporarily relieved. The issue of strategy now broke up the triumvirate of Lloyd George, Churchill, and Curzon who were leading the struggle in the cabinet for conscription. It was not a matter of westerners against easterners, but a bitter feud among the easterners, which caused the breach.

Given the deteriorating situation in the Balkans, the cabinet felt it must do something there. The question was what to do. Should Britain make a fresh attempt at Gallipoli, where stalemate had been reached, or abandon that operation and try to rescue Serbia by throwing all available forces into Salonika? Churchill, feeling his whole reputation at stake, clung to Gallipoli. Curzon staunchly supported him. Lloyd George, as ever, regarded Gallipoli as a blunder and argued strongly for Salonika. In the conflict that ensued, the conscriptionist front in the cabinet disintegrated.

[2] At this time Solicitor-General.

Diary, 26 October 1915

Went to London on October 25. . . . Told Lloyd George I was in town and he wired me to come to breakfast [on the 26th]. He was alone. Asked whether the Conference—with F. E. Smith and Churchill—had come to any conclusion. He replied impatiently "Oh! no. It's like all the other conferences: they settle nothing." "The fact is", he continued, "we are all at sixes and sevens. There's no clean-cut division such as the 'Chronicle' and the 'Daily News' imagine. I wish there were. If it were only a conflict between those who are for an energetic conduct of the war and those who aren't; between those who would put every man into the war who is capable of bearing arms and those who would restrict the number; between those who would disregard the claims of industry and those who put these first, then the matter would be comparatively simple. But it isn't like that; there are all sorts of cross currents and the result is hopeless confusion". "Not much of a 'conspiracy' then["] I said. "Conspiracy!", he exclaimed, "it's not conspiracy; it's chaos".

Then he went on to explain the different lines taken by various members of the Cabinet. Churchill hotly and persistently in favour of action at the Dardanelles even now, feeling his whole reputation and career to be at stake on that issue (I disputed this and he agreed it was an exaggeration; he was young and would outlive that error); Curzon strongly taking the same line; [Lord] Selborne[3] I think also the same; Grey very fair, saying it was a military question on which military opinion must prevail, but personally inclining to the Serbian alternative; Balfour hesitating and quite unable to make up his mind. Churchill on the other hand had a definite *parti pris* and wasn't open to argument. "When I told him so he retorted that I equally had made up my mind the other way. And", he added, "in a way it's true; I am definitely for the Serbian alternative. To begin with we are committed to it and if we didn't mean to pursue it with all our strength we ought never to have touched it at all. Further I am afraid if we hang back it may lead to a serious difference with the French. They have thrown themselves into the enterprise with great enterprise and spirit not too closely reckoning the risks. They are a chivalrous people and the desperate straits of a small and gallant people appealed to them as they appeal to me. If we fail them there will be resentment and bitterness. Already the 'Temps' is pointing out that no British soldiers are taking part in the operations in

---

[3] Conservative (of Liberal Unionist background); Minister for Agriculture in the Asquith coalition.

which the French are already engaged. When Millerand, the French War Minister, came over to consult on this very matter the other day a Committee of the Cabinet was appointed to meet him of which I was a member and we came to an agreement with him satisfactory to him. When we reported this to the Cabinet there were immediate protests, Churchill crying out 'this will never do', Curzon chiming in; and the whole thing had to be gone into again, ending in the usual compromise. When we reported this to M. Millerand and asked if it would satisfy him he merely answered '*Que voulez vous*', with an enormous shrug of the shoulders—meaning it would have to suffice if it was the best he could get. Afterwards when the matter was further discussed in the Cabinet nobody could agree as to what the agreement really meant, one side contending that it meant really the same thing as the original agreement, the other that it meant something quite different". "And there you have it" said Mr. Lloyd George. . . .

The decision taken by the Cabinet is to send six of the best Divisions to the Eastern theatre of the war. If they are in time they will go to Serbia; if they are not they will go to Gallipoli. What is "being in time"? Lloyd George is convinced that the Gallipolists are determined they shall not be in time, and in any case will say they are not. That, he said, was he believed the reason why our troops were being kept back at the base [Salonika] and are taking no part in the operations with the French. Yet it was almost certainly too late to use the new troops to any effect at Gallipoli. They could not reach Gallipoli till towards the end of November and it would take a week or ten days to disembark them. . . .

Obviously the ground of conflict within the Cabinet had shifted and I remarked this to Lloyd George. He admitted that it was no longer so much a question of Conscriptionist and anti-Conscriptionist as of Gallipolist and anti-Gallipolist. He admitted also that there could not now be question of a General Election on the Conscription issue, but he thought there might on the issue of the manning of the Army—i.e. as between the 30,000 men a week demanded by Kitchener and the 20,000 which the anti-conscriptionists were willing to concede—i.e. between an army in the field of 70 Divisions and one of 50 Divisions—and he proposed to hold on to the Parliament Act and not allow the legal term of Parliament to be extended till this question had been settled. "I should go in for a short election", he said, "a week or 10 days" and take a vote in the trenches, as was done in the American Civil War.

We had not finished our conversation when at 10 o'clock he was told the Secretary for Scotland, Lord Balfour of Burleigh, was waiting for him at the Munitions Office, having been appointed at 10.15. However he had to go and I walked to the Office with him. He explained that 90,000 men on the Clyde were threatening to strike because out of 20 men heavily fined for absenting themselves from work 3 had elected to go to prison rather than pay and their release was demanded pending an enquiry into the original grievances which had caused them to absent themselves. "That would mean", said Lloyd George, "that the Munitions Act would become a dead letter. Yet it is my last resource *short of Conscription*."

8. The Political Crisis (II), November 1915-January 1916

The events of the next few weeks completed the destruction of the triumvirate. Asquith set up a new war committee of the cabinet in which Churchill was not included. Churchill promptly resigned from the government and joined his regiment in France. Thereafter it was only a matter of time before the Gallipoli expedition was wound up. By 20 December the principal evacuations had been completed without loss—a stinging rebuff for Curzon, who had prophesied appalling casualties, and a great strengthening of Bonar Law's position against him. Lloyd George had apparently won the struggle within the easterners, but it was a hollow success. Serbia was past helping, and nothing was done with the troops which were sent to Salonika.

These events did not long relieve Asquith from torment. With Gallipoli settled, Lloyd George was free to resume the attack over conscription. His support was still formidable. He retained considerable backing among Conservative back-benchers. And thanks to the Upper House, he could as a last resort force an appeal to the electors, who were expected to vote overwhelmingly for conscription.

Yet as far as the cabinet was concerned, Lloyd George's position had suffered considerably. In quarrelling with Curzon and Churchill he had lost his closest allies. He had antagonised Bonar Law some months back, when the posts in the new coalition were being apportioned. And he was viewed with profound suspicion by the more upright Tories, like Balfour and Long. Carson, who might have proved a valuable ally, had rashly resigned in October in protest against the government's failure to aid Serbia. So even though many Conservative ministers supported Lloyd George's stand over conscription, they had little time for him personally. As for the Liberal and Labour members of the government, they found his views and his character equally distasteful.

Was Lloyd George simply to defy this front of disapproval among the leading men of the parties, appealing from them to their supporters and to the country at large? He was in a powerful position to do so. But such a course, though it might be heroic, might also prove suicidal. Lloyd George was rarely at his best when faced with such a choice. During the next two months he revealed an instability and loss of grip which displeased Scott.

James Bone[1] to C.P.S., 1 November 1915 (Extract)

I have had a talk with Seton-Watson[2] about the situation. His account of the meeting of the cabinet with Joffre sounds like a scene in a melodrama. He says that Joffre stamped and beat the table with his hand and flatly accused Grey of slackening about the war. It was only at the end that the Cabinet came round to his view about the possibility that Serbia could yet be saved. Asquith, Grey and Kitchener all against an expedition. I was told by another source that one part of the agreement was that the Dardanelles is to be evacuated and so they are not to wait for [General] Monro's report.[3] Seton-Watson says that everyone who has seen Grey says that he has quite lost his nerve and thinks the war is lost. . . . I don't know what his authority is but Seton-Watson's story is that efforts were made to prevent Joffre meeting Lloyd George; that Joffre did not go to Lloyd George's house as published but that Lloyd George saw him at the luncheon at the French Embassy. From another source I am told that Lloyd George did not know till the last moment whether he would be asked to the council or not. But you will know, of course. Among men like Seton-Watson there is complete despair about Asquith and Grey.

Diary, 1 and 2 November 1915

Saw Lloyd George for a few minutes on Monday morning [1 November] . . . —he was called off almost at once to see the Prime Minister to whom he said he had written a strong letter—and again at breakfast next day. H. Spender, however, came in not long after we had begun. I walked to the Munitions Office with Lloyd George but hadn't much time for talk altogether. The main points were

(1) As to Gallipoli and the Serbian expedition and Joffre's visit in relation to them. Joffre succeeded where "poor Millerand" had failed and been superseded partly in consequence. George described him as an alert, vigorous man not at all like the heavy and impassive person he is made to look in his photographs, full of vitality and with a very "good" face, kindly and humane and expressing force and steadiness but not great ability. He spoke to the Cabinet (apparently some others were also

[1] London editor of the *Manchester Guardian*.
[2] R. W. Seton-Watson, leading authority on Balkan affairs.
[3] Monro had just been placed in command of the Gallipoli expedition, and was to report on whether or not the undertaking should be abandoned.

present as Lloyd George mentioned the Russian Ambassador) for 40 minutes with great feeling and urged both the honourable obligation of intervention on behalf of Serbia and its military usefulness. He urged not only that all available forces should be sent to Salonika, but that Gallipoli should be abandoned. He had always been against the Dardanelles expedition and he was strongly of opinion that once the Germans were in a position to attack with their heavy guns the place would be untenable. To the objection that evacuation would involve great loss of prestige he replied that this was not the case so long as the force was merely removed to another place in the same area and this was really our opportunity.

Our active participation in the Serbian relief expedition was agreed to, but I gathered that nothing was really settled as to Gallipoli.

(2) As to Compulsion. He said that at his interview with the Prime Minister on the previous day Asquith had practically conceded his point and would say that if the present recruiting campaign failed "other measures" would have to be taken, but I gathered that this would be a pretty vague announcement. Lloyd George indeed has evidently ceased to press the question of compulsion strongly and said more than once that the Manchester Guardian was quite right in saying that the question of men was not the vital one, but the question of the direction of the war. He had indeed clearly changed his ground and now told me that he had told the Prime Minister that he could not remain a member of the Cabinet unless Kitchener were superseded. In words the Prime Minister had agreed to this, in discussion with himself and two other Ministers; yet the moment he was gone each turned and asked the other "Will he do it?" The fact is[,] concluded Lloyd George[,] "he is a soft-nosed torpedo", "he lacks the steel point".

In conversation, while H. Spender was present, he enlarged on Kitchener's shortcomings and the absolute need of clearing out a lot of the chief men both at the War Office and at the Front. I think he wants, as War Minister, to do it himself.

On 2 November Asquith made an important, but enigmatic, speech on recruiting. He said that he firmly believed that the Derby scheme would succeed and the voluntary system be saved; and further that conscription could only be carried with general consent. These points satisfied the opponents of conscription. But he also warned solemnly that if a substantial number of unmarried men failed to enlist he would consider the Derby scheme a failure and bring them in by other means. This constituted a great advance towards conscription.

In the discussion with Scott which follows, Asquith stresses the voluntary aspect of his speech: the number of men already enlisted calculated against the number needed (although he rather leaves this ground in point 4). But supporters of conscription were not concerned with the number needed: only with the number available. *Their assumption was that by one means or another all those available must be enlisted; and on 2 November, Asquith had accepted this position. Hence the loopholes which he told Scott he had left himself soon proved to be non-existent.*

Diary, 5 November 1915

Went up by the night train on [November] 4 to see if I could get Lord Derby to modify the scheme, for which Long and his officials are responsible, by which the Local Government authority, in the small and great municipal areas alike[,] is made the body to appoint an Appeal Committee entrusted with large discretionary powers. Found Long quite reasonable and ready to modify the scheme in any way desired, but Lord Derby hopelessly muddled and with no grasp whatever of the essential points, merely declaring, in his good-natured way, that all would be well, that he had various (perfectly vague) ideas for improving the scheme in his head, that the matter was difficult and must evolve by degrees. Meanwhile he goes on making one mistake after another. [Sir Jesse] Herbert[4] said that had been his experience all through and his Committee were in despair.

When I expressed to Asquith a doubt whether Lord Derby was equal to his task he merely remarked that he had the best intentions, but unfortunately was short of brains. My visit was therefore practically fruitless except in giving me a clearer insight into the character and quality of the central control. I had thrashed out with Herbert a scheme which would have made it possible to set things fairly right, but it was useless.

I had about half an hour with Asquith on the part of his speech on Tuesday which dealt with compulsion and recruiting. The chief points he made were

(1) That it was a mistake to suppose that Kitchener had asked for 70 Divisions or 30,000 men a week. He had mentioned 70 Divisions as a maximum with which he could deal not as the minimum which he required.

(2) Further, 30,000 men a week were *not* required in order to repair wastage. Even half that number would be an exaggeration.

(3) He had in his speech spoken of our having nearly a million men

[4]Chief Liberal organiser.

in France. The exact number he believed was 980,000. That was the number which French had under his command when he made the recent attack. Some of them had now been moved on. There were, besides, the troops in the Dardanelles, in Mesopotamia, in the colonial garrisons and in the Home Defence force. It was an amazing achievement and if any one had suggested such a thing as possible a year ago he would have been set down as a lunatic.

(4) No definite number could be stated for the size of our army or the weekly quota of recruits. All you could say was that the number should represent the available surplus after the essential services of the nation in other directions had been provided. He had himself always carefully avoided naming any figure whatever.

His task in the Cabinet had not been an easy one with "*acharnés* advocates*" of compulsion at one end of the table and the "*acharnés* opponents*" at the other. He had deliberately, and he was sure rightly, played a waiting game and at last had succeeded in discovering a formula which had brought the two sides together. (I chanced upon Lloyd George in the street and walked with him to his office. He confirmed this and said the words used by the Prime Minister had been those agreed on on the day I saw him before. There had only been one dissentient extremist in the Cabinet on each side).

(5) He still regarded compulsion as out of the question because it would involve conflicts which would at once ruin recruiting and instead of getting more men you would get many less. (Kitchener he said agreed as to this "so far as he understands—so far as he is capable of understanding; he is an Oriental"). He was anxious that this point should be more strongly insisted on in the press.

(6) I asked, at the beginning of our conversation[,] how soon the work of the present recruiting scheme was to be completed and he said by November 30. I said that was impossible—that there was an immense work of revision needed in "starring" the "unstarred" and "unstarring" the "starred"[5] and that this would take much time. He entirely agreed, but said that on November 30 we should take stock and see how things were going—that was all.

(7) I also asked whether Lord Derby was justified in saying that, before married men who signed on were called upon to serve, compulsion would be applied to the unmarried if they held back. He said his words on this point in his speech had been very carefully chosen and

[5]Men employed in certain occupations were "starred", on the grounds that their work was of national importance and so they ought not to enlist; but which occupations should come into this category was sometimes a matter of dispute.

they did not amount to that. He had left himself "an ample loophole"!

Before I left he spoke of Greece. . . .[6] I put it to him in case there were a strong popular movement in support of Venizelos and against the King should we be justified in intervening in its support? He said, in that case, yes, but to intervene except in support of a real popular movement would be folly. Carson's policy I said. Yes he said and "that is his measure as a statesman". "It is a policy of the nursery". "It ought never to be forgotten against him."

In the following diary-entry, Scott's dating seems to have gone slightly astray. He dates the entry "13 and 14 November 1915". But he refers to events on three days, Saturday, Sunday, and Monday. On the calendar these would correspond to 13, 14, and 15 November. Yet events which in the first paragraph he attributes to the Monday he later dates 14 November. Most probably he got the days of the week right and the dates wrong, i.e. 14 November is a mistake for 15 November.

The "Ted" referred to in the first sentence is Scott's son E. T. Scott, who was on active service. He was married to a daughter of J. A. Hobson.

Diary, probably 13-15 November 1915

Spent most of Saturday and Sunday with Ted who was staying with the Hobsons. Spent Sunday evening with Garvin at the Matthews, saw Mrs. Churchill and Sir Jesse Herbert Monday and lunched with Lloyd George.

The interesting thing about Hobson was that, though he is an active member of the Union of Democratic Control, I could not find anything in his general view with which to disagree. Germany must be beaten and must not be allowed to profit by her aggressions. Belgium must not only be liberated but indemnified. His chief concern was to replace force by law after the war and the essential condition of this was that Germany should be a party to such an international arrangement which otherwise would resolve itself into a league against the Central Powers, with competitive armaments and a revived Balance of Power, Germany ever striving to detach Russia from the League in which ultimately she might succeed.

[6]The Allies had hoped that Greece would intervene on Serbia's side, and Venizelos, the Greek Prime Minister, had favoured this course. But on 5 October, while Allied forces were landing at Salonika, King Constantine overthrew Venizelos and replaced him by a neutralist Prime Minister.

Garvin also was extraordinarily moderate—loathes war, treated as nonsense the talk of crushing Germany and held that all that was needed was so to defeat her that she might find war wholly unprofitable. From the time of Frederick the Great she had grown by successive aggressions; this time she must learn her lesson. She must find the means of progress within her own borders and in peaceful intercourse outside.

He spoke with admiration of Churchill—his insight, his immense industry, his knowledge of war and eye for the essential. That McKenna should go on to the War Council and he go off it he regarded as ridiculous. Churchill had wanted to resign again and again and he had succeeded in holding him back, but he agreed that now he was right.

He spoke rather sadly of Lloyd George of whom he had seen a good deal lately—blamed him for quarrelling with his own party. The Labour men, the Irish and the Radicals all now against him. A man should always stick to his own party because there lies his influence. What was the use of Lloyd George breaking with the "Daily Chronicle" and "Daily News" and cultivating the "Daily Mail" and "The Times". He seemed lately to have lost nerve as well as influence and, whereas Churchill had gained in force and character, he had lost. On the new War Council he was in a minority of one. Asquith and Balfour both belonged to the other camp in the Cabinet, McKenna was his sworn enemy, Bonar Law had a serious grudge against him for preventing him being Chancellor of the Exchequer in the Coalition Government when Lloyd George took the Munitions Office.[7] In putting McKenna in and keeping Bonar Law out Lloyd George made the mistake of his life. McKenna was overjoyed, "trod upon air" and ever since had been counter-working George. He had acquired an extraordinary influence over Asquith largely by saving him the trouble of thinking. It was the influence of a narrow, second-rate, efficient business mind with ready-made solutions over a much more powerful but cold, indolent, and self-indulgent nature. In fact we were now living under a McKenna régime. It was a wretched position for Lloyd George and he ought not to have accepted it. But he seemed to have lost his old self-confidence and courage and could no longer take risks.

November 14 [probably an error for 15 November]. Lunched with Lloyd George. He was not very illuminating. . . .

We spoke of the new War Committee and I said I thought it a bad

[7]At the time the coalition was being formed, Lloyd George had played an active part (at Asquith's instigation) in persuading Bonar Law to relinquish his claim to the Exchequer, which Lloyd George was vacating. Law had ended up only as Colonial Secretary, a post hardly appropriate to the leader of the Conservative party.

one and that he would stand alone on it. He did not dispute this. Had not much hope of Bonar Law, but thought it might be worth while to try to conciliate him. Balfour no better than Asquith. Of McKenna he spoke with great bitterness. He regretted having put him into his present great post—a service which he since repaid by persistent hostility. Bonar Law he agreed would have been far better. "But we thought", he said, ["]that he would let us in for tariff reform". By "we" I think he meant the present company and I'm afraid that when we discussed the matter at the time of his transfer to his new office I too hastily took that view. I said I thought it was a mistake and that it would have been far more difficult for Law to adopt Protection in any form than for McKenna who had in fact sold the pass,[8] and in any case he would have had the whole Liberal party against him. Yes, he said, and now McKenna has given away the whole principle of Free Trade.

He agreed as to the wholly unsatisfactory composition of the War Committee of the Cabinet. If Churchill had been on it instead of McKenna that would have made all the difference. He said he had doubted whether to go on himself or to let Churchill take his place and he did not know if he would not do that yet—but of course he did not really mean that: it was too late and if he knew himself he would know that he never refused or resigned the place of power. . . .

Mrs. Churchill. Called in the morning to say good-bye to Churchill.[9] He had gone to see the King and while I was speaking to "Teddy Marsh", his secretary, Mrs. Churchill came out and asked me in. She was full of courage but looked as if she had nearly cried her eyes out. She thanked me for what we had written of Churchill's resignation and when I said every word of it was true even so much of praise nearly broke her down. I asked her to tell him that we might want him at home again sooner than he expected.

Sir Jesse Herbert. Saw him for a few minutes and found that, as I expected, Lord Derby's announcement of the day before as to contingent compulsion of the unmarried did not mean nearly so much as it seemed to mean; that there was no idea of compelling all unmarried men, not exempted for cause shown, to enlist before any married men were called upon[,] and that in point of fact Lord Derby and his Committee had been at work all the morning discussing (1) what proportion of the unmarried should be regarded as adequate before starting on the married, (2) after they had started on the married how far

[8]McKenna's first budget had included tariffs on certain imports.
[9]Churchill was departing to France to join his regiment.

they should go with them before getting more of the unmarried. As to (2) it was decided that the proportion of enlistments in each of the 2 classes should be the same. As to (1) they were still debating.

Scott lunched with Lloyd George again on 26 November, Weizmann and Herbert Samuel also being present. The talk was mainly of Palestine and Weizmann's role in munitions production. But the following observations on the condition of Russia are interesting as showing that few people saw the war as clearly and consistently throughout as they subsequently liked to remember.

Diary, 26 November 1915 (Extract)

As to the war George made a frank confession of error in regard to Russia. "You know", he said, "I was very pessimistic. I was wrong". He attributed the recovery of Russia largely to the superior quality of her men. The Germans he thought were giving way under the continued strain, particularly the older men of the new levies. Over-feeding and over-drinking were all very well in early manhood, but told severely later, whereas the Russian person was inured to hardship and accustomed to the climate. He thought too that the *moral* of the Germans was suffering as they plunged deeper and deeper into the country and yet all their victories brought them no decision. Whatever the reason the fact was that the Russians were now able with a comparatively small force to hold up the Germans on the Riga front.

Lloyd George spoke confidently of the coming revolution—apparently his information was partly derived from the Russian delegates at the Munitions inter-allied Conference of the last few days. . . . It was no longer a question of whether but only of when, whether during the war or after the war. It was openly spoken of in Russia and the authorities dared not interfere. The soldiers would certainly deal with the matter. As for the Tsar he was a very poor creature. Probably he was a good deal safer in camp than he would be at St. Petersburg,[10] but he did not count for anything in the actual conduct of the campaign. The Russians had now some very able generals.

Diary, 11-15 December 1915

Went to London primarily on Garvin's invitation to meet his proprietor Major Waldorf Astor M.P.—a charming person, quite young and full of enthusiasm and good-will.

[10] The Tsar had taken command of the Russian armies on 5 September.

Saw Hobhouse and Garvin on Saturday evening [11 December]. We all three agreed that the most pressing needs of the situation were to get rid of Kitchener and substitute Lloyd George as Secretary of State for War giving Kitchener an honorific position. Garvin told me the whole story of the Cabinet conflict about Salonika. He was rather sad about Lloyd George who he thought had suffered from his recent intimate association with Lord Northcliffe—had lost faith and with it courage.

He lamented also what he described as his "breach with 'the Chronicle'[''']. I said I did not know he had broken with the "Chronicle", as I had met Donald at Walton Heath only a fortnight ago—quite friendly. He said George had resented Donald's failure to support him on his great scheme to buy out the brewers and had transferred his patronage to the "Daily Mail" which the "Chronicle" had duly resented. As I still did not understand he said "Well, you can't give the same tips to two papers[''']. I said I never dreamt of using information got in that way except as a guide to judgment and he said neither did he.[11]

On Sunday [12 December] went by appointment to see Lloyd George at Walton Heath. Met him starting out to walk before lunch with Northcliffe[12] who had arrived unexpectedly. Talked with the ladies till they returned. Lady Northcliffe, a silly little woman, said one interesting thing, no doubt repeating her husband—viz. German-Turks have now brought a light railway and 6 inch water-pipe to within 20 miles of the Suez Canal.

For half an hour before lunch and half an hour after Lloyd George sat to Augustus John for his portrait, a powerful but rather murderous effigy, which Mrs. Lloyd George repudiated but Lloyd George declared correctly translated his inner being during the last week or two.

After that an hour's walk with him myself over the heath. Found him highly pessimistic and unhelpful. Anticipated disaster at Gallipoli, perhaps at Salonica. Declared himself powerless, but could suggest no means of mending matters. Kitchener firmly entrenched and defending himself warily. Asquith anxious to get rid of him like all the rest, but shrinking from action. When Monro's report came recommending evacuation of Gallipoli seized opportunity to send Kitchener out and

[11]Though this may sound a trifle self-satisfied, in Scott's case anyway it was true. The staff of the *Manchester Guardian* were periodically infuriated to learn that they had been beaten into print with information which Scott had possessed for several days.

[12]The text says "Norcliffe", and refers to his wife as "Lady N.", but it is pretty clearly Northcliffe who is being discussed.

Admiral Lord Fisher in 1905

ir Edward Carson

Balfour

Bonar Law

hoped to keep him out, but one day Kitchener wired he was coming back next day and Asquith had not nerve to bid him go to Egypt instead. Kitchener had done a dreadful thing on his journey. Allowed King of Greece to extract from him that he had advised in favour of evacuation of Salonica and virtually promised that it should be evacuated. Repeated this error in Rome. When charged with this by George in Cabinet declared it was a lie. But you can't trust what he says—they all feel that.

Told me the whole story of the long struggle and complicated indecision of the Government on the question of Salonica. After Serbia's defeat it had been definitely decided to evacuate and Lloyd George was alone in the Cabinet in opposing it. This would have involved the resignation of the French Government which was absolutely committed to it and a severe blow to the entente cordiale. Viviani,[13] Millerand, Joffre and finally M. Thomas, the French Munitions Minister[,] had all been over here about it. Finally Thomas turned the scale. It came to this at last that Thomas told them that for Frenchmen it was a question of honour, but that for us apparently that sort of consideration did not count. (But I could see, in talking to Asquith later, that he had always been opposed to the expedition on the ground that it was undertaken too late—he did not explain why it was not undertaken earlier—and regarded it as a useless and very dangerous adventure).

Lloyd George himself had an acute passage of arms with Kitchener. "Then you propose", he said, "that we should withdraw our forces from Salonica under the protection of the Greek army and with a guarantee of safety from the Germans. So it seems that you and the Germans want the same thing", on which Kitchener turned red and Asquith white.

As to himself Lloyd George said he meant to stick to his post. He declared he would not accept the Secretaryship for War even if it were offered him with Kitchener still in a position—as e.g. Generalissimo after the model of Joffre—to hamper him. He had had experience enough of that sort of conflict in his present office. He was quite conscious that when disaster came the War Committee of 5 would have to bear the blame, but he meant to stick to that galley and sink or swim with it.

After this I thought I might as well go home.

I had a long talk again next day [13 December] with Garvin both during the lunch at Astor's house and afterwards. He was discouraged by my report of Lloyd George's purely negative attitude, quite un-

[13]French Premier, June 1914 to October 1915.

characteristic of him, and divined, as I had also in my own mind, that there was something at work in him which he had not told us. I think I partly came upon it in a curiously intimate conversation I had with Bonar Law next day when, mistaking the drift of something I had said, he remarked gravely on a tendency in Lloyd George to have an eye to his own safety. If George had become conscious of this feeling against him it would make it impossible for him to do anything which might seem to justify it. Garvin concluded that nothing could at present be done except to "create an atmosphere" by cautious but a good deal more significant criticism of the conduct of the war.

After parting with him I thought any way I would go to see Donald and try to do something to heal the breach, if there were one, between him and George. I found him unexpectedly friendly to George and in complete agreement with the view that he is the only man to succeed Kitchener. . . . Anyway that Donald, despite any small grievances, declared George to be, in his opinion, the biggest man in English politics and that he was prepared to back him was satisfactory and encouraging.

I saw Lloyd George for a few minutes again on Monday [13 December] about midday by his request—he has a curious habit of asking one to see him again as though he felt he had not quite said all he wanted to say—and walked with him from his office to the Cabinet at Downing Street, but he only emphasized some old points.

He asked me, however, to go and see Franklin Bouillon who was in London to organize an inter-Parliamentary Committee for consultation and exchange of information on the War.[14] I saw Bouillon for a few minutes afterwards and arranged to go to breakfast with him next morning. He is leader of the party of the Left in the French Chamber which comprises 1/3 of the whole Chamber and represents there much the same tendencies—dissatisfaction with the conduct of the war and determination to bring about greater decision and energy through changes in the political leadership—as Lloyd George does here. . . . He was much impressed at the way in which apparently everybody here took the war and spoke in particular of the almost unseemly levity with which Asquith and some other Ministers with whom he had been dining on the previous evening turned to their game of Bridge after

[14]Bouillon, a French politician of some importance (and a one-time contributor to the *Manchester Guardian*), subsequently earned a modicum of praise from Lloyd George in his *War Memoirs* (2-volume edition, Odhams, London, 1938, p. 1602), where he is described as "confident, ebullient, flamboyant", a man of courage and assurance, and the driving force behind Paul Painlevé when he was Premier of France in 1917.

dinner—it was not the thing so much as the whole tone, as though people were not being killed every hour, that jarred.

Asquith evidently shared the repulsion, as when I mentioned Bouillon's name next day he urged me to place no confidence in him, called him an "adventurer" and the tool of Caillaux[15]—although he tried to qualify the effect of this denunciation a little, afterwards. . . .

On Tuesday [14 December], after breakfasting with Bouillon, met Seton-Watson at Reform Club. His whole mind was concentrated on getting rid of Grey whom he blamed for all our failures in the Balkans, and he gave me a long paper which he thought we might possibly publish attacking Grey's policy ever since the death of King Edward and more especially before and since the war. I said I thought it much more important to get rid of Asquith and Kitchener.

In the afternoon saw Balfour at the Admiralty and broached the subject of Kitchener. He was extremely friendly but cautious and reticent. . . . He did not question the desirability of superseding Kitchener, but evidently felt the difficulties.

Bonar Law whom I saw next day was just the opposite. When I apologised [for] raising questions which perhaps I was not entitled to raise he at once begged me earnestly to speak with perfect freedom. Like Balfour he did not dispute the need for superseding Kitchener but like [him] also was impressed by the difficulties. In regard to Asquith he pressed me to say if I was quite clear I wanted to get rid of him and when I said I was remarked that the difficulty was to know whom to put in his place. It must[,] he said, in the present condition of parties in Parliament be a Liberal. So far as he was concerned he would be glad to serve under Lloyd George, but there was no other Liberal minister whom he would look at. Then as to Lloyd George he indicated that there was a little change of feeling in his party, that he had shown a certain instability and lack of judgment of late and they were on the whole more disposed to put up with Asquith. Evidently they were not inclined to press matters.

Asquith whom I saw in his room at the House afterwards was quite frank about Kitchener. He insisted strongly on the great hold which he had gained on public confidence not only in this country but abroad and in the Colonies and on the danger of giving a shock to confidence by any overt supersession of Kitchener. But he said he hoped to attain much the same end by different means. Munitions had already been

[15] Joseph Caillaux, discredited ex-Premier of France, was widely (and with good reason) suspected of pro-German sympathies—which makes this remark pretty strong abuse on Asquith's part.

taken from his control. Now the General Staff had been greatly strengthened and a man of first rate capacity put at its head in Sir William Robertson.[16] The Quartermaster General staff had also I gathered been strengthened, so that Kitchener was being reduced more or less to the position of a figure-head. It did not seem very convincing since what is needed is initiative, but he was clearly afraid to go further.

Earlier Scott had had a number of interviews with Lloyd George on the subject of Weizmann, whose work (of "vital importance" according to Lloyd George) in munitions production was, he claimed, being severely hampered by Lord Moulton, the Director General of Explosive Supplies in the Ministry of Munitions, and his chief assistant K. B. Quinan. Lloyd George had talked quite freely on 26 November about Moulton's "incompetence, vanity and obstructiveness" but felt ill-equipped to deal with him, "frankly admitting the difficulty of his position as a non-expert at the head of an expert department. Moulton he said talked his head off and when he had eloquently demonstrated that everything was right he (Lloyd George) had nothing to reply." Lloyd George "had appointed Sir Frederic Nathan as consultant to the department in order to act as a check on Moulton", but this had produced little effect. Moulton and Quinan had actually prevented Weizmann from attending a conference in Paris on munitions questions arranged by the French authorities. This time they had gone too far:

The same morning [15 December] I breakfasted with Lloyd George and brought Weizmann. . . . Lloyd George gave an amusing account of his encounter with Lord Moulton and his chief assistant, Sir F. Nathan being also present. He had been furious about the withholding of Weizmann's passport which he had handed to them to be visa'd and which they then refused to return, told them it was monstrous to treat a distinguished scientific man who was giving his best service to the country in that way and ended up by saying "if you offer me your resignation I shall accept it", but they didn't offer it. What evidently had enraged him particularly was that they should treat Weizmann, as a Jew and a foreigner, in a way they would not venture to treat a man in a different position. That is the generous side of Lloyd George.

Afterwards he talked in a delightfully irresponsible way about the way to end the war. It was nonsense to talk about "crushing" Germany; it was neither possible nor desirable. The best thing that could

---

[16]Robertson's career was unique in the army. Starting as a private, he had risen through the ranks to become in 1913 director of military training at the War Office (where he had anticipated the German attack through Belgium and the dangers awaiting a British force there), and in January 1915 had become chief of staff of the British Expeditionary Force. Strategically Robertson was a dogged, taciturn westerner.

happen would be that when the two sides were seen to be evenly matched America should step in and impose terms on both. Poland would otherwise be an insoluble difficulty; only so could an autonomous Poland be established. It would be useless for America to intervene now, but when both sides were exhausted her intervention might be decisive. "There", he concluded, "I think I've talked enough treason". It was difficult to say exactly how far he was talking seriously or only "in the air". It was a sort of divination.

Churchill to C.P.S., 19 December 1915 (Extract)

I was very sorry indeed not to see you before leaving. It was kind of you to call: and I read with much pleasure your fair and thoughtful article in the Manchester Guardian.

I am determined not to return to the Government unless with proper executive power in war matters; and as this is not a likely condition to arise I intend to devote myself to my old profession and absorb myself in it.

Whatever the weakness of Lloyd George's personal position, the logic of his stand on conscription was irresistible. If the Liberals in the cabinet rejected his demand, the Conservatives would have to take his side. But anyway, Asquith had practically sold the pass when, in order to persuade married men to volunteer, he had promised that he would get the single men into the army one way or another.

At the end of 1915 the timetable ran out. The results of Lord Derby's appeal were not deemed satisfactory. Asquith thereupon announced that he would conscript single men, so fulfilling his pledge and preserving the voluntary system for the married. The Conservatives accepted this as, for the moment, a sufficient measure of conscription; so, in the now uncertain mood which had so irritated Scott, did Lloyd George. The Liberals, with the sole exception of Simon, consoled themselves with the half-survival of voluntary recruiting. The Labour party resolved to oppose the measure, but eventually allowed its representatives to stay in the government. Only the Irish Nationalists, as a party, remained quite unreconciled, even though Ireland was exempted from the measure: they, with a handful of Liberal and Labour representatives, voted against the bill in Parliament. Outside, Scott continued his opposition.

Hobhouse to C.P.S., 30 December 1915

I had a long and unsatisfactory talk with McKenna yesterday. He takes the compulsion of single men as settled, and regards his refusal to resign as a sort of triumph over George's attempt to force a Khaki election. Evidently there is no solid resistance anywhere to the George-Northcliffe influence and we may take it that the Cabinet will be more and more run by the Times. [H.] Dore[17] has fine spun theories of the decision being contingent and so on, but from McKenna's manner I am clear that the essential point is settled. They stole a march on us by dividing the interests of the married and single.

C.P.S. to Hobhouse, 30 December 1915 (Extract)

What a nasty trick Asquith is playing us on the compulsion question. The whole thing is a political dodge and what he is really aiming at all through is not to do the best possible for the army, but to keep his party together and himself in power. At least that's how it looks to me. It's a duel I believe between him and Lloyd George and he means to dish Lloyd George by accepting compulsion and to prevent secessions by making the dose as homoeopathic as possible. But there is no sincerity about the whole proceeding and no serious consideration of the country's needs. He certainly is a champion in the arts of chicane. And the worst of it is that in its own small way it succeeds.

C.P.S. to Bonar Law, 2 January [1916][18] (Extract)

You were so good in allowing me to speak with you freely the other day, that I am venturing to trouble you with a few personal lines. I am deeply concerned at the decision informally announced to apply a measure of compulsion without waiting to see if the facts justify it. Personally I have been prepared to accept compulsion on condition that the voluntary system had been honestly tried out and had failed to supply the men needed for the war and who could be spared from industry and that the number of eligible men remaining was worth troubling about. But these conditions, which are essential if the nation is not to be disastrously divided[,] have not been fulfilled. . . . I can imagine no adequate reason for pressing for an immediate decision. The one commonly assigned is that so long as the Parliament Act Amendment Bill is not passed an election can be forced before the end of the month and that the married men would be interested parties. That seems to me indefensible.

[17]Of the *Manchester Guardian*'s London staff.
[18]Bonar Law Papers.

It would excite strong and it seems to me justifiable resentment and it is bound to create deep division and possibly resistance, and this for no substantial object.

Bonar Law to C.P.S., 4 January 1916[19]

I have your letter of the 2nd inst. which I confess I have read with a good deal of disappointment. I do not know whether you have had any opportunity of seeing the figures, but they are to me absolutely conclusive that the pledge given by the Prime Minister necessitated the compulsion of the single men who have not attested.[20]

Put in a nutshell these are the facts. . . . [At the end of the Derby canvass] while it is quite true, as you say, that a good many of those who had not attested would not be available for service; yet after making every possible allowance it is quite certain that the number who did not attest must have been much greater than would have justified the Prime Minister in saying that his pledge did not require compulsion to be used towards them.

You must remember also that it is not merely a question of the pledge, for if the Prime Minister had not at the beginning of the Derby campaign made this statement about the unmarried the evidence is quite conclusive that there would not have been any effective response to the appeal.

It is of course said that among the 650,000 [unattested] are all the lame, halt, blind, etc. but that does not seem to me at all likely. Even in my own limited experience, I know that those who felt sure that they would be rejected as medically unfit were the first to attest; and as regards those not canvassed, it seems to me certain that since the country was so agitated by the campaign the great bulk of them must have known of the movement and must have deliberately refrained.

In my opinion, therefore, to have delayed to take action now would really have shown a half-heartedness in carrying on the war for the responsibility of which I could not have shared. . . .

If you are in town at any time I shall be very glad to have another conversation with you on the whole subject.

[19]Bonar Law Papers.
[20]Under the Derby scheme, men were asked to "attest" their willingness to serve in the forces as and when they were required.

C.P.S. to Bonar Law, 6 January 1916[21]

Thank you for your letter. I should like very much to see you again as you kindly suggest and will take the earliest opportunity.

I don't feel the least sure that Lord Derby's residual figure, when it came to be tested and analysed, would have shown more than a negligible minority of unattested single men, and I do feel pretty certain that the minority could in any case have been rendered negligible by compelling every unattested single man to come before a tribunal to justify himself.

If *after* that had been done the remnant was not found to be negligible the case for compulsion would have been enormously strengthened and we might have avoided any very serious division. As it is I fully expect that if the attempt is made to enforce military service on angry men there will be bloodshed at home as well as abroad and very grave labour troubles besides.

Can that yet be avoided? It is the only thing I care about now.

Scott's expectation of physical resistance to conscription proved wildly astray. After all, he himself was assuming that all but a "negligible minority" of eligible men must be drawn into the services one way or another; so that his insistence that no one should be conscripted while lesser forms of coercion and cajolery remained unexhausted—though perhaps involving an important issue of principle—seemed of little political significance. With the pass of free service already so far sold, few were prepared to risk bloodshed in defence of what remained.

So, although Scott returned to London to continue the battle, he found little encouragement awaiting him there—least of all from those who were supposed to be leading the resistance. (It is doubtful if Scott was ever able to feel the same again about Simon after the conversations which follow).

John Dillon to C.P.S., 7 January 1916 (Extract)

The threat of a general election—and the conviction was/is universal, that an election on the issue of the present Bill would result in the Conscriptionists sweeping the country—caused a very large number of radical and labour members opposed to the Bill to support the Government. And of course the fact that only 45 members from Great Britain could be got to vote against the Bill is a serious fact which must modify the opposition.

[21]Bonar Law Papers.

Diary, 10-11 January 1916

Came to London (Sunday night, January 9) in order to see what could be done in order (1) to get the results of the Derby canvass tested and analysed so as to ascertain the real number of apparent defaulters (2) to have as many of these defaulters as possible attested.

Called in morning on Dillon, who had asked to see me, at Bath Club. Defended action of Irish party in voting against Bill on first reading. Redmond had been very doubtful and anxious about it but he (Dillon) had felt it to be necessary for the Nationalists to make their protest and not to lay themselves open to the charge of selling their principles. But he had been doubtful as to the policy of challenging a division. [J. H.] Whitehouse[22] had consulted him about it, but he had declined to take any responsibility. It was not their affair, as Ireland was excepted from the Bill. Whitehouse had looked for a much better division. He had counted on 100 English members, or not less than 70[,] and had derided Dillon's estimate of 30 to 40 which proved to be right. Severe pressure put on individual members by the Whips who said that if the minority exceeded 150 Asquith would dissolve, that the Tories would then come back with a big majority, Asquith would be ejected, "end of a great career", Tory Government for 20 years. Such *disjecta membra* of exhortation Dillon heard going on all day as he prowled through the Lobbies. In the result not only did the mass of the opponents crumble, but the leaders themselves who had come to curse stayed to bless. Charles Hobhouse[23] the chairman of the anti-conscriptionist Committee presided at 2 o'clock at one of its meetings and 2 hours later spoke for the Bill. [J. M.] Robertson did much the same.

As to the future action of the Irish party Dillon was not yet clear, but the view was crystalising in his mind that they would not press their opposition. The division had shown a large preponderance of Irish over Liberal and Labour votes against the Bill and this in regard to a non-Irish Bill could not be continued. Redmond was much more nervous about the matter than he. There was no chance he agreed of defeating or delaying the Bill. The aim of the Tories would be, with Lloyd George's assistance, without an election to oust Asquith and put Bonar Law in his place. Carson would come back and he and Lloyd George, between whom there was a sinister alliance, would dominate the Government and Bonar Law would be wax in their hand. Carson was a powerful personality without judgment—much more reckless

[22]Liberal M.P. and opponent of conscription.
[23]Liberal ex-minister.

even than Lloyd George. That would be a desperate position for the Irish.

As to my particular plan for rendering Compulsion unnecessary he fully approved but doubted whether Lord Derby could be trusted to put it through; "bluffness could be made a very good cover for adroitness" and he did not at heart want to succeed.

Spoke regretfully of the degeneracy of Lloyd George. On the principle of *Noscitur a sociis*[24] he said it was lamentable to see the sort of man with whom he had now surrounded himself and with whom he was to be seen in frequent conference in the tea-room—Dalziel and Booth, Chiozza Money[,] an adventurer on the make[,] and Markham —a sort of lunatic.[25]

Called on Bonar Law at Colonial Office by appointment at 2, he having evidently made his usual frugal lunch in his own room on a cup of coffee. Very friendly as before, and trying to be fair but evidently strongly biased in favour not only of passing the Compulsion Bill but of applying it—reluctant therefore to contemplate any measures which should render its application unnecessary. Evidently looked forward to compulsion of married men as sequel to compulsion of single and thought married men would not regard threat of compulsion as serious unless it had been actually applied to single men. Was evidently prepared for extreme measures in case of organized resistance. Asked if I did not think a general election would be justified in case of either obstruction in the House of Commons to passing of Compulsion Bill or of hostile labour action such, for example, as a strike in the Welsh coal-field. Spoke of the need in such a case of proclamation of martial law. "It would be better to shoot 100 men" in suppressing a strike than to lose thousands in the field as a consequence of it. Firmness essential. [J. H.] Thomas, the railway men's representative in the House of Commons[,] had actually reproached Lloyd George for "weakness" in his handling of the Welsh miners and said that their present threatening attitude was the consequence of his having conceded all their demands.

I put it to him that if such a catastrophe was likely to be the result of the application of compulsion was that not the strongest possible reason for doing everything we could to render it unnecessary. He agreed in words, but found reasons against any definite steps such as I suggested in the testing of the Derby figure of supposed single "slack-

[24]"A man is known by the company he keeps".
[25]Sir J. H. Dalziel, F. Handel Booth, L. Chiozza Money, and Sir Arthur Markham were all "ginger" Liberals, highly critical of Asquith and sympathetic to Lloyd George.

ers" which could only be done with the co-operation of the War Office, who alone possessed some of the essential information, and the re-starting of the canvass which in turn demanded Lord Derby's initiative.

He would not admit even the possibility of bringing down the figure of "single slackers" to the promised "negligible minority"—said a "negligible minority" after the Bill had been passed would have to be a different, i.e. much smaller, thing to what might have been re-garded as a "negligible minority" before—he gave no sort of reason for this arbitrary view—and obviously did not wish to reopen a question which he regarded as satisfactorily settled. He also said that even if the total of single slackers were small their distribution might be "patchy" and thus would give rise to local discontent—a meticulous objection which showed how hard put he was to find reasons. . . .

I had urged these steps, he said, in the interest of national unity, but might not national unity be equally imperilled by refusing to adopt compulsion which a majority of the nation desired—ignoring the obvious fact that the only possible way of securing national union is to refrain from raising or pressing *any* controversial issue which can pos-sibly be avoided and that this is the sole ground on which the Coalition Government exists.

The union of parties, however, he was anxious to maintain and was prepared to make all possible concessions in regard to safeguards against the compulsion of labour in order to win back the adherence of the Labour party and to retain its representatives in the Govern-ment. Henderson had been urged by the Government not finally to decide as to persisting in his resignation until he saw the Bill in its final shape. The Labour members had been invited to propose any amend-ments they desired for the protection of labour and assured that they would be considered in the most friendly spirit. It had also been decided, with Lloyd George's concurrence, to repudiate publicly any intention on the part of the Government to use the powers of the Compulsion Bill for the direct conscription of labour—i.e. as I understood him, of compelling men not engaged in Government work to undertake it under penalty of being sent into the army.

Bonar Law expressed disappointment at the attitude of the Man-chester Guardian and seemed to have great difficulty in understanding my position as being perfectly willing to accept compulsion on adequate evidence of its military necessity and the failure of the voluntary system and total unwillingness to accept it without that. . . .

Later in the afternoon saw Asquith in his room at the House of

Commons. He struck me as anxious and nervously excited and he walked rapidly round about the room nearly all the time—perhaps a quarter of an hour—that I was with him, like a trapped animal. To me he seemed a beaten man.

I raised no general topic, but spoke exclusively of the practical steps needed if the application of the Compulsion Bill was to be rendered unnecessary and his "pledge" fulfilled without it. . . . I told him Lord Derby's initiative would be needed if the Joint Recruiting Committees were to be got to work again and he . . . said he would speak to Lord Derby. I said it would be difficult to get the work taken up again by volunteers and that if it were to be properly done and quickly paid men would have to be employed and asked if Party funds might be used where needful. He said "Certainly—as much as you like—within reason" and on that we parted.

As to the number of men who might be considered a "negligible minority" he would not commit himself. I asked would 100,000? "Oh! no", he answered, "much less". 50,000? I asked. Even that he seemed to think too high a figure.

Saw Simon twice—at the House after I left Asquith and next morning at breakfast at his house.[26] At the House he was full of the next day's debate on 2nd reading of Bill. [W. C.] Anderson, Chairman of Labour Party in House and an able man[,] would move rejection and would make a good strong speech. He himself would speak next day before dinner so as not to be howled at by the Tory bloods coming back with their skins full of wine—also he added next day that he didn't want to come right up against Asquith whom it was painful to him to oppose and who would no doubt wind up the debate, and that by speaking early he would get a better report in the papers. In any case he expected a much worse reception than on first reading, partly because he was then in the position of making a personal explanation to which the House always lends a hearing, partly because there was then curiosity as to what he would say and that would have worn off. He seemed to me much too full of these little sensitivenesses which don't consort with the vigour of the fighting man. It was all an intellectual exercise to him and he had none of the joy of battle.

Agreed that the Division would be worse because the Irish would not poll so strong, but thought the debate on his side would be better because there would have been more time to get up the case. Asked if I thought he was right in the course he had taken and evidently needed a little encouragement which I tried to give. Said his object had been to

[26]Simon had resigned from the government rather than accept any form of conscription.

prevent the further extension of the compulsory principle. He did not expect to defeat or seriously threaten the Bill, but would take the risk of the Government going to a dissolution. Thought the Tory threat of forcing dissolution largely bluff. It would not suit them to dissolve unless they saw their way to a Tory majority clear of all other parties. No more Coalitions for them. But they could not in decency oppose Liberals and Labour men who had voted with them and they would not win *all* the seats of Liberals and Labour who voted against them.

Called attention to the fact that no out-and-out conscriptionist— neither Lloyd George nor Curzon—had backed the Bill. They would no doubt later decry it as a weak measure and ask for the real article. He proposed in his speech to challenge them to say whether they would be satisfied not to apply compulsion to the married men. If married men saw it would be their turn next they would not be so keen to ask for compulsion for the unmarried. Much admired Saturday's leader in Manchester Guardian (by L. T. Hobhouse) pointing out effect of Bill in imposing indirect compulsion of labour. Believe this inherent in any form of forced military service. Was so used in every conscriptionist country. No amendment of the Bill could effectively guard against it. Should point this out in his speech. . . . His policy in Committee would be to concentrate on points of substance—no niggling amendments.

At breakfast next morning Simon was in the same depressed mood. He "hated his task", felt very much his isolation, once more "hoped he was right". Should disappoint some of his supporters later. Unfortunate that so many of them were "cranks" (I defended the crank as a robust person with convictions). Should go through with the business to end of Committee stage, then accept result and end on conciliatory note, but no indication of this should be given till the last. Should stand by his supporters. He would not "Hobhouse them".[27] Regretted had no effective debating support. Otherwise could have done much better in second day's debate on first reading. As it was one day would have been better for them. The Speaker hostile. Took the view that they were only entitled to speakers roughly in proportion to their numbers as shown in the division, i.e. about 1 to 4. That might not matter so much if he would call the right men. Some of his supporters he feared would make foolish speeches. Rehearsed points of his speech for that afternoon which would be mainly a "debating" speech dealing with the points made on the other side. His points seemed to me too much in the nature of dialectical scores and I urged him to simplify and go more to

[27]See above, p. 169.

the root of the situation—the destruction of unity and the legitimate anxiety of Labour. He agreed. Incidentally he mentioned that [David] Shackleton[28] had been sent specially to report on the Trades Union Congress last year at Bristol and had come back deeply impressed with the strength and sincerity of the anti-compulsion feeling.

Later in the morning called by appointment on Lord Derby at Derby House. Found him in his usual hearty mood, anxious to be conciliatory and fair but at heart opposed to any re-opening of the Recruiting campaign or testing of the figures of his Report. Said he would do anything the Government asked him, but could only re-open canvass by joint recruiting committees if the Cabinet decided it should be done. Satisfied his figures substantially correct. Nobody could doubt that he had tried to make canvass a success; it would have been for him a personal triumph. On the question of military urgency said 300,000 men needed at once to supply arrears due to wastage, *in addition* to the 250,000 men who had enlisted for immediate service in the course of the Canvass.

Then saw Sir Jesse Herbert, chief Liberal Agent, who was strongly sympathetic to the scheme for rendering application of Bill unnecessary and assured me I should find his chief [John] Gulland, the Chief Whip, equally keen. When, however, I went across to No. 12 Downing Street to see Gulland I found him very much the reverse. He was in a very bad temper about a paragraph in the Manchester Guardian's London Correspondence alleging that great pressure on Liberal members had been used by the Whips not to vote against 1st reading of the Bill and that the threat had been used of a dissolution in case the number so voting exceeded 150. He absolutely denied that pressure had been used by him. Probably true that no direct pressure had been used on individuals, but that is another matter.

I think also he regarded the re-opening of the Canvass as a concession to the minority with whom he was angry. Said that as to getting the information needed as to the persons actually attested that was a matter for the War Office. There were difficulties but he would be glad to act on any suggestions made to him—a polite way of saying he would take no trouble himself. I said if he really wanted the thing done the only way was to find out exactly what the difficulties alleged by the War Office were and show them how they could be met. He said he would go over to the War Office and try. Thought it not much good to re-open the Canvass. This had in many cases been practically completed and he showed me some returns. I urged that even where it had

[28]One-time trade unionist and Labour M.P., now National Health Insurance commissioner.

the refusals and conditional refusals might now be re-canvassed with good results. He did not deny it, but was obviously quite indifferent. Unless therefore the Cabinet will decide to re-open the Canvass and the Prime Minister will galvanise the Chief Whip into life nothing effective will be done.

Scott can hardly have enjoyed the foregoing series of interviews (during which, it is worth noting, he had made no attempt to contact Lloyd George). By the time he left London, he can have been in no doubt that opposition to conscription was hopeless. This only increased his fears that another great Liberal ideal might soon be crushed—free trade. It seemed that tariffs might be employed not only for economic purposes, which would be bad enough, but as a weapon of foreign policy: to create a barrier permanently excluding the enemy powers from the comity of nations.

C.P.S. to Hobhouse, 20 January 1916 (Extract)

I wish I could have a talk with you about trade policy after the war. Two dangers are clearly ahead of us. One is the virtual surrender of free trade under various specious pleas and a vast extension of the policy of the McKenna import duties. The other is an economic war definitely directed against Germany and which of course will be made the ground and justification for every infraction of principle and every concession to trade interests. I can't reconcile myself to either unless we are forced to accept these evils in order to avert worse.

At the same time it is plain that we have got to make ourselves independent of all foreign powers for the essentials alike of war and of industry and this must involve special measures to meet the special needs and it will be difficult to prevent these from being made a cover for Protection. Of course the real remedy is a great improvement in education, especially technical and scientific education and the application of these to industry. But that will take time and there is at present no sign whatever of any interest in education—quite the contrary: it is treated with growing contempt.

Meanwhile Protection is handy and if the Tories come in, as they probably will, in alliance with the reactionary Liberals headed by Lloyd George, Protection and a Trade War no doubt we shall get. What I am anxious about is that we should put up a good fight against them. I don't say we may not be forced to make concessions which before the war we should have entirely refused, but I should like to limit these to proved necessities and to maintain rigorously the general ground of principle. It will be jolly difficult and the ground will have to be carefully chosen.

C.P.S. to Hobhouse, 25 January 1916 (Extract)

This question of tariffs and a customs union after the war cuts pretty deep. . . . the question of Free Trade, which we used to think so vital, is really subordinate and comparatively trifling by the side of those others. I hate the very thought of the permanent division and hostility in Europe which they contemplate and if that is all we have to look forward to I feel as if the future had little interest for me and I had rather get out of it. It isn't the material loss or even the prospect necessarily involved of future wars and bloodshed; it is the enthronement in Europe—that is practically in the civilized world—of the spirit of hatred and revenge. I had rather take almost any material risk than accept that.

On his next visit to London, Scott found himself still encountering a measure of resentment as a result of his unrepentant stand against conscription.

Diary, 28(?) January 1916[29]

To London by night train primarily in order to see Lloyd George about Munitions. Weizmann having achieved complete success in large scale production of acetone, essential ingredient for cordite (projectile)[,] eager to push on with experiments in production of toluol essential for high explosives. Some expense involved. Lord Moulton obstructive. . . . Lloyd George keenly interested . . . and promised to act.

Lloyd George quite friendly but rather cross at first about line taken by "Manchester Guardian" in opposition to Conscription Bill and particularly as to risk involved to industrial liberty. Derided Labour opposition as proceeding only from small and noisy group and as virtually negligible. Pointed to moderate attitude of Labour Congress then being held as proving his point and would not listen to suggestion that this had been largely brought about by the concessions made in the Bill and the strong assurances given. All this he regarded as unnecessary.

In regard to the War he was as usual strongly pessimistic. Thought

[29]Scott's dating is not quite precise, but pretty certainly he travelled down on the night of 27 January and had all the interviews recorded here on the 28th.

revival of Russian strength apparent only (ignoring the actual success in the Caucasus). Germans were only biding their time till spring came. They could not advance through miles of mud. Believed impossible to break through on the West. 600,000 men lost in last two attempts. Another attempt would no doubt be made but it also would fail. The only chances open to us that he could see were (1) to help Russia in the East, not with troops of which she had plenty but with our big guns, or (2) to attack Turkey in the direction of Alexandretta, so securing at least Syria, Palestine and Mesopotamia. For this purpose troops would have to be massed in Egypt. Reverted to the suggestion he had thrown out when I last saw him of a possible intervention by the United States when both sides were getting exhausted. Said he had seen Colonel House[30] and implied that House had given some encouragement to the idea.

As to the position of parties at home he thought there would be a regrouping (1) of the "real Tories", among whom he reckoned Asquith (2) of the Radicals. I asked "In which camp will you be found". He answered "In the Radical of course. Don't you make any mistake about that", and he went on to expatiate on the failure and unhappiness of [Joseph] Chamberlain, who remained a Radical essentially to the last— rather a different tone to that which he adopted some weeks ago at Walton Heath, when he first spoke of the impending breach with his party.

When we first met he remarked it was a long time since he had seen me and as we parted he said he was glad I had come. In fact I should not have done so but for the Munitions business.

After breakfast called at No. 10 to see if I could fix an appointment with Asquith. He saw me at once. At first very crusty—almost rude. No doubt angry at strong opposition of Manchester Guardian to Compulsion Bill and its support of Simon in his secession and of the Labour case against the Bill. Thawed afterwards and parted with civility. . . .

[In the late afternoon Scott saw Runciman:] He said tremendous fight going on in Cabinet as to size of army. The "70 Divisions" scale had been made a fetish by part—the majority I gathered—of the Cabinet (Bonar Law, however, he admitted was "very reasonable") and he thought he and McKenna would have to resign. McKenna was preparing a report for the Cabinet on the financial side of the matter and he on the commercial side.

In the evening supped with Hobhouse at his house and afterwards

[30]President Wilson's personal representative to the European governments.

had an hour with Garvin at his. Garvin not at all hopeful as to any reconstruction of the Government. Asquith had played his game with extraordinary dexterity. Had won over Balfour and with his support was in a stronger position than ever. Bonar Law was an excellent man but not a leader. He always tended to take on the colour of the men with whom he was acting. At one time he became almost a second Balfour. Now he was assimilating Asquith.

With Lloyd George, of whom he once had great hopes, he was deeply disappointed. His vanity and self importance were ruining him. One after another he had alienated every leading member of the Cabinet—Balfour, with whom he was once intimate, Asquith and McKenna with both of whom he was at enmity and now Bonar Law. At the same time he had fallen out with his own followers. He had become a sort of Ishmael.

9. *The Outcasts: February-March 1916*

As Garvin's remarks—just quoted—make plain, Asquith's troubles were for the moment in abeyance. With the conscription problem on one side and Lloyd George practically isolated in the cabinet, the Prime Minister seemed secure.

Two men, both out of office, threatened his ease; and Scott was active in their behalf. Lord Fisher was yearning for the power he had tossed away the preceding May when he resigned as First Sea Lord (although he insisted to Scott that he had been dismissed). Now he launched a vigorous campaign against the men directing the navy: Balfour, the First Lord of the Admiralty, and Sir Henry Jackson, the First Sea Lord. Fisher managed to convince Scott and a handful of others that the country was in serious naval danger. The government remained unmoved.

Churchill also was fretting at his powerlessness. In December it had seemed a dramatic gesture to resign office and join his regiment in France. But it had taken him further than ever from the direction of the war. To regain his former power, he must resume a place in politics. Here Churchill hesitated. Returning to the House might ultimately bring him back to office, but initially it would take him only to the opposition benches. The role of opposition leader rarely attracted him; and the prospects of an opposition were especially dim at this moment. Carson had got nowhere since resigning from the government in October. And Lloyd George had refrained from leaving.

For the moment, the causes of Churchill and Fisher merged. Returning to England on leave, Churchill took up the issue of the country's naval danger, and made a dramatic plea in Parliament for Fisher's recall. The appeal fell flat. Neither outcast was well-placed to aid the other. Each had an unexpiated blunder standing against his name: Churchill by inaugurating the Dardanelles operation, Fisher by deserting his office. Each had a reputation for waywardness and instability. After their spectacular feud a year before, this unheralded rapprochement only confirmed the distrust with which they were regarded.

In reading the descriptions of Asquith which follow, it might be remembered that they come from a devoted critic—and one who was rather self-indulgent in *expecting Asquith to overlook the criticisms which Scott's newspaper was levelling against him.*

Diary, 7-8 February 1916

To London in morning [of 7 February]. Called by appointment on Lord Fisher at 3 at his house in Berkeley Square. Stayed about 3/4 of an hour. He was full as usual of vigour and shouted his conversation so that everybody in the house might have heard every word if they had chosen, but was evidently anxious and rather depressed and looked older than when I saw him last. . . .

Was impressed with Asquith's astuteness. A man who could induce his own party to accept compulsory service and the Opposition to accept Coalition could do anything. A third achievement was the capture of Bonar Law.

He repeated an anecdote told of Mrs. Asquith, who, now that Asquith had weathered the Conscription storm, declared in triumph "God alone can turn Henry out of office". . . .

After leaving Lord Fisher called at Treasury. McKenna engaged all afternoon with Ribot, French Minister of Finance. Appointed to see me about 7. I at once opened up about Lord Fisher. McKenna said quite decidedly he would not be safe as First Lord—he needed some check. In his two years at the Admiralty he himself had never had any difficulty in this—never had a wrong word with Fisher. Fisher easy to guide if properly handled. A man of warm feeling and strong attachments. Did not think Balfour would have him back.

I put it to him that the safety of the country should come before all else and that it was a clear duty to utilise Fisher's great powers. Balfour might take some other great office—the Foreign Office for instance so as to release Grey for the rest he absolutely needed—and he might go back to the Admiralty himself. He said he could not leave his present post.

He admitted Grey's need of rest. He was suffering from a microbic disease of the eyes (of the retina I think he said) which the doctors said could be arrested—not cured—only by two years of complete rest to the eyes. Balfour, however, would not be nearly so good for the office. Spoke in the warmest terms of Grey (towards whom Garvin says he now stands in much the same intimate relation that he did a short time since towards Asquith). He was splendid and much misunderstood. I agreed that he had certain great qualities and for that reason was worth saving for the country. I could, however, get no further. . . .

I asked if he thought he and Runciman would be able to stay in the ministry or if the concessions as to the size of the army which they required would be refused. He said he did not know. The War Office had made some concessions and might make more. He should know by the end of March. He should not prepare his Budget till he knew what size of Army he must budget for.

Speaking of National Economy he said nothing would be gained by the imposition of very heavy taxation—e.g. a 10/- in the pound income tax. It would cause rather violent industrial changes and throw a good many people temporarily out of work, whose industry would be lost to the nation till they could be absorbed again. His present system of continuous borrowing on short-dated loans—Treasury Bills and Exchequer Notes—was working with admirable smoothness and, together with the proceeds of taxation[,] was giving him all the money he needed to pay his way. People either invested what money they had in this way themselves or they put it in the Banks and the Banks invested it. He believed he was getting all the money there was to be got. Heavier taxation would make the burden less *after* the war, but would not help now.

Called on Garvin at his house later in the evening. He agreed strongly as to the need of bringing Fisher back, but did not throw much light on the means by which this was to be accomplished. Fisher had made every possible mistake in his handling of the situation at the time of his resignation and since. He saw no immediate prospect of his re-instatement. Asquith had played his cards with extreme adroitness and was in a stronger position than ever. He and Balfour exactly suited each other and Asquith had set himself, with great skill and persistence[,] to win over Bonar Law in which he had been successful. Thus when on the appointment of General Robertson as Chief of the General Staff, which involved taking the general control of the War out of Kitchener's hands, there was a prospect that Kitchener would resign, Asquith had offered the reversion of the Secretaryship of State not to Lloyd George but to Bonar Law.

Breakfasted with Lloyd George [on 8 February]. He was full of Fisher's praises—the only man who had shown originality and genius during the war— but had nothing practical to suggest as to his recall. Did not think Balfour would ever have him back. He would be much too disturbing and Balfour loved a quiet life. He and Asquith exactly suited each other in that respect. As long as the Germans were not actually defeating us they thought everything was going on splendidly. It never occurred to them that our business was to be working and planning to defeat the Germans. The Germans at least gave the impression of clear thinking and method; we still had no general plan, neither had the French. When he asked about this, when in Paris with Bonar Law a week ago, was told that he was just too soon; they had had one meeting to consider the subject and in about a fortnight they might be able to tell him.

Six weeks had been wasted by a subcommittee of the War Committee, consisting of McKenna, Austen Chamberlain and the Prime Minister, in deciding whether we should have an army of 50 divisions or of 70 divisions. Finally decided to have 70, but this conclusion had no relation to the use to which this army was to be put—whether e.g. there was to be a big offensive or a series of small offensives or whether they were simply to stand on the defensive. . . .

He was sending 300 heavy guns to Russia and the French a large supply of rifles. The problem was how to get them in. The railway to the open port west of Archangel ought to have been finished long ago. Eighteen months in which to make it and a British firm of contractors could probably have made it in 4. But Russians had refused to employ them and decided to do the work themselves. Administration corrupt. Wanted pickings for themselves. . . .

Diary, 18 February 1916

Breakfast with Lloyd George. He was poorly and came down very late. . . . did not go to Munitions Office and decided to take a long week-end at Walton Heath. He looked worn and old. While we were talking Captain [Arthur] Lee M.P., one of his Parliamentary Secretaries[,] came in to discuss serious dispute and prosecution of strike-leader of Woolwich munitions workers and I did not leave till nearly 11.30. . . .

[Lloyd George] expressed his profound dissatisfaction with the whole conduct of the war. He sent for [J. T.] Davies, his Secretary, and told him to put up various papers relating to his own part in relation to this and told me he was going at Walton Heath to consider his whole position with a view to possibly resigning his place in the Cabinet. Carson was ineffective as leader of an Opposition because of his constant ill health and absence, but he and Carson and Churchill (who would return) would together make an effective Opposition.

[After breakfast Scott "went straight on to see Lord Fisher". *Inter alia* Fisher "mentioned that Northcliffe had been reported to him on good authority as hostile to himself and opposed to his resuming office." Scott "thought this unlikely and decided to see North-cliffe."]

Telephoned Northcliffe for appointment, also Bonar Law. Saw Bonar Law at 2 and Northcliffe at 3.

Put it strongly to Bonar Law that in existing circumstances—unfortunately I could not explain how grave I knew them to be—it was wrong to leave a great contriving and energetic mind like Fisher's unused, but he confessed himself more than ever opposed to his reinstatement. We talked round the subject for some time, but I got no further. It was pretty plain that, as reported, he had come completely under the Asquith influence. He asked me if I had seen Balfour and, when I said I had not, thought I should do so. He remarked that, much as he was attached to Balfour, he never could feel intimate with him and found Asquith more approachable. Not that Asquith was really frank. "I tell you", he had said to Asquith[,] "all that is in my mind, but I am sure *you* do not tell me all that is in yours". Asquith's was an extraordinarily astute mind. The simple fact, I have no doubt, was that Asquith had gone out of his way to be agreeable to him.

Saw Northcliffe in his room at the "Times" office and stayed an hour. During the latter part of the time Robinson, his editor, was present. I found Northcliffe far from hostile to the reinstatement of Lord Fisher. Indeed he appeared actively favourable to it. "But what can I do", he asked. "We have already sailed as near the wind as we can if we are to escape prosecution under the Defence of the Realm Act, with which we are being constantly threatened and in order to escape which I have a very clever counsel to advise me". At the same time it was evident he did not like Fisher who distrusts him and probably showed it. He spoke of Fisher's Malay blood and said the taint inevitably came out in certain aspects of his character. He made the extraordinary statement that Fisher had the mind of "a servant" in his attitude towards great people, especially Ministers. I repudiated this though I said it was true he did not feel equal to grappling with their arts and called himself "a babe" in this relation. "There you have it" said Northcliffe, accepting this, absurdly enough, as confirmation of his reading.

Robinson's tone as to Fisher's reinstatement was quite different and when I asked him pointblank if he were in favour of it, admitted that he wasn't. Probably therefore the report which reached Fisher later that Northcliffe is really hostile may be regarded as correct.

Afterwards called at Admiralty to try if I could see Balfour. His Secretary, M. Smith, when he found what I wanted to see him about, being a strong anti-Fisherite, dutifully did his best to put me off.

Balfour had a Board meeting at 5 but asked me to come at 6.30. He was gracious as always and seemed in no sort of hurry and I stayed an hour. I said that of course I should not have dreamt of coming to him at any ordinary time but when the country's safety was at stake one could not stand on ceremony, that it was no case of Fisherite and anti-Fisherite and I wanted to put aside the whole of that disgusting controversy, in which view he expressed his cordial concurrence.

He asked what were the particular dangers which I had in mind and against which I wished to guard. I think he was afraid I knew too much. I said . . . the whole situation which was known to be critical because of the great exertions which the Germans had almost certainly been making and their very large construction resources. Fisher was the greatest driving force we possessed, had worked wonders in the way of construction . . . and would do it again. He was what the Americans called a "hustler" and hustle was just now vital. If Fisher could get things through 50 per cent quicker than anybody else was that a gain to be neglected?

Balfour admitted the force of this and began very characteristically to count up on his fingers the points in favour of Fisher, beginning with "One—hustle", no doubt with a view to a mental equation—a balance of pros and cons. The process did not seem perfectly convincing and I think he was a little shaken, for at last he broke out "Well, if he came back I think I should have to go." I protested against this and urged that he could control Fisher all right.

Finally we reverted to the question of preparations and he said that, though very likely Fisher could get more done, they were doing all they could and that was a great deal. . . . Balfour gave me a cordial good-bye and said he would not fail to take account of all I had said.

In the course of the conversation I had suggested his seeing Fisher and I wrote a letter pressing this point.

Diary, 23 February 1916

Met Weizmann at National Liberal Club (10.30) and took him to Munitions Office to see Lloyd George. Saw him alone first. He was due at Cabinet, but stayed half an hour. . . .

I said he must not dream of leaving the Government, he could not be spared from his present job. But he was evidently still considering the matter and expressed profound dissatisfaction with the Government. "Would you believe it?", he said, "they have still no plan for the spring campaign. We are meeting today to consider it". . . .

Before returning to Manchester thought I would try to see McKenna and was lucky in finding him at the Treasury. He was very cordial and interesting and kept me for an hour.

[The talk was mainly about the naval danger, regarding which Fisher had thoroughly infected Scott. But this led by stages to a discussion of wider political questions. Scott urged that the navy should "come not only first, but immeasurably and unquestionably first and everything else should give way to it. . . . Every ship-yard worker should be recalled both from the munition factories and from the army —and miners as well." The account goes on:]

He cordially agreed, but that he said means a thorough and consistent policy and how are you going to get it? There is only one man who could impose it. That was the Prime Minister. But he added "that is not his way". Yet who was there to take his place? Balfour was the most likely successor but he agreed that he would be no improvement. Bonar Law had a certain limited Parliamentary gift but lacked force of character and grasp of mind. I said Lloyd George would have been accepted a short time ago. He said "yes", but he was now discredited— had shown great lack of judgment and steadiness of aim and had failed also as an administrator; had no persistence and no practical capacity; could *do* nothing himself but only talk about things and get other people to do them. At the same time he admitted his great qualities— his energy his zeal and public spirit. In regard to munitions he had been wildly extravagant ordering recklessly far more than we could possibly use and actually hindering output by ordering too much. He could never see that the available productivity of the country was a strictly limited quantity and that fixed capital could not be turned into goods. He was in any case now out of the running as a possible Prime Minister.

The navy should come absolutely first; goods to pay our way second; the army third. This had been our traditional policy. Unhappily a majority of the Cabinet now put the army first. The army was an old Tory interest. Perhaps that partly accounted for it. I said he and Runciman, who represented the opposite view, would I hoped hold on in the Cabinet and not resign as they had threatened to do. He said he should only remain if his Budget proposals were approved. Already trade was being strangled. He would agree to its further strangulation up to the point at which we could still hold out till we were prepared to make peace; he would not agree to our being forced to stop the war because trade was strangled. . . . By diverting so enormous a proportion of shipping to war purposes we were in fact engaged in most effectively blockading ourselves. He could not understand the mentality of his colleagues who could not see these things which to him seemed elementary and self-evident. He thought "private life was the place for him". . . .

Diary, 29 February-3 March 1916 (Extract)

Rather a mixed time from Tuesday midday to Friday afternoon. Saw a great deal of Lord Fisher almost always at the Duchess of Hamilton's flat in Cleveland Row where she took part in the conversations—a capable and beautiful woman entirely devoted to his interests. He lives in an atmosphere of intrigue in which he does not appear to play a very skilful part. A very foolish thing he had done was to send for T. P. O'Connor in order to propound to him in all seriousness a wild idea which he had conceived of making Redmond Prime Minister[,] and a good deal of my time was taken up with seeing O'Connor and pressing on him by every means in my power the obligation of a deadly secrecy as to the revelations which Fisher had also unfortunately made to him as to the naval peril—a hard task for a born journalist.

In the course of conversation he [presumably O'Connor] mentioned the dead-set now being made against Lloyd George, and, as illustrating this, that Geoffrey Howard, a person of consideration and one of the Whips, had said to him that Lloyd George was "now being found out". Donald too, of the "Chronicle", one of his friends, had spoken of the impression that he was "a muddler" and how he himself had noticed the confused litter on his table, and the contrast between that and the absolute tidiness of McKenna's. George too notoriously never answered a letter.

Another by-work was to see Weizmann and, on his behalf, Dr. Addison and Sir F. Nathan in order to try to remove or mitigate the difficulties in the practical working and organization on the great scale of his acetone process which were preying upon him and destroying his working power. Spoke also to Lloyd George as to need for giving him a more permanent and assured position.

Diary, 6-8 March 1916

Went to London by morning train [on 6 March] in order (1) to see Churchill, (home on leave and announced to speak in debate on Navy Estimates on Tuesday) and let him know the facts in regard to short-comings (2) to urge Fisher to be at once reconciled, (3) to hear from

Loreburn as to progress in regard to Peers' memorial.[1] Met Hobhouse at lunch at hotel and went straight on to Fisher.

Had an agreeable surprise in finding that both my first two objects had already been accomplished. Churchill had called on Fisher and frankly asked that, as the only real ground of difference between them —the question of the Dardanelles—had been eliminated, they should again be friends. Fisher had cordially responded and they were now completely reconciled. Fisher had also of course fully informed Churchill as to naval situation. He was enthusiastic about Churchill, foretold that he was the inevitable Prime Minister and declared that the only course open to him was to remain in England, take the lead of an independent Opposition and "stand by that box (the one on the table of the House) day by day and hour by hour" to insist on the instant and paramount needs of the navy. He became quite dithyrambic on the subject, but said that Mrs. Churchill differed from him and insisted that Churchill should go back to France. Churchill, though much inclined to agree with Fisher's view, had not made up his mind and finally it had been decided—as Fisher put it, no doubt putting his own colour on the matter—that I should "arbitrate" and he had sent me a telegram to Manchester that morning accordingly. My arrival therefore (I had left before the telegram arrived) appeared to be opportune. It would be a great sacrifice to Churchill to throw up his position and salary in the army, as he had no money and had had to borrow in order to provide for his wife while he was away. As for himself he would certainly serve under Balfour at Admiralty if desired—would sweep a crossing in Berkeley Square if it would help to win the war.

Went on to see Churchill at 41 Cromwell Road and stayed more than an hour. We discussed his course of action and Mrs. Churchill came in and joined in the discussion. He had just been selected by the General for the command of a Brigade and she was anxious he should take this up. I urged that on political grounds there could be no question that he would be more useful in Parliament—that as regards the navy there was not a day to be lost in making good the great and acknowledged deficiencies and the whole movement for that and also for vitalising the army, as to which he had strong views, would collapse if he left. He and Lloyd George and Carson were the only three men in the front rank with the instinct for action and capacity for carrying on a great war. Carson was ill, George was for the time being under a cloud and Churchill alone remained. Mrs. Churchill was evidently un-

[1] A proposed memorial by a number of influential peers to the Prime Minister, stressing the gravity of the naval situation. Ultimately the scheme foundered.

easy but acquiesced and Churchill virtually decided to resign his commission.

He then read me the full notes for his speech [the next day] which wound up dramatically with the demand for the recall of Lord Fisher. He was satisfied with it himself and said if it were the last he was ever to deliver he would be content to stand by it and that was the final test. I found nothing to object to, but Mrs. Churchill thought it went at one part rather too much into details which had better not be made public. Churchill said he thought he had better give the Prime Minister notice of what he meant to do (and he would no doubt inform Balfour) so that it might not be said he had taken the Government by surprise. He had asked to see the Prime Minister that afternoon, but had not yet had an answer. In any case Asquith was coming to dinner and he could tell him then that he meant to ask for Fisher's recall, but was not anxious to say more and so bring down protests.

He was not aiming at anything for himself but only at getting what was necessary done. Six months abroad had "cleaned" him. He had come in contact with the crude realities of life and escape from the atmosphere of scheming and intrigue. Had learned to see things more simply. He had missed the means of self-expression, but on the whole the time of absence had been one of the most contented of his life. He seemed to me indeed stronger and saner than before he went out.

Called at Bath Club to consult Dillon but found he was in Ireland. Saw T. P. O'Connor at his flat and we both wired Dillon urging him to attend next day's debate, but he replied impossible. Sinn Feiners very active and malignant. O'Connor afterwards showed me a bundle of cuttings from their press making venomous attacks on the Parliamentary party. Young Davitt had gone over to them.

If naval reverse *should* endanger or destroy the Ministry I asked O'Connor if he thought it possible that the Irish party might take part in a new Ministry. He himself thought it would be very desirable, had indeed thought that they might have had a representative—himself I gathered, as representing an English constituency—in the Coalition Government, but Dillon—who was the determining force in all these matters—had been irreconcilably opposed. As for Churchill he thought they could trust him, but they could not trust Lloyd George. On a recent occasion when they—Redmond, Dillon and himself—had gone to see George (on the question of the taxation of whisky I think he said) he had been very offensive, had said they could do without the help of Ireland and that one county in Wales had done more than all Ireland for the war. They had left him without shaking hands.

March 7. Called on Churchill after breakfast. . . .

He had told the Prime Minister what he meant to say about Fisher, but nothing more, not desiring to provoke remonstrance. He evidently felt he was in for a serious enterprise, said he knew he should have to face obloquy, but once launched on an enterprise he could never hold back. This needed more courage than the war of the trenches. He had not yet finally decided whether to stay or return to France. It would partly depend on how things went today. He wished he could be here a week hence for the Army Estimates. He had a good deal to say on the Army administration which was in many ways old-fashioned and un-enterprising. Our Army telephones for instance—a vital matter—were mere toys compared to the German.

In afternoon went to hear debate at House and sat just behind Fisher in the special Gallery for which O'Connor kindly procured me a ticket. Balfour long and dull. Churchill rather nervous and the House, quite unprepared and a good deal puzzled[,] gave him little support. But he stuck gallantly to his task amid frequent interruptions from someone just behind him (I think Macnamara[2]) and from Balfour sitting just across the table on the Treasury Bench, who writhed visibly with irritation. The close calling for Fisher's return was dramatic, but here again the House was unprepared and puzzled. Only on the confession of labour shortage and on the failure to attack Zeppelins in their sheds did he carry the House completely with him.

March 8. Called after breakfast on Churchill at his house. Found Lord Fisher already there and deep in debate with Churchill and his wife on the question of to stay or not to stay. I felt I had not on the previous day given sufficient weight to the question of military duty or propriety. Fisher was for ignoring this altogether; Mrs. Churchill all the other way.

Finally Churchill decided that he would write at once to Lord Kitchener stating (1) that he desired to be relieved of his command so soon as this might be convenient on the ground that he felt that political duty demanded his presence in the House of Commons (2) that he also desired an immediate extension of leave for a week or 10 days. Further he was to request that a copy of this letter might be sent to the Prime Minister. He was quite clear that his proper course was to remain, but only in so far as this might be possible consistently with a strict observance of military propriety. Mrs. Churchill was quite satisfied and Fisher acquiesced.

Fisher's appointment to meet the War Council was at 11.30 and we

[2]T. J. Macnamara, Liberal M.P. and Parliamentary Secretary to the Admiralty.

drove away together. I got to Downing Street at a few minutes past 11, on the chance of just catching the Prime Minister before the Council, but he fixed 4 o'clock.

Asquith. He then saw me at once. His manner was pretty cold. He sat in the middle of the long Cabinet table and the chair placed for me was at the end of the same side about five yards off. He was silent and grim. There was nothing rude this time in his reception but it was sufficiently repellant. So I started out at once on what I had to say and talked continuously, as he did not seem inclined to assist[,] for 5 or 10 minutes, quite a little speech in fact in which, having fortunately considered what I should say, I was able to feel entirely unembarrassed.

I said I was glad he had not been able to see me sooner as a great part of what I wanted to say had now already been said by Churchill. I shared the anxiety which he expressed. I ought perhaps to say that I knew he had come to England with no thought of anything except of taking the usual tri-monthly officers' leave—that he had not even known that the Naval estimates were coming on, that when he did know he at first intended only to speak on the question of the air-war and that it was only later, as information reached him which he regarded as grave, that he had decided to make a different kind of speech. That I was quite sure the speech was made in no spirit of hostility to the Ministry, or to himself personally, or to Mr. Balfour. That in regard to the proposal to recall Lord Fisher it appeared to me that this would have a great effect in allaying anxiety in the country, that this anxiety was very real and widespread, that of course there could be no question of displacing the Ministry since no other Ministry was at this time possible, but that it was important the country should have full confidence in the Ministry and Lord Fisher's return would do much to strengthen confidence. That Balfour was big enough and disinterested enough to ignore any question of personal dignity or feeling and to act solely in the interest of the country. ("Quite true" interjected the Prime Minister). That if a naval check, or misfortune[,] should take place and Lord Fisher should not have been recalled an insistent demand might arise for his immediate reinstatement, but if he had been he would share the responsibility. Finally that it seemed to me wrong that at a time of national stress and danger so great a force alike of invention and of execution should remain unused.

Then at last he began to reply. Fisher had been there that morning at the War Council and they had heard what he had to say. What did it amount to? His answer was a contemptuous ejaculation (commonly expressed in writing as "Pish" or "Pshaw") and gesture, casting thumb back over shoulder as though to get rid of dirt. Then he broke out on them both rising in his seat and marching to and fro. As for Churchill's speech it was a piece of the grossest effrontery. Did I know that only 3 months ago when Fisher was appointed as head of the Inventions Department both Churchill and his wife had been furious and had denounced it as an outrage, so much so that Mrs. Churchill had almost cut him and his wife and would not speak to him. And now suddenly Churchill professed to have discovered Fisher's extraordinary merits and called for his reinstatement. It was a piece of "impudent humbug." Why when Churchill and Fisher were together they did nothing but quarrel and Fisher's resignations were a perpetual worry of his life. He had resigned 8 times before the last time. Then he actually deserted his post and went away at a time too of some anxiety. Had he not gone there would, said Asquith, have been no Ministerial crisis and no Coalition. "He deserved to be shot", shouted Asquith, "and in any other country he would have been shot." This was known in the navy and his recall now would be deeply resented.

Then he quieted a little. I admit, he said, that he has valuable qualities. He is a constructor, very fertile and ingenious. He is the creator of our own navy—and to a very large extent also of the German navy. He is not a strategist; he would be no use in command of a fleet. He had a touch of genius, but his temper was ungovernable and he was "a little mad."

I suggested that, besides being an inventor, he was also an executant —that he had an extraordinary power of getting things done and quoted Churchill's enthusiastic testimony to that effect. "Oh! yes", Asquith replied, "he has no doubt what the Americans call 'hustle' " and then went on to say that there was nothing extraordinary about him in this and that others could do and were doing quite as well. . . .

Before leaving I raised the further question of Free Trade. The "Times" and some other papers had stated that at the approaching Conference of the Allies in Paris arrangements would be made for a common policy after, as well as during[,] the war and this appeared to me wholly illegitimate and a usurpation of the functions of Parliament. He replied that the question would certainly be raised, but that it could not possibly be settled. The consent of the various Powers represented would be needed[,] and serious questions would arise as to our future relations not only with at present enemy countries but also with present neutrals. What for instance would be thought of a preferential duty for Russian wheat as against American wheat? Pressure would undoubtedly be brought to bear on us by our protectionist allies to modify our fiscal arrangements so as to come into line with them. It ought, I suggested, to be strongly resisted. Why should we be the party to make concessions. We were under no obligations. We had done far more than we had bargained to do in the war, far more than could possibly have been expected of us. The obligation, if any existed, was all the other way. "Yes", he said, ["]and but for this everyone of them would have had to make peace long ago and on unfavourable terms. The boot is on the other leg". He had relaxed during the interview—even smiled—and we parted with an informal good-bye.

Afterwards, thinking it might be as well that Churchill should know how matters stood with the Prime Minister, I called at Cromwell Road before going back for my train. Churchill had not come back from the House, but I saw Mrs. Churchill who was grateful.

As to the Prime Minister's statement about constant quarrels between Churchill and Lord Fisher and Lord Fisher's repeated resignations she said all this took place only after the Dardanelles question had come up to divide them. Really the two men were sympathetic in temperament and admired each other.

Diary, 22-24 March 1916

Went up by breakfast train Wednesday [22 March], returned Friday afternoon. Saw Lord Fisher each day, Mrs. Churchill Wednesday and Thursday. Found Lord Fisher very low about Churchill's departure. Said that after I had gone, on the day it had been decided that he should ask to be relieved of his command, there was a battle royal between Churchill and his mother on the one hand who were for and his wife and sister-in-law on the other who were against the letter being sent and that the opposition prevailed.

Mrs. Churchill told me that what really happened was that Churchill agreed not to send the letter at once, but to take another day for consideration and to discuss the matter with Carson whom they would visit in motoring to Dover, that Carson was ill, pessimistic and unhelpful, that Churchill remained unshaken, that the letter was posted at Dover just before Churchill went on board the torpedo despatch-boat and that he also left her a statement for the P.A. [Press Association] announcing his speedy return to political life which, however, she was to submit to the Prime Minister before sending it in. When, however, she returned to London late next day, she found that Churchill had wired to the P.M.[3] withdrawing for the present his letter and Bonham

[3] The text clearly says "P.A.", but this seems to be a slip for "P.M."

Lloyd George. The Augustus John portrait described by C. P. Scott as a 'rather murderous effigy'

C. P. Scott in old age

Carter [Asquith's private secretary] was on her door-step eager to intercept the statement for the P.A. Evidently the P.M.[4] was excessively anxious to prevent Churchill from taking any further action. Although he had abused Churchill to me like a pick-pocket he had been all friendliness and suavity to him and had made no difficulty whatever about his being relieved of his command if and when he desired it. So there the matter rests.

When, however, I was with Mrs. Churchill on Wednesday afternoon, Major "Archie" Sinclair came in just returned on a week's leave from France—he is a nice young chap of 25, a great friend of the family—and gave Mrs. Churchill a letter from Churchill with one enclosed for me. In this he said his resolution to return was quite unshaken but that the time was a question of preparation and of opportunity. Saw Mrs. Churchill again next day and told her I was clear he ought to return at once and I proposed to write to him to that effect. She did not object. She explained that by "opportunity" she took him to mean *military* opportunity, as e.g. when his Brigade went for a month's rest 6 weeks hence, or in case he should be offered a Brigade and declined it. Fisher intensely anxious for his return and furious that he should ever have gone. Begged me to write as strongly as possible.

Fisher was exceedingly interesting on the subject of Tirpitz's resignation[5]—or rather summary dismissal, as he put it—which he interpreted unhesitatingly as implying the abandonment of the policy of immediate naval attack and as therefore a great piece of good fortune for the Government and still more for the country. Tirpitz, who had built up the fleet and who had been preparing "surprises" for us for the last 18 months, would never have consented not to put it to the test. . . . Tirpitz was a brave and resolute man, Capelle, his successor, Fisher compendiously described as a "naval Balfour". He was amusing about Tirpitz. I've a good mind[,] he said, to write to him and say "Well, old chap, here we are together at last in the same boat, both the victims of the politicians". . . .[6]

[Scott saw McKenna the "next day", which was presumably Thursday 23 March:]

[4] The text clearly says "P.A.", but this seems to be a slip for "P.M."
[5] Tirpitz had resigned as German Minister of Marine because the government, fearing American intervention, would not agree to his policy of unrestricted submarine warfare.
[6] Fisher was as good as his word. On 29 March he wrote Tirpitz a letter beginning "Dear Old Tirps" and ending "Yours till hell freezes", and containing expressions like: "What a time we've been colleagues, old boy!", "we did you in the eye over the battle cruisers", and "*I don't blame you for the submarine business.* I'd have done the same myself". See A. J. Marder (ed.), *Fear God and Dread Nought*, vol. 3 (Cape, London, 1959), p. 334.

I did not ask him how things were going in the Cabinet as to the Military estimates and the size of the Army to be budgeted for, but Fisher told me McKenna had told him that he expected he (McKenna) and Runciman would be out of office in 3 weeks, which looks as though he were standing to his guns. He received me with the greatest cordiality which, as the paper has lately been very critical of the Government, looks as though he were much of the same mind.

With Lloyd George, with whom I lunched on Thursday I had no conversation of any interest, as Colonel Repington, the military correspondent of the "Times", was there and it was impossible to talk freely (George lets his Secretary, Davies, make his engagements and then forgets them and makes others. Probably Repington was as much bored as I was. However I of course left him to do the talking).

In the course of the conversation one or two interesting points, however, emerged. George said that the Germans were still producing more ammunition than the English and French together, that they were able to produce it in such quantities as to be able to carry on a continuous great offensive like that at Verdun without trenching upon stocks, that we were not yet able to do that but he hoped we should be able by the end of May or beginning of June, that in consequence that would be the earliest time at which we in turn could undertake a big offensive. I suggested that the German failure at Verdun was not a great encouragement to us to make a similar attempt, but Repington appeared to attach small importance to that.

Repington asked George whether the present Russian offensive was part of a concerted strategy and George said it was not: they were acting entirely of their own motion. Further he said they had not enough ammunition to carry it through. Russians were known gamblers and this movement was a gamble for immediate success.

Directly after lunch George had to go to the House to answer questions. I went in his motor and with him to his room, but he had to leave almost immediately. I had at the outside 5 minutes in which to speak to him about Weizmann who is much the most essential man in his department, who has worked so far practically for nothing, whose inventive genius has not only saved the country 9 or 10 millions in money but has secured it essential munitions in quantities otherwise unobtainable at any price. He cannot go on any longer without some security in the present and some assurance of at least a modest recompense in the future. I could hardly get George to give his mind to the matter at all and all I could get out of him was that it was really a matter for the Treasury and that he should not oppose anything to which McKenna agreed.

When I saw McKenna a little later I found a wholly different spirit. He had already realised Weizmann's value and was resolved that he should have his reward. . . . He showed in fact the real business spirit which in George had been signally lacking. It was not merely time which had lacked.

This scrap of conversation with Fisher may conclude the episode of the Churchill-Fisher rapprochement:

There had been immense curiosity to find out where Churchill had obtained his information.[7] (He had got something a good deal more authentic and detailed than Lord Fisher could give him. I myself had seen an official paper in his hand of which he said "I must not show this even to you"). Lloyd George had been suspected[,] and all sorts of traps had been laid by the Prime Minister's women folk, who asked innocent questions to find out if there had been communication between Churchill and Lloyd George.

Lord Fisher knew the person and told me.

[7] That is, information about the naval situation.

10. *Conscription Again, April 1916*

Asquith had survived the challenge from Churchill and Fisher with relative ease. But he was soon presented with a new threat from Lloyd George. It sprang from the latter's long-standing dissatisfaction with the conduct of the war; but Lloyd George still hesitated to leave office on such general grounds, particularly if he lacked the support of the leading Conservatives. The conscription issue lay to hand as the best method of obliging the Conservative ministers to go along with him.

The first conscription bill in January had applied only to single men. Now there was a powerful movement among the Conservative rank and file, directed by Carson, to bring married men into the net as well. Asquith was due to make a statement on recruiting in the House of Commons, and Carson put down a challenging motion. If Lloyd George left the government on this matter and threw in his lot with the Conservative rebels, the bulk of Tory ministers would be hard put to it not to follow suit.

So acute did the crisis become that on successive days Asquith had to inform a disgruntled House of Commons that he could not make his promised statement. Yet at the last moment he managed once again to save his government. He made a series of concessions—amounting in the end to full conscription—which satisfied the Conservative ministers and also Lloyd George. Once more Lloyd George revealed that, however severe his discontents, he would not leave the ministry alone.

Three points need to be borne in mind when reading Scott's narrative.

(1) There was a fundamental dichotomy between his attitude and Lloyd George's on the question of resignation. Scott was quite happy to see Lloyd George leave the government and head an opposition, even if this did not cause Asquith immediately to fall from power. Lloyd George's interest was in office, not opposition. He would only quit the government if by so doing he ensured its collapse and his own prompt reinstatement.

(2) Scott was so chagrined by Lloyd George's final about-turn on the issue of resignation that he failed to notice the humiliation to which Asquith had been driven. Asquith's position was severely undermined when he was forced to accept

a further measure of conscription—something he clearly found repugnant and had earlier said he would not implement.

(3) Scott wrote up his narrative not day-by-day, but in a single account at the end of the week. Hence his story of the early stages of the crisis is slightly coloured by his knowledge of what was to come. Still, he usually kept daily notes as the basis for his narrative, and the element of hindsight is not great.

Diary, 13-20 April 1916

Went to London mainly in order if possible to get Weizmann's position and compensation settled. . . . but the political crisis caused by Lloyd George's threatened resignation supervened and nothing was finally settled.

I had wired to Lloyd George asking to see him on Friday [14 April] but getting no reply before leaving early on Thursday called at the Munitions Office and stumbled upon him on my way to enquire. He told me of his strong and increasing dissatisfaction with the conduct of the war and his intention to bring matters to a head by resigning if a measure of general compulsory service were not adopted on the lines of the motion of which Carson had given notice for the following Wednesday[,] after the Prime Minister had made his promised statement on Tuesday as to the intentions of the Government based on the report of the Cabinet Committee.

He repeated and developed this statement at breakfast next morning [14 April], adding that he was going to meet Sir W. Robertson Nicoll, Editor and proprietor of the "British Weekly", at Sir George Riddell's house that afternoon to discuss his position and he pressed me to come, as he said he would like me to meet Nicoll. I had no particular desire to do so but went. Nicoll a pawky Scotchman, with extraordinarily deliberate utterance, conveying the impression of deep wisdom, and the most highly developed Aberdonian accent I have heard. He delivered himself with caution but finally came down decidedly on the side of resignation and Sir George Riddell (owner of "News of the World" the most widely circulated of all the weeklies and Lloyd George's landlord at Walton Heath) concurred.

As we walked away I urged Lloyd George in any speech he might make after resignation to be extremely restrained and generous in tone. He said he might not be able quite to trust himself if interrupted and provoked, so he thought he would write a letter (presumably to the Prime Minister) which could be published and would be free from this danger. He would like me to see the letter and give an opinion on it. Would write it on Sunday morning [i.e. 16 April] and asked me to come to lunch on that day at Walton Heath and go through it with him.

When I got there no letter of course had been written. One of his Parliamentary Secretaries, Colonel Arthur Lee, Unionist M.P. for the Fareham Division of Hampshire, came to lunch and his private Secretary, Davies, was also there. After lunch we had a discussion as to his intended action and both Lee and I agreed that he would be of far more use outside the Cabinet than in it and that the great need of the day was an Opposition strong enough and independent enough to influence the Government and if needful to take part in a reconstruction. Then Lee left and George retired with Davies to write his letter. Not long after Davies reappeared and announced that George had gone to sleep in the midst of his composition. Half an hour later when George re-appeared and tea came in he announced that, on waking from his sleep, everything had suddenly seemed clear to him, all doubt and hesitation had passed away and he was resolved to take his stand and to resign if his terms were rejected.

Meanwhile a telephone message had come that Lord Stamfordham, the King's private Secretary[,] wished to see him on behalf of the King, 6.30 was appointed and we all drove off, George in the greatest spirits, to Downing Street, where I left him. Stamfordham's mission was to urge him on behalf of the King to reconsider his position of which the King had been informed—I gathered through Bonar Law. Stamfordham placed before him the obvious considerations of maintaining the Coalition, standing together in face of the enemy etc., to all of which George replied that he would be most happy to act upon them "but for the oath I have taken to serve his Majesty faithfully"—a reply which appears to have considerably non-plussed the worthy Stamfordham, who is not, George says, a brilliant person.

He [George] asked me to come back to sleep and I stayed on for three days. I telephoned to Mrs. Churchill, whom I had seen on Thursday afternoon, that I thought George had really made up his mind to go out and she replied "Thank God!" Everything of course would have been made easy for Churchill's return if he could have joined George and Carson in leading an effective Opposition. Then she asked "Is he happy?" and when I said "thoroughly, since he made up his mind" she was satisfied.

Next day[1] she telephoned me that the War Office had sent word to her that Churchill was returning that evening, having been summoned

[1]Presumably Monday, 17 April.

along with other Members at the front to take part in the division on Carson's motion, and later Churchill telephoned to ask me to come and see him. I went after dinner and had an hour with him and explained the situation. Mrs. Churchill, his mother and sister-in-law (he shares the house at 41 Cromwell Road with his brother) also there. He was much excited and entered enthusiastically into the idea of an independent Opposition which I had previously discussed with him in correspondence. . . .

On Sunday evening George had dined alone with Bonar Law and reported him to be in a state of the greatest bewilderment and alarm. The whole of the Unionists in the Cabinet, except Balfour, were in favour of universal compulsory military service and, if George went out on that, they would have to go out with him. Even Balfour would have to go with his friends. There would be an end therefore of the Coalition and a complete break-up of the Government.

Next day (Monday) [17 April] there was a Cabinet. It met informally at the House at 4.30, adjourned to Downing Street at 5.15 and broke up at 6.15, George and some others staying on. I waited for George till shortly before 8 when he came out for a few minutes and then returned to No. 10. He told me nothing had been settled, that the Committee of the Cabinet appointed to report on Recruiting (consisting of Asquith, Bonar Law, McKenna and Chamberlain) . . . had been dissolved and its report scrapped, that another Committee, consisting of Asquith, Balfour, himself, Bonar Law and Lord Crewe, had been appointed and he was now hurrying back to join in its discussion.

When I returned later I found him in a quite different temper. He had in fact proposed a compromise and he gave as his reasons for doing so (1) that he did not wish to alienate more than he could help his radical supporters and he wished it to appear that he had not insisted on conscription pure and simple, but had been willing to do his best to compromise; (2) that it was "either too soon or too late" for him to force his resignation—he did not develop this thesis—; (3) a personal motive—that, though munitions were coming in fast already, in two months time they would be coming in very much faster and then his possible successor would receive the credit which properly belonged to him. Perhaps this is what he meant by the time being "too soon," and the "too late" was that it would have been easier to go out when Carson went out. He had more than once before spoken somewhat in this sense.

In any case it was plain that he was no longer forcing the situation and trying to get out of the Government for the sake of getting out.

Previously he had said that his real motive was dissatisfaction with the whole conduct of the war and a desire to avoid further responsibility for this and to recover his independence and right of public criticism—that the question of conscription was in fact only the occasion and not the cause of his intended resignation. On this ground I could join with him, because, in relation to the vast issues of the war and the right conduct of it, the question of extending compulsion a little further or a little less far became quite subordinate. By consenting to compromise George had reversed this order of importance and had made compulsion the dominant issue and the conduct of the war subordinate. The fact is that, though he has again and again talked of resignation and threatened it, he has always shrunk at the last moment. Unconsciously he may be partly influenced by the fact that he has no independent means. He several times spoke of this more or less laughingly, but as he also said that he had received from an American Agency an offer of £5,000 for 10 political articles the pressure of circumstance was not too severe.

After that, though desperate efforts were made by his friends, by Lee and by Churchill especially, to keep him up to the mark, the game was lost and to all intents and purposes the Prime Minister had once more won and Mrs. Asquith's declaration that "God alone can turn Henry out of office" was again justified.

It now became a question only of how far George would consent to go. Henderson, on behalf of the Labour members[,] refused to accept his first compromise terms—i.e. the immediate passing of a Bill for general compulsion to come into force automatically a month hence unless meanwhile the full number of men required (50,000 per month) were forthcoming from among the unattested married men alone—and proposed a slight modification—i.e. that the Bill should not be passed now but only at the end of the period of grace in case the required number of men had not been forthcoming. Asquith agreed to accept this and George could not easily decline. Had he done so the bulk of the Unionists in the Cabinet would have gone with Henderson and Asquith and perhaps two—Curzon and Selborne—would have come out with George. That would have been quite a good result as no one wanted to break up the Government at once.

Churchill made a final effort on Wednesday [the 19th] to bring George up to the sticking-point and called in Lord Fisher to assist by giving evidence of the real danger of the naval situation, but in vain. I left them closeted at the Munitions Office, glad to escape from this atmosphere of futile intrigue.

Scott has made no mention up to this point of how he spent Saturday, 15 April. It passed in a number of interviews not directly connected with the political crisis. Two deserve to be preserved here: that with McKenna, because of McKenna's accurate prediction of the course Lloyd George would take; and that with Carson, because it seems to be Scott's first encounter with the Ulster leader. Scott was not the first Liberal to find Carson at close quarters much less villainous than expected—or perhaps than Carson, by his public conduct, wanted people to believe.

Among the other people whom I saw were (1) McKenna. I lunched with him at his house on Saturday besides seeing him at the Treasury. We talked mainly about Weizmann, but also discussed Lloyd George. McKenna expressed absolute scepticism as to his resigning. I said I was not at all sure about that this time. But he was right. His main concern is of course the economic situation as to which he differs wholly from Lloyd George.

(2) Carson. Called on him twice at his house in Eaton Place—first in order to ascertain his views about the return of Churchill and the formation of an independent Opposition[,] and secondly in order to come to some understanding on matters of policy in case, as then seemed likely, the Opposition were formed. He was cautious as to Churchill's return. Thought he should be careful in the choice of an opportunity, but inclined to think that if George came out that would constitute so great a change in circumstances as to give ground for his return to active political life. In regard to policy he agreed that the crushing of Germany was out of the question and he had no sympathy with the proposal to wage an economic war against her after the war of arms was over—the point as to which I was most concerned. . . .

I was a good deal attracted and impressed by him—his directness, sincerity and a kind of high disinterestedness, partly connected perhaps with the depression which dogs him and his sense of impending doom. He constantly spoke as if death were near and remarked that people made too much of death. What did it matter if a man should die at 62 (his present age) or at 72? I told him he wasn't going to die and that there were things he had first to do. He was the only man who could settle the Irish question. That had to be settled before we could get on with the building up of the new England. He agreed cordially that that was the great task before us after the war and that a beginning might be made even during the war. "I'll talk to you about the Irish question", he said, "any day you like." "And what's more", he added, "with Redmond, if you like, along with you."

I had a curious sense of the foreigner in him. English politics seemed to be more or less alien to him, as though he approached them from the outside, and at heart he seemed to me a good deal more remote, more completely an Irishman than, for instance, Dillon, who on social subjects and in foreign politics is a keen and active Liberal.

Disagreement between Scott and Lloyd George about the course the latter ought to be taking once more placed a strain on their relations.

It is only possible to guess at the paragraph in the Manchester Guardian *to which, in the following letter, Lloyd George takes exception. But probably it was a statement by the paper's Political Correspondent (on 20 April 1916) that Lloyd George had practically no personal following in the House, that he was disliked by many Liberals and distrusted by the Conservatives, and that his dealings with Labour over the Munitions Act had made him widely unpopular in that quarter also.*

Lloyd George to C.P.S., 20 April 1916

Having regard to the talks we have had the last few days when you urged me to come out to lead an Opposition to the Coalition Government—surely this paragraph is unnecessarily offensive. Why should you go out of your way to disparage my personal influence if you think I can serve the Country by my personal intervention?

[P.S.] I happen to know that McKenna supplied the paragraph and I mean to raise the question in public.

C.P.S. to Lloyd George, 20 April 1916[2]

Of course I knew nothing of the paragraph—I did not get back to Manchester till today—and was infinitely annoyed at its appearance. Had I been here it would of course have gone into the W.P.B. . . .

It's no use to apologise but I should like you to know that I dissent wholly from the observations and that I have steadily held and said that you are and will remain a great power in the State and one which I hope and believe will be turned to its great good.

We can't well publish your telegram in the form in which it is sent.[3] It would do neither you nor us any good. But of course if you think it worth while to write us a letter we shall gladly publish it.

[2]Lloyd George Papers.
[3]This telegram does not seem to have survived.

11. The Guns of Easter, April-May 1916

Events in Ireland momentarily brought that country to the centre of the stage. On Easter Monday, 23 April, the Sinn Fein leaders staged an insurrection in Dublin. The rebellion was speedily suppressed by British forces, and many of the instigators were summarily tried and executed. But despite the apparent futility of the uprising, it was recognised as constituting a landmark in Irish history—and in the history of Anglo-Irish relations.

The Easter Rising changed the whole nature of the "Irish problem", as it appeared to British statesmen. Up to that point the Irish Nationalists, supported by British Liberals, had been demanding a measure of regional self-government within the British connection. The problem had been the exaggerated devotion to the "union" of most Conservatives, plus the special difficulty of Ulster. But now southern Ireland, in moving towards Sinn Fein, was embracing its own fanaticism. Sinn Fein's object was a united Ireland (including Ulster) under a Dublin government. The link with Britain would be utterly severed, carrying with it the implication (a very potent one in wartime) that Ireland might one day ally with Britain's enemies. No British government, including a well-disposed Liberal government, would countenance such a proposal. So Liberals like Scott, though desperately concerned to solve the Irish question, found themselves losing touch with the Irish situation.

Among those who were shocked by these events into a measure of agreement were Carson and Redmond, the opposed leaders of Ulster and Nationalist Ireland. Yet they recognised that, even if at one, they lacked the power to attain a settlement. A solution could only be achieved—if then—by a British government laying down its terms and enforcing them impartially on all sections, in Ireland and at Westminster. This Asquith was not prepared to do (nor Lloyd George after him). Asquith was only interested in a solution which commanded the prior assent of the contending parties. As no such solution existed, his attitude doomed Ireland to frustration and further bloodshed.

Diary, 9-10 May 1916

In afternoon [of 9 May] went to House of Commons to meet Redmond by appointment. Heard Churchill (suddenly and unexpectedly returned) make speech . . . in which he threw out a feeler for a new departure in Ireland and for a settlement by consent of the two Irish parties.

Discussed this afterwards with Redmond. He was warmly in favour of it, but said the difficulty would be for either him or Carson to propose any terms which the other could look at. It would be necessary for terms to be *imposed* on them both. Threw out a suggestion that one of the Dominion premiers might be called in for the purpose and given statutory powers. I gathered that he had proposed this to Carson who had not been altogether hostile. But it would be useless for the leaders to agree if they could not carry their followers.

Saw him and Dillon next day, but they were preoccupied with the debate on the Dublin executions and I got no further. Both anxious that conciliation proposals should be ventilated.

May 10. Breakfasted with Lloyd George. He did not resent my leader on his Bangor Speech.[1] Seemed in excellent spirits, relieved perhaps at having got over the "crisis" and still finding himself where he was before. I said I regretted his decision, but he justified it on the ground that the conscription issue was one which would have divided him from his political friends. He should prefer to resign on the conduct of the war. He might yet do so. Still felt he might be more useful outside the Cabinet than in it. On the other hand he had evidently made up any personal differences with Asquith who he said had been quite pleased with his speech the cleverness of which he had commended and had congratulated him on getting through "without wetting his feet". Apparently has made up his differences also with Moulton whose department he specially selected for commendation. His attitude towards the Government still critical. It was still without a plan for the war and merely [waited?] on the Germans.

Afterwards saw Churchill at his mother's house in Brook St. He was in great spirits and full of plans. Said he had made a successful speech at the secret session and thought his yesterday's suggestions had

[1]Lloyd George had once more spoken out strongly for conscription, justifying it on democratic grounds as akin to compulsory taxation and education. He had also made a furious attack on the Liberal *Daily News* for its criticisms of him.

"caught on". Intended to speak again on 3rd reading of Military Service Bill. . . . also to develop his conciliation proposals for Ireland. His yesterday's speech had been practically unprepared. He had consulted Carson before making it. He intended to press for immediate revision of the Register. It was a scandal that numbers of people should be disfranchised at bye-elections and there ought at least to be the possibility of a General Election on a revised register. Said he was not now seriously anxious about the navy, but did not explain why he had changed his mind.

Lunched with Carson alone—his wife had an engagement. Still very much depressed. Said he felt as if he had a nail through his heart. Rejoiced at Churchill's return. If George had come out he and Churchill "with such little help as I could give" would have been formidable in Opposition. There could be no question of providing an alternative Cabinet, but they might influence the Government and help to reconstruct it. There ought to be the possibility of a general election.

He was quite ready for a settlement of the Home Rule question, but this could not be reached by direct negotiation between the two Irish parties. It must be imposed. A great statesman was needed. There must be no raking up of old controversies; otherwise he should have to retaliate and then passion would be roused and there would be an end of compromise.

Diary, 22-26 May 1916

Went to London primarily in order to press for C. E. Montague's release as press delegate to proceed to Russian front, if possible with commission. Also to take steps in Weizmann's affair and consult on Irish question. . . .

Took Weizmann to breakfast with Lloyd George on Thursday [25 May] in order to explain to him latest remarkable developments of the work and the difficulties and delays caused by Lord Moulton. Lloyd George at once determined to call on Moulton and the heads of explosives and propellant departments to meet him and Weizmann and have the matter out.

Before Weizmann arrived Lloyd George told me he had been asked by Prime Minister to go to Ireland as Chief Secretary, but had declined. He had agreed, however, to do his best to negotiate an agreement between the Irish parties.

Immediately afterwards saw Dillon (with whom I had also had some conversation on the previous day at the House of Commons) at his club. He was deeply impressed by the seriousness of the situation in Ireland. The executions had converted the Sinn Fein leaders from fools and mischief-makers, almost universally condemned, into martyrs for Ireland. Redmond had been far too complaisant and had largely lost his influence in Ireland. Unless some big measure of appeasement were now brought forward there was danger that the Nationalist party would be broken up and Nationalist Ireland would be divided between the Sinn Feiners and the O'Brienites[2] who were now striking an attitude of ultra-patriotism. He himself might be compelled to break with Redmond, deeply as he should regret it, unless Redmond took a stronger stand. Everything would depend on the attitude which the Prime Minister took, but he agreed with me that Asquith would move not one step beyond the point to which he was driven and that with him the whole question was one of pressure. He told me that when he and Redmond had gone to see him on the previous day he judged at once by Asquith's expression that he had come to no sort of decision. His manner was weak and he gave the impression of a man "who had run up against a snag" and didn't know how to get round it. Dillon appears to have spoken pretty emphatically, as George said next morning that he had been "positively rude".

In the afternoon I went to the House and heard the Prime Minister's halting statement. I met Dillon afterwards in the Lobby and never saw a man look so black with suppressed passion. He was furious with Asquith, if possible still more furious with Redmond. His interpretation of the whole position was that Carson was to have his way, that no pressure was to be put on Ulster and that if they [i.e. the Irish Nationalists] did not agree to the terms thus placed before them, they were to be told that they had wrecked all efforts at conciliation and must accept the consequences. "And to think", said Dillon, "that Redmond got up and said that if the negotiations failed, it would be through no fault on our part", which was much the same as to say that we would make no effective stand at all.

I did not pursue the matter then but, after . . . having a long talk with Churchill on the Terrace[3] and dining at the Club, went to the

---

[2]Followers of William O'Brien, former Nationalist M.P. but now estranged from the party.

[3]Churchill, the diary records subsequently, "was evidently pleased with the reception given to his recent speech" and "hoped we should give it to be clearly understood that he intended now to stick to his post in Parliament."

Office to write my leader, and decided to wait to resume the matter with Dillon, after he had slept upon it, next (Friday) morning.

[26 May:] Dillon was going down to Lewes early to visit some of the Irish prisoners, of whom he said there were 2000 now in England, so I joined him at breakfast at his club. He still maintained fully the position he had taken on the previous day though he had got over his first anger and had gone so far as to consent to see Asquith in company with Redmond and one or two others and to lay before him his view of the situation. But he refused to be a party to negotiation under the conditions contemplated. I told him that, after seeing him on the previous day, I had had a few minutes conversation with Lloyd George and had told him that to my mind it was no use to try to make a settlement with Redmond and without Dillon, that Dillon was much the more powerful of the two in Ireland and would have the last word to say. (I did not tell him that George's reply had been "Well, he can wreck the negotiation if he chooses; but it is their last chance.") Dillon replied that he intended in point of fact to act as just such a reserve force and then he went on to tell me some very private matters. He evidently did not trust Lloyd George. If I remember rightly he called him "a slippery snake". He had spoken in the same sense before—when I had spoken of him as a possible Chief Secretary he repudiated the suggestion as utterly out of the question. . . .

I asked him what definitely would be his own solution. He said the Home Rule Act for Nationalist Ireland with such modifications as the circumstances made necessary and "some trimming". . . . Ulster would have to be omitted from the settlement and as to what should be accepted as constituting Ulster some concession might be made as compared with those offered at the Buckingham Palace Conference [in 1914]. On the other hand the Irish members must be retained in full numbers at Westminster in order to mark clearly to the Irish people the provisional character of the arrangement come to and also in view of the purely interim character of the vitally important financial adjustments. It was essential that the substance of Home Rule should be granted now; if they waited till after the war there would no longer be the same fear [i.e. in England] either of Ireland or of America.

He spoke with some admiration of Asquith's visit to Dublin at the height of the excitement. He had run a real risk of his life, especially at the hands of the women and he, Dillon, had warned him to dispense with no precautions. Feeling was intense and German secret agents were active in fomenting disaffection.

The facts were not half known in England. As an example of the

kind of things that went on he told of the experience of the Alderman
of his own ward who was shut up for 23 hours along with 26 other men
"in a room the size of my study", without room even to lie down—
another "black hole"—and from which they were not permitted to
emerge and as I gathered, nothing to eat. There were some further
sickening details. . . .

12. Fisher on Jutland, June 1916

While Lloyd George struggled with the problems of Ireland, another event briefly occupied the centre of the stage.

The only major naval engagement of the war, the battle of Jutland, was fought on *31 May 1916*. Hitherto the British had failed to lure the German fleet into action. But on that day it was learned that the German navy was putting to sea. The British fleet set out to intercept in two parts: the main force under the commander of the fleet, Sir John Jellicoe, and a battle-cruiser squadron under Sir David Beatty. (A third force, consisting of destroyers, was detained at Harwich in case of a German raid on the British coast).

Beatty was the first to encounter the Germans—although he did not realise that the force he had sighted was the advance guard of the entire German fleet. Although temporarily separated from one of his main cruiser squadrons, he immediately attacked, and suffered substantial losses. Realising that he was in contact with the whole naval might of Germany, he then withdrew at top speed towards Jellicoe. The Germans (now unaware of their danger) set off after him. They then came in sight of Jellicoe's force, and promptly turned and fled.

Jellicoe pursued, but cautiously. The speed of the German withdrawal had left him uncertain of his enemy's whereabouts, and he was fearful of being lured into a trap of mines and torpedoes. Briefly, he encountered the Germans again; then lost them for good. During the night they were able to slip past him and return to port.

Jellicoe had achieved his primary object. He had kept his fleet intact and forced the Germans to abandon the high seas to him. He had not achieved his secondary object of annihilating the German navy.

In terms of the vast forces involved, Jutland was virtually a non-battle. This it was bound to be, given that neither side was willing to fight on the other's terms, and that neither commander succeeded in imposing his own terms of battle on his adversary. For a British public thirsting for decisive victory, this was profoundly disappointing. Two things made it worse. British losses were much the heavier. And the first news the public had of the encounter was a communiqué from the Admiralty detailing their own losses but saying nothing of the Ger-

*mans' (which were not then known). In an effort to correct the unhappy impres-
sion thus created, the Admiralty appealed to Churchill to write an account of the
battle which would show it as a British victory. Churchill was in a sense well
qualified for the job, as a former First Lord and a master of English prose. But
he was also an outspoken critic of the Admiralty, so that their need to call on
him for assistance was not reassuring.*

Diary, 5 June 1916

Came to London to ascertain view taken by Fisher and Churchill of
naval battle of May 31 of which first news was published late on Friday
June 2. . . .

Saw Fisher Monday [5 June] at 4 and Churchill at 6. Fisher fully
informed. Had seen all the telegrams and documents which Balfour
had given to Churchill on Friday when he asked him to issue his famous
report on the battle and which Churchill had brought to Fisher in
order to obtain his assistance in drawing up the report issued to the
press on Sunday. Fisher held that the result of the battle was virtually
a defeat because even assuming the German losses to be equal to our
own that was a wholly unsatisfactory result of an encounter between
forces so unequal. He made the following criticisms:

1. Timing of our forces was bad. It was all wrong for our battle-
cruisers to be 2 hours ahead of the fast battleships (Queen Elizabeths)
and these 2 hours ahead of the battleships. A rendezvous ought to have
been fixed by the Admiralty and no one section of the Fleet should have
allowed itself to become seriously engaged till it was adequately supported.

2. For this the Admiralty was to blame. It was their business, since
they alone had, or could have, complete information to see that the right
dispositions were made. "Strategy", he said again and again[,] "belongs
to the Admiralty; tactics to the Admiral". . . . The Admiralty were
now boasting that Jellicoe had for the first time had a perfectly free
hand. He ought not to have had a perfectly free hand because he
could not know as much as the Admiralty knew of the facts of the situation.

3. Beatty blundered. He is not a very clever man, though a very gallant sailor. It had been Fisher's intention at the time when he resigned
to recall him to a post on the Board of Admiralty and put De Robeck,
who so distinguished himself at Gallipoli, in his place. He was justified
in engaging the German battle-cruisers because he was in a superiority
of one (6 to 5 I think) but the moment the German battle-fleet ap-

peared on the scene he should have retired on Jellicoe's advancing force. There is neither sense nor real courage in allowing yourself to be engaged by a superior force if you can yourself be in superior force[,] and the real [courage] is shown in running away. If it be said that the Germans would not have followed and our battle-fleet would then have failed to come up with them, well at least we should have been no worse off than before and should have saved valuable ships and lives. Beatty had no right to sacrifice them. The name he gave to him is "Balaclava Beatty" which sums up the whole thing in 2 words.

He blundered further in allowing at a particular stage his weaker ships to lead (armed only with the 7 inch guns). They were like rabbits against dogs and moreover got in the way of his own fire. To complete his mistakes he allowed the Germans to manoeuvre him so that he had the sun in his eyes.[1] It was the battle of Coronel and Cradock's errors all over again. The inferior force recklessly engaged, the sun on the wrong side and—I think he added—the weaker ships in the way.

4. When Jellicoe came up with the battleships the Germans quite rightly retired. The only mistake they made was in not doing it quite soon enough. The havoc then made by our 15 inch guns showed how vastly superior was our force.

5. But they ought never to have been allowed to get back. Why was it that the moment the whole German battle-fleet was known to be out we did not send our 60 destroyers from Harwich and the Channel, all our submarines and our six fast mine-layers with their 70,000 mines and cut off the German fleet from its base? Mines, destroyers, submarines should have been arranged line on line. It was a tremendous opportunity lost.

6. The Germans also perhaps missed an opportunity, for when our fleet retired to its base rather damaged they might have made a most effective raid and even landed troops on our coast or behind our lines in France. . . .

Incidentally he mentioned that Robinson, the Editor of the *Times*[,] had been to see him. He had explained the whole matter to him fully and he had gone away declaring himself thoroughly convinced, but he had not been allowed by Northcliffe to write accordingly.

He mentioned also that Lloyd George's intention, if he obtained

[1]Among a number of dubious points made by Fisher, this is the most puzzling—unless Scott misunderstood, and so misreported, him. Certainly Beatty was placed at a disadvantage by the sun. But this was because the sun was behind him, not in front. For the major part of the engagement it was not strong enough to dazzle the Germans, and by silhouetting Beatty's ships made them an ideal target for German gunnery.

power, was to concentrate the direction of the war in a War Council of
three.

CHURCHILL

Churchill was much less interesting. When I got there Colonel Hankey,
Secretary to the War Committee, was with him taking note of the
papers he wished to be included in the Dardanelles papers promised by
Asquith for publication. Afterwards a flying man came in and then
Lord Wimborne.

Churchill himself was in a frivolous mood. As soon as Hankey was
gone he produced his most recent efforts in water-colours which he
evidently much admired and they really were quite gay and sunshiny,
contrasting them with some earlier ones and pointing with pride to the
improvement. Mrs. Churchill came in and we chaffed him vigorously
but without effect. He marched up and down the room descanting on
the fix the Dardanelles papers would put various eminent persons into
—Jackson, Kitchener, Balfour all "up to the neck" in the business—
and doubting whether Asquith when he came to see them would
venture on publication, yet how after giving his promise could he
avoid it? But all the time he had his eye on the pictures and stopped
every now and then at the far end of the room to survey them with
critical satisfaction—a queer creature.

The interesting part of the conversation was his detailed account of
the way in which it had come about that he and not the Admiralty had
issued on the Sunday the first considered report on the naval action.
When the first news was published on Friday evening he went at once
to see Masterton Smith, Balfour's Secretary and an old friend of his
own, at the Admiralty. Smith suggested that he should write an appeas-
ing commentary in order to relieve the alarm caused by the first bald
statement of British losses and to put the matter in a more favourable
light for neutrals. Churchill said he was not the person to do this and
moreover he had not the official information needed. Smith then told
him—presumably he obtained or had already received Balfour's authority—that he could see all the telegrams and have all the information
in possession of the Admiralty. On this Churchill took the papers, said
he would consider the matter and let Smith have his answer by 4
o'clock next day.

On returning he told Smith that he could do nothing except on
Balfour's express request. Smith thereupon went in to Balfour and
came back to say that Balfour begged he would make the desired state-

ment, that he (Churchill) was the best person to do it because he was known as a critic of the Admiralty and his views therefore, in so far as they were favourable, would carry the greater weight. He did not tell me that Fisher had assisted him.

He maintained and I entirely agreed with him that, having been definitely requested by the Admiralty he was bound to comply. Mrs. Churchill—who always takes the wifely point of view that he should consider his own interest and keep out of scrapes—maintained rather hotly the opposite view. Lloyd George, whom Churchill had consulted, had advised compliance, but I afterwards found that he had never dreamt of the report being issued in Churchill's own name and had assumed that Balfour merely desired him to draw it up. He was amazed, like everybody else, to find that Churchill had been employed to do the Admiralty's work. "It is just", he said to me, "as though McKenna were to come to me and say 'look here; this loan of mine is not going well. Will you, being known as having had differences with me, please issue a report to say that it isn't really going as badly as it seems and that after all it is doing better than the last German loan' ". The whole proceeding in his view showed an abject state of mind at the Admiralty and would do more than anything which had yet happened to discredit it.

Fisher's view also was that the Admiralty were in a state of panic, having confidence neither in themselves nor in the fleet.

Churchill's final conclusion also was that, though he had acted from a sense of obligation and had incurred violent abuse (from "Daily Mail" and "Morning Post") for what he had done, yet if, with Machiavellian astuteness, he had sought to discredit the Admiralty he could not have done better.

As to the war in France he was strongly opposed to our undertaking a great offensive. We could not get through the elaborately prepared German positions. We might create a salient; with good luck we might convert the salient into "a sleeve". But when we advanced up this "pipe" we should be met at the end by fresh positions and fresh troops and be attacked at the same time from both flanks. It would be better to let the Germans try the same game; it might almost be worth while to open a way for them.

13. Lloyd George, the War, and the War Office, June-July 1916

While visiting London on the Jutland issue, Scott took the opportunity for further conversations with Lloyd George. They reveal the complete impasse which the latter had reached. Nothing about the war situation pleased him. He was dissatisfied with the circumstances of Russia, whose victories he (rightly) considered illusory; with the conduct of the Admiralty by Balfour, and—by implication—with Asquith for supporting Balfour; with the strategy of launching offensives on the Western Front (this on the eve of the battle of the Somme); with Britain's military leaders for implementing that strategy; and with the Liberal party for supporting the military against himself.

Yet in concrete terms he had little to offer. He could not spare shells for the Russians. His support for the Salonika expedition fell on deaf ears, yet he seemed not to dissent from the view that Britain must attack somewhere so as to sustain French morale. And he could offer no suggestions for reconstructing the government or putting life into the war effort.

Diary, 6-8 June 1916

Breakfasted with Lloyd George next day [i.e. 6 June]. Churchill also there. Lloyd George very hot about the conduct of the Admiralty. Balfour got first news of battle on Wednesday afternoon when Parliament was still sitting. He implored Asquith to tell nobody, neither the Cabinet nor the War Committee. Thus the War Committee was not even summoned. The first which George heard of the matter was by rumour on Friday afternoon. He sent over to the Prime Minister for information before going down to Walton Heath, but got none, and it was only by keeping his Secretary in London till the last train that he was able to get the news that night. Otherwise the first he would have seen of it would have been in the newspapers next day—and that though he is a member of the War Committee.

Saw him 2 or 3 times again at Ministry of Munitions before and after the news received on Tuesday [6 June] of the fatal accident to Kitchener. Discussed

1. War Prospects. Speaking generally he declared that as things stand "we are losing the war if indeed we have not already lost it". He went on to discuss the position in detail.

(a) Russian front. Minimised importance of recent Russian successes on the Galician sector. Was positive that their munitions are quite inadequate in spite of published statements to the contrary. [Albert] Thomas, French Minister of Munitions, just returned from Russia, had told him that Russian production of shells which a few months ago had been 60,000 a day had dropped—from what cause he could not explain—to about 30,000. They promised to pull it up again. We were now producing 1,200,000 a week (thus we were producing in a day more than they were producing in a week; very little was coming through from Japan and America by the Siberian railway) but could not spare many to Russia. In heavy guns also they had fewer for their 1,000 mile front than we for our 100 mile.

(b) Western Front. [W. M.] Hughes, the Australian premier, had just returned from Verdun and reported that the French had lost there 300,000 men. The men suffered frightfully in the trenches from the terrible German artillery fire and came out dazed and broken. It was folly to suppose that we could break through the German lines. Our generals were largely incompetent. At Ypres where we had just lost 5,500 Canadians in the German attack the General in command was a man over 70 and a "slobbering" dotard. He had massed the men in the front trenches and the Germans simply slaughtered them with shell-fire without their being able to do anything. We should never do any good and had no chance to win the war until there had been drastic changes in the higher command.

(c) Salonica. The French were strong for an attack and a military deputation was now in London to discuss the matter. The Cabinet were all against it except himself who had been a Salonicist all through. Curzon had led the opposition in the Cabinet that day (Thursday)[1], but they had selected him [i.e. Lloyd George] to meet the deputation and when he protested that Curzon as representing the Cabinet's view was the right man, they insisted that he could put the Cabinet's case most persuasively just because he shared the French view. "If ever there is a difficult job", said George, "they give it to me; but if ever there is one which carries power they refuse it. I am getting a little tired of it."

[1] 8 June.

2. French Feeling. Thomas reported that there was a growing feeling in France that we were not bearing our fair share of the burden of the war. For political reasons therefore he was strongly in favour of our attempting speedily a great offensive. Otherwise he feared there might arise "a deep unacknowledged distrust". Russia and England can last; France is getting very tired.

3. The political outlook. When we discussed the matter at breakfast George had nothing particular to suggest towards bringing about a reconstruction of the Government and putting life into the conduct of the war. The Liberal party in his view had, so far as the war was concerned, become the Conservative party. Any criticism of the War Office or the Admiralty or their official heads was regarded by the Liberals in Parliament as an indirect attack on the Prime Minister and they had become a positive hindrance to any reform. But he had no remedy to suggest. "Still flapping about" was Churchill's commentary as George left the room before us.

During 6 June, a new element was thrown into the situation. Kitchener was drowned, leaving the post of War Secretary vacant. In the early part of the war Kitchener had seemed the obvious saviour of the nation. And for considerable sections of the public—though hardly for the well-informed—he had retained much of this aura to the end.

Only one other man had gone any way since 1914 towards assuming the mantle of possible saviour. In this sense Lloyd George was Kitchener's obvious successor. But the post of War Secretary had lost most of its power: in part to Lloyd George himself as Minister of Munitions, in part to the military head of the War Office, Sir William Robertson. Was it worth Lloyd George's while to succeed Kitchener, seeing that he would be surrendering control of munitions and having to share direction of the war with military experts he profoundly distrusted? On the other hand, could he risk letting someone else take the post, especially on the eve of a great battle? This dilemma now came to dominate the political stage.

4. The Successor to Kitchener. Saw Lloyd George again on Tuesday afternoon [6 June] at Ministry of Munitions on news of the loss of the "Hampshire" with all on board. Put it to him that he ought to succeed Kitchener as Secretary of State. He said he would like to if he had the full powers ordinarily attaching to the office, but the most important of these—the power of appointment to the higher commands—had been taken from Kitchener and given to Robertson on his appointment as Chief of the General Staff at the War Office and this was in writing. He doubted if Robertson would part with this, still more if the Prime

Minister would put pressure on him to do so. He was afraid of the soldiers and Robertson was indispensable.

On the other hand he would not dream of taking the post without the power. The soldiers would crawl before the man who they knew had the ultimate power over them and treat anyone who had not with contempt. He would of course not dream of exercising such authority without giving the utmost weight to the opinion of his technical adviser, but he must exercise a certain discretion and it was easier for a civilian head, free from all personal associations, to be quite impartial than for a soldier. No steps had been taken or would be taken, however, for some days to fill the vacancy. He spoke strongly on several occasions of the need for a new spirit at the War Office and for rather extensive changes of personnel. Told story of (I think) General Rawlinson—"old Rawley"—of whom it was currently said in the army that every time he lost an engagement he received a step in promotion. He had only to lose one more in order to be Commander-in-Chief.

5. Ireland. So far as the leaders on both sides were concerned the thing was settled, but there was doubt as to their followers and they had gone over to Ireland to deal with them. While I was there a message came that Colonel Craig[2] was coming over from Ireland to see him.

Churchill, whom I met next day [7 June], was strongly of opinion that the War Office could no longer be refused to Lloyd George if he desired it, whatever might have been the case a few months ago when, on Robertson's appointment, Kitchener threatened to resign, and the reversion to his post was offered by Asquith to Bonar Law. Kitchener's death would weaken Asquith's position. Balfour, his main support in the Cabinet, was somewhat discredited and Lloyd George's position had been considerably strengthened by his victory in the Cabinet on the question of compulsory military service.

Ran across T. P. O'Connor in the hall of the Ministry of Munitions on Wednesday afternoon [7 June]. He had just been seeing George and was greatly excited about the position in Ireland which he declared had been ruined by Maxwell and martial law.[3] "Before the Executions", as he rhetorically put it, "99 per cent of Nationalist Ireland was Redmondite; since the executions 99 per cent is Sinn Fein". He could find no words strong enough with which to denounce the folly of the whole proceeding and Maxwell himself he described as a wooden-headed

[2] Carson's chief lieutenant in opposing Home Rule, and organiser of Ulster's resistance.
[3] Sir John Maxwell, Commander-in-Chief in Ireland, had by his "severity in executing the leaders of the uprising destroyed any last hopes that remained of conciliating Ireland". (R. R. James).

soldier full of stupid little airs who had been sent back from Egypt because he had neglected to make any trenches. He said it would be desperately hard work now to induce the Nationalist rank and file to accept the terms offered as a temporary settlement of Home Rule at once with six Ulster counties excepted, though it would be folly to reject them. The O'Brienites were denouncing them, but happily there were still 3 weeks before the matter could come up in Parliament and sanity might by that time have been recovered.

Saw [Lord] Rosebery[4] twice—first on Wednesday . . . and again on Thursday. He strongly advised that Lloyd George should take the War Office, coming to an understanding with Robertson. I told this to Lloyd George who was a good deal impressed. I also told him the story which Churchill had repeated that Robertson, with his customary strength of language, had described Lloyd George as "the only live man in that set of bloody fools"—meaning the Cabinet—which greatly entertained Lloyd George and at least showed that Robertson was a man who would be ready to work with him.

Diary, 13-17 June 1916

Lloyd George wired late Monday evening (June 12) asking me to come and see him as early as possible on Tuesday morning. Met him and Churchill at lunch and again next morning at breakfast [i.e. 13 and 14 June]. Said he was certain War Office would be offered him but he would not take it except on condition that it carried the full ordinary powers of the Secretary of State which had been largely withdrawn from Kitchener—especially the ultimate power of appointment to the higher commands. There were no set of men more insolent than the soldiers if they knew you had not power none more subservient if they knew you had. (Churchill, who had not at first understood that this power had been withdrawn from Kitchener and given to Robertson, entirely agreed). He would not dream of accepting the mere semblance of power. On the other hand he did not think he could remain in the Ministry if somebody else were put over his head at the War Office and he had intimated as much to the Prime Minister.

We parted to reflect on the situation and when we met next morning Lloyd George challenged me at once to say what I thought. I said it was difficult for me to judge without knowing exactly what service he thought he could render at the War Office, that the one thing that was clear was that the matter ought to be decided solely on the ground of

[4] Former Liberal Prime Minister, now in the political wilderness.

the national interest and without any regard to personal gains or losses —that simplified it. They both hastened to agree.

Broadly speaking George's view was that the inevitable standpoint of the professional soldier needed correction—that it was almost impossible for them to disregard, as they ought to be disregarded, professional tradition, and personal associations, ruthlessly to scrap the incompetent or less competent men at the top and boldly to tap the new reservoir of high ability and growing experience which the war had given us. Moreover there was a no doubt unconscious but none the less ever present tendency on the part of the man at the top not to lift into inconvenient prominence other men who might come to overshadow him, and this also had to be guarded against by the civil head of the War Office who was outside all such considerations. He quoted the case of General Birdwood[5] who had done so brilliantly at Gallipoli. When he came back he was designed for some quite unimportant post. The Australians, who were devoted to him, insisted on his commanding their new Army of 4 Divisions. But after all he was only allowed to command two Divisions. The steady promotion of Rawlinson ("old Rawley") after repeated failures was another example of personal and professional favouritism.

These arguments appeared to me valid, apart even from the personal factor in the present case—the force of energy and imagination and the resourceful brain which Lloyd George would bring to bear. . . .

At breakfast [on the 14th] he told us, what he must also have known on the previous day,—he was called out hastily during lunch to see Bonar Law who was leaving immediately for France for the "Economic Conference"—that Bonar Law had agreed that he had first claim on the War Secretaryship and had said he was perfectly right to insist on the restoration of the normal powers attaching to the Office; that he himself would accept it only on those terms; and that he would consent to no one other than George being preferred to himself for it. "Then", remarked Churchill, "you have all the cards in your hand". (When, however, I saw Lloyd George next day—Wednesday—at his office he told me he had "understood" Bonar Law to say this, but that Asquith understood Bonar Law's position differently).

He was clear that for him the alternative to the War Office with full powers was resignation—not immediately, because he could not resign on the personal question, but on the first opportunity he could make. He could not resign on the previous occasion when Churchill and I

[5] General Officer Commanding Australian Imperial Force.

had both wished him to because his munitions work was unfinished. The structure was complete, but it was like a house with the roof indeed on but doors and windows lacking and an appearance of the utmost confusion. Now it was all complete and, though it was not yet producing the full output, it would do so speedily with no further change.

Carson also, on personal grounds[,] would like him to come out but agreed it was his duty to stay in if he could get the War Office with full powers. He should despair of the Ministry if George left it.

Personally that [i.e. resignation] was the course he [Lloyd George] should prefer and he should go out to fight. Asquith perfectly understood that. He had already 5 very rich men—3 Liberals and 2 Unionists —who were prepared to back him financially to an almost unlimited extent, to run elections and the usual party machinery. Churchill and I both deprecated pushing matters to this point. . . . I suggested that it would be simpler and perhaps not less effective to keep Asquith and sterilise him. If Lloyd George could force a reconstruction of the Ministry he would dominate it whoever was Prime Minister. . . .

"What about Ireland?" asked Churchill. "Oh", said Lloyd George, "the newspapers are all at sea about that. The real opponents of a settlement are the Bishops. They hate Home Rule and always have hated it, because they know it would weaken their power. It is a struggle of Carson and Redmond combined against the Bishops", and he went on to say how Colonel Craig, that arch-Orangeman, had been over from Ireland the other day, and had admitted that Home Rule would break the power of the priests. What a commentary on the old cry that Home Rule spells Rome Rule.

Redmond had declared that if the proposed settlement were defeated he should resign and go out of politics.

He spoke highly of Devlin and said he had "no ambition". I said "How splendid!" Churchill looked a little queer and came back to the point later when we were alone. I said I meant selfish ambition; it confused things so. . . .

After breakfast the inevitable Lord Reading appeared and went off with George. Churchill and I stayed on a little. He complained of the virulence and injustice of the newspaper attacks. . . . He was a little sore that George never said a word in his defence. It would be easy for him and would have a great effect. However he trusted a good deal to the publication of the Dardanelles papers to vindicate him.

Speaking of the development of the war he said he had always been at a loss to justify the German enterprise against Verdun and had now come clearly to the conclusion that it was a capital mistake. The old Napoleonic maxim of strategy was to attack the enemy at his strongest point; if you won there all the rest followed. Now the conditions were changed. The greatly increased power of the defensive had made it almost hopeless to break through at the enemy's strongest point and the thing to do was to concentrate an overwhelming force at one of his weaker points. This was what the Germans had done against the Russians last spring and what the Russians were doing against the Austrians now. It was what we might have done at Gallipoli if Kitchener had not vetoed the dispatch of an army at the outset. The naval attack was not the original design, it was a later second-best.

Three other conversations during these days deserve to be noticed.

One was with T. P. O'Connor, "just back from Ireland". According to O'Connor "the state of feeling in Ireland was such that it might be impossible to get any terms accepted". The executed men—" 'murdered' was the common word"—had all become saints and heroes, and O'Connor described a miracle attributed to one of them. Also he said there was a revival of the murder clubs, and neither Redmond's life nor his own was safe.

The other two conversations were brief enough to be quoted in full:

MRS. ASQUITH

Met her on platform at Paddington on my way to see Ted at the Oxford hospital. Greeted me with effusion. Who did I think should be Minister of War? I said Lloyd George seemed the natural person. "Was he not too much of a pressman—too much mixed up with the press—the Northcliffe press? How would it be if the Prime Minister took the office himself? There was very little in it now. Perhaps Mr. George would not care for it on the Kitchener terms." I assured her he would not—a queer woman. She probably revealed the Prime Minister's astute design.

ROSEBERY

Saw Rosebery on Tuesday afternoon. He was not keen on Lloyd George. Should be/was against any change which would diminish Robertson's powers. Thought the best arrangement would be to make Robertson Secretary of State like Kitchener.

By the end of July, Lloyd George's attempts to redeem the Irish situation had foundered.

He had developed a scheme with attractive features for both Ulster and the south. The fundamentals were: (1) immediate Home Rule for Ireland outside the six north-eastern counties; (2) full Irish representation to continue at Westminster; (3) the whole situation to be reconsidered at the end of the war. This satisfied the Irish Nationalists. It straightway gave Home Rule to most of Ireland; and although it divided Ireland it did not—technically—do so permanently, because the agreement was only for the duration. (The element of impermanence was symbolised by continued Irish representation in the House of Commons, which was crucially important for the Nationalists). On the other hand it also satisfied Carson, because it both excluded Ulster from Home Rule during the war, and contained no automatic provision to include Ulster in a Home Rule Ireland at the end of the war.

But the Conservative diehards in the government, dismayed at the imminence of Home Rule, rebelled. They threatened resignation unless the carefully-balanced terms were modified in a way unacceptable to southern Ireland. Asquith weakly gave in, thus causing the whole scheme to founder.

Lloyd George—according to his colleague Addison[6]—was indignant at Asquith's surrender, but he did not admit this to Scott. It is possible to guess why. The obvious corollary of his condemning Asquith's conduct was that he himself should resign. Once again he was unwilling to do so.

C.P.S. to Lloyd George, 5 July 1916[7] (Extract)

Is it politically possible to spare Casement's life?[8] I think it would be in the highest degree politically expedient. His health was quite broken by what he went through in the dreadful Putumayo business and I think he is at least as much off his head as the religious fanatic who murdered Sheehy Skeffington[9] and two other men and who—rightly I think—is not going to be hung.

I write to you because you have a freer mind than anybody else and because you have been chosen by the Cabinet as pacifier of Ireland and ought to be listened to on such a matter.

Diary, 27 July 1916

Breakfasted with Lloyd George. Discussed the Irish question for a few

---

[6]C. Addison, *Four and a Half Years* (Hutchinson, London, 1934), vol. I, p. 234.
[7]Lloyd George Papers.
[8]Casement had been captured after landing from a German submarine, and was sentenced to death for high treason.
[9]Irish journalist killed by a lunatic British soldier.

minutes alone. Then Lord Reading came in which did not matter, then Sir Nevil Macready, the Adjutant General, which did. Both had come to discuss the case of a well-known lady who in respect to a young officer had combined the parts of Potiphar's wife and Uriah the Hittite.[10] Sir A. Markham, who had taken up the case for the injured officer, had arrived with me, but was seized with an attack of angina which disabled him till after breakfast.

On the Irish question Lloyd George said he was prepared to resign if it would have been any good and the Prime Minister would have done the same, but the Unionists were united and the Government would have been broken up.[11] There were two questions at issue—(1) whether the exclusion of Ulster should be definite or only provisional. This was largely a matter of words, since all agreed Ulster could not be forced. (2) Retention of the Irish members [in the House of Commons] in full numbers till final settlement. Here the Unionists undoubtedly went back on the Agreement. None of them had in the first instance realised the effect of this, but the moment it was pointed out the condition was seen to be impossible. You could not justify giving Home Rule to five-sixths of Ireland and retaining the full Irish representation, though it was not for him to point this out in the first instance. The mischief was in the delay. If the terms had at once been embodied in an agreed Bill the Unionists could not have gone back on it. The terms afterwards offered—i.e. reduction in number of Irish members (presumably only from the Home Ruled part of Ireland) as provided by the Home Rule Bill[,] with right of return in full numbers whenever the final settlement came up—were perfectly fair and would have been accepted if the Irish had really wished for settlement. Dillon had always been against it and was delighted to seize the opportunity of destroying it.

[10]Mrs. Cornwallis-West, a prominent lady in Welsh landed society, had conceived a great passion for a young wounded soldier of upright character and humble origin. When he had courteously rejected her advances, she had used her position in the social hierarchy to damage his career. The military authorities had readily done her bidding, but other forces had intervened, among them Sir Arthur Markham, a mortally-ill Liberal M.P. Hence a considerable scandal ensued, as a result of which the commanding officer of the Welsh battalion was removed from his command, and the Quartermaster-General, Sir J. Cowans, was (though retained in his post on account of his distinguished war service) informed of the government's displeasure at his conduct.

[11]This seems a strange remark. Nothing, apparently, could be more obvious than that if Asquith and Lloyd George should resign the government would break up. Yet the statement is worth noting, as a clear indication of Lloyd George's attitude to resignation. He viewed it as a threat he might employ in order to bring cabinet colleagues to heel. But if the manoeuvre did not work and he seemed in danger of losing office, he simply withdrew the threat. As a result, his threats of resignation no longer carried any weight.

I pointed out that both (1) and (2), but especially (2), were essential for carrying the settlement in Ireland; they marked and secured its strictly provisional character. But Lloyd George would not listen to this. Obviously he was bent on justifying himself for going back on the terms agreed upon.

Directly after breakfast saw Dillon. He did not complain strongly of George, except that, as usual, in his endeavour to be too artful he had over-reached himself. The failure was the nemesis of his method of negotiation. For his own part he (Dillon) had made it absolutely clear from the beginning that the retention of the Irish members in full force was the *sine qua non* of any provisional agreement whatever. George's error was in not securing the formal consent of the Cabinet to the written terms before offering them to the two Irish parties as a basis of settlement. Instead he obtained the personal assent of a certain number of influential men—these I think he said included Crewe, Long, Lansdowne and Balfour—and he intended to use this as "a blunderbuss" to force the assent of the Cabinet. He assured the Nationalists that he should resign if he were not supported and that the Prime Minister would do the same. Finally I asked him whether he thought there was still room for any constructive proposals, and he was clear that at present there was not.

I ran across O'Connor afterwards at the National Liberal Club, and he took much the same view as Dillon, except that he was obviously much more sorry for the failure of the negotiations as he had hoped more from them. He added that he thought Lloyd George had done his best.

Lunched with Churchill, but there were ladies present and I had only a few minutes alone with him before lunch. Asked him whether it was true as asserted by the "Chronicle", that Lloyd George had taken [the War] office, after all, on the "Kitchener" terms, and he said it was not. Letters had been exchanged and Lloyd George had received assurances which he regarded as satisfactory. It is doubtful, however, whether these are free from ambiguity, or give Lloyd George the powers he desired.[12]

The only other points of any consequence referred to by Churchill were: (1) He regretted that Lloyd George had not lifted a finger to get him appointed Minister of Munitions after he had himself got all he wanted at the War Office, though, as he said several times, George remained perfectly friendly and even cordial. (2) He was doing very

[12]Scott's assumption was correct. Lloyd George had not secured his point regarding the powers of the War Secretary.

nicely in journalism—earning at present at the rate of £20,000 a year. He had a contract to write 12 articles for which he was to receive £6,000—monthly articles on the progress of the war, I gathered, in addition to the general articles he was writing for the "Sunday Pictorial". This was quite comfortable and left him ample leisure to pursue his pictorial studies. As before, he displayed a number of his latest efforts which were profusely praised by the ladies—Lady Churchill and Lady "Kitty" Somerset. His wife was much more reticent.

14. Murmurings Before the Storm, October 1916

Some of the foregoing entries suggest, on Scott's part, a mounting impatience with Lloyd George. True, Scott never ceased to see him as potential leader of the nation. What irked him was Lloyd George's reluctance to make a sustained bid for the leadership if it meant endangering his own position.

The Irish débâcle brought this feeling to a head. On a matter like conscription, Scott had applauded Lloyd George's intention to challenge the government even though doubting the particular cause for which he was contending. But Ireland was a cause dear to Liberal hearts. Lloyd George's failure to stand by his own proposals came to rankle very deeply with Scott.

Insult was soon added to injury. In September Lloyd George indulged in a reckless interview with an American journalist, designed to forestall a peace initiative by the U.S. government. The interview was noteworthy for its condemnation of outside interference, its use of sporting metaphors to describe the war, and its commitment to the policy of a fight "to a finish—to a knock-out". The contrast between this jingo talk and Lloyd George's pusillanimity over Ireland would not be lost on Scott. So when Scott visited London—after a break of several months—in October, he did not cross Lloyd George's threshold. Instead he had long interviews with two of Lloyd George's devoted adversaries in the Liberal ranks, Gulland (the chief whip) and McKenna.

Meanwhile Lloyd George had given annoyance in a quite different quarter. On 28 September he was fiercely attacked by the right-wing Morning Post. The paper accused him of not sticking to his desk at the War Office and of paying too many and too active visits to France. It then observed darkly that the army was perfectly well aware of what had taken place during Lloyd George's recent visit to France (when, it was widely believed, Lloyd George had spoken disparagingly of Britain's generals to French military leaders); and it warned that if this sort of "gaffe" was repeated "we shall feel it our duty to publish the facts of the occurrence."

Lloyd George issued a public rejoinder that the Morning Post's accusations were "the invention of an ill-conditioned mind in search of mischief", and that he had gone to France on the pressing invitation of Haig and the French Commander-in-Chief.

Diary, 2-3 October 1916

Monday, October 2. Came up from Bedford after seeing Ted. . . .

After lunch met Arnold Rowntree[1] at Reform Club. He brought request from old Mr. Rowntree that I should invite friendly editors and a few others[,] such as [G. Lowes] Dickinson and Hobson, to a Conference to discuss peace terms and to take action. Said I did not think that any fruitful proposals could be made apart from our allies and that the war position was not yet such as would enable us to exact the minimum which these would require. That as to the journalists any appearance of concerted action would defeat itself and he would do better to approach the Editors separately.

Met Gulland also at the club and asked him the meaning of the "Morning Post's" attack on Lloyd George. He said that what had happened was that Lloyd George had seen Foch and had spoken to him very freely about the shortcomings of our generals, particularly in the Artillery[,] adding that if only we had generals like the French there would soon be a change in the aspect of affairs. Foch, a good deal perturbed, reported these remarks both to Joffre and to Haig. Result Haig furious and Joffre refused to see George unless Haig also were present.[2]

Later in the afternoon saw McKenna by appointment at the Treasury and asked him what was the meaning of Lloyd George's most mischievous reported interview with representative of an American press agency in which he was stated to have denounced in advance any attempt on the part of the United States to bring about peace negotiations and declared for war to all extremities. (I pointed out in extenuation that the worst things were interpolations of the interviewer, but McKenna would not hear of that. He had no doubt George had passed the whole thing—very likely written it interpolations and all. He himself always wrote the whole of the alleged interviews and did not even see the interviewer who merely supplied a little decorative framework).

I said I saw two possible explanations of this outburst (1) that Lloyd George wished to cover up his false step with Foch and gain credit for vigour with the army (2) that there was a strong division of

---

[1]Liberal M.P., Quaker, and social reformer.
[2]Haig wrote in his diary for 15 September 1916 on this matter: "Unless I had been told of this conversation personally by General Foch, I would not have believed that a British Minister could have been so ungentlemanly". A fortnight later Haig was visited by the editor of the *Morning Post*, who "has a commendable dislike of the politicians." See *The Private Papers of Douglas Haig* 1914-1919, edited by Robert Blake (Eyre and Spottiswoode, London, 1952), pp. 167-8.

opinion in the Cabinet and George was trying to commit the country to his own views and to bounce his opponents out of their position. McKenna did not contradict either assumption, but proceeded to denounce George with vigour. The views he had expressed were in any case purely personal views and had no sort of sanction from the Cabinet. Since the publication of the interview there had been no meeting of either the Cabinet or of the War Committee, so he could not tell what would be said about it. There was no redress for such things. The fact was that George ought to be "suppressed"; there was nothing else for it.

I remarked that there was only one person who could do that. Yes, said McKenna, the Prime Minister is the person to do it, but unfortunately he doesn't want to. "Not that he believes in Lloyd George", he added hastily, "not a bit". And what good can come of that sort of wild talk about the war, he asked. It won't recommend him to the army, or to those at home who are concerned for the men in the army. They don't want an indefinite war, but a reasonable peace. They have no desire needlessly to sacrifice their lives or the lives of those dear to them. . . .[3]

As for his affront to America it was sheer lunacy. Lloyd George thought he could say what he liked and nothing would happen because the war profits reaped in the U.S. were so great. But you could never be sure and you might easily go too far. "I need not tell you", he added, "that for my department his action is most injurious. I am in the position now of borrowing from America two million pounds a day". . . .

And then he went on to express his satisfaction that I shared his view and to say handsome things about the influence of the "Guardian".

Lloyd George was not prepared to overlook criticisms of his "fight to a finish" interview. Scott gave him the opening for a sharp riposte by allowing the Manchester Guardian to publish a somewhat one-sided account of the French response to the interview; but Lloyd George went too far in suggesting that the source of the communication was not what it appeared.

Robert Dell (Paris correspondent of the "Manchester Guardian") to W. P. Crozier, 11 October 1916 (Extract)

The United Press interview with Lloyd George has caused great

[3]McKenna went on to make a rather cruel and slighting remark about Lloyd George which it has not been thought necessary to reproduce here.

annoyance here; Briand[4] is very angry about it. Lloyd George's habit of running over uninvited to Paris has already made him unpopular in official circles; it is said that he interferes too much with everything and everybody. Now he is posing as the mouthpiece of the Allies. The general public has not taken very much notice of the interview; the French press gave a summary of it, but there has hardly been a word of comment, no doubt because the Government has asked for silence. So far, however, as the interview has made an impression, the impression is deplorable. To say to France just now that time does not count is not exactly tactful.

[Dell's letter above formed the basis of a report ("From Our Correspondent, Paris, Friday") in the *Manchester Guardian*.]

Lloyd George to C.P.S., 16 October 1916

I have just read the note in today's Manchester Guardian which *ostensibly*[5] comes from your "Paris Correspondent". I have no objection to the "Guardian" attacking me or anything I say or do; but it is not quite consistent with the traditions of the "Guardian" to utterly misstate facts in order to discredit someone they do not approve of.

All the French newspapers of every shade of opinion have not merely published my interview but commented upon it, and that favourably. Papers of such divergent views and value as the "Debats", "Figaro", Clemenceau's paper, Pichon's paper, the "Journal", "Petit Journal", the "Patrie", and several others—I can supply you with a list—have all published, commented and approved enthusiastically.

I know your *so-called*[5] "*Paris*[5] Correspondent". There is no difficulty in detecting him: he always gives himself away by the sentence he invariably inserts in every criticism of my actions or views derogatory to my personal influence. I have no right to ask for agreement, but I think I could certainly claim from the "Guardian" fair treatment.

C.P.S. to Lloyd George, 18 October 1916

I was glad to get your letter because it gives me the opportunity of correcting a misapprehension and also of telling you, what you probably know, that it is always painful to me to find myself in opposition to you.

[4] The French Foreign Minister.
[5] Scott has underlined these words. It may be surmised that they caused him considerable displeasure.

As to the letter of our Paris correspondent in Monday's paper of which you write it was of course precisely what it professed to be. If any member of our staff here should propose to masquerade as our Paris correspondent he would know what would happen to him. We don't do these things. As to our Paris man himself I have always found him honest, capable and well-informed. Of course he may make mistakes like anybody else, but he is intimate with important people and, to the best of my belief, he has no sort of animus against you. There is a good deal of opinion which does not find expression in the newspapers and I did not feel justified in suppressing his report.

That is the whole story.

Lloyd George to C.P.S., 19 October 1916

Your correspondent stated specifically that there were hardly any comments in the French Press. I gave you the names of leading newspapers in which I had actually read favourable reports. The fact that he had talked to Frenchmen who disapproved of the interview surely does not justify his making, or the "Manchester Guardian" publishing, a misleading statement of that kind. I never complained of your disagreeing with my views or my expression of them: that would be an impertinence on my part. But I think I have a right to complain of gross misstatements.

I feel confident that if you had the information which I have as to what has been and is going on you would have approved entirely of my interposition. Do you think the Prime Minister would have made so emphatic a statement in his speech unless he had information which induced him to believe that it was essential that it should be made clear, especially after your articles and your London correspondent's notes, that I spoke the mind of the whole of the Cabinet?[6]

C.P.S. to Lloyd George, 22 October 1916

As soon as I got your first letter I wrote to our Paris Correspondent and asked him for explanations on the question of fact, but have not yet heard from him.

[6] Asquith, in a highly-praised statement in Parliament on 11 October, had warned against "faltering purpose or wavering counsels" leading to a patched-up compromise "masquerading under the name of peace"; and he had demanded "adequate reparation for the past and adequate security for the future." But (as the *Manchester Guardian* had pointed out next day) there was nothing in his statement that constituted a public warning to neutrals not to attempt mediation—the main point of the Lloyd George interview.

Some day when you can spare time I should like very much to hear from you what, broadly, you have in your mind as the necessary conditions for the conclusion of peace. When last you spoke of the matter, now a good many months ago,[7] I agreed thoroughly with the general view which you expressed, but conditions have changed a good deal since then and it is perhaps possible now to look forward with more assurance. It would be a great help to know what you are now feeling in the matter.

C.P.S. to Hobhouse, 22 October 1916 (Extract)

I have another letter from George. I think I must see him soon and have it out with him on the question of policy, so that we may know where he stands and where we stand in relation to him. Hobson thinks he means by the "knock out" the crushing of Germany not the attainment of agreed terms, however adequate[,] and wrote us a long and strong letter on that assumption which we couldn't publish. But we must really get to know.

Lloyd George to C.P.S., 23 October 1916

Of course I am always happy to have a talk with you. Let me know when you are coming up.

I saw our Ambassador in Paris on Friday, and he told me the French were delighted with the naughty interview. Briand, whom I also saw, was very grateful for it; and Grey has just sent me a telegram which has just arrived from Spring Rice, our Ambassador in America, saying: "Lloyd George's interview had a most excellent effect here".

[7] Probably a reference to the conversations in which Lloyd George had looked forward to an American peace intervention as the only way out of a stalemate war. See above, pp. 164-5 and 177.

15. A Question of Alternatives, November–December 1916

With Lloyd George suffering the disfavour of such diverse papers as the Morning Post *and the* Manchester Guardian, *Asquith's position seemed impregnable. Somehow his government had survived internal upheavals which would have destroyed a dozen other Prime Ministers. His opponents outside the government had made little headway. Within, he had snared Balfour, and (thanks to Lloyd George's waywardness) had received Bonar Law's support almost without having to work for it. Meanwhile Lloyd George's disruptiveness and threats of resignation were, through frequent repetition, ceasing to impress.*

Yet despite appearances, Asquith's days as Premier were numbered. Internal politics might be his forte. But they were ceasing to serve as a substitute for success in the war. Wherever Englishmen looked abroad, nothing seemed to have been accomplished. In important respects the military situation was deteriorating. The mood of press and Parliament, where not openly disaffected, was slipping into despair.

It was the existence of this mood which gave importance to the parliamentary upset in early November known as the Nigeria debate. No great question was at stake: only the sale of captured enemy property in Nigeria. The government, including the Conservative leaders, decided to offer it for sale both to British subjects and to neutrals. A large section of back-bench Conservatives, led by Carson, revolted against this decision, and voted that it should be offered only to British subjects. The government survived the division. But this powerful manifestation of Conservative disaffection caused the party leaders to think again.

Scott had no sympathy for the petulant nationalism manifested by the revolters. But he did share their underlying dismay at the government's conduct of the war. The following letters, although out of sequence, may be placed here as revealing his fundamental attitude to the mounting political crisis:

C.P.S. to Hobhouse, 25 November 1916 (Extract)

I'm awfully sorry to hear about the Flu—an enemy almost as barbarous and relentless as the German. This Rumanian business is horrible—the fourth little state to go down in the dust on our side and no finger raised to help[1]. . . . The crass stupidity of the military chiefs and incompetence of the Government are enough to make one despair.

C.P.S. to Hobhouse, 28 November 1916

I enquired about your movements last night because I wanted to send you this leader for your consideration. It was written under a growing sense of the futilities of the present conduct of affairs—witness the increasing sea-peril and the hideous disaster of Rumania—Ireland also—the fumbling half-and-halfness, more irritating than any resolute action, of our dealings with Greece, the long trifling with the military situation at Salonica—it is the same all round.

Of course there is the question of an alternative. It must almost inevitably be Lloyd George with Asquith possibly as Lord Chancellor and Balfour in some purely honorary office. But terms would have to be made with Lloyd George—e.g. the reinstatement of Fisher and in some degree at least of Churchill—and perhaps I ought to have a heart-to-heart conversation with him before taking any decisive step.

I enclose also the notes (too prolix, but they give the facts) of my visit to London last week[2]. . . .

I had been feeling bad about George, but thought much better of him again after hearing what he had to say. Of course he has from our point of view great defects of temperament and outlook, but it is a question of alternatives and of the immediate use of his practical and efficient qualities for a definite purpose.

I have a growing conviction that with the present men we shall *not* win the war and that the utmost we can hope for is a draw on bad terms. Hindenburg has changed the whole aspect of affairs for the Germans.[3] George *might* do something of the same sort for us. What do you think?

P.S. . . . There is no doubt that [what] we say will be widely noted which makes the responsibility the greater. I got a wire last night from the Central News to say they had been instructed to wire the whole of

[1] Rumania, having entered the war on the Allied side in August 1916, was now being overrun by the Germans.
[2] See below, pp. 234-240.
[3] In August 1916, following his successes as Germany's Commander-in-Chief on the Eastern Front, Field-Marshal von Hindenburg had been made Chief of the General Staff.

our War leaders and "Student [of the War]" articles to America, and asking permission.

Diary, 20-22 November 1916

Lord Fisher. Saw him Monday afternoon [20 November] at Duchess of Hamilton's flat, she, as usual, taking part. Congratulated him on the remarkable reception he had received at the Mansion House a few days before. He said Asquith also had shown him particular attention coming right across the room to greet him very cordially. Mrs. Asquith, on the other hand, who was with him had cut him dead—"looked at the ceiling" said the Duchess—whereas on the last occasion when he had seen her she had almost fallen into his arms. Perhaps his response had not been adequate.

Discussing the political situation and the possibility of a reconstruction of the Government he said he thought the critical point was the position of Bonar Law with whom there was growing dissatisfaction in his own party and I found this confirmed by everyone to whom I afterwards spoke. . . .

Churchill. Went in after dinner on Monday and had a couple of hours alone with him at his house. He was evidently suffering acutely from his enforced inactivity. "What fools they are", he said, smiting the arm of his chair. "They could get more out of me now in two years of war than in a hundred afterwards". I urged him to make a business of Parliament and make himself a figure there, but he said the papers (with the exception of the Manchester Guardian) would not report him and on the contrary ill natured remarks were always made, as that "there were few members present and no one troubled to come in" or "what a contrast with old days when his rising was the signal for the House to fill" and so on. Therefore he preferred to find his public in the press. Then at least every word he wished to say was printed and it took him no longer to write an article for the "Sunday Pictorial" for which he got £250 than to prepare a speech which was not reported. After Xmas he meant to start a new series of articles in which there would be some very plain speaking.

At present he was the best abused man in the country. He was determined, however, to stick it out. He could effect nothing by going back to the Army so he must just "wait in that chair"—a large and comfortable one—till his chance came. The mistake he had made was in not allowing enough for the power of the press, at a time of suspended party activity, to attack and ruin an individual. He had great hopes from the forthcoming report of the Dardanelles Committee which he had reason to believe would go far to clear him on that issue. Altogether he was in a chastened frame of mind and said he "had learnt a great deal" by his recent experience.

Speaking of the possibility of a reconstructed Ministry he said no change would be material which did not involve a change in the Premiership. Lloyd George, "with all his faults", was the only possible alternative Prime Minister. I asked if in case George formed a ministry he could count on being included. He said he thought so—that George would desire it and that it would be in his interest. Would he bring back Fisher? Of that he did not seem quite sure. He agreed that Fisher ought in the public interest to be utilised and, in his rhetorical way— he was making quite splendid speeches to me all the evening—said "he is like a great castle: the walls have crumbled, but the keep still stands". But Fisher, if he went back as First Sea Lord to the Admiralty would need some one to restrain him and prevent him from acting vindictively against individuals.

I asked about Bonar Law and he instantly agreed that that was the key—from the point of view of a change in the Ministry—of the position. Bonar Law had been losing ground steadily to Carson[,] and his friends were constantly coming to him and telling him he must do something to maintain his position in preparation for the time when, after the war, he would once more have to come forward as leader of the Unionist party. The charge against him now was that he was a mere echo of Asquith. Hence the vigour with which he asserted himself the other day against Carson on the Nigeria question. The effect had been to divide Carson's party. Carson on that occasion had pursued the traditional Tory practice—"The appeal of the Liberal was to principle[,] of the Tory to prejudice"—another rhetorical flower—and not too much should be made of the fact that Carson had taken his stand accordingly. (This was intended I think to placate my own condemnation of Carson for his part in this affair). . . .

Lloyd George. Breakfasted with Lloyd George Tuesday and Wednesday [21 and 22 November]. On Tuesday[4] he was alone and I had a good talk with him, but Davies came in before we had quite bottomed things. So he agreed that I should come again next day, but then Davies and Dr. Addison (his old factotum at the Munitions Department) were there and we got of course no forrader. [We breakfasted] at his new flat in St. James's Court to which he said he had been compelled to retire through the pressure of War taxation. He had not,

[4]The text says "Monday", but this seems to be an error for Tuesday.

as I had supposed[,] left No. 11 Downing Street, but had put down his rather expensive household there and only used it occasionally. His Parliamentary Secretary, Colonel D. Davies,[5] had "found him" this flat "and between ourselves", said George, "he has paid for and furnished it". Davies had the flat adjoining. He is a nice chap, very painstaking I should say, but certainly not brilliant. Odd that George [should] care to place himself under this obligation. A little too much like the lack of sensitiveness shown in the Marconi affair. (There is a rumour going about—I should hope quite unfounded—that North-cliffe has some information about this which he holds over George *in terrorem*).

I had felt a strong disinclination to see Lloyd George because of his violent outbreak, in his interview with an American journalist, against America as a possible peace-maker and for an indefinite continuance of war to the death (to say nothing of a rather insolent letter he wrote me at the time). The violence it appears was at least in part calculated and George himself appeared a good deal better than his words. He said he had positive and documentary evidence that Gerard, the U.S. Ambassador at Berlin[,] had gone to America with a proposal to Wilson that he should propose mediation and Wilson would be under very strong temptation to do this in order to conciliate German-American opposition to his re-election which would probably turn the scale. Once mediation were proposed it would have been very difficult to refuse, and once the war was stopped it would have been impossible to resume it. But the time for a settlement was for us extremely unfavourable and for the Germans favourable. Presumably he meant that the cohesion of the Allies—already somewhat insecure—would be broken and we ourselves should have to choose between continuing the war alone and accepting an inconclusive and wholly unsatisfactory peace. He did not explain why he had thought it necessary to use such violent language or why he rather than the Prime Minister or the Foreign Secretary should have felt called upon to make this declaration.

Speaking of his administration at the War Office he said that, while Liberal papers were attacking him he was in fact fighting the battle of civilian control. He gave two examples, both important.

(1) When in France, having doubts as to the effectiveness of our system of communication, he suggested to General Haig that this was really work for an expert civilian, Haig strongly objected. George then made an offer that he should appoint a great railway expert from

[5]Welsh landowner and Liberal M.P.

England and that Haig should appoint a soldier to be approved by George from his staff and the two should have full power to inspect the whole system and to report. Haig agreed and in a fortnight the report came that instead of everything being right, as the soldiers vowed, everything was wrong. The roads were being destroyed by the enormous traffic, the railways were quite inadequate and were being used to an extent far beyond their capacity. A serious breakdown might be expected. Besides this 70,000 motors were being used to do work which should largely be done by tramways and railways, at a great expense. . . . Within a few days a serious breakdown duly occurred. Haig was convinced. [Eric] Geddes, the expert employed, was put at the head of the communications.[6] He asked for 200,000 tons of rails and 60,000 wagons. It was impossible to supply the quantity with our existing resources and steel works and furnaces had to be ordered which will take a year to construct. A truly amazing example of military incompetence.

Incidentally this matter was the cause of a useful rupture between George and Northcliffe. Northcliffe, who was in France[,] was got hold of by the generals and wrote George an insolent letter threatening him with attack and exposure if he did not discontinue his interference.

(2) George made similar representations to Sir William Robertson on the subject of the vast department of army clothing, but was told that clothing for soldiers could only be controlled by a soldier. George remarked that officers did not appear to go to an army clothier for their clothes, but Robertson was firm. Then came the exposure of grave scandals in the clothing department. Robertson was obliged to give way and Lord Rothermere[7] was appointed. (The selection was Robertson's and Lloyd George accepted it. He knows nothing about clothing, but is a good business man and free from all suspicion of having interests of his own to serve to which any one in the trade must have been exposed).

A third revolution is probably impending. "I shall probably soon want a new Q.M.G." said George, the present Quartermaster-General being in George's opinion greatly implicated in the horrid Mrs. Cornwallis-West scandal and having connived at a gross injustice to

[6]Born in India and educated in Edinburgh, Eric Geddes had decided in his youth to try his luck in the U.S.A., where he had spent four years as a brakesman on a railroad, a lumberman, and a labourer in a steel works. Later he had moved to India where he had become involved in railway management. By 1914 he was back in Britain and deputy-manager of the North Eastern railway. Between Lloyd George and himself there was immediate rapport.
[7]Press magnate, brother of Northcliffe.

a young officer whom it was his duty to defend.[8] This was the case which poor Markham took up strongly just before his death. He [Lloyd George] talked quite openly about this on the second morning giving the whole history. It was an extraordinary example of the corrupt and perverse standards of conduct current in the old military and "Society" circles.

He told an analogous story of the attempted dismissal of one of the less exalted officers in France because he had at last refused to tolerate the presence of a scandalous woman who broke all rules by means of the intervention of certain of the more exalted ones. This also I gathered was likely to lead to a clearance. Evidently in both cases George was acting with justice and courage. . . .

As to the military situation George had nothing cheerful to say. He had always been an "Easterner" and did not believe in the possibility of a break-through on the West where we had already lost 400,000 men as against the French 200,000 for larger gains. He had raised questions as to the reasons for this—he did not specify with whom—and this was made the ground of another attack on him (I gathered that he referred to that in the "Morning Post").

On the other hand the situation in Rumania was full of danger. The Rumanian artillery was wholly inadequate, (the list he had seen was "fit for a museum") and no adequate steps had been taken to meet the danger. So long ago as September 2, when the Rumanian army was in its first course of apparent victory in Transylvania, he had warned Robertson of the danger of a heavy German counterstroke and 2 days later he sent him a written memorandum (of which he showed me a copy) pointing out that Hindenburg might be expected to cut the losses at Verdun, to give ground slowly on the Somme, making us pay his price, and to concentrate a strong striking force against Rumania which she would be unable to resist, and he urged that we should do all in our power to assist her. The reply was that this could not happen because the passes were difficult, winter was approaching and before the Germans could do anything effective they would be blocked. George pointed out that there were excellent roads across them and a railway, but Robertson was obdurate and nothing was done. Now, 10 weeks later munitions were on their way to Archangel and the Allies had agreed to send a joint force of 90,000 men to Salonica—too late. . . .

On the Wednesday there was some talk about Munitions (Dr. Addison having come over to discuss the nice question of the recruitment of munitions workers by the ex Munitions Minister) and in-

[8]See above, p. 223. The Quartermaster-General was in fact reprimanded, but not replaced.

cidentally of the new Minister of Munitions.[9] Neither George nor Addison spoke very respectfully of him. He was "rattled", "anything rattled him", he was nervous in grappling with labour difficulties, sought cover as was the manner of his race, grew hollow-cheeked under the strain. All the same he may very well be handling labour more prudently than George did.

George himself seemed buoyant as ever, but I fancy he also is not exactly enjoying himself. Asked by Addison who was to be the new "Food Dictator" he said nothing had been settled and added quite seriously "I think the job would rather suit me—to provide for the food of the people, instead of this bloody business".

Dillon. After breakfast on Tuesday had a long talk with Dillon at his club. . . . Speaking of the possibilities of Ministerial reconstruction Dillon agreed strongly that Bonar Law was the weak point in the Coalition. He was an ambitious but not a clever man and Carson was undermining his position. Their relations had undergone a remarkable change since the time before the war. Hence Bonar Law's resolute attitude on the Nigeria question which had had the effect of strongly dividing the Carson following. Nominally this was 120 strong, but only about half had gone with him in the division. None the less, excluding the 15 official Unionists who voted with the Government, he carried with him an actual majority of the Unionists taking part in the division.

As to the action of the Irish on the occasion he said it was of course not taken on the merits, as to which they were with the Government, but purely for tactical reasons. There had been much discussion about this. He and Devlin had favoured a vote against the Government because if after Redmond's strong Waterford speech they had been content merely to abstain it would at once have been said that the declaration of opposition to the Government was mere words and that in fact they were still at its tail. Redmond, however, was in favour of abstention only. But when the matter was referred to a party meeting it was practically unanimous for the stronger policy. A humorous incident was that 4 Unionists who were on their way into the Lobby to vote against the Government beat a hasty retreat when they saw the Irish trooping in.

As usual Dillon was deeply concerned in the war from the point of view especially of the protection of the smaller nationalities, and now of Rumania. The Salonica Expedition he complained had never been taken seriously by our military chiefs. "We know more about them in

[9]This was E. S. Montagu, a Jew, who had been a member of the Liberal government since 1910, and before that was Asquith's private secretary.

Ireland", he said, "than you do here, from our experience of the way in which they can and do thwart and defeat in detail the instructions which nominally they accept". It has been so in regard to Salonica and he told how a young Irish officer returning from Salonica when asked why the railways needed for an advance had not been made said of course they had not because obviously there was no intention to advance. . . .

Balfour. I had a short interview with Balfour on Wednesday afternoon, charming and friendly as usual. I put to him the extreme difficulty we should be in if the nitrate fleet from Chile should be attacked and held up by the new ocean-going submarines, as this was our sole source of supply of an absolutely essential article for the making of high explosives. He said the point was new to him and he thought we had an alternative supply from Sweden. He called in Bartholomew, one of the Junior Sea Lords, and questioned. Bartholomew retired and came back with the information that it was as I said and Chile was the sole source of supply. . . .

After breakfast on Wednesday I walked away with George's Parliamentary Secretary, Colonel Davies[,] and he opened out about Churchill. "Didn't I think he had had his chance? And when a man had had his chance and missed it ought he not to be set aside?" It was so in the army. If a man had failed and been superseded he was not given another appointment. To do so would be to "lower the morale of the Army". Did not the same principle apply in civil life and would it not "lower the morale" of civil life to do otherwise? He seemed to have got it all by heart and gave me the impression of having been stuffed by the soldiers. Churchill he said was "anathema in the Army". Evidently he feared that if George lent a hand to Churchill he might incur a share of the unpopularity. "The Chief is too good-natured" he said. The Chief was clearly all the world to him.[10]

As the foregoing conversations recognised, Bonar Law was now the key figure in the situation. He had survived Carson's challenge on the Nigeria question, but it had constituted a threat to his position which pulled him up short. He was unlikely to do as well the next time he was challenged from this quarter; so he determined that there should be no next time. He allowed himself to be reconciled with Lloyd George.

This was the end for Asquith. On 25 November Lloyd George and Bonar Law put to him proposals for instituting a new War Council to exercise supreme direction of the war; its members were to be Lloyd George, Bonar Law,

[10]For the subsequent breach between David Davies and Lloyd George, see Frank Owen, *Tempestuous Journey* (Hutchinson, London, 1954), pp. 378-82.

and Carson (but not Asquith). On 3 December, after a week of mounting pressure, Asquith went far towards accepting this proposal (though not agreeing to these particular members). That evening he issued a notice that the government would be reconstituted—which involved the resignation of ministers. But next day he back-pedalled. He wrote Lloyd George a two-part letter. In the first part he complained of a hostile leader in The Times *as reason for doubting the workability of the scheme. In the second he outlined what he considered the substance of the proposals, stressing the new War Council's accountability to himself. Lloyd George replied that he had not read* The Times *(he also remarked to Scott on the good press he had received), and said that he accepted Asquith's statement of the proposals in letter and in spirit.*

But Asquith was now thoroughly disenchanted. Later on 4 December he wrote to Lloyd George again, rejecting the scheme on the grounds that the War Council must include the Prime Minister. Lloyd George received this letter on the morning of the 5th. Now quite certain of Bonar Law's support, he broke off relations with Asquith. This rendered the latter's position hopeless. Without Lloyd George and Bonar Law, he had no chance of reconstituting his government on a workable basis. So he resigned.

Hobhouse to C.P.S., 2 December 1916 (Extract)

I pass to the questions raised by your draft leader and the Times of today. The plan is now quite clear. There is to be a Lloyd George Government getting rid of Asquith Balfour Grey and Lansdowne. Balfour I think ought to go, but the chief benefit of his departure would have been that we could have had a McKenna Fisher combination at the Admiralty. This has been evaded by Balfour and is now impossible[11]. . . . What we *know* we shall get from the Times Government is the dismissal of all the moderating element. I have no more respect than you for Asquith, but Grey is another matter. He represents a negotiated peace—to which in my belief we shall ultimately be driven. But it will be a defeat to be *driven* to it, a success to compass it by our own efforts. George combines the most pessimistic view of the condition of the war with the most extreme view of the victory to be aimed at. What policy can he show that would have succeeded better than that of the Government? Had he a definite policy as to (a) Gallipoli, with regard to which I remember his exaggerated pessimism in June 1915 (b) Salonica (c) Greece. He has been on the War Council throughout. Is there evidence that he has pressed for a saner more

[11]Balfour had just strengthened his position by creating Jellicoe First Sea Lord in place of Sir Henry Jackson. Beatty had succeeded Jellicoe as commander of the fleet.

consistent more rational policy? All we *know* is that when for a moment a negotiated peace on favourable terms to us seemed possible he killed it,[12] and that on his own showing to you at a time when he was anticipating an unfavourable turn of events. What we may be sure further is that a George-Northcliffe ministry will be for a policy of "thorough" at home and particularly in Ireland. We shall have conscription there and probably another rebellion. We may also have a serious anti-war labour movement at home.

The difficulty I admit is to defend Asquith. He is never one thing or another, but if he yields to George, taking Grey with him, the last remnant of liberalism and moderation vanishes from the Government.

Hobhouse to C.P.S., 3 December 1916 (Extract)

The more I think about Lloyd George's plan the more I feel that the only *real* thing that it means is a tightening of the screw of conscription. This I believe to be a fatal mistake because Russia is the real reserve of men, and the men now taken in England are more and more the skilled young munition workers. Secondarily the scheme also means *guerre à l'outrance*, less regard for America and other neutrals, no negotiations, no regard to our real power to win out and out.

None of the triumvirate have any claim to our confidence as conductors of operations. George among any government officials is a by-word for neglect and inefficiency. Law has made no name. Carson has no experience. The capable man is McKenna whom they won't have because he knows too much of our real condition to push conscription hard. I suspect the delays in obtaining decisions refer mainly to "man-power" and mean the resistance of Asquith and McKenna to a further turning of the screw which they know to be dangerous to the nation.

Diary, 2-5 December 1916

Saturday December 2. George wired asking me to see him next day at Walton Heath. Went to London in afternoon. Called on Fisher (who was in bed with a cold) in the evening. "Well," he said, "Lloyd George is packing up. Bonar Law has dished him". . . . He was deeply disappointed at Jellicoe's having consented to give up the command of the Grand Fleet and become First Sea Lord. There had been a great

[12] Presumably a (somewhat exaggerated) reference to Lloyd George's "naughty interview" with the American correspondent.

struggle. Jellicoe had been 3 days in London and held out. Then Balfour spent 3 days with him at the Fleet and he gave in. Lady Jellicoe was in distress. Jellicoe, she wrote him, had it in writing from Balfour that Beatty's appointment as his successor had not been made on his (Jellicoe's) recommendation. Beatty was a real danger and might ruin all. . . .

He gave me a copy of his letter of protest and regret to Jellicoe and asked me to let Lloyd George see it. He had shown it to Massingham and, at his urgent request[,] had allowed him to show it to Runciman. Runciman declared that Balfour was an element of weakness in the Cabinet not in naval matters only.

Sunday December 3. Lunched with Lloyd George at Walton Heath and talked with him before and after and drove back to War Office with him. He had not expected to return to London that day, but had received a summons from the Prime Minister—who had actually returned (motored back) from Walmer Castle, to which he had gone on Saturday for his inviolable weekend—to meet him at Downing Street. It appears by the bye that he had gone to Walmer with the Quartermaster-General—the man who was so compromised in the Cornwallis-West scandal that George thought his dismissal inevitable.

He explained his position and in some degree his policy. Had decided not to go on on present footing which was hopeless. Prime Minister conceived his function as that of Chairman of a Committee. He came to Cabinet meetings with no policy which he had decided to recommend, listened to what others said, summed it up ably and then as often as not postponed the decision. It was a futile method of carrying on a war. What was needed was a very small Committee of say 3 with very large powers, sitting day by day and controlling everything connected with the war at home as well as abroad. He had pressed this view on the Prime Minister and at the same time offered his resignation and he showed me the letter. He suggested himself, Carson and Bonar Law as members of the Committee. The Prime Minister not to be a regular member and he made no mention of a Labour representative. When I remarked that this was rather a tall order for the Prime Minister and that he might well regard it as inconsistent with his position, Lloyd George replied that there were precedents—that neither Salisbury, nor Gladstone, nor Lord Liverpool had endeavoured, in addition to the ordinary work of the Premiership, directly to supervise the conduct of war; that in a war of the present magnitude it would be doubly difficult; that the Prime Minister could not attend the War Committee every day and often twice a day; that moreover he would be liable to add continually to the numbers of those summoned regularly to the Committee even though not formally members of it, as he had done in the case of the present Committee, and that the new Committee would end by being very much like the old.

The difficulty about Carson was his demand for conscription in Ireland. He would have to abandon this. He (Lloyd George) would not countenance conscription till after Home Rule had been brought into operation. Then Ireland having been put politically on the same footing as the rest of the Kingdom must accept the same treatment. He was in favour generally of a conciliatory policy towards Ireland in regard to all the exceptional measures recently adopted. . . .

He admitted that the [new War] Committee might, if it took the domestic side also of the war under its control[,] have grave difficulties with Labour and suggested that, in this connection, Henderson might be able to render important assistance.

When I urged in regard to Churchill that his ability ought to be utilised and employment found for him, he replied that the difficulty with him was his egotism. In the Dardanelles affair our failure was primarily due to his eagerness to do the whole thing off his own bat and his reluctance to wait for the cooperation of the land forces and thus to share the credit of success with Lord Kitchener.

When I remarked to Lloyd George that he might be accused of always making trouble and attacking the Prime Minister, he admitted that he was the disruptive element in the Cabinet, but was of opinion that he had really done the Prime Minister a service, as if he had not goaded him to action he would have come to disaster long ago.

Lloyd George told me Northcliffe wanted to see me, so after leaving him I called at Northcliffe's house. I doubt if Northcliffe had asked to see me or anyway if he remembered doing so. He was interested in some things I told him—he did not know e.g. whom George designed for his War Committee—but couldn't bear not to be telling long stories himself all the time, so I just let him run on—a thoroughly egotistical person. He was very keen about Carson. Robertson he said was a wooden sort of person, but he couldn't speak highly enough of Haig.

People kept coming in—first Curtin, his American spy, with his latest article which Northcliffe glanced at and passed, and then his brother Leicester Harmsworth, M.P., who stayed on. Northcliffe was very civil, showed me the room where various 18th century literary notabilities had held conclave and engravings of them, and presented me with a copy of his book.

Later he telephoned to me to Nottingham Place to tell me that the Unionist members of the Cabinet who had held a meeting that afternoon it had been decided [sic] that Bonar Law should support Lloyd George—a quite useful piece of information[13]. . . .

Afterwards called on Fisher. . . . Asked me to show his letter to Jellicoe to Lord Northcliffe, which I did not do. He wanted me to show it also to Bonar Law as well as to Lloyd George and pressed me about Lloyd George. I did afterwards give one of the copies—he had a whole sheaf—to Lloyd George which probably did him no good. His habit of letting off steam in letters—very extraordinary compositions on which, like other great men in regard to things which are outside their scope, he specially prides himself—has probably given his enemies exactly the handle they needed in order to block his return to office and power.

Monday, December 4. Saw Lloyd George at War Office by appointment, 12.30. He confirmed Northcliffe's statement as to result of Unionist conclave on previous day. All ministers asked to resign and Prime Minister had a free hand in reconstructing his Government. Nobody need accept office again unless he approved of the terms arranged as to the War Committee and its powers. I remarked that these would be difficult to formulate as they were to be so stringent and far-reaching and asked if he were presenting them in writing. He said he was and that [Colonel] Hankey, the secretary to the War Committee, was drafting them. "He is entirely with us". Congratulated himself on "a very good press" that morning, but said "Chronicle" was all wrong. Reflected the views of the military people. Shortly before this Robertson and another—I think the Quartermaster-General—had arrived and George said he would see me again later.

Then saw Fisher again for a few minutes. He gave emphatic warning, which I afterwards conveyed to Lloyd George[,] about Hankey. He was extravagantly loyal to his immediate chief and would sell his best friend in the interest of his chief. In fact, said Fisher, he has sold me, for he told a direct lie in the Dardanelles enquiry in order to shield the Prime Minister. "A Napoleon in capacity". . . . But [Fisher] remained convinced that George would be "diddled" by Asquith.

Lunched with Dillon at Bath Club. Found him in pretty full

---

[13]Two comments are called for here:

(i) It was unusual for Scott to write such an ill-constructed sentence.

(ii) Precisely what was decided at the meeting to which Northcliffe referred has been disputed ever since. But Bonar Law and his colleagues did decide that the government should resign, which certainly strengthened Lloyd George's hand against Asquith.

possession of facts of situation. On previous Sunday[14] George had sent for him and O'Connor to see him at Walton Heath and had opened his mind very freely to them. His idea then was to resign and appeal to the country in a regular campaign of speech-making and he had asked Dillon for his advice on this plan. Dillon said he had absolutely declined to give any advice at all or express an opinion. The responsibility was far too great and the consequences of the complete exposure of the Government which would be involved might be far too serious.

As to the proposed triumvirate, or War Committee of 3, he did not believe such an arrangement, if attempted, could last because nothing could deprive the Prime Minister and Cabinet of their constitutional power. But it might serve as a half-way house. The only effective arrangement was a new Ministry putting new forces in power. Under the proposed arrangement Asquith would be the rallying point of all enmities against Lloyd George. Asquith had made no enemies—his whole study had been to conciliate everybody. George had of necessity made many. The thing would break down. The Prime Minister was an extremely artful person, and he told a story—with a deprecating smile at the indiscretion—of a recent experience of O'Connor's when the Prime Minister had solemnly said to him: "I will never betray Ireland so long as I remain Prime Minister—and I shall remain". But he betrayed us all the same observed Dillon grimly.

If a transfer of power was needed the British Constitution in its beautiful elasticity had provided for it in the premiership. The Prime Minister was the effective repository of power and there was no occasion to seek any other weapon.

Incidentally he remarked: "You will have to give up your friend Churchill. There is something wrong with him. He has gone down of late like a stone. I met him in the Lobby the other day and he said, with an air of the deepest conviction, 'There is nothing for it but to make peace.['] I replied that he couldn't expect me, as an Irishman, to share that view. Once in for a fight our way was to go through with it". "I was painfully reminded", Dillon added, "of the fate of his father. How any man could have written such a life as he has done of his father and then take such a course as he has passes comprehension.['']

Dillon, as I have long felt, is the last of the great Liberals of the last century—of the tradition of Gladstone and Campbell-Bannerman—and I told him so. He seemed rather to like the accusation.

Saw Lloyd George again at 5.30. Told him Fisher's view of Hankey

[14]Presumably 25 November.

—whom he knew intimately—as Asquith's man and that he should be on his guard. Urged him to be stiff in his terms since he had nothing to lose, but the contrary, by their rejection. They involved the degrading of the Prime Minister and of all the other members of the Cabinet who were to be reduced to comparative insignificance and he couldn't expect these to be otherwise than hostile to him.

He said he admitted all that and it had been strongly represented to him by others of his friends. But he had made up his mind, having made his proposal, to go through with it, though nobody would be better pleased than himself if it were rejected and his final resignation were accepted. Lord Derby had just been saying much the same things to him and he had given him the same answer.

I urged him to press for Bonar Law's appointment to the Admiralty (so as to make possible Fisher's reinstatement). He inclined to Curzon. He was expecting momentarily to be sent for by the Prime Minister in order to continue their discussion of terms and if possible conclude agreement. But the summons never came.[15]

Tuesday December 5. Saw Lloyd George at War Office at 11.30. He was much angered and excited. Said he had just received a letter from the Prime Minister going back completely on his previous undertaking and that in consequence he had determined at once to send in his resignation (that is really his refusal to re-enter the Ministry) and he showed me the letter which was in the act of being typed by his secretary.

He also showed me a letter he had received from Asquith on the previous day in which he recapitulated formally the terms of the agreement which they had reached on the previous afternoon and allowed me to take a copy of these. The letter was quite short, on one side of a sheet of note-paper and in two paragraphs. The second and longer paragraph was the material one recapitulating the terms.[16] The first I did not copy—or even read—as Lloyd George said (evidently quite sincerely) "Oh! that relates to another matter and is of no conse-

[15]It should be noted that Scott did not write up his final account of these events until the end of the week, by which time much water had passed under the bridge. This consideration particularly applies to his account of the following day.
[16]Copy by C.P.S. of the second paragraph of Asquith's letter:
"The suggested arrangement was to the following effect: the Prime Minister to have supreme and effective control of policy. The agenda of the War Committee would be submitted to him: its Chairman would report to him daily: he can direct it to consider particular topics or proposals and all its conclusions will be subject to his approval or veto. He can of course at his discretion attend meetings of the Committee." Scott added: "I [i.e. Lloyd George] accepted in letter and in spirit."

quence".[17] Now he received from Asquith a letter making entirely different proposals, viz: that he, Asquith, should be a regular member of the War Committee, that he should appoint the other members at his discretion and that the Committee should not be restricted to 3. George was obviously taken completely by surprise and very indignant. In his reply he remarked caustically that this was only another illustration of the indecision and vacillation on the part of the Prime Minister which had proved so ruinous in the conduct of the war and that he had no alternative now but to withdraw from the Ministry.

I saw him again at the War Office in the late afternoon. In the meanwhile the Unionist members of the Cabinet—largely influenced no doubt by Carson as leader of the formidable "ginger" group of Unionists in the House—had followed suit with George[,] and Asquith, faced by the complete break-up of the Coalition, had sent in his own resignation to the King and advised him to send for Bonar Law. Bonar Law had agreed to form a Ministry if it would make it easier for Asquith to be a member of it. Asquith however declined. Balfour urged him not to stand out, pointing out that he himself had been Prime Minister, but had not refused to serve under Asquith in a War Government. When Asquith persisted in his refusal Bonar Law declined to go on and the King sent for Lloyd George.

This is the substance of what Lloyd George told me when I saw him in the afternoon. He then had Carson and Bonar Law closeted with him and came out to speak to me. It was then his intention to ask all the Liberal members of the late Cabinet—except of course Asquith who had already declined—to join the new Ministry and the only doubt in his mind was whether he should send a collective or individual invitations. Finally he said to me he would send individual invitations.

I pressed him to give Lord Fisher a place in the new Administration. He said he was afraid he could not give him office, though he would consider the matter, but suggested that he should be given a place on the War Committee—possibly he did not mean a place as full member, but as a member ad hoc.

[17]Note by C.P.S.:

This was the paragraph, afterwards read by Asquith at the Reform Club meeting [on 8 December], in which he called attention to the offensive leader in Monday's "Times" and said that if that were the interpretation to be put on the arrangement he could not go on. Lloyd George had treated this statement as not concerning him and as immaterial and had simply replied on the second, or material part of the letter that he accepted the arrangement as there stated "in letter and in spirit".

Two comments are called for regarding the incident, just recounted, of Asquith's 4 December letter.

(1) Did Lloyd George on the 5th really believe "quite sincerely" that the first paragraph of the letter related to "another matter" and was "of no consequence"? Why then did he go to such trouble not to show it to Scott? Certainly its contents do not bear out his interpretation—and Scott (when he subsequently learned what the first paragraph contained) must have seen this, or he would not have recounted the incident in such detail.

Apparently Lloyd George on 5 December was concerned to persuade Scott (and perhaps himself) that, now the breach had come, it was Asquith's fault. Asquith, he wanted to show, had gone back on an agreement he had confirmed in writing the day before. The second part of the letter, taken alone, might seem proof of this. The whole letter pointed in precisely the opposite direction: that Asquith had been moving towards the rejection of Lloyd George's proposal. It seems strange—given that Scott had so often urged him to make the break—that Lloyd George should have taken such trouble to convince Scott that Asquith was the disrupter.

(2) On scrutiny, even the second paragraph of Asquith's letter suggests that by 4 December he was hardening against Lloyd George's scheme (as outlined to Scott on the 3rd). Asquith stipulated that he was still to have "supreme and effective control of policy", was to see the war cabinet's agenda in advance, was to receive a report from the chairman daily and approve or veto all decisions, and could attend meetings at his discretion. This was a considerable remove from the body Lloyd George had foreshadowed to Scott: a "very small Committee [of Lloyd George, Bonar Law, and Carson] . . . with very large powers . . . controlling everything connected with the war at home as well as abroad." Why then did Lloyd George tell Asquith on the 4th that he accepted the Prime Minister's version in letter and in spirit, instead of holding out for his full terms? Perhaps he recognised that, with the question of personnel unresolved, he could afford to lower his terms and still keep them ultimately unacceptable to Asquith. But another possibility suggests itself: that once more his nerve was failing him, and that (as in April) he was preparing on 4 December to be satisfied with a three-quarter loaf, rather than hold out for the whole loaf if it meant taking the plunge of resignation.

Either way, Lloyd George had once again become so involved in the intricacies of negotiation that he was losing sight of the larger issue: that the position of war director was his by right of attainment, with the premiership the only office appropriate to such a position; and that to be satisfied with less was to perpetuate an intolerable situation, as to convert Asquith into a figurehead Prime Minister would be to create an unworkable one.

Yet it is possible to appreciate Lloyd George's doubts and hesitations. He had not been born to power and office. No person of his background had hitherto become Prime Minister. There was no clear line of advance laid down for him to follow. It is little wonder that ambition and the sense of destiny conflicted with a painful awareness of what usually happened to people like himself when they forgot their place. The contrast between Lloyd George and Churchill—the latter with his unimpaired self-confidence and unashamed ambitiousness—is in part a contrast of character; partly it reflects the differences in their background and inheritance.

Wednesday [6 December]. Lunched with Dillon at the Bath Club. He thought Asquith was right to reject the terms offered him. To accept them would have been to degrade the office of Prime Minister. The only way in which a democracy could successfully carry on war was by appointing a virtual dictator. The fluidity of the British constitution makes that easy. The Prime Minister should assume supreme command. It is essential for the civil power to control the soldiers. Asquith had taken the very opposite view. The folly of this had been exemplified in Ireland. The Irish were all dangerous.

Afterwards saw Gulland, the Liberal whip. He took the same view as Dillon. The position of the Prime Minister under the proposed arrangement would have been intolerable. He denounced George as an intriguer and for his misstatements in the press—also the "Times" for its "lying leader" on Monday.

Here Scott's narrative of the events surrounding Asquith's fall comes to an end. Scott wrote:

"I remained in London till Saturday, but was laid up with a bad cold and though I was able to write the leaders, I did not see Lloyd George again."

Was illness the only thing which kept Scott and Lloyd George apart during these days when the new government was being formed? Certainly Scott wrote to Hobhouse on 9 December: "I've been laid up the last 3 days with a beast of a cold." But if Lloyd George had summoned him to discuss the apportionment of posts, would sickness have kept him away? The point is that, to all appearances, he received no summons. Some months later he wrote regarding Lloyd George and these days: "up to the point where I got flu and heard nothing from him". (Diary, 28 September 1917).

Scott at this stage was an embarrassment to Lloyd George. Although not wanting office for himself, Scott was deeply concerned that certain other people should receive posts: Churchill, Fisher, and the Liberals who had served with Asquith—note his reference to individual, not collective, invitations. Lloyd George, who had hedged when Scott raised these matters, did not intend to offer posts to any of these gentlemen. (Only Samuel among Liberal ex-ministers was asked to join, though others had already made it clear that they would refuse if asked). Hence conversations with Scott could only prove a complication for Lloyd George. It may be surmised that he preferred to avoid such complications. So Scott kept his sickbed unmolested, and returned to Manchester without again seeing the new Prime Minister.

By the time he boarded the train, much that Scott had striven for had been accomplished. Asquith was as dead politically as he had long desired, and Lloyd George was securely in his place. But clearly the new ministry, with its large Conservative predominance and absence of certain key figures, did not fulfil all his hopes. And the uncertainty remained about how Lloyd George would measure up to his opportunities, and how his Liberal heritage would fare while he was about it. In Scott's mind, hope warred with misgiving.

C.P.S. to Hobhouse, 9 December 1916 (Extract)

I hope that on the whole you approve the line we have taken. Events succeeded each other so fast that one was presented with a new situation each day and in dealing with these one had to take a line and it was hardly possible to make all the reservations one would have liked.

Hobhouse to C.P.S., 9 December 1916 (Extract)

I have followed your leaders with some apprehension and awe (I confess). The case could not have been better put, tone and spirit were in the best possible contrast to the "Times". I could not have taken the same line myself, but I hope, with trembling, that you are right. I admit (and I find others who are not Georgian doing likewise) that it is impossible to defend the Asquith government. To go on with it meant certain defeat. Lloyd George I regard as kill or cure. He may land us in even worse disaster, or he may win. The point in his favour is that he will take decisions. The point against him is that he appears to have no grasp of facts, to be incapable of taking account of two aspects of policy at the same time, to be unscrupulous and morally somewhat blunted, and to be incapable of the rudiments of organisation. To this has to be added that he associates himself with two men who have given not the smallest proof of any statesmanlike capacity or quality. All this may be balanced by the fact (if it turns out a fact) that they will agree, and therefore decide things. At least I hope so.

As to home politics we should I think make up our minds from the outset that all George's suggestions of big democratic schemes are moonshine. No *democratic* scheme of George's has ever come off. . . .

I should be happier if I thought we should have no more personal dealings with a man who appears personally disloyal and untrustworthy.

Since writing the first part of this I see from the Observer that Milner is to be Minister without portfolio i.e. I imagine one of the inner council.[18] I confess this doubles and trebles all my apprehensions. You see there is no talk of Fisher, and Churchill is of course left out. I am glad Balfour is to be at the Foreign Office. He may be as good there as he was bad at the Admiralty—but can you conceive the actual working of a War Council that does not include the Foreign Secretary? I fancy we shall see the whole scheme disintegrate as George's schemes do. Have George and Carson already diverged?

Lloyd George to C.P.S., 12 December 1916

Your article yesterday was tip-top and most encouraging to a poor fellow who has undertaken the biggest task that has ever fallen on the shoulders of a British Minister. . . .

But what on earth makes you say today that the predominant flavour of the present administration is Unionist? Half the acting Cabinet is Lib.-Lab., the other half Unionist, the President still considering himself to be an infinitely better Liberal and Democrat than four-fifths of the men who now constitute the official Opposition. . . .

I do wish you would put that right, because I know how anxious you are, apart from your old friendship for me, to see that I, in common with the rest of God's creatures, shall at least get fair treatment.

When are you coming up to town? I want to see you.

I did my best to persuade Gordon Hewart[19] to take the Home Office: I was so anxious that it should be held by a Liberal. But he refused, and insisted on the Solicitor-Generalship. However, that is a temporary appointment.

On 18 December 1916 President Wilson made a fresh peace initiative. He called on the belligerents to state their peace terms, claiming that the objects of both sides in the war were the same. His timing (like his phraseology) was unfortunate. The German government had just demanded that the Allies agree to a settlement of the war or else it would launch against them unlimited submarine warfare. And it was difficult for Lloyd George to talk about a negotiated peace just at the moment when he had acceded to power in order to put more vigour into the conduct of the war. But even so, here was an important test of Lloyd

[18]In place of Carson. [19]Liberal M.P. for East Leicester.

George's liberalism: was he now prepared to respond more positively to President Wilson's approaches, and to define specific objectives in the war rather than pursue the unlimited goal of a "knock-out" victory?

James Bone to C.P.S., "Urgent", 21 December 1916

Have seen George. He says Wilson's note is a German move and that we will not declare terms. He urges you strongly if you do not see with him in this not to take a line till he has seen you tomorrow. He is very anxious about tonight's leader that the Manchester Guardian does not oppose Government.

Bone to C.P.S., 21 December 1916

George was extremely anxious that the Manchester Guardian should not back Wilson's proposals. He said that they knew, absolutely knew, that it was put forward at the inspiration of Bernstorff[20] and he implied that America had done a deal with Germany. I asked him why, even if that were so, we could not state our outside terms for either we wanted unconditional surrender or terms, and if terms why not state them. He replied that this was the best of all times for Germany to state her terms and the worst of all for us to do so. He said with emphasis that we would be every day in a better position and Germany's would be worse. Germany was selling at the top of her market. Wilson's note was meant to embarrass us. He said it was impossible for us to state definitely our terms just now. He spoke of the tone of the note which he described as almost insulting, especially the passage where it said that the aims of the belligerents were identical. He hoped very much that you would hold your hand till you saw him, and not accept Wilson's suggestion and support it. He was not very convincing, but that might be probably because he could not speak frankly enough to me.

C.P.S. to Lloyd George, 24 December 1916[21]

I have a long telegram today from Walter Lippmann[22] in response to a request from me for his interpretation of the real meaning of the President's Note. . . . His reply comes to this that pro-Germanism has nothing whatever to do with the note, as Wilson owes nothing, unless

[20]Count von Bernstorff, German ambassador at Washington. [21]Lloyd George Papers.
[22]Distinguished American political commentator.

it be resentment, to German-Americanism in politics which the election effectually disposed of.

Wilson's real motive he says is to carry American opinion solidly with him in case, as a result of the failure of Germany's peace move and the then probable resumption of submarine ruthlessness, America should have to choose between acquiescence and war with Germany. If he goes to war with Germany he wants the American people to know that the main specific objects of the war are such as they approve. Otherwise Lippmann evidently thinks he may be unwilling to come in.

If that be a correct interpretation may it not be worth while to go a certain distance in defining our terms—as for instance by demanding the restitution (with compensation for damage) of all European territory occupied by Germany and her allies? If, *per impossible*, Germany accepted that, there would be other terms to follow relating to Alsace-Lorraine, Trieste and Constantinople. That at any rate seems to be the kind of line which Wilson desires in order to enable him to bring America whole-heartedly into the War.

C.P.S. to Hobhouse, 9 January 1917 (Extract)

I feel all you say [about Lloyd George] and I try to be on my guard. This will be the more necessary now that he is more powerful, but he knows, or should know by this time, that we don't purchase information by support. Still one can't help feeling that it's more difficult to oppose a man just after he has been rebutting all your arguments to his own satisfaction if not to yours, and that's a very good reason for not seeing him too often.

Just now I want if I can to find out if he really has a plan for the war this spring that holds out reasonable hopes apart from attrition. Also I want to challenge him definitely about Fisher. I should not feel I had done my duty till I had done everything in my power in regard to this. A third matter that I want to bring before him is the necessity—in case he contemplates the possibility of the war running into 1918—of at once setting to work to provide the machinery for extracting nitric acid—an indispensable element in all explosives—from the air instead of deriving our whole supply from the Chilian nitrates at an enormous cost in shipping and exposed to deadly risks. . . . Till I've got these things off my mind I must run the risk of George's allurements which I admit to be curiously potent at times, though not in all circumstances.

16. A Prime Minister and his Problems (1), January-February 1917

Lloyd George, when he succeeded to the premiership, entered upon an ominous inheritance. The Russian monarchy, and with it the whole eastern resistance to Germany, were collapsing. The question of how the western Allies were to advance their cause militarily was still unsolved: were they to resume the offensives which had achieved so little in 1916, and if so where? Meanwhile, the Germans were unleashing unrestricted submarine warfare against Britain, and the Admiralty under Carson and Jellicoe (now First Lord and First Sea Lord respectively) were helpless to combat it. There were political problems facing Lloyd George too: his dependence on the Conservatives, his relations with the rising force of Labour, and his attitude to the Liberal party.

Scott was deeply concerned with these and other issues. He saw the submarine offensive as ground for urging the recall of Fisher—with whom, and about whom, he had many conversations. (It has not been thought necessary to reproduce most of them here). These availed nothing. The government was not prepared to take on Fisher in a dominant capacity, and could not see him functioning in a subordinate one. The fact that Jellicoe still addressed him as "Sir", as Fisher told Scott, clearly obviated the latter possibility.

Scott was happier in pressing, on Weizmann's behalf, for a definite statement by the government in favour of making Palestine a national home for the Jews. (Again the entries on the subject have been considerably pruned). Scott records that when Neil Primrose, the chief government Liberal whip, asked Lloyd George on 26 January 1917: "What about Palestine?", Lloyd George replied with a smile: "Oh! We must grab that; we have made a beginning."

The other issue which profoundly concerned Scott was Lloyd George's political intentions. On this matter Lloyd George offered him repeated assurances. They never quite allayed Scott's misgivings.

Diary, 26-30 January 1917

Lloyd George. Breakfasted Friday [26 January] with Lloyd George at No. 11 Downing Street. . . .

Speaking of the progress and prospects of the War he insisted strongly on the serious danger from the internal condition of Russia. Anything might happen. The murder of Rasputin by Prince Dimitri(?)[1] had had an extraordinary sequel. The Prince had been banished but the *whole* of the royal family—brothers and sisters and cousins and aunts—had petitioned for his recall. The Czar had absolutely refused in these words—"He is not the only assassin among you". This message of course dictated by the Czarina.

Whether the relation between Rasputin and the Czarina was an immoral one is matter for speculation just as the conduct of Marie Antoinette under a similar charge is matter of speculation. But there is no doubt as to the character of Rasputin or his extraordinary influence over the Czarina and through her over the Czar, a weak man in love with her and at times violently in love. Rasputin's influence partly superstitious, partly sexual (origin of his influence with Czarina that she believed him to have cured her son). The most amazing stories current of his relations with the great ladies of the Court one of which —in which 8 ladies of the Court were subject to a gross and indecent indignity in respect of Rasputin—Lloyd George repeated. When asked if this could be true Rasputin replied "Of course it is true: I did it to teach them humility as Christ did to the objectors against Mary Magdalene". It all recalls the 10th century rather than the 20th, but may have the gravest political consequences.

The Czar one day does the right thing; the next day under the Czarina's influence he undoes it. Rasputin was a pro-German reactionary and the Czarina is the same. She is mad at the murder of Rasputin. It is believed that the reactionaries are doing their utmost to stir up a revolution in order to make this an excuse for breaking the compact of London and making a separate peace. The Army leaders and the Duma—now working together!—are doing their utmost to prevent one.

If the feud is carried much further it may end in the assassination of the Emperor, in which case the Grand Duke Nicholas, now in the Caucasus—an able and open-minded man who knows how to choose able men to help him and whose word can be relied upon—would become either Regent to the young heir, or Emperor. It is believed that in the last resort, if there were any sign of a military revolt, the Court party would not scruple to call in the Germans to suppress it.

[1]Actually Prince Yusupov.

Henderson and Labour Party.[2] It had been said that he had made up to Henderson; on the contrary Henderson had come of his own motion to him (on the Thursday) and asked what he meant to do about the representation of Labour in the Ministry. Replied that when [the Asquith] Coalition was formed had advocated the inclusion of *two* representatives of Labour in Cabinet instead of one and intended now considerably to increase the representation of Labour in the Ministry.

Free Trade. Topic turned up several times in course of conversation. I told him it would be a serious matter if he abandoned it and would make an effective bar between him and the Liberal party of the future. He retorted that Free Trade had already been abandoned (a) in McKenna's budget which imposed import duties on manufactures without any countervailing excise, (b) at the Paris Economic Conference.[3] At the same time declared that, as he had often told me, he was determined to remain a Liberal and would not follow Chamberlain's example. The old hide-bound Liberalism was played out; the Newcastle programme [of 1891] had been realised. The task now was to build up the country. He held to all the essential principles of Liberalism and was most anxious to avoid a split in the party. Liberals in the country dreaded this—especially he was informed Scotch Liberals were keenly anxious to avoid it. When I said that if he wished to avoid a split he must stick to Free Trade he mocked at this, evidently regarding Free Trade as part of the played-out programme of a hide-bound Liberalism. . . .

Duration of the War. He evidently did not think we could get through either on the West or on the East this year, but thought that if Germany were well hammered this year and knew that we were prepared and able to continue the attack with undiminished force next year the German Generals might report that the game was up. Incidentally he said that he thought the Russians were holding up some $\frac{3}{4}$ of a million of the enemy with perhaps $\frac{1}{2}$ a million in reserve. The weight of the war must fall on the Allies in the West. . . .

The Asquith Controversy. All sorts of charges had been made against him in relation to his action towards Asquith which led up to the change of Government. Asked if I thought he should say anything about this in his speech at Carnarvon. He had a complete and documented defence. I strongly advised him to let the matter alone. People

[2] Henderson had been included as Labour representative in Lloyd George's five-man War Cabinet, along with the Conservatives Bonar Law, Curzon, and Milner.

[3] This conference of the Allies in mid-1916 had foreshadowed a high tariff policy after the war in the event of a stalemate peace.

were not bothering about it. If Asquith, who was to speak first, should touch on it (which I did not believe he would) he might of course then reply. He seemed on the whole to agree, though evidently hankering for the assault.

Went to see Garvin in the evening. He said Asquith had been misled by his friends who assured him that George could not form a Ministry. When asked what would happen if George failed "Then", he replied, smiting the table, "he will have to come back on my terms".[4]

Saw Weizmann in morning [of 27 January] about Palestine question. . . . Memorial was being prepared on whole question. Very important to obtain American Jews' support. It would be unanimous if they could be assured that in the event of a British occupation of Palestine the Zionist scheme would be considered favourably. Now was the moment for pressing the matter when British troops were actually on Palestinian soil.

Lord Haldane.[5] Lunched with him. . . .

Haldane spoke quite dispassionately of the extraordinary persecution to which he had been subjected. His life was threatened and he had been actually assaulted in the streets and even now had to be followed by detectives.

Sunday [28 January].

Lloyd George. Afterwards at Lloyd George's invitation motored with Mrs. Lloyd George from Downing Street to Walton Heath. We picked up Henderson on the way. Saw very little of [Lloyd George] alone as in addition to Henderson, Donald of the "Chronicle" (who seems to have composed his differences with Lloyd George) came over from his house close by and the Shipping Controller (Sir Joseph Maclay). . . .

Walking with Henderson in the garden we discussed the report (not yet published) of the Speaker's Committee [on electoral reform] of which Henderson was a member. Lloyd George said he had received it that day but had not yet read it through. He said the Government would introduce a Bill embodying the recommendations of the Report and then leave it to the decision of the House. The majority of the Committee advised enfranchisement of women over 30 or 35. Lord Robert Cecil, a great suffragist, had said on that that he did not care if

[4] Although similar views are attributed to Asquith by a number of sources, they all have him employing the same words (with different degrees of emphasis); which may suggest a common source.

[5] Haldane had been driven from office in May 1915 on account of his alleged pro-Germanism.

they only enfranchised women over 50 so that women were en-franchised. As to Proportional Representation Lloyd George said he would apply the principle all round or not at all. He had not, however, yet seen exactly what the Report recommended.

As to passing a Reform Bill now his difficulty was that if the Bill were carried he would be morally estopped from dissolving till it could come into operation which would take some time. . . . Question would arise shortly whether the Life of this Parliament should again be extended. Why not just let it lapse and get rid of Snowden, MacDonald and the other extremists[6] who derived undue importance in the eyes of neutral States from the fact of their being M.P.s? He should not hesitate to hold an election on the existing register, however imperfect; at least a House elected on it would be more representative than the existing one. Henderson rather cold-watered this suggestion. Very doubtful whether either Snowden or MacDonald would be defeated. Certainly no trade unionist would be found to stand against MacDonald. If returned after a contest their importance would be greatly increased and they might become a real difficulty in the House of Commons. George was more sanguine, but when I asked what about a possible conflict at the polls between Georgians and Asquithians admitted that that was a difficulty. Henderson said the situation would be quite different if conflict took place on a question of substance relating to the War and after a challenge. Then he could safely appeal to the country. . . .

Incidentally George said he was pleased with the results of most of his outside appointment to business men, but was rather disappointed with Neville Chamberlain.[7]

As I was saying good-bye to Mrs. George, she said "We think now that perhaps you were right in advising Mr. George to resign 18 months ago".

Carson. Saw him by appointment [on 29 January] at 10.30 at Admiralty. Deeply impressed by Submarine peril. Had been constantly at work at it ever since took office. For days after he first became acquainted with the facts could not sleep at nights for anxiety. The West Atlantic he was informed was swarming with submarines. It was not merely the torpedo but the mine that made the danger. Mine-laying submarines followed immediately in the wake of our mine-sweepers and undid their work. Had little doubt the Laurentic, just reported lost, had been sunk by mine at the entrance to Lough Swilly. Merchantmen difficult to control. Their captains often would not con-

[6]i.e. opponents of the war.
[7]Director of National Service, December 1916 to August 1917.

form to instructions and persisted in following their accustomed course. One had been sunk the other day 20 miles out of the course prescribed for it.

Immediately on taking office had established a special anti-submarine Committee of the Admiralty which met daily and included the best experts he could discover with an Admiral at the head of it. This ought to have been done 18 months ago.

I urged that Fisher should be appointed as head of this Committee. He said opinions differed strongly about Fisher. Personally was not in a position to judge. He liked what little he had seen of him and admired his force and energy. . . . I said public were becoming alarmed now that the losses were regularly published (he condemned the previous suppression) and if a remedy were not speedily found would insist on recall of Fisher. He agreed and said it would be better to anticipate that rather than that George should have his hand forced. It was a question for George and he should conform to his decision.

C.P.S. to Hobhouse, 4 February 1917 (Extract)

I thought I had done rather well about Fisher. George was favourable, as you know, and Fisher made a practical proposal—that he should be Chairman of the Submarine (destruction) Committee under Jellicoe— which would have given him just the position needed. Carson was quite willing if Lloyd George desired it. Now I hear from Fisher that Garvin persuaded him to unfold his plans—which are extensive and drastic— to Jellicoe and that Jellicoe shies furiously. It is a great mistake tactically, and means I fear that Fisher will now be installed only if Jellicoe fails signally, which would mean superseding Jellicoe.

17. *A Prime Minister and his Problems (II), February-March 1917*

In addition to problems of war and politics, Lloyd George had inherited an especially threatening situation in Ireland—although he was not himself guiltless in its being so.

Without a powerful government initiative the Irish problem admitted of no solution. Ulster was immovable in its refusal to come within the jurisdiction of a Dublin parliament, and was happy to sabotage Home Rule for south as well as north. And the Irish Nationalists, who had once spoken for southern Ireland in the British Parliament, now moved in a twilight world, uncertain of the allegiance of their "followers" and so unable to attract the attention—or even merit the deception—of British statesmen.

Yet the necessary initiative from the top was not forthcoming. Lloyd George had risked his neck once in seeking an Irish solution. He was not inclined to do it again—least of all now that Conservative support meant so much to him.

Diary, 26 February-1 March 1917

Went to London Sunday night [25 February] primarily to see Lloyd George about Irish question at Dillon's request. Found he had gone on Saturday to France. He returned late on Tuesday and I stayed on to see him.

Monday [26 February]. Saw Dillon in morning at his Club. . . .

The insurrectionary movement was steadily gaining strength and the younger men were leaving the constitutional party and going over to it. If nothing were now done to check this movement he was convinced that Ireland would have to move forward through more blood. The constitutional party had made their last effort in the Partition compromise and when they had almost ruined themselves for that it was thrown over. He personally had always been against it and did not believe they could have carried it in Ireland, but had supported it for the sake of party unity. When they did carry it and it was repudiated by the Government the people began to say they were powerless and that the Government just wiped their boots on them. This coming on the top of Carson's appointment first as Attorney General and now to an even more important position had gravely shaken their position. There was no feeling against Carson personally; the people rather admired him for his courage and success and repeated the old saying about the Battle of the Boyne "Change leaders and we'll fight you again". They meant to follow his example of relying on armed force.

Dillon was very bitter against Lloyd George for his share in this shabby transaction. In negotiation with him he (Dillon) had laid down 2 conditions before assenting to Partition compromise: (a) Irish members to remain in full numbers in Parliament—to which Carson agreed (b) guarantee that compromise, if accepted, should be put through. George replied that he would feel bound in honour to support it at all costs. The Cabinet had not formally sanctioned it, but he felt certain they would and if they did not he would resign and he believed Asquith would also resign. "Now", said Dillon to him, "we are getting to business". In spite of which, I remarked, he broke faith. "He did worse", said Dillon, "he not only broke faith, but he prevaricated. The excuse he made for himself was that he offered to resign, but Asquith would not accept his resignation!" (Lloyd George, when I saw him afterwards[,] put a slightly different complexion on this). Then came the Maxwell regime which ruined everything. "A bloody ruffian" said Dillon to George. "No a bloody ass" George replied.

The prospect now Dillon regarded as extremely menacing. The only chance he saw of avoiding fresh violence and worse disasters was to carry out a proposal to which [H. E.] Duke [the Irish Secretary] had assented, to appoint at once a Statutory Commission for the purpose of putting the Home Rule Act into force "with such modifications as the changed circumstances may demand", particularly in the matter of finance. The Nationalist party would take no responsibility for such a settlement and it would have to be adopted without further reference to Parliament or debate. It would at least prevent worse trouble.

In the evening dined with the Leverton Harrises[1] at Grosvenor Street to meet the American Ambassador [W. H. Page]—an able man with a great deal of American humour, simplicity and kindliness. Mrs. Harris said he was the only U.S. Ambassador whom the President entirely trusted. No other people at dinner except Dr. Page and his wife.

After the ladies had gone Dr. Page came over to talk to me and began with some very kind things about the Manchester Guardian and its recent American Supplement. Practically everybody who counted

[1]F. Leverton Harris was Parliamentary Secretary to the Ministry of Blockade.

in the States was familiar with the Manchester Guardian, not as a rule from seeing the paper itself, but because it was so largely quoted. . . .

The two great impediments to closer relations between Great Britain and the United States [were] (1) the Irish (2) the supercilious arrogance still remaining in a large part of our governing class. He expressed himself much more mildly and tentatively than that—aloofness, lack of sympathy and comprehension, stand offishness were more the sort of phrases he used. The full expression and concentration of it all rises to one's mind in the person of Curzon. The Irish exercised an influence out of all proportion to their numerical strength by playing on the divisions of domestic parties. They were the permanent difficulty. The Germans were only a temporary one. In the 3rd generation they were completely absorbed. . . .

Speaking very seriously and with premeditation he said that in his view England with her Dominions constituted one vast group of the English-speaking race, the United States the other. They were approximately equal in population, the States at present somewhat the larger, the British group possibly the larger in the future. They were alike in fundamentals and he looked forward to their acting as one in the future of the world. That was the thing that mattered. . . .

Lunched with Garvin [on 27 February]. He thought temper of Ulster had greatly hardened since the Dublin rising and in view of the subsequent growth of Sinn Fein and the present temper of Ireland which the Orangemen regarded as confirming all the evil they had ever thought. Impossible that they should now accept proposal for a Statutory Committee to put Home Rule at once into operation, even with such modifications and safeguards as the Committee might think needful. . . .

As to Fisher whose return to the Admiralty, in whatever position, he had ardently advocated, he now despaired.

Speaking of George's eccentric "War Cabinet" he said that of course Milner and Curzon were the only two, besides George himself, who counted, and of these Milner was by far the more useful and influential—a man of immense industry and personally very charming. As to Curzon he was really impossible to work with because of his incurable arrogance and opinionativeness. He was of course an able man and had given his proofs of that; also he was not a shallow man, but equally not a deep one; he saw a little way below the surface, but not a long way—into the second layer, but never into the third one—a specious man therefore, but an unsafe one. He told a good story of Lloyd George and Curzon. Curzon was receiving some distinguished person from, I think, one of the minor Allied nations. "He treated him", said Lloyd George, "exactly as if he had been a Basuto chief".

Wednesday [28 February]. Telephoned after breakfast to Lloyd George's secretary, T. H. Davies,[2] to ask when I could see George, who had returned from France late the previous evening. Replied asking me to come along at once. Found Lloyd George ready to go out and we walked round the Park. I spoke at once of the fresh Irish arrests. George said the Government had positive information of a fresh Sinn Fein conspiracy. That communications were going on with Germany and that arrangements were being made for 2 German ships to land arms on the West coast. There was to be a rising but conditionally on the landing of 10,000 German troops. The letter making this proposal had been intercepted; they were now awaiting with interest the German reply.

I asked what he thought of the proposal (of which I understood Duke, the Irish Secretary, was the author and which Redmond was prepared to accept) for appointing a statutory committee with full powers to put the Home Rule Act into force with such modifications as the changed conditions might be thought to demand, and he replied that "he was rather favourably inclined to it". But the moment was not propitious and he strongly urged that the debate on Ireland on O'Connor's motion, fixed for next week, should be postponed till after the Colonial Conference when—especially if Hughes[3] were here—a Home Rule atmosphere would prevail. . . . If he had to speak next week he might have to say something he had rather not say "and which would be irrevocable" viz. that Ulster had as much right to be governed in her own way as the rest of Ireland. I said I would tell Dillon what he said. . . .

I asked if he proposed to do anything in regard to the differential treatment of the Countess Markievicz, as compared with the other leaders of the [Easter] rising and who had now to choose between solitary confinement and association with the lowest female criminals and prostitutes whereas the other (male) leaders had been allowed to associate with each other. He clearly was not and merely remarked that he thought "a little solitary confinement would do her no harm".[4]

[2]Presumably a mistake for J. T. Davies.   [3]Billy Hughes, the Australian Prime Minister.
[4]The Countess Markievicz (born Constance Gore-Booth) was the product of an upper-class, Protestant, Anglo-Irish family, but became an ardent Sinn Fein rebel. She was sentenced to death for her part in the Easter Rebellion, but the sentence was commuted to imprisonment "on account of her sex". She did not accept Lloyd George's prescription of solitary confinement, however, and struck up a lively friendship in prison with an American female criminal known as Chicago May.

Afterwards saw Dillon at his club. He said it was quite impossible to postpone the debate. It would ruin their position in Ireland. . . . As to the plea put forward by George that Ulster had as good a right to be governed in her own way as the rest of Ireland that struck at the very root of the claim for Home Rule based on the ground that Ireland is a nation. . . . Moreover Ulster herself did not want a divided Ireland. She wanted a united Ireland but united on the existing basis and no other. To accept the position that Ireland was not a unity was to repudiate Home Rule.

The issue of strategy makes a brief but telling appearance in the following conversation between Lloyd George and a member of the Italian government. So does Lloyd George's inconstancy in dealing with it.

A month earlier Lloyd George had tried to persuade the Italians to launch an offensive, with British and French assistance, against the Austrians. He had failed. Hence he had fallen back on the policy of an offensive on the Western Front—to be conducted, however, not by the British generals he distrusted, but by the new French commander General Nivelle. Lloyd George even went to great lengths to place the British army under Nivelle's direction.

This was a classic example of Lloyd George's inability to keep means and ends separate. He had originally become hostile to Haig because the British commander was addicted to offensives in the west. Now he was encouraging a particularly inept western offensive so as to outmanoeuvre Haig. And in the interview that follows, the only comfort he has to offer his harassed Italian visitor is that an Allied offensive in France may relieve the danger to Italy—just as earlier it had been argued, against himself, that attacks on the Western Front might relieve pressure on Serbia and then Rumania.

Thursday [1 March].

Breakfast with Lloyd George to meet Signor Bissolati whom he described as Italian Minister for War, but I rather think he is Minister of Munitions. . . . This was evidently Bissolati's first interview with Lloyd George and it was a little out of the way that George should have invited me to be present. Bissolati had two main subjects to bring forward: (a) the grave impending menace of an Austro-German attack, (b) Italy's desperate need of coal. . . .

The Italian command had positive information of two great concentrations, one of Austrians on the Isonzo front, the other of Austro-Germans on the Trentino front. George asked for the sources of information. Bissolati replied it came from spies and prisoners—the usual sources. Bissolati anticipated an advance on the same line as last year's Austrian attack which had nearly succeeded. . . . and he begged for assistance in men and in guns. He read a letter—I did not catch from whom, but probably from the Italian Foreign Minister—pointing out the great *political* importance of our fighting side by side in the crisis of Italy's fate. Then even if defeat came Italy would never forget that we had stood by her and the tie between the two countries would be permanently strengthened.

George asked what was the earliest time at which the attack could take place. Bissolati said the winter had been unusually severe with an exceptional fall of snow and he did not think it possible the advance should take place earlier than the one of last year—i.e. in May. George replied that in any case the combined spring attack of the French and English armies must take place. If it succeeded the Germans would have no men to spare for an advance on Italy; if it failed we should at least have fulfilled our promise to the French and they would not complain; the combined attack in full force would have been made and we should be more free to dispose of our forces. He reminded Bissolati that when quite recently in Rome he had himself actually suggested giving assistance, but the offer had been coldly received.[5] Then it would have been easy to tell the French that Italy had asked for help and it had been promised. Now to detach troops on the eve of the attack in the West would look like desertion. Moreover the army had made up its mind now for the big attack. They said "here we have sat before this ditch for 2 years; now we mean to go over it". It was part of British doggedness. . . .

[5] The offer however had been one of support for an Italian *offensive*.

18. The Outsiders, March 1917

Scott's next visit to London produced an interesting conversation with Lloyd George in which the Prime Minister discussed war aims, incidentally revealing the strength of his feeling against Turkey. In addition, Scott had encounters with three prominent individuals now thrust out of office: Asquith (or more accurately his wife), Churchill, and Haldane. The third encounter proved considerably more peaceful than the other two.

Diary, 15-16 March 1917

To London by night (Wednesday) [14 March] on invitation from Lady Granard to meet Asquith at lunch [on the 15th]. . . . Lunched with Countess of Granard. Very friendly greeting from Asquith—also from Mrs. Asquith who stayed talking with me the whole time till we went in to lunch. She treated me rather like the wanderer returned—effusive but reproachful. "What do you think now (i.e. after the Government's breach with Lancashire on the Indian Import Duties) of your friend Northcliffe?" was almost her first deliverance. I said he was not at all my friend and I had only met him twice in my life. "Oh! but you worked with him. He got you to help him in his conspiracy". I could only reply that it might well happen that I sometimes agreed with Lord Northcliffe, though it was not often, but that if so it was not by any concert and that in fact I paid very little attention to Lord North-cliffe's proceedings. The explanation probably did not convince, but she wound up on a friendly note. "You must come to lunch with me next week—or the week after".[1]

Breakfasted [on 16 March] with Lloyd George (Sir William Robertson,[2] Chairman of Scottish Liberal Federation also present). . . .

[On war aims:] The destruction of the Turkish Empire was one of the great objects of the war. These objects were broadly three—(1) The destruction of militarism—i.e. of reactionary military govern-

[1]There is no record that Scott did.   [2]Not the military leader of the same name.

ment. (This had already come about in Russia as a direct result of the war and could not have been brought about in any other way. The same thing would happen in Germany). (2) The establishment of popular government as a basis of international peace. (3) The destruction of the barbarous domination of the Turk. This was in course of accomplishment. We were already at Gaza in the land of the Philistines which the Turks—appropriately—were defending. . . .

Robertson asked what about Ireland. Lloyd George replied that Carson was at present in a very accommodating temper. He was not easy in his mind as to the part he had played in the past and its consequences and was hard at work endeavouring to contrive a scheme. He himself could not go a step beyond Carson but, with Carson's backing, he could defeat any other opposition in the Cabinet, though he might have to shed one or two of its members. . . .

Lunched with Churchill. He could talk of nothing but Dardanelles Report and the forthcoming debate on it in the House. 4 dispatch boxes full of printed papers. Knew his way backwards through every line of them. Report curiously careless and inaccurate. Showed me several errors on which he would score heavily. The omissions in the censored Report were all to his disadvantage. Read me part of his speech for Tuesday. As I want to see him back as an effective force in political life which is not so rich in ability as to spare him asked him before leaving how he stood with George and what he thought of George's future. Said he thought George would follow in the path of Chamberlain. I agreed that there was danger of that especially because of his growing protectionism. "Oh! he is a thorough protectionist" said Churchill. . . .

[Churchill] added reflectively that he might have gone a long way with George if George had wanted him. I asked why George had not asked him to join his government. Churchill: "Oh! he professed that he had tried, but the Tories would not let him. He did not behave well to me". I asked if he might not join yet. Churchill: "Not in any subordinate capacity—only in one of the chief posts." "The War Office?" Churchill: "Yes, that would do very well". Derby[3] he added was no good. I gathered, however, that he had no expectation of any such opening and that his eyes were turned in quite another direction—as leader of a Liberal opposition.

Had tea with Haldane who takes the blows of fate in a much more philosophic spirit—bears no rancours and works hard to make himself useful in such ways as are still open to him in spite of the—as it seems to me—extremely unjust attacks from the Jingo press which have cut

[3]Now Secretary of State for War.

short his official career. Having read the account he had given me of his
diplomatic mission to Berlin [in 1912] and his War Office administration
I had come to the conclusion that he had honestly and efficiently striven
to prevent war and at the same time had, within the limits open to him,
effectively prepared for it, and that his reward was a signal example of
national ingratitude. I told him so. He smiled in his curiously impassive
way and remarked "There is a precedent (he quoted it but I have forgotten the name); only he was impeached". . . .

I asked if he still looked forward to taking his place in politics or
whether the law would claim him. He quoted with approval the saying
of another ex-Lord Chancellor that no man who had been Lord
Chancellor for 3 years would ever want to resume the office. He was
at present very busy with various kinds of war-work, as well as with
the problem of education. When his war-work was over he hoped to
devote himself entirely to education. . . .

19. Red Prelude, March 1917

At last, in March 1917, the Russian monarchy was overthrown. To Scott, this was "a wonderful and glorious event".[1] Lloyd George welcomed it also. The French Revolution was one of the periods of history which engrossed him, and like many others he was quick to draw analogies between 1917 and 1789-93. He hoped that the overthrow of the Romanovs, like the fall of the Bourbons, would replace a corrupt autocratic regime by a nation in arms hurling back the invader.

But Scott had misgivings about Lloyd George's attitude. Would the Prime Minister's Conservative companions allow him to remain sympathetic to the revolution? Scott saw it as his duty to keep Lloyd George up to the mark.

Diary, 17 March 1917

Went on Saturday afternoon to Walton Heath in order to introduce a young Russian, Vladimir Rosing . . . (a singer of European reputation, barrister, land-owner, ardent Radical-Socialist politician, married to an English wife) who was desperately anxious to see Lloyd George in connection with the great news just come of the Revolution in Russia. George kindly sent his official car and we came back in it along with Lord Reading who had been over to golf with George.

Rosing was eager to enlist George's sympathy with the liberation movement in Russia and to obtain a speedy and emphatic expression of British sympathy. We had tea on the veranda (it was a brilliant day) and George was most sympathetic. At tea he did most of the talking rejoicing in the great change and discoursing on the extreme difficulties he had encountered in his dealings with the fallen Government —how he had sent hundreds of big howitzers and they then demanded more and bigger, but never made use of the greater part of either consignment. And the same with motor waggons for transport. Those first sent were said to be too heavy for the roads and those sent afterwards were left to rust at Tsaritse Selo. A military officer was sent to

[1]C.P.S. to Hobhouse, 21 March 1917.

concert measures. With much trouble an agreement was reached. But as soon as the off.cer got back to Russia he was superseded and the agreement with him. It was impossible to help them. Now all would be different.

After tea we walked up and down the lawn for $\frac{1}{2}$ an hour Rosing with Lloyd George and I with the Lord Chief. Rosing did a good deal I think to kindle George's enthusiasm and he was eager for a warm response to be made from England to Russia's great stroke for liberty. He asked for (1) a prompt expression of sympathy from the House of Commons, (2) a deputation of Labour men to Russia (3) a much more effective British propaganda in Russia. George agreed to all three.

Rosing naturally was delighted and conceived an immense admiration for George.

The British government, in order to defeat the Turks, was rousing against them two powerful forces: the Arab peoples who were subject to Turkish overlordship, and the Zionists who saw in the Turkish-owned territory of Palestine their own national home. It is doubtful if anyone in the British government paused to ask whether, once the Turks had been expelled, the interests of Arabs and Jews would remain the same. This applied even to Sir Mark Sykes, the much-travelled Conservative M.P. who was chief adviser to the Foreign Office on Near Eastern policy, and who was both a champion of Arab independence and an ardent Zionist.

C. Weizmann to C.P.S., 20 March 1917

The Zionist negotiations with Sir Mark Sykes are entering upon their final stage. . . .

[A]lthough Sir Mark is very keen on the Zionist scheme I cannot help feeling that he considers it somewhat as an appendix to the bigger scheme with which he is dealing—the Arab Scheme. Of course I quite understand that the Arab position at present is much more important from the point of view of the immediate prosecution of the war than the Jewish question which requires rather a long view to appreciate its meaning, but it makes our work very difficult if in all the present negotiations with the Arabs the Jewish interests in Palestine are not well defined. . . .

I feel therefore that our negotiations must be placed very soon on a more definite practical basis and the plan I have outlined in my short letter to you before, namely, that I should accompany Sir Mark to the East, enter there into negotiations with the leading Arabs from

Palestine and see what can be done almost immediately in the way of acquisition of land in the Palestinian territory already occupied by the British. It is of the utmost importance that we should *be there* as soon as possible, that the Palestinian people and Jews at large should realise that we mean business and mean to carry it out at once. . . .

I have just this minute received your very kind letter. . . . Yes, the events in Russia are tremendous and it is certainly the very best thing which could have happened, let us hope that the situation will soon clear itself and not get out of the control of the provisional government.

C.P.S. to Hobhouse, 25 March 1917 (Extract)

Don't you feel the Russian revolution rather stirring in your bones and making the growing invasion of personal liberty here more intolerable? The coldness with which this tremendous movement of political and spiritual emancipation was received by a great portion of our press and society—bitterly felt by Russians resident here—seems to show how far we have drifted from the tradition of liberty.

I feel that perhaps we ourselves have not fought hard enough against the real persecution of the conscientious objector. See the enclosed touching letter from your cousin [the Quaker Stephen Hobhouse] sent me today by Lady Courtney (which please return).

20. *Some Liberal Causes, April 1917*

Scott was not slow to act on his own suggestion, just quoted, that he should be more active in defence of personal liberty. His next visit to London found him much occupied with issues like electoral reform, conscientious objectors, Ireland, Palestine, and a League of Nations. Some of these conversations cover familiar ground and do not need to be reprinted here; but it is worth noting that on every issue which he raised with Lloyd George, except for Palestine, he made little headway. Writing to Hobhouse just after this visit he called Lloyd George's proposals for Ireland "a bare makeshift to tide over the immediate difficulty and spare us the shame of a revolted Ireland at the moment of the Peace Conference." And he concluded the letter by raising the larger issue of individual freedom. (Clearly by this time Scott has retreated some way from that enthusiasm for state organisation of the whole resources of the nation which he had expressed two years earlier):

C.P.S. to Hobhouse, 9 April 1917 (Extract)

There is another matter it seems about time for us to tackle—the inordinate and seemingly unrestricted demands of the ⎰War Office and
⎱army
the threat of the extension of the compulsory principle to the whole life of the nation in industry. It would be better and more effective to make a stand *before* intolerable and suicidal demands are made than after. There are signs of revolt. See the report of the Clerks and Shopmen's Union in Leeds and Sugden's letter in today's Manchester Guardian.

Diary, 3 April 1917

Breakfasted with Lloyd George and had arranged for Weizmann also to come. Hoped we might have been alone, but Sir George Askwith[1] and

[1]Chairman of Government Arbitration Committee.

273

some ladies were also there and the inevitable Chief Justice looked in and carried off Lloyd George for a few minutes.

Lloyd George opened fire on me the moment we sat down on the subject of Proportional Representation. . . . Evidently his mind had hardened since he spoke on the subject in the House and said he had "no opinion" about it. He argued very strongly that it was "a device for defeating democracy"[,] the principle of which was that the majority should rule[,] and for bringing faddists of all kinds into Parliament and establishing groups and disintegrating parties—all the usual commonplaces; while he evidently did not realise that the single member system might easily—as it had already been known to do—give a majority of seats to a minority of voters the country over. I argued the matter and chaffed him about his autocratic tendencies, but it was pretty plain he would be quite definitely hostile.

We afterwards discussed the question of Palestine, he and Weizmann doing most of the talking. He said it was to him the one really interesting part of the war. Of the various possible solutions he said he was altogether opposed to a condominium with France, to which Weizmann was no less hostile. "What about International control?" he asked. Weizmann said that would be a shade worse as it would mean not control but mere confusion and intrigue. "What about joint control with America?" Weizmann said he could accept that. The two countries would pull together. "Yes", said George, "we are both thoroughly materialist peoples"—a remark, as I suggested, obviously dictated by the conscious superiority of the Celt.

Weizmann spoke of the great change which the Russian revolution had produced in the feeling of the Russian Jews in England. He was confident he could get a couple of thousand volunteers from among the 30,000 Russian Jews in London. . . .

Before leaving I raised the question of the Conscientious Objectors and suggested that, as those that were left had now given ample proof of their genuineness, there could be no object in further penalising them. George replied that he had no sympathy with men who when their fellow countrymen were in danger of starvation would not do work on the land to help to save them. So much he must exact, but he imposed no other condition. It looked to me like a possible way out.

His parting word was as usual cordial. "When shall you be in London again? Come to see me when you can just to keep me straight!"

After breakfast called on Bryce and arranged with him for the publication in Manchester Guardian of his scheme for a Peace League after the War. He and some others had been working at it for more than a year, but he had delayed publication till the prospect of peace seemed more hopeful. Now the coming in of America made the moment seem opportune[2]. . . .

[2]As a result of the resumption by Germany of unrestricted submarine warfare, President Wilson had asked Congress the day before for a declaration of war.

21. *Some Leading Conservatives, April 1917*

In the course of his next visit to London, Scott spent an uncharacteristic amount of time with prominent Conservatives. His conclusion seems to have been that Carson (as seen earlier) was considerably better than Liberals usually took him to be, that Milner was much as expected, and that Curzon if anything was rather worse.

On the other hand, there could be little doubt that Carson was the least effective of the trio as a minister. His rather nerveless handling of the naval danger was revealed in his dependence on his professional advisers, and perhaps it is not surprising that soon after the interview Lloyd George elevated him to another position.

One of the most illuminating parts of the discussion is Carson's account of how Lloyd George's war cabinet functioned, as seen by the head of an important department who was not a member of it.

Diary, 19-21 April 1917

To London Wednesday night [18 April]. Saw Weizmann in the morning and Carson afterwards. . . . [A]sked Carson as to submarine struggle. He was not encouraging. We were not destroying them more rapidly and no means of countering them had been found. People had urged adoption of system of convoys. They had tried it and convoyed 4 Norwegian ships by destroyers. Two were sunk. On the other hand, though they estimated the German output of submarines at 3 a week, he admitted that Fisher might be right in putting it at 5.

As illustrating the dangers of the submarine war he mentioned that Balfour on his way to America had been held up for 2 days before starting while a fresh passage had to be swept clear of mines laid by the submarines. Then the weather was such that the escorting destroyers had their bridges washed away. There were 3,000 Canadian women and children on board Balfour's ship.

Went on to speak of Irish question. He was prepared to do all he could to bring about a compromise, but there were very strict limits to his powers and the moment he went beyond them his people in Ulster would throw him over and choose another leader. As it was by going as far as he did with Lloyd George he had lost half his friends and would have to seek a new seat—in Belfast. The object of his policy was to bring North and South together, but it could only be done tentatively. What he should propose—he was of course speaking in confidence—was that the Home Rule Act should be brought into operation and certain counties, which he would call X, should be excluded with power to vote themselves in—he did not say whether by bare majorities or something more. [And] that the Members for the excluded counties should be constituted an Ulster Council with certain statutory powers viz: (1) to deal with all private bills in concert with the Irish Parliament (2) to apply to the excluded counties any legislation adopted by the Irish Parliament for the rest of Ireland. He thought this might be the beginning of a real cooperation.

He spoke very warmly of George as a War Minister and political leader and said that, if once the Irish question were "out of the way", he saw no reason why he should not permanently act with him (according to Garvin Carson is fundamentally a democrat).

I agreed as to George's qualities of courage, decision and prescience, but remarked on his lack of consecutiveness and power of organization and expressed doubts as to the working of the *War Cabinet*. Carson admitted that in the first instance the absence of collective control by a Cabinet of the heads of the great departments had led to confusion, but said that a system of control had been developed which was now working extremely well and was, for war purposes, incomparably better than the old Cabinet system, though he admitted that, after the war, we should have to go back to a Cabinet system, but the Cabinet should be much smaller—12 or 14. There was no justification for a Cabinet of nearly double that number.

To show me the working of the present War Cabinet he sent for (1) an Agenda paper, as circulated to all the principal heads of departments (2) a copy of the minutes taken at a meeting of the War Cabinet and also circulated to all the departments whom any part of the business transacted concerned. On the Agenda paper (of some 15 items) there was a rough time-table as an indication to the ministers and others concerned of the time when their presence *might* be required, though of course the indication was far from precise and, though the War Cabinet worked very hard (straight on from about 11.30 to about 7.30

277

daily) they could not depend on getting through the whole of the agenda. The persons notified to attend varied from 3 or 4 to about a dozen and generally included the head of more than one of the great departments as well as permanent officials or officers of the services and experts.

The minutes, which of course are not taken at all at Cabinets,[1] were very complete and circulated in print, so that it was apparent exactly what business and instructions had been given to any department concerned. The whole arrangement appeared to be effective and businesslike, but I remarked that it appeared to place the great officers of State in an extremely subordinate position. Carson did not altogether dispute this, but said that on the other hand it relieved them of unnecessary attendance and enabled them to get on with the work each of his own department far more efficiently, particularly having regard to the vast increase of public business owing to the war and to the constant multiplication of departments since the war.

Saw Weizmann [on 20 April] after breakfast at Nottingham Place and then called by appointment on Philip Kerr,[2] one of the new "liaison" officers domiciled in the "Garden Suburb" at 10 Downing Street. He is one of "Milner's kindergarten" and edits the "Round Table". . . .

To my surprise I found he was quite a good Liberal—a good Scotch Liberal, as he described himself. He was keen about the future of Lloyd George, whose defects he clearly recognised and was eager "to save his soul" for Liberalism. What George needed was "a rod of principle" to keep him straight which if somewhat lacking in him at present might be supplied if only he could be put in the right relations with real Liberals. Though not easily open to individual persuasion he was very sensitive to "atmosphere". The difficulty I remarked was to find the people to create the atmosphere. I looked in vain for them among the Liberal members of the late Government who the longer they remained in office the more rapidly they shed their Liberalism. He was constrained to admit the difficulty.

Met Milner by appointment (at his request) and had tea with him at his office in Whitehall Gardens. He was very agreeable, but somehow not impressive—struck one rather as an academic than as a man of

[1]Scott means cabinets of the sort that had existed until Lloyd George took power. He did not realise that even when this sort of cabinet was resumed the practice of keeping minutes would continue.

[2]Lloyd George's private secretary since 1916; before that much concerned in imperial (especially South African) affairs.

affairs. Spoke of himself as outside party—almost it would seem outside politics. . . .

We discussed Lloyd George and he did not dissent from my view of his qualities and defects. Spoke strongly of his merit as a War Minister, but when I said I feared he might be lost to Liberalism because he did not know the meaning of liberty he looked a little puzzled which perhaps was natural as he is in the same case himself. He enquired, in the true academic manner, what I thought of the popularity of the Government as to which he felt unable to form any opinion himself. I could say no more than that I could see no present desire to change it[,] there being no very available alternative and the Government having given the impression of far greater energy and resource in the prosecution of the war. But that on the other hand George's autocratic methods had gone far to alienate him from the Liberal party and still more from the vital forces of Labour. It was in this connection that we discussed Lloyd George and his future. . . .

Went on from Milner to see Curzon by appointment at his house—a gorgeous abode at 1 Carlton House terrace where in marble halls one was received and escorted by numerous flunkeys apparently of military age.

I had asked to see him about Persia, of whose independence he was a few years ago a courageous champion when Grey was giving it away on all hands to Russia. I thought that now that, under the Revolutionary Government, Russian pressure was withdrawn and all projects of expansion renounced there was at last a chance for Persia and that British policy should conform to the new conditions and become actively friendly and constructive. The moment I spoke of the change in Russian policy Curzon became rigid and sitting up in his chair proceeded to explain thus *"ex cathedra"* (speaking on end for I think a good half-hour) that it was a delusion to suppose there was any real change and quite unsafe to build upon it, that all the talk of the revolutionaries about peace and the rights of subject peoples would come to nothing, that the commanders and officials on the frontiers would go on just as before and that, for us, the only practical result of the revolution was a reduction of 50 per cent in the efficiency of the Russian armies and the probable great prolongation or loss of the war.

In proof of this view he said that as soon as the official declaration of disinterestedness in the prosecution of the war was published we had enquired as to the bearing of this on the question of Constantinople and on our pledge to make its surrender to Russia part of the terms of peace. Does it mean, we asked, that you renounce that object and that

279

our pledge is cancelled? "Oh! no, no," was the reply[,] "nothing of the sort. Impossible that we should surrender the object of our secular ambition." "What then is the meaning of the official declaration". "Oh! something had to be said to satisfy the revolutionists—that is all". Curzon did not explain who the "We" of this conversation are, but it could only be the Russian Embassy—that is the representatives of the old order, who profess adhesion to the new, but are really utterly opposed to it, as also it was obvious is Curzon. In fact, instead of welcoming the profound change—which he utterly failed to understand—in the whole spirit of Russian internal and external policy induced by the Revolution and its immense assistance to a sound British policy, he actually regretted it.

I gathered that an arrangement had been come to—Curzon let this out, though of course it is very secret—for the surrender of the whole "neutral zone" in Persia to British influence and its addition to the existing British zone, of whose total inadequacy Curzon spoke in strong terms.[3] This probably as part of the bargain about Constantinople and the division of spoils. It was evidently in consequence of this that General Sykes[4] had been dispatched with a considerable force from India and is now careering about the whole of Southern Persia. Curzon said expressly that this force had been sent in order "to balance the Russian Cossacks in the North".

In fact a nice little agreement had been made with the late Russian Government for the division of Persia between the two powers now friendly and for the consequent abolition of the neutral dividing zone, and it was plain that Curzon was much annoyed at the check given to this nice arrangement and intended to hang on to it as long as he could.

He had nothing whatever to say about Persian liberties, except that he gave it as a reason for not supporting the "Nationalists" that they were now all pro-German. When we became allies of the Russians they gave up all hope of help from us and said there was nothing to choose between us and them—apparently with very good reason.

The whole conversation was profoundly illuminating and unsatisfactory. And Milner and Curzon are now at the centre of power and the determiners of policy. . . .

He was very friendly and when I got up to leave escorted me with pomp to the door.

[3] The original convention between Britain and Russia in 1907 had divided Persia into three zones of influence: a Russian, a British, and (in between) a neutral zone.
[4] General Officer Commanding Southern Persia since March 1916 (when he had been sent in command of a column to restore order in south Persia).

22. Death of a Party, April-June 1917

Scott's visits to London at this time were dominated by the problem of Ireland. He had a number of other interesting interviews: with Churchill, still chafing at his exclusion from office; and with General Smuts, then establishing an international reputation. But the travail of the Irish Nationalist party was moving to a finale, and Scott could not view these events unmoved.

The Irish Nationalists were now without a raison d'être. *Their function had been to extract concessions from the British Parliament, through their voting power therein plus the sympathy of a section of British M.P.s. The newly-dominant forces in Ireland rejected these methods. They believed that Ireland must achieve self-government not by gift of Britain but by its own action—that is by asserting independence without regard to the attitudes or enactments of Westminster. Hence the Nationalists were functioning in a vacuum. In an attempt to keep up with Irish opinion, they had to raise their demands beyond the tolerance of British governments. But by continuing to make demands of British governments, they only furthered their alienation from Irish opinion.*

The North Roscommon by-election in February 1917, and the South Longford by-election on 10 May, revealed to what extent the Nationalists were losing their hold on Ireland; in both instances they lost seats to Sinn Fein. When the second of these results came in the Nationalist leader, John Redmond, was (with an almost fearful inappropriateness) trying to regain his shattered health by taking the waters at Bath.

Diary, 30 April-4 May 1917

To London Monday morning [30 April] at Lloyd George's request. He was, however, unable to see me till Wednesday morning. . . .

Saw Dillon in morning [of 1 May] at his Club. Very gloomy as to situation. No arrangement yet reached with Lloyd George. Lloyd George was "in a great stew" on the matter. Had sent for him and Devlin and O'Connor to come and see him last Sunday at Walton

281

Heath. He and Devlin had refused, but O'Connor went. O'Connor very sanguine as to result and George pressed again for interview. Finally sent word was coming to London himself and asked them to meet him at Downing Street. Dillon still refused (he holds that George played him false in the autumn negotiation and broke his pledges, so will hold no further negotiation) but Devlin very reluctantly went. Interview stormy. . . . No result.

The fact was that opinion in Ireland had greatly hardened. All the young forces were going over to Sinn Fein and the demand now was for Dominion Home Rule[,] and partition [of Ireland] in any shape was scouted. . . . There was at present in Ireland no real desire for [a settlement] among the rising forces. There was a sheer fighting spirit abroad largely unreflective and irresponsible which took the shape simply of antagonism to England. Ireland had never had the discipline of responsibility. The Home Rule Act had been hung up too long and enthusiasm for it had disappeared. The people were now saying they had only to hold out in order to get something much better. The Roscommon by-election[1] was very dangerous. The Sinn Feiners had lots of money and 50 motor cars. . . . If the Nationalists lost this election he did not see how they were to survive.

Breakfasted with Lloyd George [on 2 May]. Dr. Addison and Lord Devonport, the Food Controller, also came shortly after me.

Lloyd George at once opened fire as to our criticism of his Guildhall speech.[2] We made light of the extra million acres he had brought into cultivation. Why had the late Government not done it? We said they had labour difficulties. Had he not had labour difficulties greater a good deal than theirs. I suggested that he himself was largely responsible for the shortage—that even quite recently agricultural labourers had been demanded by the War Office. "And who stopped them from going?" he said. Then he went on to indicate that his policy of "all for the army" had been quite changed and that as to the latest demand of 500,000 more men by July his view was that, so far from this being the way to win the war, it was the way to lose it—almost the words used in the Manchester Guardian.

This was before the others came in. . . .

Talk general during breakfast. Directly after[,] George moved into the next room and took me apart to explain the Irish situation. Carson was his difficulty. Both he and Craig were personally quite ready to concede county option which would settle the whole business, but both said they would be denounced by their followers as traitors and

[1] Presumably an error for South Longford.   [2] On agricultural policy.

couldn't do it.[3] "I promised them", said Carson, "that I would see them through and I can't desert them". Bonar Law said that if Carson went out he must go out and that meant the complete break up of the Government. . . .

Lloyd George explained his plan to me in detail, partly after breakfast partly in subsequent conversations. It was

(1) Home Rule Act to be brought at once into operation.

(2) The "clean-cut" for the 6 counties provisionally.

(3) A Council for all Ireland consisting of

(a) the 16 members for the excluded counties

(b) a similar number to be appointed by the Dublin Parliament.

(4) This Council to have power to apply to the whole of Ireland any legislation within the competence of the Dublin Parliament on which both sides are agreed.

(5) Revision on generous terms of the financial clauses of the Home Rule Act (Lloyd George said there would be no difficulty here. The Unionists were not interested in the question of finance.)

(6) The Amending Bill, after 2nd reading, to be referred to a "Speaker's Committee" representing all parties in the House, with power completely to overhaul the Home Rule Act.

(7) The Settlement to be provisional for 5 years certain or 3 years after the end of the war.

(8) The full Irish representation to continue in the Imperial Parliament during this period in order to mark the provisional character of the settlement.

He asked me to see the Irish members and find if they were still obdurate. . . .

Devonport, evidently bored at the conversation, hoped we had settled the affairs of the nation. There was some talk about food control. George thought compulsory rationing inevitable, but the difficulty was to adjust it to the varying needs of manual and sedentary workers. Neither he nor Devonport—who did not at all impress me—could suggest a solution. . . .

Called after breakfast on O'Connor at his flat. He was conciliatory but had not much to say. Said his own position was intermediate between Dillon and Redmond. Redmond was desperately anxious to settle; he had leant too much towards England and had lost Ireland; Dillon on the other hand had lost England in order to hold Ireland. No doubt of the two his policy was best, but with skill both might be held.

[3] County option was resisted by Ulster because it would give to the south two counties with very large Protestant minorities (about 45% of the whole).

. . . Incidentally he mentioned that Lloyd George had admitted to him that it was a good thing we had *not* got conscription in Ireland and that its labour forces were free to produce food and ships.

Went to lunch at the Savoy with Smuts—a very charming person, perfectly simple, sincere and modest.[4] Like other South Africans he never forgets the part the Manchester Guardian played in the [Boer] War and the Settlement. He spoke of the time after the War when he was in England endeavouring to secure a settlement on the basis of responsible government. Campbell-Bannerman he said was the one man on whose support he felt he could absolutely rely. I asked about Churchill. Yes, he said, Churchill was good, but Campbell-Bannerman was like a rock. The other day he had told the Imperial War Conference (I think this was the body, but it was on an occasion of the kind) that whenever they were commemorating England's great men they must never forget to set up a statue to Campbell-Bannerman.

It was very noticeable how all through the conversation (I was with him for well over an hour at lunch and after; we took our place at a small table reserved for him in the middle of the big room, packed with people, where in ordinary officer's khaki, without a scrap of decoration —gold or red tab—he might have passed for the least distinguished of the soldiers present) he identified himself completely and naturally with Britain and British interests, always speaking of "us" in connection with any issue of war or policy and evidently thinking as well as speaking in terms of the larger unity to which he applies the term of Commonwealth rather than Empire. And this was made the more interesting and significant by the slightly foreign accent—rather like that of a Welshman—in which he spoke. Obviously a very big man, and I was interested to find, when I saw Asquith afterwards, how strongly he was impressed. . . .

After leaving Smuts saw Lloyd George for a few minutes at No. 10. He said he was not going to France till late that night (the papers all announced that he had already gone) and asked me to look in at 6 or 7 after I had seen some of the other Irishmen.

Then called on Carson at Admiralty. . . . still deeply depressed about submarine war.

[4]Smuts had fought against Britain in the Boer War, but then had participated in the settlement which made South Africa a self-governing dominion within the empire. At the time of this meeting with Scott he was representing the South African government (in which he was Minister of Defence) at the Imperial War Conference and in the Imperial War Cabinet. So inspiring were his speeches and his personality (at a time when inspiration was badly needed) that he was soon invited, while remaining a South African minister, to stay on in Britain as a member of Lloyd George's war cabinet.

Went on to the House and saw first Devlin and then Dillon alone in Redmond's room which they kindly cleared of numerous inhabitants for the purpose. Both held fast to "county option". I did not feel at liberty to expose George's full plan, but went as far as I could. They paid no attention to the Irish Council proposal, Dillon in particular treating it as irrelevant and mere "trimmings". . . .

On getting home and thinking the matter over I felt the full possibilities of the Irish Council scheme had certainly not been brought home to the Irishmen and that above all Redmond had not been and could not be adequately consulted, so I wrote George accordingly. . . .

After breakfast [on 3 May] called on Churchill at his request at his house. Found him in a state of almost frenzied excitement, walking up and down the room, cursing and swearing freely, at the news just published of the torpedoing of a British ship by a German aeroplane. The invention he said was ours and dated from 9 months before the war. He had taken it up warmly realizing its possibilities, but there had been some departmental obstruction. Still progress was made and soon after the war the thing was ready. By a miserable error, without any authority from him, it was used *once* at the Dardanelles to sink a Turkish transport. Thus for no adequate purpose the secret of a priceless invention was given away to the Germans who had now adapted and applied it. . . .

He could hardly bring himself to talk of anything else, till we drove away together to the War Office where he had an appointment, but I managed at last to get a little talk with him on the state of parties. He was evidently pleased with the results of his recent speeches in the House and said the tone of the House had altered and become very friendly to him. His tone was rather bitter in speaking of Lloyd George whom he had evidently come to consider as his destined antagonist. At the same time when I said I thought it a great pity that the political character of the ministry was so one-sided and that he with other Liberals ought to be in it he said he had had no personal quarrel with Lloyd George and was evidently quite ready for that solution. There is a sort of hungry look about him in these days and he evidently feels his political isolation bitterly.

Had intended returning to Manchester that day but felt that no stone must be left unturned in order, if by any means possible[,] to get a settlement of the Irish question, or at least an approach towards it which might ease the situation, and after some conversation with Hobhouse decided to see Asquith before going in order to see if George, in case he decided to put pressure on his Unionist colleagues, could depend on freedom from attack and, if needful, active support from the Liberal members of the late Government.

Saw Asquith by appointment [on 4 May] at his house in the morning. . . . Asquith, at first a little icy, thawed rapidly when he found I had something serious to say and aimed at conciliation. I did not feel at liberty to explain fully Lloyd George's policy and made it absolutely plain that I came to him solely on my own initiative. I told him that I understood that the scheme for which he and Lloyd George were responsible [in 1916] and to which Redmond and Carson had agreed but which the Unionists had rejected had now been accepted by them and something more besides but that the Irish leaders now refused it, and I asked him if he had any plan in mind which could help. He said Lloyd George "had not done him the honour to consult him either directly or indirectly on the subject" and that "I had now told him a great deal more than he knew before". I said it was not for me to convey information and that I thought it very wrong of George not to have approached him. I asked if he would be willing to meet George on the matter if George desired it and he said that certainly he would.

Then he went on to say that his own idea had been that there should be a conference of representatives of all the political parties—not of the Irish parties only—with Smuts to represent the Empire, to discuss the matter and see if an agreement could not be reached (very like Lloyd George's idea of a "Speaker's Conference"). On that I left him.

He came with me to the hall and stopped me for a minute or two there to speak of the position on the Western front. The recent French attack had he said been grossly mismanaged and was a failure. Nivelle had been practically superseded by the appointment of Pétain to the French War Office, and his policy reversed.[5] Pétain's policy was "to stick his toes tight in the mud"—that is to put the French army practically on the defensive. "That", said Asquith, "might be quite right[']. But if so the French must take on again the part of the line which we had recently taken over from them. We had five armies actively engaged and none in reserve. That was a very dangerous position, as Smuts had urged. He did not mean to say there were no reserves for drafts and the like, but no large organized reserve. Incidentally he spoke in the highest terms of Smuts, who he said was a man of first-rate ability, head and shoulders above the rest of the Dominions representatives, of whom evidently he thought very little.

I don't know whether this little incident was intended as an ex-

[5]Following the collapse of the Nivelle offensive (amidst severe mutinies in the French army), Pétain was appointed General-in-Chief of the French forces in Nivelle's stead.

pression of friendliness and a sort of return of information for that which I had given, but his manner was certainly very friendly—for him almost cordial.

The reason for Asquith's initial iciness towards Scott can perhaps be deduced from the following letter, written by the Liberal academic Gilbert Murray who was a strong supporter of Asquith.

Gilbert Murray to C.P.S., 5 May 1917[6]

Before making up my mind, with pain and reluctance, to give up a paper which I have taken in and admired for over twenty years, I think I ought to send you a line of remonstrance about your constant cavils and sneers at Mr. Asquith.

    Liberalism is very much down in the world now. And you have your share in the responsibility for that fact. You doubtless approve of the present government, at any rate in the present circumstances.

    I do not complain of that. I have never yet attacked Lloyd George and I do not wish to throw away any element of possible strength to liberal causes in the future. . . . I want to keep Liberalism together, and with that purpose in view to soothe down the natural indignation felt by most Liberals against the people who intrigued Mr. Asquith and all the other Liberal leaders but one out of power. I believe it is possible to keep some sort of peace and preserve some sort of unity among liberals, but only on certain conditions. And one of them is that the successful Georgites do not go on sneering at those whom they have turned out. Another is that they and their leader do not fall entirely under the sway of their anti-Liberal supporters and colleagues.—But, to do the Guardian justice, it has in the main been alive to this second point.

    [P.S.] I do not argue the question of Mr. Asquith's merits as a leader because on that point we should not agree. I merely wish you to realize that the tone of your leading articles and London letter sometimes puts an almost intolerable strain on the patience of many who are accustomed to regard themselves as good Liberals and admirers of the Manchester Guardian.

C.P.S. to Gilbert Murray, 6 May 1917[7]

I have so great an admiration for your work and for all I have known of

[6]Gilbert Murray Papers.   [7]Gilbert Murray Papers.

your public attitude that your letter distresses as well as surprises me. It would be a real help if you would point out to me some of the passages in our leading articles and London Letter to whose tone you so strongly object. . . . We have, of course, never had the smallest desire either to sneer or to cavil, and if anything written in the paper can bear that interpretation I should be glad to have it pointed out.

Scott was back in London on 8 May, still seeking for an Irish settlement. He breakfasted with Lloyd George on the 9th, but Sir S. Sinha, one of the Indian representatives at the Imperial War Cabinet, was present and the talk was mainly about Indian reform. On this matter, Lloyd George was firm that the ultimate aim must be dominion status: "India must be regarded as 'a partner' in the Imperial Commonwealth and everything must work up towards that. Englishmen must get it into their heads that Indians were not just 'natives' to be governed, but members of 'a more ancient and in some respects a finer civilisation', with a religion of their own worthy of all respect." As for immediate reforms, Lloyd George proposed to set up a commission at once to consider the whole question. "Sinha spoke of the danger of delay in introducing reforms. 'It might be the same for you in India as in Ireland if you wait too long.'"

After breakfast Scott had a few words with Lloyd George on Ireland, urging him to contact Redmond. Lloyd George "said he knew nothing as to how Redmond was or where he was".

The next day, 10 May, Scott told Lloyd George of his encounter with Asquith, relating Asquith's "placable disposition" and readiness to meet the Prime Minister. Lloyd George said "he would gladly meet him either alone or with Bonar Law on his side and anyone Asquith liked to bring on the other" — which sounds as though Lloyd George saw meetings with Asquith as formal negotiations between rival powers. Scott succeeded in convincing him that a meeting à deux would be "much more unconstrained and fruitful", and E. S. Montagu's residence was thought of as a meeting place. Scott's narrative continues:

Diary, 10-11 May 1917

I then went to Asquith's house in Cavendish Square and told him what Lloyd George proposed and asked him if he would meet him as suggested. He was a little stiff in manner, but said at once that he would do so "if George wished it. But the approach must come from him". I said George did wish it.

Went back to Lloyd George after lunch and reported Asquith's acceptance and specifically of their meeting at Montagu's. Lloyd George

said he would write at once to Montagu and arrange a day. . . . I said I
found that Redmond was at Bath taking the waters (Dore had ascer-
tained this) and asked if he would like me to see him. He said he very
much would and that I should place the whole plan before him, including an increased subvention and larger fiscal autonomy. . . .

Got to Bath about 5 and went to Pump Room Hotel where by good
luck I found Redmond was staying. Sent up a note to Redmond to say
I should like much to see him and he came down to the lounge before
dinner and talked to me for about half-an-hour. Met again after dinner,
but his wife and a friend were there so there was only polite conversation. He asked me to meet him at the pump room next day [11 May]
and we went on from there to a quiet place in the public garden and
walked there for over an hour.

On both occasions he was emphatic in his rejection of the "Irish
Council" scheme and would hardly listen to my explanation of it. I
told him of George's readiness to make liberal financial arrangements—
for education among other things. He had got the impression through
Devlin that the Ulster section of the Council were to have the spending
of the money for education which he said would not be for a moment
tolerated by the Bishops. I said I had not at all understood that the
Council were to have any administrative powers. . . . But his mind
evidently was closed on the whole project. His view was that the proper
method of accommodation with Ulster was to include it under the
operation of the Home Rule Act and then to give to Ulster a majority
in the Senate. So far as he was concerned they might have the whole
Senate. I remarked that the Senate would have no veto on Finance,
which was the matter about which Ulster was most afraid. He said that
was so, but he would even give the Irish Senate powers over finance.
There was almost nothing he would not concede for the sake of conciliation and unity.

The news of the result of the South Longford election had come in
just before I arrived on Thursday afternoon [i.e. the 10th]. Redmond
was of course deeply concerned. It was a direct challenge to the
authority and representative character of the Nationalist party. The
letter of Archbishop Walsh published on the evening before the poll
and placarded everywhere after there was no time to answer it was a
stab in the back which had no doubt turned the scale, but quite apart
from that the result was serious enough. It had been hitherto a solidly
Nationalist constituency, they had the Bishop on their side and nearly
all the priests, the town of Longford had been an active recruiting
centre and the wives and mothers of the enlisted men went about wav-

ing both the Irish flag and the Union Jack and cheering for the Khaki, and they had "a fierce mob" too on their side which broke the Sinn Feiners' heads with bottles—and yet they could not win! The election was turned by the voters in the country districts. There the young men had all gone over to Sinn Fein and they took their fathers to the poll and threatened that if they did not vote for the Sinn Feiner they would not work for them.

The Nationalist party would now have seriously to reconsider its whole position. After such a blow they could not sit down and wait to be shot at. Some decisive action must be taken. He thought they would have to resign their seats in a body and either challenge re-election or else simply retire from political life and leave Sinn Fein and the British Government face to face. Then perhaps both Ireland and the Government would discover what they had lost. . . . Ireland must be brought to her bearings and compelled to make her choice between constitutional methods and revolutionary. He had asked Dillon and Devlin to come to see him on Sunday when he should consider with them the whole situation. He himself should return to London on Tuesday.

As to the Government their best plan was to mark time. Duke had had a scheme for appointing a strong non-partizan committee . . . with instructions to draw up a *modus vivendi* and to put it in force, a committee of five to arbitrate on any doubtful points. The scheme was well worth reviving. Here for George "lay the path of safety". He begged me to assure Lloyd George that he had no sort of personal animus against him. . . . On the contrary he liked Lloyd George. "Give him my love" he said.

The true policy for Ireland he said was Dominion Government, or something like it, for the whole of Ireland with a subordinate assembly, on the Canadian model[,] for Ulster, taking the whole province, and for Munster too if she wanted it. But when he suggested this the Bishops were irreconcileably opposed. They feared for their appointments—"jobs" was I think the word he used, i.e. patronage. I remarked that a Dominion status would imply control of military forces and power to impose duties. He said this was so, but they made no claim to the first and though the second ought in principle to belong to them, it was not really a practical question, because for Ireland to enter on a tariff war with Great Britain would be suicide.

He spoke with deep regret of the failure of his policy of active co-operation of Ireland in the war as a means of national reconciliation. The crass stupidity and obstruction of the military authorities and their refusal to allow Irish patriotism to be in any way appealed to had gone far to destroy the movement at first full of promise, but even so it might have succeeded if the war had lasted only a year. After that hope failed. Then came the rebellion and a complete change of sentiment as a result of the executions. . . .

Returned to London by afternoon train and saw Lloyd George before dinner. Explained Redmond's view of the situation and conveyed his suggestion of a non-partizan Committee. George rather liked this but said it would be impossible to give it the final decision. Asked me to come up again next week and I said of course I would if it would be any use. Gave him Redmond's personal message which pleased him a good deal. . . .

Scott was soon back in London on Irish business. He found that, even in terms of personalities, no progress was being made. Redmond might continue to feel respect for Lloyd George, but his chief lieutenant did not: the following passage relates one of the rare encounters between Dillon and the Prime Minister. Equally the conference which Scott had arranged between Lloyd George and Asquith had borne no fruit.

Incidentally, Scott's initial dating which follows—"Monday, May 15"—is in error. Probably he boarded the train to London on Monday evening, 14 May, and conducted the interviews on Tuesday the 15th.

Diary, 15 May 1917

Monday May 15. To London by night in response to Lloyd George's suggestion that I should see his letter to Redmond before the draft was finally settled.

Called in morning on Dillon. He said position in Ireland "perfectly devilish". Nationalists could not answer for the country; nobody could. If the Sinn Feiners found a capable leader "they would wipe the floor with us". He said he had met Lloyd George the other day behind the Speaker's chair and said to him "Well you have destroyed the Parliamentary party, as I told you you would". Lloyd George: "That's a bad thing for the Empire". Dillon: "Yes; damned bad" and on that we parted. (Lloyd George afterwards referred to an unpleasant passage he had had with Dillon—evidently this one—, as significant of his cross-grained and unfriendly attitude). . . .

Lloyd George occupied all day with almost continuous War Cabinet. Saw him for a few minutes in late afternoon. Asked at once "What about Asquith? Was he any good?" "Oh!" said George, "he's perfectly sterile". Had no suggestion of any sort to make beyond the impracticable one of referring the question of the government of Ireland to a Conference of Colonial premiers. I told him they had one and all declined, none of them caring to embroil themselves with their Orange constituents,[8] except Smuts who could not take on the task alone, but he still went on mumbling about it. He always was barren of suggestion, but doubly so now.

On the substantive question which George tentatively approached of whether, in case of need and if pressure had to be put on one or other of the Irish parties in order to impose a settlement[,] George could look for support from the Liberal Opposition Asquith was entirely unresponsive. Evidently the interview at Montagu's house had been very unfruitful. George did not conceal his disgust and said Montagu had also been struck with Asquith's total failure to give any help or suggestion. . . .

The rest of Scott's time in London was spent hammering out with Lloyd George the proposed letter to Redmond, and discussing it with the Irish leaders. The letter began by setting out the government's proposals for Ireland (as out-lined by Lloyd George in conversation earlier—see above p. 283). If these were not acceptable, it suggested the summoning of a Convention of all Irish parties. north and south, to seek an agreed solution. The Convention proposal was taken up eagerly by Redmond, and Lloyd George was "immensely pleased and ex-cited" at the prospect. Yet in the end, after lengthy sessions, the scheme proved barren. The divisions in Ireland were too deep for Irishmen—under no compulsion from Britain—to agree.

This was a particularly happy phase for Scott in his relations with Lloyd George, for he believed that he had got the Prime Minister moving towards an Irish solution—and Lloyd George was outspokenly grateful for his assistance. But in view of the negligible outcome of their endeavours, it has not been thought necessary to reproduce Scott's long and detailed account of these events.

C.P.S. to Hobhouse, 27 May 1917 (Extract)

Would you like to see my two last lots of notes? I can't remember if you have seen the first, so I send both.

I keep vowing to go no more to London, which plays the devil with my work, but it has been difficult lately to keep out.

I enclose a friendly letter too from Gilbert Murray.[9] He had little it

[8]That is, extreme Protestant supporters of Ulster.
[9]This does not seem to have survived.

seems to complain of. Strange that he should have made such a song.

The fundamental difference in our positions is that he believes in Asquith and is a good party Liberal and I don't and rejoice to see the Liberal party leaders on the way to be purged by a little adversity. Shall we ever want to see them back in power again?

Diary, 21 June 1917

To London for meeting of "Propaganda Committee" on Thursday morning. Appointed by Lloyd George to control [John] Buchan[10] and his whole rather extensive department of war propaganda in neutral, allied and enemy countries. This was its second meeting. Members Lord Northcliffe (in his absence in America Lord Beaverbrook)[,] Lord Burnham,[11] Donald of the "Chronicle" and myself.

Went to the House and had a long talk with Dillon. He said Redmond was in Ireland and very much broken. His brother's death[12] following on the break-down from which he had only partly recovered, the result of many years of anxiety and overwork (especially during the past 2 years) had prostrated him. His doctor prescribed 6 months complete rest, without even letters; and his wife wished him to retire altogether from political life. . . .

[10]Director of Information under the Prime Minister.
[11]Managing proprietor of the *Daily Telegraph*.
[12]Redmond's brother William had been killed in action in Flanders.

23. Stockholm, June-August 1917

In mid-1917 Lloyd George made a number of controversial appointments. In June he sent Lord Northcliffe on a special mission to the U.S.A. And in July he brought two wandering Liberals into his government: E. S. Montagu, who had regretted at length his failure to join the new ministry the previous December, and who now became Secretary of State for India; and Churchill, whose hunger for office was at last appeased when he became Minister of Munitions. Northcliffe's appointment was widely deplored; and the elevation of the other two was unpopular with Conservatives (and with many Liberals).

At the same time the government sustained a heavy self-inflicted loss. In Auggst Arthur Henderson was obliged to resign. He had been brought into the war cabinet purely as a representative of Labour. He now found the roles of cabinet minister and Labour spokesman incompatible. His resignation constituted (despite continued Labour representation in the government) a long step in Lloyd George's alienation from the Labour party.

What caused the breach was the deteriorating situation in Russia. A constitutional government, now under the leadership of Kerensky, was still in existence. But central authority was collapsing in Russia, power in the cities was passing to the "soviets", and the expected military revival had not occurred. Henderson, having spent June 1917 in Russia, had first-hand knowledge of the situation and was gloomy about the prospect. Lloyd George placed greater reliance on the optimistic reports of C. Nabokoff, the ill-informed Russian chargé d'affaires in London.

What brought Henderson's differences with the rest of the war cabinet to a head was a proposal to hold an international socialist conference in Stockholm. The proposal came from the Russian socialists (especially the Petrograd soviet); the object was for socialists of all nations—including the warring nations—to confer on war aims. Initially Lloyd George approved of the idea, believing that British delegates must attend to keep the Russian representatives out of the German embrace. But in June and July the Russian war effort finally collapsed, and with it went his enthusiasm for the revolutionary spirit in general and for Russian socialists in particular. He turned against the Stockholm conference, alleging that the newly-formed Kerensky government in Russia was hostile to it.

This brought Lloyd George into line with the three Conservative members of the war cabinet (Bonar Law, Curzon, and Milner), who did not believe that British socialists should confer with their German counterparts in mid-war, and who anyway deplored everything that had happened in Russia since March. But Henderson remained immovable in support of the conference. He believed that if Russia was to be kept in the war, Britain must preserve its links with the Russian socialists (even at the cost of meeting German socialists as well). But clearly he was getting into deep water by his attitude. The more "patriotic" elements in the Labour party looked askance at the Stockholm proposal, whereas the anti-war section supported it whole-heartedly—not because they wanted to keep Russia in the war, but because they saw the Stockholm meeting as a step towards closing down the war altogether. For a cabinet minister to align himself with this section on any issue seemed highly anomalous.

The Labour party called a conference for 10 August to decide for or against Stockholm. Henderson made it clear that he intended to speak in support of the proposal. This brought him into sharp conflict with the Conservative members of the war cabinet on 26 July, while Lloyd George was absent in Paris, and with the Prime Minister on his return. Ultimately it caused Lloyd George to dismiss Henderson.

At the Labour assembly, Henderson not only argued strongly for sending delegates to Stockholm, but refrained from reading out (as he had been asked to do by Lloyd George) a message from the Russian government apparently dissociating itself from the proposed conference. Lloyd George thereupon demanded his resignation. Scott had actually been present when Lloyd George received the Russian government's message, and initially he accepted the Premier's view that Henderson had acted badly in concealing what seemed to be a clear decision against the conference by Kerensky. Later, as more information became available, Scott came round to Henderson's view that this was not the case: that the message owed more to Nabokoff's inspiration than to any decision by the Russian government, and so deserved no more attention than Henderson had given it.

Diary, 27-28 June 1917

To London for Propaganda Committee and to see Lloyd George. Lloyd George at Walton Heath recovering from neuralgia and preparing Glasgow speech. (Mrs. George told me that for the first time in his life he was bothered with head-ache and she didn't like it). Dined with him at No. 10 just before he started—a frugal meal of beans and bacon. Milner came in in the middle of it and carried him off for some last words, so there wasn't much time to talk.

I told him my allegiance had been severely shaken by his appointment of Lord Northcliffe[,] but he defended himself with vigour partly on the plea that Dr. Page when consulted had welcomed the proposal "enthusiastically", partly and quite frankly on the ground—which obviously was the determining motive—that it was essential to get rid of him. He had become so "jumpy" as to be really a public danger and it was necessary to "harness" him in order to find occupation for his superfluous energies. I had to do this, said Lloyd George[,] "if I was to avoid a public quarrel with him". . . .

On Thursday [28 June] saw . . . [Michael] Farbman[1] on his return from Russia. He dwelt on (1) the growth in the power of the extremist socialists owing to mistrust of the war aims of the allies and which if it continued would result in civil war (2) the desperate economic situation produced by the immense depreciation of the paper currency—this was rapidly becoming worthless, the peasants therefore refused to part with produce for payment in paper and there was thus danger of famine in the midst of plenty, (3) the worn-out condition of the railways and rolling stock which aggravated this and was rapidly destroying the means of communication.

Diary, 9-11 August 1917

Went up Thursday morning [9 August] and saw McKenna. . . . Discussing the political situation he said Tories were finding out that they could not trust Lloyd George. "We all felt that". He denounced the policy of the 9d. [subsidised] loaf. The £40,000,000 it would cost would be raised by further inflation of the currency which would mean a further depreciation in its purchasing power. Thus what the purchaser gained at one point he would lose at all others. (This would of course not be the case if the money were raised by taxation, but he did not contemplate that). Said he had always regarded the 5/- income-tax as a maximum. If we went much beyond that the additional tax would become unproductive by destroying capital and depressing industry.

[Scott then called on Robert Donald on a matter concerning the Propaganda Committee. Also present was Lord Beaverbrook, proprietor of the *Daily Express* and a devoted adherent of Bonar Law.]

Leaving with Beaverbrook he told me that he was the first to inform Bonar Law of Churchill's appointment as Minister of Munitions, a curious commentary on Lloyd George's methods. He also mentioned

[1]Occasional special correspondent for the *Manchester Guardian* in Russia.

that he owns a majority of the shares of the "Express", which is regarded as Bonar Law's organ.

Calling afterwards at Downing Street to get appointment with Lloyd George I ran across Curzon at the door. He spoke of changed attitude of Russian Government as to Stockholm Conference which it no longer desired. I said if this were really so it of course made all the difference (but I did not quite believe him). . . .

Breakfasted with Lloyd George [on 10 August]. Montagu also there. Discussing Stockholm Conference and meeting that day of Labour Conference to decide whether it would send representatives he said both he and Bonar Law were originally in favour of British Labour being represented at the Conference in order to comply as far as possible with the wishes of the Russian Government, at that time dominated by the "Soviet"—Soldiers and Workmen's Committee. But Soviet was no longer dominant and Kerensky now regarded the Conference as a distraction and a hindrance. (This corresponded with Curzon's statement and no doubt represented information of Foreign Office). If it met in September that was just the time when Russia ought to be making her great military effort and it would be disastrous for the soldiers then to say "no, we won't fight; we'll wait to see what comes of the Stockholm Conference".

In confirmation of this and as we were talking a despatch was brought in from Nabokoff, the Russian *Chargé d'Affaires*, conveying a telegram just received from his Government to say that the present Russian Government "disinterested itself"—i.e. in diplomatic jargon "wiped its hands of"—the Conference which expressed the policy not of the Government but only of a party. George gave instructions that this should at once be communicated to Henderson and—as he afterwards told me—requested him to read the material part to the Labour Conference.

Incidentally—and with significant emphasis—he said to me "You must give up hope of peace this year". We had hoped that, with combined pressure on all fronts, it might be possible; it is no longer possible.

Then he went on to enlarge on the stupidity of the soldier, obviously including Haig. All the men who had made reputations in the War were civilians or civilian-trained. Beginning, I said, with Geddes who saved the situation for Haig.[2] Yes, he said, and yet "that strange creature Northcliffe" assailed me furiously for bringing Geddes in, and for many weeks I never saw or spoke to him. In fact till 48 hours

[2] See above, pp. 236-237.

before the change of Government I had no communication with him. Then, seeing what was impending[,] he came to me. And yet people say that I conspired with him to upset the Government or that he used me to upset the Government. Yes, said Montagu[,] that is his way; he gets word of something that is going to happen, writes it up and then claims that he did it. . . .

"What", George asked of Montagu, "is the attitude of your late Liberal colleagues towards you since you joined the Government?" "Absolutely cold", Montagu replied; ["]they don't speak to me. One might have supposed that when a Liberal with a progressive policy took the place of a rather hide-bound Conservative [i.e. Austen Chamberlain] in a very important office, they would have been pleased. But not at all. They regard me as a deserter and accuse me of ingratitude. They say that 'Asquith made me' and that is true and I like and admire him, but is that any reason why I should not try to serve the nation?" "I shall never forget it" he murmured bitterly.

"Yes", said Lloyd George, "their view of a Government is as a sort of family concern in which they hold the shares and McKenna is General Manager. That is what Liberalism means to them. What else do they now stand for? What else does Liberalism mean for them?" I said that at least it might be supposed to mean Free Trade. But that he said was given away in McKenna's Budget. The departure may have been small in itself, but it gave away the whole principle. I said that of late they had spent their time in giving away Liberal principles and that if in the providence of God Lloyd George had turned them out a year sooner it would have been better for Liberalism. . . .

Called on George at breakfast time [on 11 August] on the chance of seeing him in order to get an explanation of the extraordinary Henderson episode of the previous day. Nabokoff, the Russian *Chargé d'Affaires*[,] had just arrived and was breakfasting with him. George asked me to wait a few minutes and then asked me to join them.

He was furious with Henderson for going back, as he alleged, on his word to the Cabinet. I represented that Henderson was one of the most muddle-headed of men and that a good deal might be set down to that, but he would hear of no excuse. He again showed me M. Nabokoff's letter which he had read out at breakfast on the previous day. This he said he had at once sent across to Henderson and had requested him to read the material part to the meeting. This Henderson had failed to do. I admitted that there could be no excuse for that. George said he had seen him on the previous day and had charged him with having deceived his Chief, his colleagues and the Conference and this after he, Lloyd George, had just defended him in the House at serious risk to his Government for having gone to Paris with Ramsay Mac-Donald without previously communicating with himself and obtaining his sanction. It was something very like treachery. He was convinced that Henderson's procedure was quite deliberate, that it was a piece of boorish ("pot house" I think was the word he used) trickery such as a half-baked workman might plume himself upon and chuckle at his own cleverness.

There was something not quite dignified in his own exasperation.

He was convinced that if the despatch had been read it would have greatly affected the decision. He showed me a telegram sent by Kerensky to M. Thomas in which it was stated definitely that the Russian Government now desire (souaient[3]) that the Stockholm Conference should not take place.[4] This, which would have clinched the matter, arrived unfortunately just too late for the Labour Conference. In the Nabokoff despatch it was merely stated that the Russian Government wrote off (disinterested itself [from]) the Stockholm Conference, but as Nabokoff now explained it could not stop it because the 4 Russian delegates had already left (two of them being members of the deputation now in this country—whom Nabokoff had refused to see).[5]

Nabokoff, whose English is in every way perfect, spoke with ardour and animation on the absolute necessity of effective military action in Russia in order to save the "honour" of the country. I remarked that its safety also might be imperilled if Riga, Kieff, Odessa fell as seemed not impossible. He said Moscow was burnt in order to defeat Napoleon; "I would gladly see Petrograd drowned—drowned in blood"—to defeat the Germans. But he refused to anticipate disaster. There would, he was convinced, be a great uprising of Russian patriotism so soon as the soil of Russia—the "sacred soil", as the people called it—was invaded. I took him for a man essentially of the old diplomatic school, though no doubt serving the Governments of the day honestly.

What sort of a man asked Lloyd George is Kerensky—an idealist is he not with a genius for action? Nabokoff assented. I asked the same question the other day, George continued, when I was in Paris—was

---

[3]Presumably the word was "souhaitent".

[4]Kerensky a few days later denied having sent such a telegram.

[5]What Nabokoff failed to point out was that the Russian government had only sent its message because of an urgent request from himself that it should do so. Did he act on his own initiative, one feels driven to ask, when he sent this request to the Russian government?

he an Asquith, or a Thomas or a Sonnino, or what was he? The answer, after a moment's reflection, was "He is none of these things; he is a St. Just". Not quite, said another of the company, for St. Just set up the guillotine. Well replied Lloyd George Kerensky may do that too—indeed he has already begun as regards the army substituting the firing-party for the guillotine.

After Nabokoff had gone he showed me the draft of a letter he had written to Henderson requiring his resignation.

He added that the only course the Government could now take was wholly to discountenance the Stockholm Conference and they would refuse passports.

There would be a statement in the House immediately.

Diary, 24 August 1917

Lunched with Churchill. Before Churchill came Mrs. Churchill remarked that Churchill no longer felt any sense of grievance against Lloyd George for having left him out in the cold so long. He had only discovered on now entering the Ministry how bitter had been the opposition to him and he felt that Lloyd George had done a courageous thing in braving it. Churchill himself when he came in remarked that all the same he did not think it would have done Lloyd George any harm to have asserted himself, but the contrary, which is probably true. He added that if he was in the Ministry at all he owed it to the Manchester Guardian. "You and Garvin were my only friends in the press and Garvin had to be very careful". . . .

"We shall hold our own in the war for this year" said Churchill rather suddenly. Mrs. Churchill, surprised, "Was there any risk of the contrary?" Churchill: "Yes; Russia might have gone right out of the war and it is impossible to say what might have been the effect of the transfer of 150 Divisions onto the Western front. Italy also might have gone out of the war". . . .

C.P.S. to Hobhouse, 28 August 1917 (Extract)

About George—I am confident he did not intentionally deceive us. I think he really thought that the old government [in Russia] had promoted Stockholm whereas the present one dissociated itself. I'm sorry to say I wasn't clear on the point myself or I might have pointed out his error and so appeased his wrath.

The worst part of the business was his display of temper. In a way it excused him because he couldn't have been so angry if he had really understood the situation. But that sort of violence may land him in great difficulties some day, and even now it has done him a good deal of harm.

Diary, 29 August 1917

Called on Nabokoff, the Russian *Chargé d'Affaires*, by appointment in the morning. . . . he kept me for nearly an hour, talking mainly on the difficulties of his position and the confusion of the Departments. His first difficulty was that he could get no clear instructions from his Government and no replies to his enquiries. He said four attempts had been made to remove him. These had failed, but he got no proper support. He was not even allowed a motor-car. He did not complain; he walked. His second [difficulty was] the almost impossibility of getting attention here. Even the Foreign Office had let him call day after day putting him off as often as 4 times running till at last he absolutely insisted on being seen. It was worse with the other departments. A reply from the Foreign Office might take a week, from the War Office he might hear in 3 months, from the India Office or Treasury never. . . . All Ministers were extravagantly overworked and over busy. The War Cabinet was as bad as the Departments. Lloyd George personally much the most live and decisive. If you could get his attention you got an immediate decision and he was very accessible. But how could he go to Lloyd George over the head of the Foreign Office? Milner and Curzon were powerful, but useless—their minds closed. Curzon still lived in the year 1902 (when [Britain[6]] sent gunboats to the Persian Gulf). . . . The only way of dealing with Curzon was to appeal to his inordinate vanity. He gave an amusing example of this. There was an Allied Conference (I forget which) and Thomas and others were there. It was a question of who should draw up the Report. Thomas was suggested. Nabokoff, in a stage whisper to Lloyd George, said "Curzon". He could see him bridle up and from that time forward discovered in him a new benevolence.

On the general situation in Russia he was pessimistic. Kerensky was tired. It was getting beyond the powers of "that consumptive and epileptic young man". Obviously his sympathies are not with the Revolution, at least in its latest developments.

I asked him as to Kerensky's real attitude towards the Stockholm Conference, but he evaded the question. When I remarked that the

[6] The text says "Russia", clearly in error for "Britain".

famous telegram dissociating the present Government from responsibility for Stockholm did not really mark any change from the attitude of the previous Government he contended that in reality it did because, though the Soviet Government, as such, had also not been responsible the Minister for Foreign Affairs had personally been a prime mover in it.[7]

After seeing Nabokoff in the morning, asked to see Bonar Law who asked me to come at once to No. 11.

Found him seated low with a mass of papers on the floor round him. "I use the floor", he said, "as my desk". He was looking very tired and sad and almost broke down when he spoke of the death of his son [in action]. "When I heard of it", he said, "I felt at first that I must give up everything. But afterwards I found I could still do my work and I have gone on doing it. But I do it mechanically. I have no longer any heart in it". . . .

He then spoke of the general political situation and asked me what I thought of the state of feeling in the country. I said I thought it restless and uneasy—that people wanted to know more clearly what was our real objective and what progress we were making towards it. He wholly agreed. I added that the only adequate solution seemed to me to be the democratic solution which would consolidate the Allies and disintegrate Germany. The best thing said on the situation was Lloyd George's declaration that with a democratic Germany we could at once talk of peace. Bonar Law "Yes, but you can't impose freedom on a nation". I said George had very skilfully avoided suggesting that and I hoped the American President, who took the same position very strongly, would equally avoid any appearance of dictation. He again cordially agreed and went on to speak warmly in praise of Lloyd George. At first, when he became Prime Minister he had thought "he would not last", but he had lasted and was as fresh and buoyant as ever. I said I thought he was a far better man for the post in time of war than Asquith. Yes, he said, far better *for war*.

---

[7]By "Soviet Government" Nabokoff presumably meant that the previous government had included representatives of the soviets.

24. *War Aims and Russian Booty, September-October 1917*

By September *1917*, *though the Bolshevik* coup d'état *was still two months away, Russia had ceased to be an effective fighting force. This, combined with the failures on the Western and Italian Fronts, placed the Allies in a gloomy position. Were they, in spite of everything, to struggle on to ultimate victory—including a settlement favourable to Russia which Russia would no longer fight to secure for itself? In general the answer was yes: the country could foresee no acceptable outcome short of victory, and this would mean victory for Russia as well.*

But a handful of people on the right of politics, probably including Milner, took a different view. They had no wish to see Russia's social upheaval extending into central and western Europe. Hence they were inclining to favour a negotiated settlement of the war. Under it, the autocratic rulers of the Central Powers would remain more or less intact; and although they would have to abandon their conquests in the west, they might keep those in the east.

Such views were abhorrent to radicals (including, ironically enough, supporters of a negotiated peace). No outcome of the war could seem worse to them than that the conservative forces in Britain and Germany should make a settlement at the expense of revolutionary Russia. Scott was strongly of this view. But once more Lloyd George's position was in doubt.

Diary, 28 September 1917

Breakfasted with Lloyd George who seemed to be quite himself again after his recent illness (ptomaine poisoning). Admitted he had had rather a bad turn. "The fact is I suppose I was a good deal run down. I have been working very hard, without a break, since the formation of the new Government".

He was alone at breakfast and started at once to talk of Asquith's speech on Wednesday on "War Aims". He was greatly annoyed at Asquith's inclusion of the restoration of Poland among the necessary conditions of peace. Who, he asked, is going to restore it? The Soviet and the Russian Government will not or cannot lift a finger[,] and are we to do the work for them. We cannot be more Russian than the Russians. If Germany is asked to surrender all her gains on the East as well as to retrocede Alsace-Lorraine, she will fight on for years and, with access to the corn-lands of Russia, she can do it. He was prepared to give up even Riga which he described as practically a German city. The whole question of policy involved had been under discussion at dinner on the previous day between him and Smuts and Churchill and he said he wished he had known I was in London and he would have asked me to be there.[1]

George, rather characteristically, was inclined to attribute Asquith's attitude in enlarging the conditions of peace to a desire to make difficulties for him, Lloyd George. . . .

He spoke of his recent visit to France when he had gone close up to the front and been shelled. He had then seen more of the reality of war than ever before—the destruction and tortured-looking German prisoners being brought in—and it had filled him with horror. He had enquired from a particularly well-informed person as to feeling in the army as to continuation of war and was told that there was complete willingness to carry on for a sufficient object, but they would not go on merely for the sake of military triumph and wanted to know definitely what they were fighting for. Asked whether this were the feeling among officers as well [as] men he replied "Yes, among the officers". In his recent conversation with Briand (whom he described as much the ablest of the French politicians) he had found him inclining very much to peace. . . .

When I saw Churchill a little later he put the other side of the [Russian] question very strongly—not as necessarily expressing his definite view, but "in order that I might have the other side before me". Evidently he did not want to dissociate himself too obviously from Lloyd George. As a matter of fact he said he had endeavoured to dissuade Asquith from taking the line he did, but in vain, Asquith having rehearsed his speech in advance to him.

Churchill advanced three main reasons for not abandoning Poland and Lithuania to Germany. (1) Whatever we might say, and say justly, now, about the military failure of Russia and the indifference and futility of the Soviet, these things were passing and to a certain extent accidental and the day would come in a few years when a reconstituted Russia, once more mistress of herself[,] would reproach us bitterly with having abandoned her in her time of difficulty and weakness and, after using her, making her pay for the war. No excuses would then be

[1] The order of paragraphs that follows has been somewhat altered from the original.

accepted. (2) It would not be safe or politic to make Germany a present of this enormous accession of military strength and population. (3) A Russia thus crippled would abandon the Western alliance which had failed her and join forces with [Germany]. Thus central and Eastern Europe would stand against England, France and Italy, with America in permanent antagonism.

I hold, he said, by the Wilson policy.

Some light was afterwards thrown on George's rather singular attitude and the possibility of his contemplating a "bad peace" by Hobhouse, who had learned from a confidential source that last year [L. S.] Amery[2] and the little group acting with him had put before the Cabinet a proposal that we should not concern ourselves in the European settlement—that Europe should be left to stew in its own juice—and that we should ride off with the German colonies and Mesopotamia. These suggestions had been rejected as they deserved, but Hobhouse traced something of the spirit of them in the analogous proposal that Russia should be left to stew in her own juice and that the Western powers should ride off with the spoils.

I went back to Manchester the same afternoon in order to discuss the situation with Hobhouse and it was dealt with in the paper.

[Other points raised during Scott's discussion with Lloyd George were:]

I congratulated him on his appointment of Churchill. It was courageous but it had done him no harm and he had a perfect right to strengthen his Government on the Liberal side where it was far too weak. He said that was true but all the same the appointment of Churchill —combined as it was with that of Montagu to the India Office—had very nearly upset his Government. On the whole he had thought it best to go for the two together and make only one fight of it. That had succeeded, but not without risk.

I said the War Cabinet even now was far too Tory. The effective members of it were Curzon and Milner, who alone were able to give the work undivided and continuous attention, both very able and very industrious, but men whom no one would tolerate before the War as members of a Government[,] and essentially reactionary. He defended Milner who he said was a progressive on social questions and always supported him in them. Carson too was by no means illiberal on these matters. I said that might be so but on the larger questions of policy and fiscal questions both Milner and Curzon were essentially reactionary and they had far too much power. Smuts might supply a whole-

[2]Strongly imperialist Conservative M.P.

some corrective, but he concerned himself only with matters affecting the war. George replied that that had been so, but he was beginning to take more part in domestic issues. . . . I assured him . . . that Smuts was perhaps the most popular man in the country.

I asked him how it came to pass that he had put two such men as Curzon and Milner into the War Cabinet of which when he was forming his Cabinet and up to the point when I got flu and heard nothing more from him I supposed that he and Bonar Law and Carson would be the leading members. He said that, failing Lord Lansdowne who wished to retire, Curzon was marked out as the inevitable leader of the House of Lords and had to be included in the War Cabinet in that capacity. He himself had wished to put Carson into the War Cabinet and Milner at the Admiralty where he would have been excellent through his administrative capacity and great industry. But there was a Tory revolt, Carson was not popular with the Cecils, Long was jealous[,] and he had to give way. Then after filling the more important posts he himself got flu and had unfortunately to leave Bonar Law to complete the administration.[3]

After that we went for a walk in the Park, Kerr joining. I had asked Weizmann to come in case George should like to see him and they had a few words downstairs and George, on Weizmann's representation of urgency, told Sutherland[4] to put down "Palestine" for the next War Cabinet.

We went to see the [bomb]-hole in the Green Park about 30 feet from the dining-room window of Lord Wimborne's House[5] where he and Churchill were dining on the Monday night and where George also would have been dining if he had not had to go that evening to France. Another tenth of a second, George facetiously remarked, in the loosing of that bomb and I should have had to appoint a new Lord-Lieutenant of Ireland and a new Minister of Munitions.

We spoke of the gross attack on George in the "Star", against which George is bringing an action for libel, and George remarked on the growth of a violent and irrational spirit of personal bitterness (Churchill and Haldane as well as he himself being instances) during the war and put it down as a result of the "unwholesome atmosphere" of wartime. . . .

Churchill. Afterwards I saw Churchill at his office. He was in a state of extraordinary excitement about an "Exchange" telegram in that

[3] The cynical will not find these very convincing explanations.
[4] William Sutherland, one of Lloyd George's private secretaries.
[5] Wimborne was Lord-Lieutenant of Ireland.

morning's papers according to which the Bulgarian ambassador at Washington had stated quite bluntly that Bulgaria would have preferred to join the Entente rather than the central powers, but that these were first to guarantee them what they wanted. Churchill interpreted this to mean (if not repudiated) that Bulgaria even now would change sides if we made it worth her while, judging that we were the winning side[,] and already in imagination he saw the two armies at Salonika wheeling into line and the Bulgarians marching on the Turks. Anything which bears on the ancient and to him deeply personal controversy of Turkey and the Dardanelles excites him violently.

Afterwards we discussed the question of Poland already referred to.

Montagu. Lunched with Montagu. Mrs. Montagu also there. Liked him better than when I met him at breakfast at George's and he talked better. But he still had something of the same furtive air and was full of anxieties first as to the success of his mission and secondly as to his political future. George he said was coming more and more under the influence of the Tories and if he should end by surrendering to the powerful forces by which he was surrounded he (Montagu) might find himself in a position of complete isolation, for already he was banned by the orthodox Liberals and neither Runciman nor McKenna would speak to him. I told him I saw no sign at present of [Lloyd George's doing] this, though of course George had no real hold on Free Trade principles, but that on the contrary all the changes he had recently made in his Government were in the direction of strengthening the Liberal element—himself, Churchill, Smuts.

I urged him not to bother his head about the future, but to go right ahead and make a success of his present task and all would be well. Garvin had told me of his timidity and depression and begged me to do all I could to encourage him, but I doubt if I succeeded. . . .

Diary, 20 October 1917

Breakfasted with Lloyd George. The new editor of the "Glasgow Herald" (Bruce?)[6] also there and two of his secretaries (Miss Stevenson and Sutherland) who had been compelled by the air raid to stay on at No. 10 till the small hours and had finished the night there.

Lloyd George came in to breakfast late—wholly exceptional with him—after his broken night. He seemed tired and was highly pessimistic. Three weeks ago he had put off the end of the war decisively to

[6]i.e. Robert Bruce, formerly assistant editor and now editor of the conservative *Glasgow Herald*

next year, as though that were a new thing that we had to make up our minds to; now he hardly less decisively put it off to 1919. Seemed to think no chance of military victory till then. I asked what he meant by military victory. Would the forcing back of the Germans to the line of the Meuse and the evacuation of a great part of Belgium be victory? He said Yes, it would, but there was no prospect of that next year. Our "Student of War" much too sanguine. He had agreed with him so far, but could not agree in this. We had only secured a corner of the Flanders ridge and the great bulk of our work was yet to do before we even approached the Flanders plain. (In the course of the conversation Bruce suggested an armistice for discussion of terms. George replied significantly "Once there was an armistice the war could never begin again".) Further the restoration to France of Alsace-Lorraine was an essential condition of peace. No French ministry could stand which gave it up. I suggested a compromise possible and that as a symbol of victory half would be as good as the whole. He did not dissent, but thought it would be about as difficult to get. Then there was the claim put forward by Asquith for the restoration of Poland. How could we restore to Russia her lost provinces if she would not fight for them. Of course if she would we should be bound to back her.

Bruce raised the question of Party action. Said the Labour party was very active on the Clyde and organising its forces everywhere, while the other two parties were restrained by the Party truce and practically doing nothing. If an election came suddenly it would find them unprepared. The Labour movement in Scotland was more formidable than in England because the Scotch Labour leaders were better educated. They got their Socialism by reading and study for themselves instead of picking it up from street-corner orators. Under Redistribution Glasgow and the industrial districts round would receive a vast addition of representation and Labour would have no regard for the Party truce.

George replied with some irritation that he was getting rather tired of the Party truce and was not sure it would not have to be broken soon. On the question of a General Election he said a new Franchise might compel a new Parliament. Asked when[,] he said about November of next year. I objected that this would not be fair if the soldiers were not back. But he said by the new clause in the Franchise Bill they could vote by proxy.

I raised the question of Ireland as the most serious now facing us and asked why the Irish Administration was allowed to enter on a course of provocative action directly opposed to the policy of the

Government. He said objection was taken on the other side that the Irish administration was not sufficiently energetic in its suppression of incipient rebellion. At the same time he admitted that the Irish situation needed better handling. The difficulty was to find the right man. Would gladly appoint him if he could be found. Could Bruce suggest another Scotsman? He could spare none of those he had got. But Bruce couldn't.

As I was leaving asked me to come to lunch on Sunday at Walton Heath.

Diary, 21 October 1917

Motored to Walton Heath in George's car which goes every morning he is there with despatches and letters etc. Picked up Megan[7] at her school and went a short walk before lunch with Lloyd George and her. We talked and when I asked her if it bored her she professed on the contrary to be deeply interested. She is 15 and has some of her father's wits. . . .

In the afternoon his whole time was taken up by Sir Eric Geddes[8] who came to discuss Admiralty affairs and stayed a good 2 hours talking hard all the time and soon after he had left by Lord Derby who came just as we were finishing tea and stayed a good hour.

Finally Donald turned up, apparently not having received a letter specially asking him not to come. He seems to act in these days as a kind of scout for Lloyd George and reported why Lord Beaverbrook had not been for 3 weeks to see Bonar Law (he runs the "Express" for him and is very thick with him) and why Lord Rothermere was "disgruntled". . . .

When I said good-bye to George who was then lying on the sofa in the other room in the throes of composing his next day's speech, he expressed much regret at the frustration of our intended walk and asked me to come again. He said rather earnestly "You know I am just where I was before and I haven't the least intention of going over to the Unionists, although my late Liberal colleagues have done their best to drive me there and there have been plenty of temptations". Then he said what he has often said before only more seriously: "It does me good to see you; it really does". In a sense it may be true, though perhaps not in the obvious sense.

Motored back to London with Mrs. George and her elder daughter.

[7] Lloyd George's daughter.
[8] Now First Lord of the Admiralty.

25. *The Prime Minister and the Generals, November 1917*

In the last months of 1917, Lloyd George's relations with Britain's military leaders deteriorated alarmingly. To understand this development, it is necessary to sketch in the background.

Lloyd George had come into office determined to end the prolonged, costly offensives on the Western Front. Instead, his first year as Prime Minister had involved him in two of the most futile of all: the attack directed by General Nivelle, which had reduced the French army to mutiny; and the nightmare British offensive in Flanders usually known as Passchendaele. For initiating the first of these, Lloyd George must bear much responsibility. For the second his responsibility was less. That is, he did not want the offensive, but he did not stop it.

Had Lloyd George employed his full authority as Prime Minister, he could have vetoed the Passchendaele operation. But in June 1917, he lacked the inner resources to employ such a veto. He had no alternative strategy to offer: Russia was a spent force, Italy had refused to attack, France needed time to recuperate, and the Salonika operation was hamstrung. If Britain was to act anywhere, the Western Front seemed the only place. Admittedly no one wanted another Somme operation: a slogging-match without clear objectives. But this was not what Haig was proposing. He offered an offensive with precise strategic aims: to turn the German flank in the north, land a supporting force from the sea, and drive the Germans out of the Belgian ports. His scheme was powerfully supported from a different quarter. Jellicoe, the First Sea Lord, warned the cabinet that unless the Belgian ports (with their submarine bases) were taken from the Germans by the end of 1917, Britain would be starved into submission.

Lloyd George probably believed neither Haig's promises nor Jellicoe's forebodings. But it was a heavy responsibility for any civilian, with so much at stake, to brush aside his expert advisers. So he argued against the offensive, but let himself be overruled. The outcome is well known. After four months of fighting and a quarter-of-a-million British casualties, the offensive had to be abandoned. The Belgian ports were no nearer being captured at the end than at the beginning. The submarine menace was meanwhile being defeated by other means.

This of course is not the whole story. If the British lost heavily, so did the Germans; and it may be argued that only by mutual slaughter was the war ever going to be won. But in the present context this is beside the point. Haig had outmanoeuvred Lloyd George by claiming that he could advance the war in a different way. Lloyd George would never have agreed to the offensive—would Haig even have proposed it?—if all that had been offered were the results achieved.

Lloyd George never forgave the military. He began a campaign against them which, though it never unseated Haig, damaged his reputation and deprived him of some of his principal supporters: to begin with Generals Kiggell and Charteris, the too-compliant heads of the Army Intelligence Service; and ultimately Robertson and Jellicoe as well. Further, Lloyd George gave public notice of his feelings in a deliberately provocative speech at Paris on 12 November 1917. In it, he deplored the constant resort to offensives in the west which yielded meagre gains while allies like Serbia, Rumania, and Italy were being overrun. And he proposed the establishment of an Inter-Allied War Council to co-ordinate strategy. (The British representative on the Council, Sir Henry Wilson, was a known critic of Haig and Robertson). This speech caused a great stir. It was seen as discountenancing operations which had cost thousands of British lives, and as criticising the military leaders who had conducted them. Scott summed up the speech as "a flank move against the Generals and the policy of men and more men, blood and more blood on the Western front.[1]"

Diary, 12-13 November 1917

Received wire late Saturday evening [10 November] from Lloyd George's Secretary asking me to meet Smuts on Monday morning "immediately on his return". Went Sunday night. Saw Smuts next morning [12 November] at Savoy Hotel. His object in seeing me was to tell me of the speech George was to deliver that night in Paris of which he gave an outline[,] and to ask for support for the policy of a combined General Staff and War Council against national particularism and the opposition of the separate General staffs and personal military jealousies. George would speak "with some brutality" in exposing our past errors and failures. It was late, but not too late, to establish a better order. The policy was one which George had constantly pressed. Actually on his visit to Rome last January he had offered that a joint offensive should be made by the Allies against Laibach, but the Italians had not responded.

[1] C.P.S. to Hobhouse, 1 January 1918.

The position in Italy was of course full of peril.[2] It was a race against time between the Western Allies and the Germans. If the line of the Piave were forced and Venice fell we should lose the base of our naval force in the Adriatic. There was no other available short of Brindisi and control of the Adriatic and of the whole eastern coast of Italy would pass to the enemy[,] who would then be in a position even to effect a landing on the Italian coast. . . .

Of the 3 members of the new Allied Military Committee Cadorna[3] was stupid but, having commanded throughout the war, knew everything. Foch he regarded as the best brain in the French army. Wilson was brilliant, but everything depended on whether he could show sufficient strength of personality. He (Smuts) had impressed upon him that now was his chance to show what he was made of, a chance that could not recur. . . .

In the afternoon went to Propaganda (Press) Committee and waited half an hour alone with Lord Beaverbrook before Carson was ready. He evidently anticipated that George might have considerable difficulties with what he called the "Bourbon" section of the Government[4] in regard to his new policy of an inter-Allied War Staff and War Council. These men hated him and had never wanted him and would like nothing better than to be rid of him. The new policy was really part of the long-drawn battle between George and Robertson in which, so far[,] Robertson had won, a dour, dogged fellow backed by the whole influence of the military professional interest and of the reactionary Tories. Of course George ought never to have been personally engaged in this conflict of civil against military control. It ought to have been fought by the Secretary of State for War and he ought only to have come in decisively as arbiter. That was the penalty he paid for having appointed Lord Derby at the War Office—"genial Judas" as he was known by his intimates, because he would sell anybody, one side as much as the other, being too stupid all the time to know that he was selling them.

Then Beaverbrook went on to give his version of the whole story of the crisis which ended in Asquith's fall. The "Bourbons" had not wanted to turn out Asquith, they wanted to turn out George and keep Asquith. But Bonar Law let them down. George, under great difficulties played his cards with extraordinary skill, but he made a mistake

[2]Under the weight of a combined German-Austrian attack the Italians had just been routed at the battle of Caporetto.
[3]Commander-in-Chief of the Italian armies.
[4]Probably Cecil, Chamberlain, Curzon, and Long.

about Derby. He bought him with the War Office, but if he had realised it, he wasn't worth the price. In the same way he secured Curzon with a promise of the War Cabinet and afterwards Milner. His master-stroke was to secure Balfour. Then the Bourbons realised that they were defeated and had to come in one by one. The last to come was Lord Robert Cecil, who "crawled in with infinite reluctance". ["]I have got the whole story written out", said Beaverbrook[,] "as I interpret it".[5] It was an interesting narrative from the inside of the Tory party by a democratic Tory and Bonar Law's special ally and instrument, but not, it seemed to me[,] to be accepted with unquestioning faith.

In morning [of 13 November] went to see Colonel House (head of the American mission recently arrived and Wilson's special agent and confidential adviser) who asked to see me, at American Embassy. He began by expressing his admiration for the "Manchester Guardian" and said he was engaged in trying to establish a counterpart in America. . . .

I asked if he had read Lloyd George's Paris speech in the paper that morning, but he had not. I said I assumed that the U.S. would come into the arrangement for an inter-Ally War Council and that her support for its principles of a common handling of the war on all fronts and of the supremacy of the statesman over the soldier would be very important. He cordially agreed and said that the U.S. would certainly come in on those lines.

I said I valued the entry of the U.S. into the War quite as much for its influence on policy and in the final settlement as for its material aid and that I believed her voice might be the deciding voice, standing as she did apart and genuinely believing in democratic ideals to which many others rendered only lip service. Our present Government was essentially a reactionary Government, and that despite the fact that George had genuine popular sympathies and would never, as he had often assured me, be able to find a political resting place among his present associates.

He very heartily agreed and went on to say that something like that was Wilson's hope and design. He was resolved, come what may[,] to keep steadily in view the moral issues of the war and to base his policy throughout on no narrow view of American interests, but with an eye to what was for the permanent interest of all the nations—for the good

[5]Beaverbrook eventually published his version of these events (in volume two of his *Politicians and the War*) in 1932. But, as Mr. A. J. P. Taylor points out after a study of both accounts, the published version did not always accord with the first draft of 1917.

of the world. I said that was the true and big way of securing American interests also and he replied that that was the President's view.

Before leaving I begged him to help to bring America's influence immediately to bear on our policy, particularly in such a matter as our relations with Russia where our stupid diplomacy was actually speculating on the disaster of a [Tsarist] restoration.

He evidently wanted me to talk rather than to talk himself and was extremely cordial.

26. Henderson and Lansdowne, December 1917-January 1918

The repercussions of Lloyd George's contest with the military leaders continued during the following months. But other issues intervened to make their claims on Scott's attention. Principal among them were the future of political parties, and the question of a negotiated peace.

(1) *The future of parties.* Scott continued to take a dispassionate view of Lloyd George's regime. He had described it to Colonel House as "reactionary"; he was now to urge Arthur Henderson to keep Labour free from it. He knew why he wanted Lloyd George in office: to win the war. He was much less confident of Lloyd George's government as the architect of a new order after the war.

Neither did Scott see Asquith and his associates as the hope of a new Britain. He placed his trust rather in an association between the radical wing of the Liberal party and the newly-vitalised Labour party. He had two objects in talking to Henderson: to keep Labour out of Lloyd George's embrace, and to keep it in harmony with reformist Liberals. On the former question he met with a ready response; on the latter he did not. Henderson talked much of radicals joining the Labour party, but said nothing about Labour and like-minded Liberals acting in association.

This omission was ominous for the future. For years to come the conflict between Labour and Liberals was to vitiate their political strength, and to make the task of Conservatism easier. The effort to persuade Labour to co-operate with left-wing Liberals was to absorb much of Scott's energies hereafter; the failure of his efforts was one reason why, from now until his death, the tide of politics was to flow against him.

(2) *A negotiated peace.* A less momentous development at this time was the publication of the Lansdowne letter. Lord Lansdowne had been Conservative leader in the Upper House, an architect of the entente with France, a strong supporter of British intervention in the war, and an early advocate of conscription. He had also played a lamentable role in wrecking Lloyd George's attempted Irish settlement in 1916. But as the war proceeded he had become appalled at the way in which traditional society was destroying itself. The flower of the younger generation was being slaughtered on both sides. Revolutions seemed imminent in

many places, victory as far away as ever. So, courageously, he sent a letter to the press (which The Times *refused to publish) arguing that if Germany could be persuaded to settle on terms agreeable to the Allies, the war should be ended by negotiation.*

Although Lansdowne was a Conservative, his views were condemned out of hand by the government and its supporters. Such welcome as he received came mainly from the left of politics (Lansdowne, it should be remembered, was not proposing a settlement at the expense of Russia). The Manchester Guardian gave him a guarded endorsement, but insisted that he was proposing a definition of war aims, not the abandonment of the war.

Diary, 11-12 December 1917

Came up for Press Advisory Committee. . . . Met Henderson by appointment (at my request) at our London Office. In writing him had said I hoped that when the Labour Party came back, in probably greatly increased force, they would form an independent party and not be represented in the Government. He said that was entirely his own opinion unless they could form a Government of their own. I was the first person who had urged this policy upon him, but since then, curiously enough, several others had done so. He was against a Coalition in peace-time, though he had been in favour of it as a war measure.

I raised the general question of the future relations of parties and said that for more than 20 years—ever since I went into Parliament— I had held that a really progressive and democratic policy could only be based on the union of the Labour and Radical parties and that it was important now, in view of a general election on the new franchise[,] to keep such a Union steadily in view, especially in the selection of candidates and of the seats to be contested. He said several (he named some half-dozen) Liberal members had already given notice to their constituents that they intended to stand as independent candidates, which probably meant that they would join the Labour Party. His policy was to enlarge the bounds of the Labour Party and bring in the intellectuals as candidates. The Labour Party had been too short of brains. There was to be a meeting next day of the joint executives of the Labour Party and the Trades Union Congress to draw up resolutions for the Nottingham Conference in January and they would appoint a Candidates selection Sub-committee which would also consider the question of the constituencies to be contested.

I asked what would be the policy as to contesting seats held by good democrats and Radicals, such as [C. T.] Needham in Manchester. He said that discrimination would be difficult and that broadly he thought the policy would be to run a Labour candidate wherever there was a tolerable chance of carrying him. There were a few Radical seats which would not be contested, but in the majority of cases he would depend on the alternative vote and on a friendly understanding between Liberalism and Labour to give each other their second choice.[1] He saw no reason why this should not be done without bitterness on either side. He thought they might run as many as 500 candidates now that members were paid and election costs so greatly reduced as they were under the Franchise Bill. They were better equipped for doing this than either of the other two great parties, because they had an existing trades union organization in every town. As to the country districts [they had] the assistance of the Cooperators, if they should decide to work with them, as, in many of the country districts ("the valleys, as we call them"), 8 out of ten households were cooperators. There was no lack of candidates—they poured in daily—the only difficulty was to secure the right ones.

But what, I asked, if an attempt should be made to seize on some excuse for a snatch election on the existing franchise? There were rather sinister indications of this in Bonar Law's and Churchill's speeches. . . . He said it would be a wicked thing if a snatch election were attempted and that it would inevitably be met by extensive labour strikes which the Labour Party would not feel called upon to take any steps to prevent. A resolution would be drawn up by the joint executives for presentation to the Nottingham Conference dealing with this matter, in which the prospect of Labour troubles in such a contingency would be not obscurely indicated. I urged that they should be careful not to give ground for the charge of an unpatriotic threat, but he said they must at least show their teeth.

Speaking of the future of the Liberal party he asked how was it possible that Lloyd George could now ever hope to lead it. Up to a year ago he might have done, but he had taken a thoroughly undemocratic attitude towards the Russian revolution (he had gone completely round in the interval of his—Henderson's—going to and returning from Russia). And how could he expect him (Henderson) ever to work with him again?

Wednesday [12 December].
George at the weekly breakfast to the 12 Liberal members of the

[1] The alternative vote was never enacted.

government at Captain Guest's house in Park Lane[2]. Arranged to meet him there . . . and I motored with him to No. 10. . . .

[One of the subjects discussed was Russia:] Trotsky was in his (Lloyd George's) opinion the biggest man the revolution had produced. He did not think much of Kerensky—a man of dreams rather than actions.

Afterwards, when we were alone, he spoke of the Lansdowne letter. I said I thought Bonar Law had made a mistake in making so much of it and describing it as "a national misfortune". He said it had been his own intention when he came back from Paris to say that "rather too much had been made of it", but on reading the letter again he felt he could not. It was really a plea for immediate peace, though it did not say so in terms. And it was singularly ill-timed. The Paris Conference had been ready to tell the Russian Government that they were prepared to discuss peace-terms with them. But then came the letter and it was felt that to do this would be taken as an acceptance of the policy of the Letter, and even House, who had been in favour of a revised statement of war aims, had felt that it would be difficult.

Speaking of Asquith's speech on the previous day at Birmingham he remarked that it reiterated the extreme demands of his previous speech as to the complete break-up of Austria and he indicated some surprise that in spite of that the Manchester Guardian should have expressed general approval of the speech. He has committed himself to the most extreme territorial demands, he said, not only as to Austria, but as to Poland. Obviously his object is to put his demands so high that any terms we can make can be represented as a failure. "My own speech at Glasgow", said Lloyd George, "remains the most moderate, practical statement of terms yet made. I can't go on repeating it, but it is on record."

He asked me, as we parted, to come and see him next Sunday at Walton Heath.

Diary, 16-19 December 1917

Came up to London on Saturday, December 15, on Lloyd George's invitation to go down to Walton Heath on Sunday. Found he had changed his plans and was staying till Sunday evening at Downing Street and wanted me to lunch there with him instead. This was very little good for my purpose as I wanted a personal discussion with him

[2] F. E. Guest, was chief Lloyd George Liberal whip.

on policy and as usual there were people at lunch—Smuts and Amery besides Kerr and the family.

He greeted me with a half-laughing reproach about our "wicked leader" of the day before on his Friday's speech [condemning the Lansdowne letter] to which we had taken rather strong exception. Davies told me afterwards that he had been much put out about it, but if so he had got over his ill-humour.

Afterwards discussing the Lansdowne letter which I defended he said that one difficulty of stating our terms was the hostile attitude of the Opposition always lying in wait for an opportunity to upset him. And, he added, the other day, but for the Manchester Guardian, they might have succeeded and they came very near.[3] All the Liberal press except the Manchester Guardian and most of the Tory press—[J. St. Loe] Strachey in the "Spectator" and [L. J.] Maxse in the "Globe"— were in a conspiracy to defeat him on his Paris speech. It was an unholy alliance of the Generals' press and the partizan Liberals "but you stood out and I think you turned the scale." "Your leaders were some of the finest I ever read". I was considerably surprised, as the whole clamour had seemed to me absurd and I had no idea that he considered himself in danger. He was evidently greatly dissatisfied with the conduct of the war—the gigantic losses (400,000 casualties since April) and the small results—and gave me strongly the impression that the war Committee had failed to control the conduct of the war. He spoke of "the Generals" in terms of impatience almost amounting to abuse.

Further discussing the Lansdowne letter he said there was all the difference in the world between Lansdowne and Wilson because Wilson postulated victory and Lansdowne did not. I asked what was to be held to constitute victory. He said we should have victory when we were manifestly dominant. I said that was only to say the same thing in different words. Then he fell back on Wilson's definition of the aim of a victorious war which was that the world should have been made a safe place for democracy. But I objected that he had never explained by what test we were to judge when that condition had been reached. Then he turned to Amery and asked him how he would define victory. Amery gave the simple and obvious reply that he should consider we were victorious when we were able to secure the terms of settlement which we considered necessary, in which I entirely concurred.

From all which it appeared (1) That George and the War Cabinet were not in effective control of the army. (2) That George had not really thought out our war aims and when he talked of victory was talking

[3] This in regard to his Paris speech—hardly a comparable issue.

rhetorically, unless he meant simply victory in the field, which may not be attainable.

A good deal of anxiety was expressed about Italy and it was plain this was one of the matters on which George and Smuts had been in conflict with "the generals" and had partly failed. It appeared that only 5 English and six French divisions had been sent, or less than 200,000 men all told. But what would be said, asked George, if it appeared that civilians had compelled the head of the General staff and the General commanding in the field to weaken their line in the West to an extent which they considered dangerous? And yet, said George, they have not the excuse that, as is generally supposed, we have taken over part of the French line. We have not yet taken over a yard.

I asked . . . about the English reserves. George said it had been decided to form "an army of manoeuvre". So, I said, we have then no strategic reserve and he admitted it.

Before lunching with George I called on Haldane. . . . He spoke a great deal of his own various activities. . . . He was Chairman also of a little Advisory Committee to the Labour Party, under Henderson's auspices, which met at the Sidney Webbs' house and of which the Webbs were the most active members. They were engaged in advising as to the programme of the party in such matters as education (in conjunction with the Workers' Educational Association) and Nationalisation of mines and railways, and also as to its election policy. It had been already decided to run 350 candidates of whom 200 should be drawn from the trades unionists and 150 from the intellectuals. Ultimately they might even be able to run 500 [and he thought more than 200 would be returned].

The question of a future Parliamentary leader had been discussed and no conclusion arrived at. Lloyd George was regarded as at present impossible. But finally Webb said "Yes—perhaps Lloyd George— after an interval". . . .

We discussed the Army chiefs. Robertson he thought "no fool", but handicapped by his lack of education. [Sir Henry] Wilson he described as "the best talker in the army" and in that way he had impressed Lloyd George. But he could not answer for him as a strategist. He had yet to prove himself. Of Jellicoe he spoke somewhat depreciatingly, "a small man intellectually" and in his wrong place at the Admiralty.

On consideration felt I could not leave London without seeing Lloyd George again. He appointed 5.45 directly after the Cabinet but Cabinet was late and meanwhile Lord Reading loafed in on no particular business and when George came out kept him chatting till at last George and I retreated into a corner when he shortly departed, leaving me only a few minutes before George had to go back.

Davies had told me that he wanted to get rid of both Haig and Robertson (but Lord Derby had said he should resign if this were done), so I put it to him at once whether it was to be either or both. He said he could do with Haig, but not with Robertson, and of the two Robertson would be the easier [to get rid of], as Haig was a great friend of Lord Derby. I said it was plain the War Cabinet were not in control of the war and that if they could not do that they ought to go and be replaced by some one who could. He said he absolutely agreed, but would rather wait to take action till Parliament was up. I asked whom he would put in Robertson's place and he said Wilson. Wilson's reports from Paris had been brilliant and showed a comprehensive view of the whole situation. I said it would be objected that he had never held high command. At least, George replied, he had commanded an Army-corps, whereas Robertson had never commanded even a brigade.

I said I wanted to talk to him more fully on the whole situation and he fixed Wednesday morning after breakfast for a walk.

In the evening met Noel Buxton[4] and [J. H.] Whitehouse at dinner at the Reform Club and they were insistent that I should meet Lord Buckmaster[5] as the best and strongest of the Liberal ex-Ministers and the best man to lead hereafter a Radical-Labour combination, and Whitehouse undertook to arrange it.

The introduction to Buckmaster which resulted from the foregoing conversation was to produce yet another attempt by Scott to reconcile Lloyd George and Asquith. Despite the doubts which (for different reasons) he entertained about them both, Scott recognised that before the war they had—in partnership—constituted a powerful force for attaining Liberal objects. Occasionally he believed that they might serve that function again. In May 1917 he had brought them together in the hope that they would do something for Ireland. Now he was deeply concerned that Britain should respond to Lansdowne's call for a definition of war aims, hoping thereby to rescue the warring powers from an apparent military impasse which was being perpetuated by the doctrine of a fight to a finish. This seemed an essentially Liberal objective, and one for which the leaders of the two Liberal sections might be expected to unite. But once again he was to run up against the inconstancy of Lloyd George, the lethargy of Asquith, and the deep personal animosity which now separated the two men.

[4]Left-wing Liberal, critical of the war.
[5]Former Liberal M.P., who had been Lord Chancellor in the Asquith Coalition but was now out of office.

Breakfasted with Buckmaster [on 19 December]. Discussed possibility of an early peace, but pointed out the difficulty raised by Asquith who always went "one better" than George in his peace conditions and was believed by George to do this deliberately in order to be able to represent any terms made by George as inadequate and such a peace as a bad peace, joining forces in this with the Tory extremists. Buckmaster seemed a good deal surprised and said he believed George was quite mistaken as to Asquith's attitude and he was extremely glad to know that he was labouring under what he believed to be a misapprehension. . . .

I suggested that it would be very desirable that George and Asquith should meet and discuss the matter and he agreed. I promised to try to arrange for them to meet as I had done before on the Irish question, when however George had found Asquith singularly unhelpful.

Went on to Downing Street, but the moment George came in from the Liberal Party breakfast at No. 12 he was met by an urgent request from the American Ambassador to see him immediately, so he asked me to come to lunch instead.

Colonel Hankey was also at lunch, but left early and I had an hour with George afterwards. I told him of my interview with Buckmaster and of Buckmaster's strong desire that he should meet Asquith. I pressed upon him the importance, in case the Germans failed in their present supreme effort,[6] of seizing the opportunity for testing the possibility of coming to terms, as if we waited for America to come in in force Italy and even France might fall out and leave us alone with America. He said he regarded military victory as necessary, *but perhaps the defeat of the present great German effort might be regarded as amounting to military victory.*

I urged that an attempt should be made to come to an understanding with the Opposition, but he said the danger here was that the moment he made any advance towards meeting the Opposition he risked the loss of the Unionist support which was essential to him. In any case he would rather not meet Asquith. He could not trust Asquith to take a disinterested and not a partizan view of the situation. . . . Moreover whatever he said to Asquith would not stop there; it would all be given to the small men around him, to McKenna and the rest. Asquith after all had a kind of intellectual bigness, though his personality was small, but these had not even that. . . .

I again pressed the absolute necessity that the War Cabinet should

[6]With Russia out of the war, the Germans were massing their forces for a mighty blow in the west intended to finish off the struggle before America could intervene decisively.

determine War Policy and that at the present moment, for instance, they should send the full assistance to Italy which they judged to be necessary. He said a beginning had already been made in dealing with the obstructions by the supersession of Charteris and Maxwell[7], the two heads of the Intelligence Department at G.H.Q., who had persistently misled Haig as to the morale of the German army and the possibility of a break-through. When Robertson got out to France he found the thing already done. In this particular matter, strange to say, Northcliffe had strongly co-operated and had written a ferocious letter to Haig threatening him with his utmost wrath if he made any difficulties —an unpleasant light this upon Northcliffe's position and secret activities. He said nothing about reinforcements for Italy. He was very severe on Robertson who had grudged every man sent from the Western front. . . .

Scott saw Buckmaster again following the above conversation with Lloyd George. The gist of the interview is given in the following letter.

C.P.S. to Hobhouse, 20 December 1917 (Extract)

I wanted to tell you before you wrote some things about my last interview (yesterday) with Lloyd George.

(1) He is in dead earnest about getting his way in war policy—i.e. on stopping the useless waste of life in attacks on the West and dealing only heavy counter-strokes, while standing on the defensive. I trust also on stopping at all cost the gap in the Italian front.

(2) For this purpose he is, as you know, about to get rid of Robertson and put Wilson in his place. He has already removed Charteris and Maxwell, the heads of the Intelligence Department at G.H.Q., whom he holds responsible for bolstering up Haig in his forward policy by utterly delusive reports as to German demoralization and approaching collapse.

(3) When I put it to him that to obtain our peace terms was to obtain victory, he persisted that military victory was necessary, but then he added, most significantly, that to defeat the impending great German attack in France and Italy, or wherever else it may take place, would in itself constitute military victory. There at last we touch earth and it becomes possible to look forward to peace negotiations even in the spring.

[7]Probably an error for Kiggell.

(4) I am endeavouring to bring about an understanding as to war aims between the two wings of the Liberal party. Hitherto Asquith has been more extreme than Lloyd George, though a large part of his followers are semi-pacifist. Lloyd George distrusts Asquith and would rather not see him, but has agreed to see Buckmaster with whom I have had several conversations, but wishes that I should be present. Buckmaster agrees, if Asquith gives permission, so it is provisionally arranged that he and I are to breakfast with Lloyd George on Friday in next week.

All this seems to show that Lloyd George is taking a more moderate attitude (though I always thought his speeches were mainly a sort of "gingering-up") and his today's speech is certainly the most moderate he has made since Glasgow. I think therefore that for the present at least we should seek to promote this new growth by sympathetic treatment, remembering especially the very great difficulties he has with his Tory allies.

Diary, 28 December 1917

We breakfasted with Lloyd George, of course alone, and stayed a long time. I was surprised to find when we left that it was 12.30. We started at once on the Austro-German peace proposals[8] and Buckmaster read out the rather fuller and somewhat less hopeful text from the "Times". "I warn you", said Lloyd George, "that I am in a very pacifist temper." I listened last night, at a dinner given to Philip Gibbs[9] on his return from the front, to the most impressive and moving description from him of what the war in the West really means that I have heard. Even an audience of hardened politicians and journalists was strongly affected. The thing is horrible and beyond human nature to bear and "I feel I can't go on with this bloody business: I would rather resign".

The generals are absolutely callous as to the gigantic casualties and order men to certain death like cattle to the slaughter. Again and again splendid men have been ordered to do perfectly impossible things, such as to advance against uncut wire with enfilading machine-gun fire. He quoted a particular instance of this which had come to his knowledge in which every officer in succession had reported to the one above him that a particular operation was impossible till at last the Brigadier

[8]Issued in response to an appeal by the Bolshevik government for a statement of peace terms.
[9]War correspondent and novelist.

reported this to "G.H.Q." "G.H.Q." curtly replied on the telephone "Tell them to obey orders". They did and the inevitable result followed. "All because probably somebody wanted to go to his dinner", said Lloyd George.

There is no personal hostility he said to Haig, who never goes near the lines himself,—only indifference—, but there is intense hostility against the abstraction called "G.H.Q.". . . .

"For some time," said George, "I have been feeling that there ought to be a re-statement of war aims, but this (pointing to the 'Times' which Buckmaster had just been reading) makes it necessary". There is a good deal of feeling in the War Cabinet toward peace. Balfour is not opposed. Milner is the most inclined to peace of anybody. Carson is nothing like so violent as he seems. In fact when you talk to him he is a very charming and reasonable person (my own experience). It is only when he makes speeches that he becomes "so crude, so raw". He seems to fancy he is counsel for the prosecution at the Old Bailey. I don't know about Curzon. He is very able, very just (he has never had sufficient credit for his Indian administration)[,] a great public servant, but he is not very accessible to new ideas. . . .

George then repeated what he had said to me as to the difficulty of his position between Tories who suspected him and a Liberal Opposition always on the look out to take advantage of him. . . . In his conflict with the Generals when he was endeavouring to assert the authority of the civil power in determining policy and to curb the unlimited demands for men and to turn the Generals' flank by establishing the inter-Allied Council and making the Paris speech[,] the "Daily News" and "Nation" joined hands with the "Morning Post" and "Spectator" in denouncing him for interfering with the soldiers and very nearly succeeded in upsetting him, while the "Manchester Guardian" was the only paper which gave him support. As a matter of fact he had carefully abstained from interfering with the discretion of the Generals in matters of strategy. What he had done was to send Haig a written memorandum of his views in which he had warned him that no serious advance could be made under present conditions in the West, that the utmost to be looked for was, at an immense expenditure of life, an advance of from 5 to 10 miles. They, on the contrary, declared they would get to Ostend. But his forecast had been almost literally fulfilled. Now they were again asking for men, more men and always more men, but he had told them that if they were going to spend them as they had spent them in 1915 and 1916 they would not get them. . . .

About this point George said I think I should like to see Asquith in

connection with the new situation and I must see him alone. There are
certain things I can tell him which throw light on the present action of
Germany the authority for which he will understand and which he and
Grey alone of the late Government will understand just as Balfour and
I are the only persons in the present Government who are in a similar
position. . . . It was then suggested that he might like to see Grey at the
same time and after a moment's reflection he at once said he certainly
would; it would be better that Grey also should be present. Grey was
a great figure and his influence would be valuable. Buckmaster at once
charged himself to bring about this meeting at the earliest time
possible. . . .

George proceeded to say that in all such negotiations the difficulty
was not with Asquith but with the smaller men about him and pre-
eminently with McKenna. McKenna was a man of narrow mind, very
competent and efficient within his limits, with very strong personal
likes and dislikes and completely dominated by these feelings. He was
a small man and yet by his persistence and his faculty for intrigue he
exercised a great and unfortunate influence. . . . It was he who, working
first directly on Asquith and then indirectly through Grey and Harcourt[,] had upset the arrangement which he, Lloyd George, had made
with Asquith before the change of Government and with which
Asquith was perfectly happy. "Believe me", he said, "there was not
the least intention of displacing Asquith and that this took place was
entirely due to his having been persuaded to go back on the agreement
he had made.["] McKenna had persuaded him that he (Lloyd George)
could not form a Ministry and that he would have to come back to
Asquith on his own terms. (Buckmaster here remarked that he personally had never been of that opinion and, when asked, had said he had
not the slightest doubt that George could form a Ministry). . . . In
regard to the decision of the Liberal members of the late Government
as a body not to serve under George[,] Buckmaster said he had himself approved that decision because if they had not done so they would
have left Asquith to bear alone the reproach of inefficiency in the
conduct of the war which was the ground of the movement against
him.

On the fundamental question of whether advantage should be taken
of the Austro-German statement of terms to advance to more formal
peace negotiations George was reserved.[10] The next step would no

[10]Note how mercurial Lloyd George is. At an earlier interview he had declined to see
Asquith; now he is anxious to do so. At the beginning of this interview he was in "a very
pacifist temper"; now he is "reserved" about peace negotiations.

doubt be that a communication would be received from the Bolshevik Government, but the Bolsheviks could not be recognised as the Government of Russia, not even as the *de facto* Government, since they were in actual control of no more than half Russia. . . .

[Scott and Buckmaster left together.] In speaking of the obstacles to cordial cooperation he said it was true that Asquith felt bitterly about Lloyd George's action who he held had "stabbed him in the back". It was a great pity also that, in forming his Government[,] George had not asked for the cooperation of his old colleagues as I assured [him] he had himself told me he intended to do. Even if they had not accepted it would have helped good feeling. As it was the fact that he had asked Samuel and him alone made the omission of the others only the more marked.

Diary, 7-8 January 1918

To London by night Sunday, January 6. A. Henderson came to breakfast at the Euston Hotel. He approved Lloyd George's war aims speech but agreed that the cold-shouldering of the Bolsheviks in their stand for the freedom of their lost provinces was a grave defect. We discussed Lloyd George's future and Henderson agreed that if he would make a real fight for an early democratic peace he might yet be reconciled with Labour and lead the English democracy. He (Henderson) would never allow his personal griefs to stand in the way, though he could not but resent bitterly the charge of treachery to the Government of which he was a member. "They say I sold myself. In that case what price did I get—the exchange of an Office of £5,000 a year for one which has never been worth to me more than £150". I told him that the exchange had at least vastly increased his influence and that as leader of the Labour party he was far away more powerful than as a member of the Government. . . .

In the evening dined with Buckmaster. He told me of his experiences after I had left him on the Friday week previous. He went straight to Cavendish Square to ring up Asquith at his place in the country but by ill-luck tumbled on Mrs. Asquith ("Margot") who insisted on ringing him up herself and then stayed in the room while he spoke and finally [demanded?] to know who were the people whom he wanted Asquith to see. So she had to be told under pledge of secrecy—but be sure you don't tell. (Her daughter)—["]She's very indiscreet"!

Under these difficulties, and Asquith not being at all responsive, he decided to see Asquith and went down that evening and spent several hours with him. He began by reading him the exact terms of the memorandum which he had drawn up at the breakfast with Lloyd George stating the purpose and reasons for which George wished to see him and Grey. Asquith was exceedingly unwilling to meet George. He gave no reason for this and said no word against George which his best friend could have resented, but it was evident to Buckmaster that it was his strong personal feeling against George which moved him. It was only on Buckmaster's strong representation that, under the critical circumstances existing, it was his duty to comply, that he finally consented to do so, but he made it a condition that Buckmaster should say that he would see George if he regarded it as "important in the national interest" that he should do so.

In the course of the conversation one of the reasons urged by Buckmaster was that the military situation was grave. "Grave!", said Asquith, "I should think it was grave! We shall be lucky if we escape without the Germans occupying the Channel ports".

Asquith undertook to communicate with Grey, but Grey was even more difficult. Buckmaster left on the Monday for Paris from which he had only just returned and knew nothing more except that Asquith had met George twice. . . .

Lord Rhondda[11] was at breakfast with George next morning [8 January] and naturally we did not get much beyond Food-control during breakfast, but I saw George for a few minutes before Rhondda came and for a quarter of an hour or so after he left.

George started at once with enquiries as to how Buckmaster had got on with Asquith and I told him exactly what Buckmaster had told me as to Asquith's reluctance. Oh! yes, he said, but Asquith's reluctance was nothing to Grey's[,] and that though Grey is one of the two men primarily responsible for the war and he surely ought to have been not only willing but eager to do anything he could towards stopping it. Do you know it was *days* before we could get him up from Northumberland. I saw Asquith first and then I insisted that I must see Grey also. I got on all right with Asquith when we met and with Grey also. I [C.P.S.] said I assumed they had agreed in substance to his statement of war-aims. "In substance!", he said, "I read every word to them and then I told them that I should state publicly that they approved".

He asked me what I thought of the statement. . . . I told him of the two points in which I had felt the speech to be disappointing: (1) the absence of any response to the effort of the Bolsheviks to save the freedom of the occupied provinces, for which they were putting up a good

[11]Minister in charge of Food Control in succession to Lord Devonport.

fight—not indeed with our weapons but with their own of a pacific offensive and driving a wedge between the German Socialists and their Government. "No", he said, "they are not. Believe me, I know". It is a make-believe and they mean to give way. "They will run like whipped hounds". . . . I merely replied that in any case it was not for us to discourage them by assuming it in advance and publicly casting them off.

(2) I regretted that he had not recognised the great advance made by Czernin [the Austrian Foreign Minister] towards our point of view in his acceptance, as against the German Chauvinists, of the policy of "no forcible annexations", making this the starting point for further approximation.[12] He made the rather lame defence that if he had seemed to play up to Czernin the Germans would at once have become suspicious of a secret understanding and called the Austrians to order. Apart from the fact that such a domestic quarrel would have been in our interest rather than against it, the rather startling fact became quite patent to me that *George did not want to defeat the German ambitions* in the occupied [Russian] provinces—that in fact he was now bent on giving effect to the policy which he would have adopted even under the Kerensky Government, if he could have carried it in his Cabinet, of paying the Germans in the East in order to square them in the West. He told me this almost in so many words (he said the Germans could not be expected to surrender their colonies and compromise in Alsace-Lorraine and get no compensation) and it seemed, in any case, the only intelligible explanation of his policy. It savours rather of the "realpolitik" of Bismarck than of Wilson's idealism which we are supposed to share. But, as George remarked at breakfast to Rhondda and as Buckmaster has even more emphatically remarked to him, "it is a difficult thing to make peace" and he is apparently seeking a road along this devious path.

I tried all Monday to get an interview with [Maximilian] Litvinoff, the designated Bolshevik ambassador, but he was very elusive.[13] On Tuesday morning he turned up at the London Office and, when he heard I was leaving, said he would like to see me when next I came up.

[12]In conversation with Buckmaster, Scott pointed out that they had both urged Lloyd George to react favourably to Czernin, and that George "had rather markedly refrained from making any response."

[13]A revolutionary from an early age, Litvinoff had fled from Russia in 1902 and eventually settled in London, where he had worked for a publisher and married an Englishwoman. Hence he was an obvious choice as Bolshevik representative in England. (He was deported nine months later).

C.P.S. to Hobhouse, 27 January 1918 (Extract)

Hertling's[14] speech was much the most uncompromising, not to say provocative, that we have had from any leading German statesman and looks to me as though he thought we were weakening and they were really on top. If there were a change of spirit of this kind in Germany it would put a stop for the present to all approaches on our side towards peace and we should have to take quite a different view of the situation and prepare ourselves accordingly.

[14]George von Hertling, Chancellor of Germany.

27. The Mood of Labour, January-February 1918

Scott's hopes that the Bolsheviks would make a serious stand against German demands on their territory were soon dashed. Instead the Lenin government signed the humiliating and punitive Treaty of Brest-Litovsk. At the same time, the intransigence of certain elements in the labour movement in Britain began to disturb Scott.

Hobhouse to C.P.S., 27 January 1918 (Extract)

I met Litvinoff at the Courtneys' yesterday, and was impressed with his utter crudity and lack of ability. His Socialism is the sort of schoolboy stuff which one has been denying for 30 years to be anything but a caricature. He tells us that Local Committees are taking all the land, and all the stock on it beyond what they judge that a man can use for himself. No compensation, but a charitable allowance to keep an ex-proprietor going for a year or two till he learns to work.

C.P.S. to Hobhouse, 30 January 1918 (Extract)

Thanks for your letter. I was much interested to hear about Litvinoff. When I was in London just after his appointment as ambassador I tried hard to see him, but he eluded me, though he might have known that the Manchester Guardian was worth getting in touch with—a slow sort of man I should think. It's not wonderful perhaps that, standing where you found him, he should feel a little out of it in this terribly "bourgeois" community. There seems to be danger that the crude extravagance and injustices of the Bolshevik economic doctrine, as applied in practice, may discredit the whole popular movement. It seems to be penetrating to some extent our own Labour extremists and there is quite a Bolshevist ring in the assumption of the Clyde men to dictate

331

national policy by means of sectional strikes. It couldn't happen if we had a genuinely progressive Government whom the workers could trust. Possibly we may get that after a General Election when the Labour Party comes back with a force sufficient to determine policy. But shall we get a General Election this autumn? And who are the men who in effect are going to guide the newly risen and rather blind giant. If it were men like [Arnold] Toynbee and [R. H.] Tawney one would feel pretty safe, but I imagine the Webbs are at present chiefly pulling the strings. I wish you would see Henderson and keep in touch with him. He is the channel through whom influence flows. He is exceedingly friendly towards the paper and admits that he has been greatly influenced by it. Shall I tell him you will call?

Diary, 3-5 February 1918

Went to London Sunday midday [3 February] in consequence of strong representations made to me by young Mather and C. Renold[1] as to the explosive conditions among the engineers of which they had evidence in their own great works. . . .

We called at Downing Street about 11 [on 4 February]. Lloyd George had arrived but was engaged with Smuts. Waited in Davies' room where Churchill also was waiting. When Smuts left Lloyd George came in and I asked to speak to him. He took me into Sutherland's room and sent Sutherland out. Put the case to him that (1) Geddes[2] was altogether wrong in refusing to meet the A.S.E.[3] separately in order to negotiate on a change in the bargain which had been made with them separately. (2) The A.S.E. men convinced that the Government were out to destroy them and would therefore yield nothing on the point of form. (3) It was not a question of the A.S.E. only but all the skilled workers would stand together and the unskilled would be very apt to throw in their lot with them. Above all it was necessary to dissociate the extreme anti-war political movement of a small minority from the industrial issue with which it was at present combined and through which it was liable to derive altogether factitious strength. Asked him to hear what Renold and Mather had to say on the facts of the situation. He said he could give them one minute but in fact gave us more like ten. . . . Finally Lloyd George after hearing what Renold and Mather had to say as to the temper of the men said he thought the

[1]See above, p. 127.
[2]Probably Sir Auckland Geddes, Minister of National Service.
[3]Amalgamated Society of Engineers.

best thing he could do was to send at once for two officials of the A.S.E. and find out exactly their position.

We afterwards went on to see G. D. H. Cole,[4] head-centre of the "Guilds" movement and employed by the A.S.E. as confidential adviser—a queer position in respect of which he has been exempted by the Government from military service. He struck me as a genuine British Bolshevist, disbelieving in Parliamentary action, disbelieving in the trades union movement and the trades unionist leaders, and waiting only till the shop-stewards movement (which is the practical application of the guilds theory or organization by workshops instead of by trades) was further developed (he said they were not ready yet) in order to use the weapon of the general strike, or some approach to it both for political and for industrial purposes.

When I suggested that Parliamentary action was the appropriate weapon and that a general election on the new franchise ought to give Labour a great accession of strength he objected that there were no leaders and no prospect of any[,] and that there was a wholly inadequate supply of candidates. The constituencies would not look at the kind of labour man who was being brought forward and as for the intellectuals they were not forthcoming—not any new ones.

Professed himself a thorough "Pacifist" (which Hobhouse afterwards told me he was very far from being at the beginning of the war) so that it would seem he was preparing, on the political side, for a stop-the-war movement by industrial pressure. At the same time he professed to be against the violence which such a movement if carried far enough would necessarily provoke. Personally I should doubt if he has the moral qualities needed for the enterprise.

Afterwards lunched with Churchill at his house. Nothing of much consequence in the general conversation. . . . As to the general situation he was clear that we were in for another year of war.

Called on Henderson in the morning [of 5 February]. He did not confirm Cole's statement as to lack of candidates, but said that the prospect for Labour at a General Election would be immensely worsened if, as seemed likely, the alternative vote were rejected from the Franchise Bill.

Called in the afternoon on Weizmann who leaves shortly for Palestine. He had heard a report that the Munitions Department wished to explore the possibilities of the Dead Sea for certain rare chemicals which they need. The Zionists have already done a good deal

[4]Left wing intellectual, prolific writer on labour questions.

in that direction and Weizmann wished to be entrusted with the work. Thought I could help him with Churchill. He told me that Smuts had left that day for Palestine, George being determined to finish off that business effectively. Smuts will no doubt report on the possibilities of an even further advance. . . .

28. The Other Intervention, March 1918

Disenchantment with Bolsheviks at home and abroad did not affect Scott's utter hostility to the policy now being contemplated: intervention by Allied forces in Russia to assist in the overthrow of the Bolshevik regime.

C.P.S. to Lloyd George, 27 February 1918[1] (Extract)

I am greatly concerned about the impending attack by Japan on Russia. If she does lay hands on Russia's Eastern province and we approve there will not be a pin to choose between us and the Germans, and it would simply make nonsense of all that Wilson has been saying. If we want America's help we ought surely to pay some heed to her policy.

C.P.S. to Hobhouse, 3 March 1918

I have to go to London tonight (Sunday). . . .

I am going up mainly in order to urge (with [Felix] Frankfurter, Editor "New Republic"—who has asked to see me and says he has a message for me from Colonel House—and with the American Ambassador, if I can see him) that America should at once take a far stronger hold on policy, not in speeches there but in council here. Things will go to the devil if she doesn't. Witness refusal of Stockholm, desertion of Kerensky, throwing of the Russian border provinces to the wolves, rejection of Czernin overtures, and now the plot only too clearly brewing for a wild-cat assault on the far-eastern provinces of Russia.

I am lunching with Lloyd George. Each time I say it shall be the last and then I go again to liberate my mind—with scant effect I fear.

[1]Lloyd George Papers.

Diary, 4 March 1918

Went to London Sunday night [3 March], returning Tuesday morn-ing[,] mainly in order to meet Felix Frankfurter who had asked to see me by desire of Colonel House. Breakfasted with him at his hotel. His message from Colonel House was that I was to take everything he had told me as to the war aims and ideals of the President which he had stated to me at our recent meeting as holding good absolutely. My own object in seeing him was to convey to Colonel House and through him to the President my strong feeling that America should at once take a much more direct and continuous part in the determination from day to day of war policy corresponding to her responsibility as now an essential Member of the Alliance. I put it to him that speeches were not enough invaluable as was the lead he [i.e. the President] had given in them to which all that is best in the democratic parties here eagerly responded. . . . I urged that he should be represented here and at Versailles by a special envoy fully possessed of his mind, speaking with authority in his name and in close and constant touch with him. Frankfurter cordially assented. . . .

Lunched at No. 10 with Lloyd George. . . . I told him what I thought about his recent appointment of pressmen (Northcliffe and Beaverbrook) to direct propaganda,[2] that Austen Chamberlain's speech represented the general view on the subject[3] and that the incident had done him great harm. He admitted this but defended the appointments on the ground of Buchan's ineffectiveness and the difficulty of finding competent men for the job. Beaverbrook was extremely clever and though he was described as a "shady financier" he was not aware of any real foundation for the charge. As for Northcliffe he was safe as long as he was occupied and "The Times" had been quite reasonable during the 7 months he had been in America. It was necessary to find occupation for his abounding energies if they were not to run into mischief. Neither he nor Beaverbrook would allow their propaganda work to be determined by their personal political views—indeed he doubted if they had any considered views—and would simply take the line which they thought likely to be most useful in the particular case.

[2]Northcliffe had been appointed Director of Propaganda in Enemy Countries, and Beaver-brook Minister of Information.
[3]Chamberlain (who was out of the government from July 1917 to April 1918) condemned the inclusion of newspaper proprietors in the ministry, and called on the government to free itself of press entanglements.

As this is not very far from being probably George's own state of mind it did not seem much use to argue the matter.

I had already written to him strongly protesting against the proposed attack, in the name of the Allies, by Japan on Vladivostok and Siberia. He evidently did not like it himself and said the only thing to be said for it was that it might cut off the food supplies which Germany hoped to draw from Siberia. He admitted that this could only be done if the advance of Japan were pushed a very long way. I urged that at least Japan should [be] put under a written obligation, which should be published, to withdraw within a stated period. I gathered that the assent of America as well as our own had been already given.

He went on to discuss the question of Ireland. He had evidently abandoned all hope of a Report from the Convention so far unanimous as to supply a basis of action for the Government. I had told him of Dillon's visit to me and he asked what Dillon thought. I said he was in great fear of Mr. Murphy[4] and the "Independent"[,] and thought that unless customs and excise were conceded to the Irish Parliament, as Murphy demanded, no settlement could be reached. "So like him", said George, "he asks for it just because he knows it can't be conceded. If that were conceded he would ask for something else". . . .

Diary, 20-21 March 1918

To London by morning train [on 20 March]. Called on Smuts at his hotel by appointment. . . .

I asked him what he thought of the project of Japanese intervention in Siberia. He said that, looking at the matter broadly he was against it. The consequences were incalculable and might be tremendous. It was the opening of the flood-gates and might prove in its ultimate consequence a greater matter even than the War. It would be the beginning of a new war. Then again the time must come when Russia would recover. What would be her feeling towards us if, in her day of weakness, we had assisted in her dismemberment?

But there was another side. I said that was exactly what I wanted to know because so far I heard no reason which did not appear to be illusory. He said that the whole situation in Siberia was still obscure but that, from information reaching the Government from various sources, the danger from the Austro-German prisoners was a real one. There were altogether 2 million of them and of these a considerable number

[4] W. M. Murphy, owner of the *Irish Independent* and founder of a commercial empire in Ireland.

were in Siberia and these were being armed and it appeared to be true that German officers, under assumed Russian names, were arriving and organizing these forces. He read me a report, apparently just received, which came from a station of the American Y.M.C.A. at the important railway junction of Karymskaya to the effect that 80,000 prisoners were being armed and officered— mostly Germans—and that accommodation was being provided for 10,000 of them in Karymskaya. No doubt they were armed by Bolsheviks. But who were the Bolsheviks? They were led no doubt by Lenin and other doctrinaire theorists who were very anti-German, at least so far as the German Government was concerned, but they also included practically the whole of the old Russian secret police and black-hundreds[5] who might naturally favour a restoration for which no doubt the Germans also were working. . . . Still all this was largely conjectural and information was defective. On the balance he remained definitely opposed.

Japan could not undertake an extensive campaign on her own resources and would have to depend on assistance in money and war material from the United States, just as we ourselves now did. The refusal of the U.S. to supply these was the real cause of delay in the launching of the expedition.

As to Ireland he regarded it as essential to settle before the Peace Conference. How could we go into the Peace Conference with "this skeleton in the cupboard" still on our hands? "We (he always speaks of 'we') had settled South Africa and we must settle Ireland". I said the crux of the whole business was Customs and Excise. Was it possible to concede them?[6] He thought a moment and said "Yes, I believe it is". I said of course there would be great alarm in Ulster, which he admitted and added that "there would have to be securities for Ulster". The question was not really very important because Ireland could not afford to quarrel with her best customer. A settlement, in any case, there must be.

Breakfasted [on 21 March] with Lloyd George. He asked if I had seen the Irishmen lately and I said not since Dillon's election as leader.[7] We discussed the old question of Customs and Excise as to which he refuses to consider any concession. He rather minimises the importance of getting a settlement before the Peace Conference and said that of

[5]Organised gangs of pro-Tsarist hooligans who, before 1914, specialised in *pogroms* against the Jews in Russia.
[6]i.e. to an Irish government.
[7]Dillon had been elected leader of the Irish Nationalists following the death of Redmond on 6 March 1918.

course if the Irish made the concession of Customs and Excise an essential condition and rejected the offer made in his letter to the Convention on that ground that would end the matter.

We talked chiefly about the project of Japanese intervention and for some time he defended it, though much less effectively than Smuts, on the ground that otherwise Germany stood to obtain control of the whole of Russia in Asia. But finally he said "Well, I don't mind telling you that I am extremely puzzled. I never knew any subject on which the best-informed opinion differed so completely. One man with years of Russian experience assures you that unless you intervene at once all is lost. The next man, equally experienced and well informed[,] is not less urgent that if you intervene you wreck everything["]. On the whole evidently he inclined to intervention taking only the short view and not troubling about Smuts' long ones.

I pressed him to reconsider the question of the Conscientious Objectors and said I thought their mishandling was beginning to be strongly resented. He made rather light of this, but admitted that the infliction now common of the maximum sentence of 2 years hard labour on men who had already served long terms for the same offence was open to objection and said he was "considering" a change in this matter.

29. The Two Offensives, March-May 1918

In March 1918 the German army, with considerable reinforcements from the Eastern Front, launched a massive offensive against the British line in France. It enjoyed great initial success. The Fifth Army was shattered, and the British driven back. (Scott's son Ted was taken prisoner). The stalemate in the west was over, and the Allied cause placed in jeopardy. In these circumstances Scott temporarily lost patience even with Ireland.

But not for long. Lloyd George chose this moment to launch a sort of offensive himself. The need for reinforcements was driving him to scrape the barrel of manpower in England. Across the Irish sea were large untapped resources of men. He decided to go and fetch them, even if it involved force. So he extended conscription to Ireland. To offset it, he offered the sop of immediate Home Rule—but a Home Rule rendered illusory by the circumstances in which he was proposing it. In the outcome Lloyd George's offensive never got under way. So formidable was the threatened resistance that, although he got Irish conscription on to the Statute Book, he never tried to enforce it. (Home Rule foundered along with it). But though still-born the scheme further damaged Britain's standing in Ireland, and Lloyd George's standing with Scott.

C.P.S. to Hobhouse, 25 March 1918 (Extract)

Many thanks for your note. I always want to see you when new situations arise and the present is serious enough. They [the Germans] haven't broken our line yet, which is something, but we are far enough I fear from having exhausted the full weight of the attack.

You may believe we are anxious about Ted. . . .

The last letter received from him was written a week ago and spoke of the lovely weather and the peace around—"not a gun to be heard"— and then the flood!. . . .

If we succeed in defeating this tremendous German onslaught I think we must then insist on a direct exchange of views so that we may know clearly where we stand. Of course if we fail and the Germans get Paris or Calais everything will be changed. No tolerable terms will be obtainable and the war may go on, mainly as a sea-war, for years. But in the other event there will be an opportunity and we mustn't let it slip.

C.P.S. to Hobhouse, 29 March 1918 (Extract)

The real tug of war has begun now and no mistake. I think the temper of the nation will rise to it. It's rather sickening about Ireland. I confess to a certain growing resentment at the way they are taking the possibility of a world catastrophe and somehow the whole Irish question looks pretty small. They are perhaps just now a good deal more comfortable than any other people in Europe.

C.P.S. to Lloyd George, 7 April 1918[1]

I am deeply concerned at the growing strength of the report that compulsory service is to be applied to Ireland. It is no part of statesmanship and must destroy all hope of a conciliatory policy in Ireland. It will double your cares and may even prove a disastrous turning point I believe in your career.

You will forgive me for saying these things, knowing that my feeling for you is not a thing of yesterday and that I will never, if I can help it, abandon faith in your future. . . .

[P.S.] My boy is "missing". He was with the Ulsters at St. Quentin.

C.P.S. to Hobhouse, 12 April 1918 (Extract)

I should like to turn out the Government on the question of conscription in Ireland, if it weren't that we can't afford a change of Government just now—still less a General Election into which the present Government are quite capable of plunging us. But any way it's impossible. Asquith will never fight for a principle.

Diary, 19-21 April 1918

Went to London Thursday night [18 April] at George's request. Saw him for a few minutes on Friday. He was all afternoon at Cabinet and came out for a few minutes and gave me tea. On Saturday he wasn't

[1]Lloyd George Papers.

well and stayed at Walton Heath but had a lot of people (including Milner just back from France) to see him so I had to wait till Sunday [21 April] to see him. Went to lunch and had an hour or so with him quietly afterwards. Kerr, on whom he evidently relies increasingly, was in the room most of the time, but it didn't much matter.

George started right away by saying he was determined to put Conscription through in Ireland. He knew there would be trouble—rioting, bloodshed, but it was better to face all that and get it over. I said if he was going in for that sort of thing any way I hoped there would be no executions. Fighting the Irishman quite understood and was ready to take knocks as well as to give them but to kill men in hot blood was one thing, to kill them in cold blood quite another. George agreed and said he had already given instructions to that effect. There were to be no judicial trials and punishments. If men were to be shot they were to be put up against a wall and shot on the spot, as happened in the Paris Commune. Kerr concurred. The executions after the Dublin rising, spread out day after day, a fresh batch every morning for breakfast, had been intolerable. George said that was what he felt also. (He did not appear in the least to realise that to shoot prisoners on the spot would be simply to execute them without trial or on the verdict of a drum-head court martial).

I objected that there was no more case for conscription now than there had been all along and that to impose it now would be to ruin the chances of an agreed settlement on Home Rule. He said on that point he was inclined to agree with me. Conscription ought to have been imposed two years ago. But it was a political necessity now if the Tories were to accept Home Rule. I objected that as a military measure it would be of little or no value. Not at all, he said. Anyway it would give us 50,000 men from Ulster and some at least from other parts of Ireland. What proportion are the Protestants to the Catholics—a third? No, said Kerr, a quarter. Well, taking 200,000 as the total recruitable number that would give us the 50,000. 5 good Divisions. How many men would you need I asked in order to hold Ireland down while you recruit them—100,000? Oh! no. 50,000? No, not that. We have about 30,000 there and they are all second-class troops. With armoured-cars and aeroplanes you don't need a great many troops. He was putting [Lord] French in command, and French was already in Ireland. He would be excellent for the job—of good judgment, an Irishman and a Home Ruler.

The question, however, was really one of principle. The control of the armed forces of the Crown by Parliament had been conceded in every proposal for Home Rule and was now being disputed. The right to levy troops was part of the same right and must be asserted at all costs. To deny it was virtually to claim independence. The demand for Dominion status was really a demand for the right of secession, since the Dominions were virtually independent States and could secede at any time if they chose. It was better to face the matter at once and go through with it. Lincoln had had the same difficulty to meet and had met it by force and he should not shrink from the same course.[2] Every argument which applied in the one case had applied in the other and his position was virtually the same as Lincoln's. Otherwise the link between Great Britain and Ireland would be merely the personal link of the Crown, as in the case of Austria-Hungary, but even in that case the army was a common concern.

I urged that at least before *applying* Conscription in Ireland he should not only pass the new Home Rule Bill into law, but also put it into operation. He said the difficulty was the Register. The new Register would not come into force till November, but he would consider the point. In any case he should press on with the Bill. Would it, I asked, be adequate? Would it go at least as far as his own Letter to the Convention? He said it certainly would. It would be a strong measure and he should put it through under the closure, as he had done the Military Service Act, in order to get over the opposition of a section of the Tories and in order to mark the fact that the two measures were strictly parallel and part of the same policy. "Yes", burst in Kerr, "I am certain that is the only policy. Make the two measures strictly coordinate and force them both through".

As Kerr is quite a good Liberal (though an opinionated and rather cranky one), and very much in George's confidence, this may be taken to show that he at least believed George to be quite sincere and not, as the Irish suspect, to be playing for a fall and using Conscription as a means of killing Home Rule. George said the Cabinet were hard at work framing the Home Rule measure and it would be ready, he hoped, in about a week. He should like to see me again then and show me the draft.

C.P.S. to Hobhouse, 27 April 1918 (Extract)

[In the next two or three months] the most critical events may be happening both in the field and in our home politics, where George is

[2] The American Civil War vied with the French Revolution as the period of history which most engaged Lloyd George's interest.

heading straight for disaster. In all probability the only way of avoiding it will be to turn out the Government.

C.P.S. to Hobhouse, 7 May 1918 (Extract)

What you tell me about the movement of troops to Ireland is sufficiently ominous, but really, if the Government mean to go through with their insane policy, the more troops they send the better. You ought perhaps to see the full notes of my last conversation with Lloyd George and I am sending the material part of them to you. His mood was then entirely reckless.

I have small hope of Asquith. He looks at every situation from the personal and party point of view and even at that in a narrow and not a big way. Is it or is it not a good chance to upset the Government? How far can I go in attacking them without getting myself into trouble? Those are the sort of questions he will ask, not How can I do even a little to avert a catastrophe? How can I best uphold the honour of the Liberal party and prove to Ireland that there are still powerful political forces in this country prepared to stake all for the sake of justice and appeasement? The only chance is that the two sets of considerations may more or less coincide.

On 7 May 1918 Major-General Sir Frederick Maurice wrote a letter to The Times *claiming that the government had misled Parliament about military matters so as to conceal its responsibility for the recent setback in France. Asquith moved in Parliament for an inquiry into Maurice's charges, but after a hostile speech by Lloyd George he was soundly defeated.*

Asquith won no credit with the Manchester Guardian *by his action. Scott was as much on Lloyd George's side in any contest with the military as he was critical of the Prime Minister on the subject of Ireland.*

C.P.S. to Lord Courtney, 10 May 1918[3] (Extract)

The Maurice affair is something of a mystery. It looks as though he were rather a foolish person who had been made use of by others. There really seemed to be no case worth enquiring into, unless it were one against Maurice. The result is to strengthen George. I don't mind that so far as the conduct of the war is concerned, because whatever his faults George is at least an incomparably better war minister than Asquith and has proved himself right exactly on the vital matter of

[3]Courtney Papers.

unity of command as to which the "Daily News" and the "Morning Post"—singular alliance!—have been perpetually nagging at or attacking him. But as to the much more difficult matter of making peace it looks as though both were about equally impotent. Asquith is discredited; George, in spite of some good intentions, is hamstrung by his associates. I almost despair of a solution until we get a new Parliament. Even a victory in the field would not greatly help us because the demand would always be for more victory. Meanwhile deadly damage may be done in Ireland and to save that I would turn the Government out without a moment's hesitation.

But it can't be done without the Irish—even if with their aid—and meanwhile they have retreated to their tents. When I last saw George 2 or 3 weeks ago he was very bloodthirsty, treated resistance to Conscription as equivalent to rebellion and sheer separatism, compared himself to Lincoln as a defender of the unity of the ₒtate and was quite ready for civil war. And meanwhile Asquith chatters about things that don't matter and not a man in Parliament, so far as appears, is ready even to attempt an effective protest.

30. Kerensky in England, June-July 1918

Constitutional, liberal government had not survived long in Russia. It had come into being with the collapse of the Tsarist regime under pressure of war in March 1917. But it too had proved unable to cope with the war. Its efforts to do so had made easy the way of the Bolsheviks, who in November had seized power in the main centres, called off the war, and imposed an autocratic regime. From that moment, Liberals and radicals everywhere were placed in a fearful dilemma. The new regime was a child of the revolution which they had welcomed. But with its highly authoritarian, undemocratic practices it was far from being the child they had looked for. Ought they then to extend it their sympathy, hoping it would mend its ways but thus contributing to its survival? Or should they offer aid to its adversaries, so perhaps restoring a constitutional government, but more likely assisting in the creation of a revived Tsarist tyranny?

The two sides of the argument were explored in the following conversation between Scott and Kerensky, the most distinguished figure in Russia's liberal interlude and now (as he was to remain for another half-century) an exile from his native land.

Diary, 26-27 June 1918

To London [on 26 June] primarily in order to meet Kerensky. Missed him in afternoon owing to misunderstanding. Saw him in the evening at Dr. Gravonski's house late, after his return from the Labour Conference where he had made his sudden and unexpected appearance. He was a good deal tired and made excuse of that for speaking in Russian, using Dr. Soskice as interpreter[,] rather than in French which would have been much handier and taken less than half the time. But I believe he is not as much at home as most educated Russians in the language.

His first proposition, laid down with emphasis, was that there must be no dealings with the Bolsheviks. They were a pure usurpation, the real Russia was wholly against them, elections everywhere would go heavily against them and they dared hold none, not even for Soviets.

At the same time being in possession of power and of the plunder of the State other parties were unable to make head against them. For that reason oppressed Russians called upon their Allies for assistance. In their view, the Bolshevik Government being without any constitutional authority, its acts had no binding force. They regarded the treaty of Brest-Litovsk as invalid and a state of war as still existing and called upon their Allies to help them to reconstitute the [Eastern] front. The only lawful authority in Russia was the Constituent Assembly forcibly dissolved by the Bolsheviks as soon as they found it contained a majority against them. This had been elected on the widest possible franchise and an Executive Council representing it still existed in Russia, though the members had to remain in hiding, and a manifesto emanating from this body was handed to me.

I questioned the possibility of bringing Russia again actively into the war, reminding him of his own declaration that Russia was exhausted and imperatively needed peace. He denied this and explained that all he had said or meant was that Russia was more exhausted than her allies and that less must be expected of her.

I also pointed out that, whatever might be the theoretical position, what in effect he was asking was that the Allies should take sides in a civil war. He urgently contested this on the ground that the Russian people were now being held down by a tyranny at least as ruthless as that of the Tsars and merely asked to be given freedom. I asked was he sure that if given a free choice they would not in many places elect for the Bolsheviks and he burst out laughing at the very thought of such a thing. I objected that foreign intervention against the Bolsheviks would in all probability throw them into the hands of the Germans whom they would call to their assistance. He replied that the Bolsheviks were already completely subservient to the Germans and were compelled to do exactly what they were told.

I remarked on the practical difficulties of effective military intervention owing to the immense distances and to the ease with which the Siberian railway could be broken[,] and suggested that it was perhaps rather to the moral and political effects of intervention that he looked than to the purely military. He said that certainly was so, that the military question was not for him but for military men (which is obviously only in a very limited sense true), that intervention once begun in the east would produce reactions throughout Russia by putting heart into the elements of resistance. Then he added, with evident significance, "If these can get no help from the Allies they will have to seek a different orientation". I understood this to mean that they would have to come to terms with the Germans (and Dr. Soskice whom I afterwards questioned agreed that that was what was meant). The intervention of which Kerensky spoke was Allied intervention which obviously could only be carried out effectively by Japan, but he made no reservations as to Japan. He attached great importance to the action of the Czecho-Slovak prisoners and to the fact that they were in control of the Siberian railway at important points[1]. . . .

Rosing, the great Russian singer, whom I saw on Wednesday evening and who has suffered as keenly as anybody from Bolshevik confiscations, was still resolutely opposed to intervention believing that it would defeat its own object and by rousing national resentment against the Allies strengthen Germany's hands.

When I saw Lloyd George at lunch next day [27 June] I found him, as I expected, quite definitely in favour of intervention. Not that he liked it, but he saw no other way of coun ering Germany in the East. He also spoke of the great importance of the Czecho-Slovak control of the railway at points which would cut off the Siberian corn-lands from Western Russia. He said the report of the presence of American troops being already in Siberia was false; none had gone. But he believed the mind of the American President was inclining towards intervention. . . .

Other noteworthy points in Scott's conversation with Lloyd George were:

(1) Lloyd George's denunciation of Clemenceau, the French Premier, "for his extreme folly in relation to the letters of the Emperor Karl" (the new Emperor of Austria who had made private overtures to Clemenceau for peace talks). Lloyd George said that Dell, the Manchester Guardian's *Paris correspondent, "was quite right in reporting that he himself was in favour of negotiation". He also condemned Baron Sonnino, the Italian Foreign Minister, "for his obstinate Chauvinism".*

(2) Lloyd George's attitude to Ireland, compared with that towards India where he seemed well-disposed to reform. In relation to Ireland "he showed extreme impatience, probably from a sense of having blundered badly. He admitted that he had had no time really to consider the matter. I pressed repeatedly the importance, from the point of view of the war[,] of settling both the Indian and the Irish constitutional problems. He concurred about India, but when as we parted I

---

[1] A body of Czech soldiers, fighting originally for Austria and taken prisoner by the Russians, had decided under Kerensky to form themselves into a separate unit and support the Allies (so as to further the cause of Czech independence). When the Bolsheviks took power they gave the Czechs permission to leave by way of Siberia, but the promise was violated and the Czechs had to seize the Siberian railway so as to effect their departure.

said 'Yes, but you'll have to deal with the Irish question too', he answered, of course half jokingly, 'the only way to deal with Ireland is for some one to open a sluice and submerge her'."

(3) An exchange between Scott and Hankey, who was present for part of the time. Scott "asked him for Lord Fisher", and received the apparently mocking reply " 'He tells me he is walking 10 miles a day and is coming back soon (to office)'." Scott noted: "People, I'm afraid, no longer take the old man seriously —a pathetic end to a great career."

Diary, 26 July 1918

Saw Dillon at his club on Friday morning [26 July]. He said a good many Nationalist members had been opposed to returning to the House of Commons, but that meant coming into line with Sinn Fein and he would never consent to that policy. He had stayed on in Ireland till he had obtained a settlement of the policy of that extraordinary body, the Conference. Although Conscription had been dropped for the present the Conference, or central body representing the Church, the Nationalists and Sinn Fein, established to oppose it remained, and it was in possession of about a quarter of a million of money. There was danger that Sinn Fein which was in a majority on the Conference would gain possession, or control, of the money, but he had succeeded in establishing the principle that all decisions of the Conference must be unanimous and there should be no voting. So now he felt safe.

It was only through his action in joining the Conference that the Bishops had been induced to come in. The Conference had saved the situation. Wild schemes were afloat and it had been seriously proposed to blow up tunnels and bridges and to burn the standing crops. The Conference had been able to restrain all this. The Sinn Fein leaders were not really so dangerous as they seemed. Valera,[2] for instance, was a schoolmaster pitchforked into a position of extraordinary prominence and power and nervously conscious of his own inadequacy. . . .

The Church itself was now completely divided. The curates everywhere had taken the bit in their teeth and the same was true of the Maynooth students[3] who equally were carried away by the spirit of Sinn Fein and openly applauded or hissed the names of the bishops according to their political views. Father Flanagan, an extraordinary natural actor, had been suspended for advocating violence. But he went

[2]Eamon de Valera, president of Sinn Fein, who had escaped execution after the Easter Rebellion because of his American passport.
[3]Maynooth was a Roman Catholic theological seminary.

about the country holding meetings and his congregation had retaliated by nailing up the doors of the Church and the Presbytery until such time as the suspension should be withdrawn.

As to the future he saw nothing for it but to mark time and wait for their opportunity. Asquith was a broken reed. He proposed a loose alliance with Labour. . . .

31. The Approach to the Polls, August–December 1918

The question of Lloyd George's political future, which had concerned Scott so long, came to a head in the second half of 1918. With the failure of the great German offensive, the tide of war turned irresistibly in the Allies' favour. This placed Lloyd George in a most advantageous position to appeal to the country. In July he set some of his associates to work on plans for an election.

At this moment, all Lloyd George's protestations that he would not leave the Liberal party and, like Joseph Chamberlain, enter into a permanent association with the Conservatives became meaningless. An election under existing circumstances—the Liberal party divided, the Conservatives predominant in the government, and the nation in a mood of extreme nationalism—was bound to benefit the Conservatives; and would only benefit Lloyd George if he meant to continue his association with them. Scott sought to confront Lloyd George with this reality, but without success. Lloyd George chose to believe that he was maintaining his links with Liberalism by making liberal-sounding speeches, without regard to their party context. Thus his addresses in Manchester in September, which to some extent were a curtain-raiser to an election, were full of excellent Liberal sentiments.

Diary, 7-8 August 1918

To London by night train [on 6 August] in order to see some people before Parliament was adjourned as to plans and prospects of a General Election. Called on Geoffrey Howard at the Liberal Central Office in Abingdon Street 10.30 [on 7 August] and discussed the whole business with him. He said no one wanted a General Election and yet we were steadily drifting towards one. There were many reasons why an Election should not be held in war time. There was no real issue. We were all practically agreed as to the prosecution of the war, and an election would only mean an orgy of anti-Germanism and alien hunting by the Tories who would easily beat the Liberals at that sort of game. The new Register was grossly defective. . . . The soldiers vote

351

was a make-believe and it would be impossible to bring home the issues to them. . . . Shortage of helpers. All the men who normally would be active at elections were either at the war or engaged on war work. Lack of candidates. The younger men who give life to a party were all away and very few of them were, like young [Frederick] Cawley, well enough known *locally* to be selected as candidates. Liberals always did badly in a War Election and he did not want one.

Neither did the Unionists. There had been a great hardening of opinion lately among Unionist party-managers against it. (This was confirmed by Gulland whom I ran across in the street as I was leaving).[1] The Unionist Managers complained that the party was all to pieces— no life, no interest. Where 200 people were summoned to a meeting 6 attended.

The Labour party also were not ready and there were serious divisions among them.

To the Irish Parliamentary party a General Election at this time would mean something like destruction. Dillon estimated that they could hold no more perhaps than 10 seats. (When I saw Dillon later he confirmed this and O'Brien, the whip, said *six*). That would mean that Nationalist Ireland would be swept by Sinn Fein. They would not attend Parliament but would set up a mock Parliament of their own and would all have to be arrested and sent to prison—a pretty position vis-à-vis the Peace Conference.

He would not object to an agreed election as between Liberals and Unionists with a time limit to the duration of the Parliament to say 6 months after conclusion of peace, except for the desperate position in Ireland. But George's game was probably to hold a khaki election without a time limit. In any case there could be no agreement with Labour. Their claims were much too high. They wanted to be placed in practically a dominant position. A good judge told him he thought if an election were held shortly they [Labour] would come back 80 strong, i.e. double their present numbers—quite as much as they are fit for yet said Howard—but they claimed far more than that. If they fought he thought Liberals would have to fight too, as otherwise our radical working men would go over to Labour in shoals and most of them we should not get back again.

As for Lloyd George he would never get a more subservient House of Commons than the present. I asked if he despaired of Lloyd George's

---

[1]The brackets have been added in this conversation. Sometimes it is not clear when Scott is talking to Howard and when to others, but as far as can be told he is talking to Howard except in the sentences bracketed.

return to the Liberal party and he said he did not altogether. He admitted that Asquith made a great mistake in not holding a General Election immediately after the formation of the 1st Coalition. He also did not defend his failure to put through the George-Carson agreement and his breach of faith with the Nationalists.

Went on to see Davies, Lloyd George's secretary. He said Lloyd George wanted to see me and he would make an appointment. When I spoke of danger for Ireland from a General Election he said point was new to him. Evidently George had not bothered about it. But from a personal point of view George needed an election in order to strengthen his position (1) Against Opposition Liberals who at present decried him as an interloper who had simply stepped into Asquith's shoes as the result of an intrigue and had no mandate from the country. This could not be said after a general election. (2) Against the Tories. At present they could upset him at any moment, because he cannot dissolve. He was in danger e.g. from Maurice and Robertson incidents. So soon however as new Register came in force his position would be stronger.

Breakfasted with Lloyd George [on 8 August]. Guest, the Liberal [Government] Whip, and Lord Reading, just back from his mission to the U.S., also there.

As to a General Election he said at once that it could not be postponed beyond the present term of the life of Parliament unless by general consent. That would transfer power of dissolution to Henderson whenever he liked to ask for it. It was true Henderson might not wish for a dissolution just now because he was not ready. But he would demand it as soon as he was ready and it could not be denied. . . .

When I said that none of the political parties wanted an Election now—Unionists, Liberals, Labour, Nationalists—he gave a mischievous look and said "You have forgotten one party" and, as I pointed at him, "perhaps the most important". Clearly, as Davies had indicated, he felt the need of a mandate. . . .

As to the results of a General Election under existing circumstances in Ireland Lloyd George expressed himself as not in the least concerned. He thought there might be advantage in having only a handful of Nationalists in the House. It would be easier to pass a Home Rule Bill over their heads and as to the Sinn Feiners he would deal with them ruthlessly.

I put it to him that Ireland, bedevilled by every Government, had some claims upon him. He was himself responsible for the fatal blow to the Constitutional party when the Asquith Coalition Government failed to put through the agreement he had himself negotiated between the Nationalists and Carson and to which both he and Asquith were alike in honour pledged. He at once said, in the most disarming way[,] "Yes, I ought to have resigned; it was the greatest mistake I have made". . . .

Discussing the prospects of a General Election he agreed with me that there was, so far as the conduct of the war is concerned, no contested issue. The Tories of course I said will fight on an orgy of anti-Germanism and the aliens hunt. The Liberals can hardly beat them on that ground though some of them seem inclined to try. (He said Samuel that afternoon had appeared to be rather on that line). Nor can there be any great fight on the fiscal issue so far as Opposition Liberals are concerned since they are already compromised. He agreed but thought an election necessary on the general grounds stated and also obviously because he wants it.[2]

Guest left before breakfast was over and I spoke a few words to him as he was going away. He said he was quite prepared for a deal with the Opposition Liberals in regard to the General Election, but his terms would be rather stiff. He had been most careful for the last 18 months to do nothing to break up the unity of the Liberal party and had strongly urged this policy on Lloyd George in spite of much provocation, for the Opposition (18)[3] elected under the party truce had constantly failed to observe the spirit of the truce and had taken every opportunity of attacking the Government. Lloyd George had about 100 Liberal supporters in the House and he should insist on no opposition to these. He should also require a very explicit pledge of support from Liberals generally for the Government in regard to the conduct of the war. For 18 months he had been sitting on a volcano and this could no longer be endured.

Had a few words with Lord Reading as we went away. He agreed with me that Lloyd George was too headstrong and too impressionable and needed to be held back if he was to be saved for Liberalism. His present associates were thoroughly bad for him.

Speaking of the Siberian and the Archangel expeditions he said their sole object was first to rescue the Czecho-Slovaks, by way either of Vladivostok or Archangel, and secondly to protect the enormous stores at Archangel supplied by the Allies. If the Bolsheviks, acting

[2]Scott noted an inclination on Lloyd George's part towards tariff protection, and reported him as saying: "We must be free to adjust our tariff as we thought best in our own interest —and the United States which was a high tariff country would have no right to complain".
[3]This may be a mistake for "Libs."

under German dictation, had not refused to allow the Czecho-Slovaks to leave quietly with their arms—and they would have been helpless if they had surrendered them—no intervention would have been necessary. . . .

Diary, 17-18 August 1918

To London Saturday afternoon [17 August], returning next day, to see Captain Walter Lippmann, formerly one of the "Editors" of the "New Republic", now on special service as representative of the American War Office. . . . Had a long talk with him Sunday evening at Savoy Hotel. He was clear that Wilson had engaged unwillingly in the Siberian adventure. Was unable to explain his motive in doing so. The last he knew about the matter was that just before he left America (on, I think he said, July 17) he had said to Mr. Baker[4] that he feared the President was being "pushed into intervention" in Siberia. "You need be under no anxiety", was Baker's answer, "he will not do it". Then when he reached Europe he found he had done it. . . .

I urged that in this matter of intervention as in others the power of America was under-estimated and her influence insufficiently exerted. He asked in what other instances. I said notably in that of the peace offers of the Emperor Karl, so insultingly and stupidly turned down by Clemenceau. Nobody here had been consulted except the Prime Minister and the King. Had Wilson been consulted? He said he believed not. I said it was preposterous, that the power of America was the decisive factor in the war and her responsibility great in proportion. She ought to be represented here by some one in the full confidence of the President and in direct and constant communication with him. He entirely agreed. . . .

He also asked, in case Germany made really reasonable proposals in the autumn, whether they would have a chance of being accepted. I said I was convinced that if the Government accepted them the mass of the people would follow them gladly, but I could not answer for the Government. Lloyd George was not really a bitter-ender and wanted to make peace in certain moods, but he was unstable, had no real hold on political principle, was swayed by his surroundings—at present bad —was largely in the hands of his reactionary associates and would make no heroic sacrifice. . . .

Lloyd George was taken severely ill during his visit to Manchester: hence the gap between Scott's meetings with him.

[4]Newton D. Baker, the Secretary for War.

Diary, 12-18 September 1918

LLOYD GEORGE IN MANCHESTER

Thursday, September 12.
Saw Lloyd George immediately after his speech at the Midland Hotel luncheon succeeding his speech at the Hippodrome. He repeated the declaration he had made in his speech that he would be no party to an extreme war policy[,] and added that the statement to that effect made in his speech that morning would be strongly resented by some of his colleagues and that he had taken risks in making it.

Wednesday, September 18.

Saw him again in his room at the Town Hall as soon as he was allowed to get out of bed. He had sent for me two days before (Monday) on receipt of the news of the Austrian note[5] but the doctor forbad the conversation and I only saw him for a moment. I gathered from Sutherland, his secretary, that what he had wanted to say was that the note did not supply an adequate basis for negotiation, for various reasons which Sutherland detailed. We wrote in the Manchester Guardian of Tuesday condemning Balfour's hasty and ill-considered speech of the previous day and on Wednesday, equally condemning Wilson's summary rejection of the Austrian approach. When I saw Lloyd George on that day the first thing he said to me was "Do you know, I am sorry to say I agree with both leaders in the 'Guardian' today and yesterday". He went on to say that there was no question of accepting the Austrian offer and he understood us to agree in that, but he did strongly object to the haste shown in its rejection, and the absence of any previous consultation. Here was a formal approach from a great Power on a vital matter. There was no need for haste in replying to it and there was great need of common and concerted action. Yet here we had first Balfour and then Wilson and Clemenceau as it were racing to be first in the field to toss it aside. . . .

Clemenceau's deliverance was only what was to be expected from him and after Balfour had led the way no complaint could be made. I said I thought Clemenceau was a little mad. "Oh!", he answered, "he is perfectly mad".

[5]On 14 September the Austrian government had issued an invitation to all belligerents to send delegates to a meeting for "a confidential and noncommittal exchange of views". The United States immediately rejected the invitation, as did Britain and France soon after.

He went on to say that though there were extremists on both sides he believed the mass of the nation was for a moderate policy which should secure our ends without unnecessary sacrifice. I of course warmly concurred and said I believed a policy at once strong for essentials, restrained and without passion would carry an overwhelming majority of the nation and he said that was his opinion. He believed that in the Cabinet he should have the support of Bonar Law for this— "He's a very sensible fellow"—and no doubt of Smuts. Of Balfour also I suggested and he concurred. "There's nothing", he said laughingly as I left[,] ["]like five days of influenza to take the violence out of a man", and then "I begin to think I am the only sensible man left".

Diary, 23-25 September 1918[6]

Saw A. E. Zimmern[7] and his chief Sir W. Tyrrell, head of the Information Department of the Foreign Office. . . . both thought President Wilson's recent rather violent demonstrations were really tactical and were intended to cut the ground from under the feet of Republicans at the forthcoming biennial election for the Senate and House of Representatives and to prevent them from going one better on the war in the present extremely warlike temper of the American people.

Zimmern had been seeing Ellery Sedgwick editor of the "Atlantic Monthly" who breakfasted with me a few days ago when his party of Journalists were in Manchester. I had told him of George's present moderate attitude on the war and of my hope that we might hold him for Liberalism. [Sedgwick] is being entertained in London by Lord Beaverbrook. Beaverbrook had laughed at the idea that George could go back to the Liberals. "We have got him", he said.

Saw Lord Lansdowne by appointment in the afternoon. He regretted that the Austrian proposal for an informal Peace Conference had been received in so hostile a spirit. Not that he desired any sort of inconclusive peace. . . .

I pressed him on the question of Ireland as having a direct bearing on the principles of an international settlement, but here he was quite hopeless and barren. I was a member he said of the Buckingham Palace Conference and Liberals and Conservatives alike were then anxious for a settlement on the basis of Partition, but my feeling since

[6]For once Scott does not specify the precise days on which the various interviews took place.
[7]Historian and educationist, now a member of the Political Intelligence Department of the Foreign Office.

then has hardened against Partition. Geography is against it and the intermixture of the opposing elements, as in Tyrone and Fermanagh. Moreover it seems to me a confession of failure. I said something would have to be done if we were to be able to face the Peace Conference and that it was for the Conservatives to take the initiative. But he had no sort of proposal to make.

C.P.S. to Hobhouse, 8 October 1918 (Extract)

Things are very much as I expected. Success at once inflames our people as it did the Germans[,] and the Americans—if one may judge by the reports (probably carefully selected) vouchsafed to us by Reuter —are hottest of any.

C.P.S. to Hobhouse, 13 October 1918 (Extract)

Isn't the [war] situation developing splendidly? Of course our people at once begin to raise their terms—not only a wild man like Frederic Harrison,[8] but a usually moderate one like Lord Sheffield[9]—see his letter in today's Manchester Guardian.

C.P.S. to Hobhouse, 28 October 1918 (Extract)

We are not out of the wood, but always remember Germany *is absolutely done* and has not a kick left in her. The defection of Austria today is the last blow. She must have peace and have it at once *coûte que coûte*.

Diary, 25-26 October 1918

To London by night. Intended deputation of Manchester Liberal Federation to Lloyd George and Asquith with a view to healing breach in Liberal party fell through owing to premature publication in "Chronicle".

In the afternoon [of 25 October] saw Lord Robert Cecil. . . . Very keen as to League of Nations which he agreed must enter into whole structure of the terms of peace. Was going to take it as subject of his inaugural address as Rector of Birmingham University next month.

Breakfasted [on 26 October] with Lloyd George. He meant to be alone (with only his women folk who don't count!) but Guest sent up

[8]The author and positivist, a strong critic of Germany.
[9]Highly-respected Liberal peer.

word to ask if he might come and he grumbled but assented. It rather prevented a heart to heart conversation as to his political position and prospects which would naturally have followed on discussion of the intended Manchester deputation. As it was we discussed (1) the Peace Negotiation (2) his position on Free Trade (3) on Ireland.

As to (1) he was hopeful—said he would bet 2 to 1 on Peace. Stated the very important fact that Clemenceau was now all for peace. He was 78 and though still in full force was at the end of his career and wanted a prompt settlement. He was himself going to Paris next day to settle with Foch and the other military chiefs the military terms of Armistice.[10] Foch a great man, not merely a great soldier, not self seeking, generous in giving credit to those acting under him, had through the war himself quietly accepted the position of subordination to which he had been relegated, was to be trusted for an honest opinion. If there were extreme demands they were likely to come from our own Admiralty. . . .

(2) In regard to his own position in relation to the Liberal Party and Free Trade he had informed his Unionist colleagues (a) that he would agree to no taxes on food, nor to Protective Tariffs generally. As to so-called "key industries" every great industry was a key to some other industry or industries and all he would do was to take measures, not by tariff but by some administrative machinery, to prevent "dumping" and by dumping he meant the selling in this country of a staple article at below the price of production, so as to disorganise industry here. But as to Protection under the name of Tariff Reform he would have nothing to do with it. He had been amused to observe that Balfour had for it a supreme intellectual contempt.

(3) As to Ireland he was still violent and uncompromising. He would not withdraw the threat of conscription. If there were Peace there would be no conscription but otherwise there would because we should need the men. I tried in vain to represent that he would not get as many men as he would have to use in getting them. Evidently it was not really a question of men but of the assertion of a principle—of the right and power of this country to determine all questions relating to the armed forces of the Crown. As to this Ireland would have to learn a lesson. Resistance would be brushed away as by the mere sweep of our arm. I said there would be bloodshed all over Ireland and that he had perhaps not considered the drastic effects, both as to politics and as to persons which would follow, but he took no heed of this and I could

[10]Since the military crisis of April 1918, Foch had been supreme commander of the Allied forces on the Western Front.

not at the time pursue the matter, but as we left the room he got rid of Guest and we had a few words alone in another room. He said there could be no question of a combination at a General Election between his party and the Liberal Opposition, but only between the Coalition Government and the Opposition. Asquith could not enter the Government as its head, but he might have a great place in it—say as Lord Chancellor.[11]

As he left he said he would like to go further into the matter with me on his return from Paris.

In the evening met Lord Buckmaster at dinner and he put the converse view—that the proper thing for George to do was to say that he had ousted Asquith and parted company with his Liberal colleagues only because of the necessities of the war, that he had not ceased to be a Liberal and that he was prepared to return to the party on the conclusion of peace and to take any position in the Government that might be assigned to him. Then he would inevitably inherit the succession to the leadership.

In the afternoon saw Weizmann who had returned 3 weeks ago from his 7 months' stay in Palestine as head of the Jewish Commission. He gave an extraordinarily interesting account of his mission, the iron wall of military routine against which he had beaten his head and how he had at last succeeded in blowing it up, his voyage of discovery in search of the Arab with whom he was to establish relations . . . at last discovered in the person of the Prince of the Hedjaz, a splendid specimen of a man surrounded by the scum of the earth[,] whom he travelled through the furnace of the desert to find. He was largely under the influence of an Englishman, [T. E.] Lawrence, one of those extraordinary adventurous travellers who assimilate themselves wholly to the people of strange lands and acquire ascendancy over them. It was he who had started the whole Arab movement of revolt and created the new Kingdom of the Hedjaz.

The great danger alike for Jew and for Arab was the Frenchman with his claim to northern Palestine (Samaria) which he was now actually administering and to Damascus where he was already intriguing and seeking by means of loans to the Arab leader to get control over him. But Damascus, Baghdad and Medina were the three necessary pillars of the Arab State and must be preserved for it.

He had been 3 weeks in England and found no one to whom he could report. Balfour had seen him for 25 minutes, tired and half

[11]Asquith had firmly rejected the proposal that he become Lord Chancellor when it had been conveyed to him a month earlier.

asleep, but had taken no step and would take none. His report had simply been pigeonholed. Yet a prompt decision on policy was vital if the future of Palestine was not to be involved in the gravest difficulty and that of the new Arab State compromised. The Arabs loathed the French and in Palestine they would be intolerable.

He begged me to get him an interview with Lloyd George. A solid hour would be needed, alone and without interruption, but it would be worth his while. I promised to do my best.

If Scott secured Weizmann his "solid hour" with Lloyd George, there is no record of it. Indeed there is no record of any further encounter between Scott and Lloyd George in 1918—even though the Prime Minister had said that, on his return from Paris, he wanted a further conversation about his political intentions. The truth was that the two men had nothing left to say on the matter. Lloyd George had made his choice: to fight side by side with the Conservatives, taking a section of Liberals with him but treating the Liberal party as such, and the Labour party, as enemies. From the moment the election was announced, the Manchester Guardian *condemned it as a fraud. As Lloyd George's path proceeded steadily downhill, the* Guardian's *denunciations rose to magisterial heights. In such circumstances Lloyd George could have no more wish to converse with the editor of the paper than he had had in the last weeks of 1916, when he was constituting his government on the predominantly Tory base which was now to provide his platform.*

Oswald Garrison Villard (editor of the New York "Nation") to C.P.S., 15 November 1918 (Extract)

While we are all heartily rejoicing that the bloodshed is over and thanking God that so much has been accomplished in the destroying of German autocracy and militarism, our hearts are very heavy when we think of the Peace Conference, realize the totally unintelligent and uninformed opinion of America, and see all our imperialistic and reactionary forces rallying and in the saddle, save for Mr. Wilson. He is unfortunately weakening steadily under pressure. It is a darker outlook than we have ever known, and we look to you liberals in England, and particularly to the Labour Party and the radical Socialists in France as our one hope. This will strike you as curious, in view of what you write me about your relying on Wilson, when we have found him a weak and unsteady reed, often disappointing and then doing perfectly magnificent public service. But we never can tell from day to day where he will stand.

C.P.S. to Hobhouse, 28 November 1918 (Extract)

I have felt myself more and more driven into opposition by the development of the true inwardness of the whole Coalition cabal which more and more reveals itself as a reactionary movement of large possibilities.

C.P.S. to J. L. Hammond, 4 December 1918 (Extract)[12]

What you tell me of the state of feeling and the growing Chauvinism is disquieting but, with a victory so unexpectedly sweeping, perhaps to be expected. The conditions in America seem to be at least as bad and partizanship rampant. Wilson will certainly have his work cut out. George who at the start meant very well (he spoke to me of his determination to stand for a just peace with obvious sincerity) has gone downhill under stress of the election.

Runciman to C.P.S., 5 December 1918 (Extract)

Your efforts in the last three weeks to raise the level of this election controversy and to preserve free Liberalism from extinction have been the most cheering influences I have struck. And I am especially grateful for your appeals for the League of Nations, which is being quietly smothered in Downing Street and Fleet Street. . . .

John Dillon to C.P.S., n.d. [December 1918][13]

What do you think of Lloyd George now.

Have not my forecasts been more than justified?

Do you remember anything more contemptible in your life experience of public affairs than George's recent election speeches. He has got pretty near the level of [Horatio] Bottomley,[14] who I am told has recently been a welcome and honoured guest at No. 10 Downing Street. . . .

According to my reports I have been beaten in East Mayo by about two thousand majority.[15] The result was brought about by a system of

---

[12] J. L. Hammond Papers. Hammond, a distinguished historian and journalist, was acting as special correspondent for the *Manchester Guardian* at the Peace Conference.
[13] The first part of the letter, including the date, is missing.
[14] Rabble-rousing journalist and politician.
[15] This was to prove an under-estimate. Dillon lost his seat to de Valera, the Sinn Fein candidate, by some 4,500 votes.

intimidation—the most ferocious and elaborately organised I have ever known of. Organised by the secret society. Armed bands were brought from other counties—400 or 500 from Clare—and the people were threatened with death if they voted for me—"The friend of England" (! ! !). If the people had been free to vote as they wished, I am quite certain I would have won *at least* two to one. Redmond[,] in his zeal for the War, allowed *all* our organisation to lapse—and we had no machine to meet this campaign of intimidation.

32. The President, December 1918

When Woodrow Wilson visited Britain on his way to the Peace Conference, he stood high in the estimation of the British left. Admittedly since America entered the war, certain of his actions had aroused misgivings: he had rejected what some thought promising overtures from the enemy powers, and had endorsed intervention in Russia. Yet he still seemed the only hope—and a considerable one—for a good peace settlement. The French appeared bent on revenge; the Italians on loot. Lloyd George, as his conduct during the election campaign had revealed alarmingly, was too unstable to be depended upon. Only American idealism, and the President as its spokesman, seemed powerful enough to counteract these forces. Scott (as he records in one of his rare diary accounts of an interview in Manchester) readily seized the opportunity to urge Wilson in the way he ought to go.

Diary, 29 December 1918

President Wilson. Asked me to call at Town Hall on his arrival in Manchester from Carlisle, on Sunday. Had nearly an hour with him alone. He was extremely friendly and talked very frankly on all the matters discussed.

Spoke of the pleasure he had had in his visit to Carlisle and of the atmosphere of extreme friendliness he had met. In speaking in the Chapel, the lineal descendant of the one where his grandfather had been minister, he said he had done something [of] which his grandfather would have entirely disapproved, but he had thoroughly enjoyed his visit.

RUSSIA

He was well pleased with his conversations with Balfour and Lloyd George and thought things were shaping well. I said I had gathered that from the reports in the newspapers. In Russia they were perhaps not going quite so well and I suggested that he had perhaps gone into that enterprise a little against his will. He said No—that was not so. He had not acted under pressure—at least not from his own people. The pressure had come from England and France, especially from France. He had approved what he regarded as the limited object of the Vladivostok expedition, namely to rescue the Czecho-Slovaks. Beyond that he had merely proposed to assist the inhabitants of the invaded district by supplying them with necessaries and by sending small detachments of troops to escort these supplies and see that they were properly distributed. He arranged to send 9000 men whom he had available and Japan agreed to send the same number. Instead of that she sent 60,000. Further when he desired to establish a depot at Harbin to act as a distributing centre for goods and to send troops to protect them he found the Japanese in possession of every available habitation —not occupying them but having engaged them. It was the same with every other point of vantage. . . . As to any further invasion he was quite opposed to it, though if the Bolsheviks attacked on the Western front they must be repelled.

I suggested that terms could probably be arranged with the Bolsheviks both in regard to the safety of those who had supported us in the Archangel and Murmansk districts and as to the Western border provinces but that we needed first of all much fuller information as to the facts, about which the Government at present knew rather less than the Press, and secondly the opening of conversations with the Bolsheviks, whether we recognised them formally as a *de facto* Government or not. Their invasion was mainly an invasion of ideas and you could not defeat ideas by armies. He entirely agreed. We had no right to interfere with the internal affairs of Russia and, provided they did not attack their neighbours, they had a right to have what internal polity they liked. His policy all through had been not to attack Russia but to help her.

GERMANY

I asked how far we were now helping Germany in regard both to food and the raw materials of industry[,] both of which were necessary if she was to avoid such internal troubles as would be entirely against our interests as well as her own. We had all had great confidence in Hoover,[1] but time passed and nothing was done. He replied that

[1]Herbert Hoover, director of various economic relief activities in Europe including the organisation of food supplies.

Hoover was indeed worthy of all confidence, but the delay was no fault of his. He was being held up by our Government, or rather specifically by Lord Reading who was in control of the matter and who refused to deal with Germany until he could do so as part of a general scheme he had in hand for the rationing of supplies all round. He (the President) fully recognised the importance from every point of view of giving speedy relief to Germany. He was inclined to take the matter into his own hands. . . .

LEAGUE OF NATIONS

He asked what bearing I thought the result of the [British] elections might have on foreign policy.[2] I said I thought very little. The greatness of the majority was no real strength to the Government—perhaps the reverse. He said Yes, when he saw Lloyd George and Balfour before leaving London they were overwhelmed at what had happened and could not get their bearings. I said the matter was really in the hands of the Government and they could do pretty much what they liked. He said he found them very favourable to his policy.

I said Lloyd George need not have descended so low in his electoral appeals in order to get his majority, that the line he had taken was not really consistent with any atmosphere in which a League of Nations could be created. He assented. I spoke of George's inconsequence as a reassuring feature in this connection. As Morley had remarked of him, he could not understand a principle; he acted on feeling, impulse, vision and his policy was not a consistent whole. I begged Wilson not to regard the result of the election as a demonstration against the policy of a League of Nations. It was nothing of the sort; the League of Nations was not in question. It was due to a great wave of emotion thrown up by the war and was at bottom an expression of pure anti-Germanism inflamed by Lloyd George's appeals. He agreed and said this was strictly analogous to what had happened in the recent Congressional elections in America.[3] They were in no degree a demonstration against his policy and there was nothing concerted about them, but every man among his supporters against whom a charge could be

[2] The election had resulted in a landslide victory for the Conservatives and the Lloyd George Liberals. The non-government parties had been routed. Asquith, Simon, McKenna, Runciman, and other prominent Liberals had lost their seats, as had Labour leaders like Henderson, MacDonald, and Snowden. In Ireland, the Nationalists had been swept away by Sinn Fein.

[3] As a result of the mid-term elections in the U.S.A., the Republicans now possessed a majority in both Houses of Congress.

brought of slackness in the war or pro-German sympathies was promptly fired.

I begged him to believe that all the better and deeper feeling of the nation was on his side and only needed to be appealed to. He said he was very glad to hear that. In point of fact it was his intention, if in the course of the Peace negotiations he found himself met by obstacles to his policy which he could not overcome, then to make a public statement, he hoped in the politest terms but still perfectly clear and frank, as to the position and to challenge the public opinion of the world.

I said I had good hopes of Lloyd George, that he responded very quickly to his surroundings and could I believed be greatly influenced by him, but he was extremely elusive and in dealing with him you had to keep an extremely bright look-out. He replied, with a twinkle, that though he liked George very much, he was quite conscious of that.

I remarked that any little influence I might myself have had with him was probably now at an end, since of late we had been steadily attacking him. He said he had noticed that, but that when George had spoken of me to him recently he had done so in the most friendly terms and appeared to bear no malice. . . .

33. Peacemaking, 1919

The problems facing the nation in the first year of peace were formidable: industrial unrest at home, Ireland utterly estranged, Russia in chaos, France desperate for security against a German recovery, Germany apparently on the brink of starvation and anarchy. One problem above others captured attention: what was to be the nature of the peace settlement? The issue seemed of the utmost importance. Allied statesmen were convinced—perhaps they were wrong—that it lay in their power to make or mar the new Europe.

To Scott the alternatives seemed clear (though in practice they proved to be less so): either it could be a peace of reconciliation, with Germany rehabilitated as a democracy and the League of Nations established as the instrument of international harmony; or a peace of vengeance, with Germany to be held in permanent subjection, and the League a victors' weapon for keeping it so. As the Peace Conference proceeded, Scott and his associates looked sometimes to Wilson, sometimes to Lloyd George, sometimes to both, to produce the first sort of peace. But in the end they sadly concluded that it was the second sort they had got. And they did not doubt that the consequences of the wrong decisions made at Paris would hang heavy on the world for generations to come.

C.P.S. to Lloyd George, 7 January 1919 (Extract)

I was delighted with Wilson when he was in Manchester, and I gathered that he was delighted with you. The combination ought to be formidable.

C.P.S. to Hobhouse, 27 January 1919 (Extract)

Things are going pretty well there [i.e. at the Peace Conference] I think. George has evidently determined to throw in his lot with Wilson and the combination is formidable. Luckily George is quite as ready to cast aside what is bad as what is good and he has now left the General Election far behind him and is well on the way—with Wilson's aid—

368

to pick up again some of his Liberal principles. He may yet emerge as a shining example of Progressive statesmanship. I thought the olive branch to the Bolsheviks must have been of Wilson's suggestion but Smuts wrote to tell me it was all Lloyd George's own and that he was quite hurt at being denied the credit.[1] The Duke of Somerset I see like the "Morning Post" regards it as an incredible betrayal, but the gay little man won't care a fig.

Diary, 21-22 February 1919

To London by night (Thursday) to see Lloyd George at his suggestion. Was to have breakfasted with him on Friday [21 February], but changed at the last moment to Saturday. Weizmann came to breakfast with me at the Euston Hotel [on the 21st]. At the crisis of his affairs. Zionist Conference from all over the world on Tuesday. Discussion at Peace Conference very shortly. . . . Strongly advised him to concentrate at the Peace Conference on getting adequate powers i.e. a satisfactory "mandate" to Great Britain and to leave all else for settlement with British, which would be comparatively easy.

After breakfast called on A. E. Zimmern at Foreign Office, who had asked to see me. He was full of a projected Committee, of which Lord Bryce was to be chairman, for collecting and collating information about Russia by bringing the witnesses (whose accounts differed so widely) together and cross questioning them. Asked me to join Committee which he said would meet only about once a fortnight. Gave doubtful reply. He also introduced me to the latest and one of the most authentic witnesses, a photographer and mechanic named Keeling 5 years in Petrograd and just returned. He reported (1) great scarcity. His own salary from Soviet was the highest paid, 1500 roubles a month and that barely kept him going. The older paper currency alone negotiable at any price in country districts. The later valueless. Barter the only profitable mode of payment. Had bought 80 lbs of flour for an old suit, as clothing was almost unprocurable.

(2) Universal discontent among workpeople owing to the general scarcity. They had hailed the second revolution with joy, but now said that, though its principles were beautiful in theory, in practice they would not work.

(3) Universal terrorism. Two people could not stop to talk in the street

[1]On 22 January 1919 Lloyd George and Wilson persuaded Clemenceau and Orlando, the Italian Premier, to agree to a conference of all Russian factions on Prinkipo island. The *émigré* Russians, however, refused to attend and the scheme lapsed.

without incurring suspicion and death was the ready penalty for all suspects. To be in possession of arms of any sort was to incur the death penalty. The returning soldiers had kept theirs for a time, but had now all parted with them under threats. Spying was everywhere and combination to resist had become impossible. Elections were farcical. Some one was put up to nominate the person it was desired by the authorities should be elected and nobody dared oppose. Keeling had been sent about a good deal as a mechanic to do repairs to places as far as 1000 miles from Petrograd and found the feeling everywhere the same among the people he met, but these of course would be mainly artizans.

He finally escaped with the utmost difficulty by walking the 60 miles to the Finnish frontier and evading the numerous guards. Finally he only got through the last one by pretending he was going to see a friend and buy tobacco (for which the people were wild)[,] promising to give some to the guard and leaving his pack as security. After all the guard thought better of it and pursued him, but he had reckoned on that and took hiding.

Later called by appointment on Lord Robert Cecil[2]. . . . He spoke with much satisfaction of the progress made with the League of Nations scheme. He admitted, however, that much remained to be done. I said it could not be regarded as securely established while Germany and Russia remained outside. Germany, he agreed, must be admitted "as soon as practicable". As to Russia he took a very despairing view. To his mind the only alternatives were intervention or some form of a dictatorship. But military intervention by the Allies on an adequate scale was impracticable. Not one of them could or would undertake it. He saw nothing for it therefore but a restoration of autocracy, not necessarily of course the old autocracy. As a matter of fact Bolshevism was itself an autocracy, a despotic form of government.

Why not, I suggested, try what can be made of the Bolshevists—start from the position as it exists today and try to build up a tolerable order upon it? The Bolshevists show signs of learning by experience and of coming to terms with the adherents of the old social order. He would not hear of this. Bolshevism in his view was impossible as a basis of society and nothing could be built on it. . . .

He spoke very seriously of the attitude of the French towards the League of Nations. They did not believe in it and took no interest

[2]Cecil was now out of the government, and was devoting himself to the establishment of the League of Nations.

whatever in it except as it might bear on the question of French military security. . . .

Lunched with Bryce. He was very strong on the Bolshevik barbarities. Thought there was ample evidence for them and that they vastly exceeded those of the French revolution. There was in truth "a sea of blood". Made no suggestions, however, of policy. Spoke of Asquith's extreme unpopularity for which he could not quite account. No doubt Lloyd George had done better in the war, but he thought Asquith would have pulled through. . . .

In the evening dined with Garvin. Found he had cooled a good deal in regard to Lloyd George. Said he had been injured by power—not in the sense of being puffed up and thrown off his balance, but he had become entranced by the handling of great affairs and by the great game of politics. He had lost his ideals and forgotten that little thing, his soul. . . .

Breakfast [on 22 February] with Lloyd George alone. He came into the big drawing-room (not nearly so nice as the dining-room at No. 11. The dining-room here even more enormous—would seat a battalion) very jolly and genial. Didn't I think him very forgiving? So I didn't judge him worthy to be a member of the Manchester Reform Club?[3] I said it was a challenge and had to be met. "I don't mind['], he said, ["]because I know that with you there's no malice. I always read what you say and sometimes I profit by it. As for the 'Daily News' and 'Nation' I never heed them because I know that in their eyes I never can do right. I know beforehand what they're going to say. But with you it is otherwise. You can say what you like. I shan't resent it" and on that we went to breakfast.

"Well," he said, "don't you think I've done pretty well at the Conference". Yes, I said, jolly well and I have been delighted at the way you have backed up the President. He went on to speak of the hopeless attitude of the French and this has become even worse since the attempt on Clemenceau.[4] His disablement a great misfortune because he had unique authority and could afford to be moderate. Wilson's attitude was a little too stiff. Some concessions would have to be made to the French—the Saar Valley coalfield for instance. I asked did he mean the use of it or the possession. Oh! the possession he

[3]Lloyd George had been chosen President of the Manchester Reform Club for the coming year. The *Manchester Guardian* had criticised this choice, arguing that his conduct towards the Liberal party at the election had called in doubt his position as a Liberal.
[4]Three days before, Clemenceau had received a bullet wound during an unsuccessful attempt to assassinate him.

answered. . . . A buffer state must also be conceded, and the country west of the Rhine—that is all Rhenish Prussia—converted into such a State. (He did not say whether with its consent or without it, but Ramsay MacDonald, whom I saw later and to whom and the Webbs he had said the same thing[,] said they none of them had any doubt that he meant this to be part of the conditions of peace and that no option would be allowed).

As to Russia he took the view that Prinkipo was "off" and that for the present we must mark time. The Bolsheviks had not agreed to the armistice which was one of the conditions of the Prinkipo conference. He was dead against military intervention, but inclined to think we must continue to supply with arms and ammunition the various independent forces opposed to the Bolsheviks.

As to Ireland he stood by the terms of the letter "which you helped me to compose in this room" which contained, along with the offer of the Convention, a far-reaching scheme of Dominion Home Rule minus Customs and Excise. The Tories had agreed to that and were surprised now to find how far they had gone. But he could take no action while the condition of Ireland remained as at present. . . .

C.P.S. to Hammond, 4 March 1919[5]

I saw Lloyd George a few days ago and am greatly concerned at his present attitude. As to the Western front he is prepared to agree (a) to the annexation by France of the Saar Valley coal-field, (b) to the conversion of all the rest of German territory West of the Rhine into a buffer State, independent of Germany. These arrangements can hardly be reconciled with the principles of "self-determination" and a "just peace" as laid down by Wilson and I can't imagine his consenting to them or the American people consenting to guarantee them. As to Russia he had quite given up Prinkipo and had nothing better to suggest than practically the status quo with continued support to the anti-Bolshevik forces.

Truly it's time the President came back!. . . .

C.P.S. to Hammond, 20 March 1919[6] (Extract)

Your last Sunday's telegram was tremendously encouraging as indicating that on the essential points in the controversy with France the

[5]Hammond Papers.
[6]Hammond Papers.

President was winning all along the line. No other paper had anything at all on the same line and, though you put the thing a little less confidently in a letter written about the same time, it seems to be working out all right. The President once described himself as the most obstinate man in the world. It's lucky!

C.P.S. to Hammond, 5 April 1919[7] (Extract)

At least if the wrong thing is done at Danzig it will not be for lack of knowledge.[8] How well Lloyd George seems to have shown up in this business. Imagination, courage—what are they not worth in a tight place. He seems to have found himself in the singular position of defending Wilsonian principles against Wilson.

By slow degrees and against great obstacles I believe a substantially just peace is emerging. What troubles me most now is the crime of the blockade.[9] There seems to be no limit to French vindictiveness and commercial jealousy. Wilson ought never to have stood it, but though he can be firm in *resistance* ("obstinate" as he says of himself) I'm afraid he isn't equally strong in action and initiative and that he is better in stating a principle than in forcing its application. George is worth two of him there.

C.P.S. to Bryce, 6 April 1919[10] (Extract)

My information from Paris (I got W. H. Dawson[11] to go out and he has had some conversation with Lloyd George) is that George is putting up a strong fight for the right policy both in regard to Danzig and in regard to the West front. He can't have everything his own way, but he is backing Wilson steadily and deserves great credit for what he has

[7]Hammond Papers.

[8]Although German in population, Danzig was in the process of being separated from Germany so as to provide the reconstituted state of Poland with an outlet to the sea. Eventually it was made a "free city" under the League of Nations, but with Poland exercising a large measure of control.

[9]The Allied blockade continued for four months after the armistice (by which time much of the German population was starving), partly because Foch was determined thereby to force Germany to accept the peace terms, partly because the Germans failed to make merchant shipping available to supply themselves with food. Thanks to an impassioned intervention by Lloyd George and better sense on the part of the German government, the blockade was effectually ended from March.

[10]Bryce Papers.

[11]The historian, who had just replaced Hammond as the *Manchester Guardian*'s special correspondent in Paris.

done. Nobody else could have done it—particularly in face of his own hot-heads and the unscrupulous press attacks.

He is showing more of the real quality of statesmanship than I ever thought him capable of. Liberals ought to back him steadily and quietly, so as not to rouse the Jingoes.

Hobhouse to C.P.S., 12 May 1919 (Extract)

I think if I had been Wilson I had rather have put a bullet through my head than signed those terms. I fear all protest is ineffectual, but every man I talk to whose opinion I value takes the same view. Tawney tells me that his fellow soldiers are especially keen. The feeling is that [it] is a real and deep breach of faith with the German Republic, and that it simply rivets conscription and militarism on us all. . . . No doubt for each detail taken alone some sort of case can be made out, but when the whole are put together it is an attempted reduction of Germany to serfdom, and it won't work. . . .

The League of Nations as formed to guarantee this settlement seems to be not an imperfect good thing but a definitely bad thing like the Holy Alliance, and Liberals ought in my judgment to refuse to go further with it.

C.P.S. to Hobhouse, 19 May 1919 (Extract)

By the bye I hear that Smuts returned to England the other day and it might be worth while to see him if he is at the Savoy. His views on the peace would be illuminating. He remarked to Weizmann, who was on the same boat, that it was not made in Heaven.

Smuts to C.P.S., 26 June 1919 (Extract)

Now that the Peace Treaty is on the point of being signed, I wish to write you a line to express my admiration for the magnificent courage and ability with which you have fought many of its reactionary provisions. I view it as a thoroughly bad peace—impolitic and impracticable in the case of Germany, absolutely ludicrous in the case of German Austria.[12] Indeed I have not been able to read the comments of the

[12]The Austrian Empire of 30 millions was shorn of its subject peoples (and some of its Germanic peoples) and reduced to a small landlocked state of six-and-a-half millions. Despite the expressed wish of what remained of Austria to be united with Germany, this was forbidden under the terms of the treaty.

Austrian delegates on our draft terms without deep emotion. I have fought this Peace from the inside with all my power, and have no doubt been able in the end to secure some small openings of hope for the future.

Diary, 5 July 1919

GENERAL SMUTS

Had some scattered conversations with Smuts on his visit to Manchester to receive his honorary degree when he was by way of being my guest.

The Peace. "I return to South Africa a defeated man". Those were his words and he explained that he had fought persistently for a better settlement but had failed. The General Election was at the root of the mischief. Lloyd George had meant well and he had been in close touch with him. He was "all right in 1917 and all right in 1918" down to the moment of the General Election. I besought him then not to commit himself, told him he was bound to win easily and that he need give no pledges. But letters came pouring in from election agents all over the country declaring that people were caring about nothing but punishments and indemnities and Lloyd George gave way. Ever since he has been tied by his pledges.

Wilson he described as "a second-rate man", he handled the whole business without adequate knowledge or resolution. But "in spite of his weakness and his folly" his ideal, he agreed with me, would remain and in time would win its way. George was unstable without any clear guiding principle "jumping about" from one position to another. Balfour was a tragedy, a mere dilettante, without force or guidance, when a strong British Foreign Minister might have saved the whole situation. Clemenceau knew clearly what he wanted from the beginning and got it.

League of Nations is our best hope, but unless put on a right footing from the first may become entirely futile. The diplomats are all against it, regarding it as a toy to amuse and mislead the public, but intending all the time to carry on their old game just as before. . . . If the League is to be effective it must meet constantly and be represented by first rate men from all the countries who are parties to it, and it must be supplied with all the detailed and confidential information which goes to the various foreign offices. Its model should be the Supreme International War Council which met at Paris during the later stage of the war and won it. . . .

The *Manchester Guardian*. He spoke very warmly of the service rendered by the paper. It was the only paper Lloyd George cared about. "It is very strange; it hasn't got a large circulation; yet it's the only paper that counts". So Smuts reported him as saying. "He doesn't mind what the others say, but when you attack him he squirms". . . .

Diary, 12-14 August 1919

Called Curzon in afternoon [of 12 August] at his request. . . . [*Inter alia* he remarked that] the worst of our recent commitments was Palestine. He was dead against the whole Zionist arrangement. The Zionists were very grasping and arrogant and even claimed to expropriate the Arabs though in numbers they were only as one to four.

Lunched with Lloyd George [on 14 August]. Sir M. Hankey was there most of the time, but that did not much matter as he is such an intimate.

We talked first about the foreign situation. I said I hoped he would put his foot down about the Archduke Joseph's usurpation and Rumania's defiance of the Peace Conference.[13] If the Peace Conference could be defied with impunity how much more could the League of Nations in whose place it now stood. The whole credit of the League of Nations was at stake. He agreed, but when I asked when he expected to take part in person again in the Conference seemed altogether doubtful, except that he "supposed he should be there to sign the Austrian Treaty".

Then he went on to talk about Russia. Thought there must be a revival of the Prinkipo proposal. Spoke highly of Lenin's ability and with enthusiasm of the organizing power of Trotsky. The way in which he had created a great army, without munitions, or factories or transport was one of the greatest achievements of the War. Said he was altogether in favour of coming to terms. Not only was our army to be withdrawn but he had given notice to Churchill that the supply of munitions now being sent would have to be the last. At the same time he thought there had been advantage in the aid we had so far given because it had compelled the Bolsheviks to come to terms with the other less extreme revolutionary parties and there was now the possibility of the rise of a more stable Government. . . .

[13]Rumania, with the indulgence of the Peace Conference, had invaded Hungary to overthrow the Communist regime of Bela Kun. But, to the Allies' dismay, the Rumanians then proceeded to occupy Budapest, eject the moderate socialist regime which had replaced Kun, and set up a reactionary government under the Habsburg Archduke Joseph.

Afterwards we got on to Ireland. Asked if I had seen Dillon lately. I said no as he had been ill for 6 months and nearly died, but I had heard from him. What policy had he. I said he wrote chiefly of the past, and what might have been. He said he thought he was a spent force and I could not deny it. He has always had a curious ill-will against Dillon. His [i.e. Dillon's] tinge of fanaticism and lack of *bonhomie* are extremely antipathetic to George. . . .

Harold Spender to C.P.S., 23 August 1919 (Extract)

I had a long talk with the Prime Minister on Ireland, and found him entirely hopeless. He said that Ireland always had hated England and always would. He could easily govern Ireland with the sword: he was far more concerned about the Bolsheviks at home. . . .

He seemed to me to have surrendered to the most extreme Anti-Irish hatred.

C.P.S. to Hobhouse, 3 September 1919 (Extract)

I'm so sorry I shan't see you before you leave. There are a lot of things I should like to talk to you about. First is it, or is it not, desirable that the American Senate should refuse to sign the Treaty? If that would mean that the Treaty would have to be revised I should say refuse by all means. But would it and could it? Of course America's signature is not necessary to its validity for the other Powers, but could a treaty to which America refused to be a party on the ground of its injustice stand? I doubt it. Not for long any way and a fresh Conference must be summoned within a year. Is that not worth playing for? France, it seems, already begins to see that her real security is the League of Nations which she has crabbed and derided.

Then what about the position of Lloyd George and the possibility of the return of Asquith? This Government is doomed. What is to succeed it? Are we to wait on the good pleasure of Lloyd George and his calculation of chances, or should he not rather be forced to make his choice and have done with tight-rope walking?

It is the measure of Scott's disgust with Lloyd George that it seems to have driven him (to judge from the following letters written to him by Loreburn) to regard even Asquith as a desirable replacement. Loreburn did not agree. He held no brief for Lloyd George—"We need a change of Government: chiefly to get rid of Lloyd George and Churchill", he wrote on 2 October; nevertheless "Lloyd

George did good work, excellent work, in ending the war." But nothing would persuade him to say a good word about Asquith.

Loreburn to C.P.S., 3 September 1919 (Extract)

I am sorry and surprised that you think Asquith a possible leader in place of Lloyd George. . . . I cannot understand your thinking him possible.

Loreburn to C.P.S., 2 October 1919 (Extract)

I have known Asquith for years and sat with him in Parliament. He will not bring the two qualities needed viz. honesty and courage but will merely talk generalities and practise shuffling and deception. You say he has no courage no imagination no initiative and is steeped in the old traditions of political management and diplomacy but that he has some dignity some prudence and moderation and will take his cue from his supporters. Who are they? They are the men who have by their blindness and incompetence and want of independence nearly ruined the country.

C.P.S. to Bryce, 26 October 1919[14] (Extract)

The weakness and folly of the Paris Conference is almost beyond belief. Not a man left among them, it would seem, after Hoover left. What an impression he produced. If only he had been President!

C.P.S. to Hobhouse, 31 October 1919 (Extract)

G. P. Gooch tells me that he has completed the life of Courtney. . . . What was so splendid about [Courtney] was his unshakable stand for principle, for which in these days hardly anybody seems resolutely to stand. Could any contrast be greater than that between his whole mentality and that of Lloyd George, which seems to have infected our whole politics?

Diary, 30 November–1 December 1919

Went to dinner with Lloyd George [on 30 November] at his new house at Cobham. The American ambassador (Davis) and his wife and Sir Eric and Lady Geddes also there[15]. . . .

[14]Bryce Papers.   [15]Geddes was at this time Minister of Transport.

[At dinner] there was a lot of chaff about Lloyd George as a "so called" Liberal and Geddes as a "so-called" Conservative, and Lloyd George recited with pride the legislative achievements of the session most of which would have been impossible but for the existence of the Coalition and several of which the Manchester Guardian, he remarked, had not condescended to notice while seizing on "peccadilloes" like the Dumping Bill. Then he sang the praises of Coalitions. Any government at present must be a Coalition, since the alternative to the present Coalition was a Labour and "Asquithian" Coalition. I said I had not the least objection to Coalition in itself, but only to surrenders of principle as a condition of forming one.

As I left he was rather extra friendly, fearing I fancy that I might have taken his chaff amiss which of course I should not dream of doing. He wore such a nice grey velveteen coat on which I complimented him.

Geddes and his wife sung a lot of not very Sunday songs—mostly roaring Scots ballads. She is fortissimo all through, but he sang with admirable mellowness and humour. The ambassador and his wife joined heartily in the choruses.

Lloyd George has placed [H. A. L.] Fisher[16] in charge of the preparation of the Home Rule Bill and asked me to go and see him before I left next day. He spoke in very warm terms of him—"another Morley" he said, most popular also and influential in the Cabinet, and a thorough Liberal—evidently his chief support on the Liberal side.

Went to see Fisher [on 1 December] by appointment at 12 o'clock. He is friendly but a little inexpressive, very unlike George's exuberance. Like everybody else in the Government he has too much on his hands and complained that there are not "brains enough" available for the tasks in hand. . . . I pressed urgently on Fisher the necessity of not pushing the [Irish] hunger-strikers to extremities. Their deaths would make any settlement impossible and that was why it would be likely to happen. There was beyond question some malign influence in the Irish Administration which *did not want* a settlement and had again and again conspired or at least succeeded in preventing it. You cannot trust your own Government. He listened and more or less acquiesced, but it needs a good deal more than that to put a bridle on the Irish Executive.

Diary, 20 December 1919

Dined with Lloyd George at Cobham, returning the same evening. He was in the midst of writing out his speech [on Ireland] for next day

16Prominent historian and Lloyd George's Minister of Education.

and was deeply impressed with the difficulty of his task and of the whole situation. I never saw him so gloomy. He revived a little after dinner when Megan played some fine old Welsh hymn tunes and he joined in in his mellow voice with the Welsh words. "I have seen a crowd of Welshmen go quite mad over that tune", he said, of one of them.

At dinner there was much discussion of the government's proposals for Ireland. Scott summed it up as follows:

All through George seemed to me to be contemplating retreat. He had to propose something, but obviously he had little faith in his own plan. Everybody in Ireland he said would be against him and unless he got support in England he could not go on.

When I remarked that at least the Government could deliver the goods as they had nothing to fear from the *House of Lords*, he said "I must deal with the House of Lords[17] next session". I objected that any change was likely to leave them stronger. He said "I think it might be rather useful as a check on the Labour Party". . . .

Bryce to C.P.S., 20 January 1920 (Extract)

What do you think of J. M. Keynes's book?[18] . . . . The condemnation of the work of the Conference as a whole is none too severe. I remember few cases in history where negotiators might have done so much good, and have done so much evil.

G. Lowes Dickinson to C.P.S., 27 January [1920] (Extract)

I saw Keynes last night, he thinks it is too late now for any remedies, and that we shall have bolshevism and anarchy from Vladivostok to the Rhine. Did ever set of men do such evil in the world as those who met at Paris? Literally, they have destroyed Europe and the whole heritage of its civilisation.

[17]i.e. with the question of House of Lords reform.
[18]*The Economic Consequences of the Peace* (Macmillan, London, December 1919), which instantly became the classic condemnation of the Peace Treaty.

34. The Future of Mr. Lloyd George, 1920

Scott came to London but little in 1920. In its early months he talked several times with ministers about the government's Irish bill. But as Lloyd George moved decisively towards repression in Ireland, Scott had no further wish to discuss the matter with him.

In a wider sense the two men now lacked grounds for discussion. On 17 March 1920, as recorded below, they talked about Lloyd George's future. Part of the conversation was on a metaphysical plane: Lloyd George believed that events shaped the course of individuals, not vice versa. Part was more down to earth: the Prime Minister hinted that he wished to resume his career as a Liberal. None of this is very illuminating. What is illuminating is the matter they did not discuss.

For months it had been an open secret that Lloyd George was planning to break with the Liberal party for good. His scheme was to enter into a permanent alliance with the Conservatives by converting the coalition into a "Centre" party. Its programme was to be negative: a crusade against "socialism", i.e. the Labour party. By March 1920 he was trying to bring these plans to fruition. On 15 March, two days before he conversed with Scott, he had held a private meeting with his Liberal associates in the government to sell them the Centre party scheme. (They had firmly resisted it). A full account of this meeting had somehow got into The Times *next day. Yet on 17 March Scott and Lloyd George managed to discuss the latter's political future without mentioning the Centre party, the conclave of Liberal ministers, or the previous day's revelations in* The Times.

It is easy to see why. Had they got on to these matters, they would have come into head-on collision. During the war it had been possible to have meaningful discussions about Lloyd George's future course, because there had been a real element of doubt concerning the choice he would make. Now there was none. So, if they talked about the matter at all, they must either quarrel or ignore the most salient facts in the situation. On 17 March they chose to do the latter.

But it is not surprising that Scott did not spend much of 1920 having such conversations.

Diary, 16-17 March 1920

Went up [late on 15 March] really to see Kerr who had asked to see me about the Irish Bill[1]. Lloyd George left word asking me to breakfast, so I stayed another day.

Saw Kerr on Tuesday morning [16 March]. He admitted the defects of the Bill, but said it was the best that could be got from the existing Government. It would at least accomplish two essential things: it would take Ulster out of the Irish question which it had blocked for a generation and it would take Ireland out of English party controversies. There would never be another special Irish Bill. . . .

In the afternoon called on Fisher in his room at the House. . . . he regarded the Bill as falling far short of the Liberal standard, but none the less judged it to be of the utmost importance that it should pass. He had no expectation that it would be accepted by Sinn Fein as a settlement and, if as was probable they refused to work it and endeavoured to set up an independent authority of their own, military government would have to go on, perhaps for 2 or 3 years till they changed their minds. In time moderate opinion and business interests would assert themselves and men would be elected who would consent to form a Parliament. . . .

He recognised that the political situation was precarious, but he did not care what happened once the Bill was passed—to Lloyd George or anybody else—and on that we parted.

Breakfasted [on 17 March] with Lloyd George—alone for some time, then Mrs. George and a lady friend came in, but as usual Lloyd George went on talking ignoring their existence and he stayed on for some time after they had gone till Colonel Hankey, secretary to the Cabinet, came in to claim him for business.

We talked partly on Ireland, partly on the general political situation. As to the Bill he said they must at all costs pass it. Nothing could be done to amend it to which Carson objected.[2] A tremendous case could be made against it on the ground of the state of Ireland—the murders and the rampant sedition. Papers had been found (in the pockets I gathered of the man who was landed from a German submarine) showing a plot for risings in England as well as in Ireland on the morrow of a German success. Carson, if he chose, could blow the Bill sky

---

[1] The bill offered a limited form of Home Rule to a divided Ireland. North and south were to have separate Parliaments, but these could unite if each side was agreeable. The south utterly rejected the measure, but Ulster eventually accepted it.

[2] Carson had been out of the government since January 1918.

high. There was already plenty of dissatisfaction on the Tory side. They couldn't reconcile themselves to a predominantly Unionist Government passing a Home Rule Bill. There had been a meeting only the day before at the Carlton Club[3] which declared unanimously (66 of them) against the Bill. Bonar Law was much concerned for the meeting was not made up only of extremists and fire eaters but [contained] a proportion of good steady-going party men.

I asked what he thought of the prospects of the Bill. He made no doubt of getting it through. If there was serious Unionist opposition in the Commons they would have to be told that if they were not satisfied with the Irish policy of this Government they must find another Government they liked better. As to the Lords he did not think they would reject the Bill if it passed the Commons. At the same time he said something about the impossibility of carrying the Bill if everybody opposed it which was not obviously consistent with this uncompromising attitude. . . .

He referred to a leader I had written in the paper of the day before on "The future of Mr. Lloyd George" and said he thought it a very good one. Didn't I think so. I warmly concurred.[4] He said he had been particularly interested in the part which dealt with the action and re-action of events and personalities, that for his part he was of those who held that the individual counted for little and was in fact the creature of circumstance. For himself he made no pretence to be among the Caesars and the Cromwells, but looking back over his recent career he could not see how at any point he could have taken a different course to that which he had chosen. Everything had concurred to force him into the position he had taken. If for instance at the beginning he had had to do with Balfour instead of Bonar Law there would have been a Unionist Government in place of a Coalition with himself as Prime Minister. And so it had been all through.

As to the future he quite recognised that Coalition could not be a permanent form of Government, but Asquith also could never form a Government. There was no life in him. He was "like a great boulder, blocking the way". Nor could he [i.e. Asquith] join with Labour. He (George) had far greater sympathy with Labour. Nor were his followers —men like Runciman and McKenna—any better. The one man in the

[3]A leading Conservative club.
[4]Included in the editorial (though one would hardly guess it from this conversation) were passages like the following: "Is it then true that in winning the war Mr. Lloyd George has lost himself—that, at least, the pre-war Mr. George, the champion of Liberalism, the great fighter for every progressive cause, has passed from us to return no more?"

Liberal ranks of any commanding personality was Grey. I asked would he serve under Grey and he at once said unhesitatingly and cordially "Certainly". I said in that case the succession would inevitably be his. He said he was not troubling about that.

In a curious way he was evidently feeling his way back to his old position in the Liberal ranks. He had been examining his past to see, if he could, where he had gone wrong and recognised only the hand of fate. Now when he looked forward reconciliation might be practicable only there was Asquith, impossible himself, blocking the way. "Well, we've had a very useful conversation. Don't desert me", he added laughingly as we parted. "Come and see me sometimes and correct my faults". When I demurred he added "Or help my best self". I think he partly meant that. He would be far happier to be a Liberal.

Diary, 10 April 1920

Went up by morning train at urgent request of Zionists who are in terror of an impending recognition of Arab Suzereignty over Palestine as part of the Emir Feyzal's Syrian kingdom. Lunched with Lloyd George and saw him alone for a quarter of an hour or so afterwards. He was leaving next morning for the Peace Conference meeting at San Remo.

Speaking of the Irish Bill he was emphatic that the Bill must be put through and that, as far as Ulster was concerned, it would be brought into operation. Of course if Sinn Fein refused to work it he could not make them. But Carson had made it a condition of his support that the Bill should be put through. He had been let down on the compromise agreement of 1916 and he would not run the same risk again. . . .

As to the Ruhr incident and the isolated action of France in occupying Frankfort he was emphatic that our hand was not to be forced in this way.[5] If France thought that she could move forward and we should meekly follow she was entirely mistaken. The present movement was the work of the Chauvinist party—Poincaré, Briand and the rest—who had overthrown Clemenceau on the accusation of weakness ("Clemenceau weak!" he interjected) and wanted to show what a truly "French" policy meant. There was no justification for these attacks on Germany. She was right down "in the mud" and helpless. I re-

[5] The French had occupied Frankfort and other German cities because the German government, in order to suppress Communist disturbances, had sent large numbers of troops into the area demilitarised by the Treaty of Versailles. (Eventually the French withdrew under British protests).

marked that the incident was not exactly encouraging for the desired Franco-British alliance. "No, indeed!" he said. . . .

In regard to Palestine he assured me there was no change of policy. "Jimmie" Rothschild had been over that morning to see him about it. At the same time he seemed to me to be fencing a little with the matter. When I asked for an assurance that no adverse step should be taken in his absence he said the whole matter would be discussed and settled at San Remo. Finally he suggested that Herbert Samuel should come there to present the Zionist case.[6]

C.P.S. to Hobhouse, 21 May 1920

This is called a forecast of the Government Bill,[7] but obviously it is just a summary of the Bill itself. . . . It looks like just a revival of the old corn law. The excuse that prices must be guaranteed because a minimum wage is fixed [for labourers] would apply, so far as I can see, in any other industry in which a minimum wage is enforced and is untenable provided the minimum is a reasonable one. How does not war breed reaction all round. What will the Coalition Liberals, I wonder, have to say to this? How incredible such things would have seemed in the days before the war!

Diary, 4 June 1920

Breakfasted with Lloyd George. The Archbishop of York[8] also there. Rumoured that he [i.e. Lloyd George] was casting about for a new Irish policy and I wanted to test this, but found him entirely occupied with plans for repression. There must, he regretted to say, be stronger measures. Crime was unpunished—29 police murdered and no one brought to justice. The force would become demoralised if this went on. It was already demoralised in Dublin. He was informed by the authorities there that if a murder took place in the street under the eyes of the police no arrest would be made.

He proposed to set up a special tribunal—a Judge to try murder cases without a jury. "What about evidence?" I asked. We have got

---

[6]Despite Scott's misgivings, the San Remo conference on the Middle East did reaffirm the promise made to the Zionists in 1917 to establish a Jewish national home in Palestine; and Samuel was appointed the first High Commissioner under the British mandate.
[7]The Corn Production Bill, proposing guaranteed prices for agriculture.
[8]Cosmo Gordon Lang.

evidence he said. "Of informers?" Yes, but not of Government agents, of men who have turned King's witness in order to save their own lives. (He instanced one and I suspect it was the only one—a boy of 17 who had been drawn, on casting lots, to fetch a gun. He went to the house, but the woman there beat him off with a spade and he shot her. He was caught and in terror confessed the whole plot.) "Would the trials be public?" Yes. "Would conviction follow only on evidence which was definite and unimpeachable?" To this he appeared also to assent. "Was there not danger that, whatever care were taken, the judgments would be impeached, that we should hear of another Bloody Assize and that there would be heavy reprisals? He had just spoken of a Sinn Fein Labour leader (Murphy, of Cork) who said bluntly that Labour wanted a settlement. Would not that stream of tendency at once be reversed?" He replied that the first need was to break up the murder gang. It had been done in previous cases, as e.g. in the case of the Phoenix Park murderers.[9] Government had always succeeded in the end and would succeed again. . . .

Speaking of President Wilson he said he thought he was the most ill-used man in public life.[10] Party feeling in America was ferocious. [Theodore] Roosevelt[11] would gladly have strung up Wilson to the nearest lamp-post and once said so to George with gesticulation and emphasis. He himself had started at Paris with a strong prejudice against him but had quickly changed his mind. Found him kindly, sincere, straightforward, but tactless, obstinate and vain. One little incident revealed him at his best. At a certain point in the negotiations Orlando, who was a highly-strung man, broke down, and resting his head on his arms on the window rail was shaken with sobs. Wilson at once went forward and took his hand. The Archbishop said that, on his recent visit to America, he was told that just the same qualities came out in Wilson's management of Princeton University—excellent ideas and motives and no skill in recommending them.

So you agree with the Times about Russia Lloyd George remarked by way of a joke.[12] Evidently he felt pretty sure of his ground in that business. The whole Cabinet greatly impressed by Krassin[13]—a far abler

[9]In 1882.

[10]Wilson had been rendered a semi-invalid by a stroke; and the U.S. Senate had failed to ratify the Peace Treaty.

[11]Republican President of the U.S.A. 1901-9.

[12]The point of the joke, presumably, was that *The Times* and the *Manchester Guardian* disagreed utterly about Russia.

[13]Leonid Krassin, "unique among the Bolsheviks in having a business training" (Sir John Maynard), was sent to London in an attempt to restore commercial relations.

ambassador said George than any ever sent to us under the old regime. He spoke to us for an hour and [a] quarter, including interpretation, or say three-quarters of an hour without, and set out the whole position in Russia with the greatest clearness and frankness. We are to see him again. Obviously nothing can be done except by opening up trade. The French need not be so anxious about the Russian gold. They will never get any of it as things stand. The only way they can get paid is by goods and by enabling Russia to develop her resources.

Nothing is to be got by encouraging the attack of Poland [on Russia]. The Poles are a hopeless set of people—"very like the Irish", he incidentally remarked. They have quarrelled with every one of their neighbours—Germans, Russians, Czecho-Slovaks, Lithuanians, Rumanians, Ukrainians—and they are going to be beaten. Trotsky[14] extremely able and would win. The Archbishop recalled how Trotsky lay kicking on his back on board ship when arrested at Halifax and how a telegram had been sent to Kerensky to ask whether he should be detained or sent back, and the answer came to send him. That casual telegram, he remarked, perhaps changed the history of Russia. "Yes, and of the world" said Lloyd George. . . .

C.P.S. to Hobhouse, 27 June 1920 (Extract)

I was so glad you fired off that last shot at Lloyd George and his betrayal of the League of Nations.[15] I had the same sort of feeling of desperate regret and disillusion when I read his reply to Asquith as when I first realised that the whole policy of the Fourteen Points had been utterly abandoned with the connivance of its author. But the fight isn't finished yet. All the decent elements in our politics will have to be rallied, largely under the leadership of the better sort of Tories, and the thing will have to be fought out continuously and in detail. Luckily even Lloyd George is committed pretty deeply in words to the policy of the League of Nations and there are limits even to his power of evasion.

[14]Commissar for War and creator of the Red Army.
[15]Under the terms of the Peace Treaties, the former German and Turkish colonies were to become "mandates", controlled by particular Allied countries but under the ultimate responsibility of the League; however Lloyd George had laid it down in Parliament that it was for the Allies, and not the League, to decide which countries were to have which mandates.

Diary, 14 July 1920

Dined at Reform Club to meet Colonel House on Sir George Paish's invitation.[16] After dinner there was no general conversation, but only a series of interrogatories. Everybody was to be free to question him and he promised to answer every question. Some interesting things emerged particularly as to the position of the President and House's relations with him. Evidently the difference between them dated from the first moment of the Paris Conference and has continued to grow so that House, before and through the war Wilson's most intimate friend and adviser, is now completely cut off from him, greatly to the President's loss.

His advice to Wilson at the very start of the Peace Conference was that "the Treaty was already half made. The terms of the Armistice, which had not only been accepted by all the Allies, but accepted after explanation and negotiation which made them the more binding, constituted the skeleton of a Treaty. It needed only to be clothed with flesh". When asked why this was not done he said he could not tell, that the President believed it had been done, that nothing would persuade him that all the "points" and the "principles" were not embodied in the Treaty. When somebody (Massingham) asked how was that possible when the discrepancies were so glaring he said again he could not tell, but so it was. It might be that, as some one suggested, he lost himself in the mass of detail. It was a calamity. I think he could have said more but refrained from loyalty to Wilson. His (the President's) illness, after his return to America, prevented him from fully stating his case, but nothing he could have said would have made the slightest difference to the Senate which was immovable in its personal hostility. Some one suggested that it might have been well if he had died and House replied emphatically "Yes it would"; there would have been an immediate and overwhelming revulsion of public feeling; he would have become a hero and a martyr. . . .

As to the future he agreed that the world would have to come back to the Wilson policy, but Wilson himself, though still influential, could never take an active part in public life again. Hoover also was not a possible leader. He was a great administrator, but extremely ignorant of politics. He had been thoroughly badly advised in his electoral campaign and his candidature for the Republican nomination had been a complete fiasco.

[16]House was now utterly estranged from President Wilson.

He had hoped that America might lead the world. Now he thought it was for Liberal England to do it. There was much more regard for liberty in England. . . .

The remarks of House just quoted are some indication of the collapse of Scott's wartime hopes. During the later years of the war, Scott had come to regard Britain under Lloyd George as no longer fit to lead the way to a better world. So he had placed his hopes on the America of Woodrow Wilson. By 1920 these hopes had foundered. Wilson was ill beyond recovery, and America had turned its back on international responsibilities. Yet there was little ground for House's belief that the Old World—ruled by Lloyd George and the Conservatives, and embarked on repression in Ireland—would redress the apostasy of the New.

Indeed the most disreputable phase in Lloyd George's administration was about to begin—the phase of "reprisals" in Ireland, whereby British forces countered the terror campaign of Sinn Fein by unauthorised and undisciplined attacks on the Irish population.

C.P.S. to Hobhouse, 4(?) November 1920 (Extract)

The conditions in Ireland are almost incredible. Curzon the other night approved the "reprisals" provided they were not extravagant. In that case they ought to be carried out officially and a line drawn as to what constitutes extravagance. But really of course the whole position is anarchic and indefensible.

C.P.S. to Hobhouse, 15 December 1920 (Extract)

I'm so glad you agreed with my leader on George's "double policy" statement.[17] I was at first inclined to damn it, but on examination felt that [there] was in it, if honestly worked, just a possibility of good, and it did not seem right to ignore that. All the same I confess my hopes are of the slenderest and I would bet almost anything that George will show himself in this as slippery as ever. In my heart I agree with almost every word of Desmond MacCarthy's onslaught this morning.

[17] The "double policy" was to encourage efforts towards peace (e.g. by granting safe conducts to Sinn Fein leaders not accused of serious crime so that they could attend discussions on a settlement), but at the same time to intensify the war against the Irish insurgents by proclaiming martial law—including the death penalty for possession of arms or harbouring rebels—in the disaffected areas.

35. Ireland Over Everything, 1921

For a year (judging from the diaries) Scott and Lloyd George did not meet. Many things had come between them; but Ireland above all. At their last encounter in June 1920, Lloyd George had been "entirely occupied with plans for repression" in Ireland. And repression had borne shameful fruit. British forces, known as the Black and Tans, had countered Sinn Fein attacks by "reprisals" against the Irish population: individuals had been assaulted or killed and the towns of Cork and Balbriggan set on fire. Lloyd George called this "taking murder by the throat". He put his seal of approval on it in a speech at Carnarvon which, to Scott, seemed his nadir. It was as well the two men did not meet.

Then, mercurial and resourceful as ever, Lloyd George abandoned ruthlessness, and sought a settlement with Sinn Fein. He arranged for a truce in Ireland while an Irish delegation, led by de Valera, came to London to negotiate. Willy-nilly, Scott found himself being drawn back into his company and his support.

Diary, 13-15 July 1921

To London by night on Tuesday. Called in the morning [of 13 July] on H. T. Cadbury at the "Daily News" office. He had written to say "he would like to talk over the present position of Liberalism and its Leadership", but he really had nothing to say beyond reporting that his father thought ill of Asquith as a leader and wanted to know what I thought. I said I was entirely of his opinion and so was practically every Liberal whose opinion I had asked, but that it wasn't much use to be off with the old love till you were ready to be on with a new, and that moreover it was an extremely difficult thing to dispossess an ex-Prime Minister from the leadership of a party except with his own good-will which at present appeared in Asquith's case to be not forthcoming.

Lunch . . . with Smuts at his rooms at the Savoy.[1] Mrs. Gillett a grand-daughter of John Bright, who is acting as his hostess in London, was also there. He was not very sanguine. Had been seeing a good deal of de Valera and the Irish delegation both in Dublin and in London and was to see them again that afternoon. Was not impressed by any of them. No big man among them. De Valera a Romantic, lacking in practical sense and capacity of handling affairs. Very difficult in consequence to deal with. Craig also very difficult. At present Ulster was on velvet. She had all she wanted and the protection of Great Britain to defend her against the rest of Ireland. If she persisted in her present irreconcilable attitude that protection would have to be withdrawn and she would have to be brought to a sense of responsibility. She could not be deprived of what she had got under the Government of Ireland Act, nor could force be used against [her], but the economic weapon might prove effective. Her prosperity depended largely on the South.

He thought Lloyd George was in dead earnest now to get a settlement, and I was struck by the tone of respect in which he spoke of his capacity. Speaking of his own part in these transactions he said the King had sent for him as soon as he landed in England. The King was then under promise to open the Ulster Parliament. He told the King that he thought it would have an unfortunate effect if he were to be identified in this way with a sectional assembly unless he were to use the occasion to address himself to the whole of Ireland. The King concurred and asked him to see the Prime Minister and obtain his approval. Lloyd George at once assented and the thing was done. The Cabinet was not consulted. . . .

Thursday [14 July]

Had expected to see de Valera, but it was his first day with Lloyd George and it could not be arranged. Met [A. D.] Lindsay[2] of Balliol at lunch. He had been over to Ireland and got into close touch with Erskine Childers[3] and the Sinn Feiners, and I gathered that he was

[1]Smuts was back in London for the Imperial Conference. As a sometime opponent of Britain and office-holder in the former South African republic, he was able to play an important role as mediator between the British government and the Irish leaders.
[2]Philosopher and classicist.
[3]Formerly a clerk in the House of Commons, Childers had fought on the British side in the Boer war and had warned against the danger of a German invasion in *The Riddle of the Sands* (1903). Then he had become a fanatical convert to the cause of Irish independence. (It was he who had commanded the yacht which landed rifles for the National Volunteers in July 1914). In July 1921 Childers was principal private secretary to the Irish delegation.

doing his best to promote an understanding between them and the Government. He shared Smuts's view of de Valera as a man without much sense of reality and obsessed by a sort of poetic vision of an ideal Ireland. He regarded the Childers-de Valera combination as unfortunate. Childers, having gone over to Sinn Fein, had applied a logical habit of mind to its idealism and by no means helped it to come to earth. He agreed also with Smuts that George had now swung round completely from the policy of force and was all for a settlement.

Friday [15 July]

Saw de Valera at his hotel in the afternoon. A whole bevy of people in the sitting-room, through which Childers showed me to the bedroom, where the great man shortly afterwards appeared. After greetings I remarked that I fancied he had a little quarrel with me for something in the Manchester Guardian (I had heard this from Denoir, a good Irishman of our London staff whose suggestion it was that de Valera would be glad to see me) and he replied with alacrity that he had and at once launched forth. . . . It appeared that his grievance was that we had denounced some of the Sinn Fein outrages as murders on a par with the murders committed by the agents of the Government. He regarded this as outrageous and spoke of the Irish Republican Army as the cream of the population, as chivalrous and honourable a force as existed anywhere in the world. I said we discriminated between acts which were really acts of war done in the open and assassinations of individuals like the Dublin murders which we certainly did utterly condemn.[4] But he would hear of no such distinction. The murders were he said executions carried out for a purpose against spies or the suborners of spies or persons convicted on evidence of similar offences. He even defended the dreadful Dublin murders on the ground that the men murdered one by one in their beds were officers of the Government secret service and Childers, who was present throughout the conversation of about half-an-hour, concurred with him. He said these men were members of the Government headquarters staff and were engaged in spying out in order to destroy the Sinn Fein headquarters staff and they had a right to kill them.

Throughout de Valera based himself on the absolute right of the Irish people to "self-determination". Their elected representatives

[4]On "Bloody Sunday" (21 November 1920) fourteen selected British officers and civilians were callously murdered in their lodgings. Allegedly they were part of a special force chosen to track down Michael Collins, military head of the Sinn Fein resistance.

were the sole lawful Government of Ireland and those who opposed them were intruders and usurpers to be resisted in every possible way. At one point in the conversation he denounced Lloyd George's Carnarvon speech as the most wicked speech ever delivered by a statesman. I said we also had strongly denounced it and that I felt so strongly on Lloyd George's practical condonation of outrage by the Government's own servants that I had since been almost completely estranged from him. But he took quite another view. What he objected to was the strong assertion in the speech of the right to coerce Ireland not the means taken for doing it. "I don't think much about that" he said. The crime was the crime of violating Irish rights not that of condoning breaches of the law by the instruments of the law. What he disputed was the validity of the law itself.

They had no desire to use force, and only used it because constitutional methods had been found to be useless. As soon as an offer to seek a settlement by other means [was made] they had accepted it and that was how matters now stood. They had refused the offer in its original form because it appeared to imply some right on the part of Great Britain to determine the nature of the settlement.

When I asked about his own [Protestant] minority he said they would present no difficulty if we did not interfere. He was a little confused on this subject at one moment saying that they were quite prepared to allow Ulster its autonomy, at another that while the minority could have fair representation it could not expect to be put on a par with the majority. One reason why he had refused the invitation to a Conference as originally proposed was that it practically put Great Britain at the back of Ulster whereas he held that the majority and minority in Ireland must settle matters between them.

I asked him in conclusion if there was any ground for the fears which had been expressed to me by Southern Unionists that neither their lives nor their property would be safe under a Sinn Fein Government. He utterly derided the suggestion. Only those whom they knew to be working against them had been attacked and where large country houses had been burnt it was because they had reason to believe that they would be used as part of the proposed "block-house" and chains of intensified coercion.

During 1921 and 1922 the war between Greece and Turkey impinged periodically on the British political scene.

The Allies had dealt harshly with Turkey in the peace settlement, the Treaty of Sèvres of August 1920 leaving it little more than a shadow of its former self. A Turkish nationalist movement under Mustapha Kemal had risen against these terms and had set about undoing them. Weary of war, the Allies had no stomach for enforcing the terms themselves, but the Greek Premier Venizelos had proposed that his country should launch an offensive against the Turks. The Allies had agreed, and Britain had advanced Greece a loan for the purpose.

During 1921 the Greeks enjoyed considerable military success. But France and Italy were losing enthusiasm for the undertaking, leaving Britain (and in particular Lloyd George) as the only devoted supporter of the Greeks.

Lloyd George to C.P.S., 23 July 1921[5]

You and I have been so hopelessly at variance of late over Irish affairs that I was afraid it would be difficult for us to meet without coming to blows! But now that the atmosphere is more serene I should very much like to see you once more. I want to talk Ireland and Asia Minor with you.

With regard to the latter. . . . I must say I feel rather sad that the Manchester Guardian should be untrue to its great traditions in the past and cast the whole weight of its great influence on the side of the Turk.

If you happen to be in town in the course of the next fortnight I shall be very glad to see you on these two questions.

Diary, 28 July 1921

Breakfasted with Lloyd George at his invitation. Sir James Barrie also there and later Austen Chamberlain.[6] . . .

He was a little reproachful that I had not been to see him before. I said I had not felt able after the Carnarvon speech. But why, he said, did you not tell me what you thought. In the course of conversation at breakfast I told him what I did think which was that the things done under his authority in 1921 were on the whole worse than those done in 1798 and that for a parallel it would probably be necessary to go back to Cromwell. He disputed that, but did not seem to mind.

Asked me what I had made of de Valera. I said a closed mind and he had surprised me by the lengths to which he was prepared to go—e.g. in justifying the dreadful Dublin murders (of the 9 Intelligence officers in their beds) as acts of State. You could not get over a position of that

[5]Lloyd George Papers.   [6]Chamberlain was now leader of the Conservative party.

kind; the only chance was to get round it, conceding everything of theoretic assumption for argument's sake and then getting on to the practical problems. That, said Lloyd George, was exactly what he had done and he had gone very far in his concessions. "I liked de Valera" he said. . . . "I made great concessions in substance and the Cabinet have gone further in supporting me than I should have thought possible". "It is the first real justification of the Coalition", I said. "Yes" he said. "It would have been utterly impossible to carry a settlement on such lines as I have proposed in face of a powerful hostile opposition using the sort of methods of attack which the 'Morning Post' uses. The great difficulty with de Valera is the question of the unity of Ireland. He insists on an all-Ireland Parliament. I pointed out that that would mean that Ulster would be out-voted by three or four to one and that Ulster would never consent to accept a tariff imposed by the South. You would then have exactly the same difficulty for yourself as I now have with you. Ulster would simply seize the custom-houses and refuse to pay. Are you prepared to use force?" De Valera admitted he was not. He thought it would be unnecessary. But he could give no adequate reason in support of that opinion. In all this Lloyd George clearly implied that he had offered fiscal autonomy. . . .

In his letter Lloyd George had reproached me with having become "pro-Turk" and forsaken the Gladstonian tradition. He had nothing really to say in support of this (which when I afterwards mentioned it to Smuts he at once treated as merely silly). I think he was a little annoyed at Toynbee's scathing exposure of the Greek massacres and he made light of them on the plea that this was merely an example of what all the Balkan peoples did.

But his real difference with us was as to the prospects of the Greek offensive, the possibility of their permanently holding their own against the Turks in Anatolia and the position consequently to be assigned to them in the permanent arrangements for the protection of the Straits and generally in the Near East. On all these points he took an extremely sanguine view, and in supporting Greece he found himself in opposition both to Italy and to France who were both in favour of making large political concessions to the Turks in return for economic monopolies and concessions. He was for giving them [i.e. the Greeks] complete control of both sides of the Dardanelles, remarking that if they misbehaved it would always be open to our fleet to "lay Athens flat". Before the last Greek offensive he had had a controversy as to quality of the Greek army and its leadership of which General Harington[7]

[7] General Officer Commanding the Army of the Black Sea.

had a low opinion, but on careful enquiry he had had to admit himself wrong and the event had proved the forecast to be correct. . . .

"Then you put your money on Greece" I said. "Yes", he answered, "I do. The Greeks are destined to be a very great people". He was in favour of leaving the Turks in full possession of Constantinople and the northern part of Asia Minor, as well as of the interior beyond the Greek zone. He would also give them full autonomy in their own land abolishing all the financial, military and railway control contemplated in the unratified Treaty of Sèvres. These were French demands who here as everywhere had an eye to the main chance—78% of the Ottoman debt was held in France. . . .

Before breakfast was over Austen Chamberlain came in and reported the substance of the Northcliffe New York interview with the alleged rebuke of Lloyd George by the King which had reached him through Lord Stamfordham.[8] Lloyd George was furious, threatened a libel action. "I have been wanting to get at him for some time". "I am not sure it is not a criminal libel" he said, and begged me to try to get him a copy of the paper in which it had appeared.

Chamberlain was extremely friendly in his manner to me and gave me the impression of being on the best terms with the Prime Minister. I spoke of de Valera's impracticable attitude and of his justification even of the worst murders, but he seemed to have made up his mind to that. I said there will be plenty to forgive and forget as the King advised and he agreed. (When I spoke to Smuts afterwards of the impression I had received he said he believed it was true that [in regard to Ireland] Chamberlain had now made up his mind to go far—that at first he had been hard to convince, saying that all his tradition was against it, but finally had become reconciled. I asked him, said Smuts, to consider the alternative—the perpetuation of strife[,] the ruin of Ireland, the embroiling of this country not only with America but with our own colonies. The policy of force must fail in the end and it would fail with disaster to us).

SMUTS

Dined with Smuts at his rooms. . . . He had been at the meeting of the Cabinet in the morning.

[8]Northcliffe was reported as saying that the King had protested to the government against the excesses of British forces in Ireland. Subsequently Northcliffe repudiated the interview. (Yet the statements he was supposed to have attributed to the King came very close to the King's actual opinion).

On the subject of Ireland he spoke again not too hopefully. Small men and a great question was again the difficulty pressing on his mind. He regarded de Valera as a man living in a world of dreams. The real crux of the situation was Ulster, yet he would recognise no difficulty in Ulster. To his mind the whole Ulster difficulty was artificial, nursed and indeed created by Britain in her own interest in order to create trouble and division in Ireland. We had only to withdraw and cease our interference and Ulster, which was just a part of Ireland like the rest, would at once fall into line. . . .

Smuts therefore was not hopeful of an early settlement. He had urged on Lloyd George that great patience would be needed, that above all forcible pressure from our side should be avoided, that ample time should be allowed for opinion in Ireland itself to develop. It might be that we should have to wait for a new negotiator—that de Valera might have to disappear. . . .

Of the Silesian question and our relations with France he took a very grave view.[9] France had of late been heading straight for a breach of the Entente. She perhaps even desired it. Her policy aimed at the economic ruin of Germany. She was resolved that the Silesian coal-field should be Polish and she was waiting only for the first presentable excuse in order to occupy the Ruhr. These were the two lungs of German economic life. If France could not gain her end without a breach of the Entente, he believed she was prepared to break it. Germany was incapable of military resistance, but she was not incapable of guerrilla warfare on the Irish model and her ruin would in the end involve France's ruin. . . .

He had been taking a close interest also in the question of the near East, of Turkey and Greece and the Straits. It was terribly difficult and complicated and he had found no complete solution. He differed from Lloyd George as to the power of Greece and thought he was staking far too much on her. If she advanced further into the heart of Asia Minor her communications would be open to guerrilla attack. Her forces were small and she had no reserves of munitions. She was living

[9]France had wished at the time of the Peace Conference to award the rich industrial district of Upper Silesia to Poland, but at Lloyd George's insistence had agreed that a plebiscite of the inhabitants should be held. When this took place in March 1921 it had resulted in a six-to-four majority for Germany, but the Poles, with French connivance, had occupied the district. Britain had made it clear that it would not condone such conduct. The French now formally warned Britain that its attitude, if adhered to, must lead to a formal rupture. Britain was in the process of sending them a sharp reply. (Ultimately a League of Nations committee resolved to divide the district, most of the population going to Germany, most of the industrial wealth to Poland).

397

on the stock left over from the war. Neither we nor France were supplying her and she had no manufacture of her own. The Greek soldier, like the Greek nation, was volatile and collapsed under a reverse. There might easily be a change of fortune. . . .

[Smuts offered three observations on Lloyd George's character:] "George believes far too much in force".

"George's weakness", said Smuts at another moment, "is that he is always considering how he will look in the eye of history—what sort of a historical figure he will cut".

And again "there is a curious element of brutality in George—something primitive."

At the same time as he was being drawn back into Lloyd George's company, Scott was becoming associated with a move by some opposition Liberals to revive the Liberal party as a crusading anti-government force. One of the leaders of this movement was Sir Donald Maclean. Maclean had been a respected but little-known Liberal M.P. until, as a survivor of the electoral débâcle of 1918, he had been chosen to lead the rump of the opposition Liberal party in Parliament during Asquith's absence. This he had done with considerable distinction during 1919, and there were those who considered it a misfortune when Asquith was returned to Parliament at a by-election in February 1920.

The revived activity of the opposition Liberals, at a time when Lloyd George was returning (at least over Ireland) to a "liberal" course, meant that Scott was once more being pulled between the contending sections of the old Liberal party. Yet ultimately there was little doubt that, at least in terms of personalities, he would adhere to Lloyd George. Renewed encounters with Asquith did not commend him to Scott. And in the matter of an Irish settlement, which meant so much to Scott, Lloyd George alone could deliver the goods and was straining every nerve to do so.

Diary, 9 August 1921

Went up to London by night at Sir D. Maclean's urgent invitation and met him at Reform Club next morning. He wanted to set out a plan for (1) bringing back Grey into active politics, (2) getting Lord Robert Cecil to declare publicly in favour of a Liberal programme,[10] (3) making this the occasion for a great Liberal rally. Grey, after much persuasion, had agreed. Lord Robert at first wanted a new middle party to be formed, but Maclean had strongly opposed this on the ground that it

[10]Cecil, having left the government at the end of the war, was now in open revolt against the coalition.

would sacrifice a great existing tradition and organization and put nothing effective in its place. Lord Robert finally convinced.

Modus operandi was for Asquith to write a letter to Grey in which the essentials of Liberal policy at this time would be set forth and that Grey should reply accepting this. Lord Robert would then concur. This exchange might be made the occasion for a gathering of a number of important Liberals, either at a public meeting or at a dinner, some of whom would certainly be recruits.

As to Grey's health it was never better. The trouble was his eyes. . . . he did not feel he could take any post involving Ministerial duties. Politically he was largely a new man. He deeply realised the futility and wrongness of the old diplomacy and was heart and soul in favour of the League of Nations. He was no less deeply moved on the question of Ireland, utterly condemning the policy of licensed official violence and as a solution going the whole length of Dominion Home Rule. It was his interest in these two questions which was bringing him back into active political life, against all his natural interests, which were in the direction of birds and fishes.

I asked What of Asquith? Was he prepared to resign the leadership? The question, Maclean said, did not at present arise. All that was being done was being done with Asquith's full knowledge and cordial support. The question of the leadership belonged to a later stage. There were people who were for putting forward McKenna on the ground that finance was now the most vital of all issues and that he was the best man to bring order into our disordered finances. I said there were people also who thought that he himself would make an effective leader. He said that question did not exist. It was outside discussion, partly, as I gathered, because of his personal relations to Asquith, partly, as he implied, for financial reasons. . . . He felt he had been made for his present job. That was enough. . . .

I asked about [Liberal party] finances and he said of course they were low. They were resolved not again to fall back on the discreditable system of the sale of honours (he had rejected £50,000 the other day from a man who was prepared to stake it on "a long shot") but on the day that the present scheme went through he believed he could collect £150,000 in free gifts. They had still in hand enough money to contest 300 seats and leave something over.

I asked what about Labour? The names he had mentioned did not suggest an advanced industrial policy. Yet social questions were more and more dominating political. There should be at least a strong attempt to understand the Labour point of view and to promote as far as possible Labour ideals. He cordially agreed, but said that sympathy could not over-ride economic facts and that nationalisation as a policy was discredited. As to electoral policy they had tried hard to come to some agreement with Labour but in vain. The leaders were ready enough but they were powerless and among the rank and file the feeling against the Liberal party was much stronger than against the Tory because it was felt that an enemy was far less dangerous than a competitor.

In the course of conversation I said I hoped Asquith did not suppose I had any sort of unwillingness to see him—that on the contrary I should be delighted to do so if at any time he wished it. Maclean said he was sure Asquith would like to see me and went off at once to the telephone to make an appointment which he fixed up for lunch.

ASQUITH

Geoffrey Howard and Violet Asquith[11] also at lunch. Mrs. Asquith away. The conversation largely a repetition of that with Maclean. One fresh and rather significant thing that Asquith said about Grey was that, though he was willing and able to take once more an active part in politics, he would not "take the first place". I repeated this to Maclean, with whom I had tea afterwards at the House of Commons, and he said that it was all right that Asquith should think so, but as a matter of fact the question was an open one. It would depend on how Grey stood the strain and the impression he produced.

What struck me most about Asquith was his immobility. He had not moved—did not really know about things; could not believe that George was really keen about the Irish question and dead set on settling it; thought if he did it would do him no good. Ireland was unpopular, he was in favour of giving her fiscal autonomy, but thought people here would resent it if her taxes were lower than ours. Had advocated great concessions to Ireland because he thought them right, but had never deluded himself as to the unpopularity of this. He had not seen de Valera and knew nothing as to his real temperament and outlook. Again thought nothing of Austen Chamberlain, wholly ignoring his sterling qualities and setting him down as a poor creature. So also of George, he could see no good in him or anything he did. All the time he laid down the law with great positiveness. Altogether a somewhat querulous and very old old man.

[11]Asquith's elder daughter (who since her marriage in 1915 was actually Violet Bonham-Carter).

In my last words with Maclean at the House he said suddenly, as if liberating his soul, "For myself I have done with Lloyd George. I could never work with him or under him". I said "that's all right for you. My position is quite different. George seems to like to keep in touch with me as representing, I suppose, a certain type of Liberalism. Whatever one may think of him he is a great force. Whatever I may count for it's my business to turn that force as far as I can to good ends". He did not dissent but said "Do you go further and call him not only a great force but a great man". At least I said he will occupy a considerable place in history. . . .

Of Asquith himself, though entirely loyal, [Maclean] said that he had evidence that he was not gaining but losing ground in the country. He had missed a great and unique opportunity by his failure to make any figure in Parliament since his return. Was it I asked consideration for him (Maclean) or indolence. Something of both said Maclean, but he evidently thought that the first was only a cover for the second.

By October 1921, one major obstacle to the success of the Irish negotiations had removed itself. De Valera had withdrawn to Ireland, leaving more tractable Sinn Fein leaders to carry on the negotiations. Principal among them were Arthur Griffith, the strong-willed journalist who had founded Sinn Fein and given it its philosophy, and Michael Collins, the "Big Fellow" who had organised the military arm of the resistance and for years had outwitted attempts to capture him.

Yet formidable differences between the two sides remained. Even at his most accommodating, Lloyd George would never concede Sinn Fein's demand for a united Ireland independent of Britain. He refused to coerce Ulster (which since 1920 had had a government of its own) into merging with the south. And he insisted that even a self-governing Ireland should retain certain links with Britain: it must take a formal oath of allegiance to the crown, and allow Britain to retain naval bases there. The fate of the negotiations depended on whether the Irish delegates would agree to modify their position on these matters.

C.P.S. to Hobhouse, 27 October 1921 (Extract)

Ireland just now overshadows everything. I had a wire this afternoon from Lloyd George bidding me to breakfast tomorrow, so am off by the midnight train. Is it a crisis? Anyway I'm glad to have a chance to see him. It will give me a chance to find out what—if *anything*—he has in his mind in case of the breakdown of the Conference. Whatever happens there must be no more Black-and-Tan business. I see some one says it is to be "real war" with *press censorship* and everything handsome.

In that case I shall certainly find myself in prison!

Meanwhile Lloyd George was learning that there was a political price to be paid for his change of policy towards Ireland: that although the more adaptable Conservatives like Austen Chamberlain were now prepared to work for an Irish settlement, there remained a section of Tories implacable in their hostility both to Home Rule and to any government which was prepared to countenance it.

Diary, 28-29 October 1921

Wire from Lloyd George October 27 to breakfast with him next morning. Went up by the night train. He was alone except for Mrs. Lloyd George and Megan, who on these occasions are treated as furniture.

He opened up at once on the rather critical nature of the situation. Tories restive, Sinn Feiners very difficult. Had gone down to the House on previous day when Hamar Greenwood[12] was to be bombarded with questions by the Tory cave in order to judge feeling of the House. Attitude towards Hamar Greenwood very bad. Towards himself better, when he also was questioned, but still bad. Decided at once to challenge opponents. Asked Austen Chamberlain in stating business for next week to leave Monday free. Then asked for debate *and a division*. Told me real danger was not in division but in abstentions. Much would depend on statement he was able to make.

Had told the Sinn Feiners he must have their reply in writing. His terms to them had been put definitely in writing and so must be their reply. He had great difficulty in bringing them to the point. He would talk to Griffith and find him quite reasonable. Then he went away and came back after consultation with quite another story. Erskine Childers was, he thought, the villain of the piece, always seeking to counterwork every approach to concession. The written reply was promised for 12 o'clock that day. It was, I gathered, to deal with the whole of the fundamental issues, the de Valera telegram to the Pope having made it necessary that these should be raised at once.[13]

He was determined if it were possible to put the negotiation through and secure peace. It might be necessary (i.e. if he met with unreasonable opposition) to have a general election and ask the people if they wanted

[12]Secretary of State for Ireland.
[13]De Valera's telegram had asserted the "independence of Ireland" and had repudiated "allegiance to the British King".

peace or not. He did not care how that might turn out for himself. He had had 14 years of Office and his present life was not a bed of roses. He had tried to get a short holiday in a remote corner of Scotland, but without the smallest success. Everything had pursued him and he had very nearly broken down at Gairloch with blood poisoning, but the King's doctor had pulled him through. "It was a dog's life". (I noticed next day at Chequers that Mrs. George spoke of his "resting" in the afternoon—evidently, as I gathered[,] by doctor's order). He now regarded himself in the light of *a judge*. If Sinn Fein refused the minimum concessions he regarded as necessary he would fight them; if the Tories refused to accept them when conceded he would fight them. . . .

A danger which he foresaw was the attitude of Bonar Law.[14] (Hammond said that Devlin reported that Lloyd George had said to him "I find I have been living in a fool's paradise". I thought Bonar Law would not recover so soon and that, when he did, he would not want to return to active political life. I was wrong in both.) He had come back quite recovered and was taking an active interest in politics. He and Carson had come to breakfast the other day. He was very reasonable and moderate up to a point. Then suddenly you touched something and he blazed up. At heart he was an Orangeman and the Orange fanaticism was there. He had brought it with him from Canada. He might at any time, in defence of what he regarded as an attack on Ulster, lead a Tory revolt.

On the other hand, if he could not get the essential conditions—allegiance to the Crown and common naval defence—from Sinn Fein there would be nothing for it, but to fight them. He should send 100,000 additional men, making 150,000 altogether in Ireland, and that he believed would be sufficient to dominate the country. I said it would not prevent the continuance of murder and outrage which would of course be extended to this country. George said that was possible and he might himself be shot (though he said he thought they would find it rather difficult) but it would have to be faced and could be dealt with. It had been tried before and had always failed. I said a renewal of outrage, miscalled war—for there could be no war where there were no organised forces—on our part would be intolerable and I did not think public opinion here would tolerate it. In any case we (in the paper) should do our utmost to see that they did not. . . .

I suggested that it might be useful if I were to see Griffith and Collins and he said he would be glad if I would do so and see him again.

[14]Law had left the government through illness in March 1921.

COLLINS

Telephoned at once to Desmond Fitzgerald, co-Secretary with Childers
to the delegation[,] and he arranged for me to see Collins at 3.30 at
Cadogan Gardens. He was still engaged at the Conference at Hans
Place. There was a series of characteristic muddles, precision not being
as yet an Irish virtue, and it was close on six before Collins turned up in
immense force at Cadogan Gardens, turned everybody, including an
unhappy typist[,] out of the room with a sweep of his arms and settled
down to talk for an hour and a quarter. The telephone rang at intervals
when he sprang upon it fiercely as an enemy and yelled a challenge that
might have split the instrument. Then Fitzgerald would appear and he
relapsed into gloomy silence till the interruption was over.

In spite of these mannerisms I found him a straightforward and
quite agreeable savage. He was intent on the question of the Government's claim to retain the Irish ports as a naval base and I could hardly
get him off that portion of the subject. (I afterwards found from Lloyd
George that it was his speciality). I pressed him on the question of
allegiance, but he was for giving nothing away. At last I had to point
out that if he had come to negotiate on the principle of claiming everything and conceding nothing he might have spared himself the trouble
of coming and might just as well pack up at once. Then he became
more moderate and evolved a constructive policy of his own. Why not
have a linking of constitutions, each country swearing allegiance to its
own constitution. But where I asked would the King come in? "Oh!
we'll find room for the King" he said.

This did not seem very promising and I pointed out that Lloyd
George was fighting their battle hard under great difficulties and had
done wonders in bringing over the Tories. He alone of all the Statesmen—Gladstone, Campbell-Bannerman, Asquith—who had taken the
Irish question in hand was in a position to "deliver the goods". He
surely had a right to expect some help from those he was helping.
"Oh!", said Collins, "I know nothing about your politics. I have only
to think of Ireland". But[,] I said[,] you have got to think of our politics
if you want to get anything done.

He went on declaiming as to the war they were making on us everywhere, in America and wherever they could in Europe. "Oh! if I had a
hundred men in Cologne[15] I would make the place untenable". And
for himself he did not care if it was to be war in Ireland. It was a great

[15]Where, under the peace settlement with Germany, Britain maintained an army of occupation.

adventure and what did one's life matter when that of one's country was at stake. At the same time he confessed he did not want war. He wanted peace. But one could not sell the honour of one's country any more than one could sell the honour of a woman. Ireland *was* a nation. Every Irishman felt it in himself. It was not a theory. "It was there". He ended up on a more rational note: "Surely it would be a discredit to us all if after coming together in conference we did not manage to agree". I left him with a renewed exhortation to study our politics a little.

CHEQUERS[16]

By the time I got to Downing Street, George and all his party had gone off for the week-end to Chequers Court. So I went down next morning [29 October] to see him. Got there about 10.30 when he was still in bed. He reads his papers and often does some writing before he gets up. He soon came down and took me for his morning walk to the lovely view-point which had been a Roman camp, with the surrounding trench still visible which Foch said he could even now successfully defend with a few machine guns. The whole place delightful in its autumn beauty, a wonderful Elizabethan house, the sunken rose-garden in front still full of bloom and masses of lavender flowering on each side of the terrace.

I reported to Lloyd George what Collins had said and of course he found no help in his suggested union of constitutions. "I must have something quite simple, direct, unequivocal, something which I can put without qualification or beating about the bush before the House of Commons". Collins was an uneducated rather stupid man, but he liked him (as I did) and if he had him and Griffith alone to deal with could settle in five minutes. . . .

I told George, as I had told Collins, that personally I did not think the question of naval bases was vastly important because a friendly and satisfied Ireland would make as little trouble about the matter as the Dominions did. But no doubt it was an essential point for the House of Commons. For the country too Lloyd George insisted.

Collins, he said, was a little uplifted. (Hammond mentioned that when he [i.e. Collins] was visiting the prisoners' camps, since the truce in Ireland, he had talked so loud and blatantly of the police he had murdered that the guards revolted and threatened to resign if they were

16 This estate had been presented to the nation in 1917 by Sir Arthur Lee (who had been Lloyd George's parliamentary secretary when he was Minister of Munitions) to serve as the official country residence of Britain's Prime Ministers.

called on to escort him again.) He fancied he had met and defeated the whole might of the Empire. But, if the necessity came, he would find out his mistake. A country which had raised six million men for a great war was not to be so easily defied. He repeated that though he hated the policy of force he would not shrink from it. He reverted once more to Lincoln. Lincoln was the only American statesman who interested him. Washington was by comparison a tame figure. But [Lincoln] had not shrunk from employing force to secure unity, though at the time he was reproached as violating democratic principle, and he would not shrink from it. . . .

I had meant to leave before lunch but he asked me to stay as the Sinn Fein reply was promised for 12 o'clock at Downing Street and the gist of it would be telephoned to him. So I stayed on. It came about half-past two. George was a good deal excited. It was better than he had feared. On the naval question there was no concession, but on the question of allegiance "a considerable advance"—not enough, George said, "but it was enough to go on with". There would be no breakdown. Now he was free to get on with his speech. In a humane mood he thought he would let off the revolters easily.[17] After all they are only children—not one man of any account among them. Besides if I were to go for them it might only excite sympathy. "But I should like to". He had got his desired ammunition.

The outcome of the negotiations remained in doubt almost to the last. The number of disputed questions—any one of which might cause breakdown—remained considerable: would the Irish delegates agree to stay within the British Commonwealth if conceded full dominion status; would they take some form of oath of allegiance to the crown; would they grant to the British navy the use of Irish ports; would they admit the right of Ulster (however constricted its boundaries) to separate existence if it persisted in its refusal to come in? In deciding on these issues, the Irish delegates had more to take into account than their own opinions: there was the probable reaction of colleagues over the water who had declined to participate in the negotiations themselves—de Valera most of all. Yet in the end, after breakdown seemed imminent, an affirmative answer was given to each question, and the agreement was signed.

Diary, 2-5 December 1921

Came up [on 2 December] by 8.30 a.m. train at Hammond's urgent

[17]Presumably the rebels against his policy in the Conservative party.

request who reported the situation almost desperate and was anxious for me to see Lloyd George. Hobhouse concurring. Met Laski[18] and Hammond at Euston and talked while Hammond had lunch. Laski reported conversation with Churchill in which Churchill was full of threats of John Bull laying about with a big stick. We had utterly broken rebellion in 16th century. Why not now with our vastly greater power? Yes replied Laski but the condition of Ireland today is the fruit of our policy then.

Hammond reported, for my information alone, terms of ⎰oath ⎱declaration which Government had proposed to Sinn Fein: to "the Free State of Ireland, constitution of Commonwealth of States known as the British Empire, and the King as its head", "Free State" being a literal translation of the Irish word for "Republic".

Lunched with Lloyd George. Alone at first (with Mrs. Lloyd George). Afterwards Sir Robert Horne[19] and Tom Jones, acting secretary to the Cabinet in the absence of Sir Maurice Hankey, came in. George looking tired. Had been up till past midnight with the Sinn Fein deputation. (Newspapers failed to discover this). He was evidently not sanguine as to the Sinn Fein reply to the written statement of terms sent to them. In that case, he said, the responsibility will rest on Sinn Fein not on Ulster. (Hammond had reported that this was his line. If the Conference was to fail it would suit him best that it should fail on Sinn Fein rather than on Ulster). We had made great concessions. Why could not Sinn Fein make some concession too? South Africa had made no difficulty about the oath—Hertzog[20] himself had taken it. Why should Sinn Fein? The fact was the Boers were a finer people. Then after we had settled with Sinn Fein we could go on to settle with Ulster. If there was no settlement there must be coercion.

I said that is all very well, but the soldiers say it will take 200,000 men. Where are you going to get them? You can't have conscription. Oh! he said no great numbers will be needed. We could blockade. He rather trifled with this suggestion, adding that if there were any outrages on loyalists we should have to send punitive expeditions. The fact is he had evidently not in the least made up his mind what he would do. But apparently he still had some hope for he begged me, whatever we did in the paper, not to encourage Sinn Fein to stand out on the question of allegiance. . . . I could only say that the form of the

[18]Harold Laski, left-wing intellectual.
[19]Conservative M.P. and Chancellor of the Exchequer.
[20]General J. B. Hertzog, Boer extremist.

oath seemed to me to matter very little. The real bond of union was moral and entirely different.

George complained bitterly of Childers. He could have settled easily with Griffith and Collins, but Childers always managed to put a spoke in the wheel. [W. B.] Spender (also an Englishman and a relative of Harold and J.A.) played exactly the same part in Ulster. . . .

I urged as we were leaving that we should get down to facts, to the actual things we wanted, and not stand on phrases and pleas of legality. Horne and Jones laughed consumedly at the idea of George as the champion of legality[,] and he joined.

In the evening I called by appointment to see Michael Collins at Hans Place. He was late and in haste to pack and catch the night train to Holyhead. I saw him for a few minutes alone and then joined him at dinner. Erskine Childers was also dining and leaving with him. I told him my reason for seeing [him] was in order that I might be able to do whatever was in my power to save the situation and he said he perfectly understood that. At the same time he appeared to be quite cheerfully contemplating failure (not necessarily a bad sign. According to Hammond it is the custom of Sinn Feiners to speak in quite a different strain to Englishmen and to Irishmen or foreign sympathisers). . . .

At dinner I urged that in their reply Sinn Fein should put their case in the best light for the British public stating quite strongly and definitely what they were prepared to accept—as e.g. common citizenship—so that Lloyd George might not be able to throw all the blame of any failure on them and exonerate Ulster.

I asked how far they could go on the question of allegiance. Childers asked Collins if he might say and Collins nodded assent. It appeared that they were not prepared to admit the Crown in Ireland at all. I pointed out that the solution which Griffith himself had put forward had been that the King should be King of Ireland as well as King of Great Britain. Yes, said Childers, but that was two years ago before the war in Ireland. Now we will not admit the Crown on any terms. The Crown would really mean the British Ministry (an absurd statement since the King could act only on the advice of his Irish Ministers as in the parallel case of the Dominions). I pointed this out, but he said the Dominions were a long way off and it would be quite different in the case of a country only a few miles away. Then it comes to this that you mean to have a Republic in Ireland in association with the British Empire. Collins assented. Then I said you expect the negotiation to break down. Collins, with emphasis: "I do".

Childers went on to descant on the total untrustworthiness of Great Britain and on the monstrous proposal to raise an army of 200,000 and "exterminate" the Irish people. I said the thing could not and would not be done. We would not tolerate it. Then you will have your work cut out, he said. I could only say to Collins that I hoped the Sinn Feiners would go to the utmost length they could. "We have done" he said. I gathered that they had accepted the Government terms on the questions of naval defence and the control of the ports and on that of the conduct of foreign affairs. Only the question of the Crown remaining.

allegiance

Saturday [3 December]

Called in the morning on Lord Buckmaster (failed to get hold of Simon or Sir Gordon Hewart who were both week-ending, or of Asquith also away, but spoke to Mrs. Asquith and arranged to visit them at Sutton Courtney).

Buckmaster very interesting and tremendously stirred up. Insisted on the need of starting from particulars not from generalities, not by laying down a principle and then trying to discover how it can be applied, but by asking what were the precise things we wanted and then devising means by which they could be attained. There might be many means. All should be explored, and if Sinn Fein would not accept the means we proposed they should be asked to suggest others. I told him I believed this was exactly what they had done in the case of the Crown and he said he thought their suggestion (I told him what Collins had said) quite feasible. The things that really mattered were naval defence and foreign affairs and if these were conceded and the unity of the Empire, with Ireland a member of it[,] also conceded, he thought the question of the Crown, which was largely an unreal question[,] could be settled. As to the common citizenship of which the Crown was regarded as the symbol that was a very vague thing. All that mattered in it could be specified and defined and could be made matter of contract.

As for the renewal of the attack on Ireland on a great scale it could not be done. Conscription for the purpose was impossible. Blockade if it could be made effectual would be inhuman. But it could not and would be futile.

He spoke of the increasing alienation between the two wings of the Liberal party and of the aggressive tactics of the Coalition Liberals at by-elections, e.g. Spen Valley.[21] He made a great onslaught on them. The Coalition which they supported had not carried a single measure which would not be approved by moderate Conservatives and on the other hand every sort of folly and wickedness had been condoned.

He himself had clearly become much more embittered since I saw him last two years ago. He said something about people who did not take a side being like a man with one foot in a punt and one on shore who did not know which way he would be pulled, which if intended as a personal reference would have been offensive. I took occasion afterwards to remark that the punt as it happened contained the fortunes of the British State and that it was not an unworthy enterprise to try to pull her into safety and prevent her from going over the lasher. He then became rather profuse in his approval of that endeavour. . . .

Sunday [4 December]

Went to Sutton Courtney to see Asquith and had a long talk with him. He received me a little coldly—perhaps it was only his usual manner—but warmed up and became very friendly later. I think he was a little puzzled at my being at the trouble of going so far to see him, not realising all one felt as to the tremendous issues at stake. His mind still works largely in the party groove.

He repeated very much what Lord Buckmaster had said. He had to make a speech to his constituents that week and would like to denounce any resumption of the terror in Ireland. But of course if he did so and the negotiations failed it would be said that he had been the cause of the failure.

Monday [5 December]

Lloyd George asked me to come to see him at 5 minutes to 10—an unusual and curiously exact hour. When I arrived he was closeted with Collins[,] and Davies told me he was due to meet the King at 10.10 before the King went down to Sandringham. At 10.10 Collins was still with him. As he came out of the Cabinet room he laid hold of me and pulled me in. He was excited and angry, said the Irish had gone back on everything—allegiance, naval securities, in fact all along the line.

[21]The Spen Valley constituency had been represented by a Coalition Liberal M.P. until his death late in 1919. The local Liberal organisation then adopted an Opposition Liberal (Simon) as their candidate, whereupon Lloyd George brought forward a candidate of his own, splitting the Liberal vote and enabling Labour to win the seat.

Agreement on these terms was impossible. Collins had refused to be a party to them[22] and said one of the others must go with Griffith, in his place, to explain and justify them; he would not. So he had come late on Sunday night by himself after the others had gone and had stayed late and returned this morning.

Then [Lloyd George] hurried off to see the King. I told Davies I would come to lunch if George wanted me and he did. T. Jones was there and I stayed with him a little after Lloyd George had gone for his short sleep before the Irishmen came at 3 (they had appointed 2.30, but, as usual, put off). Jones was deeply discouraged. He said he agreed entirely with me on the Irish question. He had loathed the reprisals and told Lloyd George what he thought of them, as I had. Lloyd George was now on his true line and deserved all possible support.

I was to have seen Lloyd George again later, but the Irishmen stayed on and on and I had my leader to write. Tea was sent in to the Conference at 5, at 7 Lloyd George[,] Austen Chamberlain and Birkenhead[23] our 3 chief negotiators retired to formulate new terms, the which were handed to the Irishmen at 7.30. They were to return at 10 and did return at 11.15. At 2.20 the Treaty was signed.

I went to lunch with Lloyd George next day [presumably 6 December]. Hamar Greenwood was also there[24]—a dreadful person, vulgar and soapy like the worst type of Methodist preacher only less sincere— his wife also, much too good for him. George was of course in great spirits but did not say much during lunch. Afterwards I saw him for a few minutes alone. He told me the decision had remained in the balance up to the very last. After they had threshed out their differences (I gathered that obligatory free-trade between Great Britain and Ireland was one of the last points conceded on the British side and that Birkenhead's form of the oath had been accepted) George said he put it to Griffith whether he could sign on behalf of all the Sinn Fein plenipotentiaries. Griffith said he could not. "Then", said Lloyd George, "I must put it to you individually". He put it to Collins. Collins hesitated, and declined. The others declined. There was a moment when Griffith stood alone. "There", said Lloyd George, "you see the difference between physical and moral courage".

[22]"Them" seems to refer to the new, unacceptable terms which the Irish were now putting forward. But the passage is not clear, Scott apparently having been carried away by the drama of the events into unwonted obscurity.
[23]The former F. E. Smith, now Lord Chancellor.
[24]As Secretary of State for Ireland during the period of "reprisals", Greenwood was the *bête noire* of radicals like Scott.

It was then that Lloyd George played his last card. Some days before (before the debate in the House on the previous Monday, Lloyd George told me) he had seen Griffith alone—"not here" said Lloyd George with a twinkle, "some way from here"—and had come to a general, informal agreement with him as to the terms on which Griffith would be prepared to settle, and it was only after he had made sure of his ground in this way that George challenged a division in the House. Before they parted George said to Griffith for clearness' sake this had better be put into writing and that was done. George now at the critical moment produced the document. "You signed this", George said, "and, knowing you to be the man you are, I am sure you communicated it afterwards to Mr. Collins. He therefore is also a party to it. I have fulfilled my part of the bargain. I took the risk of breaking my party. You in Ireland often bring against us in England the charge of breach of faith. Now it is for you to show that Irishmen know how to keep faith". (Griffith, said Lloyd George[,] seemed a little surprised when the terms were read. So evidently he had not kept a copy himself). That settled it. An extraordinary example of skill and foresight in negotiation. The words I have quoted stuck in my mind. I think they are almost exact. All signed.

At parting I congratulated Lloyd George warmly and he responded. "To think", he said, "that we have succeeded at last in the task we have both worked at for more than thirty years". He was jubilant.

Lloyd George had achieved a great Liberal objective: he had disposed of Ireland as a problem in British politics. But he had not, as he believed, gone further and brought peace to Ireland. The settlement split Sinn Fein, between those who would accept the three-quarter loaf which had been secured, and those who would accept nothing less than their full demands. Civil war broke out, and within a few months Collins, Griffith, and Childers (but not de Valera) were all dead. This was a bitter experience for Scott: another Liberal dream (like women's suffrage, which seemed only to have produced hordes of Conservative voters) gone sour as soon as it was attained. Scott referred little to the new wave of bloodshed in Ireland. But in a letter to Margot Asquith on 31 August 1922 he did make the remark: "Who could have believed that, having got rid of us, the Irish would start a terror of their own?"

36. The State of Parties, January-March 1922

1921 had ended heroically for Lloyd George. 1922 began dangerously. He had achieved a great triumph over Ireland, but the prestige it brought him proved transitory. And it caused him to bring on himself a major political setback.

Lloyd George wanted his association with the Conservatives to become permanent. The best way of cementing it was to hold another election as their ally, and his Irish success seemed to have provided him with the opportunity. The leading Conservatives, including Austen Chamberlain and Balfour, were agreeable. So in January 1922 Lloyd George set election arrangements in motion.

At this point he was stopped in his tracks by a surge of resistance from the Conservative rank and file. Their spokesman was Sir George Younger, the party manager. Younger sent to Conservative organisations a statement of reasons against holding an election at this time. Lloyd George tried to laugh off his action, but in February Younger returned to the attack, calling for the coalition to be wound up and the Conservatives to resume their independence. Lloyd George was irate, and demanded that the Conservative leaders bring their mutinous subordinate to heel. Younger was appropriately rebuked, but by then the damage was done. The Prime Minister's election plans had foundered, and it was now evident that large numbers of Conservatives no longer had any use for him. But Lloyd George would not recognise this. Whatever he might tell Scott, he wanted the Conservatives as allies for the future, and refused to admit that not all of them reciprocated his feelings.

The threat of an election also produced a flurry of activity among the Liberal and Labour parties, who saw in Lloyd George's difficulties the prospect of electoral benefits. But the damaging rivalry between the two parties persisted, and Scott made no headway in trying to bring Labour to an accommodation with the Liberals.

Meanwhile, the situation in Europe remained threatening. Lloyd George was using all his efforts to achieve reconciliation tehre. But always he ran up against France's fear of a recovered Germany. To offset it, he offered Briand, the French Premier, a British guarantee of French territory against invasion, if in return France would prove more amenable. This proposal caused much dissent at home.

413

To many Liberals (but not Grey) it looked like a revival of the "entangling alliances" which they thought had brought on the war. Anyhow the proposal fell through. Briand was thought by the French Chamber to be too susceptible to Lloyd George's blandishments, and he was replaced by the intransigent Poincaré. This boded ill for the forthcoming conference at Genoa, where Lloyd George was to make a final effort to settle the affairs of Europe.

Yet in one respect Lloyd George was himself the chief intransigent. He still improvidently backed Greece against the resurgent might of Turkey, which was now making short work of the Greek offensive. Other governments were prepared to recognise that Greece lacked the capacity to impose on the Turks the harsh peace terms which the victors had laid down but did not themselves intend to enforce. Lloyd George was not.

Diary, 18-20 January 1922

To London Tuesday night [17 January]. Breakfasted with Lloyd George Wednesday (my request). He was alone (except for Mrs. Lloyd George, and a Welsh lady friend who did not utter) and did not seem in a hurry. Davies came in at a quarter to 11 to announce arrival of the Greek Archimandrite.

He started on Poincaré and his Paris interview. Reports in press that it had gone off in the most friendly manner all wrong. Poincaré made of course the conventional references to our gallant ally etc., but interview the reverse of cordial—"almost hostile". Poincaré pressed for reciprocal obligation of defence in place of the guarantee of French territory offered to Briand—i.e. for a military alliance. Lloyd George emphatically refused. "If that is what you ask", I said[,] "you may regard the Cannes offer as withdrawn". France in that case must face isolation. . . .

I said I hoped the whole proposal would now lapse. But he said Germany was in favour of it as putting some restraint on France. . . .

The difficulty in the whole matter was not with France, but with the French Chamber which did not really represent France. It was, as M. Briand had said, "a one-legged Chamber"—i.e. one whose members had been elected primarily because they had suffered in the war. It reflected the war mind.

I asked him what he was going to say in his Saturday's speech and he proceeded to give an outline. It was to be an out-and-out Liberal speech. [1] First a peace-policy—peace for all Europe and restoration. This was essentially a Liberal policy, but it had also been the policy of the biggest and most enlightened Conservatives and represented their higher tradition—Canning, Pitt in his best day, Salisbury, Peel. [2] Secondly Free Trade. The Safeguarding of Industries Act[1] did not represent a policy; it was an incident designed to meet an emergency. To Free Trade as a policy he should hold fast. [3] The speech would on Labour subjects be anti-socialist in the sense in which Liberalism was anti-socialist—that is it would be opposed to rash experiments and in favour of giving full play to individual effort. [4] As to the Reform of the House of Lords I suggested that he might reform it as much as he liked provided he did not repeal the Parliament Act. But he said the Parliament Act, in his view, was not good enough. Nothing had been accomplished under it, not even Home Rule. . . . Three whole sessions had to be spent in forcing a Bill through and the last two of them were sterile. The process exhausted and wearied Parliament and prevented it from embarking on other tasks. . . . He was in favour of a joint session of the two Houses, [and] of a smaller House of Lords (not less than 200) . . . so elected as normally to secure a Conservative majority of 60 or 80, so that a corresponding majority in the House of Commons would be able at once to have its way. He thought a majority of 100 in the House of Commons ought always to be able to have its way. . . . The motto of his speech would in fact be "Peace, Retrenchment and Reform".

If the Tories objected to the programme thus set forth he should not mind. He should tell them they were of course at liberty to break the Coalition whenever they liked, but that they must give him a little warning. The real danger for him had been that the break should be immediate before he had had time to make any fresh combination. But Sir George Younger had kindly relieved him of this risk by definitely committing the whole Tory party against an immediate election and he had watched his proceedings with entire composure. He was playing his (Lloyd George's) game.[2]

As to the prospects of a General Election his impression was that the temper of the country was Conservative, that there was indifference, almost lethargy, disillusion, a desire to be let alone. If the Coalition broke up the Tories very likely would win. He should not mind. (I had taken the opposite view—that people were sick of war and the war spirit and recognised that safety lay only in a policy of justice[,] good-will and reconciliation, that there was a strong drift towards free-trade and generally for the healing measures for which Liberalism stands).

[1]This Act protected a small range of British industries, usually from German competition.
[2]Lloyd George's reasoning at this point is difficult to follow—assuming he was doing anything more than making a virtue of necessity.

As for himself, he could of course carry Wales, Scotland also he thought and a good part of the North of England, especially Lancashire. If he could do that Liberals elsewhere would have to fall into line. He thought too that he might be able to gain support from Labour. They preferred him to Asquith. They knew his sympathies were democratic, that he was for the "under-dog". They could work with him where they could not work with the regular party Liberals. They regarded him as being to a certain extent outside party and he did not therefore come under the ban of their standing feud with the Liberals.

Churchill—now his second in command of the Liberal Coalition organization—he incidentally remarked was not a Liberal; his sympathies were all with the Imperialists. But he was sound on free trade, almost fanatical.

But he should like, in any break-up, to carry Austen Chamberlain with him, and Birkenhead, and even Curzon—yes even old Curzon who had been quite decent of late. . . . Thus were plans shaping themselves in his scheming brain. It almost looked as though Churchill and Bonar Law were to be left to lead the Tory party. . . .

Sir Donald Maclean. Lunched with him at the Reform Club (on his invitation). He was full of confidence as to Liberal prospects at a general election. There was a strong Liberal movement in the country, men who had left us were coming back, good candidates were pouring in and, if only we had a little more time, we should make a big fight. (I assured him I did not think there could be an election before May). There must be no compromise with the Coalition. We must go right ahead. (I fully agreed). The Central Office was putting everything it knew in money and effort on the election. We ought to come back fully 100 to 120 strong. Lord Gladstone[3] was in charge of all the arrangements at the Central Office. His name and his experience as chief whip were invaluable. When asked to take the position he had at once and without a moment's hesitation assented.

I spoke of the almost universal distrust of Asquith as leader. He admitted it, but said (which may be true) that the objection was not so much to Asquith as to "his ladies".[4] But Asquith must still take the

[3]Between 1899 and 1914 Gladstone had been successively Liberal chief whip, Home Secretary, and Governor-General of South Africa.

[4]Presumably a reference to Asquith's wife Margot rather than to his daughter Violet, whom Maclean on an earlier occasion (9 August 1921) had described as "not only a very able but a very fine woman. It was an immense credit to her to have come quite clean and clear through the indescribable mess that surrounded her mother". (Margot Asquith was in fact her step-mother). Maclean incidentally had denied that Asquith took much notice of his wife's opinions.

position of leader. Grey would help powerfully to gain popular confidence and the utmost use must be made of him. He would now take a much more active part. . . .

Lord Gladstone. I saw Lord Gladstone on the same subject at the Liberal Central Office next day. He was even much more sanguine than Sir Donald Maclean and looked forward to an actual majority in Parliament of Liberals and Labour combined. We must broaden our programme and make our first object the restoration of Europe and a European peace. We must do our best to come to terms with Labour. In 1906 he had agreed with Ramsay MacDonald on a policy of give-and-take constituency by constituency. That was not possible now, but there might be partial and tacit understandings, when the time came, not to spoil each other's game.

He took much the same view as Sir Donald Maclean as to Asquith and an even stronger one as to Mrs. Asquith. I asked if nothing could be done to prevent her lecturing in America on the eve of the election. He said he had already spoken several times on the subject and was going to see her again that day when he should have something very strong to say.

Like Sir Donald Maclean he attached great importance to the return to active politics of Grey. He was the antithesis of George and where George attracted by resource and daring he would inspire confidence by his high character and known disinterestedness and by the straightforwardness and stability which Englishmen loved.

Diary, 28 February–2 March 1922

Accepted invitation to dine with the Astors to meet Mr. Balfour on his return from the Washington Conference, February 28. Went to London Monday night [27 February]. Arthur Henderson came to breakfast [on the 28th] at Nottingham Place. I wanted to discuss with him possibilities of the next Government in view of the apparent likelihood of a heavy Coalition defeat at the General Election. Asked him how many candidates the Labour party were running. He said 400, he hoped 420. They expected to carry 200-220 seats. The independent [Asquithian] Liberals he believed had now about 200 candidates in the field but hoped nearly to double the number before the election. They might win anything up to 150 seats. That would give to Liberals and Labour together a clear majority of the now reduced membership of the House.

I asked him if he had considered how in that case a Government

should be formed. He said he had not. I said there were various possibilities. (1) A Coalition Government of Liberals and Labour. I presumed that was out of the question. He said it was. (2) A Labour Government resting on Liberal support. Was that possible or would Labour insist on a clear majority of the House before taking office. At first he said it would insist and could not consent to hold power at the pleasure of the Liberal party. Then he changed his mind and said it might take office under these conditions provided there were a perfectly clear agreement in advance on the programme[,] session by session[,] to cover the whole four years. And he added that there was one thing on which Labour would in any case insist—a Bill, such as the Labour party had introduced session after session and the Liberal party had invariably shelved, for the prevention of unemployment. He admitted this was a difficult problem but it would have to be tackled. . . .
(3) There was the possibility of a Liberal Government with independent Labour support. He saw no objection to this in principle. Whether it were practicable would depend on the result of the general election. (4) A Coalition Liberal, or Lloyd George Government with support from various quarters—from Conservatives like Chamberlain and Birkenhead, from independent Liberals and from a section of Labour. Henderson said there were signs that George thought he might be able to split the Labour party. That was a delusion. But when I put it to him that it might be easier for the Labour party as a whole to work with George, supple as he was and not so definitely a Liberal party man as Asquith, than with Asquith, he admitted that that was so. "But", he added, "can we trust him?"

I raised the question of the competence of the Labour party to man an administration, especially the Foreign Office and the Exchequer. Their resources he thought were much greater than was commonly supposed[,] but it was noticeable that he relied mainly on men who have yet to be elected. . . .

Wednesday [1 March]

Breakfasted at Reform Club with Sir Donald Maclean. The moment I broached the subject of future political relations he burst in rather eagerly with "There will be no approach to Lloyd George" and I had to explain that I was not thinking about him but about the kind of Government that might be formed assuming that independent Liberalism and Labour had, as seemed likely, a majority as the result of a general election.

I told him of Henderson's view that a Liberal Government supported by Labour subject to a preliminary agreement on policy might be possible[,] and he also thought it might be possible, though difficult. The chief difficulty which he foresaw was on questions of expenditure. A Liberal Government would insist upon rigid and detailed economy, as contrasted with profligacy qualified by the "axe" of the present Government. They would go right back to the Gladstonian policy of saving the pence and even the ha'pence. . . . Labour on the other hand would make all sorts of demands on the public purse in support of its social policies.

He went on to talk about Grey who he thought had been misunderstood.[5] He said he was *not* in favour of an exclusive military guarantee to France, but of a series of protective guarantees, of which that to France should be only one. That, I said, was of course quite a different matter, but no one would have inferred it from his speeches. . . .

Speaking of the row between Lloyd George and Sir George Younger he said Sir George Younger "had saved the Tory party".

Lunched with [Herbert] Sidebotham[6] at the Reform Club. He said he had resigned from the "Times" because his work as a "Student of Politics" was persistently cut. He had complained and received apologies and assurances, but the thing went on. I asked if Northcliffe interfered much with the work of the office. He said his method was the singular one of making a detailed criticism (sometimes quite to the point) of the paper each day and circulating it among *all* the members of the staff. On the "Daily Mail" the process was carried a step further and the document was posted up, so that the office boys could enjoy the criticism of the various members of the staff. On leaving the "Times" he had intended to take only an engagement with a weekly paper and for the rest to trust to "free-lance" journalism, but the "Chronicle" had offered him a big salary and he went there.[7] They were greatly overstaffed with three men to write one or two leader notes. . . .

Had tea at the National Liberal Club with J. M. Hogge, one of the two Independent Liberal Whips.[8] I said I wanted to get the unofficial Liberal view. "Then you don't regard me as official" he said, which I certainly didn't. He was obviously in a pretty active state of revolt

[5] i.e. on the subject of a British guarantee to France against aggression.

[6] Until a few years before, one of the most able members of the *Guardian*'s staff.

[7] The *Daily Chronicle* was at that time under the control of Lloyd George.

[8] A Liberal M.P. since 1912, Hogge had established himself as an outspoken critic of the party leaders. Following the 1918 election, the Independent (Asquithian) Liberals in Parliament had elected him whip, clearly as a criticism of the way the party was being led by Asquith.

against his party leaders and regarded the return of Asquith to Parliament as a source of weakness. He and Sir D. Maclean had up to that time run the party in the House of Commons with vigour and some success, but after Asquith came back Maclean was a changed man and all the steam was taken out of him. Asquith did no work but Maclean could decide nothing, as before, and had to refer on all occasions to Asquith.

At Abingdon Street[9] he and Sir D. Maclean had shared a room, but suddenly Lord Gladstone was appointed and for six weeks he waited before he was even offered a chair. So in the House: Gladstone had taken possession of what had been the Independent Liberal Whips' room. He himself had been elected as Whip by the unanimous choice of the party in Parliament—the only Whip ever so appointed—but Asquith had selected [George Thorne] for the post and the difficulty was only got over by their being both appointed.

These domestic grievances had rankled, but evidently there was a much more general difference. Hogge and, I gathered, the Radical end of the party generally are quite without prejudice against Lloyd George and would take him back tomorrow if he would cut his Tory connections. Eight or ten of them had actually arranged a dinner at the Ritz to meet Lloyd George. Then something happened which obliged it to be put off, and since then Lloyd George had made no sign that he wished the invitation to be repeated. As to the party leaders neither Asquith nor Grey were he thought any good. Sir Donald Maclean was far better. The men who had done all the real fighting were now ignored. The party meeting the other day was an almost absurd example. Instead of putting the whole of their little party in Parliament to the front they were relegated to the back rows[,] and ornamental people who had not done a stroke of work took their place. Lady Emmott, who was nobody, was asked to move a vote of thanks while Mrs. Wintringham, their excellent first lady member, was left in her back row. Thus Mr. Hogge.

In the evening went to a small dinner and crush at the Astors "to meet Mr. Balfour". Took in Mrs. Snowden.[10] She entirely dissented from Henderson's view as to the administrative and political competence of the Labour Party, of whose executive she is a member, effectively to man and run a Government. They are not yet even a tolerable Opposition and have everything to learn. She had told them so in the party executive and they had not liked it.

[9] Headquarters of the Liberal party.
[10] The forceful, rather tactless wife of Philip Snowden.

Churchill, who sat next to her[,] was friendly and amusing. Repudiated the legend that he had wasted 100 millions in Russia;[11] "it was only 40". Was quite impenitent as to his part in that nefarious business. . . .

Thursday [2 March]

Breakfasted with Lloyd George. To my remark that there seemed to be rather a blaze in the heather[12] he replied "I should think so. But if they think that I am going to take my orders meekly from the Tory party they are very much mistaken. I have told Chamberlain and Balfour that unless Sir George Younger is publicly disowned I resign, and, what's more, I've put it in writing". Chamberlain is speaking on Friday and Balfour—"more important"—on Tuesday. After that I shall know what to do.

I said I supposed it was largely a Tory revolt against his leadership and an attempt to reconstitute the party on an avowedly Tory basis, rather than a difference on definite grounds of policy. He said that was so, but there was in fact also resentment on particular grounds of policy. In their hearts the more hard-bitten Tories disliked the Irish policy and the new Egyptian policy and the Indian policy. They distrusted Chamberlain because of his Radical past. Balfour was perhaps the only man who could hold them. Balfour and Chamberlain were both now practically Liberals. Balfour, for instance, was in matters of foreign policy far more Liberal than Grey. He did not believe that Grey had been misunderstood and had really changed in his outlook. He was just where he had been in 1914. . . .

He went on to speak of the Boulogne interview with Poincaré[13]. . . . I never spoke so strongly to any French statesman as I did to him, warning him that French policy was utterly alienating British opinion.[14] If he did not go to Genoa we should go without him. We should enter into economic arrangements with the other Powers. "Economic leads to political, and political to you know what". . . . "The little man put up no fight and gave way at every point". He merely emphasized the points already conceded to Briand to which of course I had no objec-

[11]Churchill had been the fiercest advocate in the government of intervening in Russia to overthrow the Bolsheviks.

[12]As a result of Younger's call for an end to the coalition.

[13]On 25 February 1922.

[14]Cf. the account of this meeting in *The Times*: "Boulogne Success. General Concord Reached. . . . both statesmen emerged smiling and vividly contented. Both of them before they left told us that the meeting was one of the most satisfactory and fruitful ever held."

tion. He even gave way a little in regard to the discussion of reparations at Genoa. . . .

I asked George if anything was said about the proposed military pact. He said not a word. For three hours we discussed Genoa and the Cannes agreement. Then Poincaré said he must go to catch his train. "I said 'What about the Pact'? and he replied 'Oh! we can discuss that another time'. That was all["]. . . .

Before leaving I spoke, as I had promised Weizmann I would, as to the urgent need of the confirmation of the British mandate for Palestine by the Council of the League of Nations at its meeting this month. He admitted it. The obstacle he said was France. She did not want a mandate herself for Syria; she wanted to annex it, as a fresh recruiting ground for native levies, like Tunis and Senegal and—as she intended—Morocco. It was part of the old obsession of German military power and expanding population. Therefore she did not want us to have a mandate for Palestine, as a precedent. I asked if he would see Weizmann and he said he would—in a fortnight.

37. Breach with Asquith, May 1922

In May, Scott's relations with Asquith came to a rupture. Asquith had long endured criticism from the Manchester Guardian *without publicly complaining. Now he turned on the paper in strong terms over a rather minor matter.*

Liberals were still divided about the proposed British guarantee to France. Asquith at an early stage had uttered a mild criticism of the proposal, but the Guardian *pressed him to do so more explicitly. He recurred to the matter in a speech at Blackpool, but a leader in the paper claimed that he had still not mad his position clear. Asquith issued a public statement that this was a "falsehood"*

Scott was outraged at what seemed an imputation against not only his· accuracy but his honesty. Moreover the incident led to an acrid correspondence between Scott and Asquith's secretary Vivian Phillipps, who complained that a Guardian *correspondent, in a subsequent interview with Asquith, had suppressed a vital passage.*

The "falsehood" incident virtually ended such relations as Scott and Asquith had maintained with each other. Occasionally letters of a formal kind passed between them. But (as far as can be told) they never met again.

Diary, 31 May 1922

Went to London Tuesday evening, May 30, at Lloyd George's request. Breakfasted with him Wednesday (9.15 as usual). He was looking well and as spry as possible. . . .

I asked what about the trouble in the Near East. Oh! yes, said Lloyd George, there is plenty. In regard to the Turk I am not only a Liberal in policy, I begin to think I am the only Liberal left, the only upholder of the Gladstonian policy. Greece must be supported. The Greek army is all right. It is money that Greece needs. Five millions was all she needed. . . . It was a mistake to suppose that the Turk was a cultivator and the Greek only a trader. The Turkish peasant just scratches the ground and gathers just enough to satisfy his own wants. The real cultivator is the Greek. . . .

423

SIR D. MACLEAN

Lunched with Sir D. Maclean at his club. Had wired offering to see him when I found I was going to London. I had heard from a common friend that he was "in despair" about the attitude of the Manchester Guardian, particularly in relation to the Asquith incident[,] and as I hate to be at loggerheads with friends for no sufficient reason obvious to myself I thought it was a good chance to get the matter cleared up.

He was extremely friendly and, to my surprise, really had nothing against me. He fully admitted that Asquith had not made the policy of the party in relation to a possible exclusive agreement with France clear at Blackpool (my whole case) and said he ought to have done so. Regretted Asquith's charge against the paper of "falsehood" for which he admitted there was no foundation. I said the outburst was unlike Asquith who was usually restrained and dignified, his chief distinction being as a great Parliamentary figure, and asked what it was that had made him so extraordinarily angry. He said Asquith had taken immense pains with his Blackpool speech and had concerted its lines with Grey and Lord R. Cecil and, when he was told that there was nothing in it on the only thing that mattered, it was more than he could bear. I fancy there was more in it than that and that Asquith's wrath had been accumulating and this was the last touch which made it boil over.

I said probably he had not read the leader, but had merely been supplied with the offending extract and then flared up. But he said No, he was sure he had read it all. It was not a sudden impulse on partial information. The sentence he quoted had infuriated him. . . .

As we parted he said he hoped that what had passed would not prevent me from meeting Asquith. I said it certainly would unless he withdrew his imputation, though I had no sort of animosity towards Asquith—quite the contrary. He said he hoped Asquith would take an opportunity of doing this.

38. Last Breakfast in Downing Street, September-December 1922

January to September 1922 were the twilight months of the Lloyd George coalition. Vigorous enough in trying to settle the affairs of Europe, it scarcely knew what to do at home for fear of disturbing its supporters.

In October, the end came abruptly. The situation in the Near East brought matters to a head. The Greek army, which Lloyd George had supported so heedlessly, abandoned its task and fled. When the Turks reached the Straits, they found only British and French forces in occupation. The attitude of the French government was uncertain. That of the British government was not. It sent martial instructions to its commander on the spot, which he prudently ignored. And it issued a grandiose appeal—clearly Churchillian in authorship—to the Dominions for assistance. Their response was not enthusiastic, but as it happened assistance was not needed. The Turks halted their advance.

Diary, 15 September 1922

Stayed a night in London on way home from Bognor. Toynbee came up from Oxford to lunch with me. Afterwards went to see Lloyd George and had half an hour with him before the meeting of the Cabinet. He threw an altogether new light on the retreat of the Greeks. Believed it had been definitely designed by [King] Constantine who cared nothing for Greek expansion, but was wholly intent on safeguarding his personal position.[1] The war had become deeply unpopular in Greece and he judged it expedient to retreat. . . . The Turks only attacked when they saw signs that the Greeks were retreating, but there was no one left to attack; "it was a blow in the void". Only at a

[1] Constantine had been driven from the Greek throne by the Allies in 1917, but had been restored by a plebiscite despite Allied opposition late in 1920 (soon after the pro-British Venizelos had been defeated at an election). Britain had indicated its displeasure by terminating financial assistance; but this had not subdued Lloyd George's enthusiasm for a Greek victory.

single point in the course of the retreat did the Greeks make any resistance and then they were successful. But the bulk of their forces kept well ahead of the Turkish pursuit and practically the whole army reached the coast and had been safely evacuated "to the islands". . . .

As to the military situation there was nothing to cause alarm. He read me a telegram which had that moment arrived from Lord Hardinge [the British ambassador] in Paris stating that the French Government had agreed to maintain, along with us, the "Neutral zone" along the whole eastern shore of the Straits and the Marmora which both belligerents had been formally forbidden in May of last year to enter with armed forces.[2] Additional troops had been sent to reinforce the small number at present acting as a corps of observation. He had given orders that if the Turks attempted to send a single transport with troops across the Straits it was to be sunk. There was no difficulty in holding the Straits. Field artillery was useless against armoured ships. I don't understand our pro-Turks, he said. I hold to the Gladstonian tradition which regards the Turk as a curse.

As to the future settlement he said he thought the Turks, flushed by success, were likely to prove extremely impracticable. . . . He would make no concessions in Europe. In fact he said, a little under his breath, "I hope to clear the Turks out of Constantinople". . . . (Evidently if he could have his way completely he would prefer to leave the Greeks in undisputed military control at least of the Dardanelles peninsula).

In the course of the conversation he complained rather bitterly of Curzon.[3] He has been laid up, he said, for four months. When he came back he went to a house in the country without a telephone. Then he moved to another with a telephone, but it was so bad that the Foreign Office could not make him hear.

Having done with the Turks I asked him when he was going to have a general election. He wasn't to be caught and answered in the same spirit "When would you like one?" "I don't care", I said. "Neither do I", he answered, and moreover I don't much care about the result. You sometimes make light of my Liberalism. Well, you will see then. In any case I must have my independence.

Then he said quickly "What is your forecast of the result of an election? What do you put Labour at?" I said 150 to 200 members.

[2] When Britain issued its appeal to the Dominions, Poincaré reversed this policy and ordered the withdrawal of French forces.

[3] Since 1919 Curzon had been Secretary of State for Foreign Affairs, but he had been at odds with Lloyd George over the conflict between Greece and Turkey.

"No", he said, "250". "And the Wee Frees?"[4] I guessed about 120. "No", he answered, "not more than 80". Then, I said, you ought to get 50 or 60 seats and in that case would hold the balance. He accepted the estimate.

It was close on time for the 4 o'clock Cabinet and I got up to go. My last words were to beg him to give all possible importance to the League of Nations in the terms of the settlement with the Turks and he agreed.

C.P.S. to Hobhouse, 4 October 1922 (Extract)

The Near East is a nightmare. I utterly distrust the Government— alike their competence and their disposition. George and Churchill I fear dominate its councils and we have a sample of their capacity in the famous Manifesto, perhaps the most heedless and ill-advised document ever issued by a responsible Government in a time of danger.

But it's no use declaiming. We've got to make the best of them.

The Greek débâcle, *and the ill-fated appeal to the Dominions, were grave humiliations for Lloyd George's government. They produced a fresh upsurge of Tory discontent, which was nearing its peak when Lloyd George visited Manchester (and Scott) on 13 October to keep a long-standing speaking engagement.*

Diary, 13 October 1922

Dined with Lloyd George at Noton Barclay's house, Mobberley Hall, on the evening before his speech at the Manchester Reform Club. He took me into another room as soon as he came down and before all the other people had arrived and I had about 20 minutes alone with him.

He burst out at once with "Well, what I wanted to tell you is that a breakup is inevitable. Whether it comes a little sooner or a little later, before the election or after it, it can't be avoided. As I told you before I hope to carry some of the other Ministers with me—Chamberlain and Birkenhead who are both really Liberals and Horne. And Churchill, who is really a Tory, will be bound to follow". He went on to speak of Chamberlain's speech at Birmingham the day before strongly recommending a continuance of coalition as showing that there was no doubt about his position.

We spoke of the question of the Freedom of the Straits and I urged

[4]i.e. the Independent or Asquithian Liberals.

strongly that there was nothing in it so far as warships were concerned and that all we need contend for at the Peace Conference was that they should be open alike in peace and war to merchant ships[,] and that there should be a sufficient demilitarised zone on both shores under international control to secure this. I added that I didn't think it would be safe to risk battleships in the Black Sea as it might be difficult to get them out again. He replied that he didn't care about their going into the Black Sea; what he wanted was that they should be able to pass the Dardanelles and threaten to bombard Constantinople if the Turks mis-behaved. . . . I said it was all right to hold the Straits till after peace was signed and the League of Nations put in control of them, but it was impossible for us to act as permanent policemen to keep the Turks in order, that what really mattered was to come to terms with Russia by agreeing to the closing of the Straits to warships passing either way. [Russia] we ought at once to recognise. He rather demurred to this. How could you recognise a State which did not acknowledge its debts and so on—really the French objections—but he did not speak with much conviction. . . .

He was in great spirits over his popular reception at Macclesfield and elsewhere on his journey.

Lloyd George and the Conservative leaders decided to outmanœuvre the dissidents in the Tory party by plunging straight into a general election. But the tactic back-fired. Chamberlain as head of the party summoned a meeting of Conservative M.P.s to the Carlton Club on 19 October to endorse the appeal to the country. He was utterly defeated. Instead, the Tory rank and file resolved to end the coalition. So Lloyd George had no alternative but to leave office; and Chamberlain loyally resigned the Conservative leadership. Bonar Law, who had come out of retirement to direct the opposition at the Carlton Club, became Prime Minister as head of a purely Conservative government.

Scott was present at Lloyd George's last breakfast in Downing Street. It should have been a noteworthy conversation. Instead, it bordered much of the time on fantasy. The reason was that Lloyd George, though rejected by the Conservative party, was determined to stick with those Conservatives still faithful to him. Yet he was concerned to prove to Scott that he was following a Liberal course. Re-conciling the two involved him in adopting two fanciful propositions: that he had voluntarily made his escape from the coalition, not been pushed out; and that the Conservatives who had gone with him were really Liberals. Scott did not argue too hard against these views: perhaps because he was trying to influence Lloyd George in a Liberal direction, but mainly out of sympathy for the fallen states-man. However, when Lloyd George tried to pass off Balfour as a latter-day

Gladstone even Scott jibbed; and he did not respond to the suggestion that he should act as mediator between Lloyd George and the opposition Liberals.

Diary, 23 October 1922

Went to London by last train Sunday afternoon [22 October] in response to wire from Lloyd George asking me to breakfast next morning (he was vacating Downing Street that evening). Mrs. Douglas-Tennant—Coalition Liberal candidate for Forest of Dean—and Major [Gwilym] Lloyd George[5] were there most of the time besides Mrs. Lloyd George.

"This is splendid", I said on meeting, "now you will be free". He agreed quite warmly and with I think a genuine sense of relief. "I feared", he said, "I might be caught in the cog-wheels and that by constant association with Conservatives I might become so bound that I could not get away". This was the first time he ever admitted to me that he had been conscious of the danger. He added: "The moment I saw my chance of escape—snap! I seized it". . . .

"Well", he said, "what do you think of the situation? What of the Wee Frees?" I said "I think nothing of the Wee Frees. They will do nothing effective so long as Asquith leads them. He is an incubus. What I am concerned about is your own position. Will you be really free?" "Absolutely," he answered. "I stand as a Liberal pure and simple." "And what of your colleagues?" "They stand as independent Conservatives. I told you I hoped to carry Chamberlain, Birkenhead and Horne with me. Well, I have carried Balfour as well". "How far will you carry them?" He took a sanguine view. Chamberlain, he said[,] is a Liberal. He sees that a tariff is now impossible. He may still go for Imperial Preference. I go for Free Trade pure and simple. Of Birkenhead he said he is a powerful intellect, a democrat. As for Horne, he is the son of a Scotch Presbyterian Minister—not much of Toryism in that. He is a Tory with a difference. He is a Gladstonian in finance. He has resisted all temptations to easy and popular finance. . . . Balfour again has become a Liberal in his old age—like Gladstone. (I remarked that the conversion in Gladstone's case had taken place a good deal earlier in life, but he took no notice of that.) It won't do to press them too hard. They must have time. It was so with the Peelites. You can't expect them to call themselves Liberals at once. Yet the Peelites supplied Liberalism with some of its most powerful intellectual reinforcement. We shall help each other. Not all the 87 minority at the Carlton

[5] Lloyd George's son.

Club will stand as supporters of the dissenting Ministers—perhaps 60 of them. If 30 are returned that will be enough. The Die-hards will probably not attack. If they do we shall retaliate. Bonar Law's seat in Glasgow is not safe. I could turn him out. (Major Lloyd George, who is the adopted Coalition Liberal candidate in Pembrokeshire, here produced a cutting from a local paper which said that the local Conservatives now felt they had made a mistake [in agreeing to support him] and intended to run a Conservative instead.)

Our great object will be to prevent the Die-hard party from getting a clear majority. A good deal depends on the Liberals. Now is their chance to save seats. At present they are attacking Coalition Liberals in 30 constituencies. We are opposing them in only two. Asquith and Gladstone are hopeless. Maclean too has been pretty bad in his latest speeches. Oddly enough my change of position is injuring the Labour prospects. [J. H.] Thomas told me that a good many of their supporters who would have voted against my Government will vote for me.

"What", I asked, "of a programme". I am speaking, he said, on Wednesday and shall declare mine. It will be out and out Liberal. Some of the Conservatives did not like my reference the other day to "Belgravia and Mayfair". They thought it smacked of Limehouse[6] and were alarmed at what I was coming to. I was obliged in my first speech to defend the record of the Coalition. Bonar Law will also this week declare his programme and I risk a prophecy to you. It will be a very advanced programme.[7] But a programme is one thing and the application of it in practice quite another. If Bonar Law gets a majority we shall have five years of reaction. . . .

After the others were gone I pressed him as to how far he was prepared to throw in his lot with the Liberal party and to give it a lead—which was his natural part. He said he saw no chance at present. It might grow easier as time went on. Cooperation in the House would help to bring the two sides together.

In the meanwhile he seems to be pretty closely bound to the Conservatives who have stood by him. There had been a dinner he told me at No. 10 on the previous evening and he ran over the list of guests which seemed to include almost every prominent name in the late Ministry. It had been a very cordial assembly. It was reported that the other side were somewhat disconcerted—had not quite realised what they were doing. "Well", said Balfour, "if they did not realise what they

[6]Where Lloyd George in 1909 had made a famous speech attacking the landed aristocracy.
[7]This prophecy proved inaccurate. Bonar Law declared for "tranquillity"

were doing that puts the last touch to their imbecility". He also mentioned with some satisfaction that Balfour had told him he was "the most powerful personal influence since Gladstone". He has in fact had a nasty fall and may naturally have been glad to lay this flattering unction to his soul.

Curzon, of whom Lloyd George had at one time had hopes[,] was not of course present [at the dinner].[8] "A weak man" said Lloyd George. Do you know at Paris he completely collapsed in face of Poincaré, who bullied him to his face. At one moment he was so over-come that he had to retire to another room where he cried and Lord Hardinge had to comfort him.

At parting he asked me how long I was staying. He wondered if I should be seeing any of the Independent Liberals. I said I was propos-ing to go back to Manchester at once. I couldn't see Asquith till he had withdrawn his insult to the paper. Was he drunk, said Lloyd George, to attack in that way "by far the most powerful Liberal paper in the country"? [Lloyd George] had evidently had it in mind that I might act in some degree as a peace-maker. . . .

Bonar Law had dissolved Parliament immediately on taking office. In the ensuing election Lloyd George occupied an indeterminate position, appealing for Conservative assistance to his hard-pressed followers yet deeply resenting attacks from the opposition Liberals. As for the vigorous policy statement which he had promised Scott, it never appeared.

C.P.S. to Hobhouse, 30 October 1922 (Extract)

As to the prospects of the election I don't put the Tory chances nearly so high as you—a clear majority of 50 (including the Chamberlainites) at the highest. More likely only a bare equality or even less, with Lloyd George and his little band (quite a little one I expect) possibly holding the balance. Anything approaching the sweep of the last election is I think impossible. The conditions for it don't exist. But of course I may be all wrong[,] and with the tremendous Conservative element of the Women's vote all ordinary calculations may be upset.

Lloyd George to C.P.S., 8 November 1922

What is the use of talking about Liberal reunion at this Election when

[8]Curzon had thrown in his lot with Bonar Law.

you have speeches like those that Grey delivered at the Free Trade Hall last night. There was his chance. Both wings of the Party in Manchester had come to an arrangement. The Coalition Leader (Rhodes) had delivered a warm and generous speech and Grey's only response is a Tory Diehard support of the Bonar Law Government and a prolonged nag at me. These men, believe me, are far too obsessed with their personal wrongs and disappointments to welcome any re-union except on the express condition that I am marooned. I am confident that my friends will not agree to this. . . .

You will forgive me for saying that I am surprised that the "Manchester Guardian" had not a word of protest against Grey's flouting of the Liberal pact in Manchester. I cannot help thinking that if I had been guilty of attacking the Independent Liberal Leaders in a speech delivered in Manchester immediately after an arrangement had been arrived at to win the two wings, I should have been admonished pretty severely in the leading *columns of the "Guardian"*. . . . Events will demonstrate even to the most prejudiced in a very short time who are the real Liberals and who are the men who simply have been using Liberalism as a vendettist weapon to avenge their own personal disappointments.

C.P.S. to Lloyd George, 15 November 1922 (Extract)[9]

First as to Grey's speech. I heard the first part, but it was delivered late (the subsidiary speeches were all taken before it) and the last part, which contained the only passage of importance, was not available for comment. Indeed I read it for the first time in print. I don't think Grey meant to be vicious, but he is temperamentally intensely antipathetic to you and above all he is outraged by what he regards as the invasion of the prerogatives of the Foreign Office. Then again he can have known nothing of the fact that the occasion was to be one of Liberal re-union. It was only made known in Manchester that afternoon and he has in these days to prepare his speeches very carefully beforehand. He might have spoken rather differently had he known. . . .

The Liberal party of the future if it is to count for anything in the life of the country will have to be not Whig or Imperialist Liberal but in the full sense Radical with strong affinities with Labour. Forgive me for saying that that is where I believe your own future to lie. On that line you will never fail of Liberal support.

[9]Lloyd George Papers.

H. A. L. Fisher to C.P.S., 12 November 1922 (Extract)

What a curious political situation! Three parties[10] practically appealing to the electorate on the same immediate programme! As for me I have long regarded the dissolution of the Coalition as inevitable. Indeed I advised Lloyd George last February to take his Liberal followers out of a Government in which it was clear that their continued presence was giving offence to the majority of the Government's supporters in the House of Commons. . . . I don't mind confessing that I am an anti-Turk. I hate to think of these ruffians being let into Europe once more.

Contrary to Scott's expectations, the Conservatives did secure an absolute majority at the election, with 345 seats. Labour made a considerable advance and, with 142 M.P.s, became the official opposition. Lloyd George's Liberal group was reduced to 60. As for the Asquithian Liberals, they did not enjoy the revival which Maclean and Gladstone had earlier anticipated and secured only 56 seats. This caused Scott to press even harder for immediate Liberal reunion. Lloyd George seemed to agree with him, but it was not certain that the two men were meaning quite the same thing.

Diary, 6 December 1922

Breakfast with Lloyd George. Only Mrs. George and Megan there (at Grigg's[11] house in Vincent Square). He plunged at once with "Well, what do you think of the results of the general election". I said I thought it was a disaster for the Liberal party worse if possible than that of 1918 because there was less excuse for it. He agreed. Reunion was essential, but how could it be attained when Grey went about almost praying for a Conservative majority? He heard that Runciman said Grey lost him his election in the 2 or 3 days that he came down to help him in his own country and his own former constituency [Berwick-on-Tweed].

He had gone as far as he could to meet the other side [i.e. since the election] offering to accept a vote of the whole party on the leadership. But that was not the right way of approaching the matter. Reunion ought to come by collaboration in the House of Commons and pressure from public opinion. . . . There ought to be a meeting of the leaders of

[10]Presumably the Conservatives, Coalition Liberals, and Independent Liberals (but not Labour).
[11]Sir Edward Grigg, formerly private secretary to Lloyd George, and returned as a Lloyd George Liberal M.P. in 1922.

the two groups to come to an understanding as to the conduct of business and to establish cooperation. After all my group is just about as strong in numbers as Mr. Asquith's and in debating power it is stronger. I cannot accept the part often proposed to me of a traitor to Liberalism who can only be taken back as penitent. As a matter of fact the record of Liberal measures passed by the Coalition Government is a fine one— the greatest measure of Irish self-government ever proposed or thought of, a very great measure of franchise extension, a remarkable temperance measure, a not insignificant measure of land reform which accepts my land valuation survey as its basis, an important international agreement as to disarmament.

At the general election the Liberals spent a great part of their strength in fighting each other. It was the hardest job I ever had and I hope never to have such another. "It was not fighting: it was fencing." You never knew from what quarter the attack would come and the conditions varied from constituency to constituency. The people who were helping each other in one constituency would be fighting in the next. If the party were united we could pull down the Government pretty much when we liked. It is a weak Government—terribly weak in debating force, as this Parliament has already shown. . . .

Asquith and his party have no positive policy, no fighting policy. That came out at the election. But for the Liberal party a fighting policy is essential. . . . The real ground of attack is the *Land*. On that the Tories would be bound to make a stand and you would have a real battle with an unanswerable case. . . .

BONAR LAW

Saw Bonar Law by appointment in his room at the House of Commons in the afternoon. He was extremely friendly and kept me for nearly an hour. Reminded me that the last time we met was at the Colonial Office during the war. My object in seeing him was to find if he would consider the introduction of P.R. or the alternative vote so as to give the Liberal party (at present in danger of being ground down between the upper and nether millstones of Conservatism and Labour) a fair standing ground on which it could hold its own. He acknowledged that the destruction of the Liberal party was the last thing he desired, but refused entirely to admit that, once reunited, it would be in any such danger. "You will have a chance", he said, "when we grow unpopular". That may happen very soon in connection with foreign affairs. . . . I know I am suspected of being pro-French and it is quite possible you may quarrel with me on that score (I admitted that I had my fears). It is true that I attach the utmost importance to maintaining a good understanding with France. I may have to choose between two evils—between a breach with France, which would mean chaos in Europe, or concessions to France which would also involve great mischiefs. . . .

He did not say he should be prepared to concede the occupation of the Ruhr [by France] as a penalty of "voluntary default",[12] but the whole drift of his statement pointed to the possible necessity of doing this. To my objection that Germany's default was certainly not voluntary he replied that he was not sure about that—that Germany might have done more, that she had not really put forth her full effort. I said she had had no encouragement to do so since no limit was put to the demands made on her. He admitted this, but did not think it affected the legal position.

As to the position of parties he said the real reason why the Conservative party had won the election was that the people were sick of the Coalition and wanted a change. The only party which could hope to establish an independent Government was the Conservative party, so people voted for it. When I came home from abroad after two years, he said, I noticed a very great change in opinion. The House was a different House. I warned Lloyd George a month before the Carlton Club meeting of this and advised him to retire while he could do so with dignity and that the longer he stayed the worse the position would be. He said he would consider the matter and speak to me again in a week. I saw at once that he did not mean to do it. He did nothing and the vote at the Carlton Club was the result. We had been very good friends up to that time and I hope we shall be again. He is the most outstanding figure in our politics, the best fighting man. Asquith is old and tired. . . .

As to the Labour party he would not admit that the Liberal party stood in any serious danger. Labour was now, he believed, at the top of the wave and would now progressively decline. It owed its present position mainly to the divisions in the Liberal party and the Coalition had done for it more in two years than it could have done for itself in twenty. Liberals had only to unite in order to reassert themselves as against Labour. . . .

[12] i.e. default by Germany in its payment of reparations to France.

39. The Iron in Liberal Souls, January-October 1923

Scott spent much effort in 1923 trying to persuade the two Liberal parties to re-unite. He encountered insuperable difficulties. Among Asquithian Liberals, Lloyd George was viewed with distrust and sometimes loathing. As for Lloyd George, he was prepared to consider reunion, but did not seem to think it his main concern. He still hankered after the coalition that was past, and to this end continued to seek alliance with such Conservatives as would have him. Their platform was hostility to Labour—which did not please Scott.

Meanwhile, France had fulfilled Bonar Law's fears. It occupied the Ruhr in order to extract the reparations which Germany was failing to pay. Liberal and Labour opinion was outraged, seeing this as equivalent to kicking a man who was down. Many Conservatives also were uneasy.

Diary, 29 January 1923

Saw Simon at his Chambers—3 to 4. Somehow, in spite of general political agreement I always feel slightly repelled by him. An affectation of cordiality which hasn't much behind it, great volubility in talking about what interests him and no attempt to talk about what interests you. An appearance of deference with no real desire to consult, except in so far as may be needful to find out what line you mean to take. Intellectually a Liberal without much of the stuff of it. A great contrast to Maclean (whom I was also to have seen, but who unfortunately was away) who has Liberalism in his bones and never thinks of himself. Talked for nearly an hour about the French occupation of the Ruhr, mainly on the question of its legality. . . . He traversed the fairly familiar grounds for asserting illegality as though they were in the nature of discoveries. . . .

Just before leaving (he had another engagement) I asked him about the Liberal position in Parliament next session and relations with Lloyd George. "I think Lloyd George is done" was about all he had to say on the subject, and, on that assumption, he was apparently not much interested in considering what relations should be established with his followers. I said I supposed these included some quite good Liberals. He said that was a matter which had been carefully examined, but I gathered without much result. He evidently took the usual rather narrow official view, though he professed to have no prejudice. There was no suggestion of a big, energetic, generous Liberal movement which would sweep the whole party together and make artificial divisions and names meaningless.

Incidentally he mentioned that he was giving up most of his law work and that after the session opened he should probably give it up altogether. In Maclean's absence[1] he is second in command [to Asquith] and he is playing for the succession. He ought not to under-rate Lloyd George, whose star is at present under eclipse, but who may yet find himself.

Diary, 8-9 March 1923

Thursday [8 March]

To London on invitation of Astors to dinner (to meet K. and Q.).[2] Left [Manchester] early on urgent invitation of Lloyd George to lunch that day. Hogge and Entwistle also there.[3] They asked my views on Liberal re-union and I gave them, but they had been at work all morning on a scheme for immediate action of their own and had the draft of an exchange of letters between Entwistle and Lloyd George, in which Lloyd George replied to definite questions put to him, practically ready. Hogge, who did not appear publicly in the matter was obviously the moving spirit. He was urgent for immediate publication. I agreed and carried off the drafts for my own use. Hogge determined to push on. Sent word for a meeting of members in favour of reunion of both sections for that afternoon at the House to be followed by a more formal one on Monday. Lloyd George evidently keen for reunion, though he put the need for immediate action on the ground that otherwise the Labour party would make all the running and the Liberal party would sink into impotence. He was prepared to go a long way in the way of conciliation but "I will not crawl. I will not crawl on my belly".

He complained bitterly of the attacks on him, particularly that by Simon. I said nothing would be gained by retaliation and Hogge

---

[1]Maclean had been defeated at the general election.   [2]Presumably King and Queen.
[3]Hogge and C. F. Entwistle were Independent Liberal M.P.s who were working, without regard to their leaders, for reunion.

warmly concurred. Said he had been expending all his energies in holding Lloyd George back. I reminded Lloyd George that after all it was he who had burst the Liberal party and that he had helped to defeat Sir D. Maclean, by far the best man on the Independent Liberal side, at the general election. He replied depreciating Maclean, but said his action had been misrepresented. It was very likely true that when he met Maclean's Conservative opponent—along with numbers of other people at a club or railway station at Edinburgh—he might have wished him success, though he had no recollection of it, but he had definitely refused, when asked, to send a message to the constituency against Maclean.

At the dinner in the evening had some talk with Lord R. Cecil, Simon, the American Ambassador and others. Lord Robert argued strongly and perversely that the French invasion of the Ruhr and all their other military proceedings could be justified under the Treaty on the ground that, though the means were military[,] the aim was commercial and that they might therefore be construed as commercial measures. Simon altogether dissented but made use of Lord Robert's opposition as a ground for not raising the question of legality (as he had repeatedly promised me he would do) in public. . . .

Lady Simon, with whom I also had some conversation, was exuberant and indiscreet. I had always suspected that the one good and courageous piece of work that Simon had done—his stumping of the country (decidedly frowned upon by Asquithian headquarters) against the Black and Tan wickedness—was largely inspired by his wife, and she now frankly admitted it. "One day", she said, "he came home with a bad cold and went to bed. I walked up and down the room crying. 'How can you lie there', I said, 'while these dreadful things are being done in my country'. Then he got up and started on his campaign and never stopped". "I always thought", I said, "that there was something electric at the back of him" and she accepted the imputation.

Friday [9 March]

Lunched with Masterman[4] whom I wanted to see as the most extreme opponent of Lloyd George and of any sort of re-union which would bring him back into the party. He went through a whole catalogue of his offences, some real mostly distorted, including his "treachery" to Asquith in upsetting him in 1916. The only fresh matter in this was the

[4]Cf. the account of this interview in Lucy Masterman, *C. F. G. Masterman* (Nicholson and Watson, London, 1939), pp. 328-330.

charge that in 1910 he was intriguing for a deal with the Tories on the basis of dropping the Parliament Bill and "reforming" the House of Lords. . . .

He was hot on the Maclean incident and would not accept the account George and Hogge had given of it. As to Hogge himself he denounced him as a sort of untouchable—a type of "the worst kind of vulgar Lowland Scot" and corrupt. He knew he had been paid as Liberal Whip which Opposition Whips customarily were not, he had no doubt he was now in Lloyd George's pay and he expected he had been paid by George at the same time that he was paid by the Independent Liberals. Lloyd George was believed still to have a very large party fund—something like a million, largely Tory money. If Lloyd George came back to the Liberal party as part of a scheme of amalgamation he and plenty of others would go out. Better fight the Liberal battle with a party uncompromised if only of three in Parliament than make such a surrender. Altogether not a very helpful attitude.

Diary, 1 July 1923

Had a long talk with Lord Gladstone (at his request) at his house, formerly Armistead's, in Cleveland Square. He had not told me what he wanted to see me about but opened up at once on the subject of Lloyd George and the Liberal party. To begin with, he said, one point might be regarded as fixed and irrevocable: for whatever reason, whether arising from his own feelings or the pressure of his (domestic) entourage, he [i.e. Asquith][5] was resolved never again to accept Lloyd George as a colleague. I said I had already understood this, but what exactly did that imply? I gathered that Asquith was not unwilling to confer with Lloyd George and had often done so on the day to day procedure and tactics in the House. He said that was so and that they met on quite friendly terms.

What Asquith refused to do was to admit Lloyd George into the "inner council" of the party. This by custom consisted, when the party was in opposition, of such persons as the leader of the party chose to summon and was a matter within his absolute discretion, just as the membership of the Cabinet, when the party was in office, was within the Prime Minister's discretion. A theory had been advanced that all ex-Cabinet Ministers had a right to be summoned, but that was not so.

[5]That "he" refers to Asquith is clear both from the context and from an account of this same conversation by Gladstone (Viscount Gladstone Papers in the British Museum).

"My father" Gladstone, who was not fond of consulting anybody, had been in the habit of discussing policy with only two or three people. Campbell-Bannerman used to summon some 8 or 9, among whom were not included the Liberal Imperialist group—Asquith, Grey etc. These differed from the Liberal party of the day on vital matters of policy—the South African war and Home Rule as an immediate issue. Later a reconciliation was effected largely through Chamberlain's action in forcing the issue of Free Trade to the front, on which there was agreement between the two sections. During the war party was in abeyance and after the 1918 election there was practically no Liberal organization till I took up my present work (at the Liberal Central) and re-established it. Lloyd George was of course not a member and he will not now be admitted.

I said I had not realised the importance attached to this inner council which seemed to be a rather fluctuating body, but was membership essential to co-operation? After all it was a practical question. Lloyd George was already consulted on a good many matters involving policy; why should he not be consulted on all matters of immediate or prospective practical importance? There was in his case no question of difference on policy as there was in that of the Liberal-Imperialists. He was as good a Liberal as any of the leaders of the Independent Liberals, or perhaps rather a more advanced one. That was not the case no doubt with all his followers in the House and these would have to choose their political associations as they pleased, but that was a matter which would settle itself and did not affect him.

Gladstone admitted this, but more was involved. There was the question of the succession. What of Sir John Simon? It was generally recognised that Asquith was no longer effective as an active leader. Was Lloyd George then to succeed him, as he inevitably must, by force of personality and past position, if once accepted and recognised as a full member of the party? That would disintegrate the party. It was not merely the other leaders who would not accept him (and he himself should decline with the rest), but in most of the constituencies there were important men who could never be brought to accept Lloyd George and who would go out of active politics if he were once more brought in in an important position.

Then there was the question of his separate organization in the constituencies with heavily subsidised agents and his rival central organization in Abingdon Street, with about double the personnel of the Independent Liberal organization, and his separate campaign fund. Yes, I said, I have often wondered about that. What does it amount to

—thousands of pounds, or tens of thousands, or hundreds of thousands? Nobody knows, he answered, but it is possible to estimate. J. M. Hogge who was formerly chief Independent Liberal Whip has gone over to Lloyd George's service. (He gave a somewhat lurid account of Hogge's proceedings and character. He was frequently drunk in the House and during the December election had gone off to Scotland with one of the House of Commons waitresses known among the House of Commons reporters as "the fairy". Throughout the election we were in terror, said Gladstone, of exposure and an awful scandal. After the election we were determined not to reappoint him as Chief Whip. Vivian Phillipps was appointed and Hogge offered the second place at a reduced salary of £600 a year instead of £800. He declined to accept it and was taken over by Lloyd George at a salary of £1000. But before that he had been a great advocate of "reunion" and very much of a Lloyd George man.) Some one suggested (before the last election in December) that Lloyd George's separate fund might amount to £5 millions. Oh! no, said Hogge, not as much as that, not more than three millions. Suppose, said Gladstone, we deduct £500,000 for his expenditure at the election and divide by half the remainder, that would still leave him with well over a million and that is not an unreasonable estimate. It is known that in one particular case £200,000 was paid for a peerage.[6] That was quite exceptional, but £100,000 or £120,000 was not unusual and the *scale* of these transactions was unprecedented. Formerly the Prime Minister's [honours] list had been based on *political* service, but this qualification was now abandoned and any sort of benevolence, with no other service at all, was accepted as a ground for conferring an honour. The system, he said, had steadily grown. Under Gladstone [himself] it was pretty severely restricted. When [George] Whiteley (member for Stockport) became chief whip[7] it had a considerable extension. The Master of Elibank, who succeeded him, went much further in raking in the shekels, and Lloyd George carried the matter to its extreme.

What is to become of this fund, said Gladstone? I don't see that we could accept it even if it were offered. It is the proceeds of corruption and we have protested against corruption. Lloyd George can do what

---

[6]Lloyd George's political fund, it was believed, had been accumulated during his premiership by awarding honours to those who made large "donations". His was not the first party fund to be enriched in this way, but in Lloyd George's case the transactions had become so numerous as to cause a public scandal. Gladstone was assuming that the Conservatives had taken half the proceeds when the coalition split up.
[7]From 1905 to 1908.

he likes with it. It is his personal fund in a sense in which no such fund ever was personal before. The best thing he could do with it would be to pension [off] his numerous agents and hand over the balance to the League of Nations. But we can't take it and are better without it. If Liberals believe in Liberalism they must be ready to pay for its necessary organization. At one General Election I had only £25,000 in hand and we got through somehow.

That was Gladstone's statement of the position. He had no way out to propose and appeared to be satisfied that the existing division should continue, or at least to see no way in which it could be bridged. I said I did not see that the position was hopeless. There was no difference of policy and admittedly Lloyd George was the most effective popular advocate of Liberalism—the only man perhaps who could really fire the party and win over the masses of unorganized voters. It seemed to me the matter must be dealt with as a practical one. There must be sufficient communication to secure unity of action both in Parliament and in the constituencies. The two sections of the party must under no circumstances oppose, but must aid each other. There must be an effective concordat. Lloyd George could not, if treated still as a power apart, dissolve his organization at once, but he might reduce it by degrees and utilise his separate fund in the constituencies in which his candidates stood. The fund itself was not in dispute. As to the question of Lloyd George's admission to the party Council it did not seem to me vital at present, but I should like to hear what Lloyd George himself had to say. For the rest time might do a good deal to ease matters. I had learned from an American source that Lloyd George, who was going to Canada next month, would go on to America and then probably to Australia (this was new to him). His importance right through the English-speaking world would be demonstrated and emphasized. If, when he came back, he threw himself, as was to be expected, into the work of Liberal advocacy in Parliament and in the country, how could he be ignored? I think Gladstone did in fact realise this and it constituted for him a problem for which he saw no solution. He wanted me, I suppose, to see his side of the case. I said I should like, in view of what he had said, to ascertain Lloyd George's.

Diary, 26 July 1923

Went to London to see Lloyd George at his invitation. Ellis Davies also at breakfast. Talk turned mainly on Welsh politics. Davies is head of the Welsh Independent Liberal organisation—a depressed little

[man], a good deal out of health. Took a discouraging view of Liberal prospects generally, but was quite ready for re-union, beginning in Wales. . . . I said that was all right as a start, but what about the adjacent district of Great Britain? He [Lloyd George] said nothing could be done till he was accepted on terms of full equality in the councils of the party. I told him what Lord Gladstone had said to me as to the permanent impossibility of that, and he said if that were so it ought to be publicly stated. While he was to be shut out [W. M. R.] Pringle[8] was actually now being put forward as the possible future Liberal leader, even in preference to Simon. At that rate the Tory party would be in power for 20 years or more and then there would be a big reaction and Labour would come in. He was blamed for keeping up relations with Austen Chamberlain, but Chamberlain was in fact a Liberal. . . . The Tory party from time to time absorbed Liberals (McKenna to wit);[9] why should not the Liberal party absorb Tories? . . .

Masterman to C.P.S., n.d. (Extract)

If Lloyd George would retire for a few years and stop writing the nonsense he is writing for the Daily Telegraph[10] and Hearst's papers in America, I think it quite possible that he might lead a United Liberal Party. But I doubt if everyone realises what is the opinion of the active Liberal Party at this time. My wife and I went down to Clay Cross in Derbyshire where I stood in the general election, to receive a presentation from the local Liberals last Saturday. The leader of them, amid the cheers of all the stalwarts representing all the mining districts, declared that if Mr. Lloyd George and the Coalitionists came back to lead the Liberal Party, he would altogether go out of politics. I believe this feeling to be common to all the constituencies outside Lancashire.

You and I have known our Lloyd George now for twenty years. . . . At the 1920 Club he tried to explain that in home and foreign affairs, he and his Liberal colleagues in the Coalition carried out everything that was desirable for the welfare of humanity. You and I know this to be a lie. Hadn't he better acknowledge that he is lying as a first step towards the union of the good old days?

[8]Liberal back-bencher, highly critical of Lloyd George.
[9]McKenna had spoken in support of Bonar Law at the 1922 election.
[10]Presumably a mistake for *Daily Chronicle*.

443

40. The New Man, October 1923

Illness forced Bonar Law to resign as Prime Minister. He was succeeded by the inexperienced Stanley Baldwin. It was not long before Baldwin's utterances began causing confusion.

The Ruhr difficulty remained unsettled. Curzon, the Foreign Secretary, had indicated dissent from France's action. But Baldwin was anxious "to restore that atmosphere of confidence between France and ourselves which had for some time been lost". So he visited Poincaré in Paris and issued a communiqué *expressing agreement with French policy.*

On home policy he also caused some raising of eyebrows. The day before Scott visited him, Baldwin addressed a Conservative gathering at Plymouth. Referring to the problem of unemployment, he said that the government was bound by his predecessor's pledge not to introduce tariffs without a mandate from the people; but he also claimed that he could see no way of combatting unemployment except by tariffs. Whether this constituted a counsel of action or inaction, no one knew.

Diary, 26-27 October 1923

Called on Baldwin at 10 Downing Street on Friday afternoon [26 October] (I had asked for an appointment). I apologised for troubling him, but he was very friendly and said he was glad of the opportunity of seeing me (I had not met him before) and he knew he could trust me.

He opened up almost immediately on the subject of the Paris interview, without any approach by me: "The first thing I said to Poincaré was 'do you trust me to mean exactly what I say. I know that was not the case with a late Prime Minister (all confidence he said to me had been lost by Poincaré in Lloyd George) because if you cannot I shall say nothing at all'.["] M. Poincaré gave the necessary assurance. "I then went on to tell him squarely what was the feeling in England— not of one party only, but the general feeling in regard to the Ruhr occupation. The occupation in time of peace of part of the territory of a neighbouring country which is not in a position to resist is resented by Englishmen. They do not like it. They may put up with it for a time for special reasons, but if it goes on much longer they will revolt against it and neither I nor anybody else may be able to restrain them". He then asked whether if passive resistance [by the Germans] ceased the conditions of the occupation would be changed and M. Poincaré assured him that they would. He declared further solemnly that France desired neither to crush nor to break up Germany. And Baldwin appears to have accepted these assurances in good faith. Hence the famous note.

He then asked Poincaré whether supposing passive resistance to have ceased he had decided on the steps which he would then take. M. Poincaré replied that he had not. It would be time enough to consider that when the occasion arose. That, said Mr. Baldwin[,] is I believe his difficulty now. He does not know in the least what to do next and so defends himself by saying the occasion has not arisen—that passive resistance has not really ceased. Either that or he is simply playing for time and is struggling to postpone any settlement till after the French elections in the spring and to conceal from the French people the fact that the pledge which was to be productive can produce nothing and that reparations are further off than ever. "It is difficult to say whether he is deceiving himself or breaking his word".

He went on to discuss Poincaré's character: "honest perhaps as honesty is understood among diplomatists, able, eloquent, persistent, limited, without constructive power, ignorant as a child of the very elements of economics".

Discussing the possibility of American cooperation he said one difficulty was the total absence of men of commanding ability. [C. E.] Hughes[1] he admitted was perhaps the best of them. "But", he said, "he is a Welshman". . . . I think he suspected slipperiness on the analogy of another prominent Welshman. He had felt this [lack of men of ability] very much when trying to settle in America the question of the British debt. Had found it impossible apparently to get any but the narrowest view taken. What had struck him was the extraordinary ignorance of the mass of the people of anything outside their own country and generally the low intellectual level.

Our present troubles in Europe were to a very great extent due to the withdrawal of America. The drafting of the Treaty postulated America's cooperation. A wholly different Treaty would have been drawn on the opposite assumption. . . .

[1]U.S. Secretary of State.

The difficulty of coming to an understanding with France arose largely from the difference in the moral outlook, the "ethos"[,] of the two peoples. Justice and fair play, I understood him to mean, did not mean quite the same thing to them.

[In the evening Scott dined with the American ambassador, and found himself placed on the right of the Duke of York, who was guest of honour:]

He told me a good tale about Northcliffe. "Latest news: Lloyd George has resigned: Lord Northcliffe has sent for the King". He thought it a very good joke, which it was.

Saturday [27 October]

Breakfasted (8.30) with Smuts at the Savoy. . . .
  I asked what he thought of Baldwin who was something of a dark horse. Was he strong and was he able? Smuts gave a somewhat qualified judgment on both points. An excellent man he said and thoroughly well meaning and honest, but lacking, he evidently thought, in judgment and drive. The Paris *communiqué* was an obvious mistake and he had just made another very grave one in allowing an absorbing and controversial domestic issue like that of Protection to be raised at a moment when all the nation's thought and effort should have been concentrated on the European problem. . . .
  He said rather an interesting thing about Keynes with whom he appears to have close relations and whom he frequently consults. Keynes had written denouncing his whole effort, as futile and misplaced. Why, he asked, do you fuss about Reparations; there can be no Reparations? Why not let France have her way and let things work themselves out to the inevitable disaster? Then it may be possible to do something and to attempt a real reconstruction. The usual fallacy of the theorist, said Smuts, who works out everything on paper. We poor people have to face the facts and do what we can step by step. . . .

41. Ramsay, November 1923- September 1924

The riddle of Baldwin's statement at Plymouth about tariffs was soon solved. He announced that he must introduce tariff protection, and—to release himself from Bonar Law's pledge not to do so—he dissolved Parliament and appealed to the country. Against him, the Liberal and Labour forces took their stand for free trade. Indeed the two Liberal parties precipitately reunited, Asquith and Lloyd George meeting and deciding to fight under a single banner. In the glow of this restored Liberal harmony, Scott found it possible for a while to look with enthusiasm on Asquith and his associates.

The results of the election of December 1923 robbed Baldwin of his majority. Conservatives secured 258 seats, Labour 191, Liberals 158. Thus the Liberals held the balance of power. What were they to do: keep Baldwin in office; or put him out and support a Labour government; or try to form a (virtually anti-Labour) government themselves, hoping for Conservative support? The Manchester Guardian came out strongly for the second course: a Labour government with independent Liberal backing. So ultimately did the Liberal leaders. One who strongly favoured this course was Lloyd George—now momentarily purged of his hankerings after a new coalition. According to the account he gave Scott, he had to overcome strong opposition from Asquith and his associates; but not all versions agree with this.[1]

Yet this experiment in minority government was doomed from the start. What rendered it hopeless was Labour's hostility to the Liberals. Once in office, Labour needed Liberal support in every division. Yet the Labour party was more concerned to crush the Liberals than to work with them. Hence during the life of the government it subjected them to unrelenting attack. It was only a matter of time before the Liberals' patience—notwithstanding their acute anxiety to avoid another election—gave way under the strain. In short, the first

---

[1]Vivian Phillipps, *My Days and Ways*, pp. 97-99, recounts a conversation with Asquith and others (but not Lloyd George) three days after the election in which, though Asquith doubted the capabilities of Labour for governing, he was in no doubt that Labour could take office if it wanted to.

Labour government was like a man sitting on the branch of a tree and sawing through the branch at the end nearest to the trunk. When the saw bit deep enough the branch would break; whereupon not only the branch but the occupant would come crashing down.

Scott strained every effort to preserve the life of the first Labour government. But even before it was formed, he was given a pretty clear warning of the fall it would prepare for itself. He corresponded with Ramsay MacDonald, the Labour leader, in December, and talked with him on 6 January, a fortnight before the vote of censure in Parliament which ejected Baldwin and opened the way for MacDonald to become Prime Minister. Thereafter, though retaining a high opinion of MacDonald as a diplomatist, Scott's personal assessment of him went steadily downhill.

C.P.S. to Simon, 30 November 1923[2]

How kind of you! Yours was the first and not least welcome letter of a kind friend. . . .

How splendidly you and our other leaders are carrying on the campaign. I don't remember ever to have seen Asquith in such fine form. And there's more than that in it—a fine spirit of generosity from you all.

C.P.S. to Ramsay MacDonald, 9 December 1923 (Extract)

I am greatly concerned as to the future of parties and as to the relation of the Liberal party to your party which will go far to determine the future of our politics.

I should be so glad if, when you have time, I might see you.

[Scott also mentioned in this letter that he had heard reports that MacDonald felt the Labour party had been unfairly treated by the press during the election. MacDonald in reply exonerated the *Manchester Guardian* from this charge, but not the other Liberal papers:]

MacDonald to C.P.S., 11 December 1923 (Extract)

I do think . . . that the way that the Daily News and the Westminster Gazette behaved [during the election] was contemptible. We expect nothing better from the Daily Mail and such miserable products. The

[2]Simon Papers. Simon apparently had written congratulating Scott on being made an honorary fellow of his old Oxford college.

result, however, of the whole fight has been to dig both deeply and broadly a ditch between Liberalism and Labour. From all over the country I hear from my friends who fought that the Liberal fight was dirtier than the Tory, and I have seen leaflets like that issued by [Sir Henry] Webb who fought [Hugh] Dalton in Cardiff, which are simply amazing in their dishonesty. The line he took was that whilst we pitied the poor German who was being asked to pay £2,000,000,000, we had no qualms in imposing a Capital Levy upon Englishmen to the extent of £3,000,000,000. Eight Liberal Leaders in my own constituency issued an appeal to the Liberals to join in the glorious work [of] defeating the Leader of the Opposition, and stating that they had an agreement with the Conservatives that after my defeat the Liberals would have a chance of getting the seat. The only merit of the thing was that it was done in public and that the Liberal Leaders had the courage to put their names to it.

Mr. Lloyd George's campaign in its gross demagogic vulgarity has also increased both the number and the value of the reasons why we should have nothing whatever to do with his Party.

I am always delighted to see you and if you would let me know when you are next in town, it would give me great pleasure to have a talk.

Lloyd George to C.P.S., 27 December 1923 (Extract)[3]

I am very anxious to have a talk with you about the interesting situation which is developing in the new Parliament. I am entirely in accord with the line you have taken in the "Manchester Guardian". The Liberal Party is very divided on the question of supporting Labour. Quite a number of the "important and influential" emphatically dislike it, but if Ramsay were tactful and conciliatory I feel certain that the Party as a whole would support him in an advanced Radical programme.

Diary, 5-6 January 1924

Saturday [5 January]

Met Lloyd George in London at his request and (after hearing part of the "Messiah" in his box at the Albert Hall) drove with him to his new house at Churt. All our talk on the way was of the new position of parties and the relations to be established between the Liberal and

[3]Lloyd George Papers.

Labour parties. He was in great spirits and exploded with joy at his final escape from Tory trammels. He did not confess to the immense mistake of that entanglement, but I think it was clearly in his mind. Now he had once more found himself—confessed that in his election tour his good spirits had verged on levity—it was a "tin-kettle" affair all through and looking to the shortness of the time that was perhaps the best way to take it. Elaborate exposition of free-trade principles [was] out of place and ineffective.

He repeated the view he had indicated when he wrote to me (he then said he entirely agreed with the line taken by the "Manchester Guardian") that the only possible course, under present conditions, for the Liberal party was to back the Labour party whole-heartedly to the full extent open to it, and in concert with it to reap a full harvest of Radical reform. There was of course strong difference of opinion within the party on this subject. Immediately after the declaration of the poll (on the Friday or Saturday I gathered; the final results came in on Friday evening[4]) there had been a meeting of the Liberal leaders. The general view, adopted by Asquith and strongly urged by Simon, was that the Tories should first be turned out by a combination with Labour[,] and Labour (if it formed a Government) as speedily as possible by a combination with the Tories, the Liberals then taking Labour's place. George strongly opposed and asked what they would do, if they did take office, being, as they would be[,] entirely dependent on Tory support. The feeling of the meeting was, however, clearly against him and so, to gain time he proposed an adjournment over the week-end. Asquith ("always ready to adjourn anything") concurred and when the meeting met again he had so far changed his position as to propose his policy of complete independence—no truck with the Tories who were to be upset at the first opportunity and non-committal towards Labour after it had formed a Government. George accepted this as a first step in the right direction. It left the question of co-operation open.

But, if there was to be cooperation for common purposes with Labour, there must be consultation. It was not merely occasional support that the Labour Government would require in divisions; the support must be continuous. The Liberal whips would have to "keep a House" for Labour, that is some 60 Liberals would have to be constantly in reserve. It was no use for the Labour leaders to say that they would ignore snap divisions; they might ignore them now and again, but no Government could afford to be placed constantly in a minority—

[4] i.e. 7 December 1923.

the conduct of business would become impossible and the Government would be discredited. Yet if the Liberals simply failed to attend this must be the consequence. Cooperation to be of use must be complete and it must be concerted.

There will of course be opposition to this on the Liberal side. Simon in particular remains entirely hostile. At the party meeting at the National Liberal Club soon after[,] Asquith adhered rigidly to his purely non-committal policy and evidently had still in mind the ulterior aim of upsetting and superseding Labour. I went to the meeting, said Lloyd George, prepared to speak, but after hearing Asquith, I determined to be silent. I should have advocated cooperation and that would have introduced disharmony. So I held my peace.

I said I thought if he took the line of cooperation strongly he would have the bulk of the party with him and Asquith could not afford to be left behind. He said he quite thought that was so.

As to the actual business of co-operation I said a great deal would of course depend on the Whips and I was afraid Vivian Phillipps, as Chief Whip, would be a serious obstacle. My own experience of him, of which I gave him the particulars, had been highly unfavourable. . . . He said his impression also was unfavourable. We went through the list of the Liberal Whips and found them a poorish lot (with a relatively bright spot in the person of Lloyd George's own son!).

As to policy he saw no difficulty. There was an ample field common to the two parties. The danger, to his mind, was not that Labour would go too fast and far, but that it would not go fast and far enough and perish of inanition. It must be prepared to take risks and Liberalism should back it in a courageous policy. The line of advance would, however, have to be carefully selected. Thus if an advance were to be made in the direction of nationalisation it would be well to begin with the easiest matter—Electricity. Electrification was not a local affair and could not be dealt with locally. It was national and so was specially adapted to [national] treatment. . . . The railways should come next as being also non-local and amalgamation had already prepared the way. Mines were a good deal more difficult.

I chaffed him about his incendiary article in that day's "Chronicle" in which he had warned Labour against the dangers of moderation. He said he meant it to be incendiary. If Labour failed through lack of courage and initiative Liberalism, which had put it in office and kept it there, would share the discredit.

The great danger to a Labour party was its extreme inexperience and consequent timidity. He expressed some doubts as to MacDonald's

451

own qualities as a leader. He had had no experience of administration even of a trades union, and he was extremely vain. (This was strongly confirmed by Mrs. Snowden at dinner. He had courage but lacked persistence. This also was confirmed at dinner by H. A. L. Fisher. They had been in India together on an Education Enquiry Commission and you never could depend on MacDonald to stick to an opinion for a week together). [In Lloyd George's view:] If they had even a couple of men of real capacity and experience of affairs, it would make all the difference. Haldane might be very useful to them. . . . He disagreed with the "Manchester Guardian" about J. H. Thomas who, on the whole, would he thought make a better Foreign Minister than MacDonald. He was very shrewd and very quick and knew how to handle men. He knew a good deal about foreign affairs and what he did not know he was not above learning. He could get up a subject with extreme rapidity and was an excellent speaker. . . . I had no idea Thomas was in such high esteem, but then to be sure he also is of Wales.

I told Lloyd George of the conquest he appeared to have made of the Asquiths and rashly told him that Mrs. Asquith had told me in a letter to me that "he had behaved very well". He fired up at once at the implied suggestion that he had ever behaved otherwise, and went on to give an interesting piece of information. Asquith himself, he said, had come to the conclusion that, at the critical moment preceding his overthrow [in 1916], he had made a mistake and that at bottom it was due to the failure of his Whips in the advice they gave him (no doubt as to the possibility that Lloyd George could form a Government) and that Asquith had said "if Illingworth had been there" everything would have gone differently. . . .

Mrs. Snowden and Mr. and Mrs. H. A. L. Fisher (neighbours) were at dinner (Snowden had gone to Newcastle to give a lecture) and the evening was spent, to a late hour, mainly in the singing of old English songs and Welsh hymns, in which Lloyd George, with his still fine tenor voice, joined with immense gusto, Mrs. Snowden playing the accompaniments and both ladies joining in.

Sunday [6 January]

Called on MacDonald by appointment at midday at his house in Howitt Street, Hampstead. Found him at work in his study with a vast litter of papers about him. He looked fagged and anxious. I hoped he had enjoyed a rest at Lossiemouth. He said he would have done but for the postman. I said he would need about six secretaries. He said he had already got three and should have to engage a fourth. Between secretaries and political journeyings he had in one month spent two years' savings. I said he would certainly have to take his ministerial salary, whatever some of his followers might say, and that living at No. 10 would cost him all that, according to Lloyd George, or more. He said he told the objectors that he meant to take it. As a matter of fact he intended to go on living in his present house and to use No. 10 for official purposes so would be at double expense. He did not expect to save anything in the first year of office; in the second he might save "the price of a glass of whisky".

I explained the position as I understood it—Lloyd George wholeheartedly with Labour both because of big reforms following on success and of the discredit (which Liberals must share) in case of failure. Of course there was division in the party. Asquith, however, could hardly afford to hang back if George gave a strong lead. For success, however, cooperation was essential. He said he was quite prepared for cooperation between the Whips. A certain amount of friendly communication between the Whips of the opposing parties had always been customary for mutual convenience, and he proposed to carry this somewhat further. I urged that communication would have to go a good deal further, as Labour would be dependent on Liberal support from day to day and in small things as well as great. He had plenty of former Liberals among his followers and one of them might perhaps serve as a channel.

He said the difficulty was the strong feeling of hostility toward Lloyd George throughout the party[,] and the people I referred to— such he presumed as [Arthur] Ponsonby and Morel—hated him even more than the rest. They felt they could not trust him. His own ex· perience bore this out in a small way. Before he went to Russia Lloyd George promised to see him through, but when the pinch came he did nothing. I said there must surely be some one less hard-bitten who could serve the purpose and he promised to find one.

One thing he was clear about—there must be an end to the flaunting of Labour's dependence [on the Liberals]. It might be tolerated once, it might be tolerated twice, but after that, if repeated, he should speak out strongly. He showed a curious sensitiveness on this and spoke with feeling, as though this were a matter of deep importance. Probably it is the matter on which his own party feels most and on which he would be most exposed to attack.

A great difficulty he said for him and his party was that they had been taken entirely by surprise and as they had not the least expectation of being called upon to take office, so they were quite unprepared for it. I expressed surprise as the possibility had been very present to our own minds. . . .

We had got so far and were on the way to go a good deal farther when MacDonald suddenly woke up and said he had unluckily a luncheon engagement in Chelsea at one o'clock which he had made just before he had got my telegram (it was then nearly one o'clock) and hastily changed his coat. I had my taxi at the door and offered to take him as I had a call to make in that region. He laughed at my excuse, but let me take him and his nice young daughter half way, talking hard all the time. As we parted he begged me to come and see him again next time I was in town.

On the way he said suddenly "there is a private matter which perhaps I ought not to mention to you, but I'll risk it". It wasn't a very big matter and related to communications from Lloyd George or rather expressions of opinion reported as his which reached them through a channel regarded by the party as quite unsuitable and much resented accordingly. Very likely, said MacDonald, Lloyd George had not in any way authorised these communications, but it was very desirable they should cease, and he would be very glad if I could make a suggestion to Lloyd George to that effect—not as from him. It all seemed rather unimportant and a further evidence of the sensitiveness of a party not yet sure of itself, and I could only say that the best way to avoid the wrong channel was to provide a right one.

By the time Scott returned to London a month later, Labour was safely installed in office. MacDonald, somewhat rashly, had taken the Foreign Office in addition to his duties as Prime Minister. Meanwhile the Liberals were becoming anxious at the complexities of their new situation as a party maintaining in power a government which considered itself at war with them.

Diary, 2-3 February 1924

Went to London Friday [1 February]. . . . Took the opportunity to see if MacDonald could see me and, when I found it would be late on Sunday before he could do so, accepted a pressing invitation from Lloyd George to spend the night with him at Churt. . . .

Motored to Churt Saturday evening [2 February]. Philip Kerr and Harold Spender also there. Had some time alone with George that evening and saw a good deal of him again next morning before leaving after lunch. I told him that I was to see MacDonald on Sunday evening at the War Office and remarked that it was very good of him, considering how full of work he must be and that he was only coming up from Chequers that evening. "Not at all", said George, "considering what he owes you. But for you he would not have been in office. You were the first to make a stand for cooperation with Labour. I only came in second". Very likely the line taken by the Manchester Guardian did help him to make up his own mind after his strong attacks on Labour to come round to its support, and there can be little doubt that his action determined that of Asquith.

I asked him a little more about the meeting of Liberal party leaders held just after the election. It was on the Sunday after the results of the election were known.[5] There were present—besides himself and Asquith—Simon, [Sir Alfred] Mond, Macnamara and [C. A.] McCurdy.[6] On that day McCurdy alone supported George in the policy of cooperation. The rest were in favour of themselves taking office, with Conservative support. (A paradoxical situation. George, the Coalitionist[,] against a virtual coalition, the Independent Liberals, its sworn antagonists, in favour). It was not till the adjourned meeting that Asquith propounded his policy, announced at the National Liberal Club, of the half-way house, or holding the balance, which George accepted as a step in the right direction and which Asquith afterwards, in his famous speech on the Address, developed into one of frank cooperation [with Labour].

But evidently George was still much exercised in his own mind as to how the thing should be worked out. He kept coming back on its difficulties from the party point of view. If Labour succeeds they get all the credit; if it fails we get the blame for putting them in power. Then again to be safe from day to day in the House they will need to be able to rely on the support of at least 120 Liberals. If 50 seceded their majority would be gone. Already, on the vote of want of confidence, there was a secession of 10 and the number will grow. How can you expect Liberals to go on continuously supporting Labour with no share in the Government? On the other hand[,] when Spender said he thought the Government would be out in six months[,] he offered to wager that they would live to bring in a King's Speech, which means at least a year. When I said that if this course was difficult from the party point of view any other would have been far worse he did not seem quite confident of that and fell back on a higher standard. If it was not

[5] Presumably 9 December 1923.
[6] Mond, Macnamara, and McCurdy had all held office in Lloyd George's government.

right from the point of view of tactics it was from that of Liberal principle and, being right, it would work out right, though it was impossible to see exactly in what way it would work out.

One of the last things he said to me was "Well, what am I to do?" I could only suggest that, in a strange and tangled situation, we should go right ahead on the simple line we had taken and make all possible allowance for the section of the party which, having been in direct conflict with Labour at the election, found it hardest to cooperate with it afterwards. The present alignment of parties was obviously unreal and there would have to be readjustments. By-elections were the most immediate difficulty and we discussed Burnley. He thought that if a moderate Labour man were brought forward there, especially a Labour Minister like Henderson, he should not be opposed, and in analogous situations they should reciprocate.[7]

There were difficulties also from the Labour point of view. His [MacDonald's] own Left wing would become clamorous. Then he must either ride for a fall, or there must be a further approximation between Labour and Liberals. Pringle for example might perhaps join them.

Lloyd George has bought a delightful little property, mainly unspoilt woodland, of about 70 acres and he took us all round and about it on a lovely morning. He joked about the coming *Revolution* against which it was to serve as a retreat, but half in earnest too. Everything would depend on the course of trade. If it were good enough to keep our great population in reasonable comfort there would be no explosion. Otherwise it might come within 10 years. Ostentatious luxury was a great provocation and it was still rampant. An actress was put on the stage the other day blazing with half-a-million pounds worth of jewels. That was a sign. . . .

MACDONALD

Returned to London on Sunday afternoon [3 February] and saw MacDonald by appointment at the Foreign Office. He arrived from Chequers almost at the same moment and saw me immediately. Three or four of the red dispatch-boxes were on the table and he opened them as we talked—asking me not to stop talking. It seemed just a little of a pose and the impression grew. He was in knickers with a rough over-

---

[7] Henderson had been defeated at the General Election, and in due course stood at Burnley. The Liberals did not oppose him, so ensuring his election. But Labour never reciprocated their action.

coat (when he came in) and treated the Foreign Office chair of state much as Balfour sometimes treated the table at the House of Commons —a curious contrast to the dignified pose of the last occupants I used to see there—first Grey and then Curzon. He seemed to find little in the dispatch boxes to interest him and we just went on talking. At the end of about an hour I made a move to go, but he gave me no encouragement and kept me nearly another three-quarters of an hour till he left himself and I went with him as far as Charing Cross station. He told me [he] was sleeping that night for the last time at Hampstead and after that should close the house and take up his quarters regularly at No. 10.

He discoursed of many things foreign and domestic, interestingly and in the most friendly way, but all too well pleased with himself, too confident and too contemptuous of all that had been done before. Was it the native vainglory of the Highlander?

As to his own position he told me he had at first made up his mind not to take the Foreign Office in addition to the Premiership, but on consideration felt that as, in view of the immense present importance and difficulty of foreign affairs[,] he must in any case inform himself very closely in regard to them it would really be more satisfactory to deal with them directly himself instead of having to get the information second-hand from the Foreign Secretary. He found the work extraordinarily interesting merely as a spectacle if only he had not to be actor as well as spectator. . . .

Relations of Parties. We do not depend only on the Liberals. The Tories are extremely friendly. On the whole they like us better than they do the Liberals. They will do nothing merely for the purpose of putting us out. Whatever party did put us out at present would pay heavily with the country. I asked how long he thought this Parliament would last. I myself had from the first given it a pretty long lease of life. It will last, he said, as long as we have work to do which does not bring us into direct conflict with the other parties. That may not be very long. It looks as though we should get through our work extraordinarily quickly. When I come to a "barren patch" and am held up on my own distinctive policy I shall dissolve—e.g. on the question of the nationalisation of mines.

As to the day to day work of Parliament I see no difficulty in the Whips—Liberal and Labour—coming to an understanding as happened when the Liberals and Irish were working together in Parnellite times. But I cannot accept a position of dependence on the Liberal party. Grey's speech on this subject the other day was extremely unfortunate, and has excited some of our people. I must keep in touch with our Left wing. They threaten, if they see any sign of political subservience, to vote against me. I admit the similar difficulty of the Liberals. The whole position is extremely difficult and delicate, particularly in the matter of by-elections, as at Burnley. Henderson is going to stand there. There ought to be no conflict there between Liberals and Labour.

I said of course we had our own party difficulties and divisions. He said he quite realised that. He understood that Simon and Pringle were the two most hostile to them among the Liberal leaders. That of course is true as regards Simon. Of Pringle I had not heard. . . .

As we were about to leave soon after half-past ten MacDonald sent for the Foreign Office telegrams and some were brought in. Among them was a long one from Mussolini strongly objecting to the independent action of Great Britain in recognising the Russian Government. He looked at it hastily and came on the words: "Italy resumes her full liberty of action". "This [is] not so good" he remarked as he closed the box, rang for a clerk and left word for Eyre Crowe[8] to see him "the first thing in the morning".

I walked with him as far as his station at Charing Cross. . . .

He spoke of E. D. Simon[9] whose maiden speech in the House he had admired. Also of his wife of whom he had heard good things. He had evidently been impressed by Simon. He gave me, on parting, the usual friendly invitation to see him again.

Diary, 21 March 1924

Dined with the Webbs alone and was to have gone on to the Parmoor's Reception of Labour M.P.s with them afterwards,[10] but Webb had still a touch of flu and they cried off. Mrs. Webb did most of the talking and he seemed rather subdued. She said she did not believe the country would stand the three party system. I said it would have to put up with three parties, though it might give one of them—presumably the Tory party—a majority over the other two. She urged that there was very little to divide the real Liberals, who alone mattered, from Labour, not enough she evidently thought to give them standing ground as a separate party. The difference between the two on the question of Socialism was not one of principle, but only of emphasis. When the

[8] Permanent under-secretary at the Foreign Office.
[9] Liberal M.P. for the Wythenshawe division of Manchester.
[10] Lord Parmoor was Lord President of the Council in MacDonald's government.

question arose in relation to any great industry the presumption on the one side would be in favour of socialisation, on the other against it. That was all. Both would be guided by experience and would proceed piecemeal. I said I thought the spirit was different as was shown by Poplar.[11] She denied that Poplarism was approved by more than a small minority of the Labour Party; on the contrary by the mass of the Party it was condemned. Then she diverged into discussion of the Minority Report of the Poor Law Commission[12] which she held would have settled the whole question of relief on a sensible and moderate basis.

The Reception at the Parmoors was rather a slender affair and I was not introduced to a single Labour member, although there were a fair number of my own acquaintance present, including Lord Olivier,[13] who seemed to be relieved to find a friend and sat down with me for quite a long time. The attendant footmen in uniform seemed more in keeping with him than with the Glasgow members, who however, it is said, avoid all such functions. . . .

Diary, 15 July 1924

To lunch with MacDonald at his invitation. J. A. Hobson also there. He had asked me ten days earlier. Then he went on tour in his constituency. Then came the bolt out of the blue, while he was still in Wales, of the explosion in France about the Chequers Conference and the terms of the invitations to the Powers.[14] He apologised for the delay and plunged at once into his defence. He was not responsible for the terms of the invitations. In point of fact he had never seen the documents before they were despatched. Not knowing French it was useless for him to see the originals and if he had seen a translation he could not have checked its accuracy—a most extraordinary statement to which Hobson and I listened in silent amazement.

There had been a general agreement between himself and Herriot in the conversations at which both Eyre Crowe and Peretti de la Rocca,

[11]Poplar was an impoverished district of London. The local council was controlled by the Labour party, and since the war it had come into conflict with the central government on a number of occasions because of its excessive provision of benefits to the poor and unemployed.
[12]Produced by the Webbs in 1909.
[13]Secretary of State for India in the MacDonald government.
[14]Poincaré had been defeated in the French elections in May, and been succeeded by Edouard Herriot. MacDonald and Herriot had a successful meeting at Chequers late in June, but an invitation which they issued to other powers to confer on reparations caused an uproar in France, as seeming to undermine the Treaty of Versailles.

the representative of the French Foreign Office[,] had been present, and he left it to them to settle together the terms of the communications to the Powers. As a matter of fact the despatch to our ambassador at Rome "was all right", because it discriminated clearly between the terms of the invitation to the London Conference and the expression of the British Government's views on the situation. It was the despatch to Belgium which confused them. As Peretti had been cognisant of all that had passed and was a party to the drafting of the despatches his subsequent behaviour in making trouble was abominable.

MacDonald then burst out into a general denunciation of the whole crew of French politicians—underhand, grasping, dishonourable. I was entertained the other day, he said, at Versailles to dinner in a room about three times as long as this—the big dining-room at No. 10, about 50 feet long. There were present about 70 ex-premiers and would be premiers—everybody, he added, in France wants to be a premier, if it is only for four days. I was seated in the middle of the long side of the table so had a good view of all the men opposite. There wasn't a good face among them. Mme Herriot, a very nice person, was seated next to me. I said to her "can you tell me if there is an honest man here, besides your husband". "Yes", she replied, "I think there are two".

He went on to say that he could have taken a stronger line in Paris if he could have counted on Liberal support, but he was certain he could not and nothing I could say in protest—in which Hobson also joined—would convince him to the contrary. He was sure they were lying in wait to trip him up. He seemed to distrust the Tories also.

He reverted again and again to this dislike and distrust of the Liberals. He could get on with the Tories. They differed at times openly then forgot all about it and shook hands. They were gentlemen, but the Liberals were cads. The only grounds he gave for this strong feeling were, first, Asquith's patronising speech at the beginning of the session in the Commons in which he had proclaimed himself and his party as the real arbiters of the situation. I pointed out to him that this speech was really addressed not to the Labour party but as consolation to his own dissatisfied followers who thought the Liberals ought to have accepted the Tory offer to put them in office instead of themselves putting Labour in power. But in vain.

The only specific charge he could bring against the Liberals' conduct in the House was of persistent talking on their front bench with the deliberate intention of putting out the Labour front bench speaker (e.g. in the case of [Robert] Richards, one of the under-secretaries, the other day in whose case it had succeeded) and generally behaving in a way to show indifference and contempt, their object being to assert their own importance and to belittle their opponents. Masterman, who sat at the end of the Liberal front bench immediately next to theirs, was a particular offender. He also complained of Lloyd George. Asquith behaved better and only talked when first spoken to. He had spoken to Masterman on the subject (according to his own account with not a little rudeness) but it had made no difference. He had hoped to establish better relations through Vivian Phillipps and had on one occasion written "with his own hand" to thank him for something which he had thought particularly nice on his part and said at the same time that he hoped it might be the beginning of better things. But the only result was that Phillipps asked him was he really serious—"as though I could not be serious when I wrote to him with my own hand".

The feeling against the Liberals was general in the party. Social intercourse had almost ceased. J. H. Thomas was perhaps now the only man who ever asked a Liberal to tea. . . .

THE LONDON CONFERENCE

Speaking of the Conference on the Dawes Report [on reparations] which was to meet next day I remarked that the French were it appeared preparing for a stiff fight and I hoped we should put up at least as stiff a one. I urged once more that in doing that he could beyond question rely on Liberal support—that Liberal opinion would in fact be entirely with him and that the Liberal leaders, even if they wished to, could not possibly disregard it. Hobson, who himself is now a member of the Labour party, was equally strong on this point, but there was no evidence that MacDonald was in any degree convinced. He said Asquith had put him in a difficulty by conceding too much in the debate.

Somewhat inconsistently he once again remarked that he saw no reason why the Government should not last for a couple of years or so—that there was plenty of good work to be done on which the two parties were in agreement to occupy at least that time. But he put all the blame for the existing bad relations on the Liberals. Hobson and I urged conciliation. Was there no one who could play the part? What about Wedgwood Benn?[15] Yes, said MacDonald[,] he is a good fellow, but not big enough. What about Pringle? He has gone curiously

[15] Highly-regarded left-wing Liberal.

461

"flat", said MacDonald, of late and no longer counts as he did. He has occupied himself chiefly of late in coaching [David] Kirkwood and the other Labour back-benchers, next to whom he sits, in making trouble and I often see him out of the corner of my eye leaning over to them and speaking behind his hand.

Nevertheless, as Hobson and I rose to go, "We need a conciliator" he said. Then you had better find seats, I suggested, for Hobson and me. . . .

Vivian Phillipps to C.P.S., 19 July 1924

Thank you for your letter of July 17th. . . .

I am interested in your postscript about the Prime Minister. There is really no ground for his suspicion that we shall not support him in resisting undue French claims. . . . Frankly, I have been disappointed in the attitude of Ramsay MacDonald to our Party during the past six months. Not only does he appear not to seek our goodwill and co-operation but on several occasions it has seemed as if he went out of his way to make it as difficult as possible for us to back him. Personally, I have always held the view, and still do so, that there is a large area of common ground in which we might co-operate with real and fruitful results, and I have not only endeavoured to bring this about by private effort in the House but I have said so publicly on more than one occasion.

Diary, 22 July 1924

Called on Vivian Phillipps who had asked to see me after I had written him. . . . I told him of MacDonald's complaints of the contemptuous attitude of our front bench and general antagonism. He said it was all nonsense, that Masterman who was regarded as the chief offender was no doubt somewhat exuberant and made remarks to his neighbours on points in the debate. He was in fact much too clever for the Labour people who got flustered if a point in their speech was taken up with an interrogation which was quite usual in the play of debate and it was quite true that Richards, one of the under-secretaries, was floored the other day and couldn't go on. He did not say, which is no doubt also true, that Masterman would not do these things nicely. He spoke of MacDonald's "womanish" sensitiveness—an aspersion on women who usually have much more control than he [i.e. MacDonald] of their nerves. I agreed to "childish". He thought that when he got up to speak all should listen reverentially. To lie back with closed eyes—a thing often done and which did not imply lack of attention—was an affront.

Personally he was on excellent terms with MacDonald and constantly consulted him, but he did not like to thrust himself upon him, though he never failed to respond when sent for. This, however, had happened less frequently for the last month or so. If he were in MacDonald's place he should make a practice of discussing the week's programme at the beginning of every week and as far as possible making common arrangements. But he doubted whether MacDonald really wanted closer cooperation. Cooperation was already too close to please some of his followers on the left wing who were committed to the assertion that there was nothing to choose between Liberals and Tories. Also any real drawing together would alarm his new recruits ([who] often prompted the left wing people in their opposition), the arriviste Liberals like Ponsonby and Trevelyan, who in those circumstances would quickly find their level. But it was a great pity, for the two parties marching, not in combination, but as he had himself expressed it (and MacDonald had thanked him for it), in step, might achieve in four years a splendid block of work.

Liberal prospects in the country were he thought improving. The Labour Government had alienated a good many minor sections, partly by their failure to fulfil electoral promises—as in the matter of unemployment—partly by their policy—e.g. on the temperance question. The Liberal campaign in the country also was now meeting with a very good response. At the general election the Labour Party were in the happy position of not having been put to the test and were helped by the good-natured desire to give them a trial.

There was no prospect of any compromise on the question of seats. Thus P. M. Oliver[16] was to be opposed in Blackley and that would mean that [J. R.] Clynes must be opposed in Platting. Triangular contests were however often less dangerous for Liberals than was commonly supposed. The public house and sporting interests were not so much pro-Tory as anti-Liberal, and were apt to go over in considerable numbers to Labour, to the relative advantage of the Liberal. Thus he himself in a straight contest in Edinburgh [in 1922] had won by only 600, but in a triangular contest at the general election [in 1923], by over 2,000—to the astonishment of the Tories.[17]

[16]Liberal M.P. for the Blackley division of Manchester.
[17]This was soon to prove a gross miscalculation. Phillipps was thoroughly defeated in Edinburgh at the general election in October 1924.

Altogether he was very friendly and amiable, but had not much to say outside the Whip's point of view.

C.P.S. to Hobhouse, 6 September 1924 (Extract)

What a fine speech MacDonald made at Geneva—wise, far-seeing and courageous. I wish we had a man in our party who could have done the like.

42. Post-Mortems and Recriminations, October 1924-March 1925

In October 1924, the Liberal support on which the Labour government rested fell from under it. The ultimate cause, as mentioned earlier, was Labour's refusal to establish tolerable relations with the Liberals. But the immediate occasion was Labour's involvement with "Communism".

On assuming office, MacDonald had formally recognised the Soviet government. He then sought to establish a trade agreement with Russia. This was not because he was "soft" on Communism, but because he was seeking a general reconciliation throughout Europe. But whereas reconciliation with Germany had become a respectable cause, reconciliation with Russia had not.

At last, after months of negotiations and near-failure, a trade "treaty" between British and Russian delegates was signed in August 1924. It immediately aroused Liberal ire, not on general grounds but because it contained the promise of a guaranteed British loan to Russia. This appeared a rash concession to make to a country which gave little sign of honouring its existing debts. So when Parliament re-assembled in October, the Liberals decided to vote against the treaty.

As it happened, the government dissolved Parliament on another issue, which arose later but came to a division earlier. The crown law officers had brought a charge of sedition against a Communist journalist, J. R. Campbell. It was a very dubious prosecution, and the government (possibly as a result of pressure from its left wing) decided to withdraw it. The Conservatives moved a vote of censure, alleging political interference in judicial matters. The Liberals tried to side-step this with an amendment proposing a parliamentary committee of investigation. But MacDonald stated that he would regard either motion or amendment as an issue of confidence. The Conservatives thereupon withdrew their own motion and voted for the Liberal amendment, so achieving the government's defeat. MacDonald promptly dissolved Parliament.

The ensuing election ended in the sensation of the "Zinoviev letter". This was an inflammatory letter to British Communists, allegedly written by Zinoviev, the head of the Communist International. (More probably it was forged, with the connivance of Conservative headquarters). In mid-campaign

465

MacDonald was sent a copy of the letter by the Foreign Office. Assuming it to be genuine, he drafted a letter of protest to the Russian government. Without consulting him further, the Foreign Office published both the Zinoviev letter and his draft protest four days before polling. It was subsequently explained that they did so in order to anticipate publication of the Zinoviev letter by the Daily Mail.

The result of the 1924 election was a sweeping victory for the Conservatives, a setback for Labour, and a total rout for the Liberals. (The result was widely attributed to the "Red letter", but this is probably an exaggeration). Among the defeated Liberals was Asquith, who had actually embraced Conservative support in his constituency to secure his position, but who nevertheless lost his seat to Labour. Most of the Liberals who did get back were supporters of Lloyd George, and this gave him, in Asquith's absence, the chance of being elected chairman of the parliamentary party. To many Liberals this was a dreadful prospect. Since Liberal reunion a year before, Lloyd George had not been cooperative. He had kept his political organisation intact, and had retained his large political fund. Admittedly Lord Gladstone had once told Scott that the Liberal party would not touch his money, but dire necessity had caused it to change its mind. The Liberal party went into the 1924 election almost penniless, and the spectacle of Lloyd George sitting on a vast fund which he would not relinquish caused great bitterness.

Other issues arose from the Liberal débâcle of 1924: the question whether the shattered party had any further cause for existence, and the problem of future Liberal-Labour relations. Scott argued strongly that a Liberal party was still required—though to do so he had to exaggerate the strength of Labour's left wing. As to the conflict of Labour and Liberals, he could only hope that reason would eventually prevail in Labour minds.

[The following letter was written during the election campaign:]

C.P.S. to Hobhouse, 23 October 1924 (Extract)

The more I think of it the more I dislike the [electoral] deal [of Liberals] with the Tories. I don't know exactly how far it has gone, but both Asquith and Simon are certainly compromised. Both, without Tory support, would probably lose their seats. I am glad we have had nothing of the kind, so far as I know, in Lancashire.

The stupidity of the dissolution was I fancy due to mistakes on both sides. The Liberal amendment was intended in the first instance as a way out for the Government. Almost to the last moment it looked as if it might serve. Then when Baldwin made his right about face in the debate by withdrawing his motion there was no time for proper consideration on either side. Asquith made an effort to smooth the Government's path by making a present of the Liberal representation on the Committee.[1] I believe opinion on the Labour side was divided as to whether or not to accept the concession, but they were already deeply committed and MacDonald had his way. Of course when Baldwin withdrew his motion Simon ought to have withdrawn his amendment but there again there were no doubt divided counsels and he has no courage. That is as far as I understand the matter, but I hope to learn more of its true inwardness by and bye.

Polling took place on 29 October. The Conservatives secured a mammoth 415 seats, bringing Baldwin back into office. Labour receded to 152. The Liberals crashed to 43.

C.P.S. to Hobhouse, 6 November 1924 (Extract)

I wish too very much that we could have a talk on the situation which is extraordinarily difficult. The difficulty lies not only in the situation itself, but in the men who are called upon to handle it. Of course given P.R. (the "alternative" vote is useless . . .) the whole situation would be immensely simplified; we could just go ahead with Liberal propaganda and organization and could make our bargain with either of the other parties later. Also we could be sure of a solid footing on which to work. As it is we are sure of nothing, least of all of our leaders. The one thing immediately needful is to rally the party on the very morrow of defeat, but Mr. Asquith has gone off to Egypt, Lloyd George is only concerned to insist on his claim to the leadership of the party in Parliament, and no general meeting of representatives of the party is to be officially called till the new year.

There is a subterranean conflict going on all the time between Lloyd George and Asquith whom he desires to supersede, but in any case to make sure of the succession. There is always I think a presumption in favour of making your strongest man leader, but where should we be with George? He is frightfully irresponsible and would be difficult to restrain, though no doubt, once leader of the party, he would have to consider any strong pressure of opinion.

But the crucial question will be our relations with Labour—that is supposing at the next election neither Tories nor Labour have a clear

[1] Asquith had proposed that additional Labour members should sit in place of Liberals on his proposed committee of inquiry into the Campbell case; but the government had refused to be mollified.

working majority. My feeling would be if possible to work with Labour, but this time on agreed terms, including P.R. But Lloyd George has become increasingly anti-Labour and I can't see him working decently well with MacDonald, though he might with one of the other Labour leaders. Meanwhile I find lots of spirit in the party and a strong desire to stand on its own bottom.

Hobhouse to C.P.S., 7 November 1924 (Extract)

My difficulty about the Liberal Party lies further back than yours. I doubt if it any longer stands for anything distinctive. My reasons are on the one side that moderate Labour—Labour in office—has on the whole represented essential Liberalism, not without mistakes and defects, but *better* than the organised party since Campbell-Bannerman's death. On the other side the Liberal party, however you divide it up, never seems any better agreed within on essentials. Of the present fragment part leans to the Tories, part to Labour, part has nothing distinctive, but is a kind of Free Trade Unionist group. The deduction I draw is that the distinction between that kind of Labour man who does not go whole hog for nationalisation on the one side and the Liberal who wants social progress on the other is obsolete. I myself have always felt it was unreal and that if we divided parties by true principles, the division would be like this

Communist	ordinary Labour	Bad Liberal	Diehards
Theoretical Socialist	Good Liberal	ordinary Tory	

But tradition and class distinctions kept many good Liberals outside Labour. Now Labour has grown so much that it tends to absorb them and to leave only the "bad" Liberals who incline to the Tories and a mass of traditional Liberals who can't desert a party of that name. . . .

For a moment fate seemed to be avoided by the decision of the Liberals on the Manchester Guardian lead to support Labour. Labour responded badly, and the Liberals then drew away and inevitably gravitated to the other side. They failed to present a third view because outside the extremists there is really no third view. Liberals may be full of fight but as against the main body of Labour what have they to fight for? Internationalism? Free Trade? Ireland, India, any particular kind of Social Reform? No, on all these there is agreement. There is really nothing, till you come up against doctrinaire Socialism, which is really outside "moderate" Labour.

468

C.P.S. to Hobhouse, 19 November 1924 (Extract)

I am almost wholly with you in regard to the position and true policy of the Liberal party. Between Liberalism as I feel and understand it and moderate Labour there is next to nothing to choose. It is only through the accident of the war and what has come after it that they have ever been divided and one strong reason for keeping the Liberal party in being as an effective organisation seems to me to be to maintain contact with Labour and keep the door open for cooperation.

But the trouble is that it is not moderate Labour which is in the ascendancy. The I.L.P.,[2] formerly a relatively small section, now dominates it and it is no doubt because MacDonald realised that moderate Labour might gravitate towards Liberalism that he has so ferociously opposed any movement in that direction.

My feeling therefore is that our proper course is exactly that which you recommended in your earlier letter—to make it our object "to maintain principles, define aims, advocate causes and let party organisation adapt itself to these"—only I should put the last part of the prescription more strongly. We've got to make the organisation a far truer image of real Liberalism and fight as hard as may be necessary to achieve that end. That may lead to apparent disunion, but there are things that matter more than union.

Of course we may not wholly succeed, but we shall achieve something. . . .

What we need of course above all is a sane but courageous social policy. There is not one of the party leaders who can be trusted to supply it. It will have to come from the body of the party—from people like yourself.

Diary, 27-30 November 1924

To London (Thursday) [27 November]. . . . Dined with Lady Courtney and sat next Mrs. Webb. She tried to persuade me that the true policy for the Liberal party now was to "permeate" Labour as the Fabians had permeated Liberalism. Permeation I suggested in that case would mean absorption[,] and that we could do much more to strengthen the moderate element in Labour by staying outside it and offering an independent alternative.

I asked why MacDonald had broken up his Government by dis-

[2]Independent Labour party, a body affiliated to the Labour party.

solving. She said they *knew* the Liberals meant to defeat them on the Russian Treaty a month later and thought it was better for them to anticipate their fate.

Saw Brailsford on Thursday.[3] He was overworked and much depressed. Had evidently disapproved MacDonald's whole attitude towards the Liberal party and his dissolution policy. For 10 months had not seen MacDonald or had any communication with MacDonald who had taken offence because early on Brailsford had made in the "New Leader" not any criticism of MacDonald, but merely some suggestions on policy. That had been regarded as an even greater offence. . . . But, while MacDonald only boycotted the New Leader, he was furious with the "Herald"[4] which perhaps was not wonderful as its editor was a Communist and perhaps hated MacDonald more than any other person in the world. I asked why the Trade Unions which paid for the paper tolerated this. He said they had nobody else to put in his place and a Committee of management of Trade Union officials would be hopeless. Moreover the "Herald" was now beginning to pay.

On Saturday [29 November] motored to Churt with Mrs. Lloyd George and her daughter-in-law. Other expected guests had fallen through so had a walk with Lloyd George and saw a good deal of him that afternoon and next morning when we went out again. Mr. and Mrs. Snowden came over after dinner with Philip Kerr who was staying with them.

Lloyd George much preoccupied with his position in the party and the threat of opposition to his appointment as leader of the party in Parliament at the party meeting next Tuesday. Finally decided to challenge a vote and to abide by the result whatever it might be. . . . I cordially agreed as for the party to take any other course would be either a confession of impotence or an acknowledgment of irreconcilable disagreement. He was evidently rather nervous and was anxious that something on those lines should be said in the paper.

I had been rather anxious as to his attitude towards the Labour party after his "never again" declaration but found that that was not very seriously meant and that he would be quite ready to cooperate—on terms. Looking back he said he felt that the real mistake of the past session had been not the putting of Labour into Office but doing so without any understanding or conditions. I confess, he said, it never

[3]Since 1922 Brailsford had been editor of the *New Leader*, organ of the I.L.P.
[4]The *Daily Herald* was at this time owned jointly by the Labour party and the Trades Union Congress; its editor was H. Hamilton Fyfe, late of *The Times*, *Daily Mirror* (editor 1903-7), and *Daily Mail*.

occurred to me that we could be treated as we were treated. I took for granted that the relations of the two parties would be analogous to those between the Irish and Liberal parties in the Home Rule period. Even as it was I should have put the proposal of cooperation a little differently at the [first] Party meeting and I had come with notes of a speech in my pocket. But Asquith did not consult me beforehand and after he had spoken I felt there was nothing for me to do but to put back my notes into my pocket and briefly to concur. Later I tried to force an understanding and in July I proposed to hold up the Labour party on the Unemployment question. MacDonald dared not then have dissolved; he was too keen about the London Conference and foreign affairs. But I was over-ruled and the party would not take the risk.[5]

When it came to the autumn his patience, I gathered, was exhausted. He certainly meant and the party meant to reject the Russian Treaty, but whether he meant to do this unconditionally or would have been ready to make terms did not clearly appear. When I said there seemed no reason why we should not have accepted the Treaty in a modified form he merely replied "Well, why did they not try". But in an earlier conversation he said something which indicated that he did not want them to get as far as to bring in a Budget in which, he said, there would have been proposals for the taxation of land. I rather think he wanted to keep the land question for himself. He is still very keen about it and is bringing out a long report. His objects are (1) to improve and modernise cultivation under *County* Committees and (2) gradually to multiply small holdings for the benefit of the agricultural labourer, who might thus be able, step by step, to rise into the position of a small farmer. But he has small hope that the party will agree to take the scheme up. . . .

Neither Lloyd George nor the other party leaders had wished to turn the Government out on the Campbell case and he thought it was a mistake on their part to have proposed an amendment. They ought simply to have voted against the Conservative motion. Asquith did his utmost to make retreat easy for the Government by the modification in the terms of the amendment proposed in the course of the debate[,] and the Government were divided as to whether to accept it. [Vernon] Hartshorn[6] told me, said Lloyd George[,] that when Thomas began by

---

[5]Lloyd George was still refusing to recognise that at no point was the first Labour government willing to be "forced to an understanding", and that throughout its life it was prepared to defy the Liberals to go ahead with any threat they might make to defeat it.
[6]Postmaster-General in the MacDonald government.

proposing that they should consider the new situation MacDonald instantly rounded on him and asked what there was to consider. Then Henderson (with his usual blundering stupidity) chimed in with an indignant "Are we then to go back on our decision", and finally MacDonald had his way. But there was great dissatisfaction among the other Ministers with MacDonald's leadership. According to Hartshorn MacDonald had really broken down in nerve after about six months of office and had gone on from bad to worse until his palpable and disastrous collapse at the close (in connection with the Zinoviev letter. Lloyd George was clear that this had a tremendous effect on the result of the election). They would not re-elect him now, but for the difficulty of finding any one else to take his place. His egotism said Lloyd George has become a disease and affects his mental stability.

Lloyd George's immediate position is obviously difficult. He is nothing if not a Radical yet circumstances have made him appear as the leader of the right wing of the party—of the "bad Liberals". I put it to him that he had really nothing in common with these people and that the only course open to him was to lead the Radicals. That is what he wants to do, but meanwhile his supporters in the party are on the Right and his opponents on the Left. Asquith who is really a Whig is accepted as a better Liberal than he. . . .

I was interested to meet the Snowdens who live close by and are frequent guests with Lloyd George. They are evidently very much on the Right of the Labour party. The "Manchester Guardian" said Mrs. Snowden "represents my views". I had some side talk with Snowden. He had evidently wholly disagreed with MacDonald's action in courting a dissolution. He would have worked cordially with the Liberal party and did not wish it to disappear, but believed that only P.R. (of which he is an advocate) could save it. If the Liberals would have supported, as I said they would, moderate and tentative measures in the collectivist direction such as Nationalisation of the railways and electric supply that would have amply sufficed as a basis of cooperation. Incidentally Lloyd George in a moment of enthusiasm declared that if the Labour party would have worked frankly with the Liberals they could have remained in office for five years.

Diary, 13 January 1925

Breakfasted with Sir Donald Maclean at the Reform Club (went up to London previous day, at his invitation). During breakfast he would only talk about the "Westminster Gazette" [whose financial position was becoming desperate] because, he said, if he started on politics he was in danger of becoming so emphatic as to be heard all about the room. . . .

[After breakfast:] We then retired to an upstairs room and he broke out against Lloyd George. A week after the last General Election there was a meeting of the Liberal party leaders. Defeat so far from depressing the party had produced an extraordinary rally of Liberal feeling. It was felt that advantage ought at once to be taken of this. Asquith (at whose house the meeting was held) was in the Chair. Lloyd George was asked to speak. He said he would rather hear others first. All were in favour of immediate and energetic action, a meeting of Liberal members and defeated candidates, Liberal peers and representatives of Young Liberals and the Women's organisations perhaps 500 in all, to set the ball rolling in the country. To everybody's astonishment Lloyd George then got up and strongly opposed anything of the kind. The Liberal party was, he said, in effect the Liberal party in Parliament and it was to these that any appeal should be made in the first instance. Finally, as a compromise it was agreed that there should be no immediate meeting, that a Convention, with much larger numbers, should be held early in the New Year and that meanwhile a Commission should be appointed to visit various parts of the country, take evidence on the subject of policy and organisation, prepare for the Convention and report to Asquith, who also selected the members of the Commission. Sir Donald Maclean was proposed as Chairman and appointed against Lloyd George's opposition. Lloyd George disliked the whole thing and fears it.

Sir Donald Maclean admitted that Lloyd George had done very good work in the House during the short autumn session, but as a leader of the party he was hopeless. Nobody trusted him, and personally he could never follow him. His followers in the House were the worst kind of Liberals. . . .

There was a splendid opportunity now for Asquith if only he would grasp it and throw himself with fervour into the conflict as Gladstone did when he was 10 years older—but would he? So far as he could see it must be a "soldiers' battle" and that was what made the coming Convention so vitally important. There was a new spirit in the party. Wherever he had gone in his travelling Commission he had found a spontaneous activity entirely new in his experience. . . .

I suggested that a Lloyd George in admitted command and, so far, with satisfied ambition might be a somewhat different Lloyd George to the scheming politician we now had to do with and that his inter-

473

est would then be to run straight: there would be penalties. But he would not even listen to the idea. Yet the day may come when circumstances may compel a choice. Meanwhile we have to be thankful for Asquith. . . .

Lloyd George to C.P.S., 30 January 1925[7]

The persistent and growing hostility of the "Guardian" to me perplexes me. I am quite at a loss to understand it. I certainly thought its distinguished proprietor was a sincere friend of mine, and there is certainly no public man in England for whom I cherish such a genuine respect and affection. That fact I know does not—and ought not—to influence his judgment when I deviate from what he regards as the true path. But in what respect have I sinned during the last three months? I am doing my best to keep the party together, and to restore its power and efficiency. I am giving the whole of my strength and such gifts as I have to that object, and the more I do it the more offensive does the "Guardian" become in its references to me. Its leading article on my Edinburgh speech was extremely unkind. As to the gibe in today's article,[8] there is no reputable paper in England would have condescended in a serious leading article to such a triviality: and that the "Guardian" should indulge in a little feminine personality of that kind is unaccountable.

I can give you many more illustrations if you need them of unmistakeable antagonism—in reports of speeches, descriptive articles, paragraphs—and even in the way my name is given in headlines!

I am frankly distressed about it because of our old friendship, but there is the fact—that there is no Liberal paper in England which treats me with less courtesy and fairness than the "Manchester Guardian".

C.P.S. to Lloyd George, 30 January 1925[9]

I'm so sorry, but indeed, indeed, no offence was meant on this occasion or any previous ones by me or, I feel confident, by any of my staff. Perhaps I am apt to presume too much on an underlying regard which I am glad to think mutual. In me it has survived some extremely trying

[7]Lloyd George Papers.
[8]This remarked on the "slight coyness" with which Lloyd George had taken an "inconspicuous seat" at the Liberal Convention. (Lloyd George replied that he had taken the seat allocated to him).
[9]Lloyd George Papers.

experiences. You know how I have hated some of the things you have done, and I have said so openly. I should never dream of a policy of pin-pricks and if, in such matters as you refer to in your letter, you have had cause for offence, however unintentional, I must ask to be forgiven.

I should like just to add that certain references to yourself which you will see in a short leader in tomorrow's paper were written before your letters to the paper and to me were read. They may therefore at least claim the merit of spontaneity.

Good luck to you in your new and difficult undertaking! I think you will pull it through.

Diary, 4 March 1925

Went to London partly for Reform Club dinner to Mr. Asquith translated[10], but chiefly to see MacDonald who had "complained very bitterly" to [Arthur] Ransome[11] that I had not kept in touch with him during the latter part of his administration and had consequently mis-understood the situation. So I wrote to express regret and asked for an appointment. Saw him in his room on Wednesday morning for about an hour. He gave a detailed history of the unhappy Campbell episode[,] which he justly described as a series of muddles and developed a sur-prising and not very credible story of a plot for the destruction of his Government. I had thought he might be offended at some plain speak-ing in the Manchester Guardian, but, on the contrary, he was exceed-ingly friendly.

The Campbell affair, he said, was an extraordinary series of muddles. First the prosecution ought never to have been brought and he said so to Sir P. Hastings the Attorney-General, as soon as he heard of it. But, he added, "as you have brought it, you must go through with it". Unfortunately Hastings imagined that MacDonald did not quite mean what he said. Next the matter came up before the Cabinet along with a great deal of other business and was discussed from various points of view. The Attorney-General was sent for but no attempt was made to interfere with his proper discretion. There was no deputation from the Left wing on the subject. That was a pure invention. Then came another muddle. Hankey, the usual Cabinet Secretary, had been unable to attend and a substitute had been employed to take the minutes who

[10]Asquith had accepted a peerage, it having become evident that he was unlikely to regain a seat in the House of Commons.
[11]Author and contributor to the *Manchester Guardian*.

took them all wrong. When Hankey brought them to MacDonald to be initialled he was in the midst of an important discussion with Herriot and the rest on the proposed London Agreement. MacDonald scolded him for bringing them at such a time, contrary to his instructions, but Hankey persisted and said he thought he should look at item 5. MacDonald, still impatient, said "Well, is it all right?" and Hankey replied "Yes, I think so". "So I just initialled it," said MacDonald, and thought no more about it. (The other members of the Cabinet all saw the minutes and no one called them in question. In fact, said MacDonald, they did not read them). A fortnight later, after the Conference was over, he went to Lossiemouth and took with him a number of papers which he had not previously had time to read, the Cabinet minutes among them. To his horror he found these gave quite a wrong account of the proceedings on the Campbell question. But it was too late to withdraw and alter them. They were already "docketed" and if anything were withdrawn a memorandum would have to be made as to the person on whose orders it had been done. So all I could do, said MacDonald[,] was to attach a note to this particular item stating that, in my view, it was incorrect. But meanwhile there had been questions in the House of Commons and it would be open to anybody to say that my note was an afterthought. There is only my word for it that it was not which people can believe or not as they please.

There was yet another blunder and muddle. At the same Cabinet meeting some military business had been dealt with and the custom is that where any Departmental matter is dealt with a copy of the minute relating to it should be sent to the Department concerned. On this occasion the communication was sent to the Admiralty, but instead of the particular minute alone the whole of the minutes were communicated including the erroneous one about the Campbell affair. The Admiralty circulated them among the Army and Navy chiefs and so the matter came to be known. It was known to Lloyd George and to Simon when the Debate came on and formed the real ground of attack.

I suggested that, however unfortunate all this might be, it did not spell defeat for the Government which was not desired by the Liberal party and could easily have been avoided. He admitted that, so far as the Campbell case was concerned, that was true. "I never", he said, "saw a more dejected looking lot of men than the Liberals as they streamed into the Lobby to join in the defeat of the Government". But, as a matter of fact[,] I knew that the fate of the Government had already been sealed, that if we were not thrown out on the Campbell case we should be on the Russian Treaty, and all I had to consider was

476

MARCH 1925

which would be for us the more favourable ground. I concluded that
we had better go at once and not later with the stigma upon us of the
censure of the House of Commons. It had come to my knowledge that
so far back as in July a compact had been made between Lloyd George
and the Tories to turn us out. The parties to it were Lloyd George,
Beaverbrook and Austen Chamberlain. But, I said, Lloyd George is not
the Liberal party and besides what reason had he to enter into any conspiracy of the kind. The Tories were eager to turn you out at any time
and no compact was needed. He had really no answer to make beyond
saying that Lloyd George had to make sure of his ground.

I said there was no more reason why the Government should be
turned out on the Russian Treaty than on the Campbell case, that there
was no objection to a treaty but only to a Government loan, or guarantee, without security, and that the way was completely open to a
compromise. He remained, however, fixed in his belief that to all
intents a death sentence had been passed and that in no case could the
life of the Government have been prolonged. With that in his mind
he said "then when I saw Asquith's notice of motion on the Campbell
case I said to myself 'that settles it' ". In the end there was confusion.
The Labour party like the Liberal party had expected that the procedure of the House would open a way of escape, but this was closed
when Mr. Baldwin at the last moment dropped his amendment and
decided to vote for the Liberal motion.

In the last days of the election which followed confusion was even
more confounded. MacDonald was deep in the concluding meetings
in his constituency and, as he admitted, greatly exhausted. He heard
rumours of an impending bombshell, but could not imagine what it
was. It never occurred to him as possible that his rough draft of a reply
to the Zinoviev letter could be published without his consent. "If you
had seen it", he said, you would have realised that it could not possibly
be regarded as a final draft for publication, covered as it was with
erasures and marginal additions. Besides, the Foreign Office officials
knew quite well that my method is to make various drafts. I always like
to begin by getting something on paper to see how it looks, and I then
work upon it. In the present case the document was not even consistent for the first sentence did not agree with the last and they were in
fact alternatives. To make the matter worse I could get no explanation
from the foreign office. They said the matter was too confidential to
telephone about and they would send a messenger. (It was I gathered
[J. D.] Gregory, the head of the Russian Department of the Foreign
Office). When the messenger came he could not explain. When I

realised the incredible thing that had happened "it simply blew me sky high". (He several times admitted that his nerves had gone all to pieces).

The party too was thrown into confusion. Some accepted the Zinoviev letter as authentic, others denounced it as a forgery. Clearly the right line was to have accepted it and pointed to the vigour of my reply as showing that I was clear of all complicity with Bolshevism, and where this was done I believe it succeeded. But there can be no doubt that the incident did us great damage.

He did not directly impute malice to the officials of the Foreign Office, but neither did he repudiate it. All he said was that if there was a villain of the piece it was Gregory. What he could not understand and what had never been explained was the failure to consult him on the telephone before publication of the draft despatch. His address was known and he could have been rung up at any moment. The foreign office heard at mid-day that the "Daily Mail" was in possession of a copy of the Zinoviev letter and was about to publish it, and his draft reply was not issued to the press till six o'clock because it was not desired that it should appear first in the evening papers. There was therefore ample time for communicating with him. I said that I understood that the irregularity was admitted generally by civil servants and that the Foreign Office itself was much upset, fearing that it would never again be trusted by a Labour Government. "No", replied MacDonald, with energy "it never will". Sir Eyre Crowe, the permanent head of the Foreign Office, he said, had become quite ill in consequence and had gone to bed. There were too many Roman Catholics high up in the Foreign Office. Gregory was one of them. . . .

He was as frank and friendly as possible at parting, begged me to come to see him whenever I was in town, but if possible to give him two or three days warning. . . .

P.S. A main object I had in seeing him was to see if he had any views as to possible cooperation, in case of emergency, with the Liberal party, but he evidently didn't want to talk about that. When I put it to him all he said was that it would be difficult, or impossible, whatever the emergency, to change the whole current of events at the last moment and that what was done at an election would be determined by what had been going on continuously before the election.

He went on to complain that in his own constituency of Aberavon the compact between Liberals and Tories was still in full force and that at every Liberal meeting the Tories were represented on the platform. In consequence he expected to lose his seat at the next election. . . .

if defeated at Aberavon it was doubtful if he would put up anywhere else. He spoke like a man who would be rather glad to be released or who at least liked to play with the idea.

He added that he believed the same thing was happening in other constituencies, but wrote afterwards to say that, on enquiry, he had found no direct evidence of this.

43. The View from the Sidelines, 1925-1928

For two decades, Scott had been in close contact with men at the centre of power. By 1925 all that had changed. The Liberals with whom he had sat in Parliament at the turn of the century were now conclusively out of office; and his hopes that they might still influence the affairs of the nation by their support for a Labour government had been dashed by the events of 1924.

Scott found himself on the fringe of politics. Churchill, now restored to the Conservative party and Chancellor of the Exchequer in Baldwin's new administration, was still pleased to see him; but they had long since lost any meeting-ground politically. MacDonald also pressed him to visit. But the intransigence of the Labour leader towards the Liberal party moved Scott to despair, so that he ceased calling. Only with Lloyd George did he still have some common ground. But Lloyd George remained an uncertain quantity as far as the Liberal party was concerned. And anyway, what did the Liberal party amount to any longer?

Lloyd George spent 1925 trying to restore his and the party's fortunes by a vigorous programme of land reform. This cut little ice, in or out of the party. What gave him his chance was the general strike in 1926. Asquith (now Lord Oxford) publicly denounced Lloyd George for failing to condemn the strike in the strong terms used by the other Liberal leaders. Lloyd George, under Scott's guidance, made a statesmanlike reply. The party declined to take Asquith's side in the quarrel, and he resigned the leadership. His principal supporters, including Runciman, went off to form a new body within the party called the Liberal Council. Lloyd George became Liberal leader, and Sir Herbert Samuel re-entered politics to direct the Liberal organisation. Great hopes were entertained for a Liberal revival. But Lloyd George and Scott recognised that revival depended ultimately on co-operation with Labour—and here no headway could be made.

Diary, 30 June-1 July 1925

Went to London for dinner given by Sir Hubert and Lady Lorn to the Radical [i.e. anti-Lloyd George] wing of the Liberal Parliamentary

Party on July 1. Brendan Bracken, manager of Eyre and Spottis-woode's, whom I did not know, had asked me to dinner to meet Churchill (who he said wanted to see me and would come any [time] that I liked) so I offered the day before the other. I thought we should have been almost alone, but there were a dozen other people. . . .

Sat next Churchill who talked incessantly. He professed himself entirely at home in the Tory party. In foreign policy it was now a peace party. In home politics he differed from it only on Protection. Its errors on that subject were only small and for his own part he always frankly admitted them. They would not go much further. . . . In-sufficient attention had been paid to his insurance scheme.[1] It was a very big thing and meant great alleviation to the risks and hardships of the working class. It would no doubt have received more notice if brought in as a separate measure, but he was obliged to include it in his Budget because of the costs it involved to the Exchequer. . . .

The Polish ambassador, whose English was imperfect and talked with Churchill and me partly in French[,] was very friendly in spite of the sins of the Manchester Guardian and pressed me to come to see him when next I was in London. Churchill, who was as rhetorical as ever in his anti-Bolshevism, argued strongly that Poland should by all means cultivate the friendship of Germany. Else, if Germany were driven back on Russian support, Poland in the end would be crushed between them. But the ambassador was not inclined to take so long a view and could only reiterate that Poland was quite ready to be friends with Germany provided only that she was asked to give nothing up.

Breakfasted next morning [1 July] with Lloyd George who could talk of nothing but his Land scheme. He has a Committee at work on it of 3 landlords, 3 farmers and 3 labourers with, if I remember rightly, 3 academics thrown in. It is a big scheme, dealing separately with the needs of town and country and I was much more impressed than when he spoke of it before. I urged him to consult Hammond who knows more than anybody else of the historical side of the matter and he promised to do so, though he was a little taken aback when I told him Hammond, though an intimate of the Manchester Guardian, was a member of the Labour Party. The "Manchester Guardian", he said[,] "reeks with Labour". He is in close touch with Asquith on the scheme and had supplied him with points for the speech he was about to make.

[1]This provided for more generous old age pensions, and introduced pensions for widows and their children and for orphaned children; but it retained the contributory system, whereby only insured persons and their dependents were eligible for benefits.

My dinner with the Radical Section of the Liberal Parliamentary party in the evening was a pretty dull affair. The mistake was made of spreading the people out so thin at the tables that they looked like a remnant and even so there were a good many vacant chairs. The redeeming feature of the evening was a speech, with fire and real conviction, from Benn . . . . a fine, straight, capable fellow.[2]

Diary, 19 October 1925

Sir Donald Maclean in Manchester for meeting of U.K.A.[3] Asked me to see him at his hotel. . . . [W]hat he wanted to speak about was the position of the party and in particular that of Lloyd George. It was known that he had a party fund of a million which he would not disgorge and on all hands people who were asked to subscribe to the Liberal million fund declined to do so till Lloyd George paid up.[4]

And this was not the worst. He was at his old game of intrigue with the Tories. Did I know anything about it? I said I had heard rumours to that effect. It was true. Garvin had told Sir Robert Hudson[5] who had told him (Maclean) that Lloyd George had approached him on the subject, representing that the Baldwin Government was a failure, that Labour was divided and incapable of governing, that the Liberal [party] was in much the same case and that the only means of forming a strong Government to face the social danger ahead was by a coalition of the moderate elements in the Liberal and Conservative parties. Would Garvin support this scheme. After a long consultation Garvin consented. He[6] anticipated serious social trouble in the spring and looked to this as the occasion for giving effect to his plan. . . .

I said I doubted whether Lloyd George would go far with his plan. The only thing to be done (short of getting rid of him, for which there was no present ground) was to watch for any signs of defection and to hit out hard at once. It was impossible that he should bring the party round to any such policy.

Personally he said he found it impossible to work with Lloyd George. I asked about Asquith. He admitted that there was no real

---

[2]Benn defected to Labour a year later, when Lloyd George secured the leadership of the party as a whole.

[3]United Kingdom Alliance, a temperance body.

[4]The Liberal party had launched an appeal for a million pounds to restore its finances. The appeal was a failure.

[5]Secretary of the Liberal Central Association.

[6]Probably Lloyd George.

reconciliation. Asquith's language in private about Lloyd George was lurid. And yet here was the country just ripe for Liberalism and only needing an energetic and sincere lead.

Diary, 13-14 November 1925

Went to London November 12. . . . Offered to call on Lloyd George if he were in town. He was at Churt and sent his car for me.[7] His secretary, Miss Stevenson, the only other person there. Had a long talk with him at and after dinner and next morning before leaving. He was of course full of his Land Scheme. He asked what I thought of the recent Manchester meeting. I told him I thought it a great success especially for a wet Saturday but that I gathered the party in the south, as represented by its middle-class elements[,] seemed to be much divided. He did not seem to care about that but spoke of the extraordinary interest shown both in Scotland and at the great meeting held in Acland's part[8] where 20 to 30 thousand collected from the villages of 10 miles round—the biggest meeting, he believed[,] ever held in the south-west of England. His chauffeur showed a moving picture of it (borrowed from the "Daily Express" photographer) on the white wall of his library.

He said he intended to put his whole strength into the movement and he had money enough to carry it on at full blast for 4 or 5 years. . . . Asquith was the only man in the party who had seemed to grasp the full magnitude of the matter. He had been twice through the Report and declared himself in principle in favour of it. But before committing himself he wanted to be satisfied that it was wise as a party move, that the country would rise to it. . . .

A doubt in my mind, he said, is whether I should not resign my position as leader of the party in Parliament. It is not possible for me to do justice both to the work in Parliament and to the agitation in the country.[9] I should like you to turn it over in your mind and let me know what you think in a few days. I said I knew quite well in the main what I thought[,] which was that it would be dangerous to give up the leadership in the House which carried with it the presumption of the leadership of the Party whenever Asquith resigned it for the simple reason that, deeply as I had on certain occasions disagreed with him, it was obvious to me that we had no one else who could lead the party effectively. . . . He gave no hint of the design attributed to him by

[7] Presumably on 13 November.   [8] Killerton in Devon.
[9] Lloyd George may also have been influenced by the fact that most of his particular supporters in Parliament were hostile to his land scheme.

Maclean of playing for the leadership of a middle party, except that he spoke of the fluidity of parties and the slenderness of the barriers at present dividing them, and of course there would be advantage in a detached position if any opportunity for reconstruction arose. . . .

On the question of finance I told him that I gathered (as Maclean had told me) that the failure of the Million pounds fund was largely attributed to his own refusal adequately to support it: "Why should we pay up when he refuses to? When he does, we will". He was supposed to have a million of party funds at his disposal with which he refused to part. On this he had several things to say. (1) He had not got a million pounds; he had (or rather the trustees of the fund had) a controlling share in several newspapers. . . . Until we took the risk of issuing Preference shares (which fortunately were well taken up by the public—largely by our own employees) there was little money available, but I managed to scrape together £50,000 for the general election and besides took over the cost of the election in Wales—another £10,000. (2) The fund is not my property to dispose of as I like; it was raised by the Liberal element in the Coalition Government and is in the hands of trustees of that party . . . and their consent is needed in its disposal.[10] It would not be given in support of any organisation hostile to the interests of this wing of the Liberal party. (3) As a matter of fact I have, since the reunion of the party[,] contributed £220,000 to its funds. I have also (perhaps foolishly) promised £20,000 a year to the Liberal Central to carry it on till the general election. Otherwise it will be bankrupt in three months. The million fund is being grossly mismanaged (I heartily concurred); Vivian Phillipps, who is now in command at the Liberal Central, is wholly incompetent (I again concurred) and some people advised me to let it die and then start afresh. But I didn't. . . .

I raised the question of future relations with Labour. What if the position of 1923 were repeated and there were a composite Liberal-Labour majority, with Labour the larger part of the compound. Should we put them into office again? Not on the same terms as before, he said; it would have to be on agreed terms as to policy and we could keep them in the cold until they did agree. If we left the Tories in office we could prevent them from doing any harm and as long as they had the offices they would not mind. They don't really want to do anything and could always plead that the Liberals prevented them. . . .

We happened to speak of P.R. as to which George evidently felt he had made a great mistake. "Some one ought to have come to me"

[10]Lloyd George did not mention that he appointed and removed the trustees.

he said, "in 1918 and gone into the whole matter. I was not converted then. I could have carried it then when I was prime minister. I am afraid it is too late now". And to think that under P.R. we might, I suppose, have now had ten safe seats in London. Yes, I said, probably more. (When I told Lady Courtney of this at lunch afterwards she mocked at him. Why she said he was in constant communication with my husband.[11] But of course it was not the general principle which needed explaining to him, but its special application to the interests of the Liberal party, as to which Lord Courtney would have been an imperfect expositor).

Diary, 8-9 December 1925

Went to London on invitation of Lloyd George and breakfasted with him on Tuesday and Wednesday [8 and 9 December]. Proposed myself for lunch on Tuesday with the Churchills as she had asked me to do next time I might be in London.

Ramsay Muir[12] also at Lloyd George's on Tuesday. Lloyd George entirely absorbed in his Land Campaign, but had nothing very fresh to say. Was anxious the first day as to the possibility of securing unanimity among the Liberal Candidates Association on his amended Land Scheme, jubilant on the second when he had secured it. Very bitter against Vivian Phillipps whose letter to the Manchester Guardian on Monday contained he said a definite falsehood, but he did not intend to enter into any controversy with him. He was a hopeless person in every way, an opinion in which Muir cordially concurred. We discussed party differences and in general terms his amended Land Scheme, which appeared to me to have alike the virtues and the vices of a compromise.

The lunch at the Churchills' where there was a small party was a purely social affair and Churchill disappeared before it was over in order to undergo some sort of electric treatment, a sort of amusement in which Lloyd George says he is apt to indulge from time to time.

I stayed a little afterwards with Mrs. Churchill who gave an amusing account of how Churchill's appointment to the Exchequer had come

[11]Lord Courtney had been such an ardent supporter of Proportional Representation that in 1884 he had resigned from Gladstone's ministry because it would not embrace the proposal.
[12]Formerly Professor of History at Manchester University, now devoting himself to the affairs of the Liberal party.

about, not a soul knowing in advance (not even Baldwin himself said Lloyd George when I repeated the story to him). It was a sudden inspiration arrived at after Churchill had entered the room. No wonder therefore that the Chief Whip whom Churchill came across as he left the Prime Minister's room was overwhelmed when he heard the news which Churchill had assumed could be no news to him. Horne was the obvious man or, failing him, Neville Chamberlain. But Baldwin was angry with Horne according to Mrs. Churchill for refusing to take the Chancellorship when he was in difficulties in forming his first Government and had been further annoyed by a memorial from a number of Tory members protesting against Churchill's appointment to any office at all. No one was more surprised than Churchill himself.

It is clear from what has gone before that Asquith (Lord Oxford) and his associates had come to the conclusion that there were many good reasons for severing relations with Lloyd George. But they blundered badly when they chose, as the occasion for repudiating him, his stand for a more moderate attitude towards the trade unions in the general strike.

C.P.S. to Hammond, 21 May 1926[13] (Extract)

Lloyd George is coming to Manchester this afternoon, "on his way" to Wales, and I am to dine with him at the Midland. There is no doubt that his position in the party is threatened. Of course journalism is not his job and he ought not to have been tempted to earn money in that way.[14] But apart from that general objection I don't think the American article is open to serious criticism, and his general plea for moderation is wholly to his credit.

Diary note, referring to the events of 21 May 1926 but written some time subsequently.

Perhaps the most serviceable thing I ever did for Lloyd George was at the time of his rupture with Oxford in May 1926.

Lord Oxford's letter to Lloyd George reprimanding him for his non-attendance at a meeting of the shadow Cabinet and for his general attitude in connection with the Coal Strike and threat of a General

---

[13]Hammond Papers.
[14]Lloyd George had written an article in an American newspaper predicting that the general strike would be a long affair. Asquith had included this among his reasons for condemning Lloyd George's attitude to the strike.

strike, and practically cutting him off from the communion of the party was written on Thursday May 20 and despatched to Lloyd George by hand. It was acknowledged by Lloyd George on the following day. He said he would "take two or three days to consider and consult" with his friends before replying, adding that he was "off to the north today". The north meant Manchester. I dined with him at the Midland and went through his proposed reply to Lord Oxford with him. It was written with considerable acerbity. I cut out everything provocative and left it full of mildness and dignity. He accepted the revision with complete good humour and has often joked about it since.

The letter was sent on Lloyd George's return to Criccieth on Monday May 24th and received in London on the following day. Lord Oxford's denunciatory letter had been sent to the press for publication about an hour previously and was published on Wednesday, May 26th. Lloyd George's reply appeared alongside of it and it was thus effectively countered.

The following recollection by Scott's son of the incident just recounted deserves to be included here.

E. T. Scott to Hammond, n.d. [? early 1932][15] (Extract)

I was present at the meeting of May 21, '26 when C.P. blue pencilled Lloyd George with almost as little regard for his feelings as he would have shown to a leader writer on trial. Lloyd George would interrupt now and then with explanations about the sharpness of the sting that was being withdrawn. But he submitted with extraordinary good humour.

Diary, 22-23 July 1927

To London Thursday night [21 July]. Breakfasted with Lloyd George Friday morning. He complained with his usual bonhommie that it was long since I had been to see him—the last time, I see, was on April 4, at his request[16]—and went on to recall the time when he came to see me "on his way to Criccieth!" a famous occasion he said which had made political history. . . . He is always very amusing on this subject and told me this time how Clifford Sharp[,] the editor of the "New Statesman", had asked him point blank "Whom did you consult". "I asked him first

[15] Hammond Papers.
[16] If Scott made a record of this encounter, it has not been preserved.

what business that was of his. Then I told him". "I thought so said Sharp".

I asked him if it was true (as [T. F.] Tweed, his secretary, had told me) that Samuel hoped for a Liberal majority over all the other parties at the next election. He did at first said Lloyd George, but I think now he realises more clearly the difficulties. I think nobody now looks for more than 250 Liberals in the new House with 150 or 200 Labour. Even that would leave only about 150 for the Tories which is hardly possible. He did not volunteer a guess himself, but evidently had very much more slender expectations. He warmly approved the policy advocated by [A. M.] Thompson[17] and the Manchester Guardian of not contesting hopeless seats by either side. If that were not done he thought the Tories might still come in with a small majority or a Liberal-Labour combination with a similar one. It would not much matter which as such a parliament could have but a short life. In the second case he would advocate a strong policy of reform and if the Bill were thrown out by the Lords, a dissolution upon it. We might be defeated, but at least the two parties would go down fighting together and that would weld them together as, in like case, the Tories and Liberal Unionists were welded. Then it would be possible for a united progressive party to arise. I suggested that that could only happen after the Labour party had shed its Left wing. He thought that when it came to the point the secession would be small.

I asked what he thought should be done if or when there was a combined Liberal-Labour majority. Should we let the Labour Party form a Government with Liberal support, as in 1923 [i.e. 1924], which personally I should prefer, or should there be a combined Ministry? He said he thought the renunciation of 1923 could not be repeated, that it was all very well for people like himself and Samuel, who had already had their share of political distinction, but that the younger men demanded openings and would lose interest if they were told there was never to be a chance of promotion. Personally he should not take part in such a Ministry . . . but he should insist on the adoption of his Land policy which in substance was that also of the Labour party. Of course there would be secessions—Simon and Runciman whose last speech showed him to be hopeless. He spoke with some bitterness of the recent action of their party.[18] They had lost us the Westbury [by-] election. A win there was the easiest thing in the world, but the whole pack of them settled down on the constituency, resolved to make it a

[17] A prominent figure in the early history of the Labour party.
[18] i.e. the Liberal Council, of which Runciman—but not Simon—was a leading member.

Liberal Council victory. They ignored Samuel to whom, as head of the Liberal electoral organisation it was their clear duty to apply and appointed their own organiser independently. . . . Then they tried to get Mrs. Lloyd George to speak and afterwards Megan, who both declined while Lloyd George himself was ignored. Finally they got the local paper to ask for Lloyd George's help which he declined till he was asked officially. He then sent a message, but it was too late. It would have been worth anything to win this election for both Beaverbrook and Rothermere, he said, were preparing to come out on the Liberal side—only, it is true, as part of their economy stunt, but that did not matter—but when Westbury was lost they drew back.

Saturday [23 July]

Lunched with Ramsay MacDonald at the Athenaeum. . . . I raised the question of Liberal-Labour cooperation and getting out of each other's way at elections where either of us had no chance. He said any sort of cooperation, for however limited a purpose, was very difficult because of the extreme hatred by Labour of the Liberal party, which went so far that many of the men in Parliament said that they would rather cooperate with the Tories than the Liberals. I said I quite understood that they should dislike us as being their only serious competitors and a standing refutation of the myth that there was nothing to choose between Liberal and Tory. He said that was partly the reason but far from the whole. They regarded us as tricky and unreliable—false friends. On critical divisions half the party went into the wrong Lobby and there were endless difficulties on simple matters of procedure where cooperation should have been easy. They had a particular dislike for Lloyd George whom they regarded as mainly responsible for the fatal division in the House which broke up the Government of 1924. They had a very low opinion also of Samuel as a dead failure in office and as responsible for some of the most extreme features of DORA.[19] There was some anti-Semitism too in relation to him and Reading and (formerly) Mond. . . .

Nevertheless I said the question was a practical one and would have to be faced if, as was probable, there was a combined Liberal-Labour majority after the election, as to the probability of which he also agreed. Either the position of [1924] must be repeated, to which Lloyd George was opposed, or there must be a joint Ministry. He said that his party were not altogether opposed to this. They felt that the Liberal party

[19] The wartime Defence of the Realm Act.

would then have given hostages and that they would have a hold upon them which they could not otherwise obtain. . . . I said Lloyd George would stand out of such a Ministry and MacDonald said he also should stand out.

As to the contesting of seats the Labour party would ask nothing better than that the Liberals should contest as many as possible of the industrial constituencies. There was general rejoicing in the Labour party when the Samuel announcement was made that 500 seats were to be contested by the Liberals. That, said MacDonald, would give us, by dividing our opponents, perhaps 20 seats that we could not win in straight contests. What the Liberals of course fear is that we should oppose them in the rural constituencies. But I may tell you that the determining factor in the whole matter will be finance. The Trade Unions Bill will absolutely cripple our resources.[20] In a couple of years we could reorganise our methods of raising money, but if there is an election, as there will be, within fifteen months, it will find us with deficits at all the local banks and no central fund whatever. We shall manage somehow by further overdrafts and local efforts, but we shall not contest perhaps a hundred seats which otherwise we should have contested.

The Government was absolutely discredited in the country. It was the feeblest and foolishest within memory and a real discredit to the country. "I see a good deal of the younger Tories", he said, "and you should just hear the things they say of the Government and the Prime Minister. They would never say such things in print or in public, but they relieve their feelings to me". As to poor Baldwin I was talking to him the other day about something and he was entirely at sea. I said "you're not well" and he said "no, I'm not very well". He is an extraordinary failure. He does not know what he wants to do and, if he did, he has no power to assert himself—the weakest prime minister within memory. . . .

I told MacDonald that he was looking well—which was only half true—that he was indispensable to his party and, as I thought, very necessary to our politics in general. But I failed to evoke a cheerful response. "Oh yes", he said, ["]I look all right and I am all right, so long as I don't exert myself, but the moment I do anything—such as going to Swansea last night, which I ought not to have done—I go

[20]After the general strike Baldwin's government passed through Parliament a Trades Disputes Bill, which *inter alia* had the effect of reducing trade union contributions to the Labour party.

flop and I'm not going on like that. I'm not going to be a dead-weight on the party."

He was very friendly and asked me, as he has done before, to let him know whenever I was in London.

Diary, 14 October 1927

To London by night. Lloyd George at Churt. Sent his car for me. Had a couple of hours with him and back to London after an early lunch. Told him I was going to see MacDonald that afternoon. We discussed possibilities of cooperation and coalition. Apart from any unforeseen turn of luck in favour of the Government he anticipated a joint Liberal-Labour majority of 80 to 100. On the question of policy we discussed the points I had recently discussed with the Webbs:

(1) Repeal of Trades Union Act. The demand is for absolute repeal and I mentioned Webb's suggestion that the Act might first be repealed and then in part re-enacted,[21] following the precedent of the Conservative Government in 1876 (of which Lloyd George was not aware). He thought there would be great difficulty about total repeal as, unlike the Government of 1876[,] we should have no power of re-enactment.

(2) Mines. He thought there need be no great difficulty about this, provided that State-management were not demanded.

(3) Finance. The proposed 2/- in the £ special tax on all unearned income over £500 a year would hit a good many of our supporters pretty hard. Still, if applied as originally proposed, to the extinction of debt in place of the Capital tax[,] he had found quite conservative financial opinion which regarded it as defensible.

As to Coalition it could only be on terms. The Labour people must not suppose that they were our only possible allies. There were plenty of progressive young Conservatives and with them also a Coalition might be made. It was stupid of MacDonald to keep on attacking the Liberals as he had done recently in "Forward". It made all cooperation difficult. In South Wales alone 8 seats could be won on an understanding between the two parties to divide them.

In the afternoon went to tea with MacDonald at his new house in Frognal with which he is immensely pleased. "It is the first time", he said, "that I have had a proper home. I shall stay here till I am carried out". It is a small house between two large ones and a small strip of garden between two very large gardens and the road in front is only a

[21]The Liberals approved some parts of Baldwin's Trade Union measure, while opposing others.

foot-way. He showed me all over and was very innocent about it. He had an aged and inexpressive housekeeper at tea, but his daughter, Ishbel, and his son, who is a candidate for the Bassetlaw Division of Nottingham, live with him.

After our previous conversation (last July) I assumed that he favoured cooperation between Liberals and Labour and even Coalition and I raised the question of agreement on policy, but soon found him not at all forthcoming. As to the Trades Union Act he said nothing would do but unqualified repeal. He would not even discuss the possibility of partial re-enactment in regard to such a matter, for instance, as "peaceful picketing". As to the Mines, it was not enough to buy out the Royalty holders; the whole industry must be nationalised by buying out the existing leaseholders and reorganising the industry under existing or fresh management in the most effective and economical way. As to finance they adhered to the 2/- surtax. It would produce not indeed £100 million a year but £85 million. . . . They would apply £20 million of this to the Sinking Fund raising it to 80 millions, the rest to social purposes.

But then, he added, at last quite blankly, there was no question of making terms with the Liberals. They would much rather make terms with the Tories. I remarked that it might be difficult to get much out of them, but he was quite sanguine; there were a number of progressive young Conservatives. He said nothing about foreign policy, as to which he might be supposed to care.

He was quite friendly to me personally and begged me, on leaving, to come again. But what, on that footing, could I have to say to him? . . .

C.P.S. to Lloyd George, 16 October 1927[22] (Extract)

There has been a change of wind at Frognal since I saw MacDonald last July. Then he spoke quite cheerfully of a possible Lib.-Lab. coalition Government. Now that dream has vanished into thin air—perhaps on the Blackpool breezes.[23] Now he says that if it is a question of cooperation his party would rather cooperate with the Tories. As he had previously drawn up a fairly stiff political programme . . . I remarked that even the more progressive young Tories to whom he looked might find this a little difficult, but he made light of the objection. His position altogether seemed to me theoretic rather than

[22]Lloyd George Papers.
[23]Blackpool had been the venue of the Labour party annual conference earlier in October.

practical and it conforms no doubt in that respect with the other purely theoretic and unreal assumption that "there is nothing to choose", from the Labour point of view, between Liberals and Tories. Such unrealities will no doubt tend to disappear in the light of the results of a general election, but, for the present at least, that seems to be MacDonald's position.

Lloyd George to C.P.S., 19 October 1927[24] (Extract)

I am not in the least surprised about the change in the Frognal weatherglass—or weather vane, as you please. I never thought Ramsay would willingly cooperate with the Liberals. He hates them. He is a compound of vanity and vindictiveness. His snobbish instincts incline him to association with Tories. But I quite agree with you that the mere idea of Tories and Socialists working together in harmony is just a dream of a man who is not recovered from a bad nervous breakdown.

As I told you at Churt, I have always thought real cooperation between Liberals and Labour was impossible, as long as Ramsay led the Socialist forces. He knows it, and I think he has quite made up his mind that his only hope of returning to office is at the head of a Labour Government, which has at any rate the toleration of conservatism. It is a sad reflection but there is no doubt that the future of progressive activities depends largely upon Ramsay's health. If he continues where he is, the prospect of the next Parliament is a dreary one for all those who want to see a real advance towards the dawn.

Diary, 7 December 1928

Dined with Lloyd George at the Midland. Talked chiefly of Liberal-Labour relations. No sort of cooperation possible in his view before or at the election. In case Tories had again a clear majority situation would be simple: we could just attack. In case of a joint Lib-Lab majority it would be more difficult. MacDonald must not imagine he could have Liberal support for the asking—that we had no alternative. Cooperation with the Tories, *on terms*, would be quite possible. Terms would have to include full maintenance of free trade and a reform of the system of voting. . . .

It should be a real coalition with a joint ministry. Able young Liberals (and there were a number of them: he mentioned Kingsley Griffith, Garro Jones and Archibald Sinclair, with [W. A.] Jowitt and

[24]Lloyd George Papers.

Norman Birkett as possible legal members) must not feel that as Liberals they had no chance of office (he himself would not take office), or they would in the end join Labour. If Labour refused then terms would have to be made with the Tories. In the end Labour would have to come to terms, because for the next 20 years or more, so long as the Liberals maintained their separate organisation, they would have no chance of a clear majority over the other two parties. They might win 100 seats at the next election, but still they would be a minority party.

On this distracted, anti-climatic note the diaries end. In part, Scott with advancing years had lost the diary habit. But mainly, he no longer had anything of importance to record. He had ceased to meet the people who mattered, or, when he did see them, to influence their actions. And he must have been getting rather tired of hearing MacDonald and Lloyd George, the leaders of the rival progressive parties, building pipe-dream coalitions on the basis of a projected alliance with the bright young men of the Tory party.

The rest of the story is soon told. Within six months of the preceding conversation with Lloyd George, Liberal prospects of revival were finally shattered. At the general election of May 1929, the Liberals secured only 59 seats. Labour, though still short of an absolute majority, came so near to it that Baldwin simply resigned and MacDonald assumed office. The Liberals were not consulted, let alone offered anything. Holding the balance in Parliament once more proved to give them no effective power.

Even so, the Manchester Guardian *hailed Labour's return to office in 1929 as full of hope for the future. But during the next two years the paper pitilessly chronicled MacDonald's failure to fulfil that hope. The débâcle of August 1931, when Labour simply abandoned office in despair, had long been foreshadowed in its columns.*

The outcome was ironical. Back in 1927, MacDonald had enthused to Scott about a possible alliance between Labour and the young, progressive Conservatives. Now in August 1931 he made an alliance with the Conservatives; but they were neither young nor progressive, and he had to abandon the Labour party in order to join them. The Liberals readily adhered to his new National government (Lloyd George at the time was temporarily incapacitated); but Scott rapidly lost enthusiasm for it, regarding it as a Tory government behind a "National" front. In this matter he was once more—and for the last time—in step with Lloyd George, whose disenchantment ran parallel to his own. Scott wrote in October 1931 lamenting that the bulk of the Liberal party "is simply delivering itself bound hand and foot to the tender mercies of the Tory party, whose prime object is to plant Protection, as a permanent policy, firmly on our necks. Lloyd George is the only man in the party who sees this and we shall back him for all we are worth."[25]

But their defeat was absolute. The Conservatives swept home to a decade of power, free trade disappeared as if it had never been, and Lloyd George—now separated even from the Liberal remnant—went permanently into the wilderness. Scott did not share their joint exile for long. He died, full of honours but with his political hopes in ruins, on 1 January 1932. The following letter—perhaps the last he ever wrote—suggests how far he was by that time divorced from the politics of his day.

C.P.S. to Hammond, 22 December 1931[26] (Extract)

The present higgledy-piggledy Government doesn't know its own mind, even supposing it had a mind. Free Trade in the sense in which we have always understood it is either a sound economic policy or it is not. Judging by results in national prosperity I should have thought it would take a lot of disproving, but the Tories are ready to play fast and loose with it and some of our own people who ought to know far better seem ready to back them up. If there is any future for the Liberal party it surely rests on the rock of Free Trade.

I am writing this from bed; being for the moment slightly disabled —nothing serious.

[25]C.P.S. to Lady Boyd Dawkins, 18 October 1931, quoted in J. L. Hammond, *C. P. Scott of the Manchester Guardian* (Bell, London, 1934), p. 299. This letter does not appear to be among Scott's papers.
[26]Hammond Papers.

Index

Index

Addison, Dr Christopher: 128, 186, 235, 238-239.
Agadir crisis (1911): 41-57, 59-60, 86.
Aliens, in wartime: 108-110.
Amery, L. S.: 305, 319.
Anderson, W. C.: 172.
Angell, Norman: 102-103, 105.
Archbishop of York (Cosmo Lang): 385-387.
Asquith coalition (1915-1916): 121-122, 132, 134, 199;
fall of: 232-252.
Asquith, H. H.
and C.P.S.: 24-26, 28-32, 121-122, 177, 190-192, 267, 286-287, 371, 379-380, 410, 423-424.
and Lloyd George: 134, 153, 157-158, 166, 204, 286, 291-292, 321-328, 360, 400-401, 439-440, 447, 452, 480, 482-483, 486-487.
and women's suffrage: 34, 58, 65, 66-67.
and naval estimates: 37, 38, 39-40, 75-77.
and Agadir crisis: 45, 47, 49, 54, 56, 59-63, 86.
as Prime Minister: 56, 60, 68, 84-85, 157, 162-163, 178, 180, 181, 183, 185, 200, 243, 246.
and Ireland: 78, 84, 203-207, 222-223, 286, 410.
and outbreak of First World War: 93-94, 103, 104.
and aliens: 109.

and drink question: 121-123.
forms coalition: 121, 141.
and conscription: 132, 134, 135, 143-144, 153-156, 165, 166, 171-172, 177, 196-197, 199-200, 217.
and conduct of the war: 152, 160-161, 163-164.
and Churchill: 190-194.
and Fisher: 190-192.
and free trade: 191-192.
and terms of war settlement: 230, 303-304, 321-328.
falls from office: 232-250, 258.
loses seat: 366.
re-elected: 398.
unpopularity of: 371, 377-378, 401.
as Liberal leader, post-war: 390, 398-401, 416-417, 419, 429, 440, 448, 473.
and Labour government: 447-451, 453, 455, 460, 466-467, 471.
loses seat and takes peerage: 466, 475.
resigns Liberal leadership: 480.
other references: 33, 69, 90, 111, 340, 344, 345, 349, 353, 418, 472.
Asquith, Margot: 61, 180, 221, 234, 267, 327, 416-417, 452.
Astor, Waldorf: 159.

Baldwin, Stanley: 28, 444-447, 466-467, 477, 486, 490, 494.
Balfour, A. J.: 28, 53, 64, 129, 130, 132, 136-137, 146, 151, 157-158,

499

272, 274, 306, 334, 360-361, 369,
376, 384-385, 422.
Pankhurst, Christabel: 57, 58, 67.
Pankhurst, Mrs Emmeline: 34-35.
Peace settlement: *see* First World
War.
Pease, J. A.: 52, 53, 69.
Pentland, Lord: 60.
Persian question: 42, 55, 56, 89,
279-280.
Phillipps, Vivian: 24-26, 423, 441,
447, 451, 461, 462-464, 484, 485.
Poincaré, Raymond: 384, 414, 421-
422, 426, 431, 444-445, 459.
Ponsonby, Arthur: 453, 463.
Press censorship: 108-109, 116.
Primrose, Neil: 42, 255.
Pringle, W. M. R.: 443, 456, 458,
461-462.

Quinan, K. B.: 164.

Rawlinson, Sir H. S.: 217, 219.
Reading, Lord (Rufus Isaacs): 73,
103, 104, 220, 223, 320-321, 353-
355, 366, 489.
Redmond, John: 64-66, 82, 90, 91,
113, 169, 188, 203-207, 220, 239,
283, 285, 289-291, 292, 293, 338,
362.
Renold, Charles: 127, 332-333.
Repington, C.: 194.
Riddell, Sir George: 197.
Ripon, Lord: 52, 53.
Roberts, G. H.: 99.
Robertson, J. M.: 169.
Robertson, Sir William: 164, 181,
216-217, 218, 221, 237, 238, 244,
311-312, 320-321, 323.
Robinson (Dawson), Geoffrey: 83,
183, 211.
Rosebery, Lord: 26, 218, 221.
Rosing, Vladimir: 270-271, 348.
Rothermere, Lord: 237, 309, 489.
Rowntree, Arnold: 227.

Runciman, Walter: 52, 53, 78, 122,
131, 134, 135, 177, 181, 185, 194,
243, 307, 363, 366, 433, 480, 488.
Russell, Bertrand: 115.
Russia
Revolution in: 159, 256, 270-271,
274, 294-295, 346.
Allied intervention in: 335-339,
346-348, 354-355, 364-365, 369,
370, 372, 376.
Conditions in, following Revolution: 296, 369-370, 371.
British relations with, post-war:
386-387, 465-466.

Salisbury, Lord: 38, 54.
Samuel, Herbert: 52, 53, 75, 78,
113, 159, 250, 354, 385, 480,
488, 489.
Scott, C. P.
character: 27-28.
career: 21, 22.
diary-keeping: 22-23, 33-34, 197,
494.
and Lloyd George: 24-29, 102,
122, 126-127, 177, 199-202, 226-
231, 232-233, 236, 250-251, 292,
296, 307, 313, 315, 321, 335-337,
340-345, 351, 354-355, 357, 361-
363, 366-367, 371, 377, 378-380,
381-387, 389-390, 394, 398, 401,
427, 432, 442, 467, 473-475, 480,
486-488, 494-495.
and Asquith: 24-26, 28-32, 121-
122, 163, 166, 177, 179-180, 287-
288, 293, 321, 340, 344-345, 377-
378, 390, 398-401, 410, 416, 423-
424, 429, 431, 447-448, 473-474,
486-487.
and Churchill: 108, 158, 187-193,
481.
and Boer War: 28-32.
and women's suffrage: 34, 65-67,
412, 431.
and naval estimates: 37, 75, 79.

Tyrrell, Sir W.: 357.

Unionist party: *see* Conservative party.

Venizelos, E.: 121, 156, 394, 425.
Villard, Oswald Garrison: 362.
Viviani, René: 161.

Walsh, Stephen: 99.
Ward, Dudley: 104.
Webb, Beatrice: 458-459, 469-470.
Webb, Sidney: 115-116, 320, 332, 372, 491.
Weizmann, Chaim: 113, 128, 159, 164, 176, 184, 186, 194-195, 197, 205, 255, 258, 271-272,

306, 333-334, 360-361, 369, 422.
Whitehouse, J. H.: 169.
William II, Kaiser: 41-42, 54, 61, 96, 98.
Wilson, Sir Henry: 311-312, 320-321.
Wilson, President Woodrow: 236, 252-254, 313-314, 355, 356-357, 362, 364-367, 368-380, 386, 388-389.
Women's suffrage: 33, 34-37, 57-59, 64-68, 258-259, 412, 431.

Younger, Sir George: 413, 415, 419, 421.

Zimmern, A. E.: 357, 369.